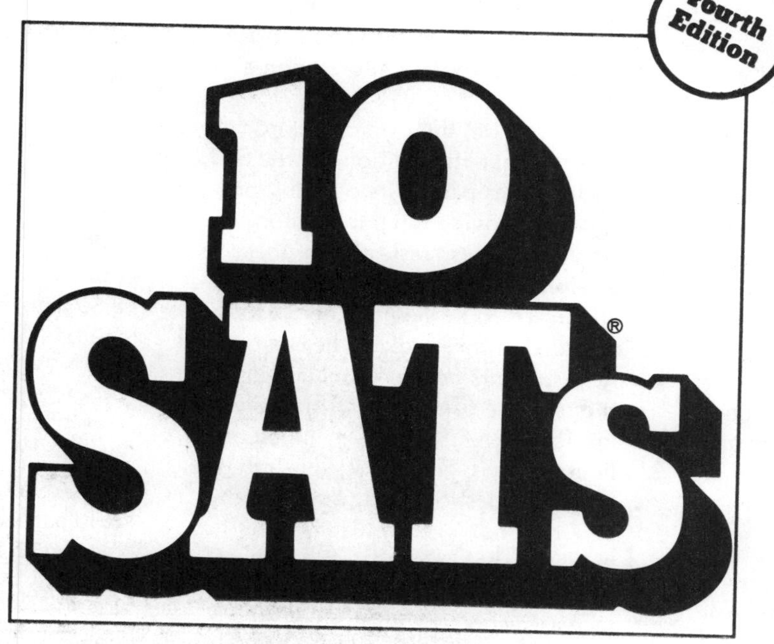

PLUS ADVICE FROM THE COLLEGE BOARD
ON HOW TO PREPARE FOR THEM

COLLEGE ENTRANCE EXAMINATION BOARD
NEW YORK

Introduction

The College Board knows that some people are uncomfortable with the prospect of taking any test, but that there is even greater anxiety before taking national standardized tests such as the Scholastic Aptitude Test (SAT). One reason that people worry about how they will do on the SAT is that they don't know what the test will be like, what it measures, or how the results will be used.

This book helps students to become better acquainted with the SAT and, therefore, reduce some of that anxiety. The following topics are included:

- What the SAT measures
- The format of the test as a whole
- The kinds of questions on the test
- How to mark the answer sheet
- How each question is scored
- Rules of good test-taking practice
- How scores are reported and used
- How to use sample tests for practice and self-scoring

This information and one sample test are also available in the booklet *Taking the SAT*, which students who plan to take the test receive free of charge from their schools. *Taking the SAT* is revised annually and contains the most up-to-date information about the SAT.

In addition, the College Board makes public five editions of the SAT each year as part of its ongoing program to provide full public information about these tests. Ten of these editions, all of which have been administered in the past few years, are included in this book. Other than to help students become familiar with the test, use of all 10 tests in preparing for the SAT probably will be of limited value. These tests illustrate the range of questions and topics on any SAT test; however, research offers no evidence that extensive drill or practice on these particular tests will increase scores significantly. The soundest preparation for the SAT continues to be serious application to regular school studies, with emphasis on academic courses and plenty of outside reading.

Although this book has been written for students and others who are planning to take the SAT, it also may be useful to parents, teachers, and individuals who have an interest in the SAT and who use its results.

If you want to write or call...

Address
College Board ATP
P.O. Box 6200
Princeton, NJ 08541-6200

Phone Numbers (Monday-Friday)

Princeton, NJ
8:30 a.m. to 9:30 p.m. Eastern time
(609) 771-7588 Registration
(609) 771-7600 Score Reports
(609) 771-7150 TDD for hearing impaired

Bay Area Office, CA
8:30 a.m. to 6:30 p.m. Pacific time
(415) 653-1564

The Admissions Testing Program (ATP) is a program of the College Board, a nonprofit membership organization that provides tests and other educational services for students, schools, and colleges. The membership is composed of more than 2,500 colleges, schools, school systems, and education associations. Representatives of the members serve on the Board of Trustees and advisory councils and committees that consider the programs of the College Board and participate in the determination of its policies and activities.

This book was prepared and produced by Educational Testing Service (ETS), which develops and administers the tests of the Admissions Testing Program for the College Board. The text of this book is adapted from *Taking the SAT*, a booklet that is shipped at the beginning of each academic year to secondary schools for free distribution to students who plan to register for the SAT. (Copies of *Taking the SAT* can be purchased for $4.00 each; 50 or more, $2.00 each.)

The College Board and Educational Testing Service are dedicated to the principle of equal opportunity, and their programs, services, and employment policies are guided by that principle.

Cover design by Bob Silverman

Library of Congress catalog card number 87-063591

Printed in the United States of America
9 8 7 6 5 4 3 2

Contents

How the Tests Are Developed

Many people are involved in the development of every new edition of the Scholastic Aptitude Test (SAT) and the Test of Standard Written English (TSWE). Questions are written by high school and college teachers and by test specialists at Educational Testing Service. Questions then are placed in an equating section of the SAT to be tried out under standard testing conditions by representative samples of students. The responses to each question are then analyzed statistically. Satisfactory questions become part of a pool of questions from which new editions of the SAT are assembled.

In developing a new edition of the SAT, test specialists and test editors review each question and reading selection on which questions are based for accuracy and to ensure balanced content of the test as a whole. Each reviewer prepares a list of answers that is compared with other reviewers' lists to verify agreement on the correct answer for each question. In addition, trained "sensitivity" reviewers eliminate any references in the test material that might be unfair or offensive to some student groups because of stereotyping, sex bias, or content that could produce negative feelings.

After the new edition has been assembled, the SAT and TSWE Committees, composed of high school teachers, college faculty, and educational administrators, review the test a final time before it is given to students. In addition to reviewing all new tests, these committees also are responsible for determining overall test specifications, recommending related research, and advising the College Board on policy matters related to the tests.

SAT Committee 1989-90

Karl M. Furstenberg, Wesleyan University, Middletown, Connecticut, *Chair*

John A. Blackburn, University of Virginia, Charlottesville, Virginia

Lloyd Bond, University of North Carolina at Greensboro, Greensboro, North Carolina

Diane J. Briars, Pittsburgh Public Schools, Pittsburgh, Pennsylvania

Anne Chapman, Western Reserve Academy, Hudson, Ohio

Marjorie M. Claytor, South Carolina Department of Education, Columbia, South Carolina

James B. Cox, Anaheim Union School District, Anaheim, California

Amy Ling, Queens College, Flushing, New York

Robert L. Linn, University of Colorado at Boulder, Boulder, Colorado

W. Jean Lockhart, Episcopal High School of Houston, Bellaire, Texas

Jose P. Mestre, University of Massachusetts, Amherst, Massachusetts

Thomas W. Rhoades, Anne Arundel County Public Schools, Annapolis, Maryland

Jacqueline H. Simmons, Paul Robeson High School, Chicago, Illinois

TSWE Committee 1989-90

William H. Thomas, Mt. Diablo Unified School District, Concord, California, *Chair*

Sandra H. Flowers, Clark Atlanta University, Atlanta, Georgia

Aida M. Ortiz-Ruiz, Hostos Community College/CUNY, Bronx, New York

Gregory L. Rubano, Toll Gate High School, Warwick, Rhode Island

Lucille M. Schultz, University of Cincinnati, Cincinnati, Ohio

A Message to Students

This book is intended to help you do your best when you take the Scholastic Aptitude Test (SAT) and the Test of Standard Written English (TSWE). It describes the tests, gives tips on test-taking strategies, and explains the different kinds of questions. Complete practice tests and answer sheets are included as well as answers and scoring directions.

Reading this book and *Taking the SAT* and taking a practice test will help prepare you for the test day. You'll probably feel more confident if you know ahead of time what to expect.

If you don't have a copy of this year's *Registration Bulletin* for the SAT and Achievement Tests, ask for one at your school guidance office. The *Bulletin* tells you how to register for the test, when and where it is given, how your scores will be reported, and other information.

About The Test

The SAT

The SAT (Scholastic Aptitude Test) is a multiple-choice test made up of verbal and math sections. The verbal questions test your vocabulary, verbal reasoning, and understanding of what you read. The math questions test your ability to solve problems involving arithmetic, elementary algebra, and geometry. These verbal and mathematical abilities are related to how well you will do academically in college. The SAT does not measure other factors and abilities—such as creativity, special talents, and motivation—that may also help you do well in college.

SAT scores are useful to college admissions officers in comparing the preparation and ability of applicants from different high schools that may vary widely in their courses and grading standards. Colleges also consider your high school record and other information about you in making admissions decisions. Your high school record is probably the best single indicator of how you will do in college, but a combination of your high school grades and test scores is an even better indicator.

You receive two SAT scores (verbal and math), each reported on a scale of 200 to 800.

The TSWE

The TSWE (Test of Standard Written English) is a multiple-choice test given at the same time as the SAT, but it has a different purpose. The TSWE is intended to be used to help the college you attend place you in an English course appropriate for your ability. The questions in it measure your ability to recognize standard written English, the language that is used in most college textbooks and that you will probably be expected to use in the papers you write in college. The TSWE is reported on a scale of 20 to 60+.

How the Test Is Organized

The SAT and TSWE are in the same test book. Each test book has six sections:

- 2 SAT-verbal sections
- 2 SAT-math sections
- 1 TSWE section
- 1 section of equating questions (verbal, math, or TSWE)

The six sections are not in the same order in every test book.

The questions in the equating section do not count toward your score. They are used for two purposes: First, representative questions from earlier editions are given again in order to set the SAT on the 200 to 800 scale. Repeating these questions makes it possible to compare scores earned at different administrations. Second, the equating section is used to try out questions for future use in the SAT. Trying out questions in advance makes it possible to assemble each edition of the SAT with the same mix of easy and hard questions. Thus, the unscored equating section is used to assemble SATs of comparable difficulty so that college admissions officers can compare SAT scores equitably.

You will be given 30 minutes to work on each section, and you are expected to remain in the testing room until all six sections have been completed. On the following pages you will find detailed explanations of each type of question as well as tips on how to make the best use of the testing time.

Preparing for the SAT

Keep Things in Perspective

In many ways, you have been preparing for the SAT during your entire school career. Doing well on the SAT is a natural result of hard work in academic courses in school and a strong interest in reading and other mentally challenging activities. If you are reading this booklet, chances are that you are seriously considering going to college. For many students, taking the SAT is one of the first steps in the college admission process and, logically, you want to do your best when you take the test. But getting ready for the SAT should be only one part of your overall plan to gain admission to college.

Surveys by major national educational organizations show that most colleges are likely to view your high school record—the courses you have taken and your rank in class or grade average—as most important. Usually this record is viewed along with your SAT scores. Indications of personal qualities such as motivation, initiative, and leadership ability may also influence colleges' decisions.

Even though SAT scores are seldom the most important factor in admissions decisions, they do carry weight, in varying degrees, with many colleges. For that reason, you should be as well prepared as possible to show your skills when you take the SAT.

You Can Prepare for the SAT: Here's How and Why

Over the long term, a good selection of solid academic courses, wide reading, and consistent hard work on your studies are the best strategies. In the short run, you should be sure that you know the format of the test:

- How it is organized,
- The kinds of questions it asks,
- The terms and concepts it uses,
- How it is timed, and how it is scored.

You should also know some basic rules of test-taking strategy, including when and why to guess, how to pace yourself, and so on. If you do not have this information you may be at a disadvantage in taking the test.

Taking the SAT provides this information. Students who have read this booklet carefully and taken the full practice test have reported greater confidence, less anxiety, and more familiarity with the test than students who did not use this booklet.

Just how much practice you may need to feel comfortable is a decision you must make. For those who want to practice with more than one sample SAT, the College Board publishes several books of sample tests, which are available from your school guidance office, your school or local library, and in bookstores. Remember, though, that practice is not likely to improve your scores dramatically. If you are nervous about taking tests, it can help you relax. But simply drilling on hundreds of questions cannot do much to help you develop the skills in verbal and mathematical reasoning that the test measures.

What about Coaching Courses?

There is a bewildering array of courses, books, and computer software programs available to help you prepare for the SAT. Some of them do no more than provide the familiarization and practice that is described in the previous section. Others are intended to help you develop your mathematical and verbal skills. These are often called "coaching" courses and we are often asked whether they work.

The vast majority of coaching courses are conducted in school, during class time or after hours, at little or no cost to students. A few commercial coaching courses are elaborate and costly. Some require as much time and effort as you might spend in a full semester course in school.

Some students may improve their scores by taking these courses, while others may not. Unfortunately, despite decades of research, it is still not possible to predict ahead of time who will improve, and by how much—and who will not. For that reason, the College Board cannot recommend coaching courses, especially if they cost a lot or require a lot of time and effort that could be spent on schoolwork or other worthwhile activities.

We are not saying they don't work. We just can't say with certainty whether a particular program or activity will work for you. We can suggest some questions to ask in deciding whether to take a coaching course, but we cannot tell you what your decision should be.

First, how much time should you devote to this activity? Your SAT scores may help distinguish you from other applicants. But so may success in an especially rigorous course, involvement in school or community activities, or demonstrating an outstanding special talent.

It is important to know that most students who take the SAT a second time have not been coached. Yet, most of these students show growth the second time—on average, 15-20 points on verbal and 15-20 points on math. Out of every 100 students who repeat the test, five will show a gain of 100 points or more on verbal or math, while one will show a drop of 100 points or more.

How much improvement beyond normal growth may result from coaching? The best available research suggests that short-duration familiarization courses (20 hours or so) improve scores on the average about 10 points on the verbal section and about 15 points on the math section. Studies of some longer-duration courses (40 hours or so) that stress work to develop the underlying skills measured by the test suggest average gains of 15-20 points on the verbal section and 20-30 points on the math section.

Keep in mind these are averages; some students improve their scores dramatically, while others show little or no gain. Some scores even go down.

Very much larger gains than these are claimed by some commercial coaching courses. Some appear based only on the scores of students who have improved dramatically on retaking the test. It is not always clear whether the reported gains are for verbal and math separately or added together. It is also not clear whether scores that drop are included in these claims.

Finally, are there tricks you can learn to beat the SAT? Some commercial coaching courses claim to teach them. Many are not tricks at all, but legitimate pieces of advice that all test takers should know and that are provided free in *Taking the SAT*. On the rare occasions that a useful trick has surfaced, the test developers who write the SAT immediately have changed the test so that the trick would no longer help. It is risky business to rely on tricks instead of using the strategies suggested in *Taking the SAT* and thinking carefully about the questions.

Our Recommendations

The College Board believes that the coaching that works best is the coaching that is most like hard schoolwork. If that is so, you should ask yourself whether you can't do just as much by studying harder and taking more demanding courses.

You can, and should, ask for advice from your parents, counselors, and teachers. Talk with your friends, too. But don't rely too heavily on anecdotal evidence, especially if it is second- or third-hand.

If you decide to consider a course, investigate it carefully. Examine carefully and ask for verification of all claims of results. Weigh the investment—both in time and in money. Be sure you know what is available from your school before you decide to pay for a commercial course.

And above all, ask what you can do in your regular schoolwork, in your leisure time on your own, or working with fellow students or adults to prepare for the SAT without distracting from other things that are important to your education and your college aims.

Know What to Expect

The best way to prepare for the test is to know what will be expected of you on the test day. To make sure you are prepared for the test, you should:

- **Read this book and *Taking the SAT*.** They have the information you will need to become familiar with all aspects of the test. As you read, note those parts that seem important or confusing. You can go back to them after you've read all the way through.
- **Study the sample questions and explanations** that begin on page 9. They will give you a good idea of the kinds of questions on the test. The more familiar you are with the sample questions, the more comfortable you'll feel when you see the questions in your test book on the day of the test.
- **Study and understand the test directions.** The directions in this book are the same as those in the test book. If you study the directions now, you will spend less time figuring them out on the test day and will have more time for answering the questions.
- **Take at least one practice test, score it, and review the questions you missed.** Take the practice test under conditions similar to those of the test day. (Suggestions for doing so are on page 30, just before the first practice test.) That way you'll already have been through a dry run before you take the test.

The Day Before the Test

Learn as much as you can about the test well before you plan to take it. Following are some suggestions for activities the day or evening before the test:

- **Review briefly the sample questions, explanations, and test directions in this book.** Hours of intense study the night before probably will not help your performance on the test and might even make you more anxious. But a short review of the information you studied earlier probably will make you feel more comfortable and better prepared.
- **Get your testing materials together and put them in a place that will be convenient for you in the morning.** Use this checklist:
  - ✓ Admission Ticket
  - ✓ Acceptable identification (You won't be admitted to the test center without it. See the *Registration Bulletin* for specific examples.)
  - ✓ Two No. 2 (soft-lead) pencils with erasers
  - ✓ Directions to the test center, if you need them
  - ✓ All the materials you will need to register as a standby, if you have not preregistered (See the *Registration Bulletin*.)
- **Spend the evening relaxing.** You'll accomplish little by worrying about the test. Read a book or watch TV, or do anything else you find relaxing.
- **Get a good night's sleep.** You'll want to feel your best when you take the test, so try to be well rested and refreshed. Set your alarm early enough to avoid having to rush, and feel satisfied that you've prepared yourself well for the test day.

Test-Taking Tips

Here are some specific test-taking tips that will help when you actually take the test.

✓ Within each group of questions of the same type, the easier questions are usually at the beginning of the group and the more difficult ones are at the end. (The reading comprehension questions are an exception. The reading passages are generally ordered easiest to hardest, but the questions that follow each passage are ordered according to the logic and organization of the passage.)

✓ If you're working on a group of questions and find that the questions are getting too difficult, quickly read through the rest of the questions in that group to see if there are more you can answer. Then go on to the next group of questions in that section. (Again, this advice does not necessarily apply to the questions immediately following a reading passage, in which case a difficult reading comprehension question might be followed by an easier one.)

✓ You get just as much credit for correctly answering easy questions as you do for correctly answering hard ones. So answer all the questions that seem easy before you spend time on those that seem difficult.

✓ You don't have to answer every question correctly to score well. In fact, many students who answer only 50-60 percent of the questions correctly receive average or slightly above-average scores.

✓ You *can* omit questions. Many students who do well on the SAT omit some questions. You can always return to questions you've omitted if you finish before time is up for that section.

✓ You *can* guess. If you know that one or more answer choices for a question are definitely wrong, then it's generally to your advantage to guess from the remaining choices. But because of the way the test is scored, random guessing with no knowledge of any of the choices is unlikely to increase your score.

✓ You get one point for each question you answer correctly. You lose a *fraction* of a point for each question you answer incorrectly. You neither gain nor lose credit for questions you omit. (See page 62 for more detailed information on scoring.)

✓ If you do not respond to any SAT-verbal, SAT-math, or TSWE questions, you will receive the minimum score for that part.

✓ Use the test book for scratchwork and to mark questions you omitted, so you can go back to them if you have time. You will not receive credit for any responses written in the test book. You must mark all your responses to test questions on the separate answer sheet before time is up on each section.

✓ Do *not* make extra marks on the answer sheet. They may be misread as answers by the scoring machine. If the scoring machine reads what looks like two answers for one question, that will be considered an omitted question. So it's in your best interest to keep your answer sheet free of any stray marks.

✓ Any four-choice mathematics question (see page 24) for which you mark the fifth answer oval, E, will be treated as an omitted question. You will not receive credit for that response.

✓ Mark only one answer for each question. To be certain that your answer will be read by the scoring machine, make sure your mark is dark and completely fills the oval, as shown in the first example below.

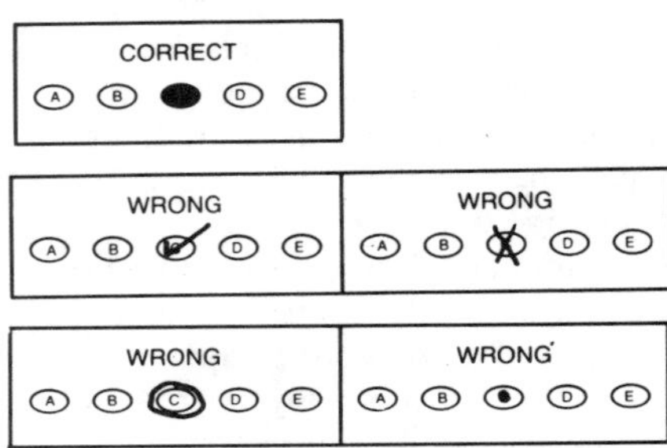

Sample Questions and Explanations

Following are sample questions and explanations for each type of question that appears on the SAT. Become familiar with the directions. You'll see them again on the test you will take.

Verbal Sections of the SAT

The verbal sections of the SAT contain four types of questions:

- 25 antonyms
- 20 analogies
- 15 sentence completions
- 25 questions based on reading passages

The antonyms usually take the least time per question, followed by analogies, sentence completion questions, and, finally, the reading comprehension questions. Individual students spend varying amounts of time working on the different types of questions. Some students can answer two or three antonyms a minute, but the same students may take longer to read a lengthy passage and answer a set of questions on it. The length of the reading passages will vary, as will the number of questions based on different passages.

Your answers to the 85 questions in the verbal sections make up your total verbal score. (See page 62.) The score report you receive will also show two subscores: (1) a vocabulary subscore, based on the antonym and analogy questions, and (2) a reading subscore, based on the sentence completions and the questions following the reading passages.

A careful balance of reading materials and words drawn from a variety of subject-matter fields helps ensure that the test is fair to students with different interests. However, no specialized knowledge in science, social studies, literature, or other fields is needed.

Antonyms (opposites)

Antonym questions primarily test the extent of your vocabulary. The vocabulary used in the antonym questions includes words that you are likely to come across in your general reading, although some words may not be the kind you use in everyday speech.

Directions: Each question below consists of a word in capital letters, followed by five lettered words or phrases. Choose the word or phrase that is most nearly opposite in meaning to the word in capital letters. Since some of the questions require you to distinguish fine shades of meaning, consider all the choices before deciding which is best.

Example:

GOOD: (A) sour (B) bad (C) red (D) hot (E) ugly

Ⓐ ● Ⓒ Ⓓ Ⓔ

You can probably answer this example without thinking very much about the choices. However, most of the antonyms in the verbal section require more careful analysis. When you work on antonym questions, remember that:

1. Among the five choices offered, you are looking for the word that means the *opposite* of the given word. Words that have exactly the same meaning as the given word are not included among the five choices.

2. You are looking for the *best* answer. Read all of the choices before deciding which one is best, even if you feel sure you know the answer. For example:

   SUBSEQUENT: (A) primary (B) recent (C) contemporary (D) prior (E) simultaneous

   Subsequent means "following in time or order; succeeding." Someone working quickly might choose (B) *recent* because it refers to a past action and *subsequent* refers to an action in the future. However, choice (D) *prior* is the best answer. It is more nearly the opposite of *subsequent* than is *recent*.

3. Few words have exact opposites, that is, words that are opposite in all of their meanings. You should find the word that is *most nearly* opposite. For example:

   FERMENTING: (A) improvising (B) stagnating (C) wavering (D) plunging (E) dissolving

   Even though *fermenting* is normally associated with chemical reactions, whereas *stagnating* is normally associated with water, *fermenting* means "being agitated," and *stagnating* means "being motionless." Therefore, choice (B) *stagnating* is the best of the five choices.

4. You need to be flexible. A word can have several meanings. For example:

   DEPRESS: (A) force (B) allow (C) clarify (D) elate (E) loosen

   The word *depress* can mean "to push down." However, no word meaning "to lift up" is included among the choices. Therefore, you must consider another meaning of *depress*, "to sadden or discourage." Option (D) *elate* means "to fill with joy or pride." The best answer is (D) *elate*.

5. You'll often recognize a word you have encountered in your reading but have never looked up in the dictionary. If you don't know the dictionary meaning of a word but have a sense of how the word should be used, try to make up a short phrase or sentence using the word. This may give you a clue as to which choice is an opposite, even though you may not be able to define the word precisely.

   INCUMBENT: (A) conscious (B) effortless (C) optional (D) improper (E) irrelevant

   You may remember *incumbent* used in a sentence such as, "It is incumbent upon me to finish this." If you can think of such a phrase, you may be able to recognize that *incumbent* means "imposed as a duty" or "obligatory." Of the five choices, (A), (B), and (D) are in no way opposites of *incumbent* and you can easily eliminate them. Choice (E) means "not pertinent" and choice (C) means "not compulsory." Although choice (E) may look attractive, choice (C) *optional* is more nearly an exact opposite to *incumbent*. Choice (C), therefore, is the answer.

Hints for Antonyms

Answering antonyms depends on knowing the uses as well as the meanings of words, so just memorizing word lists is probably of little value. You're more likely to improve your performance on antonyms and other kinds of verbal questions by doing things that help you to think about words and the way they are used. So, it would be a good idea to:

✓ Read books or magazines on subjects with which you're not already familiar. This will give you an idea of how familiar words can have different meanings in different contexts.

✓ Use a dictionary when you come across words that you don't understand. This will help to broaden your vocabulary and could improve your performance on the tests.

Analogies

Analogy questions test your ability to see a relationship in a pair of words, to understand the ideas expressed in the relationship, and to recognize a similar or parallel relationship.

Directions: Each question below consists of a related pair of words or phrases, followed by five lettered pairs of words or phrases. Select the lettered pair that best expresses a relationship similar to that expressed in the original pair.

Example:
YAWN : BOREDOM : : (A) dream : sleep (B) anger : madness (C) smile : amusement (D) face : expression (E) impatience : rebellion

Ⓐ Ⓑ ● Ⓓ Ⓔ

The first step in answering an analogy question is to establish a precise relationship between the original pair of words (the two capitalized words). In the example above, the relationship between *yawn* and *boredom* can best be stated as "(first word) is a physical sign of (second word)," or "(first word) is a facial expression of (second word)." The second step in answering an analogy question is to decide which of the five pairs given as choices best expresses a similar relationship. In the example above, the answer is choice (C): a (smile) is a physical sign of (amusement), or a (smile) is a facial expression of (amusement). None of the other choices shares a similar relationship with the capitalized pair of words: a *dream* is something that occurs when you are asleep, but it is not usually thought of as being a sign of *sleep* as, for example, closed eyes or a snore might be; *anger* denotes strong displeasure and *madness* can refer to rage or insanity, but neither word is a physical sign of the other; an *expression* is something that appears on a *face*, but a *face* is not a sign of an *expression*; *impatience* may lead to *rebellion* or be characteristic of a rebellious person, but *impatience* is not a physical sign of *rebellion*.

For the analogy below, state the relationship between the original pair of words and then decide which pair of words from choices (A) to (E) has a similar or parallel relationship.

SUBMISSIVE : LED : : (A) wealthy : employed (B) intolerant : indulged (C) humble : humiliated (D) incorrigible : taught (E) inconspicuous : overlooked

The relationship between *submissive* and *led* can be expressed as "to be submissive is to be easily led." Only choice (E) has the same relationship: "to be inconspicuous is to be easily overlooked." To be *intolerant* is not to be easily *indulged*, to be *humble* is not to be easily *humiliated*, and to be *incorrigible* (or incapable of being reformed) is not to be easily *taught*. With regard to choice (A), the statement "to be wealthy is to be easily employed" is an expression of opinion and not an expression of the relationship between the words according to their dictionary meanings.

Practice describing verbal relationships. Below are some examples of the kinds of relationships that could be used.

SONG : REPERTOIRE : : (A) score : melody (B) instrument : artist (C) solo : chorus (D) benediction : church (E) suit : wardrobe

The best answer is choice (E). The relationship between the words can be expressed as "several (first word) make up a (second word)." Several (songs) make up a (repertoire) as several (suits) make up a (wardrobe).

REQUEST : ENTREAT : : (A) control : explode (B) admire : idolize (C) borrow : steal (D) repeat : plead (E) cancel : invalidate

The best answer is choice (B). Although both of the capitalized words have similar meanings, they express different degrees of feeling; to (entreat) is to (request) with strong feeling as to (idolize) is to (admire) with strong feeling. To answer analogy questions, you must think carefully about the precise meanings of words. For instance, if you thought the word "entreat" meant only "to ask" instead of "to ask urgently," you would have trouble establishing the correct relationship between *request* and *entreat.*

FAMINE : STARVATION : : (A) deluge : flood (B) drought : vegetation (C) war : treaty (D) success : achievement (E) seed : mutation

The best answer is (A). The relationship can be stated as (famine) results in (starvation) as a (deluge) results in a (flood). None of the other pairs of words expresses a causal relationship. (C) is close, since a *treaty* often follows a *war,* but we do not think of a war "causing" a treaty in the same way that a famine "causes" starvation.

AMPLIFIER : HEAR : : (A) turntable : listen (B) typewriter : spell (C) platter : eat (D) camera : feel (E) microscope : see

The best answer is choice (E). An (amplifier) magnifies in order to help a person (hear) in the same way that a (microscope) magnifies in order to help a person (see). Note that, in (A), while a *turntable* is part of a larger mechanism that allows a person to *listen,* the choice is not as good an answer as (E) because a *turntable* does not magnify anything. Choice (D) is also wrong for a similar reason: a *camera* produces pictures that may make a person *feel* something, but a *camera* does not magnify in order to help a person *feel.*

Some choices may have relationships that are close but not parallel to the relationship in the original pair. However, the correct answer has *most nearly* the same relationship as the original pair. Look at the following:

KNIFE : INCISION : : (A) bulldozer : excavation (B) tool : operation (C) pencil : calculation (D) hose : irrigation (E) plow : agriculture

On the most general level, the relationship between *knife* and *incision* is that the object indicated by the first word is used to perform the action indicated by the second word. Since "a (knife) is used to make an (incision)," "a (bulldozer) is used to make an (excavation)," and "a (hose) is used for (irrigation)," there appear to be two correct answers. You need to go back and state the relationship more precisely. Some aspect of the relationship between the original pair exists in only one of the choices. A more precise relationship between *knife* and *incision* could be expressed as: "a knife cuts into something to make an incision" and "a bulldozer cuts into something to make an excavation." This relationship eliminates *hose : irrigation* as a possible answer. The best answer is choice (A).

Remember that a pair of words can have more than one relationship. For example:

PRIDE : LION : : (A) snake : python (B) pack : wolf (C) rat : mouse (D) bird : starling (E) dog : canine

A possible relationship between *pride* and *lion* might be that "the first word describes a characteristic of the second (especially in mythology)." Using this reasoning, you might look for an answer such as *wisdom : owl,* but none of the given choices has that kind of relationship. Another relationship between *pride* and *lion* is "a group of lions is called a pride"; therefore, the answer is (B) *pack : wolf,* since "a group of wolves is called a pack."

Hints for Analogies

✓ State the relationship between the two capitalized words in a sentence or phrase as clearly as you can. Next, find the pair of words that has the most similar or parallel relationship. Don't be misled by choices that merely suggest a vague association. Be sure that you can identify a specific relationship.

✓ Always compare the relationship between the pair of capitalized words with the relationship between the pair of words in each of the choices. Don't try to set up a relationship between the first word in the original pair and the first word in each of the five choices.

✓ Think carefully about the meanings of words. The words in analogy questions are used according to their dictionary definitions or meanings closely related to their dictionary definitions. The better you know the precise meanings of words, the less trouble you'll have establishing the correct relationships between them.

✓ Don't be misled by relationships that are close but not parallel to the relationship in the original pair. The correct answer has a relationship that is most nearly parallel to the relationship between the capitalized words.

Sentence Completion Questions

Sentence completion questions test your ability to recognize relationships among parts of a sentence. Each question has a sentence with one or two words missing. Below the sentence, five words or pairs of words are given. You must choose the word or set of words that best fits with the other parts of the sentence. In sentence completion questions, you have to know the meanings of the words offered as choices and you also have to know how to use those words properly in the context of a sentence. The sentences are taken from published material and cover a wide variety of topics. You'll find that, even if you're not familiar with the topic of a sentence, there's enough information in the sentence for you to find the correct answer from the context of the sentence itself.

Directions: Each sentence below has one or two blanks, each blank indicating that something has been omitted. Beneath the sentence are five lettered words or sets of words. Choose the word or set of words that, when inserted in the sentence, best fits the meaning of the sentence as a whole.

Example:
Although its publicity has been ----, the film itself is intelligent, well-acted, handsomely produced, and altogether ----.

(A) tasteless . . respectable (B) extensive . . moderate (C) sophisticated . . amateur (D) risqué . . crude (E) perfect . . spectacular

● (B) (C) (D) (E)

The word *although* suggests that the publicity gave the wrong impression of the movie, so look for two words that are more or less opposite in meaning. Also, the second word has to fit in with "intelligent, well-acted, handsomely produced." Choices (D) and (E) are not opposites. The words in choice (B) are somewhat opposite in meaning, but do not logically fulfill the expectation set up by the word *although*. Choice (C) can't be the correct answer, even though *sophisticated* and *amateur* are nearly opposites, because an "intelligent, well-acted, handsomely produced" film isn't amateurish. Only choice (A), when inserted in the sentence, makes a logical statement.

For a better understanding of sentence completion questions, read the following sample questions and explanations.

Nearly all the cultivated plants utilized by the Chinese have been of ---- origin; even rice, though known in China since Neolithic times, came from India.

(A) foreign (B) ancient (C) wild (D) obscure (E) common

To answer this question, you need to consider the entire sentence—the part that comes after the semicolon as well as the part that comes before it. If you only consider the first part of the question, all five choices seem plausible. The second part of the sentence adds a specific example—that rice came to China from India. This idea of origin supports and clarifies the "origin" mentioned in the first part of the sentence and eliminates (C), (D), and (E) as possible answers. The mention of Neolithic times makes (B) harder to eliminate, but the sentence is not logical when (B) is used to fill in the blank because the emphasis in the second part of the sentence—country of origin—is inconsistent with that in the first—age. Only choice (A) produces a sentence that is logical and consistent.

The excitement does not ---- but ---- his senses, giving him a keener perception of a thousand details.

(A) slow . . diverts (B) blur . . sharpens (C) overrule . . constricts (D) heighten . . aggravates (E) forewarn . . quickens

Since the sentence has two blanks to be filled, you must make sure that both words make sense in the sentence. If you look for grammatical clues within the sentence, you will see that the word *but* implies that the answer will involve two words that are more or less opposite in meaning. If you keep this in mind, you can eliminate all of the choices except for (B) *blur . . sharpens*. Only the words in choice (B) imply opposition. Also, "sharpens his senses" is consistent with the notion that he has a "keener perception of a thousand details."

They argue that the author was determined to ---- his own conclusion, so he ---- any information that did not support it.

(A) uphold . . ignored (B) revise . . destroyed (C) advance . . devised (D) disprove . . distorted (E) reverse . . confiscated

The logic of the sentence makes it fairly easy to eliminate choices (B), (D), and (E). The first word in choice (A), *uphold*, and the first word in (C), *advance*, seem all right. However, the second word in choice (C), *devised*, does not make sense in the sentence. Why would an author who wished to advance his theory devise information that did not support it? Only choice (A) makes a logically consistent sentence.

She is a skeptic, ---- to believe that the accepted opinion of the majority is generally ----.

(A) prone . . infallible (B) afraid . . misleading (C) inclined . . justifiable (D) quick . . significant (E) disposed . . erroneous

The words to be inserted in the blank spaces in the question above must result in a statement that is consistent with the definition of a skeptic. Since a skeptic would hardly consider the accepted opinion of the majority as *infallible, justifiable,* or *significant,* you can eliminate choices (A), (C), and (D). A skeptic would not be afraid that the accepted opinion of the majority is misleading; a skeptic would believe that it was. Therefore, choice (B) is not correct. Only choice (E) *disposed . . erroneous* makes a logical sentence.

Hints for Sentence Completions

✓Read the entire sentence carefully; make sure you understand the ideas being expressed.

✓Don't select an answer simply because it is a popular cliché or "sounds good."

✓In a question with two blanks, the right answer must correctly fill both blanks. A wrong answer choice often includes one correct and one incorrect word.

✓After choosing an answer, read the entire sentence to yourself and make sure that it makes sense.

✓Consider all the choices; be sure you haven't overlooked a choice that makes a better and more accurate sentence than your choice does.

Reading Comprehension Questions

The reading comprehension questions on the SAT test your ability to read and understand a passage. The test generally will have one passage taken from each of the following six categories:

Narrative:	novels, short stories, biographies, essays, etc.
Biological Science:	medicine, botany, zoology, etc.
Physical Science:	chemistry, physics, astronomy, etc.
Humanities:	art, literature, music, philosophy, folklore, etc.
Social Studies:	history, economics, sociology, government, etc.
Argumentative:	the presentation of a definite point of view on some subject

Each passage contains all the information you'll need to answer the questions that follow it.

Several types of questions are asked about the passage. Some ask about the main idea of a passage. Some ask about those ideas that are stated directly in the passage. Some ask you to recognize applications of the author's principles or opinions. In some questions you must make an inference from what you have read. And in others you must evaluate the way the author develops and presents the passage.

Following are a sample passage, sample questions, and explanations of each of the questions.

Directions: The passages below are followed by questions based on their content. Answer the questions following each passage on the basis of what is stated or implied in that passage and any introductory material that may be provided.

Any survey of medieval town life delights in the color of guild organizations: the broiders and glovers, the shipwrights and upholsters, each with its guild hall, its distinctive livery, and its elaborate set of rules. But if life in the guilds and at the fairs provides a sharp contrast with the stodgy life on the manor, we must not be misled by surface resemblances into thinking that guild life represented a foretaste of modern life in medieval dress. It is a long distance from guilds to modern business firms, and it is well to fix in mind some of the differences.

In the first place, the guild was much more than just an institution for organizing production. Whereas most of its regulations concerned wages and conditions of work and specifications of output, they also dwelt at length on noneconomic matters: on a member's civic role, on his appropriate dress, and even on his daily deportment. Guilds were the regulators not only of production but of social conduct.

Between guilds and modern business firms there is a profound gulf. Unlike modern firms, the purpose of guilds was not

first and foremost to make money. Rather, it was to preserve a certain orderly way of life—a way which envisaged a decent income for the master craftsmen but which was certainly not intended to allow any of them to become "big" businessmen. On the contrary, guilds were specifically designed to ward off any such outcome of an uninhibited struggle among their members. The terms of service and wages were fixed by custom. So, too, were the terms of sale: a guild member who cornered the supply of an item or bought wholesale to sell at retail was severely punished. Competition was strictly limited and profits were held to prescribed levels. Advertising was forbidden, and even technical progress in advance of one's fellow guildsmen was considered disloyal.

Surely the guilds represent a more "modern" aspect of feudal life than the manor, but the whole temper of guild life was still far removed from the goals and ideals of modern business enterprise. There was no free competition and no restless probing for advantage. Existing on the margin of a relatively moneyless society, the guilds were organizations that sought to take the risks out of their slender enterprises. As such, they were as drenched in the medieval atmosphere as the manors.

Following are sample questions about this passage. You may be asked to identify the main idea or primary focus of the passage. For example:

1. The author is primarily concerned with

(A) analyzing the origins of the guild system
(B) explaining the relationship between manors, fairs, and modern business firms
(C) depicting the weaknesses of the guilds' business practices
(D) stressing the historical evolution of guilds to modern business firms
(E) discussing some differences between medieval and modern business practices

The answer to the question is (E). The passage compares medieval business practices, as represented by the guilds, with modern business practices. The author describes the guilds and suggests some ways in which they differ from contemporary business organizations. The most concise statement of what the author intends to discuss in the passage is made at the end of the first paragraph in lines 8-10. Choice (A) is incorrect because the passage does not mention the origins of the guild system. Choice (B) is unacceptable because the author's main comparison is not between manors, fairs, and modern business firms, even though all are mentioned in the passage. Choices (C) and (D) are slightly harder to eliminate. Readers who think that the author is criticizing the guilds by pointing out the ways in which they differ from modern business enterprise are mistaken; there is no evidence in the passage to suggest that the author wants either to praise or to criticize the guilds. Choice (D) mentions the author's main concerns—guilds and modern business firms—but is incorrect because the passage does not deal with the evolution from medieval to modern practices.

Another type of question asks about details stated in the passage. Sometimes this type of question asks about a particular phrase or line; at other times, the part or parts of the passage referred to are not as precisely identified. For example:

2. According to the passage, modern business enterprises, compared to the medieval guilds, are

(A) more concerned with increasing profits
(B) influenced more by craftsmen than by tradesmen
(C) more subordinate to the demands of consumers
(D) less progressive in financial dealings
(E) less interested in quantity than quality

To answer this question, locate the parts of the passage that compare guilds and modern business—the beginnings of the third and fourth paragraphs. Lines 19-20 suggest that the foremost purpose of modern firms is to make money. Lines 34-37 indicate that "free competition" and "restless probing for advantage" are central to modern business enterprise. Choice (A) is the most appropriate answer among the choices given. There is no justification in the passage for any of the other choices. Some people might argue from their own experience or opinion that (C) is a possible answer. However, since the question says, "According to the passage . . .," the answer must be based on what is stated in the passage.

Some questions ask you to make inferences based on the passage. For example:

3. It can be inferred that the guilds were organized as they were because

(A) life on the manors was boring and drab
(B) technical improvements were still improbable
(C) they stressed preservation and stability, not progress
(D) people in medieval times were interested in advancing individual liberty
(E) social status was determined by income

This question is not answered simply and directly in the passage itself, but the passage gives you information to draw on. In the third paragraph, the author notes that the purpose of guilds "was to preserve a certain orderly way of life" and that guilds were specifically designed "to ward off . . . uninhibited struggle among their members." In the fourth paragraph, the author states that the guilds "were organizations that sought to take the risks out of their slender enterprises." From these statements and the comparisons between guilds and modern business firms that the author makes elsewhere in the passage, choice (C) is the most reasonable conclusion to draw. Choice (A) is stated in the passage, but is not related to the purpose of the organization of the guilds. The statement about technical progress made in lines 31-32 weakens the plausibility of the inference in (B). The passage doesn't provide enough information to justify the inferences made in (D) and (E). This is a fairly easy and straightforward inference question. You may be asked others that will require somewhat more sophisticated reasoning processes.

Other types of questions ask you to apply information in the passage to situations that are not specifically mentioned in the passage or to evaluate the author's logic, organization, attitude, tone, or language. Following is an example of one type of question that asks you to apply information given in the passage.

4. According to the passage, which of the following would LEAST likely be found in a guild handbook?

(A) The fees a master guildsman should charge
(B) The bonus a member would receive for record sales
(C) The maximum number of hours a guildsman would be expected to work
(D) The steps a new shipwright would follow to become a master craftsman
(E) The organizations to which a member should contribute as an upstanding citizen

To answer this question, you must decide which of the five choices is <u>least</u> likely to have been included in a guild handbook. The passage does not mention a handbook, but it does provide enough information about the areas of business and personal life that the guilds attempted to regulate to enable you to make reasoned judgments. The passage suggests that (A), (C), and (E) would definitely be included in such a handbook and that (D) would be a logical area of concern and regulation for a guild. Choice (B) seems to be the least likely area of regulation and is, therefore, the correct answer. In fact, the statements made in the passage about the purpose of the guilds—to enable all master craftsmen to earn a decent income and to discourage ruthless competition among members—suggest that offering a bonus for record sales would indeed be an unlikely activity for a guild to engage in.

The question below is another type of evaluation question.

5. With which of the following statements concerning modern business firms would the author be most likely to agree?

(A) They make rules concerning appropriate business practices for employees.
(B) They permit the free play of price in terms of service and sales.
(C) Their main concern is the stability of profit levels.
(D) Their aim is to discourage competition among independent manufacturers.
(E) They are organized in such a way that cooperating monopolies will develop.

Paragraphs three and four provide information about the author's characterization of modern business practices and support choice (B) as the correct response. Choices (A), (C), and (D) are more true of guilds than of modern business firms. There is little or nothing in the passage to support (E) as the answer; the author stresses the competition rather than the cooperation of modern businesses. When answering such questions, remember to read the question carefully and to look for evidence in the passage to support your choice. In this question, for example, you are not asked which of the statements about modern business is true or which of the statements you agree with, but which one the author is most likely to agree with based on what he or she has written in the passage. Sometimes questions that ask for the <u>most</u> likely or <u>least</u> likely answer require you to make careful distinctions between choices that are partly correct and those that are more complete or more accurate.

Hints for Reading Comprehension Questions

✓Read each passage carefully. Follow the author's reasoning. Notice attitude, tone, and general style.

✓You may want to mark an important fact or idea, but don't waste too much time underlining or making notes in the margin of the test book. Try to get a sense of the principal ideas, facts, and organization of the passage.

✓A passage with a subject that is familiar or interesting to you may be easier for you than a passage that is about an unfamiliar subject. If a passage seems too difficult, you might want to skip it and go on. You would be omitting only a few questions and saving yourself time. You can always return to that passage if you finish before time is up for that section of the test.

✓You might want to read the questions before you read the passage so that you have a sense of what to look for. But if the content of the passage is familiar, looking at the questions before you read the passage might be a waste of time. Try both methods when taking the sample test in this booklet and see if one approach is more helpful than the other.

✓Answer questions on the basis of what is *stated* or *implied* in the passage. Don't answer questions on the basis of your personal opinion or knowledge.

✓Read all of the choices before you choose your answer.

✓Answer the question that is asked. Don't pick one of the choices simply because you know it's a true statement.

✓Make sure the answer you choose is the best among the choices given. Don't be misled by choices that are partially true.

✓In answering questions about the main idea of the passage, don't be distracted by statements that are true according to the passage but that are secondary to the central point.

Mathematical Sections of the SAT

Some questions in the mathematical sections of the SAT are like the questions in your math textbooks. Other questions ask you to do original thinking and may not be as familiar to you. The questions are designed for students who have had a year of algebra and some geometry. Many of the geometric ideas involved are usually taught in the elementary and junior high years, but a few of the questions involve topics that are first taught in high school geometry. Most of the questions are classified as arithmetic, algebra, or geometry, and there is approximately an equal number of each type.

When you take the SAT, remember to use the available space in the test book for scratchwork. You are not expected to do all the reasoning and figuring in your head.

Following is a review of some specific words, phrases, and concepts you should know. Sample questions and explanations follow the review. The two types of questions that appear in the mathematical sections are explained separately.

Mathematics Review

Some Mathematical Concepts with Which You Should Be Familiar

Arithmetic—simple addition, subtraction, multiplication, and division; percent; average; odd and even numbers; prime numbers; divisibility (for example, 24 is divisible by 8 but not by 5)

Algebra—negative numbers; simplifying algebraic expressions; factoring; linear equations; inequalities; simple quadratic equations; positive integer exponents; roots

Geometry—area (square, rectangle, triangle, and circle); perimeter of a polygon; circumference of a circle; volume of a box and cube; special properties of isosceles, equilateral, and right triangles; 30°-60°-90° and 45°-45°-90° triangles; properties of parallel and perpendicular lines; locating points on a coordinate grid

Words and Phrases You Should Know

When You See:	Think:
Positive Integers	1, 2, 3, 4, . . .
Negative Integers	−1, −2, −3, −4, . . .
Integers	. . . , −4, −3, −2, −1, 0, 1, 2, 3, 4, . . .
Odd Numbers	±1, ±3, ±5, ±7, ±9, . . .
Even Numbers	0, ±2, ±4, ±6, ±8, . . .
Consecutive Integers	n, n + 1, n + 2, . . . (n = an integer)
Prime Numbers	2, 3, 5, 7, 11, 13, 17, 19, . . .

Arithmetic and Algebraic Concepts You Should Know

Odd and Even Numbers

Addition:
- even + even = even
- odd + odd = even
- even + odd = odd

Multiplication:
- even × even = even
- even × odd = even
- odd × odd = odd

Percent

Percent means hundredths or number out of 100, so that $\frac{40}{100}$ = 40 percent and 3 is 75 percent of 4 (because $\frac{3}{4} = \frac{75}{100}$ = 75 percent).

Some Percent Equivalents:

$\frac{1}{10} = 0.1 = 10\%$

$\frac{1}{5} = 0.2 = 20\%$

$\frac{1}{2} = 0.5 = 50\%$

$\frac{1}{1} = 1.0 = 100\%$

$\frac{2}{1} = 2.0 = 200\%$

Note: To convert a fraction or decimal to a percent, multiply by 100.

General Method of Converting a Fraction $\frac{a}{b}$ to a Percent:

$\frac{a}{b} = \frac{x}{100}$

$x = 100\left(\frac{a}{b}\right)$

Example: $\frac{3}{4} = \frac{x}{100}$

Therefore, $x = 100\left(\frac{3}{4}\right) = 75$

$\frac{3}{4} = \frac{75}{100} = 75\%$

Percents Greater Than 100

Problem: 5 is what percent of 2?

Solution 1: $\frac{5}{2} = \frac{x}{100}$

$$x = \frac{500}{2} = 250$$

Therefore, 5 is 250 percent of 2.

Solution 2: "5 is what percent of 2?" is equivalent to

$$5 = \frac{x}{100} \cdot 2 = \frac{2x}{100}$$

$$500 = 2x$$

$$x = 250$$

This solution is a fairly direct translation of the question into an algebraic statement as follows:

$$\underbrace{5}_{5\ =}\ \text{is}\ \underbrace{\text{what percent}}_{\frac{x}{100}}\ \underbrace{\text{of 2?}}_{\cdot\ 2}$$

Note that saying 5 is 250 percent of 2 is equivalent to saying that 5 is $2\frac{1}{2}$ times 2.

Problem: Sue earned \$10 on Monday and \$12 on Tuesday. The amount earned on Tuesday was what percent of the amount earned on Monday?

An equivalent question is "\$12 is what percent of \$10?"

Solution: $\frac{12}{10} = \frac{x}{100}$

$$x = \frac{1{,}200}{10} = 120$$

So, $\frac{12}{10} = \frac{120}{100} = 120\%$

Percents Less Than 1

Problem: 3 is what percent of 1,000?

Solution: $\frac{3}{1{,}000} = 0.003 = 0.3\%$ or $\frac{3}{10}$ of 1 percent

Problem: Socks are \$1.00 a pair or 2 pairs for \$1.99. The savings in buying 2 pairs is what percent of the total cost at the single pair rate?

Solution: At the single pair rate, 2 pairs would cost \$2.00, so the savings is only \$0.01. Therefore, you must answer the question "\$0.01 is what percent of \$2.00?" Because $\frac{0.01}{2.00} = \frac{0.5}{100}$, the savings is 0.5% or $\frac{1}{2}$ of 1 percent.

Average

The most common mathematical meaning of the word *average* is the arithmetic mean. The average (arithmetic mean) of a set of n numbers is the sum of the numbers divided by n. For example, the average of 10, 20, and 27 is

$$\frac{10 + 20 + 27}{3} = \frac{57}{3} = 19$$

Unless otherwise indicated, the term *average* will be used on the mathematical portion of the SAT to denote the arithmetic mean. Questions involving the average can take several forms. Some of these are illustrated below.

Finding the Average of Algebraic Expressions

Problem: Find the average of $(3x + 1)$ and $(x - 3)$.

Solution: $\frac{(3x + 1) + (x - 3)}{2} = \frac{4x - 2}{2} = 2x - 1$

Finding a Missing Number if Certain Averages Are Known

Problem: The average of a set of 10 numbers is 15. If one of these numbers is removed from the set, the average of the remaining numbers is 14. What is the value of the number removed?

Solution: The sum of the original 10 numbers is $10 \cdot 15 = 150$. The sum of the remaining 9 numbers is $9 \cdot 14 = 126$. Therefore, the value of the number removed must be $150 - 126 = 24$.

Finding a Weighted Average

Problem: In a group of 10 students, 7 are 13 years old and 3 are 17 years old. What is the average of the ages of these 10 students?

Solution: The solution is *not* the average of 13 and 17, which is 15. In this case the average is

$$\frac{7\,(13) + 3\,(17)}{10} = \frac{91 + 51}{10} = 14.2 \text{ years}$$

The expression "weighted average" comes from the fact that 13 gets a weight factor of 7 whereas 17 gets a weight factor of 3.

Finding the Average Speed in Distance-Rate-Time Problems

Problem: Jane traveled for 2 hours at a rate of 70 kilometers per hour and for 5 hours at a rate of 60 kilometers per hour. What was her average speed for the 7-hour period?

Solution: In this situation, the average speed is:

$$\frac{\text{Total Distance}}{\text{Total Time}}$$

The total distance is $2(70) + 5(60) = 440$ km. The total time is 7 hours. Thus, the average speed was $\frac{440}{7} = 62\frac{6}{7}$ kilometers per hour. Note that in this example the average speed, $62\frac{6}{7}$, is not the average of the two separate speeds, which would be 65.

Squares of Integers

n	1	2	3	4	5	6	7	8	9	10	11	12
n^2	1	4	9	16	25	36	49	64	81	100	121	144

n	−1	−2	−3	−4	−5	−6	−7	−8	−9	−10	−11	−12
n^2	1	4	9	16	25	36	49	64	81	100	121	144

Signed Number Properties

positive × positive = positive
negative × negative = positive
negative × positive = negative
$-(a - b) = b - a$
$(-x)^2 = x^2$
If $x < 0$, $x^2 > 0$

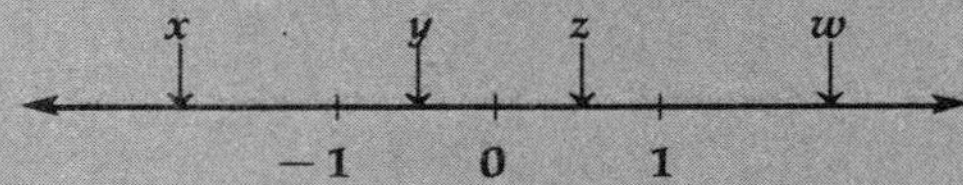

On the number line above: $x < y$ — For example, $-2 < -\frac{1}{2}$

$y^2 > 0$

$z^2 < z$ — For example, $(\frac{1}{2})^2 < \frac{1}{2}$

$x^2 > z$ — For example, $(-2)^2 > \frac{1}{2}$

$z^2 < w$

$x + z < 0$

$y - x > 0$

Note: Unless otherwise indicated, in all questions involving number lines, the numbers on the number line increase from left to right. Similarly, in questions involving the x and y axes, numbers to the right of the y axis are positive and numbers above the x axis are positive.

Factoring

$x^2 + 2x = x(x + 2)$
$x^2 - 1 = (x + 1)(x - 1)$
$x^2 + 2x + 1 = (x + 1)(x + 1) = (x + 1)^2$
$x^2 - 3x - 4 = (x - 4)(x + 1)$

Geometric Figures

Figures that accompany problems in this test are intended to provide information useful in solving the problems. They are drawn as accurately as possible EXCEPT when it is stated in a particular problem that the figure is not drawn to scale. The following examples illustrate the way figures can be interpreted.

Example 1

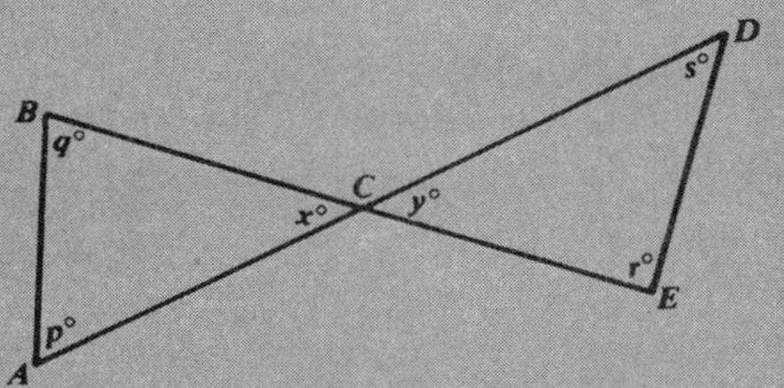

Since AD and BE are line segments, ACB and DCE are vertical angles, and you can conclude that $x = y$. You should NOT assume that $AC = CD$, that $p = 60$, or that the angle at vertex E is a right angle even though they might appear that way.

Example 2

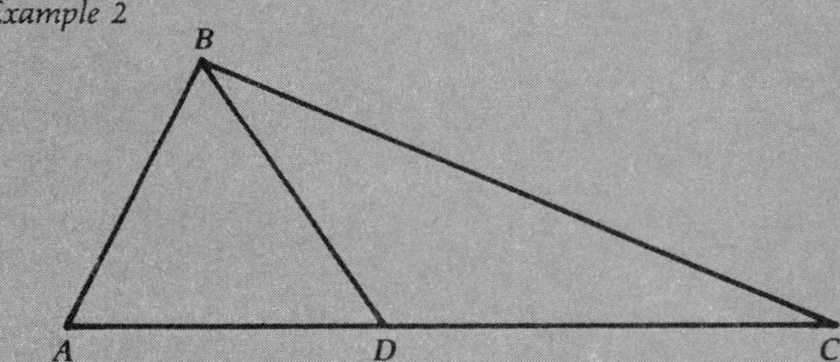

Note: Figure not drawn to scale.

Although the note indicates that $\triangle ABC$ is not drawn to scale, you may assume that:

(1) ABD and DBC are triangles.
(2) D is between A and C.
(3) ADC is a straight line.
(4) Length $AD <$ length AC
(5) Measure $\angle ABD <$ measure $\angle ABC$

You may not assume the following:

(1) Length $AD <$ length DC
(2) Measure $\angle BAD =$ measure $\angle BDA$
(3) Measure $\angle DBC <$ measure $\angle ABD$
(4) $\angle ABC$ is a right angle.

Example 3

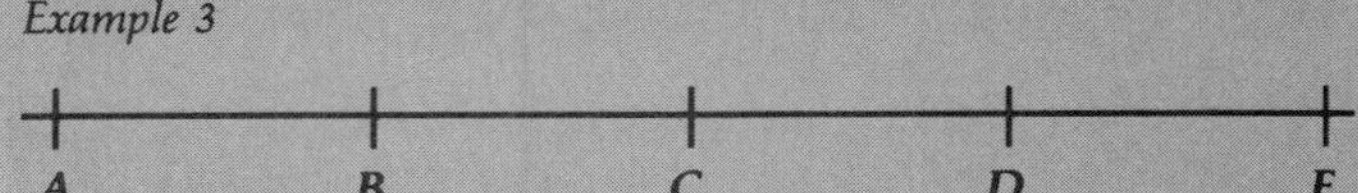

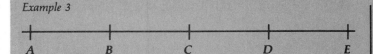

Note: Figure not drawn to scale.

Given: $AC = 10$, $AE = 18$, $BC = 6$

The figure above is not drawn to scale. However, the lengths of three of the line segments are given, and these lengths can be used to determine the lengths of certain other segments. For example,

$$AB = AC - BC = 10 - 6 = 4$$

$$CE = AE - AC = 18 - 10 = 8$$

However, from the information given, it is not possible to determine the length of either CD or DE.

In general, even when figures are not drawn to scale, the relative positions of points and angles may be assumed to be in the order shown. Also, line segments that extend through points and appear to lie on the same line may be assumed to be on the same line, as illustrated in the three figures above. The note that a figure is not drawn to scale is used when specific lengths and degree measures may not be accurately shown.

Geometric Skills and Concepts

Properties of Parallel Lines

1. If two parallel lines are cut by a third line, the alternate interior angles are equal.
   For example:

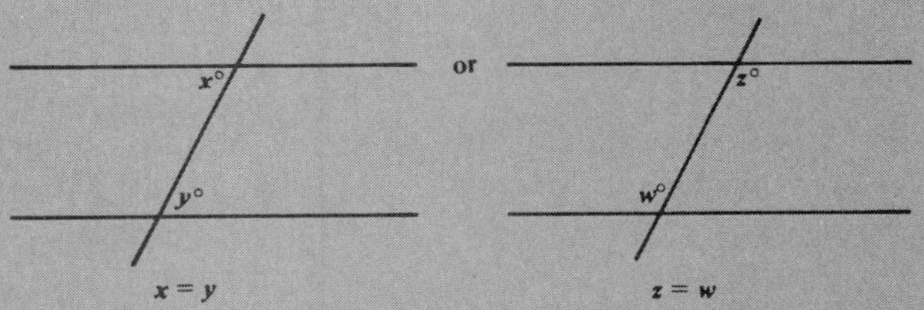

2. If two parallel lines are cut by a third line, the corresponding angles are equal.
   For example:

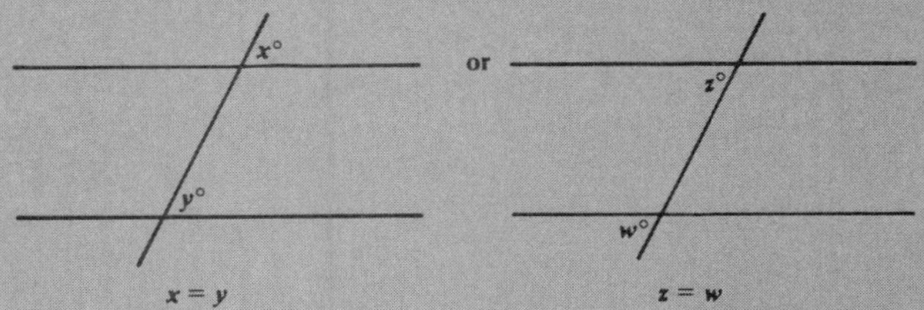

Note: Words like "alternate interior" or "corresponding" are generally not used on the test, but you do need to know which angles are equal.

Angle Relationships

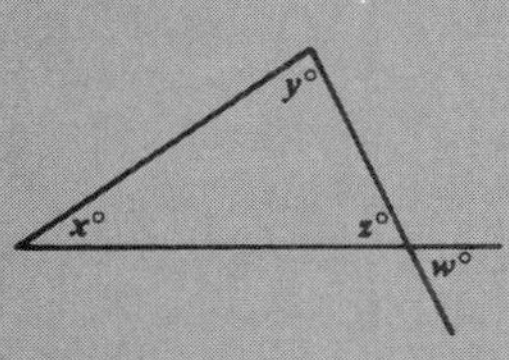

$x + y + z = 180$
(Because the sum of the interior angles of a triangle is 180°)

$z = w$
(When two straight lines intersect, vertical angles are equal.)

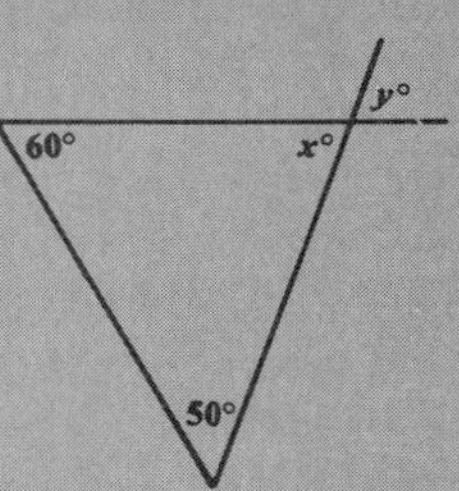

$y = 70$
(Because x is equal to y and $60 + 50 + x = 180$)

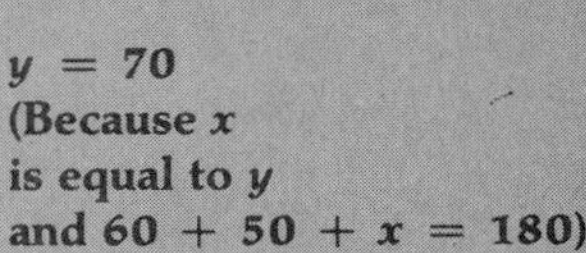

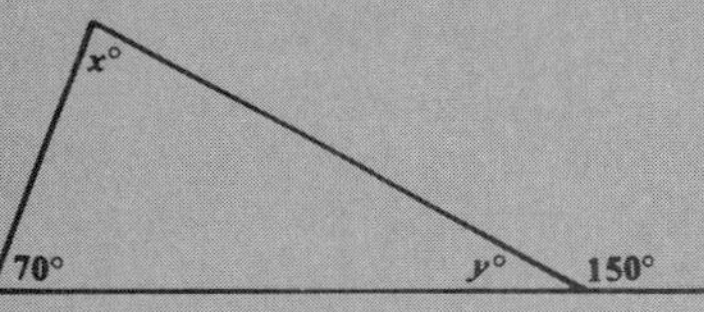

$y = 30$
(Because a straight angle is 180°, $y = 180 - 150$)

$x = 80$
(Because $70 + 30 + x = 180$)

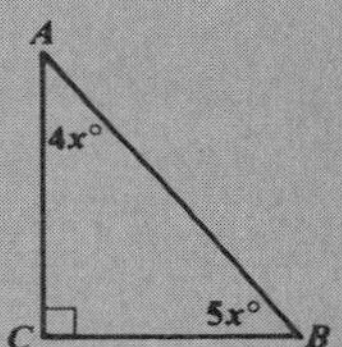

$x = 10$
(Because $4x + 5x = 90°$) Also, the length of side AC is greater than the length of side BC (Because $\angle B$ is greater than $\angle A$)

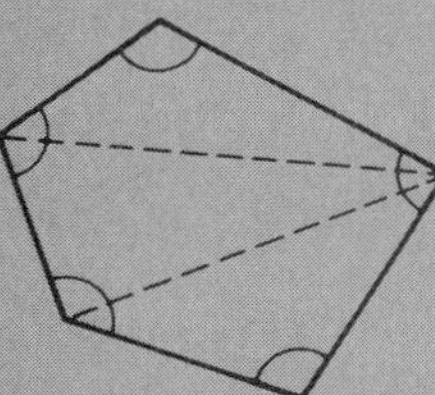

The sum of all angles of the polygon above is 3 (180°) = 540° because it can be divided into 3 triangles, each containing 180°.

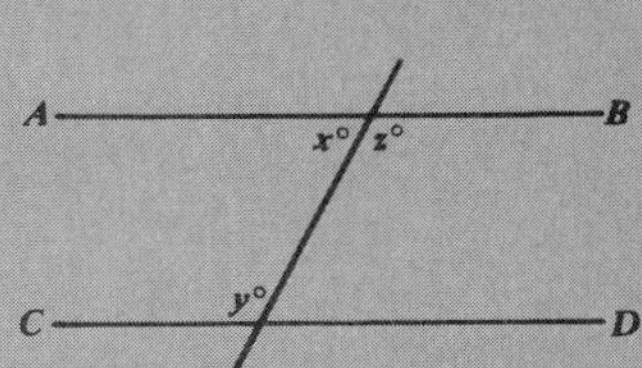

If AB is parallel to CD, then $x + y = 180$
(Because $x + z = 180$ and $y = z$)

Side Relationships

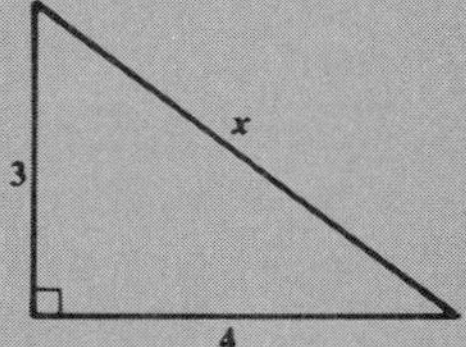

$x = 5$
(By the Pythagorean Theorem,
$x^2 = 3^2 + 4^2$
$x^2 = 9 + 16$
$x^2 = 25$
$x = \sqrt{25} = 5$)

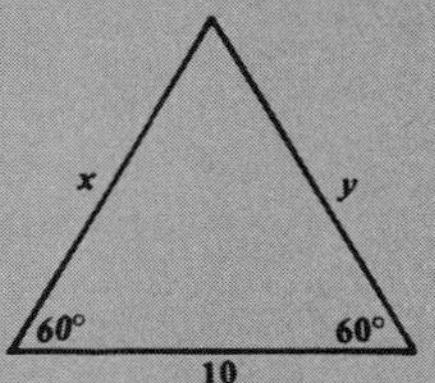

$x = y = 10$
(Because the unmarked angle is 60°, all angles of the triangle are equal, and, therefore, all sides of the triangle are equal)

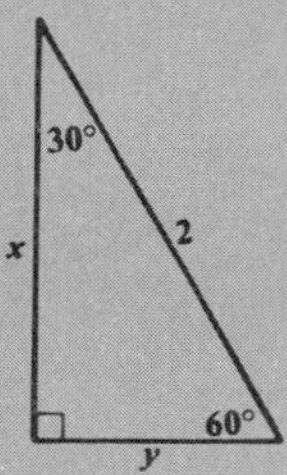

$y = 1$
(Because the length of the side opposite the 30° angle in a right triangle is half the length of the hypotenuse)

$x = \sqrt{3}$
(By the Pythagorean Theorem,
$x^2 + 1^2 = 2^2$
$x^2 = 3$
$x = \sqrt{3}$)

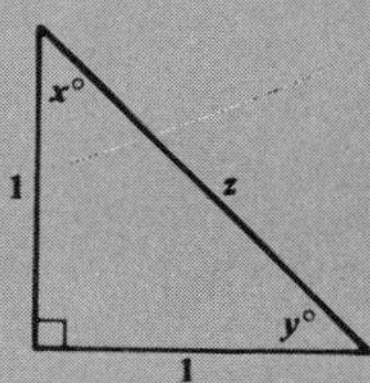

$x = y = 45°$
(Because two sides are equal, the right triangle is isosceles and angles x and y are equal. Also, $x + y = 90$ which makes both angles 45°)

$z = \sqrt{2}$
(Because $1^2 + 1^2 = z^2$)

Area and Perimeter Formulas

Area of a rectangle = length × width = $L \times W$
Perimeter of a rectangle = $2(L + W)$

Examples:

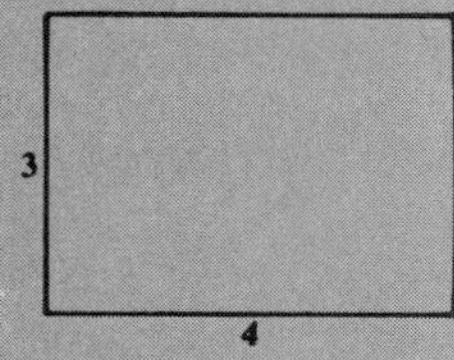

Area = 12

Perimeter = 14

Area = $(x - 3)(x + 3) = x^2 - 9$

Perimeter = $2[(x + 3) + (x - 3)] = 2(2x) = 4x$

Area of a circle = πr^2 (where r is the radius)
Circumference of a circle = $2\pi r = \pi d$ (where d is the diameter)

Examples:

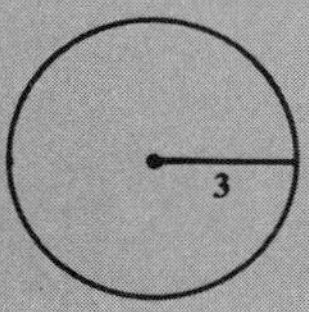

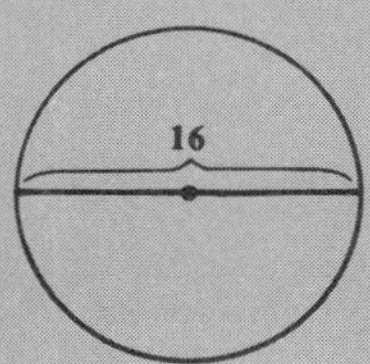

Area = $\pi(3^2) = 9\pi$
Circumference = $2\pi(3) = 6\pi$

Area = $\pi(8^2) = 64\pi$
Circumference = $\pi(16) = 16\pi$

Area of a triangle = $\frac{1}{2}$(base × altitude)

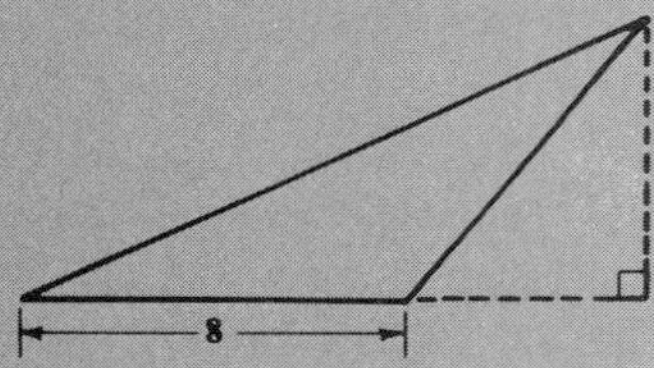

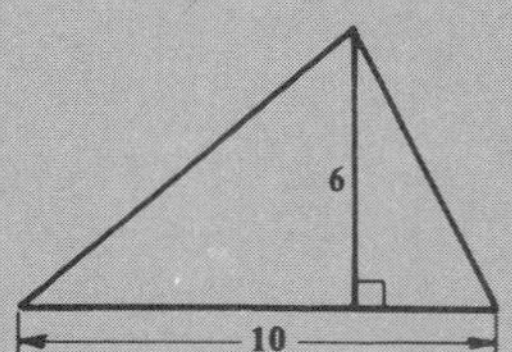

Area = $\frac{1}{2} \cdot 8 \cdot 6 = 24$

Area = $\frac{1}{2} \cdot 10 \cdot 6 = 30$

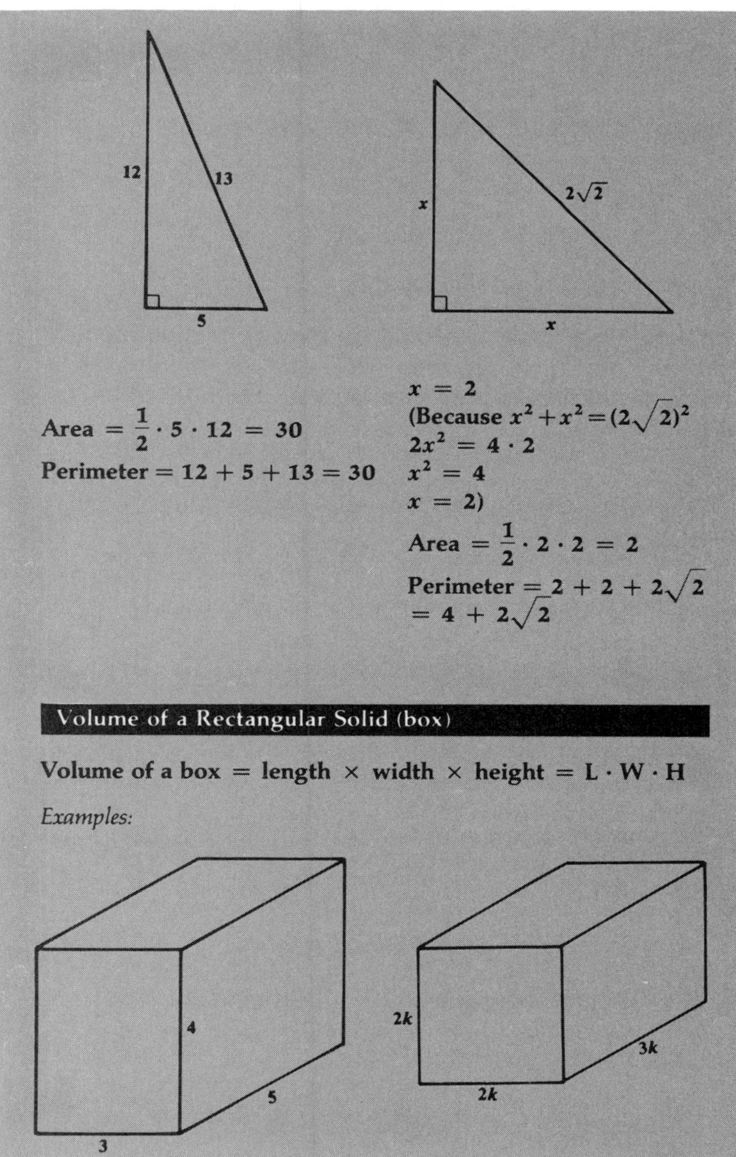

12
13
5
x
$2\sqrt{2}$
x
Area $= \frac{1}{2} \cdot 5 \cdot 12 = 30$
Perimeter $= 12 + 5 + 13 = 30$
$x = 2$
(Because $x^2 + x^2 = (2\sqrt{2})^2$
$2x^2 = 4 \cdot 2$
$x^2 = 4$
$x = 2$)
Area $= \frac{1}{2} \cdot 2 \cdot 2 = 2$
Perimeter $= 2 + 2 + 2\sqrt{2}$
$= 4 + 2\sqrt{2}$
Volume of a Rectangular Solid (box)
Volume of a box = length × width × height = L · W · H
Examples:
4
5
3
2k
3k
2k

Volume $= 5 \cdot 3 \cdot 4 = 60$ Volume $= (3k)(2k)(2k) = 12k^3$

Two types of multiple-choice questions are used in the mathematical sections of the SAT:

1. Standard multiple-choice questions (approximately two-thirds of the math questions)

2. Quantitative comparison questions (approximately one-third of the math questions)

The formulas and symbols given in the directions that follow appear in the test book. Learning them now will help you when you take the actual test.

Standard Multiple-Choice Questions

Directions: **In this section solve each problem, using any available space on the page for scratchwork. Then decide which is the best of the choices given and fill in the corresponding oval on the answer sheet.**

The following information is for your reference in solving some of the problems.

Circle of radius r:
Area $= \pi r^2$;
Circumference $= 2\pi r$
The number of degrees of arc in a circle is 360.
The measure in degrees of a straight angle is 180.

Triangle: The sum of the measures in degrees of the angles of a triangle is 180.

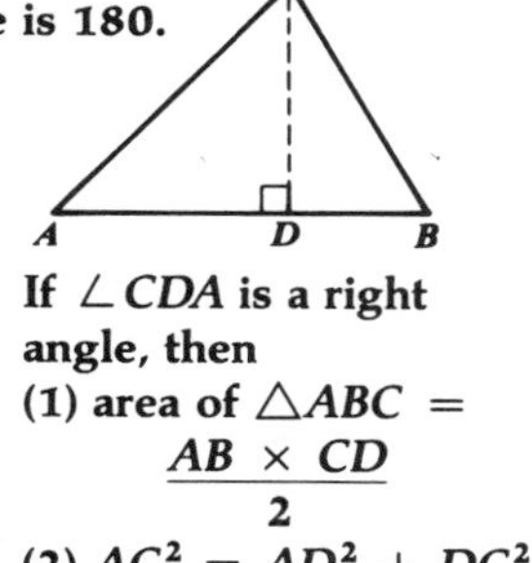

If $\angle CDA$ is a right angle, then
(1) area of $\triangle ABC = \frac{AB \times CD}{2}$
(2) $AC^2 = AD^2 + DC^2$

Definitions of symbols:

= is equal to	**≦ is less than or equal to**
≠ is unequal to	**≧ is greater than or equal to**
< is less than	**∥ is parallel to**
> is greater than	**⊥ is perpendicular to**

Note: **Figures that accompany problems in this test are intended to provide information useful in solving the problems. They are drawn as accurately as possible EXCEPT when it is stated in a specific problem that its figure is not drawn to scale. All figures lie in a plane unless otherwise indicated. All numbers used are real numbers.**

The problems that follow will give you an idea of the type of mathematical thinking required. First, try to answer each question yourself. Then read the explanation, which may give you new insights into solving the problem or point out techniques you'll be able to use again. Note that the directions indicate that you are to select the *best* of the choices given.

1. If $2a + b = 5$, then $4a + 2b =$

(A) $\frac{5}{4}$ (B) $\frac{5}{2}$ (C) 10 (D) 20 (E) 25

This is an example of a problem that requires realizing that $4a + 2b = 2(2a + b)$. Therefore, $4a + 2b = 2(2a + b) = 2(5) = 10$. The correct choice is (C).

2. If $16 \cdot 16 \cdot 16 = 8 \cdot 8 \cdot P$, then $P =$

(A) 4 (B) 8 (C) 32 (D) 48 (E) 64

This question can be solved by several methods. A time-consuming method would be to multiply the three 16s and then divide the result by the product of 8 and 8. A quicker approach would be to find what additional factors are needed on the right side of the equation to match those on the left side. These additional factors are two 2s and a 16, the product of which is 64. Yet another method involves solving for P as follows:

$$P = \frac{\overset{2}{\cancel{16}} \cdot \overset{2}{\cancel{16}} \cdot 16}{\cancel{8} \cdot \cancel{8}} = 2 \cdot 2 \cdot 16 = 64$$

The correct choice is (E).

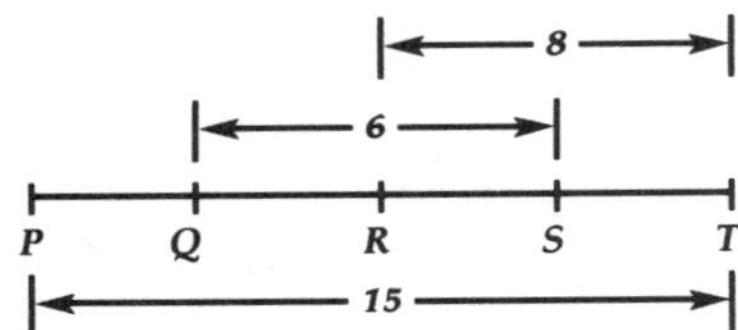

Note: **Figure not drawn to scale.**

3. In the figure above, if R is the midpoint of QS, then $PQ =$

(A) 1 (B) 2 (C) 3 (D) 4 (E) 5

The figure for this question is not drawn to scale so it is important to solve the problem using the given information rather than estimating lengths visually. It may be helpful in questions like this to write lengths you have determined on the figure. Since R is given as the midpoint of QS and the figure shows the length of QS to be 6, we know that $QR = RS = 3$, so the length of ST will equal 5 as shown in the following figure.

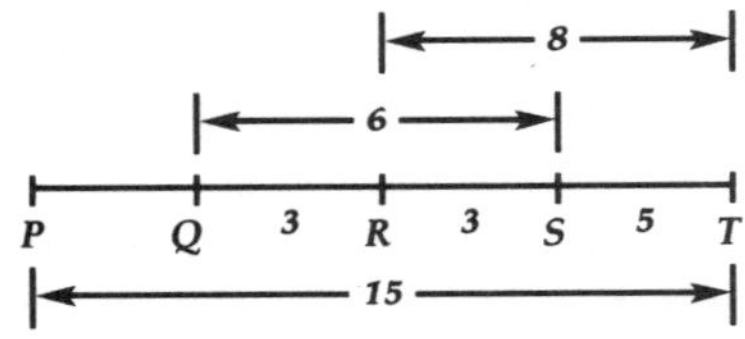

Since $QT = 11$, subtracting 11 from the total length of 15 gives the length of PQ as 4. The correct choice is (D).

4. If the average of seven x's is 7, what is the average of fourteen x's?

(A) $\frac{1}{7}$ (B) $\frac{1}{2}$ (C) 1 (D) 7 (E) 14

Don't get caught up in the wording of this problem, which might lead you to choose (E) 14. The average of any number of equal numbers such as x is always x. Since you are given that the average of seven x's is 7, it follows that $x = 7$ and that the average of fourteen x's is also 7. The correct choice is (D).

5. The town of Mason is located on Eagle Lake. The town of Canton is west of Mason. Sinclair is east of Canton, but west of Mason. Dexter is east of Richmond, but west of Sinclair and Canton. Assuming all these towns are in the United States, which town is farthest west?

(A) Mason (B) Dexter (C) Canton (D) Sinclair (E) Richmond

For this kind of problem, drawing a diagram may help. In this case, a line can be effectively used to locate the relative position of each town. Start with the statement "The town of Canton is west of Mason" and, using abbreviations, draw the following:

From the remaining information, place the other towns in their correct order:

W R D C S M E

The final sketch shows that the town farthest west is Richmond (R) and the correct choice is (E).

6. If each time the symbol $\sim$ is used it can represent either of the arithmetic operations $+$ or $\times$, which of the following could be the result of $1 \sim (2 \sim 4)$? (In this expression, the second $\sim$ need not represent the same operation as does the first $\sim$.)

I. 7
II. 8
III. 9

(A) I only (B) II only (C) I and II only (D) II and III only (E) I, II, and III

In questions of this type, statements I, II, and III each should be considered independently of the others. Determine whether or not *each* of the statements is true, that is, whether or not the number given could be the result of $1 \sim (2 \sim 4)$. You may want to mark each statement as true or false and then examine the answer choices.

This particular problem involves working with a newly defined symbol. If $\sim$ represents $+$ in both positions, the expression becomes $1 + (2 + 4)$ which has a value of 7. Therefore, statement I is true. If $\sim$ represents $\times$ in both positions, the expression becomes $1 \times (2 \times 4)$ which has a value of 8, so statement II is true. Finally, by using $\sim$ as $+$ and then $\times$ the expression becomes $1 + (2 \times 4)$ which has a value of 9 making statement III true. Since I, II, and III are true, the correct answer is choice (E).

It is possible to eliminate answer choices (A), (B), and (D) after determining that statements I and II are true. At that point, it may have been worthwhile to guess one of the remaining choices, (C) or (E), if you were not sure which is correct.

7. If a car travels X kilometers of a trip in H hours, in how many hours can it travel the next Y kilometers at this rate?

(A) $\frac{XY}{H}$ (B) $\frac{HY}{X}$ (C) $\frac{HX}{Y}$ (D) $\frac{H+Y}{X}$ (E) $\frac{X+Y}{H}$

You can solve this problem by using ratios or by using the distance formula.

Using the ratio method, X kilometers is to H hours as Y kilometers is to $\square$ hours, where $\square$ represents the amount of time required to travel Y kilometers:

$$\frac{X}{H} = \frac{Y}{\square}$$

$$X\square = HY$$

$$\square = \frac{HY}{X}$$

The correct choice is (B).

8. If 90 percent of P is 30 percent of Q, then Q is what percent of P?

(A) 3% (B) 27% (C) 30% (D) 270% (E) 300%

Writing an algebraic equation for this percent problem not only simplifies the work, it also helps you organize your thoughts. "90 percent of P is 30 percent of Q" can be written as $0.90P = 0.30Q$ (or $\frac{9}{10}P = \frac{3}{10}Q$). "$Q$ is what percent of P" tells you to find $\frac{Q}{P}$ and express it as a percent. $\frac{Q}{P} = 3$ and, therefore, Q is 300 percent of P and the correct choice is (E). (See pages 15-16 for a review of percent.)

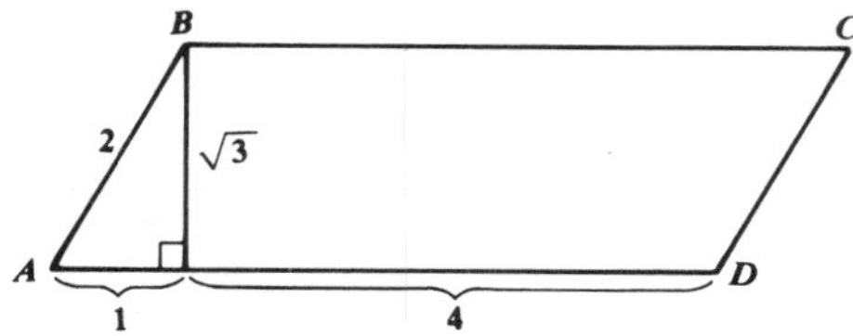

9. The figure above shows a piece of paper in the shape of a parallelogram with measurements as indicated. If the paper is tacked at its center to a flat surface and then rotated about its center, the points covered by the paper will be a circular region of diameter

(A) $\sqrt{3}$ (B) 2 (C) 5 (D) $\sqrt{28}$ (E) $\sqrt{39}$

The first step in solving the problem is to realize that the center of the parallelogram is the point of intersection of the two diagonals; thus, the diameter you are looking for is the length of the longer diagonal AC. One way to find AC is to think of the additional lines drawn as shown in the following figure.

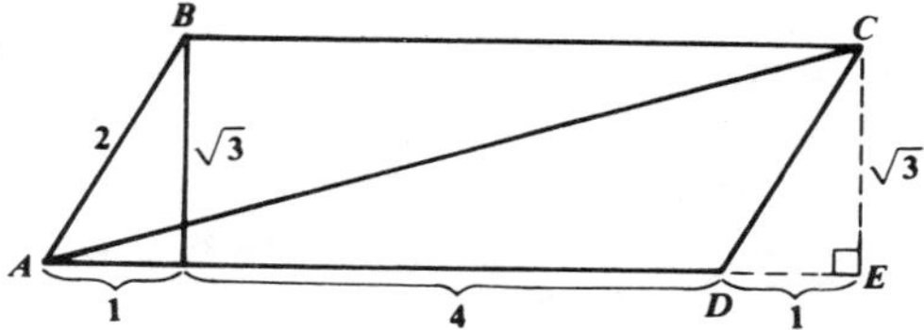

The triangles at each end are congruent (equal in size and shape), so the lengths of DE and CE are 1 and $\sqrt{3}$, respectively. AEC is a right triangle; therefore, the Pythagorean Theorem can be used in solving the problem:

$$AC^2 = CE^2 + AE^2$$
$$AC^2 = (\sqrt{3})^2 + (6)^2 = 3 + 36 = 39$$

The diameter AC is $\sqrt{39}$ and the correct choice is (E).

10. A number is divisible by 9 if the sum of its digits is divisible by 9. Which of the following numbers is divisible by 45?

(A) 63,345
(B) 72,365
(C) 99,999
(D) 72,144
(E) 98,145

It would be very time-consuming to divide each choice by 45. In order for a number to be divisible by 45 it must be divisible by both 9 and 5. Choices (A), (B), and (E) are divisible by 5, but choices (C) and (D) are not. So you can eliminate choices (C) and (D) immediately. You are given that a number is divisible by 9 if the sum of its digits is divisible by 9. The sum of the digits in choices (A), (B), and (E) are 21, 23, and 27, respectively.

Of these choices only 27 is divisible by 9. The correct choice is (E). Your scratchwork for this problem might appear as follows:

(A) 63,345 ~~21~~
(B) 72,365 ~~23~~
(C) ~~99,999~~
(D) ~~72,144~~
(E) 98,145 (27)

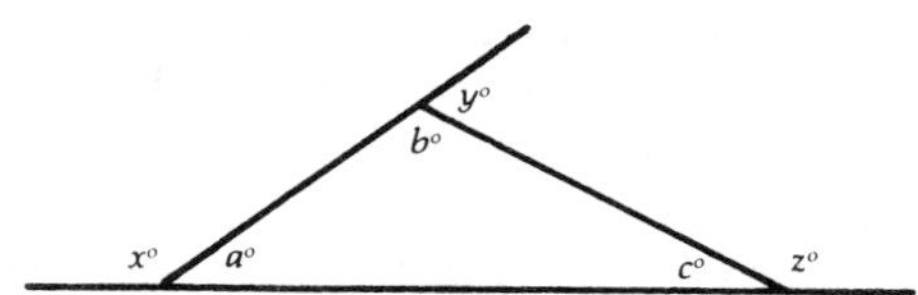

11. In the figure above, $x + y + z - (a + b + c) =$

(A) 360
(B) 180
(C) 90
(D) 0
(E) −90

It may first appear that the correct answer cannot be determined from the information given. However, since each pair of adjacent angles forms a 180° angle (for example, $x° + a° = 180°$), the sum of all lettered angles is $3 \cdot 180°$, or 540°. This means that

$$x + y + z + (a + b + c) = 540.$$

Since a, b, and c are the degree measures of the angles in a triangle, their sum must be 180. Therefore,

$$x + y + z + 180 = 540$$

$$\text{so that } x + y + z = 360$$

The desired result is then obtained as follows:

$$x + y + z - (a + b + c) = 360 - 180 = 180$$

The correct choice is (B) 180.

Quantitative Comparison Questions

Quantitative comparison questions emphasize the concepts of equalities, inequalities, and estimation. They generally involve less reading, take less time to answer, and require less computation than regular multiple-choice questions. Quantitative comparison questions may not be as familiar to you as other types of questions. Therefore, understand the directions ahead of time. Be careful not to mark answer option E when responding to the four-choice quantitative comparison questions.

Directions: Each of the following questions consists of two quantities, one in Column A and one in Column B. You are to compare the two quantities and on the answer sheet fill in oval

A if the quantity in Column A is greater;
B if the quantity in Column B is greater;
C if the two quantities are equal;
D if the relationship cannot be determined from the information given.

AN E RESPONSE WILL NOT BE SCORED.

Notes: 1. In certain questions, information concerning one or both of the quantities to be compared is centered above the two columns.

2. In a given question, a symbol that appears in both columns represents the same thing in Column A as it does in Column B.

3. Letters such as x, n, and k stand for real numbers.

	EXAMPLES Column A	Column B	Answers	Explanations:
E1.	2×6	$2 + 6$	● Ⓑ Ⓒ Ⓓ Ⓔ	**(The answer is A because 12 is greater than 8.)**
E2.	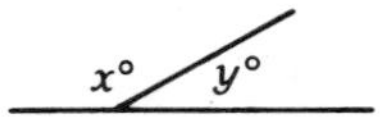 $180 - x$	y	Ⓐ Ⓑ ● Ⓓ Ⓔ	**(The answer is C because $x + y = 180$, thereby making $180 - x$ equal to y.)**
E3.	$p - q$	$q - p$	Ⓐ Ⓑ Ⓒ ● Ⓔ	**(The answer is D because nothing is known about either p or q.)**

To solve a quantitative comparison problem, you compare the quantities in the two columns and decide whether one quantity is greater than the other, whether the two quantities are equal, or whether the relationship cannot be determined from the information given. Remember that your answer should be:

A if the quantity in Column A is greater;
B if the quantity in Column B is greater;
C if the two quantities are equal;
D if the relationship cannot be determined from the information given.

Problems are clearly separated and the *quantities to be compared are always on the same line as the number of the problem.* (See example 2 on page 23.) Figures and additional information provided for some problems appear *above* the quantities to be compared. The following are some practice problems with explanations to help you understand this type of question.

	Column A	Column B
1.	$(37)(\frac{1}{43})(58)$	$(59)(\frac{1}{43})(37)$

Because the numbers in this problem are fairly large, it may save time to study the multipliers first before attempting the calculations. Note that (37) and $(\frac{1}{43})$ appear in both quantities; thus, the only numbers left for you to compare are 58 and 59. Since $59 > 58$, the quantity on the right is greater and the correct choice is (B).

Figures are also included in some questions that appear in the quantitative comparison format.

Column A **Column B**

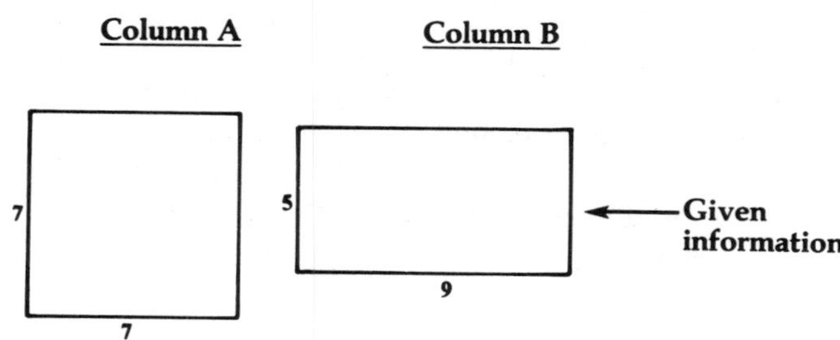

2. **The perimeter of the square** **The perimeter of the rectangle** ← **Quantities to be compared**

It can be assumed that the units used to indicate measures in a given problem are the same in all figures in that problem unless otherwise stated. The correct choice is (C) because the perimeter of the square is $4 \cdot 7 = 28$ units and the perimeter of the rectangle is $(2 \cdot 5) + (2 \cdot 9) = 28$ units.

Column A **Column B**

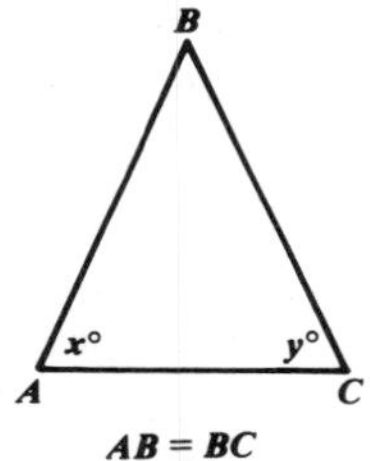

$AB = BC$

3. x y

Since $AB = BC$, the angles opposite AB and BC are equal and, therefore, $x = y$. The correct choice is (C).

Column A **Column B**

4. $\sqrt{2} - 1$ $\sqrt{3} - 1$

For any positive number x, the symbol $\sqrt{x}$ denotes the positive square root of x. The fact that $\sqrt{3} > \sqrt{2}$ leads to the conclusion that $\sqrt{3} - 1 > \sqrt{2} - 1$. The correct choice is (B). Note that $x^2 = 9$ has two solutions, $x = 3$ or $x = -3$. However, $\sqrt{9} = 3$, not ± 3.

Column A **Column B**

5. $x + 1$ $2x + 1$

Because both expressions contain a "1," the problem is one of comparing x with $2x$. When you compare algebraic expressions, a useful technique is to consider zero and negative numbers for possible values of the unknown.

$2x > x$ for positive values of x
$2x = x$ for $x = 0$
$2x < x$ for negative values of x

The correct choice is (D), as the relationship cannot be determined from the information given. If you had been given that x was positive (that is, $x > 0$), the correct choice would have been (B) because $2x$ would be greater than x.

Column A **Column B**

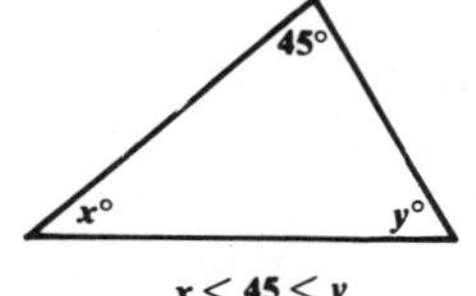

Note: Figure not drawn to scale.

$x < 45 < y$

6. y 90

Because the sum of the angles of a triangle is 180, $x + y + 45 = 180$ or $x + y = 135$. Since $x < 45$, it follows that $y > 90$. The answer is (A). In this problem you should not try to determine the answer from the appearance of the figure because the note indicates that the figure is not drawn to scale.

Column A **Column B**

$x \neq 1$

7. $\frac{x^2 - 1}{x - 1}$ x

The condition $x \neq 1$ (read x is not equal to 1) is given because the algebraic fraction in Column A is not defined for $x = 1$ (the denominator becomes zero). The solution of this problem involves simplifying the fraction in Column A as follows:

$$\frac{x^2 - 1}{x - 1} = \frac{(x + 1)(x - 1)}{x - 1} = x + 1$$

Therefore, the quantity in Column A is equal to $x + 1$. Since $x + 1$ is always greater than x, the answer is (A).

Column A	Column B
8. Area of a triangle with altitude 4	**Area of a triangle with base 5**

To answer this question, you need to know how to find the area of a triangle. To find the area of a triangle, you need to know the length of a base and the altitude to that base. You can't find the "area of a triangle with altitude 4" without knowing the base, so the area of such a triangle could be any number depending on the length of the base. Likewise, you can't find the "area of a triangle with base 5" without knowing the length of the altitude. Since you can't tell anything about the two areas, the correct choice is (D).

The Test of Standard Written English

The questions on the TSWE measure skills that are important to the kinds of writing you will do in most college courses. In particular, the questions test your ability to recognize the use of language essential to a finished piece of writing—writing that would be considered acceptable by most educated readers and writers of American English.

The TSWE questions ask you to recognize several aspects of language usage.

Use of basic grammar—for example, subject-verb agreement, agreement of pronouns with the nouns to which they refer, and the correct use of verb tense.

Sentence structure—for example, distinguishing between complete and incomplete sentences and recognizing when the connections between parts of a sentence are clear and when they are not.

Choice of words—for example, recognizing when words or phrases should be revised to make the meaning of a sentence clear or to make the language consistent with what is normally expected of educated writers.

The questions do not ask you to define or to use grammatical terms, nor do they test spelling or capitalization. In a few questions, punctuation marks like the semicolon or apostrophe are important in arriving at the correct answer, but these questions primarily test the structure in which the punctuation appears.

The best way to prepare for the TSWE is to get regular practice in writing and rewriting your own prose, paying particular attention to clarity and effectiveness of expression. You should also try to gain experience in reading the prose of skilled writers on a variety of subjects, noticing especially how the writers use language to create meaning. As with the SAT, reading the sample questions and explanations and taking the practice test provided in this booklet will help you prepare for the TSWE. After you've taken and scored the sample test, look carefully at the questions you missed. Talk over those questions with your teachers and other students and look up the portions of your textbooks that discuss the problems in wording, sentence structure, and grammar that were most difficult for you.

As you begin the TSWE section, you will see the following directions:

The questions in this section measure skills that are important to writing well. In particular, they test your ability to recognize the use of language that is clear, effective, and correct according to the requirements of standard written English, the kind of English found in most college textbooks.

The TSWE is made up of approximately 50 questions of two types. You will see the following directions for the first type of question:

Directions: The following sentences test your knowledge of grammar, usage, diction (choice of words), and idiom.

Some sentences are correct.

No sentence contains more than one error.

You will find that the error, if there is one, is underlined and lettered. Assume that elements of the sentence that are not underlined are correct and cannot be changed. In choosing answers, follow the requirements of standard written English.

If there is an error, select the one underlined part that must be changed to make the sentence correct and fill in the corresponding oval on your answer sheet.

If there is no error, fill in oval Ⓔ.

Example: **Sample Answer**

Ⓐ ● Ⓒ Ⓓ Ⓔ

The other (A) delegates and him (B) immediately (C) accepted the resolution drafted by (D) the neutral states. No error (E)

As you can see from the example, this type of question consists of a sentence in which four short portions are underlined and lettered A, B, C, and D followed by a fifth underline, "No error," lettered E. Sometimes the underlined portion of the sentence is only a single word, as in (B) and (C) above. In other cases, a group of words or a phrase is underlined, as in (A) and (D).

For each question, you must decide whether one of the underlined portions must be changed to make the sentence acceptable in standard written English. In the example above, (B) must be changed because the pronoun *him* is incorrect. If you imagine leaving out the words *The other delegates and*, you can see the error more easily. You would change *him* to *he* and write *he immediately accepted.* The pronoun *him* is not appropriate to refer to the person performing an action. Therefore, the correct answer to the example is (B) because that is the portion that needs to be changed to make the sentence correct. Changes could be made in the other underlined portions of the sentence, in the example, but none of them is necessary to make the sentence acceptable.

In some sentences of this type you could imagine changes in parts of the sentence that are not underlined. However, you should focus only on possible changes to the underlined words. Notice that if none of the underlined portions needs to be changed, the correct answer is (E). By choosing (E) as the answer, you are indicating that the sentence is correct as written.

Most questions of this type test your ability to recognize problems in basic grammar or in choice of words. A few questions also test problems in sentence structure. To give you a better sense of the variety of problems tested, a few more sample questions follow. Keep in mind the following suggestions as you work through the sample questions.

- ✓ For each question, read the entire sentence carefully but quickly.
- ✓ Go back over the sentence, looking at each underlined portion to see whether anything needs to be changed to make the sentence correct.
- ✓ If you find an error, mark the oval on your answer sheet with the same letter as the underlined portion with the error.
- ✓ If you don't find an error, don't waste time searching for one. Mark the oval for (E), No error, on your answer sheet to indicate that you believe the sentence is correct as written.
- ✓ In general, you should be able to move quickly through these questions since they do not involve much reading. Put a mark next to any question you want to return to and move on to the next question.

The four sample questions that follow are based on questions that originally appeared in the TSWE. They are arranged in order of increasing difficulty. Together, the example question and the four samples should give you a sense of the difficulty level of the questions you will be asked.

1. One of the goals of (A) women's organizations is to encourage (B) programs that will improve (C) the quality of life for (D) working parents. No error (E)

Probably the first impression you get from reading the sentence is that nothing is really wrong with it. But before you make a final decision, you should look at the sentence again, especially at the underlined portions. The (A) portion, *goals of,* seems correct; *of* is the appropriate preposition for the context. The (B) portion, *is to encourage,* is a little more complicated but also seems correct; *is* is the appropriate verb to use with *one* and *to encourage* is all right following *is,* even though *encouraging* might be nearly as good. In (C), *will improve* is appropriate with the subject and has the correct tense for the context. In (D), the preposition *for* is used correctly.

Even though your analysis probably would not be as extensive as this, you should do something fairly similar, quickly checking each underlined portion of the sentence to make sure that each is acceptable as written. For some portions, you might have been able to think of another way of writing the sentence, even a way of improving it a little, but you probably decided that no changes were necessary in the underlined portions. At this point, you should have been able to decide on (E), No error, as the correct answer. Keep in mind that some of these questions are correctly answered with (E).

2. Probably (A) the best-known baseball player of all time, (B) Babe Ruth established a record for lifetime home runs that has been broke (C) only (D) by Hank Aaron. No error (E)

You may have noticed when you read the question for the first time that *broke* in (C) should be changed to *broken.* But if you didn't see the error immediately, or if you were not sure of it, you should have looked at the sentence again, especially at the underlined portions. In (A), *probably* is the appropriate adverb, in (B) *of all time* is an acceptable idiom and is used correctly, and in (D) the adverb *only* is acceptable. But in (C), *broke* is clearly incorrect and needs to be changed to make the sentence acceptable in standard written English. The complete and correct verb for this part of the sentence is *has been broken.* With *has been,* the only possible form of the verb *break* that can be used is *broken.* The correct choice is (C).

3. Many travelers claim having seen the Abominable
A
Snowman, but no one has proved that
B
such a creature actually exists. No error
C D E

The answer is (A). In the context of this sentence, the verb *claim* requires the expression *to have seen; claim having seen* is not idiomatic in American English and is therefore not acceptable. The word *but* at (B) provides a link between the two major parts of the sentence and appropriately suggests a contrast between the ideas they present. The expression at (C), *such a creature,* and the adverb *actually* at (D) are correct although other expressions and adverbs could be substituted.

4. The commission investigating the accident at the
A
laboratory was less interested in why the experiment
was conducted than in whether they were conducted
B C
properly. No error
D E

This question is more difficult than the previous ones. You should be sure to look carefully at the underlined portions when you read the sentence. In (A), *investigating* is correctly used to describe the activities of the commission. In (B), *than in* correctly introduces the second part of the comparison that begins with *less interested in.* Good usage requires the repetition of *in* for appropriate parallel structure. In (D), *properly* is correct as an adverb modifying the verb immediately before it. But in (C), the pronoun *they* is plural, and it is therefore the incorrect pronoun to refer to *the experiment*, which is singular. The version of the underlined material in (C) should read *it was.* Choice (C) is the correct answer.

You will see the following directions for the second type of question on the TSWE.

Directions: In each of the following sentences, some part or all of the sentence is underlined. Below each sentence you will find five ways of phrasing the underlined part. Select the answer that produces the most effective sentence, one that is clear and exact, without awkwardness or ambiguity, and fill in the corresponding oval on your answer sheet. In choosing answers, follow the requirements of standard written English. Choose the answer that best expresses the meaning of the original sentence.

Answer (A) is always the same as the underlined part. Choose answer (A) if you think the original sentence needs no revision.

Example: **Sample Answer**

Ⓐ ● Ⓒ Ⓓ Ⓔ

Laura Ingalls Wilder published her first book and she was sixty-five years old then.

(A) and she was sixty-five years old then
(B) when she was sixty-five years old
(C) at age sixty-five years old
(D) upon reaching sixty-five years
(E) at the time when she was sixty-five

This type of question presents you with a sentence and four possible revisions of it—(B), (C), (D), or (E). The (A) version is always a repetition of the underlined portion of the original sentence. The underline in the original sentence tells you how much of the sentence will be revised in the other versions that are presented to you.

The example above is a sentence in which the connection between the two major ideas is weak. The use of *and* to join the two clauses suggests that the ideas are of equal importance in the sentence, but the wording and the ideas in the clauses themselves suggest that the first idea should actually be the major point of the sentence and that the second should be secondary to it. Versions (B), (C), (D), and (E) all begin with more appropriate connecting words, but (B) is the only one in which the second idea of the sentence is clearly, concisely, and idiomatically expressed. Therefore, (B) is the correct choice.

The directions tell you to look for the most effective sentence. In some questions you may find a version of the original sentence that has no grammatical errors but does not express the ideas of the sentence as effectively as another version. For other questions you may be able to think of a version you consider better than any of the choices given. In either case, you should select the version that is the best of those presented.

This type of question is primarily concerned with problems of sentence structure. But you'll also need to consider basic principles of grammar and word choice to decide which of the versions makes the clearest and most effective sentence. For example, some versions will be grammatically incorrect or the ideas in the sentence will be presented so awkwardly or imprecisely that they cannot be considered acceptable.

You'll get a sense of the problems tested in the questions from the discussion of the sample questions provided here. You'll have an idea of the range of difficulty found in the questions, since the sample questions given here are arranged in order of increasing difficulty. You'll also notice that this type of question will usually require more time than the first type of TSWE question described. To learn as much as possible from the sample questions, read carefully the directions that precede the example question above and approach the questions with the following suggestions in mind.

✓ In each question, read the original sentence carefully but quickly. Note the underlined portion of the sentence because that is the portion that may need to be revised. Remember that the portion with no underline stays the same.

✓ Keep in mind the portion of the original sentence that stays the same when you read through each of the versions presented.

✓ Decide which version seems best. If you can't decide between two choices, go back and read each version you have chosen in the context of the entire sentence.

✓ If you still feel uncertain about your answer, put a mark next to that question in your test book and note which versions you thought might be correct. You can return to the question later if you have time.

1. <u>Althea Gibson was the first Black American to win major tennis championships and played in the 1950s.</u>

(A) Althea Gibson was the first Black American to win major tennis championships and played in the 1950s.
(B) Althea Gibson, being the first Black American to win major tennis championships, and playing in the 1950s.
(C) Althea Gibson, playing in the 1950s, being the first Black American to win major tennis championships.
(D) Althea Gibson, who played in the 1950s, was the first Black American to win major tennis championships.
(E) Althea Gibson played in the 1950s, she was the first Black American to win major tennis championships.

Here the original sentence is entirely underlined, so you can expect the versions that follow to be revisions of the whole sentence.

This question is fairly easy. You may have been able to decide which version of the sentence was best simply by reading through all of the choices. However, to help you feel more certain of your choice and to help you understand more fully how the decision can be made, it's worth looking separately at each version. The (A) version, the same as the original sentence, has a problem similar to the one in the boxed example: *and* does not adequately convey the relationship between the two clauses in the sentence. The (B) version has the same problem and an additional one: the use of *being* and *playing* makes it an incomplete sentence. In the (C) version, *playing* seems at first to have corrected the original problem of relationship between parts of the sentence, but the use of *being* gives the second idea no more importance than the first and also makes this version an incomplete sentence. In (E), you can see that a comma is used improperly as a means of connecting two independent clauses. Thus, (D) is the only acceptable version. In (D), the major point appears in the main part of the sentence and receives most emphasis, while the less important point appears in the *who* clause and so is emphasized less.

You won't need to analyze questions of this type in this much detail. You'll be able to decide by reading through each version and looking closely at one or two of them. But you should use this approach for the questions that are most difficult for you, especially the ones you miss on the sample TSWE.

2. After placing the meatballs in a pan, the cook sautéed them until they were brown <u>and then let them simmer</u> in the sauce.

(A) and then let them simmer
(B) then they were simmered
(C) and then simmering it
(D) then letting them simmer
(E) and then the simmering was done

You should have read the original sentence quickly, noting that the portions not underlined will remain the same in all versions of the sentence. The original sentence and choice (A) may have seemed plausible, but you should have gone on to the other versions before making a final decision. In the (B) version, the unexpected shift from the *cook* as subject to *they* (the meatballs) is awkward and somewhat confusing. The (C) version uses *simmering* where *simmered* is needed to parallel *sautéed.* Furthermore, the pronoun *it* does not seem to refer back to anything named earlier in the sentence. In the (D) version, the use of *letting* rather than *let* again neglects the parallel with *sautéed.* The (E) version is wordy and, like the (B) version, involves a shift in which a passive construction replaces a more appropriate active one and in which the action is described without reference to the person responsible for it. Therefore, the best version of the sentence in this case is the original one, and the correct choice is (A).

3. Being as it was a full moon, the tides were exceptionally high when the storm struck.

(A) Being as it was a full moon,
(B) With the moon as full,
(C) Due to there being a full moon,
(D) The moon was full,
(E) Because the moon was full,

The problems immediately apparent are in wording. Version (A), like the underlined portion in the original sentence, uses *Being as,* an expression considered unacceptable in standard written English. In addition, the indirect *it was* construction introduces unnecessary wordiness. Version (B) itself seems acceptable, but leads the reader to expect a construction ("as it was") different from the one that follows in the rest of the sentence. In version (C), *due to* is used in a way that is considered unacceptable usage, and *there being* introduces unnecessary wordiness. Version (D) itself is acceptable but, when combined with the rest of the sentence, results in the unacceptable joining of two independent clauses with a comma. This sentence needs an expression that is acceptable in good written English and that accurately reflects the relationship between the first and second parts of the sentence. Version (E) solves the problem—the word *because* indicates that the fullness of the moon was causally related to the high tides described in the second part of the sentence—so (E) is correct.

4. The Dutch had been trading with Asia since the sixteenth century, their ships have visited Persia and Japan.

(A) century, their ships have visited
(B) century while their ships had visited
(C) century, but their ships had been visiting
(D) century, when their ships visited
(E) century, where their ships were visiting

The original sentence and the (A) version present two problems. First, two independent statements are joined by a comma, with no indication of the relationship between them. Second, the tense of the verb *have visited* is not consistent with the tense of *had been trading* earlier in the sentence. The (B) version may appear to be acceptable, but the relationship between the ideas in the sentence is not the one implied by *while* and the use of *while* makes the sentence illogical. Similarly, the (C) version appears plausible, but the contrast implied by *but* is not appropriate to the relationship between the two parts of the sentence. The (D) version corrects both of the problems presented in the original sentence and is more logical than either (B) or (C). Notice that the tense of *visited* is consistent with the earlier verb *had been trading.* It suggests that Dutch ships had traveled to Persia and Japan in the sixteenth century, and that such travel was part of a process of Dutch trade with Asia that continued until some later, unspecified time. Version (E) resembles (D), except that *where* is substituted for *when* and *were visiting* for *visited.* Since the connection with *century* is clearly one of time rather than place, the use of *where* is not appropriate. Furthermore, the use of *were visiting* would imply emphasis on visits occurring over a period of time. Such emphasis is not called for because the purpose in this part of the sentence is to describe the point at which the Dutch began trading with Asia. Therefore, (D) expresses most effectively the ideas in the two parts of the sentence as well as the relationship between them. The correct choice is (D).

Practice Test

The practice SAT that follows is the edition given on May 7, 1988 (except for the TSWE, section 4, given on December 6, 1986). It includes only five of the six sections that the test contains. The equating section has been omitted because it contains questions that may be used in future editions of the SAT and does not count toward the scores. The practice test will help you most if you take it under conditions as close as possible to those of the test:

- Set aside two-and-one-half hours of uninterrupted time, so that you can complete the entire test at once.
- Sit at a desk or table cleared of any other papers or books. You can't take a calculator, a dictionary, books, or notes into the test room. (See the *Registration Bulletin*.)
- Allow yourself only 30 minutes for each section of the test. Have a kitchen timer or clock in front of you for timing yourself on the sections.
- Tear out the practice answer sheet on page 31 and fill it in just as you will on the day of the test.
- Read the instructions on page 33. They are reprinted from the back cover of the test book. When you take the test, you will be asked to read them before you begin answering questions.
- After you finish the practice test, read "How to Score Your Practice Test," on page 62.

(Cut here to detach.)

COLLEGE BOARD — SCHOLASTIC APTITUDE TEST and Test of Standard Written English — Side 1

Use a No. 2 pencil only. Be sure each mark is dark and completely fills the intended oval. Completely erase any errors or stray marks.

1. YOUR NAME: (Print) ______________________ Last ______ First ______ M.I.

SIGNATURE: ______________________ **DATE:** ___/___/___

HOME ADDRESS: (Print) ______________________ Number and Street

______________________ City ______ State ______ Zip Code

CENTER: (Print) ______________________ City ______ State ______ Center Number

IMPORTANT: Please fill in items 2 and 3 exactly as shown on the back cover of your test book.

FOR ETS USE ONLY

2. TEST FORM (Copy from back cover of your test book.)

3. FORM CODE (Copy and grid as shown on back cover of your test book.)

0	A	J	S	0	0	0
1	B	K	T	1	1	1
2	C	L	U	2	2	2
3	D	M	V	3	3	3
4	E	N	W	4	4	4
5	F	O	X	5	5	5
6	G	P	Y	6	6	6
7	H	Q	Z	7	7	7
8	I	R		8	8	8
9				9	9	9

4. REGISTRATION NUMBER (Copy from your Admission Ticket.)

Seven columns, each: 0 1 2 3 4 5 6 7 8 9

5. YOUR NAME

First 4 letters of last name | First Init. | Mid. Init.

Each column: A B C D E F G H I J K L M N O P Q R S T U V W X Y Z

6. DATE OF BIRTH

Month	Day		Year	
Jan.				
Feb.				
Mar.	0	0	0	0
Apr.	1	1	1	1
May	2	2	2	2
June	3	3	3	3
July		4	4	4
Aug.		5	5	5
Sept.		6	6	6
Oct.		7	7	7
Nov.		8		8
Dec.		9		9

7. SEX

Female

Male

8. TEST BOOK SERIAL NUMBER (Copy from front cover of your test book.)

Start with number 1 for each new section. If a section has fewer than 50 questions, leave the extra answer spaces blank.

SECTION 1

Questions 1–50, each: A B C D E

SECTION 2

Questions 1–50, each: A B C D E

Q1362-04

I.N. 575008 — 110VV58P3720

COLLEGE BOARD — SCHOLASTIC APTITUDE TEST and Test of Standard Written English **Side 2**

Use a No. 2 pencil only. Be sure each mark is dark and completely fills the intended oval. Completely erase any errors or stray marks.

Start with number 1 for each new section. If a section has fewer than 50 questions, leave the extra answer spaces blank.

	SECTION 3	SECTION 4	SECTION 5	SECTION 6
1	Ⓐ Ⓑ Ⓒ Ⓓ Ⓔ	Ⓐ Ⓑ Ⓒ Ⓓ Ⓔ	Ⓐ Ⓑ Ⓒ Ⓓ Ⓔ	Ⓐ Ⓑ Ⓒ Ⓓ Ⓔ
2	Ⓐ Ⓑ Ⓒ Ⓓ Ⓔ	Ⓐ Ⓑ Ⓒ Ⓓ Ⓔ	Ⓐ Ⓑ Ⓒ Ⓓ Ⓔ	Ⓐ Ⓑ Ⓒ Ⓓ Ⓔ
3	Ⓐ Ⓑ Ⓒ Ⓓ Ⓔ	Ⓐ Ⓑ Ⓒ Ⓓ Ⓔ	Ⓐ Ⓑ Ⓒ Ⓓ Ⓔ	Ⓐ Ⓑ Ⓒ Ⓓ Ⓔ
4	Ⓐ Ⓑ Ⓒ Ⓓ Ⓔ	Ⓐ Ⓑ Ⓒ Ⓓ Ⓔ	Ⓐ Ⓑ Ⓒ Ⓓ Ⓔ	Ⓐ Ⓑ Ⓒ Ⓓ Ⓔ
5	Ⓐ Ⓑ Ⓒ Ⓓ Ⓔ	Ⓐ Ⓑ Ⓒ Ⓓ Ⓔ	Ⓐ Ⓑ Ⓒ Ⓓ Ⓔ	Ⓐ Ⓑ Ⓒ Ⓓ Ⓔ
6	Ⓐ Ⓑ Ⓒ Ⓓ Ⓔ	Ⓐ Ⓑ Ⓒ Ⓓ Ⓔ	Ⓐ Ⓑ Ⓒ Ⓓ Ⓔ	Ⓐ Ⓑ Ⓒ Ⓓ Ⓔ
7	Ⓐ Ⓑ Ⓒ Ⓓ Ⓔ	Ⓐ Ⓑ Ⓒ Ⓓ Ⓔ	Ⓐ Ⓑ Ⓒ Ⓓ Ⓔ	Ⓐ Ⓑ Ⓒ Ⓓ Ⓔ
8	Ⓐ Ⓑ Ⓒ Ⓓ Ⓔ	Ⓐ Ⓑ Ⓒ Ⓓ Ⓔ	Ⓐ Ⓑ Ⓒ Ⓓ Ⓔ	Ⓐ Ⓑ Ⓒ Ⓓ Ⓔ
9	Ⓐ Ⓑ Ⓒ Ⓓ Ⓔ	Ⓐ Ⓑ Ⓒ Ⓓ Ⓔ	Ⓐ Ⓑ Ⓒ Ⓓ Ⓔ	Ⓐ Ⓑ Ⓒ Ⓓ Ⓔ
10	Ⓐ Ⓑ Ⓒ Ⓓ Ⓔ	Ⓐ Ⓑ Ⓒ Ⓓ Ⓔ	Ⓐ Ⓑ Ⓒ Ⓓ Ⓔ	Ⓐ Ⓑ Ⓒ Ⓓ Ⓔ
11	Ⓐ Ⓑ Ⓒ Ⓓ Ⓔ	Ⓐ Ⓑ Ⓒ Ⓓ Ⓔ	Ⓐ Ⓑ Ⓒ Ⓓ Ⓔ	Ⓐ Ⓑ Ⓒ Ⓓ Ⓔ
12	Ⓐ Ⓑ Ⓒ Ⓓ Ⓔ	Ⓐ Ⓑ Ⓒ Ⓓ Ⓔ	Ⓐ Ⓑ Ⓒ Ⓓ Ⓔ	Ⓐ Ⓑ Ⓒ Ⓓ Ⓔ
13	Ⓐ Ⓑ Ⓒ Ⓓ Ⓔ	Ⓐ Ⓑ Ⓒ Ⓓ Ⓔ	Ⓐ Ⓑ Ⓒ Ⓓ Ⓔ	Ⓐ Ⓑ Ⓒ Ⓓ Ⓔ
14	Ⓐ Ⓑ Ⓒ Ⓓ Ⓔ	Ⓐ Ⓑ Ⓒ Ⓓ Ⓔ	Ⓐ Ⓑ Ⓒ Ⓓ Ⓔ	Ⓐ Ⓑ Ⓒ Ⓓ Ⓔ
15	Ⓐ Ⓑ Ⓒ Ⓓ Ⓔ	Ⓐ Ⓑ Ⓒ Ⓓ Ⓔ	Ⓐ Ⓑ Ⓒ Ⓓ Ⓔ	Ⓐ Ⓑ Ⓒ Ⓓ Ⓔ
16	Ⓐ Ⓑ Ⓒ Ⓓ Ⓔ	Ⓐ Ⓑ Ⓒ Ⓓ Ⓔ	Ⓐ Ⓑ Ⓒ Ⓓ Ⓔ	Ⓐ Ⓑ Ⓒ Ⓓ Ⓔ
17	Ⓐ Ⓑ Ⓒ Ⓓ Ⓔ	Ⓐ Ⓑ Ⓒ Ⓓ Ⓔ	Ⓐ Ⓑ Ⓒ Ⓓ Ⓔ	Ⓐ Ⓑ Ⓒ Ⓓ Ⓔ
18	Ⓐ Ⓑ Ⓒ Ⓓ Ⓔ	Ⓐ Ⓑ Ⓒ Ⓓ Ⓔ	Ⓐ Ⓑ Ⓒ Ⓓ Ⓔ	Ⓐ Ⓑ Ⓒ Ⓓ Ⓔ
19	Ⓐ Ⓑ Ⓒ Ⓓ Ⓔ	Ⓐ Ⓑ Ⓒ Ⓓ Ⓔ	Ⓐ Ⓑ Ⓒ Ⓓ Ⓔ	Ⓐ Ⓑ Ⓒ Ⓓ Ⓔ
20	Ⓐ Ⓑ Ⓒ Ⓓ Ⓔ	Ⓐ Ⓑ Ⓒ Ⓓ Ⓔ	Ⓐ Ⓑ Ⓒ Ⓓ Ⓔ	Ⓐ Ⓑ Ⓒ Ⓓ Ⓔ
21	Ⓐ Ⓑ Ⓒ Ⓓ Ⓔ	Ⓐ Ⓑ Ⓒ Ⓓ Ⓔ	Ⓐ Ⓑ Ⓒ Ⓓ Ⓔ	Ⓐ Ⓑ Ⓒ Ⓓ Ⓔ
22	Ⓐ Ⓑ Ⓒ Ⓓ Ⓔ	Ⓐ Ⓑ Ⓒ Ⓓ Ⓔ	Ⓐ Ⓑ Ⓒ Ⓓ Ⓔ	Ⓐ Ⓑ Ⓒ Ⓓ Ⓔ
23	Ⓐ Ⓑ Ⓒ Ⓓ Ⓔ	Ⓐ Ⓑ Ⓒ Ⓓ Ⓔ	Ⓐ Ⓑ Ⓒ Ⓓ Ⓔ	Ⓐ Ⓑ Ⓒ Ⓓ Ⓔ
24	Ⓐ Ⓑ Ⓒ Ⓓ Ⓔ	Ⓐ Ⓑ Ⓒ Ⓓ Ⓔ	Ⓐ Ⓑ Ⓒ Ⓓ Ⓔ	Ⓐ Ⓑ Ⓒ Ⓓ Ⓔ
25	Ⓐ Ⓑ Ⓒ Ⓓ Ⓔ	Ⓐ Ⓑ Ⓒ Ⓓ Ⓔ	Ⓐ Ⓑ Ⓒ Ⓓ Ⓔ	Ⓐ Ⓑ Ⓒ Ⓓ Ⓔ
26	Ⓐ Ⓑ Ⓒ Ⓓ Ⓔ	Ⓐ Ⓑ Ⓒ Ⓓ Ⓔ	Ⓐ Ⓑ Ⓒ Ⓓ Ⓔ	Ⓐ Ⓑ Ⓒ Ⓓ Ⓔ
27	Ⓐ Ⓑ Ⓒ Ⓓ Ⓔ	Ⓐ Ⓑ Ⓒ Ⓓ Ⓔ	Ⓐ Ⓑ Ⓒ Ⓓ Ⓔ	Ⓐ Ⓑ Ⓒ Ⓓ Ⓔ
28	Ⓐ Ⓑ Ⓒ Ⓓ Ⓔ	Ⓐ Ⓑ Ⓒ Ⓓ Ⓔ	Ⓐ Ⓑ Ⓒ Ⓓ Ⓔ	Ⓐ Ⓑ Ⓒ Ⓓ Ⓔ
29	Ⓐ Ⓑ Ⓒ Ⓓ Ⓔ	Ⓐ Ⓑ Ⓒ Ⓓ Ⓔ	Ⓐ Ⓑ Ⓒ Ⓓ Ⓔ	Ⓐ Ⓑ Ⓒ Ⓓ Ⓔ
30	Ⓐ Ⓑ Ⓒ Ⓓ Ⓔ	Ⓐ Ⓑ Ⓒ Ⓓ Ⓔ	Ⓐ Ⓑ Ⓒ Ⓓ Ⓔ	Ⓐ Ⓑ Ⓒ Ⓓ Ⓔ
31	Ⓐ Ⓑ Ⓒ Ⓓ Ⓔ	Ⓐ Ⓑ Ⓒ Ⓓ Ⓔ	Ⓐ Ⓑ Ⓒ Ⓓ Ⓔ	Ⓐ Ⓑ Ⓒ Ⓓ Ⓔ
32	Ⓐ Ⓑ Ⓒ Ⓓ Ⓔ	Ⓐ Ⓑ Ⓒ Ⓓ Ⓔ	Ⓐ Ⓑ Ⓒ Ⓓ Ⓔ	Ⓐ Ⓑ Ⓒ Ⓓ Ⓔ
33	Ⓐ Ⓑ Ⓒ Ⓓ Ⓔ	Ⓐ Ⓑ Ⓒ Ⓓ Ⓔ	Ⓐ Ⓑ Ⓒ Ⓓ Ⓔ	Ⓐ Ⓑ Ⓒ Ⓓ Ⓔ
34	Ⓐ Ⓑ Ⓒ Ⓓ Ⓔ	Ⓐ Ⓑ Ⓒ Ⓓ Ⓔ	Ⓐ Ⓑ Ⓒ Ⓓ Ⓔ	Ⓐ Ⓑ Ⓒ Ⓓ Ⓔ
35	Ⓐ Ⓑ Ⓒ Ⓓ Ⓔ	Ⓐ Ⓑ Ⓒ Ⓓ Ⓔ	Ⓐ Ⓑ Ⓒ Ⓓ Ⓔ	Ⓐ Ⓑ Ⓒ Ⓓ Ⓔ
36	Ⓐ Ⓑ Ⓒ Ⓓ Ⓔ	Ⓐ Ⓑ Ⓒ Ⓓ Ⓔ	Ⓐ Ⓑ Ⓒ Ⓓ Ⓔ	Ⓐ Ⓑ Ⓒ Ⓓ Ⓔ
37	Ⓐ Ⓑ Ⓒ Ⓓ Ⓔ	Ⓐ Ⓑ Ⓒ Ⓓ Ⓔ	Ⓐ Ⓑ Ⓒ Ⓓ Ⓔ	Ⓐ Ⓑ Ⓒ Ⓓ Ⓔ
38	Ⓐ Ⓑ Ⓒ Ⓓ Ⓔ	Ⓐ Ⓑ Ⓒ Ⓓ Ⓔ	Ⓐ Ⓑ Ⓒ Ⓓ Ⓔ	Ⓐ Ⓑ Ⓒ Ⓓ Ⓔ
39	Ⓐ Ⓑ Ⓒ Ⓓ Ⓔ	Ⓐ Ⓑ Ⓒ Ⓓ Ⓔ	Ⓐ Ⓑ Ⓒ Ⓓ Ⓔ	Ⓐ Ⓑ Ⓒ Ⓓ Ⓔ
40	Ⓐ Ⓑ Ⓒ Ⓓ Ⓔ	Ⓐ Ⓑ Ⓒ Ⓓ Ⓔ	Ⓐ Ⓑ Ⓒ Ⓓ Ⓔ	Ⓐ Ⓑ Ⓒ Ⓓ Ⓔ
41	Ⓐ Ⓑ Ⓒ Ⓓ Ⓔ	Ⓐ Ⓑ Ⓒ Ⓓ Ⓔ	Ⓐ Ⓑ Ⓒ Ⓓ Ⓔ	Ⓐ Ⓑ Ⓒ Ⓓ Ⓔ
42	Ⓐ Ⓑ Ⓒ Ⓓ Ⓔ	Ⓐ Ⓑ Ⓒ Ⓓ Ⓔ	Ⓐ Ⓑ Ⓒ Ⓓ Ⓔ	Ⓐ Ⓑ Ⓒ Ⓓ Ⓔ
43	Ⓐ Ⓑ Ⓒ Ⓓ Ⓔ	Ⓐ Ⓑ Ⓒ Ⓓ Ⓔ	Ⓐ Ⓑ Ⓒ Ⓓ Ⓔ	Ⓐ Ⓑ Ⓒ Ⓓ Ⓔ
44	Ⓐ Ⓑ Ⓒ Ⓓ Ⓔ	Ⓐ Ⓑ Ⓒ Ⓓ Ⓔ	Ⓐ Ⓑ Ⓒ Ⓓ Ⓔ	Ⓐ Ⓑ Ⓒ Ⓓ Ⓔ
45	Ⓐ Ⓑ Ⓒ Ⓓ Ⓔ	Ⓐ Ⓑ Ⓒ Ⓓ Ⓔ	Ⓐ Ⓑ Ⓒ Ⓓ Ⓔ	Ⓐ Ⓑ Ⓒ Ⓓ Ⓔ
46	Ⓐ Ⓑ Ⓒ Ⓓ Ⓔ	Ⓐ Ⓑ Ⓒ Ⓓ Ⓔ	Ⓐ Ⓑ Ⓒ Ⓓ Ⓔ	Ⓐ Ⓑ Ⓒ Ⓓ Ⓔ
47	Ⓐ Ⓑ Ⓒ Ⓓ Ⓔ	Ⓐ Ⓑ Ⓒ Ⓓ Ⓔ	Ⓐ Ⓑ Ⓒ Ⓓ Ⓔ	Ⓐ Ⓑ Ⓒ Ⓓ Ⓔ
48	Ⓐ Ⓑ Ⓒ Ⓓ Ⓔ	Ⓐ Ⓑ Ⓒ Ⓓ Ⓔ	Ⓐ Ⓑ Ⓒ Ⓓ Ⓔ	Ⓐ Ⓑ Ⓒ Ⓓ Ⓔ
49	Ⓐ Ⓑ Ⓒ Ⓓ Ⓔ	Ⓐ Ⓑ Ⓒ Ⓓ Ⓔ	Ⓐ Ⓑ Ⓒ Ⓓ Ⓔ	Ⓐ Ⓑ Ⓒ Ⓓ Ⓔ
50	Ⓐ Ⓑ Ⓒ Ⓓ Ⓔ	Ⓐ Ⓑ Ⓒ Ⓓ Ⓔ	Ⓐ Ⓑ Ⓒ Ⓓ Ⓔ	Ⓐ Ⓑ Ⓒ Ⓓ Ⓔ

9. SIGNATURE:

FOR ETS USE ONLY	VTR	VTFS	VRR	VRFS	VVR	VVFS	WER	WEFS	M4R	M4FS	M5R	M5FS	MTFS	
	VTW	VTCS	VRW	VRCS	VVW	VVCS	WEW	WECS	M4W		M5W		MTCS	

YOUR NAME (PRINT) ______ LAST ______ FIRST ______ MI

TEST CENTER ______ NUMBER ______ NAME OF TEST CENTER ______ ROOM NUMBER

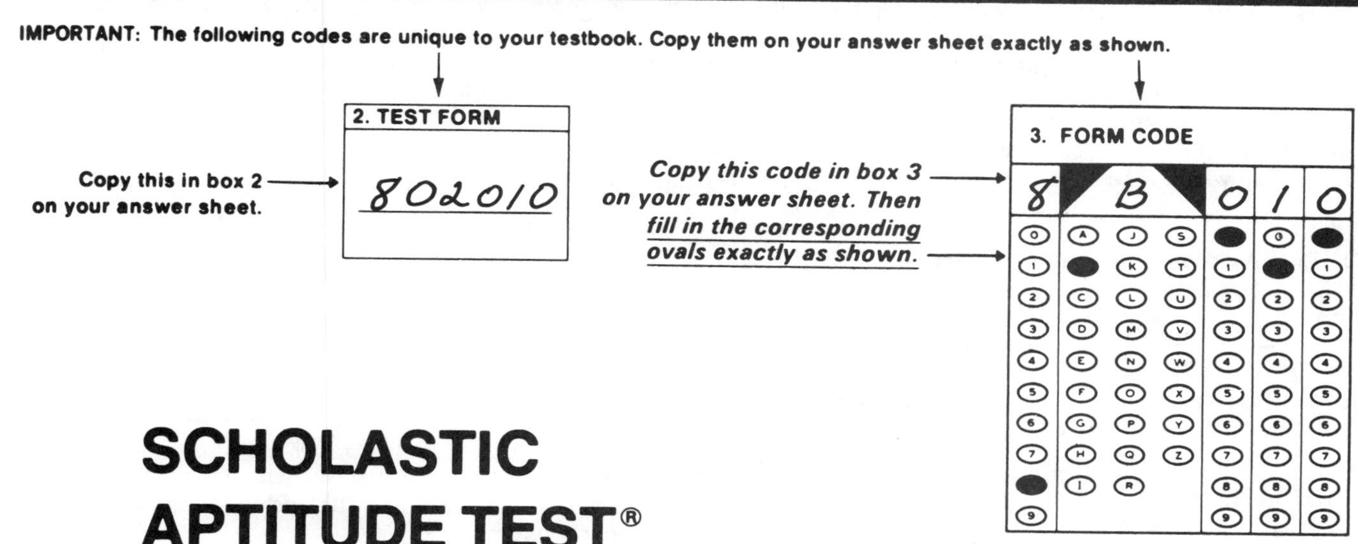
IMPORTANT: The following codes are unique to your testbook. Copy them on your answer sheet exactly as shown.

Copy this in box 2 on your answer sheet.

2. TEST FORM

802010

Copy this code in box 3 on your answer sheet. Then fill in the corresponding ovals exactly as shown.

3. FORM CODE

8B010

SCHOLASTIC APTITUDE TEST®

and Test of Standard Written English

You will have three hours to work on the questions in this test book, which is divided into six 30-minute sections. The supervisor will tell you when to begin and end each section. If you finish before time is called, you may check your work on that section, but you are not to work on any other section.

Do not worry if you are unable to finish a section or if there are some questions you cannot answer. Do not waste time puzzling over a question that seems too difficult for you. You should work as rapidly as you can without sacrificing accuracy.

Students often ask whether they should guess when they are uncertain about the answer to a question. Your test scores will be based on the number of questions you answer correctly minus a fraction of the number you answer incorrectly. Therefore, it is improbable that random or haphazard guessing will change your scores significantly. If you have some knowledge of a question, you may be able to eliminate one or more of the answer choices as wrong. It is generally to your advantage to guess which of the remaining choices is correct. Remember, however, not to spend too much time on any one question.

Mark all your answers on the separate answer sheet. Mark only one answer for each question. Since the answer sheet will be machine scored, be sure that each mark is dark and that it completely fills the oval. In each section of the answer sheet, there are spaces to answer 50 questions. When there are fewer than 50 questions in a section of your test, use only the spaces that correspond to the question numbers. Do not make stray marks on the answer sheet. If you erase, do so completely, because an incomplete erasure may be scored as an intended response.

You may use the test book for scratchwork, but you will not receive credit for anything written there.

(The passages for this test have been adapted from published material. The ideas contained in them do not necessarily represent the opinions of the College Board or Educational Testing Service.)

DO NOT OPEN THIS BOOK UNTIL THE SUPERVISOR TELLS YOU TO DO SO.

SECTION 1	Time—30 minutes 40 Questions	For each question in this section, choose the best answer and fill in the corresponding oval on the answer sheet.

Each question below consists of a word in capital letters, followed by five lettered words or phrases. Choose the word or phrase that is most nearly opposite in meaning to the word in capital letters. Since some of the questions require you to distinguish fine shades of meaning, consider all the choices before deciding which is best.

Example:

GOOD: (A) sour (B) bad (C) red (D) hot (E) ugly

Ⓐ ● Ⓒ Ⓓ Ⓔ

1. DRENCH: (A) extend (B) heat (C) search (D) dry out (E) pull apart

2. STIMULATE: (A) record (B) suppress (C) criticize (D) assemble (E) illuminate

3. CIVIL: (A) rude (B) inefficient (C) shy (D) lazy (E) proud

4. RUPTURE: (A) immensity (B) clamor (C) dejection (D) scrutiny (E) union

5. GROUNDLESS: (A) familiar (B) symmetrical (C) well-founded (D) deeply appreciated (E) carefully executed

6. BUNGLE: (A) resist firmly (B) behave honestly (C) speak respectfully (D) endure bravely (E) handle competently

7. OSTENTATIOUS: (A) dutiful (B) implausible (C) modest (D) at odds with (E) in awe of

8. VIGILANT: (A) unobtrusive (B) misleading (C) tardy (D) corrupt (E) inattentive

9. CAPITULATION: (A) fragmentation (B) impossibility (C) mediocrity (D) resistance (E) elegance

10. MUTABILITY: (A) absentmindedness (B) contentiousness (C) constancy (D) complexity (E) hardiness

Each sentence below has one or two blanks, each blank indicating that something has been omitted. Beneath the sentence are five lettered words or sets of words. Choose the word or set of words that, when inserted in the sentence, best fits the meaning of the sentence as a whole.

Example:

Although its publicity has been ----, the film itself is intelligent, well-acted, handsomely produced, and altogether ----.

(A) tasteless. .respectable (B) extensive. .moderate (C) sophisticated. .amateur (D) risqué. .crude (E) perfect. .spectacular

● Ⓑ Ⓒ Ⓓ Ⓔ

11. Scientists have discovered that our sense of smell is surprisingly ----, capable of distinguishing thousands of chemical odors.

(A) rigid (B) inert (C) erratic (D) keen (E) innate

12. With these ---- sites as evidence, it would be ---- to draw definite conclusions as to the places typically selected as settlements by the people of the Neolithic age.

(A) imperfect. .feasible
(B) few. .unsound
(C) complete. .ridiculous
(D) abundant. .presumptuous
(E) scattered. .prudent

13. Alice Walker's prize-winning novel exemplifies the strength of first-person narratives; the protagonist tells her own story so effectively that any additional commentary would be ----.

(A) subjective (B) eloquent (C) superfluous (D) incontrovertible (E) impervious

GO ON TO THE NEXT PAGE

14. The importance of science in the practical affairs of modern societies is recognized even by its detractors, but, surprisingly, its positive influence on culture is often ----, even by its ----.

(A) despised . . adversaries
(B) ascertained . . partisans
(C) conceded . . beneficiaries
(D) nullified . . assailants
(E) questioned . . champions

15. True to her altruistic beliefs, Natalie ---- the ---- attitude of her colleague that a client represented nothing more than a source of income and an opportunity for advancing one's professional reputation.

(A) applauded . . conscientious
(B) condoned . . aggressive
(C) lamented . . mercenary
(D) adopted . . egotistical
(E) belittled . . magnanimous

Each question below consists of a related pair of words or phrases, followed by five lettered pairs of words or phrases. Select the lettered pair that best expresses a relationship similar to that expressed in the original pair.

Example:

YAWN : BOREDOM ::
(A) dream : sleep
(B) anger : madness
(C) smile : amusement
(D) face : expression
(E) impatience : rebellion 

16. NUTRIENTS : FOOD :: (A) oxygen : air (B) earth : plants (C) diet : health (D) disease : symptom (E) moon : night

17. LIE : UNTRUTHFUL :: (A) steal : punished (B) exaggerate : retold (C) proofread : erroneous (D) pardon : forgiving (E) pray : kneeling

18. SHELL : WALNUT :: (A) coating : candy (B) peel : banana (C) icing : cake (D) loaf : bread (E) root : tree

19. RENOVATE : BUILDING :: (A) revoke : contract (B) rejuvenate : age (C) restore : painting (D) repeat : sentence (E) relinquish : possession

20. APPLAUSE : OVATION :: (A) performance : audience (B) sleep : nightmare (C) disrespect : homage (D) cure : medicine (E) disturbance : tumult

21. ANNUL : MARRIAGE :: (A) rebuke : criticism (B) hire : application (C) void : check (D) reject : hospitality (E) warn : danger

22. BLUEPRINT : BUILDING :: (A) score : music (B) letter : alphabet (C) chapter : segment (D) clothes : closet (E) prologue : novel

23. NEOPHYTE : EXPERIENCE ::
(A) oppressor : persecution
(B) traitor : loyalty
(C) genius : intelligence
(D) mediator : disagreement
(E) comedian : amusement

24. PROGENITOR : LINEAGE :: (A) prototype : inventor (B) heir : legacy (C) sibling : family (D) founder : dynasty (E) pioneer : frontier

25. MAXIM : TERSE ::
(A) tirade : calm
(B) proclamation : haughty
(C) definition : verbose
(D) cliché : trite
(E) eulogy : deceased

GO ON TO THE NEXT PAGE

The passages below are followed by questions based on their content. Answer the questions following each passage on the basis of what is stated or implied in that passage and any introductory material that may be provided.

For some very small animals, survival means existing in a state that conventional biology defines as death. These common but little-known life forms simply dry up, shriveling into wrinkled kernels. In this state they neither eat nor breathe, nor move. Digestion stops. Nervous systems shut down. All metabolism ceases. For periods of weeks, months, and even years, the little kernels merely endure.

But with the return of moisture, they revive. Within minutes the desiccated kernels absorb enough water to swell back to their normal proportions, and all of the hundreds of biochemical processes that make for life, at least as it is conventionally defined, begin again. Shrunken lumps of organisms that may have spent ten years in a bottle on a laboratory shelf virtually spring back into action when wetted, writhing and wriggling in a Petri dish, or literally crawling off the microscope slide in search of food.

Most introductory biology books teach that life cannot exist without water and that life is characterized by the various chemical processes that are summed up in the word "metabolism." And most biology books say that when metabolism ceases, death ensues. Are these books wrong? At the least, they seem to neglect an astonishing biological ability, a genuine form of suspended animation, possessed by scores of species that can be found by the billions in almost every habitat on earth.

26. Which of the following is the primary concern of the author?

(A) Redefining the significance of death
(B) Giving specific examples of animals that do not die
(C) Calling into question traditional definitions of life and death
(D) Announcing the discovery of a new species of animal
(E) Attacking biology texts as erroneous and inadequate

27. According to the passage, in conventional biology, the most important criterion for life is an organism's ability to

(A) communicate (B) reproduce (C) move
(D) metabolize (E) excrete

28. Which of the following does the author imply about life and death in the passage?

(A) Water can bring some forms of life back from death.
(B) Death does not necessarily occur when biochemical processes cease.
(C) Death does not occur as long as breathing continues.
(D) Life can be extended after death in laboratory environments.
(E) Suspended forms of life are quite vulnerable.

GO ON TO THE NEXT PAGE

The reading passages in this test are brief excerpts or adaptations of excerpts from published material. The ideas contained in them do not necessarily represent the opinions of the College Board or Educational Testing Service. To make the text suitable for testing purposes, we may in some cases have altered the style, contents, or point of view of the original.

This passage is from the beginning of a short story published in 1899. Hadleyburg is an imaginary town.

It was many years ago. Hadleyburg was the most honest and upright town in all the region round about. It had kept that reputation unsmirched during three generations, and was prouder of it than of any other of its possessions. It was so proud of it, and so anxious to insure its perpetuation, that it began to teach the principles of honest dealing to its babies in the cradle, and made the like teachings the staple of their culture thenceforward through all the years devoted to their education. Also, throughout the formative years temptations were kept out of the way of the young people, so that their honesty could have every chance to harden and solidify, and become a part of their very bone. The neighboring towns were jealous of this honorable supremacy, and affected to sneer at Hadleyburg's pride in it and call it vanity; but all the same they were obliged to acknowledge that Hadleyburg was in reality an incorruptible town; and if pressed they would also acknowledge that the mere fact that a young man hailed from Hadleyburg was all the recommendation he needed when he went forth from his natal town to seek for responsible employment.

But at last, in the drift of time, Hadleyburg had the ill luck to offend a passing stranger—possibly without knowing it, certainly without caring, for Hadleyburg was sufficient unto itself, and cared not a rap for strangers or their opinions. Still, it would have been well to make an exception in this one's case, for he was a bitter man and revengeful.

29. The main purpose of the passage is to
    (A) describe the general appearance of Hadleyburg as well as its special qualities
    (B) introduce the civic officials of Hadleyburg and account for their behavior
    (C) present Hadleyburg's reasons for establishing honesty as a principle
    (D) analyze Hadleyburg's pride in its reputation
    (E) establish the general character of Hadleyburg and its residents

30. The author's tone in the passage is best described as one of
    (A) moral indignation
    (B) hearty approval
    (C) impatient condescension
    (D) apparent objectivity
    (E) amused dismissal

31. It can be inferred that the author is preparing to describe
    (A) the actions of an individual from Hadleyburg who is different
    (B) the reasons for Hadleyburg's indifference to the opinions of strangers
    (C) the motivation of outsiders who sneer at the people of Hadleyburg
    (D) why the citizens of Hadleyburg behave as they do
    (E) the effect of one individual on Hadleyburg

GO ON TO THE NEXT PAGE

Homeric Heroes and Heroines

That there had once been a time of heroes and heroines few Greeks early or late ever doubted. They knew all about these epic figures: their names, their genealogies, and their exploits. Homer was the most authoritative source of information about them, but by no means the only one. Unfortunately, neither Homer nor other early Greek poets had the slightest interest in history as we understand it. The poets' concern was with certain events of the past, not with their relationship to other events, past or present, and in the case of Homer, not even with the consequences or dates of those events. The outcome of the Trojan War, the fall and destruction of Troy, and the fruits of Greek victory would have been of prime importance to a historian of the war. But Homer, the poet of the *Iliad*, was indifferent to all that; he gives no indication of the date of the Trojan War other than "once upon a time."

The participants in these events, the heroes and heroines, were central. Such figures are ubiquitous, of course. Every age has them, and that is misleading, for the label "hero" or "heroine" conceals a staggering diversity of substance. These figures always seek honor and glory. But few of the heroic figures of history or of literature from the fifth century B.C. to our own time actually shared the single-mindedness of their Homeric counterparts. For the latter, everything pivoted on honor and virtue: strength, bravery, physical courage, prowess. Conversely, there was only one weakness, one unheroic trait, and that was cowardice and the consequent failure to pursue heroic goals.

32. According to the passage, early Greek poets were most concerned with which of the following?

(A) Portrayal of heroic virtue
(B) Proof of military exploits
(C) The dates of past events
(D) The causes of the Trojan War
(E) The connection between past and present events

33. By saying that for Homer the Trojan War began "once upon a time" (line 17), the author implies that Homer's treatment of past events is

(A) historically imprecise
(B) morally neutral
(C) highly formulaic
(D) excessively prosaic
(E) wholly fictional

34. The primary focus of the second paragraph is on the

(A) deficiency of modern heroic figures in comparison to those presented by Homer
(B) specific problems encountered by historians studying ancient Greece
(C) distinctive qualities of Greek mythical heroes and heroines
(D) misrepresentation of human nature through the use of labels such as "hero" and "heroine"
(E) evidence that ancient Greek myths were based on historical events

35. It can be inferred from the passage that the author believes that Homeric heroic figures in general differ from post-Homeric heroic figures in which of the following ways?

I. They seek honor and glory.
II. They demonstrate courage.
III. They pursue heroism with unwavering determination.

(A) I only (B) II only (C) III only
(D) I and II only (E) I, II, and III

Henry Adams—scion of a family that included two American Presidents—felt himself out of place in the post-Civil War America political scene that was his inheritance. Adams entitled his autobiography *The Education of Henry Adams*—and if we assume that an education means the acquisition of skills and the mastery of tools designed for intelligent reaction in a given context, it would appear that Henry Adams' failure in American political society was a failure in education. Society wanted quick success and cared only for enough intelligence to support the drive. Society cared nothing for political mastery, and commonly refused to admit it had a purpose beyond the aggregation of force in the form of wealth. The effect of these implicit and pervasive attitudes on Adams as a young man was immediate, but it took him longer to articulate the problem. For such a society, any education was too much; and an Adams—with the finest education of his times—was clearly useless. The question was not, then, Adams' failure, but society's inability to make use of him: its inability to furnish a free field for intelligent political action. Washington was full of wasted talent—of able young people desperately eager to be of use, but no one knows what talent could have accomplished, because talent was never

GO ON TO THE NEXT PAGE

given a chance without being at the same time severely hampered.

The discovery—that he was to be wasted whether he was any good or not—was all the more bitter to Henry Adams because he had three generations of conspicuous ability and conspicuous failure behind him. Every Adams had ended as a failure after a lifetime of effort—marked by occasional and transitory success—to handle political power intelligently. Their intelligence they had kept; none had ever desired power for the mere sake of having it. An Adams met issues, accepted facts and developed policy, and never took public issues lightly.

Thus it is that many great individuals, if seen as examples of intellectual biography, seem either pawns of, or parasites upon, the society that produced them. Something of the sort is true, with different emphases, of Walt Whitman, Henry James, and Herman Melville. All outsiders from the life they expressed and upon which they fed, they stand out too much from their native society. If all knew the ignominy of applause from the wrong people, for the wrong thing, or for something not performed at all, it only accented their own sense of eccentricity and loneliness. That is how Adams stood out, without much applause—ignominious or otherwise—eccentric and lonely. But within him, as within the others, was an intelligence ruling actions that were direct, bold, and, at their best, terrifyingly sane.

36. The author is primarily concerned with describing

(A) Henry Adams' weaknesses as a commentator on nineteenth-century America
(B) the reasons for Henry Adams' failure in American political society
(C) the insensitivity of politicians in post-Civil War America
(D) the formal education of three generations of Adamses
(E) Henry Adams' life in comparison to those of other nineteenth-century writers

37. The author apparently believes that post-Civil War American society was

(A) lax and decadent
(B) confused and fragmented
(C) vengeful and hypocritical
(D) greedy and impatient
(E) disenchanted and depressed

38. With which of the following statements regarding Henry Adams would the author most likely agree?

(A) A perception of inherited public responsibility sharpened his disillusionment.
(B) His frustration with Washington politics rendered him ineffectual as a reporter of his times.
(C) A failure of vision more than a failed education accounted for his difficulties.
(D) He should have been more resolute and persistent in forging a political career.
(E) His expectations of success were unrealistic in view of his cynicism about the era.

39. According to the passage, many talented young people who went to Washington to serve in the post-Civil War government were

(A) appalled by society's greed
(B) hampered by their inadequate educations
(C) rendered ineffectual by the political power structure
(D) scorned for having intellectual and social pretensions
(E) trapped in a polarized political community

40. It can be inferred from the passage that the author believes Henry Adams possessed which of the following qualities?

I. A consuming desire for fame
II. A clear understanding of politics
III. A strong sense of moral accountability

(A) III only
(B) I and II only
(C) I and III only
(D) II and III only
(E) I, II, and III

IF YOU FINISH BEFORE TIME IS CALLED, YOU MAY CHECK YOUR WORK ON THIS SECTION ONLY. DO NOT TURN TO ANY OTHER SECTION IN THE TEST. **STOP**

SECTION 2 Time—30 minutes 25 Questions

In this section solve each problem, using any available space on the page for scratchwork. Then decide which is the best of the choices given and fill in the corresponding oval on the answer sheet.

The following information is for your reference in solving some of the problems.

Circle of radius r: Area $= \pi r^2$; Circumference $= 2\pi r$
The number of degrees of arc in a circle is 360.
The measure in degrees of a straight angle is 180.

Definition of symbols:

$=$ is equal to	$\leqq$ is less than or equal to
$\neq$ is unequal to	$\geqq$ is greater than or equal to
$<$ is less than	$\parallel$ is parallel to
$>$ is greater than	$\perp$ is perpendicular to

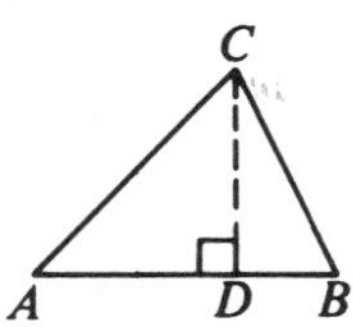

Triangle: The sum of the measures in degrees of the angles of a triangle is 180.
If $\angle CDA$ is a right angle, then

(1) area of $\triangle ABC = \frac{AB \times CD}{2}$

(2) $AC^2 = AD^2 + DC^2$

Note: Figures that accompany problems in this test are intended to provide information useful in solving the problems. They are drawn as accurately as possible EXCEPT when it is stated in a specific problem that its figure is not drawn to scale. All figures lie in a plane unless otherwise indicated. All numbers used are real numbers.

1. If $2x - 6 = 10$, then $3x - 6 =$

(A) 0
(B) 8
(C) 11
(D) 18
(E) 24

2. $\frac{6 \times 10^3}{2 \times 10^2} =$

(A) 3
(B) 4.5
(C) 20
(D) 30
(E) 40

Questions 3-4 refer to the following graph.

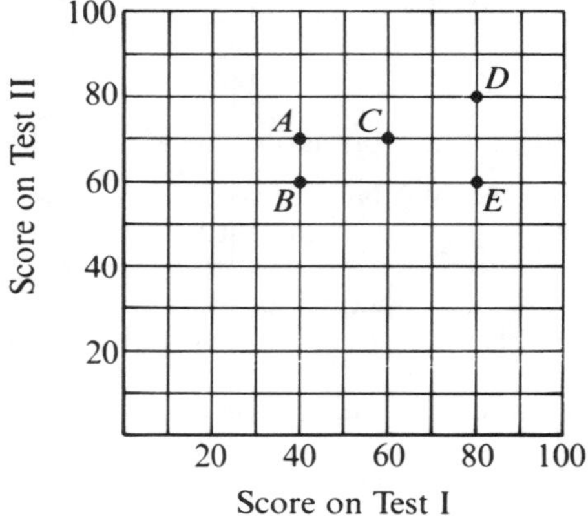

3. For which student was the change in scores from test I to test II the greatest?

(A) A
(B) B
(C) C
(D) D
(E) E

4. What was the average (arithmetic mean) of the scores of the 5 students on test II ?

(A) 60
(B) 65
(C) 68
(D) 70
(E) 72

GO ON TO THE NEXT PAGE

5. If $\frac{2+3}{x} = \frac{2+x}{3}$, which of the following could be a value for x?

(A) -3
(B) -1
(C) 3
(D) 5
(E) 15

6. If $x = 16$, then $x^2 - \sqrt{x} =$

(A) 24
(B) 28
(C) 144
(D) 248
(E) 252

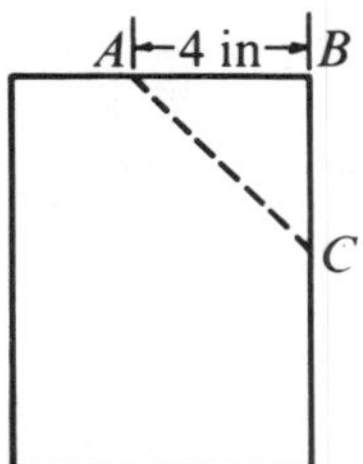

Figure I

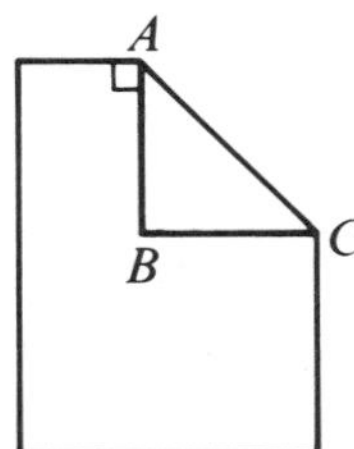

Figure II

7. The rectangular piece of paper represented in Figure I above is folded on dotted line segment AC so that the folded paper is represented by Figure II. If the length of AB is 4 inches, what is the length of BC, in inches?

(A) 2
(B) 4
(C) 5
(D) $4\sqrt{2}$
(E) $4\sqrt{3}$

8. If a, b, and c are three consecutive integers, which of the following must be true?

I. At least one of these integers is divisible by 2.
II. One of these integers is divisible by 3.
III. One of these integers is divisible by 4.

(A) I only
(B) II only
(C) III only
(D) I and II
(E) I and III

9. Expressed as a sum, $8 - 9 - (-10) - 4 =$

(A) $8 + (-9) + (-10) + (-4)$
(B) $8 + 9 + 10 + (-4)$
(C) $8 + (-9) + 10 + (-4)$
(D) $8 + (-9) + (-10) + 4$
(E) $8 + 9 + (-10) + 4$

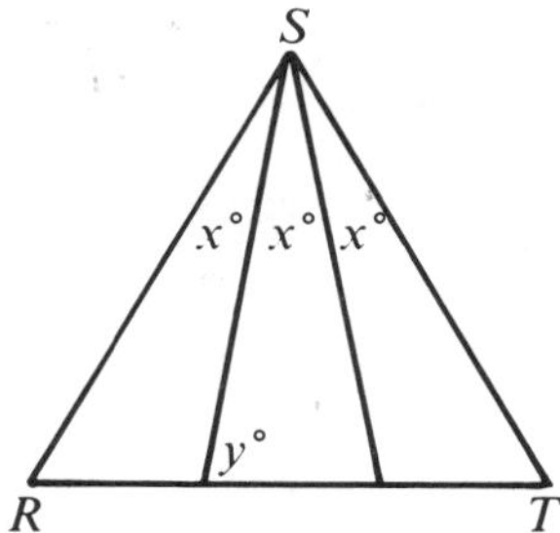

10. In the equilateral triangle RST above, y equals

(A) 60
(B) 70
(C) 75
(D) 80
(E) 85

11. The average (arithmetic mean) of three numbers is 23. If one of the three numbers is 8, what is the sum of the other two?

(A) 15
(B) 38
(C) 47
(D) 54
(E) 61

12. A "weather watch" camera is set so that its shutter opens every 31 seconds. At this rate, approximately how many times does the camera's shutter open in 1 hour?

(A) 12
(B) 91
(C) 116
(D) 1,200
(E) 1,860

13. If x and y are positive integers, $x^2 + y^2 = 25$, and $x^2 - y^2 = 7$, then $y =$

(A) 3
(B) 4
(C) 5
(D) 9
(E) 16

GO ON TO THE NEXT PAGE

14. If horizontal line segment AB is perpendicular to line segment CD at point O and if line segment EF bisects $\angle AOD$, which of the following could be the value of $\angle COF$?

(A) 60
(B) 45
(C) 40
(D) 30
(E) 20

15. If $\frac{a}{b} = \frac{5}{9}$ and $\frac{b}{c} = \frac{3}{5}$, then $\frac{a}{c} =$

(A) $\frac{1}{9}$

(B) $\frac{1}{5}$

(C) $\frac{1}{3}$

(D) $\frac{5}{9}$

(E) $\frac{3}{5}$

16. How old was a person exactly 1 year ago if exactly x years ago the person was y years old?

(A) $y - 1$
(B) $y - x - 1$
(C) $x - y - 1$
(D) $y + x + 1$
(E) $y + x - 1$

17. A, B, C, and D are points on a line, with D the midpoint of segment BC. The lengths of segments AB, AC, and BC are 10, 2, and 12, respectively. What is the length of segment AD?

(A) 2
(B) 4
(C) 6
(D) 10
(E) 12

Q R
P T S

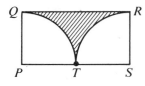

18. In rectangle $PQRS$ above, arcs QT and RT are quarter circles with centers at P and S, respectively. If the radius of each quarter circle is 1, what is the area of the shaded region?

(A) $1 - \frac{\pi}{4}$

(B) $2 - \frac{\pi}{2}$

(C) $2 - \frac{\pi}{4}$

(D) $\frac{\pi}{4}$

(E) $\frac{2}{3}$

19. A baseball team has won 10 games and lost 5 games. If the team wins the next k games, it will have won 80 percent of all the games it played. What is the value of k?

(A) 2
(B) 3
(C) 6
(D) 8
(E) 10

A, B, C, D, E, F, G

20. How many three-letter arrangements, such as DCA, can be formed using the letters above if the first letter must be D, one of the remaining letters must be A, and no letter can be used more than once in an arrangement?

(A) Five
(B) Six
(C) Nine
(D) Ten
(E) Twelve

GO ON TO THE NEXT PAGE

21. For all numbers x, let $\boxed{x}$ be defined by $\boxed{x} = x^2 - 1$. Which of the following is equal to the product of $\boxed{3}$ and $\boxed{4}$?

(A) $\boxed{12}$

(B) $\boxed{11}$

(C) $\boxed{10}$

(D) $\boxed{9}$

(E) $\boxed{7}$

22. If r_1 and r_2 are the radii of two circles and if $2 \leqq r_1 \leqq 7$ and $3 \leqq r_2 \leqq 9$, then the greatest possible difference between the areas of these circles is

(A) 32π
(B) 40π
(C) 49π
(D) 77π
(E) 81π

23. A blend of coffee is made by mixing Colombian coffee at $8 a pound with espresso coffee at $3 a pound. If the blend is worth $5 a pound, how many pounds of the Colombian coffee are needed to make 50 pounds of the blend?

(A) 20
(B) 25
(C) 30
(D) 35
(E) 40

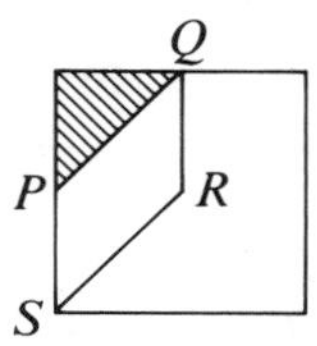

24. In the figure above, $PQRS$ is a parallelogram, and P and Q are the midpoints of adjacent sides of the square, as shown. If the area of the shaded region is 2, then the perimeter of $PQRS$ is

(A) $4 + 4\sqrt{2}$
(B) $2 + 4\sqrt{2}$
(C) $4 + 2\sqrt{2}$
(D) 4
(E) 16

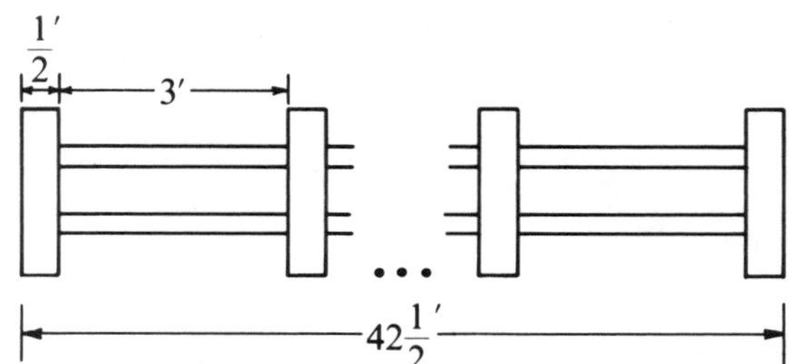

25. The figure above shows part of a $42\frac{1}{2}$-foot fence in which $\frac{1}{2}$-foot wide vertical boards are arranged 3 feet apart. How many vertical boards are needed for the entire fence?

(A) 10
(B) 11
(C) 12
(D) 13
(E) 14

IF YOU FINISH BEFORE TIME IS CALLED, YOU MAY CHECK YOUR WORK ON THIS SECTION ONLY. DO NOT TURN TO ANY OTHER SECTION IN THE TEST. **STOP**

SECTION 3 Time—30 minutes 45 Questions

For each question in this section, choose the best answer and fill in the corresponding oval on the answer sheet.

Each question below consists of a word in capital letters, followed by five lettered words or phrases. Choose the word or phrase that is most nearly opposite in meaning to the word in capital letters. Since some of the questions require you to distinguish fine shades of meaning, consider all the choices before deciding which is best.

Example:

GOOD: (A) sour (B) bad (C) red (D) hot (E) ugly

(A) ● (C) (D) (E)

1. EXCESS: (A) response (B) modification (C) concealment (D) shortage (E) slenderness

2. DETESTABLE: (A) measurable (B) mature (C) agreeable (D) expensive (E) colorful

3. PREDETERMINED:
(A) not encountered before
(B) not decided in advance
(C) not essential
(D) imperfect
(E) undesirable

4. COINCIDE: (A) diverge (B) hesitate (C) intend (D) remove (E) excite

5. VAPORIZE: (A) decrease (B) progress (C) immobilize (D) condense (E) dilute

6. DRAWBACK: (A) festivity (B) proposal (C) tabulation (D) sketch (E) asset

7. UNSUNG: (A) dramatic (B) explicit (C) concentrated (D) celebrated (E) reconciled

8. CONVIVIAL: (A) flexible (B) patient (C) perceptive (D) unkempt (E) unsociable

9. EFFERVESCENT: (A) old (B) flat (C) lawful (D) coarse (E) bent

10. UNEXPURGATED: (A) delayed (B) constructed (C) mishandled (D) extinguished (E) censored

11. PARITY: (A) ruthlessness (B) indecision (C) inequality (D) unpreparedness (E) forfeiture

12. ASCENDANCY: (A) act of clemency (B) proof of disloyalty (C) insecurity (D) subjugation (E) obligation

13. JETTISON: (A) recover (B) regress (C) endure (D) obstruct (E) subdue

14. QUERULOUS: (A) uncomplaining (B) disorganized (C) conventional (D) faithful (E) timid

15. PITHY: (A) rambling (B) fine (C) gracious (D) congruent (E) isolated

GO ON TO THE NEXT PAGE

Each sentence below has one or two blanks, each blank indicating that something has been omitted. Beneath the sentence are five lettered words or sets of words. Choose the word or set of words that, when inserted in the sentence, best fits the meaning of the sentence as a whole.

Example:

Although its publicity has been ----, the film itself is intelligent, well-acted, handsomely produced, and altogether ----.

(A) tasteless. .respectable (B) extensive. .moderate (C) sophisticated. .amateur (D) risqué. .crude (E) perfect. .spectacular

● Ⓑ Ⓒ Ⓓ Ⓔ

16. The athlete's insistence on self-discipline had become ----; rarely, it seemed, did he allow himself even a minor indulgence.

(A) dilatory (B) obsessive (C) spontaneous (D) infectious (E) unemotional

17. All female red *Colobus* monkeys leave their natal troops, but because these females are ---- by young females from other troops, the practice has little effect on troop size and composition.

(A) joined (B) replaced (C) ignored (D) influenced (E) rejected

18. Some travelers from the United States experience culture shock when they suddenly find themselves in a place where "yes" may mean "no," where a fixed price is ----, where laughter may signify ----.

(A) alterable. .joy
(B) unchangeable. .insult
(C) sovereign. .merriment
(D) incalculable. .harmony
(E) negotiable. .anger

19. According to Burgess, a novelist should not ----, for sermonizing has no place in good fiction.

(A) invent (B) offend (C) inform (D) preach (E) distort

20. The archaeologist enjoyed the ---- life she led while gathering artifacts; she never stayed at any one site long enough to get bored.

(A) stealthy (B) nomadic (C) clamorous (D) indiscreet (E) rustic

21. Medieval illuminated manuscripts are too ---- for exhibition except under rigorously controlled conditions of light, temperature, and humidity, and thus are ---- the majority of art lovers.

(A) intricate. .imperceptible to
(B) immaculate. .idolized by
(C) fragile. .available to
(D) valuable. .scorned by
(E) vulnerable. .inaccessible to

22. The artistry of cellist YoYo Ma is essentially ----; the melodic line rises ----, imbued with feeling and totally lacking in apparent calculation.

(A) carefree. .stiffly
(B) reserved. .involuntarily
(C) lyrical. .passionately
(D) detached. .carefully
(E) deliberate. .methodically

23. The Supreme Court's reversal of its previous ruling on the issue of States' rights ---- its reputation for ----.

(A) sustained. .infallibility
(B) compromised. .consistency
(C) bolstered. .doggedness
(D) exacerbated. .inflexibility
(E) dispelled. .vacillation

24. Denise was astounded to hear that her brother, whom she knew to be quite ----, was described as taciturn and aloof by his colleagues at the university.

(A) insular
(B) placid
(C) anguished
(D) vacuous
(E) garrulous

25. Because they are ---- to take the financial loss that results from providing drugs for ---- markets, pharmaceutical manufacturers often do not produce needed drugs for rare diseases.

(A) proud. .small
(B) eager. .known
(C) prone. .nebulous
(D) loath. .limited
(E) reluctant. .expanding

GO ON TO THE NEXT PAGE

The passages below are followed by questions based on their content. Answer the questions following each passage on the basis of what is stated or implied in that passage and any introductory material that may be provided.

Of Lucy Terry and the man she married, historian George Sheldon has written, "In the . . . lives of Abijah Prince and Lucy Terry is found a realistic romance going beyond the wildest flights of fiction." Lucy Terry, born in Africa around 1730, was five years old when she was brought to Deerfield, Massachusetts, a little town standing on the northernmost edge of a vast hostile territory that stretched between the British colonies and French Canada. By the time she married Abijah Prince in 1756, she had won fame for a ballad she had written ten years earlier, at sixteen, about a surprise attack by Indians outside of Deerfield. Her rhymed description of "The Bar's Fight" appears to be the first published poetry by an Afro-American and has been called the most accurate surviving report of the event.

Abijah Prince had distinctions of his own: for four years he served in the militia during the French and Indian struggle known as King George's War. He later gained his liberty and obtained his wife's freedom. He owned farms in Northfield, Massachusetts, and in Guilford, Vermont; by his own application to George III of England and the governor of New Hampshire, he became one of the original grantees and founders of the town of Sunderland, Vermont, where he also owned a farm.

In addition, two of the Princes' sons served in the American Revolution, but not even patriotism and wartime service could provide immunity from bigotry in early America. In 1785 property on the farm at Guilford was destroyed by a wealthy White neighbor. Abijah, nearly eighty, stayed at home, and Lucy crossed the state to carry her protest to the governor's council. The men on that council, who were not unmindful of the political influence of her wealthy antagonist, listened to her argument and on June 7, 1785, found in her favor. Never before had a Black woman in America reached so high into the sources of power and met with such success.

Lucy Terry was to appear once more in public to claim her rights to equal justice. This case concerned a boundary dispute with a neighbor who claimed part of her Sunderland property. Abijah had died in 1794, and so Lucy entered Vermont's Supreme Court advised by Isaac Ticknor, United States senator, jurist, and for many years Vermont's governor. Opposing counsel was Royall Tyler, later chief justice of the Vermont Supreme Court. There is uncertainty about the identity of the judge who presided, but there is no uncertainty about what he said to the party in whose favor he ruled. He stated that Lucy Terry "made a better argument than he had heard from any lawyer at the Vermont bar." Again, Lucy Terry had been unafraid to confront the most powerful—and she had won.

26. The primary purpose of the passage is to

(A) describe what made Lucy Terry and Abijah Prince important
(B) explain the events that led to the Princes' marriage
(C) examine what motivated Lucy Terry in her search for justice
(D) analyze the reactions of two Afro-Americans to the American Revolution
(E) compare the accomplishments of Lucy Terry to those of Abijah Prince

27. It can be inferred from the passage that, from her youth to her later years, Lucy Terry was recognized for her

(A) bravery in exposing unjust practices
(B) ability to use words eloquently and effectively
(C) talent for creating literary texts
(D) gift for extemporaneous public speaking
(E) skill in organizing people quickly and efficiently

28. The passage indicates that during his lifetime Abijah Prince was all of the following EXCEPT a

(A) member of the militia in a colonial war
(B) husband who secured his wife's freedom from slavery
(C) landowner in several different communities
(D) cofounder of a town in Vermont
(E) soldier in the American army during the Revolution

29. Which of the following specifically disregarded the rights of the Prince family?

(A) A colonial governor of New Hampshire
(B) A judge of the Vermont Supreme Court
(C) A United States senator
(D) Their neighbors in Northfield
(E) A resident of Guilford

30. The passage suggests that the author would agree most fully with which of the following statements about Lucy Terry?

(A) She received extensive legal training from prominent attorneys.
(B) She urged her children to speak out on local issues.
(C) She was a pioneer in a variety of fields.
(D) She was by nature eager to help others.
(E) She was a characteristic figure of her era.

GO ON TO THE NEXT PAGE

Geological and geophysical studies of the Earth's crust reveal the dominance of vertical movements during the formation of the continents. Water-deposited sediments now exposed in outcrops many thousands of meters above sea level, uplifted plateaus, and downwarped sedimentary troughs all point to dramatic vertical movement. Rocks of all ages can be found in continental areas, some 3,000 to 4,000 million years old, almost as old as the Earth and the solar system itself, and probably representing a very primitive crust.

More recently scientists have been unraveling the history and structure of the two-thirds of the Earth's crust that is covered by deep water. Their studies indicate that the deep ocean floor has a fabric that implies large-scale horizontal movements during its evolution. In addition, it is probably true that no part of the deep-sea floor is more than 200 million years old. Thus, this two-thirds of the Earth's outermost skin has been formed within less than 5 percent of geologic time.

Using seismic techniques involving refraction, marine geophysicists have learned that the oceanic crust is remarkably thin—6 or 7 kilometers in thickness compared to the 35 kilometers typical of continental areas. A study of rocks dredged from the ocean floor revealed that they were all basalts, or simple derivatives of basalts, comparable to those extruded by volcanoes on Hawaii. Continental basalts are similar to those on the ocean floor, but form only a small proportion of the continental crust. Clearly, the structure and the composition of the Earth's crust beneath the ocean are much simpler than are those of the continental crust.

In 1960 Professor Harry Hess postulated that the thin oceanic crust is derived directly from the Earth's mantle (the dense, hot material below the crust) by partial melting and simple chemical modification. Hess suggested, moreover, that this crust is constantly being created from the mantle at midocean ridge crests and reabsorbed back into the mantle in the deep trenches that lie mostly at the margins of the Pacific. If the oceanic crust forms at ridge crests at one centimeter per year, the resulting sideways "spreading" would have been sufficient to produce the Atlantic basin within the past 200 million years. In terms of the Earth's history, the ocean basins are young, short-lived entities, and the seemingly permanent continents have been passively drifting apart and coming together as the ocean floors spread.

The realization that most earthquake activity occurs along a narrow belt of mountain systems at the boundary of the spreading seafloor corroborated Hess's thesis. Indeed, the currently accepted geological picture shows new seafloor continuously forming at the midocean ridges, old floor plunging into the deep ocean trenches, and this seafloor activity pushing the Earth's rigid crustal plates into a motion that, over time, has radically changed the positions and shapes of all the continents.

31. The passage is primarily concerned with which of the following?

(A) Reporting a controversy that has arisen among marine geophysicists
(B) Portraying a prominent geologist who has made an important discovery
(C) Outlining the new field of seismic geology
(D) Describing a recently advanced theory of geological processes
(E) Countering a prevailing theory about how the Earth was formed

32. According to the passage, in which of the following respects do the oceanic and continental crusts differ?

I. Age
II. Thickness
III. Compositional complexity

(A) I only
(B) II only
(C) I and II only
(D) II and III only
(E) I, II, and III

33. According to the passage, the age of the Earth's oceanic crust is

(A) not more than 200 million years
(B) approximately 667 million years
(C) between 1,000 million and 2,000 million years
(D) between 3,000 million and 4,000 million years
(E) greater than 4,000 million years

34. Which of the following discoveries, if it were made, would constitute the most significant evidence against Harry Hess's thesis?

(A) The continents once had very different configurations from those they have now.
(B) More earthquakes occur at the ocean's boundary than in the midst of the continents.
(C) The Atlantic basin crust contains rocks different in composition from, and much older than, any previously known to be there.
(D) Basaltic rock is more prevalent in the continental crust than was formerly suspected.
(E) The Earth's mantle extends much deeper beneath the oceanic and the continental crusts than was formerly suspected.

GO ON TO THE NEXT PAGE

35. The passage offers information to answer all of the following questions EXCEPT:

(A) Approximately how old is the Earth?
(B) Approximately how thick is the oceanic crust?
(C) What is the basic cause of the ocean floor's movement?
(D) What is the effect of earthquake tremors on the oceanic crust?
(E) What happens to oceanic crust that plunges into the deep oceanic trenches?

Each question below consists of a related pair of words or phrases, followed by five lettered pairs of words or phrases. Select the lettered pair that best expresses a relationship similar to that expressed in the original pair.

Example:

YAWN : BOREDOM :: (A) dream : sleep
(B) anger : madness (C) smile : amusement
(D) face : expression (E) impatience : rebellion

Ⓐ Ⓑ ● Ⓓ Ⓔ

36. HAMMER : CARPENTER :: (A) stone : mason
(B) brush : painter (C) music : violinist
(D) suspect : detective (E) bracelet : jeweler

37. EXPEL : SCHOOL :: (A) deny : entrance
(B) banish : country (C) reject : offer
(D) extricate : safety (E) abandon : enemy

38. SALUTATION : LETTER ::
(A) greeting : conversation
(B) message : telegram
(C) goodwill : feeling
(D) address : location
(E) agreement : debate

39. PEPPER MILL : GRINDING ::
(A) scale : weighing
(B) grease : moving
(C) detergent : scrubbing
(D) engine : fueling
(E) spice : seasoning

40. FACTION : POLITICS ::
(A) geography : history
(B) war : peace
(C) sect : religion
(D) taxes : income
(E) duel : honor

41. EGOISM : SELF ::
(A) escapism: daydreamer
(B) materialism : possessions
(C) capitalism : economics
(D) symbolism : artist
(E) isolationism : society

42. SPY : WATCH :: (A) admire : extol
(B) hoard : save (C) design : build
(D) study : learn (E) bargain : reduce

43. ARBORETUM : TREES ::
(A) stadium : spectators (B) theater : tickets
(C) museum : artworks (D) pasture : cows
(E) library : shelves

44. CONFLAGRATION : FIRE ::
(A) misdemeanor : crime
(B) metropolis : city
(C) matrimony : spouse
(D) sedative : sleep
(E) controversy : peace

45. FLACCID : FIRMNESS ::
(A) weathered : exposure (B) dreadful : fear
(C) amorphous : form (D) stagnant : stillness
(E) cavernous : space

IF YOU FINISH BEFORE TIME IS CALLED, YOU MAY CHECK YOUR WORK ON THIS SECTION ONLY. DO NOT TURN TO ANY OTHER SECTION IN THE TEST. **STOP**

SECTION 4

Time—30 minutes
50 Questions

The questions in this section measure skills that are important to writing well. In particular, they test your ability to recognize the use of language that is clear, effective, and correct according to the requirements of standard written English, the kind of English found in most college textbooks.

Directions: The following sentences test your knowledge of grammar, usage, diction (choice of words), and idiom.
Some sentences are correct.
No sentence contains more than one error.

You will find that the error, if there is one, is underlined and lettered. Assume that elements of the sentence that are not underlined are correct and cannot be changed. In choosing answers, follow the requirements of standard written English.

If there is an error, select the one underlined part that must be changed to make the sentence correct and fill in the corresponding oval on your answer sheet.

If there is no error, fill in oval (E).

Example:

The other (A) delegates and him (B) immediately (C) accepted the resolution drafted by (D) the neutral states. No error (E)

Sample Answer

(A) ● (C) (D) (E)

1. For (A) the past three years, the puppet troupe has went (B) to schools throughout (C) the state to present programs that teach (D) children about Black history. No error (E)

2. Of all (A) the written sources from which history can be (B) reconstructed, diaries are undoubtedly (C) the more (D) entertaining. No error (E)

3. Diplomatic relations between (A) Great Britain and Iceland improved once (B) it (C) had agreed to (D) observe the fishing restrictions. No error (E)

4. When (A) Zora Neale Hurston began to write (B) short stories in the late (C) 1920's, she initiated (D) the second stage of the Harlem Renaissance. No error (E)

5. A stunt man often is able for working (A) only two weeks a month (B) because of (C) the injuries he suffers on the job (D). No error (E)

6. If there is (A) funds budgeted for purchasing (B) new books, your request will probably (C) be approved (D). No error (E)

7. Many scientists are convinced that (A) individuals who have been working at (B) asbestos in their jobs (C) are likely (D) to develop health problems. No error (E)

8. For the recent exhibition, the museum acquired (A) a rock from (B) a volcano that has erupted (C) more than (D) two thousand years ago. No error (E)

GO ON TO THE NEXT PAGE

9. Some researchers have theorized (A) that there may be (B) a connection between hormones with (C) the body's ability to (D) heal damaged organs. No error (E)

10. Whether (A) relaxing with visitors or lecturing to (B) an audience, the mayoral candidate freely (C) offered her opinions on all subjects (D). No error (E)

11. According to (A) recent reports, more women are working (B) as the manager (C) of small business firms than ever (D) before. No error (E)

12. Although (A) the language of *The Canterbury Tales* seems strange (B) to us, it reflects (C) the language talked (D) in Chaucer's time. No error (E)

13. To a much greater extent (A) than is generally (B) realized (C), the economy of the United States relies on (D) agriculture. No error (E)

14. Gustave Flaubert is thought to be (A) one of (B) the three or four writers which (C) were influential in (D) the creation of the modern realistic novel. No error (E)

15. Even with (A) a calculator, you must have a basic understanding of (B) mathematics if one expects (C) to solve complex problems correctly (D). No error (E)

16. In the last decade, some college graduates will have defaulted (A) on federal loans for (B) their (C) education by declaring (D) bankruptcy. No error (E)

17. In their (A) report to the treasurer and I (B), the members of the subcommittee argued in favor of (C) establishing (D) a library. No error (E)

18. Because (A) eighteenth-century literature is filled up with (B) references to (C) Greek mythology, it often intimidates those who have not studied (D) ancient myths. No error (E)

19. There is (A) a number of reasons, both (B) economic and ecological, for (C) Oregon's desire to limit (D) population growth. No error (E)

20. A deer herd can be expected (A) to double in size every two or (B) three years until (C) its territory becomes crowded (D). No error (E)

21. Those interviewed said that they (A) excepted (B) the principle of equal employment and believed that every effort should be made (C) to end (D) sex discrimination. No error (E)

22. Even though (A) she had the impressive title of (B) executive assistant, her salary was lower (C) than a secretary (D). No error (E)

23. The similarities between (A) the two societies Heyerdahl studied (B) tend to (C) support his theory that the origins of the Polynesians were in (D) South America. No error (E)

GO ON TO THE NEXT PAGE

24. To learn more about Hispanic culture, we invited a lecturer who had spoken frequently with regard to the life of early settlers in Santa Fe. No error
(To learn more = A; lecturer who = B; with regard to = C; the life of = D; No error = E)

25. In the nineteenth century, a number of occupations came to be viewed as unsuitable for women or incompatible with her work in the home. No error
(In = A; came to be viewed = B; unsuitable for = C; her = D; No error = E)

Directions: In each of the following sentences, some part or all of the sentence is underlined. Below each sentence you will find five ways of phrasing the underlined part. Select the answer that produces the most effective sentence, one that is clear and exact, without awkwardness or ambiguity, and fill in the corresponding oval on your answer sheet. In choosing answers, follow the requirements of standard written English. Choose the answer that best expresses the meaning of the original sentence.

Answer (A) is always the same as the underlined part. Choose answer (A) if you think the original sentence needs no revision.

Example:

Laura Ingalls Wilder published her first book and she was sixty-five years old then.

(A) and she was sixty-five years old then
(B) when she was sixty-five years old
(C) at age sixty-five years old
(D) upon reaching sixty-five years
(E) at the time when she was sixty-five

Sample Answer

26. This year's Puerto Rican Day parade being more impressive than last year's.

(A) being more impressive than last year's
(B) it was impressive, more so than last year
(C) which was more impressive than the one last year
(D) was more impressive than last year's
(E) by far more impressive than the last

27. Changing to the metric system means using grams rather than ounces, liters rather than quarts, and to using kilometers rather than miles.

(A) to using kilometers rather than miles
(B) to the use of kilometers rather than miles
(C) kilometers rather than miles
(D) replacing miles with kilometers
(E) to kilometers rather than miles

28. It was not until the sixteenth century that chairs became common, before that time a chair was an authority symbol.

(A) common, before that time a chair was an authority symbol
(B) common; before that time a chair was a symbol of authority
(C) common; in prior times a chair was a symbol of authority, however
(D) common because earlier chairs were considered authority symbols
(E) common in that earlier they were authority symbols

GO ON TO THE NEXT PAGE

29. The two carpenters are building their own shop, which is satisfying to them.
    (A) The two carpenters are building their own shop, which is satisfying to them.
    (B) Building their own shop, this is satisfying to the carpenters.
    (C) The two carpenters find that building their own shop is a satisfying experience.
    (D) The two carpenters, who are building their own shop, which is satisfying.
    (E) A satisfying experience, the carpenters are building their own shop.

30. When Robert E. Lee was well past forty, he competed with his sons in high jumping.
    (A) he competed with his sons in high jumping
    (B) him and his sons were competing in high jumping
    (C) he and his sons have competed in high jumping
    (D) he was in competition in high jumping with his sons
    (E) competition with his sons in high jumping took place

31. Josh was relieved to find his lost keys walking along the street in front of his apartment building.
    (A) Josh was relieved to find his lost keys walking along the street in front of his apartment building.
    (B) Much to his relief, Josh found his lost keys walking along the street in front of his apartment building.
    (C) Walking along the street in front of his apartment building, Josh's lost keys were found by him, much to his relief.
    (D) Josh, relieved to find his lost keys, while walking along the street in front of his apartment building.
    (E) Walking along the street in front of his apartment building, Josh found his lost keys, much to his relief.

32. It is not easy to arrive at a single set of values in a pluralistic society, where it has divergent views that challenge conventional thinking.
    (A) where it has divergent views that
    (B) in which divergent views
    (C) whereby divergent views
    (D) and the reason is if the views of those diverging
    (E) because in it the views of those diverging

33. The steel industry, under pressure to give women equal job opportunities, and changing its all-male image.
    (A) and changing its
    (B) by changing its
    (C) is changing their
    (D) but changing their
    (E) is changing its

34. The patient recovered quickly and was quite ill earlier in the week.
    (A) The patient recovered quickly and was quite ill earlier in the week.
    (B) The patient recovered quickly, earlier in the week he was quite ill.
    (C) The patient's recovery was quick after being quite ill earlier in the week.
    (D) The patient, who was quite ill earlier in the week, recovered quickly.
    (E) The patient, who recovered quickly, being quite ill earlier in the week.

35. Foreign correspondents are like birds of passage, resting for a few weeks, then flying off again to a new place.
    (A) then flying off again
    (B) after which again they fly off
    (C) then they fly off again
    (D) when once again they fly off
    (E) but soon they are flying off again

36. Hoping to add a touch of humor to his mother's birthday party, Jim gave a huge box to her containing a very small gift.
    (A) Jim gave a huge box to her containing a very small gift
    (B) given to her by Jim was a huge box containing a very small gift
    (C) she was given a huge box containing a very small gift by Jim
    (D) Jim gave her a huge box containing a very small gift
    (E) Jim gave a very small gift to her contained in a huge box

37. Alice Walker, one of America's best-known writers, she has published both poetry and prose.
    (A) writers, she has published
    (B) writers, has published
    (C) writers, and publishing
    (D) writers since publishing
    (E) writers when she published

GO ON TO THE NEXT PAGE

38. Justice Thurgood Marshall, who was appointed by Lyndon Johnson, is the first Black American to serve on the Supreme Court.

    (A) Justice Thurgood Marshall, who was appointed by Lyndon Johnson, is the first Black American to serve on the Supreme Court.
    (B) Justice Thurgood Marshall being the first Black American to serve on the Supreme Court and was appointed by Lyndon Johnson.
    (C) Being the first Black American to serve on the Supreme Court, Justice Thurgood Marshall was appointed by Lyndon Johnson.
    (D) Justice Thurgood Marshall is the first Black American to serve on the Supreme Court and was appointed by Lyndon Johnson.
    (E) Justice Thurgood Marshall is the first Black American to serve on the Supreme Court, and he was appointed by Lyndon Johnson.

39. The turning point in the battle of Actium clearly was Cleopatra, who was fleeing.

    (A) Cleopatra, who was fleeing
    (B) Cleopatra, in that she fled
    (C) Cleopatra's flight
    (D) when Cleopatra was fleeing
    (E) that Cleopatra took flight

40. Today's fashion designers must consider both how much a fabric costs and its wearability.

    (A) its wearability
    (B) is it going to wear well
    (C) if it has wearability
    (D) how well it wears
    (E) the fabric's ability to wear well

Note: The remaining questions are like those at the beginning of the section.

Directions: For each sentence in which you find an error, select the one underlined part that must be changed to make the sentence correct and fill in the corresponding oval on your answer sheet.

If there is no error, fill in oval Ⓔ.

Example:

The other (A) delegates and him (B) immediately (C) accepted the resolution drafted by (D) the neutral states. No error (E)

Sample Answer

Ⓐ ● Ⓒ Ⓓ Ⓔ

41. The pamphlet from the insurance company reported that good drivers change (A) lanes cautiously, are constantly (B) alert, and react swift (C) when (D) danger threatens. No error (E)

42. Many readers of Leon Damas's poetry do not realize (A) that much (B) of his work was inspired by (C) the sounds and rhythms of (D) African music. No error (E)

GO ON TO THE NEXT PAGE

43. If Carol had not warned her guests about (A) the flooded (B) streets, they might have ran (C) into difficulty on the way (D) to her house. No error (E)

44. Members of the Parti Québécois were threatening seceding (A) from Canada, for (B) they (C) considered their interests to be different from (D) those of English-speaking Canadians. No error (E)

45. The idea of romantic love is often (A) thought to originate (B) in (C) the Middle Ages and to have resulted from (D) a misinterpretation of Ovid's writings. No error (E)

46. The good politician, like most (A) other perceptive people, learns (B) more from their (C) opponents than from (D) supporters. No error (E)

47. Either the manager or (A) the customer-relations representative are (B) supposed to (C) respond to complaints about (D) damaged goods. No error (E)

48. The friendship between (A) Alicia and Karen developed when (B) she agreed (C) to help with (D) the preliminary design for the new municipal building. No error (E)

49. Recent protests against (A) nuclear power plants have (B) much in common with (C) some of the social protests of the preceding (D) two decades. No error (E)

50. The supply of oak, hickory, and birch logs are (A) sufficient to keep (B) the family warm, even if (C) this winter is as cold as the last one (D). No error (E)

IF YOU FINISH BEFORE TIME IS CALLED, YOU MAY CHECK YOUR WORK ON THIS SECTION ONLY. DO NOT TURN TO ANY OTHER SECTION IN THE TEST. **STOP**

SECTION 5 | Time—30 minutes 35 Questions

In this section solve each problem, using any available space on the page for scratchwork. Then decide which is the best of the choices given and fill in the corresponding oval on the answer sheet.

The following information is for your reference in solving some of the problems.

Circle of radius r: Area $= \pi r^2$; Circumference $= 2\pi r$
The number of degrees of arc in a circle is 360.
The measure in degrees of a straight angle is 180.

Definition of symbols:
$=$ is equal to
$\neq$ is unequal to
$<$ is less than
$>$ is greater than
$\leq$ is less than or equal to
$\geq$ is greater than or equal to
$\parallel$ is parallel to
$\perp$ is perpendicular to

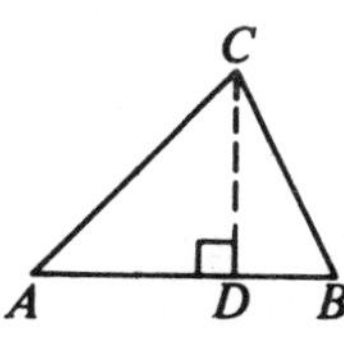

Triangle: The sum of the measures in degrees of the angles of a triangle is 180.
If $\angle CDA$ is a right angle, then

(1) area of $\triangle ABC = \frac{AB \times CD}{2}$

(2) $AC^2 = AD^2 + DC^2$

Note: Figures that accompany problems in this test are intended to provide information useful in solving the problems. They are drawn as accurately as possible EXCEPT when it is stated in a specific problem that its figure is not drawn to scale. All figures lie in a plane unless otherwise indicated. All numbers used are real numbers.

1. $9(7 + 3) - (2 \times 10) =$

(A) 46
(B) 70
(C) 169
(D) 280
(E) 3,780

2. Carol has 5 more than twice the number of goldfish that Mark has. If Mark has 2 goldfish, how many does Carol have?

(A) 6
(B) 7
(C) 9
(D) 12
(E) 14

3. If, in a given year, February 24 falls on a Saturday, what day of the week is February 12 of that year?

(A) Monday
(B) Tuesday
(C) Wednesday
(D) Thursday
(E) Friday

4. Which of the following is equal to $2^3 \cdot 2^2$?

(A) 2^5
(B) 2^6
(C) 4^5
(D) 4^6
(E) 4^9

GO ON TO THE NEXT PAGE

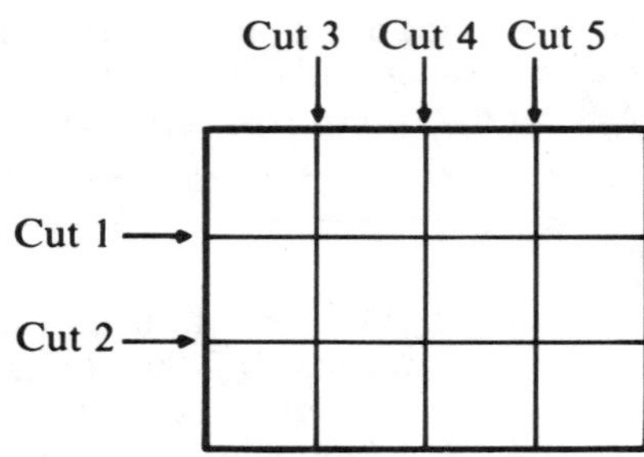

5. The figure above represents a rectangular cake in a pan. The cake has been sliced into 12 square pieces by 5 straight cuts, each cut extending from one side of the pan to the opposite side of the pan. What is the minimum number of additional such cuts needed to halve each of the 12 pieces if the pieces remain in the pan as shown?

(A) 2
(B) 3
(C) 4
(D) 6
(E) 12

6. The symbol □ represents one of the four fundamental operations of arithmetic; b and c are different integers; and $b \neq 0$. If $b \square c = c \square b$ and $b \square 0 = b$, then the symbol □ must represent

(A) + only
(B) × only
(C) + or ×
(D) −
(E) ÷

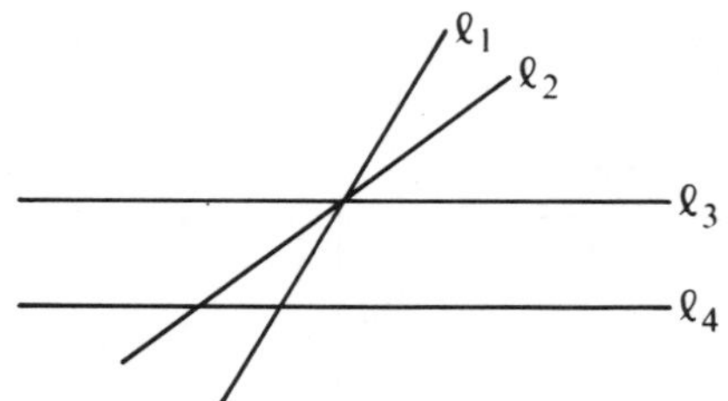

7. In the figure above, $\ell_3 \parallel \ell_4$. If ℓ_5 (not shown) is another line in the same plane as ℓ_1, ℓ_2, ℓ_3, and ℓ_4, what is the <u>least</u> number of points at which ℓ_5 can intersect these four lines?

(A) None
(B) One
(C) Two
(D) Three
(E) Four

GO ON TO THE NEXT PAGE

Questions 8-27 each consist of two quantities, one in Column A and one in Column B. You are to compare the two quantities and on the answer sheet fill in oval

- A if the quantity in Column A is greater;
- B if the quantity in Column B is greater;
- C if the two quantities are equal;
- D if the relationship cannot be determined from the information given.

AN E RESPONSE WILL NOT BE SCORED.

EXAMPLES

	Column A	Column B	Answers
E1.	2×6	$2 + 6$	● Ⓑ Ⓒ Ⓓ Ⓔ
E2.	$180 - x$	y	Ⓐ Ⓑ ● Ⓓ Ⓔ
E3.	$p - q$	$q - p$	Ⓐ Ⓑ Ⓒ ● Ⓔ

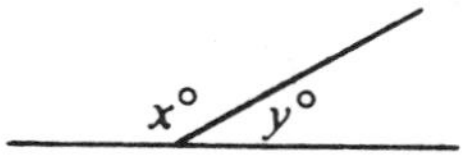

Notes:

1. In certain questions, information concerning one or both of the quantities to be compared is centered above the two columns.
2. In a given question, a symbol that appears in both columns represents the same thing in Column A as it does in Column B.
3. Letters such as x, n, and k stand for real numbers.

	Column A	Column B
8.	$\frac{1}{2} - \frac{2}{5}$	$\frac{1}{2} - \frac{2}{3}$

r, s, and t are the degree measures of the three angles of a triangle.

	Column A	Column B
9.	$r + s$	t

$n > 0$

	Column A	Column B
10.	$0.42 \times n$	$0.042 \times 10n$

$\frac{3}{a} = \frac{b}{4}$

	Column A	Column B
11.	ab	12

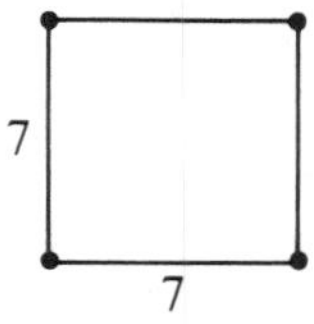

Figure A

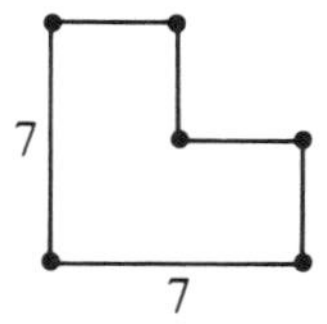

Figure B

In Figures A and B, pairs of line segments that meet at a point are perpendicular.

	Column A	Column B
12.	The perimeter of Figure A	The perimeter of Figure B

Questions 13-14 refer to the following graph.

YIELD OF CROP P
AT VARYING TEMPERATURES
AND LIGHT INTENSITIES

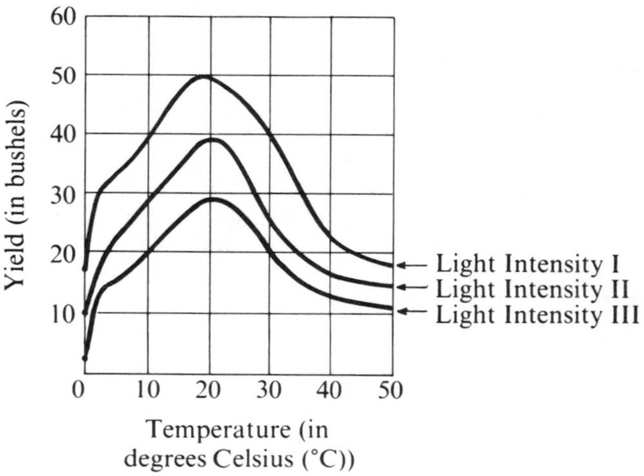

	Column A	Column B
13.	For the temperature range shown, the highest yield, in bushels, of crop P at light intensity II	45

At light intensity III, for the temperature range shown, the highest yield, in bushels, of crop P is H and the lowest is L.

	Column A	Column B
14.	$H - L$	30

GO ON TO THE NEXT PAGE

5

SUMMARY DIRECTIONS FOR COMPARISON QUESTIONS

Answer: A if the quantity in Column A is greater;
B if the quantity in Column B is greater;
C if the two quantities are equal;
D if the relationship cannot be determined from the information given.

AN E RESPONSE WILL NOT BE SCORED.

	Column A	Column B

$x = 4$
$y = -4$

15. $x - y$ | $2x$

Questions 16-17 refer to the following definition.

If a, b, and c are integers, and if $a \leq b \leq c$, then the "funnel" of $\{a, b, c\}$ is defined to be the least integer greater than c that is a multiple of both a and b. For example, the funnel of $\{2, 3, 10\}$ is 12.

16. The funnel of $\{2, 4, 12\}$ | 16

17. The funnel of $\{4, 6, 8\}$ | The funnel of $\{3, 5, 7\}$

$x = 2y + 3 - 2y + 2 - y + 1 + y$

18. x | 5

$S = \{3, 6, 9, 12, 15\}$
$T = \{6, 12, 18, 24, 30\}$

s represents one of the numbers from S.
t represents one of the numbers from T.

19. $s - t$ | 0

$p + r = 19$

$r < \frac{19}{2}$

20. p | r

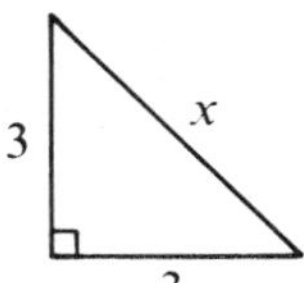

21. x | 5

	Column A	Column B

One card is picked at random from 20 cards numbered 1 through 20.

22. Probability that the card has a two-digit number | Probability that the card has a one-digit number

---

1 liter = 1,000 milliliters

23. $\frac{1}{3}$ of a liter | 333 milliliters

Line segments RS and TU are parallel and have the same length. M is the midpoint of RS.

24. Length of MT | Length of MU

$a + b + c = 15$
$b + c + e = 21$
$a + e = 12$

25. The average (arithmetic mean) of a, b, c, and e | 7

$y - x = 1$

26. $y^2 - x^2$ | 1

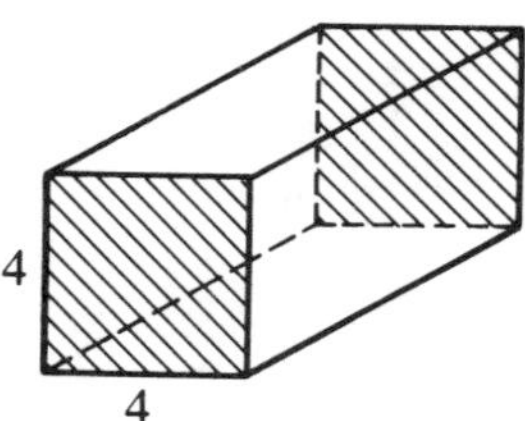

Points P, Q, R, and S (not shown) are the centers of the four unshaded rectangular faces of the rectangular solid.

27. The area of square $PQRS$ | 16

GO ON TO THE NEXT PAGE

Solve each of the remaining problems in this section using any available space for scratchwork. Then decide which is the best of the choices given and fill in the corresponding oval on the answer sheet.

28. A room in the shape of a rectangular solid has a floor area of 108 square feet. If the volume of the room is 1,296 cubic feet, what is the height of the room, in feet?

(A) 6
(B) 8
(C) 12
(D) 16
(E) 18

29. If v, w, x, and y are consecutive even integers and $v < w < x < y$, then $x + y$ is how much greater than $v + w$?

(A) 2
(B) 4
(C) 6
(D) 8
(E) 10

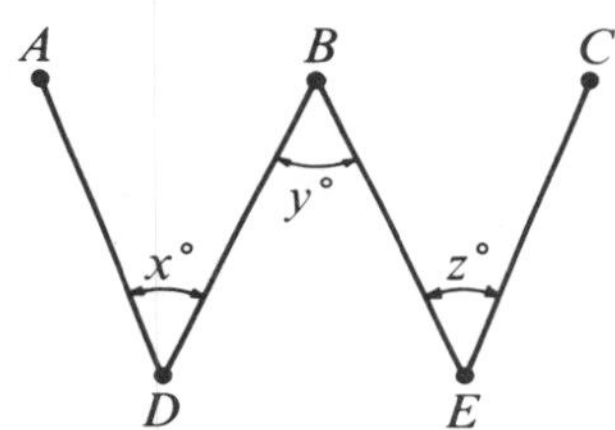

Note: Figure not drawn to scale.

30. In the figure above, $x = y = z$ and $AD = BD$. Which of the following must be true?

I. $AD \parallel BE$
II. $DB \parallel EC$
III. Points A, B, and C lie on the same line.

(A) I only
(B) III only
(C) I and II only
(D) II and III only
(E) I, II, and III

31. If 1 can of brand X cat food feeds 3 kittens or 2 grown cats, then, at this rate, 10 cans of brand X cat food will feed 12 kittens and how many grown cats?

(A) Eight
(B) Nine
(C) Ten
(D) Eleven
(E) Twelve

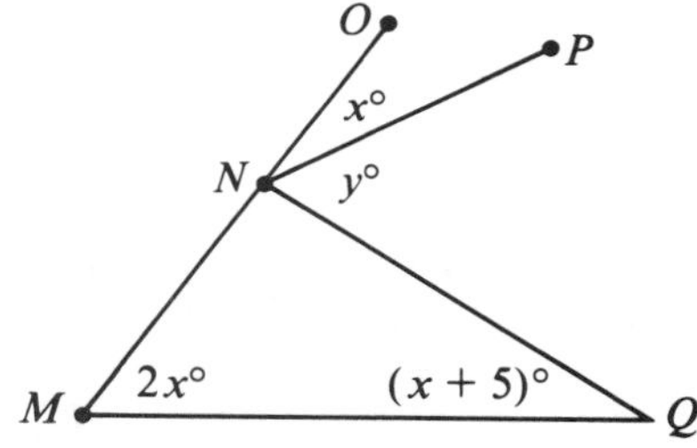

32. In the figure above, N lies on line segment MO. Which of the following gives y in terms of x?

(A) $2x$
(B) $2x + 5$
(C) $3x + 5$
(D) $90 - x$
(E) $180 - 3x$

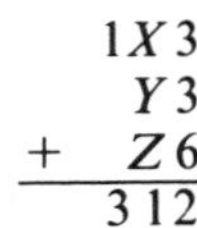

33. In the addition problem above, which of the following could be the digit Z?

    I. 1
    II. 5
    III. 8

    (A) II only
    (B) III only
    (C) I and II only
    (D) II and III only
    (E) I, II, and III

x increased by 10% of x yields y.
y decreased by 50% of y yields z.
z increased by 40% of z yields w.

34. According to the statements above, w is what percent of x?

    (A) 10%
    (B) 33%
    (C) 77%
    (D) 81%
    (E) 100%

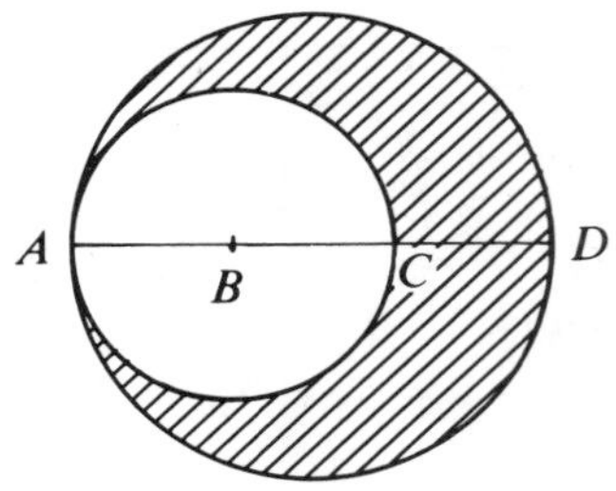

35. In the figure above, AC and AD are diameters of the small and large circles, respectively. If $AB = BC = CD$, what is the ratio of the area of the shaded region to the area of the smaller circle?

    (A) 1 : 1
    (B) 3 : 2
    (C) 4 : 3
    (D) 5 : 4
    (E) 9 : 4

IF YOU FINISH BEFORE TIME IS CALLED, YOU MAY CHECK YOUR WORK ON THIS SECTION ONLY. DO NOT TURN TO ANY OTHER SECTION IN THE TEST. **STOP**

Answers to Practice Test Questions and Percentage of Students Answering Each Question Correctly

Section 1—Verbal			Section 2—Mathematical			Section 3—Verbal			Section 4—TSWE			Section 5—Mathematical		
Question number	Correct answer	Percentage of students answering the question correctly	Question number	Correct answer	Percentage of students answering the question correctly	Question number	Correct answer	Percentage of students answering the question correctly	Question number	Correct answer	Percentage of students answering the question correctly	Question number	Correct answer	Percentage of students answering the question correctly
1	D	95%	1	D	81%	1	D	95%	1	B	89%	1	B	92%
2	B	87	2	D	89	2	C	85	2	D	75	2	C	92
3	A	83	3	A	88	3	B	90	3	C	65	3	A	80
4	E	67	4	C	76	4	A	68	4	E	80	4	A	79
5	C	63	5	C	80	5	D	78	5	A	89	5	B	68
6	E	56	6	E	85	6	E	59	6	A	84	6	A	75
7	C	51	7	B	72	7	D	58	7	B	72	7	C	64
8	E	27	8	D	59	8	E	45	8	C	78	8	A	74
9	D	24	9	C	76	9	B	33	9	C	63	9	D	76
10	C	30	10	D	53	10	E	30	10	E	72	10	C	67
11	D	91	11	E	60	11	C	36	11	C	64	11	C	72
12	B	63	12	C	64	12	D	30	12	D	84	12	C	65
13	C	46	13	A	58	13	A	22	13	E	59	13	B	83
14	E	33	14	B	72	14	A	33	14	C	54	14	B	73
15	C	14	15	C	48	15	A	14	15	C	54	15	C	79
16	A	83	16	E	55	16	B	84	16	A	75	16	C	49
17	D	83	17	B	38	17	B	74	17	B	56	17	B	45
18	B	85	18	B	35	18	E	84	18	B	53	18	A	67
19	C	68	19	E	33	19	D	92	19	A	64	19	D	61
20	E	56	20	D	32	20	B	80	20	E	61	20	A	56
21	C	62	21	B	27	21	E	60	21	B	31	21	B	61
22	A	47	22	D	23	22	C	49	22	D	41	22	A	49
23	B	31	23	A	19	23	B	34	23	E	36	23	A	35
24	D	23	24	A	14	24	E	28	24	C	36	24	D	26
25	D	20	25	D	17	25	D	22	25	D	48	25	B	28
26	C	72				26	A	48	26	D	93	26	D	30
27	D	91				27	B	36	27	C	82	27	B	09
28	B	80				28	E	81	28	B	60	28	C	57
29	E	55				29	E	58	29	C	83	29	D	54
30	D	33				30	C	33	30	A	76	30	C	41
31	E	65				31	D	54	31	E	58	31	E	22
32	A	75				32	E	50	32	B	70	32	B	15
33	A	46				33	A	75	33	E	63	33	D	26
34	C	30				34	C	27	34	D	64	34	C	09
35	C	17				35	D	25	35	A	66	35	D	07
36	B	65				36	B	94	36	D	80			
37	D	37				37	B	88	37	B	91			
38	A	17				38	A	70	38	A	61			
39	C	29				39	A	64	39	C	46			
40	D	35				40	C	46	40	D	42			
						41	B	45	41	C	63			
						42	B	39	42	E	69			
						43	C	38	43	C	64			
						44	B	19	44	A	65			
						45	C	26	45	B	54			
									46	C	41			
									47	B	50			
									48	C	52			
									49	E	50			
									50	A	38			

Notes: The percentages for the SAT-verbal and SAT-mathematical sections are based on the analysis of the answer sheets for a random sample of juniors and seniors who took this test in May 1988 and whose mean scores were 434 on the SAT-verbal sections and 479 on the SAT-mathematical sections.

The percentages for TSWE are based on the analysis of the answer sheets for a random sample of all students who took this test in December 1986 and whose mean score was 41.

How to Score Your Practice Test

Before you can find out what your scores are on the College Board 200 to 800 scale, you need to determine your verbal, mathematical, and TSWE raw scores. The steps for doing so for each section of the test and a scoring worksheet are provided below and on page 63. Use the table on page 61 to determine your correct and incorrect answers for each section.

Determining Your Raw Scores

SAT-Verbal Sections 1 and 3

Step A: Count the number of correct answers for section 1 and record the number in the space provided on the worksheet. Then do the same for the incorrect answers. (Do not count omitted answers.) To determine subtotal A, use the formula:

$$\textbf{number correct} - \frac{\textbf{number incorrect}}{\textbf{4}} = \textbf{subtotal A}$$

Step B: Count the number of correct answers and the number of incorrect answers for section 3 and record the numbers in the spaces provided on the worksheet. To determine subtotal B, use the formula:

$$\textbf{number correct} - \frac{\textbf{number incorrect}}{\textbf{4}} = \textbf{subtotal B}$$

Step C: To obtain C, add subtotal A to subtotal B, keeping any decimals. Enter the resulting figure on the worksheet.

Step D: To obtain D, your raw verbal score, round C to the nearest whole number. (For example, any number from 44.50 to 45.49 rounds to 45.) Enter the resulting figure on the worksheet.

SAT-Mathematical Sections 2 and 5

Step A: Count the number of correct answers and the number of incorrect answers for section 2 and record the numbers in the spaces provided on the worksheet. To determine subtotal A, use the formula:

$$\textbf{number correct} - \frac{\textbf{number incorrect}}{\textbf{4}} = \textbf{subtotal A}$$

Step B: Count the number of correct answers and the number of incorrect answers for the *five-choice questions (questions 1 through 7 and 28 through 35)* in section 5 and record the numbers in the spaces provided on the worksheet. To determine subtotal B, use the formula:

$$\textbf{number correct} - \frac{\textbf{number incorrect}}{\textbf{4}} = \textbf{subtotal B}$$

Step C: Count the number of correct answers and the number of incorrect answers for the *four-choice questions (questions 8 through 27)* in section 5 and record the numbers in the spaces provided on the worksheet. To determine subtotal C, use the formula:

$$\textbf{number correct} - \frac{\textbf{number incorrect}}{\textbf{3}} = \textbf{subtotal C}$$

Note: Do not count any E responses to questions 8 through 27 as correct or incorrect. Because these four-choice questions have no E answer choices, E responses to these questions are treated as omits.

Step D: To obtain D, add subtotal A, subtotal B, and subtotal C, keeping any decimals. Enter the resulting figure on the worksheet.

Step E: To obtain E, your raw mathematical score, round D to the nearest whole number. (For example, any number from 44.50 to 45.49 rounds to 45.) Enter the resulting figure on the worksheet.

TSWE: Section 4

Step A: Count the number of correct answers for section 4 and record the number in the space provided on the worksheet. Then do the same for the incorrect answers. (Do not count omitted answers.) To determine your unrounded raw score, use the formula:

$$\textbf{number correct} - \frac{\textbf{number incorrect}}{\textbf{4}} = \textbf{total unrounded raw score}$$

Step B: To obtain B, your raw TSWE score, round A to the nearest whole number. (For example, any number from 34.50 to 35.49 rounds to 35.) Enter the resulting figure on the worksheet.

SCORING WORKSHEET FOR THE PRACTICE TEST

SAT-Verbal Sections

A. Section 1:	________ no. correct	− ¼	(________) no. incorrect	=	________ subtotal A
B. Section 3:	________ no. correct	− ¼	(________) no. incorrect	=	________ subtotal B
C. Total unrounded raw score (Total A + B)					________ C
D. Total rounded raw verbal score (Rounded to nearest whole number)					________ D

SAT-Mathematical Sections

A. Section 2:	________ no. correct	− ¼	(________) no. incorrect	=	________ subtotal A
B. Section 5: Questions 1 through 7 and 28 through 35 (5-choice)	________ no. correct	− ¼	(________) no. incorrect	=	________ subtotal B
C. Section 5: Questions 8 through 27 (4-choice)	________ no. correct	− ⅓	(________) no. incorrect	=	________ subtotal C
D. Total unrounded raw score (Total A + B + C)					________ D
E. Total rounded raw math score (Rounded to nearest whole number)					________ E

TSWE

A. Section 4: Total unrounded raw score	________ no. correct	− ¼	(________) no. incorrect	=	________ A
B. Total rounded raw TSWE score (Rounded to nearest whole number)					________ B

Finding Your College Board Scores

Use the table on page 65 to find the College Board scores that correspond to your raw scores on this edition of the SAT. For example, if you received a raw verbal score of 32 on this edition of the test, your College Board score would be 390. If your raw mathematical score were 22, your College Board score would be 430 for this edition. If your raw TSWE score were 31, your College Board score would be 44 for this edition.

Because some editions of the SAT may be slightly easier or more difficult than others, statistical adjustments are made in the scores to ensure that each College Board score indicates the same level of performance, regardless of the edition of the SAT you take. A given raw score will correspond to different College Board scores, depending on the edition of the test taken. A raw score of 40, for example, may convert to a College Board score of 450 on one edition of the SAT, but might convert to a College Board score of 480 on another edition of the test. When you take the SAT, your score is likely to differ somewhat from the score you obtained on the practice test. People perform at different levels at different times, for reasons unrelated to the test itself. The precision of any test is also limited because it represents only a sample of all the possible questions that could be asked.

Reviewing Your Performance

After you have scored your practice test by following the directions on page 62 and above, analyze your performance.

Asking yourself these questions and following the suggestions can help:

- Did you run out of time before you finished a section? Reread pages 9 through 30. The suggestions in them may help you pace yourself better.
- Did you make careless mistakes due to haste? You may have misread the question, neglected to notice the word "except" or "best" in the directions, solved for the wrong value, or reversed column A and column B in your mind.
- Were there questions you omitted that you might have gotten right if you had guessed? Did you lose points because of random guessing? Reread page 8 to determine when guessing might be helpful.
- Did you spend too much time reading directions? You should be familiar with the test directions so you won't have to spend as much time reading them when you take the actual test.

How Difficult Were the Questions?

The table on page 61 gives the percentages of a sample of students who chose the correct answer for each question. (These students obtained a mean SAT-verbal score of 434, mean SAT-mathematical score of 479, and mean TSWE score of 41.) These percentages will give you an idea of how difficult each question was.

For example, 63 percent of this group of students answered question 5 in verbal section 1 correctly. However, only 30 percent selected the correct answer for question 10 in section 1. In other words, question 5 was easier than question 10 for the students who took this edition of the SAT.

After the Test

Receiving Your Score Report

About six weeks after you take the SAT and TSWE, you will receive your College Planning Report, which will include your scores, your percentile ranks, and interpretive information. With this report, you'll receive a booklet, *Using Your College Planning Report*, which provides advice on how to use your scores and other information to help you with your college planning.

SAT Question-and-Answer Service

If you take the SAT on one of the dates for which the SAT Question-and-Answer Service is available, you may order the service when you register for the test or anytime up to five months after the test. You will receive a copy of your test questions and answer sheet, a list of the correct answers, and scoring instructions. See the *Registration Bulletin* or *Using Your College Planning Report* for additional information on how to order this service. (The service does not apply to the TSWE or equating questions.)

SCORE CONVERSION TABLE
Practice SAT and TSWE

Raw Score	College Board Scaled Score		Raw Score	College Board Scaled Score		Raw Score	College Board Scaled Score
	SAT-Verbal	SAT-Math		SAT-Verbal	SAT-Math		TSWE
85	800		40	450	600	50	60+
84	780		39	440	590	49	60+
83	760		38	430	580	48	60+
82	750		37	430	570	47	60+
81	740		36	420	560	46	60+
80	730		35	410	550	45	59
79	720		34	410	550	44	58
78	710		33	400	540	43	56
77	700		32	390	530	42	55
76	690		31	390	520	41	54
75	690		30	380	510	40	53
74	680		29	370	500	39	52
73	670		28	370	490	38	51
72	660		27	360	480	37	50
71	660		26	350	470	36	49
70	650		25	350	460	35	48
69	640		24	340	450	34	47
68	630		23	330	440	33	46
67	630		22	330	430	32	45
66	620		21	320	420	31	44
65	610		20	310	410	30	43
64	600		19	310	400	29	42
63	600		18	300	400	28	41
62	590		17	290	390	27	40
61	580		16	290	380	26	39
60	580	800	15	280	370	25	38
59	570	790	14	270	360	24	37
58	560	770	13	270	350	23	36
57	560	760	12	260	340	22	35
56	550	750	11	250	330	21	34
55	540	740	10	250	320	20	33
54	540	730	9	240	320	19	32
53	530	720	8	230	310	18	31
52	520	720	7	230	300	17	30
51	520	710	6	220	290	16	28
50	510	700	5	210	280	15	27
49	500	690	4	210	270	14	26
48	500	680	3	200	260	13	25
47	490	670	2	200	260	12	24
46	480	660	1	200	250	11	23
45	480	650	0	200	240	10	22
44	470	640	−1	200	230	9	21
43	470	630	−2	200	220	8 or below	20
42	460	620	−3	200	210		
41	450	610	−4 or below	200	200		

A Sample Score Report

A sample score report for a fictional student is provided on pages 67-68. The report has six major parts:

1. Identification Information
   This is the information that will be used to identify your record, which is stored at Educational Testing Service. If you have any questions about your report, call or write to the College Board's Admissions Testing Program at the address given on page 2.

2. Test Scores
   The next section shows your most recent test scores. SAT scores are shown both as specific numbers and as score ranges to help illustrate that the test cannot measure your abilities with perfect accuracy (see "How Precise Are Your Scores?" on page 69).

3. Summary of Test Scores
   This section summarizes your test scores and includes all of your scores from any Admissions Testing Program tests (SAT or Achievement Tests) that you have taken at any time while in high school.

4. Educational Background
   This information comes from the Student Descriptive Questionnaire (SDQ), which you fill out when you register to take the test. It describes your high school course work, summarizes your grades, and gives your grade point average and class rank.

5. Plans for College
   This section includes information about your plans for future study that you reported in the Student Descriptive Questionnaire.

6. Colleges and Scholarship Programs That Received a Score Report
   This information about the institutions to which you have your scores sent includes addresses, telephone numbers, application and financial aid deadlines, and the basis for admissions decisions.

ADMISSIONS TESTING PROGRAM
The College Board

COLLEGE PLANNING REPORT

SCORE REPORT FOR MARGARET K WRIGHT 60600

1

Sex	Birth Date	Social Security No.	Telephone No.	Registration No.	Ethnic Group	U.S. Citizen	Report Date
F	3/15/73	123-45-6789	111-222-3333	7654321	White	Yes	12/15/90

High School Name and Code	First Language	Religion
JEFFERSON MEMORIAL HIGH SCHOOL 555555	English only	Methodist

2

TEST SCORES — NOVEMBER 1990 SCHOLASTIC APTITUDE TEST

Test	Score	Score Range (200 300 400 500 600 700 800)	Percentiles: College-bound Seniors National	State
SAT V	480	<<<>>>	68	56
SAT M	500	<<<<>>>>	57	42
TSWE	49		66	51

See the reverse side of this report for more information about these scores.

3

SUMMARY OF TEST SCORES							Achievement Tests				
Test Date	Grade Level	SAT Verbal	SAT Verbal Subscores: Reading	Vocabulary	SAT Math	TSWE	Test Date	Grade Level	1	2	3
Nov 90	12th	480	45	49	500	49	Jun 90	11th	EN 450	BY 500	M1 550
May 90	11th	460	44	47	480	46					

4

EDUCATIONAL BACKGROUND (REPORTED ON STUDENT DESCRIPTIVE QUESTIONNAIRE 11/90)

Courses	Years	Honors	Average Grade	Course Work and Experience
ARTS AND MUSIC	4	Yes	A	Acting/Play Production,Dance,Drama App, Perform Music,Photography/Film,Studio Art
ENGLISH	4	Yes	B	Amer Lit,Comp,Grammar,Other Lit, Speaking/Listening
FOREIGN LANGUAGES	2		B	French
MATHEMATICS	4+	Yes	A	Algebra,Geometry,Trigonometry,Calculus, Computer Math
NATURAL SCIENCES	2		B	Biology,Chemistry
SOCIAL SCIENCES	4		A	U.S. Hist,U.S. Govt,European Hist,World Hist, Other
COMPUTER EXPERIENCE				Programming,Math,Word Processing

Grade Point Average A-   Class Rank Second tenth

5

PLANS FOR COLLEGE (REPORTED ON STUDENT DESCRIPTIVE QUESTIONNAIRE 11/90)

Degree Goal	First Choice of Major	Certainty of First Choice
Bachelor's	Arts: Visual and Performing	Very certain

Other Majors Listed	Requested Services
Dramatic arts Art (painting, drawing, sculpture) Engineering/Engineering Technologies	Educational planning Part-time job

Preferred College Characteristics	College Programs and Activities
Type: 4 yr,Public,Private Size: Up to 1,000,10,000 to 20,000, Over 20,000 Setting: Large city,Suburban Distance from home: Undecided Other: Coed,On-campus housing	Art Dance Drama/Theater

Advanced Placement or Exemption Plans
Art,Math

6

Colleges and Scholarship Programs That Received a Score Report

FOR THE NOVEMBER 1990 TEST ADMINISTRATION

A score report has been sent to the colleges and scholarship programs listed below. The information about the colleges is from *The College Handbook*. For more information about these and other schools, consult the *Handbook* or other materials available in your high school or library and talk with your counselor. Contact the colleges for application materials and additional information.

If you want to have your scores sent to other colleges and scholarship programs, complete an Additional Report Request Form. You received one of these forms with your Admission Ticket. Your high school counselor has additional forms.

1234
City College of Art
3030 West Street
Hill, California 90512
(213) 123-4567

BASIS FOR ADMISSION DECISION: School achievement record is very important. Interview, school and community activities and recommendations are considered.

ADMISSION APPLICATION DEADLINE: Closing date is August 27. Notification is on a continuous rolling basis.

FINANCIAL AID APPLICATION DEADLINE: No closing date; priority date is March 1. Notification is on a rolling basis starting on April 1.

1489
State University
89 Central Street
Center City, Texas 34567
(901) 678-9534

BASIS FOR ADMISSION DECISION: School achievement record, test scores and recommendations are important. Interview and school community activities are considered.

ADMISSION APPLICATION DEADLINE: Closing date is August 1. Applications received by April 1 are given priority. Notification is on a continual rolling basis.

FINANCIAL AID APPLICATION DEADLINE: Closing date is April 1. Notification is on a rolling basis beginning January 30.

7632
St. Michael's College
110 Hilford Street
Bankster, Ohio 06010
(101) 987-6734

BASIS FOR ADMISSION DECISION: School achievement record and test scores are very important. School and community activities and recommendations are important. Interview is considered. Achievement Tests are required of all applicants.

ADMISSION APPLICATION DEADLINE: Closing date is February 1. Notification begins on or about April 15.

FINANCIAL AID APPLICATION DEADLINE: Closing date is February 1. Notification date is April 1.

1920
Alma Mater
645 Southwest Street
Deerfield, New York 10310
(904) 272-6243

BASIS FOR ADMISSION DECISION: School achievement record and test scores are very important. School and community activities and recommendations are important. Interview and school community activities are considered.

ADMISSION APPLICATION DEADLINE: Closing date is January 15. Notification date is April 15.

FINANCIAL AID APPLICATION DEADLINE: Closing date is April 1. Notification date is April 10.

MARGARET K WRIGHT
1234 TIGERLILY LANE
CHICAGO IL 60600

SAT and TSWE Scores

SAT Scores are reported on a scale of 200 to 800. You receive separate scores for the verbal and math sections of the SAT. SAT-verbal subscores (reading comprehension and vocabulary) are on a scale of 20 to 80. TSWE scores are reported from 20 to 60+. The tests have no passing or failing scores, and they are not scored on a curve—this is, the scores of other students who took the test with you had no effect on your score.

What Do Your Percentile Ranks Mean?

The percentile ranks on your score report allow you to compare your scores with those of other students. A percentile rank tells you the percentage of students in a given group whose scores were below yours. Remember that the same score can have a different percentile rank for different groups, depending on the ability of the group. (For example, a runner whose time ranks in the 80th percentile when compared with the junior varsity track team might rank in the 50th percentile when compared with the varsity team, which usually has faster runners.)

Percentile ranks on your score report compare your scores with those of "College-bound Seniors/National": all seniors who took the test any time while in high school, and with "College-bound Seniors/State": all seniors in your state who took the test any time while in high school.

How Precise Are Your Scores?

When you consider your scores, keep in mind that no test can measure your abilities with perfect accuracy. If you took a different edition of a test or the same edition on different days, your score probably would be different each time. If you were to take a test an infinite number of times, your scores would tend to cluster about an average value. Testing specialists call this average your "true score," the score you would get if a test could measure your ability with perfect accuracy. To measure how much students' obtained scores vary from their true scores, an index called the standard error of measurement (SEM) is used.

For the SAT, the SEM is about 30 points. About two-thirds of those taking the test score within 30 points (or one SEM) of their true score. If your true score is 430, for example, the chances are about 2 out of 3 that you will score between 400 and 460 (430 plus or minus 30).

You should think of your scores in terms of score ranges rather than precise measurements—a 400 SAT score, for example, should be thought of as being in the 370 to 430 range. This will help you realize that a a small difference between your score and another student's on the same test does not indicate any real difference in ability. College admissions officers also are advised to look at scores this way.

Will Your Scores Go Up if You Take the Test Again?

As indicated above, you are not likely to get exactly the same score on a test twice. Improving your score a great deal also is unlikely. Some students who repeat tests do improve their scores, but, on the average, these increases are small.

The *average* increase for a junior who takes the SAT again when a senior is about 15-20 points for the verbal score and 15-20 points for the math score. About two out of three students who retake the test improve their scores, but the scores of about one student in three go down. About one student in 20 gains 100 or more points, and about one in 100 loses 100 or more points. Students whose first SAT scores are low are more likely to achieve score gains. Students whose initial scores are high are less likely to achieve score gains.

If you repeat a test, your earlier scores will still appear on your score report. Colleges evaluate multiple scores on the same test in different ways. Some look at all the scores on your report; others use just the highest, most recent, or an average.

Who Receives Your Scores?

A score report will be sent to your high school if you provide your high school code number when you register for the test. Reports also will be sent to all colleges and scholarship programs whose code number you give.

The College Board may use your scores and descriptive information for research, but no information that can be identified with you is ever released without your consent.

How Do Colleges Use Your Score Report?

Your SAT scores give college admissions officers an idea of how well you have developed some of the abilities you will need to do well in college courses. The scores also help them to compare you with students from schools with different grading standards. Admissions people know that although your high school grades are the best *single* indicator of your readiness to do college work, a combination of your high school grades and your SAT scores provides a better indicator than either one alone.

Some colleges also use Achievement Tests in making admissions decisions or for course placement, or both. The TSWE is a placement test designed to identify students who may need help in developing their writing skills. Your college may use it to help place you in the freshman English course that is right for you.

Colleges vary in the way they use test scores, but few, if any, make admissions decisions based on scores alone. Therefore, low or high scores should neither discourage you nor make you overconfident. Admissions officers usually consider the descriptive information on your score report as well as other information sent by you and your school.

Different colleges value different qualities in applicants: One college may be looking for leadership potential, while another may place more weight on various extracurricular activities. Some colleges have open admissions policies and admit almost all applicants. Some will admit students who have particular qualities, even if the students' grades and scores indicate they will have to make an extra effort. Whatever your scores, remember that probably there are many colleges that could meet your needs and where you would be happy.

COLLEGE BOARD — SCHOLASTIC APTITUDE TEST and Test of Standard Written English Side 1

Use a No. 2 pencil only. Be sure each mark is dark and completely fills the intended oval. Completely erase any errors or stray marks.

1. YOUR NAME: (Print) ______ Last ______ First ______ M.I.

SIGNATURE: ______ **DATE:** ___/___/___

HOME ADDRESS: (Print) ______ Number and Street

______ City ______ State ______ Zip Code

CENTER: (Print) ______ City ______ State ______ Center Number

IMPORTANT: Please fill in items 2 and 3 exactly as shown on the back cover of your test book.

FOR ETS USE ONLY

2. TEST FORM (Copy from back cover of your test book.)

3. FORM CODE (Copy and grid as shown on back cover of your test book.)

4. REGISTRATION NUMBER (Copy from your Admission Ticket.)

5. YOUR NAME

First 4 letters of last name | First Init. | Mid. Init.

6. DATE OF BIRTH

Month | Day | Year

Jan. Feb. Mar. Apr. May June July Aug. Sept. Oct. Nov. Dec.

7. SEX

Female

Male

8. TEST BOOK SERIAL NUMBER (Copy from front cover of your test book.)

(Cut here to detach.)

Start with number 1 for each new section. If a section has fewer than 50 questions, leave the extra answer spaces blank.

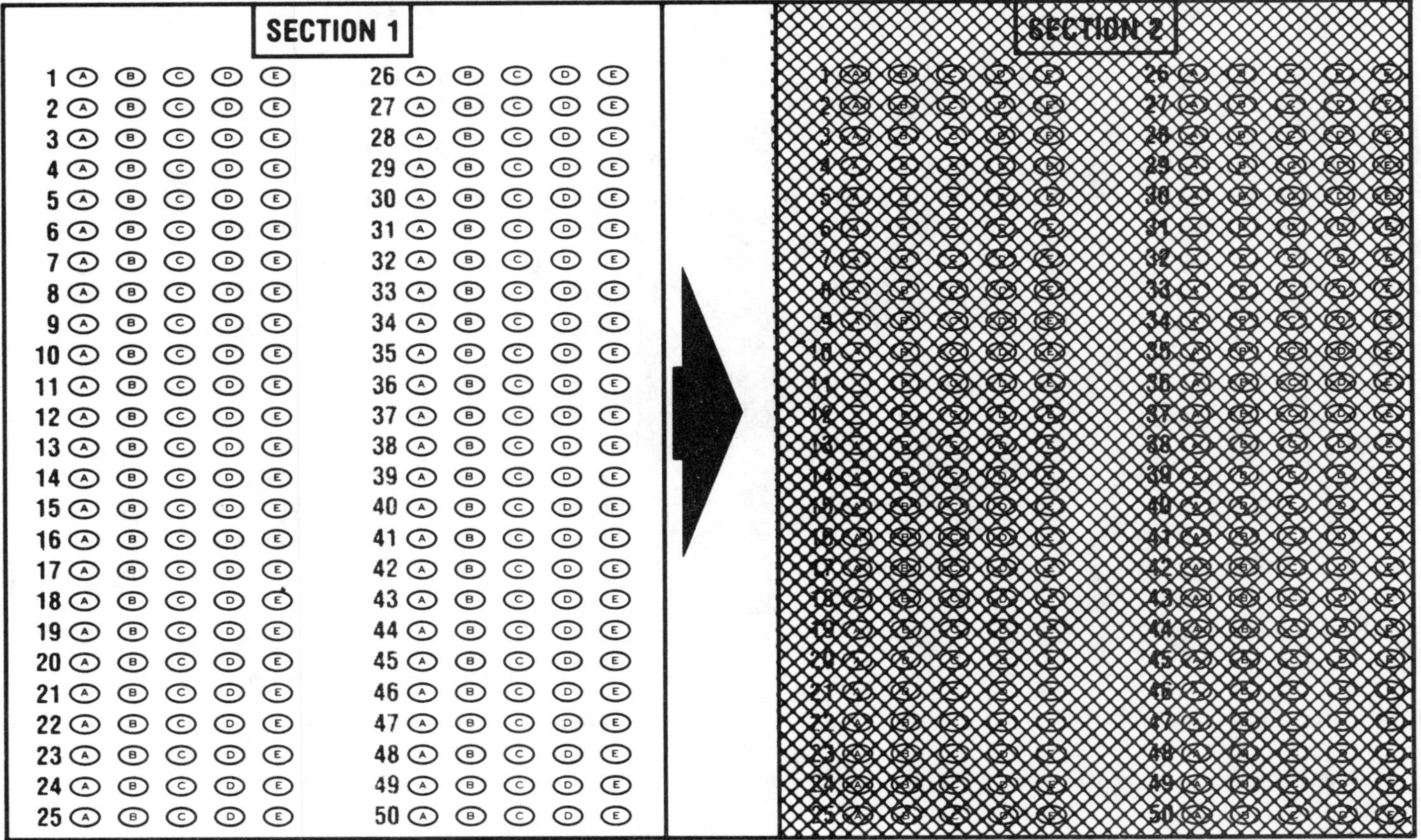

SECTION 1

SECTION 2

Q1362-04

I.N. 575008 — 110VV58P3720

COLLEGE BOARD — SCHOLASTIC APTITUDE TEST and Test of Standard Written English Side 2

Use a No. 2 pencil only. Be sure each mark is dark and completely fills the intended oval. Completely erase any errors or stray marks.

Start with number 1 for each new section. If a section has fewer than 50 questions, leave the extra answer spaces blank.

SECTION 3	SECTION 4	SECTION 5	SECTION 6
1 Ⓐ Ⓑ Ⓒ Ⓓ Ⓔ	1 Ⓐ Ⓑ Ⓒ Ⓓ Ⓔ	1 Ⓐ Ⓑ Ⓒ Ⓓ Ⓔ	1 Ⓐ Ⓑ Ⓒ Ⓓ Ⓔ
2 Ⓐ Ⓑ Ⓒ Ⓓ Ⓔ	2 Ⓐ Ⓑ Ⓒ Ⓓ Ⓔ	2 Ⓐ Ⓑ Ⓒ Ⓓ Ⓔ	2 Ⓐ Ⓑ Ⓒ Ⓓ Ⓔ
3 Ⓐ Ⓑ Ⓒ Ⓓ Ⓔ	3 Ⓐ Ⓑ Ⓒ Ⓓ Ⓔ	3 Ⓐ Ⓑ Ⓒ Ⓓ Ⓔ	3 Ⓐ Ⓑ Ⓒ Ⓓ Ⓔ
4 Ⓐ Ⓑ Ⓒ Ⓓ Ⓔ	4 Ⓐ Ⓑ Ⓒ Ⓓ Ⓔ	4 Ⓐ Ⓑ Ⓒ Ⓓ Ⓔ	4 Ⓐ Ⓑ Ⓒ Ⓓ Ⓔ
5 Ⓐ Ⓑ Ⓒ Ⓓ Ⓔ	5 Ⓐ Ⓑ Ⓒ Ⓓ Ⓔ	5 Ⓐ Ⓑ Ⓒ Ⓓ Ⓔ	5 Ⓐ Ⓑ Ⓒ Ⓓ Ⓔ
6 Ⓐ Ⓑ Ⓒ Ⓓ Ⓔ	6 Ⓐ Ⓑ Ⓒ Ⓓ Ⓔ	6 Ⓐ Ⓑ Ⓒ Ⓓ Ⓔ	6 Ⓐ Ⓑ Ⓒ Ⓓ Ⓔ
7 Ⓐ Ⓑ Ⓒ Ⓓ Ⓔ	7 Ⓐ Ⓑ Ⓒ Ⓓ Ⓔ	7 Ⓐ Ⓑ Ⓒ Ⓓ Ⓔ	7 Ⓐ Ⓑ Ⓒ Ⓓ Ⓔ
8 Ⓐ Ⓑ Ⓒ Ⓓ Ⓔ	8 Ⓐ Ⓑ Ⓒ Ⓓ Ⓔ	8 Ⓐ Ⓑ Ⓒ Ⓓ Ⓔ	8 Ⓐ Ⓑ Ⓒ Ⓓ Ⓔ
9 Ⓐ Ⓑ Ⓒ Ⓓ Ⓔ	9 Ⓐ Ⓑ Ⓒ Ⓓ Ⓔ	9 Ⓐ Ⓑ Ⓒ Ⓓ Ⓔ	9 Ⓐ Ⓑ Ⓒ Ⓓ Ⓔ
10 Ⓐ Ⓑ Ⓒ Ⓓ Ⓔ	10 Ⓐ Ⓑ Ⓒ Ⓓ Ⓔ	10 Ⓐ Ⓑ Ⓒ Ⓓ Ⓔ	10 Ⓐ Ⓑ Ⓒ Ⓓ Ⓔ
11 Ⓐ Ⓑ Ⓒ Ⓓ Ⓔ	11 Ⓐ Ⓑ Ⓒ Ⓓ Ⓔ	11 Ⓐ Ⓑ Ⓒ Ⓓ Ⓔ	11 Ⓐ Ⓑ Ⓒ Ⓓ Ⓔ
12 Ⓐ Ⓑ Ⓒ Ⓓ Ⓔ	12 Ⓐ Ⓑ Ⓒ Ⓓ Ⓔ	12 Ⓐ Ⓑ Ⓒ Ⓓ Ⓔ	12 Ⓐ Ⓑ Ⓒ Ⓓ Ⓔ
13 Ⓐ Ⓑ Ⓒ Ⓓ Ⓔ	13 Ⓐ Ⓑ Ⓒ Ⓓ Ⓔ	13 Ⓐ Ⓑ Ⓒ Ⓓ Ⓔ	13 Ⓐ Ⓑ Ⓒ Ⓓ Ⓔ
14 Ⓐ Ⓑ Ⓒ Ⓓ Ⓔ	14 Ⓐ Ⓑ Ⓒ Ⓓ Ⓔ	14 Ⓐ Ⓑ Ⓒ Ⓓ Ⓔ	14 Ⓐ Ⓑ Ⓒ Ⓓ Ⓔ
15 Ⓐ Ⓑ Ⓒ Ⓓ Ⓔ	15 Ⓐ Ⓑ Ⓒ Ⓓ Ⓔ	15 Ⓐ Ⓑ Ⓒ Ⓓ Ⓔ	15 Ⓐ Ⓑ Ⓒ Ⓓ Ⓔ
16 Ⓐ Ⓑ Ⓒ Ⓓ Ⓔ	16 Ⓐ Ⓑ Ⓒ Ⓓ Ⓔ	16 Ⓐ Ⓑ Ⓒ Ⓓ Ⓔ	16 Ⓐ Ⓑ Ⓒ Ⓓ Ⓔ
17 Ⓐ Ⓑ Ⓒ Ⓓ Ⓔ	17 Ⓐ Ⓑ Ⓒ Ⓓ Ⓔ	17 Ⓐ Ⓑ Ⓒ Ⓓ Ⓔ	17 Ⓐ Ⓑ Ⓒ Ⓓ Ⓔ
18 Ⓐ Ⓑ Ⓒ Ⓓ Ⓔ	18 Ⓐ Ⓑ Ⓒ Ⓓ Ⓔ	18 Ⓐ Ⓑ Ⓒ Ⓓ Ⓔ	18 Ⓐ Ⓑ Ⓒ Ⓓ Ⓔ
19 Ⓐ Ⓑ Ⓒ Ⓓ Ⓔ	19 Ⓐ Ⓑ Ⓒ Ⓓ Ⓔ	19 Ⓐ Ⓑ Ⓒ Ⓓ Ⓔ	19 Ⓐ Ⓑ Ⓒ Ⓓ Ⓔ
20 Ⓐ Ⓑ Ⓒ Ⓓ Ⓔ	20 Ⓐ Ⓑ Ⓒ Ⓓ Ⓔ	20 Ⓐ Ⓑ Ⓒ Ⓓ Ⓔ	20 Ⓐ Ⓑ Ⓒ Ⓓ Ⓔ
21 Ⓐ Ⓑ Ⓒ Ⓓ Ⓔ	21 Ⓐ Ⓑ Ⓒ Ⓓ Ⓔ	21 Ⓐ Ⓑ Ⓒ Ⓓ Ⓔ	21 Ⓐ Ⓑ Ⓒ Ⓓ Ⓔ
22 Ⓐ Ⓑ Ⓒ Ⓓ Ⓔ	22 Ⓐ Ⓑ Ⓒ Ⓓ Ⓔ	22 Ⓐ Ⓑ Ⓒ Ⓓ Ⓔ	22 Ⓐ Ⓑ Ⓒ Ⓓ Ⓔ
23 Ⓐ Ⓑ Ⓒ Ⓓ Ⓔ	23 Ⓐ Ⓑ Ⓒ Ⓓ Ⓔ	23 Ⓐ Ⓑ Ⓒ Ⓓ Ⓔ	23 Ⓐ Ⓑ Ⓒ Ⓓ Ⓔ
24 Ⓐ Ⓑ Ⓒ Ⓓ Ⓔ	24 Ⓐ Ⓑ Ⓒ Ⓓ Ⓔ	24 Ⓐ Ⓑ Ⓒ Ⓓ Ⓔ	24 Ⓐ Ⓑ Ⓒ Ⓓ Ⓔ
25 Ⓐ Ⓑ Ⓒ Ⓓ Ⓔ	25 Ⓐ Ⓑ Ⓒ Ⓓ Ⓔ	25 Ⓐ Ⓑ Ⓒ Ⓓ Ⓔ	25 Ⓐ Ⓑ Ⓒ Ⓓ Ⓔ
26 Ⓐ Ⓑ Ⓒ Ⓓ Ⓔ	26 Ⓐ Ⓑ Ⓒ Ⓓ Ⓔ	26 Ⓐ Ⓑ Ⓒ Ⓓ Ⓔ	26 Ⓐ Ⓑ Ⓒ Ⓓ Ⓔ
27 Ⓐ Ⓑ Ⓒ Ⓓ Ⓔ	27 Ⓐ Ⓑ Ⓒ Ⓓ Ⓔ	27 Ⓐ Ⓑ Ⓒ Ⓓ Ⓔ	27 Ⓐ Ⓑ Ⓒ Ⓓ Ⓔ
28 Ⓐ Ⓑ Ⓒ Ⓓ Ⓔ	28 Ⓐ Ⓑ Ⓒ Ⓓ Ⓔ	28 Ⓐ Ⓑ Ⓒ Ⓓ Ⓔ	28 Ⓐ Ⓑ Ⓒ Ⓓ Ⓔ
29 Ⓐ Ⓑ Ⓒ Ⓓ Ⓔ	29 Ⓐ Ⓑ Ⓒ Ⓓ Ⓔ	29 Ⓐ Ⓑ Ⓒ Ⓓ Ⓔ	29 Ⓐ Ⓑ Ⓒ Ⓓ Ⓔ
30 Ⓐ Ⓑ Ⓒ Ⓓ Ⓔ	30 Ⓐ Ⓑ Ⓒ Ⓓ Ⓔ	30 Ⓐ Ⓑ Ⓒ Ⓓ Ⓔ	30 Ⓐ Ⓑ Ⓒ Ⓓ Ⓔ
31 Ⓐ Ⓑ Ⓒ Ⓓ Ⓔ	31 Ⓐ Ⓑ Ⓒ Ⓓ Ⓔ	31 Ⓐ Ⓑ Ⓒ Ⓓ Ⓔ	31 Ⓐ Ⓑ Ⓒ Ⓓ Ⓔ
32 Ⓐ Ⓑ Ⓒ Ⓓ Ⓔ	32 Ⓐ Ⓑ Ⓒ Ⓓ Ⓔ	32 Ⓐ Ⓑ Ⓒ Ⓓ Ⓔ	32 Ⓐ Ⓑ Ⓒ Ⓓ Ⓔ
33 Ⓐ Ⓑ Ⓒ Ⓓ Ⓔ	33 Ⓐ Ⓑ Ⓒ Ⓓ Ⓔ	33 Ⓐ Ⓑ Ⓒ Ⓓ Ⓔ	33 Ⓐ Ⓑ Ⓒ Ⓓ Ⓔ
34 Ⓐ Ⓑ Ⓒ Ⓓ Ⓔ	34 Ⓐ Ⓑ Ⓒ Ⓓ Ⓔ	34 Ⓐ Ⓑ Ⓒ Ⓓ Ⓔ	34 Ⓐ Ⓑ Ⓒ Ⓓ Ⓔ
35 Ⓐ Ⓑ Ⓒ Ⓓ Ⓔ	35 Ⓐ Ⓑ Ⓒ Ⓓ Ⓔ	35 Ⓐ Ⓑ Ⓒ Ⓓ Ⓔ	35 Ⓐ Ⓑ Ⓒ Ⓓ Ⓔ
36 Ⓐ Ⓑ Ⓒ Ⓓ Ⓔ	36 Ⓐ Ⓑ Ⓒ Ⓓ Ⓔ	36 Ⓐ Ⓑ Ⓒ Ⓓ Ⓔ	36 Ⓐ Ⓑ Ⓒ Ⓓ Ⓔ
37 Ⓐ Ⓑ Ⓒ Ⓓ Ⓔ	37 Ⓐ Ⓑ Ⓒ Ⓓ Ⓔ	37 Ⓐ Ⓑ Ⓒ Ⓓ Ⓔ	37 Ⓐ Ⓑ Ⓒ Ⓓ Ⓔ
38 Ⓐ Ⓑ Ⓒ Ⓓ Ⓔ	38 Ⓐ Ⓑ Ⓒ Ⓓ Ⓔ	38 Ⓐ Ⓑ Ⓒ Ⓓ Ⓔ	38 Ⓐ Ⓑ Ⓒ Ⓓ Ⓔ
39 Ⓐ Ⓑ Ⓒ Ⓓ Ⓔ	39 Ⓐ Ⓑ Ⓒ Ⓓ Ⓔ	39 Ⓐ Ⓑ Ⓒ Ⓓ Ⓔ	39 Ⓐ Ⓑ Ⓒ Ⓓ Ⓔ
40 Ⓐ Ⓑ Ⓒ Ⓓ Ⓔ	40 Ⓐ Ⓑ Ⓒ Ⓓ Ⓔ	40 Ⓐ Ⓑ Ⓒ Ⓓ Ⓔ	40 Ⓐ Ⓑ Ⓒ Ⓓ Ⓔ
41 Ⓐ Ⓑ Ⓒ Ⓓ Ⓔ	41 Ⓐ Ⓑ Ⓒ Ⓓ Ⓔ	41 Ⓐ Ⓑ Ⓒ Ⓓ Ⓔ	41 Ⓐ Ⓑ Ⓒ Ⓓ Ⓔ
42 Ⓐ Ⓑ Ⓒ Ⓓ Ⓔ	42 Ⓐ Ⓑ Ⓒ Ⓓ Ⓔ	42 Ⓐ Ⓑ Ⓒ Ⓓ Ⓔ	42 Ⓐ Ⓑ Ⓒ Ⓓ Ⓔ
43 Ⓐ Ⓑ Ⓒ Ⓓ Ⓔ	43 Ⓐ Ⓑ Ⓒ Ⓓ Ⓔ	43 Ⓐ Ⓑ Ⓒ Ⓓ Ⓔ	43 Ⓐ Ⓑ Ⓒ Ⓓ Ⓔ
44 Ⓐ Ⓑ Ⓒ Ⓓ Ⓔ	44 Ⓐ Ⓑ Ⓒ Ⓓ Ⓔ	44 Ⓐ Ⓑ Ⓒ Ⓓ Ⓔ	44 Ⓐ Ⓑ Ⓒ Ⓓ Ⓔ
45 Ⓐ Ⓑ Ⓒ Ⓓ Ⓔ	45 Ⓐ Ⓑ Ⓒ Ⓓ Ⓔ	45 Ⓐ Ⓑ Ⓒ Ⓓ Ⓔ	45 Ⓐ Ⓑ Ⓒ Ⓓ Ⓔ
46 Ⓐ Ⓑ Ⓒ Ⓓ Ⓔ	46 Ⓐ Ⓑ Ⓒ Ⓓ Ⓔ	46 Ⓐ Ⓑ Ⓒ Ⓓ Ⓔ	46 Ⓐ Ⓑ Ⓒ Ⓓ Ⓔ
47 Ⓐ Ⓑ Ⓒ Ⓓ Ⓔ	47 Ⓐ Ⓑ Ⓒ Ⓓ Ⓔ	47 Ⓐ Ⓑ Ⓒ Ⓓ Ⓔ	47 Ⓐ Ⓑ Ⓒ Ⓓ Ⓔ
48 Ⓐ Ⓑ Ⓒ Ⓓ Ⓔ	48 Ⓐ Ⓑ Ⓒ Ⓓ Ⓔ	48 Ⓐ Ⓑ Ⓒ Ⓓ Ⓔ	48 Ⓐ Ⓑ Ⓒ Ⓓ Ⓔ
49 Ⓐ Ⓑ Ⓒ Ⓓ Ⓔ	49 Ⓐ Ⓑ Ⓒ Ⓓ Ⓔ	49 Ⓐ Ⓑ Ⓒ Ⓓ Ⓔ	49 Ⓐ Ⓑ Ⓒ Ⓓ Ⓔ
50 Ⓐ Ⓑ Ⓒ Ⓓ Ⓔ	50 Ⓐ Ⓑ Ⓒ Ⓓ Ⓔ	50 Ⓐ Ⓑ Ⓒ Ⓓ Ⓔ	50 Ⓐ Ⓑ Ⓒ Ⓓ Ⓔ

9. SIGNATURE: ______________________

FOR ETS USE ONLY	VTR	VTFS	VRR	VRFS	VVR	VVFS	WER	WEFS	M4R	M4FS	M5R	M5FS	MTFS
	VTW	VTCS	VRW	VRCS	VVW	VVCS	WEW	WECS	M4W		M5W		MTCS

TEST 2—FORM CODE 4I

SECTION 1 Time—30 minutes 40 Questions

For each question in this section, choose the best answer and fill in the corresponding oval on the answer sheet.

Each question below consists of a word in capital letters, followed by five lettered words or phrases. Choose the word or phrase that is most nearly opposite in meaning to the word in capital letters. Since some of the questions require you to distinguish fine shades of meaning, consider all the choices before deciding which is best.

Example:

GOOD: (A) sour (B) bad (C) red (D) hot (E) ugly

1. DURABLE: (A) barely perceivable (B) easily destroyed (C) impudent (D) conclusive (E) outlandish

2. SLUMP: (A) upsurge (B) unification (C) clear view (D) desolate area (E) unexpected arrival

3. DISPUTE: (A) alleviate (B) affirm (C) enervate (D) answer caustically (E) inquire curiously

4. PROFANE: (A) happy (B) guarded (C) future (D) new (E) holy

5. RETROGRADE: (A) insolvent (B) cautious (C) spinning (D) moving forward (E) hindering success

6. DEBILITATE: (A) abbreviate (B) isolate (C) invigorate (D) infuriate (E) decorate

7. BALM: (A) residue (B) irritant (C) tinge (D) proper dose (E) weak solution

8. DEPLORE: (A) celebrate (B) disclose (C) intervene (D) accumulate (E) implore

9. PROPENSITY: (A) punctuality (B) aversion (C) ability to guess (D) lack of courage (E) grace in movement

10. DAUNT: (A) execute thoroughly (B) express carefully (C) hearten (D) debate (E) plead

GO ON TO THE NEXT PAGE

Each sentence below has one or two blanks, each blank indicating that something has been omitted. Beneath the sentence are five lettered words or sets of words. Choose the word or set of words that, when inserted in the sentence, best fits the meaning of the sentence as a whole.

Example:

Although its publicity has been ----, the film itself is intelligent, well-acted, handsomely produced, and altogether ----.

(A) tasteless. .respectable (B) extensive. .moderate (C) sophisticated. .amateur (D) risqué. .crude (E) perfect. .spectacular

● Ⓑ Ⓒ Ⓓ Ⓔ

11. Because management ---- the fact that employees find it difficult to work alertly at repetitious tasks, it sponsors numerous projects to ---- enthusiasm for the job.

(A) recognizes. .generate (B) disproves. .create (C) respects. .quench (D) controls. .regulate (E) surmises. .suspend

12. Eratosthenes' maps were ---- by the ---- state of exploration in his time, but they fit the facts then known.

(A) enhanced. .traditional
(B) disorganized. .stagnant
(C) limited. .primitive
(D) refuted. .flourishing
(E) determined. .exaggerated

13. Never forgetting his education as a preacher, Burwell often interrupts the narrative with ---- commentary, eager that his readers ---- the moral.

(A) romantic. .ignore (B) prophetic. .discredit (C) bombastic. .disregard (D) apathetic. .heed (E) didactic. .grasp

14. The training center, clean and regimented, is ---- to those seeking the ---- once associated with boxing.

(A) convincing. .chaos
(B) disappointing. .seediness
(C) surprising. .austerity
(D) refreshing. .camaraderie
(E) inspiring. .ambition

15. Of ---- disposition, she spoke very little, even when in the company of her good friends.

(A) an amiable (B) a benign (C) a carping (D) a taciturn (E) an inhumane

Each question below consists of a related pair of words or phrases, followed by five lettered pairs of words or phrases. Select the lettered pair that best expresses a relationship similar to that expressed in the original pair.

Example:

YAWN : BOREDOM :: (A) dream : sleep (B) anger : madness (C) smile : amusement (D) face : expression (E) impatience : rebellion

Ⓐ Ⓑ ● Ⓓ Ⓔ

16. CLOTH : MILDEW :: (A) wood : timber (B) insect : termite (C) flower : mushroom (D) iron : rust (E) antidote : poison

17. CRITIC : JUDGMENT :: (A) satirist : ridicule (B) doctor : rejection (C) writer : relaxation (D) miser : generosity (E) exile : patriotism

18. ZOO : ANIMAL :: (A) safari : guide (B) supermarket : shopper (C) herd : cattle (D) river : stream (E) museum : painting

19. FATHOM : DEPTH :: (A) mile : hour (B) volume : space (C) porthole : window (D) knot : speed (E) port : starboard

20. OFFHAND : FORETHOUGHT ::
(A) furtive : secrecy (B) voluntary : coercion (C) ingenious : talent (D) artistic : success (E) fanciful : elaboration

21. OPAQUE : LIGHT ::
(A) dense : weight (B) buoyant : air (C) hot : radiation (D) watertight : dampness (E) brilliant : illumination

22. AMORPHOUS : SHAPE :: (A) obvious : evidence (B) humble : belief (C) nondescript : classification (D) momentary : fame (E) ambiguous : obscurity

23. SYBARITE : LUXURY ::
(A) hermit : seclusion
(B) student : school
(C) employee : office
(D) mathematician : complexity
(E) official : expectation

24. ANNEX : BUILDING :: (A) addendum : book (B) scenario : play (C) program : computer (D) landscaping : park (E) duplex : apartment

25. BOAST : SPEAK :: (A) shout : utter (B) blare : hear (C) stumble : fall (D) stare : see (E) swagger : walk

GO ON TO THE NEXT PAGE

Each passage below is followed by questions based on its content. Answer the questions following each passage on the basis of what is stated or implied in that passage.

From the beginning, this trip to the high plateaus in Utah has had the feel of a last visit. We are getting beyond the age when we can unroll our sleeping bags under any pine or in any wash, and the gasoline situation throws the future of automobile touring into doubt. I would hate to have missed the extravagant personal liberty that wheels and cheap gasoline gave us, but I will not mourn its passing. It was part of our time of wastefulness and excess. Increasingly, we will have to earn our admission to this spectacular country. We will have to come by bus, as foreign tourists do, and at the end of the bus line use our legs. And if that reduces the number of people who benefit every year, the benefit will be qualitatively greater, for what most recommends the plateaus and their intervening deserts is not people, but space, emptiness, silence, awe.

I could make a suggestion to the road builders, too. The experience of driving the Aquarius Plateau on pavement is nothing like so satisfying as the old experience of driving it on rocky, rutted, chuckholed, ten-mile-an-hour dirt. The road will be a lesser thing when it is paved all the way, and so will the road over the Fish Lake Hightop, and the one over the Wasatch Plateau, and the steep road over the Tushar, the highest of the plateaus, which we will travel tomorrow. To substitute comfort and ease for real experience is too American a habit to last. It is when we feel the earth rough to all our length, as in Robert Frost's poem, that we know it as its creatures ought to know it.

The reading passages in this test are brief excerpts or adaptations of excerpts from published material. The ideas contained in them do not necessarily represent the opinions of the College Board or Educational Testing Service. To make the text suitable for testing purposes, we may in some cases have altered the style, contents, or point of view of the original.

26. According to the author, what will happen if fewer people visit the high country each year?
    (A) The characteristic mood of the plateaus will be tragically altered.
    (B) The doctrine of personal liberty will be seriously undermined.
    (C) The pleasure of those who do go will be heightened.
    (D) The people who visit the plateaus will have to spend more for the trip.
    (E) The paving of the roads will be slowed down considerably.

27. The author most probably paraphrases part of a Robert Frost poem in order to
    (A) lament past mistakes
    (B) warn future generations
    (C) reinforce his own sentiments
    (D) show how poetry enhances civilization
    (E) emphasize the complexity of the theme

28. It can be inferred from the passage that the author regards the paving of the plateau roads as
    (A) a project that will never be completed
    (B) a conscious attempt to destroy scenic beauty
    (C) an illegal action
    (D) an inexplicable decision
    (E) an unfortunate change

GO ON TO THE NEXT PAGE

Sergeant Blake was a man to whom memories were an encumbrance and anticipations a superfluity. That projection of consciousness into days gone by and to come, which makes the past a synonym for the pathetic and the future a word for circumspection, was foreign to Blake. With him the past was yesterday; the future, tomorrow.

On this account he might, in certain lights, have been regarded as fortunate. For it may be argued with great plausibility that reminiscence is less an endowment than a disease, and that expectation in its only comfortable form—that of absolute faith—is practically an impossibility; whilst in the form of hope and the secondary compounds, patience, impatience, resolve, curiosity, it is a constant fluctuation between pleasure and pain.

Sergeant Blake, being entirely innocent of the practice of expectation, was never disappointed. To set against this negative gain there may have been some positive losses from a certain narrowing of the higher tastes and sensations which it entailed. But limitation of the capacity is never recognized as a loss by the loser therefrom: in this attribute, moral or aesthetic poverty contrasts plausibly with material poverty, since those who suffer do not mind it, whilst those who mind it soon cease to suffer. What Blake had never enjoyed, he did not miss.

29. The passage is primarily concerned with

(A) recounting Blake's past
(B) evaluating Blake's personality
(C) showing Blake's interaction with other characters
(D) pondering Blake's future behavior
(E) justifying the author's philosophy of life

30. The author's statement that Sergeant Blake could be "regarded as fortunate" (line 9) is

(A) a sincere expression of esteem for Blake's character
(B) an ironic recognition of the advantages of Blake's limitations
(C) an obviously false statement intended to amuse
(D) a contradiction of what the author later says about Blake
(E) an indication of the author's belief in the power of fate

31. The author states that thinking about the future is an activity that

(A) distinguishes humans from animals
(B) is restricted to those with absolute faith
(C) has no beneficial effects
(D) results in moral or aesthetic poverty
(E) subjects one to emotional turmoil

GO ON TO THE NEXT PAGE

Literary study in the United States has reflected the taste of the majority while leaving unturned the forgotten pages of our national literature. The intellectual flexibility inherent in a multicultural nation has been stifled in classrooms where emphasis on British-American literature has not reflected the cultural amalgam of our country.

The literary disenfranchisement of particular groups is evidenced by the lack of serious study given to oral literature. American oral literature is characterized by its stylistic freshness relative to more commonly studied forms and by the variety of its metaphors and choice of subject. The corn grinding song of the Navajo is typical. Of course, when languages have widely dissimilar structures, translations are rarely faithful. Yet the picture of a rainbow moving across the plains to the waiting corn and, by symbolic correlation, of humanity's utter dependence upon rain is vivid even in translation. Rain is a positive metaphor among the Navajo: a welcome guest, for example, is often compared to a thundershower. Some of the experiential complexities which seem inexpressible in English are less so in other American languages which are not limited by spatial and temporal priorities of syntax. Without using extensive description, the Navajo poet created an epiphany, intense and fleeting, much like the Japanese haiku.

Black slaves also had a moving oral tradition: consider the poetry of the spirituals and animal fables, the latter usually conveying a lesson in survival in a hostile environment. Furthermore, Yiddish stories once told in the ghettos of Europe provided inspiration for such contemporary American writers as Bellow and Malamud, yet these stories are largely ignored because they are untranslated.

The common argument that the nature of an original is obscured by translation has little validity. An original translation introduces a new work. If the translation is of high quality, it is relatively unimportant whether or not it is an exact duplicate. Moreover, translations provide the vitality of heterogeneous literary influences for aspiring writers. Schoolcraft's compendium of Chippewa poetry resolves the translator's dilemma by presenting two translations of each song. The first is a literal presentation, the second captures the "feel" of the original. This technique is not practical for longer works, however.

Traditional forms of verse—epic, pastoral, metrical romance—do not include the Chippewa medicine songs, war songs, and dream songs. This is not to argue that these categories should supplant traditional genres but that traditional literary modes do not exhaust human artistic potential.

32. Which of the following titles best describes the content of the passage?

(A) Who Is to Blame for the Intellectual Rigidity of American Classrooms?
(B) Wellsprings of Talent in Contemporary American Literature
(C) The Need to Reconsider Traditional Verse Forms
(D) A Plea for the Neglected Pages of Our Literature
(E) The Translator's Dilemma

33. According to the author, those who criticize the value of literature in translation do so on the grounds that

(A) oral literature cannot be subjected to literary analysis
(B) translation is not practical except in short poems and stories
(C) the feeling of the original is often distorted
(D) traditional works are more generally appealing
(E) English speakers will not appreciate works translated from languages of dissimilar structure

34. The author implies that the traditional study of verse forms should be

(A) temporarily relegated to a minor position in favor of fresher forms
(B) supplanted by vital new modes of native American poetry
(C) modernized for use in contemporary classrooms
(D) supplemented by other forms from American literature
(E) subjected to exhaustive categorization so that it will be more meaningful

35. The author cites Bellow and Malamud as examples of authors who

(A) were inspired by an oral tradition
(B) overcame the indifference of American audiences
(C) are a source of motivation to young writers
(D) are not widely translated
(E) convey lessons in survival in a hostile world

GO ON TO THE NEXT PAGE

36. What the author says about Schoolcraft's technique in presenting Chippewa poetry in translation suggests which of the following situations?

(A) Depicting a scene by presenting a photograph, then an artist's rendering
(B) Writing a novel in which characters' desires are contrasted with actual events
(C) Presenting a concert in which a classical piece is played by a marching band
(D) Presenting a drama first as a stage play, then as a motion picture
(E) Illustrating a magazine article with caricatures accompanied by descriptive captions

---

In 1816, I was consulted by a young woman presenting general symptoms of disease of the heart. Owing to her stoutness, little information could be gathered by application of the hand and percussion. The patient's age and sex did not permit me to resort to the kind of examination I have described earlier [that is, direct application of the ear to the chest]. I recalled a well-known acoustic phenomenon: namely, if you place your ear against one end of a wooden beam the scratch of a pin at the other extremity is most distinctly audible. It occurred to me that this physical property might serve a useful purpose in the case with which I was then dealing. Taking a sheaf of paper I rolled it into a very tight roll, one end of which I placed over the precordial region, whilst I put my ear to the other. I was both surprised and gratified at being able to hear the beating of the heart with much greater clearness and distinctness than I had ever done before by direct application of my ear.

I saw at once that this means might become a useful method for studying, not only the beating of the heart, but likewise all movements capable of producing sound in the thoracic cavity, and that consequently it might serve for the investigation of respiration, the voice, rales, and even possibly the movements of a liquid effused into the pleural cavity or pericardium.

37. It can be inferred from the passage that the patient's stoutness was a handicap to the author because the stoutness

(A) inhibited the production of sound when the chest was tapped in a prescribed manner
(B) prevented the use of pressure to find tumors and other growths in the chest
(C) caused wheezing and other chest noises that interfered with diagnosis
(D) precluded the use of more strenuous methods of diagnosis
(E) muffled the sounds of the chest so that they could not be detected by an ear placed on the chest

38. The use of the sheaf of paper as described in lines 14-16 had which of the following immediate effects?

(A) It intensified the author's concern for the patient.
(B) It allowed the diagnosis of irregular heartbeats.
(C) It opened the way for research into medical applications of wood and paper.
(D) It amplified the sounds the author wished to hear.
(E) It allowed the author to analyze the patient's respiration rate.

39. The author's tone is best described as

(A) ecstatic (B) compassionate (C) arrogant (D) apprehensive (E) objective

40. The main purpose of the passage is to

(A) characterize the inventiveness of nineteenth-century physicians
(B) describe how a medical instrument was first devised
(C) explain an unusual cure for a common ailment
(D) call for investigation of the heart and lungs
(E) reveal the difficulties of early medicine

IF YOU FINISH BEFORE TIME IS CALLED, YOU MAY CHECK YOUR WORK ON THIS SECTION ONLY. DO NOT TURN TO ANY OTHER SECTION IN THE TEST. **STOP**

SECTION 3	Time—30 minutes 25 Questions	In this section solve each problem, using any available space on the page for scratchwork. Then decide which is the best of the choices given and fill in the corresponding oval on the answer sheet.

The following information is for your reference in solving some of the problems.

Circle of radius r: Area $= \pi r^2$; Circumference $= 2\pi r$
The number of degrees of arc in a circle is 360.
The measure in degrees of a straight angle is 180.

Definition of symbols:

$=$ is equal to	$\leq$ is less than or equal to
$\neq$ is unequal to	$\geq$ is greater than or equal to
$<$ is less than	$\parallel$ is parallel to
$>$ is greater than	$\perp$ is perpendicular to

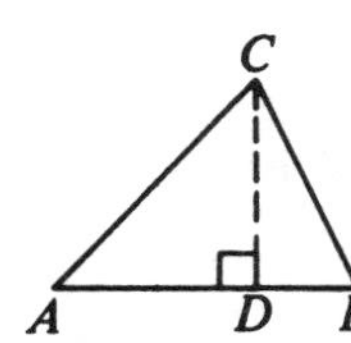

Triangle: The sum of the measures in degrees of the angles of a triangle is 180.
If $\angle CDA$ is a right angle, then

(1) area of $\triangle ABC = \dfrac{AB \times CD}{2}$

(2) $AC^2 = AD^2 + DC^2$

Note: Figures that accompany problems in this test are intended to provide information useful in solving the problems. They are drawn as accurately as possible EXCEPT when it is stated in a specific problem that its figure is not drawn to scale. All figures lie in a plane unless otherwise indicated. All numbers used are real numbers.

1. If $k = -1$, then $k + k^2 + k^3 + k^4 =$

(A) -4 (B) -2 (C) 0 (D) 2 (E) 4

2. At 9:00 a.m. the temperature of a solution is $-20°$C. This temperature rises at a uniform rate and at noon the reading is $0°$C. What will be the temperature of the solution at 3:00 p.m. on the same day, if it continues to rise at the same rate?

(A) $-20°$C
(B) $-10°$C
(C) $0°$C
(D) $10°$C
(E) $20°$C

3. If the sum of x and $x + 1$ is greater than 7, which of the following could be a value of x?

(A) -4
(B) 0
(C) 1
(D) 3
(E) 4

Questions 4-5 refer to the following definition.

For all positive numbers p, where $p \neq 1$, define p^* by the equation $p^* = \dfrac{p+2}{p-1}$.

4. If $p = 4$, then $p^* =$

(A) $\frac{6}{5}$ (B) $\frac{3}{2}$ (C) $\frac{5}{3}$ (D) 2 (E) 3

5. If p is positive and $p \neq 1$, then $\frac{1}{2}\left(\frac{1}{p^*}\right)$ is equal to which of the following?

(A) $\dfrac{p-2}{p+1}$

(B) $\dfrac{p-1}{2(p+2)}$

(C) $\dfrac{2(p-1)}{p+2}$

(D) $\dfrac{p+2}{p-1}$

(E) $\dfrac{2(p+2)}{p-1}$

GO ON TO THE NEXT PAGE

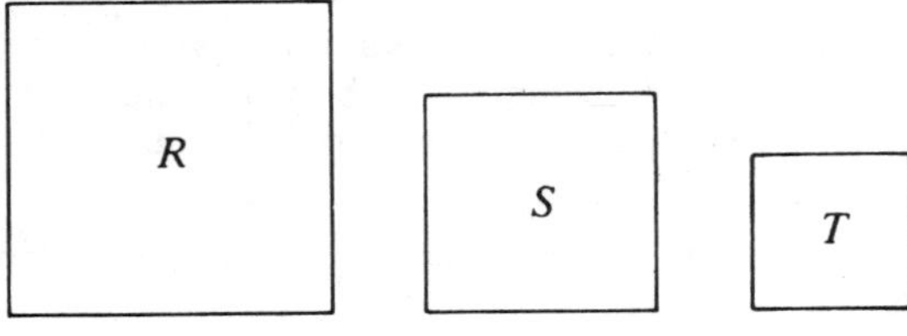

6. Three squares R, S, and T are shown above. The area of R is twice the area of S, and the area of S is twice the area of T. If the area of S is 1, what is the sum of the areas of all three squares?

(A) $2\frac{1}{2}$

(B) $3\frac{1}{2}$

(C) 4

(D) $5\frac{1}{4}$

(E) 6

---

7. If $40{,}404 + x = 44{,}444$, then $40{,}404 - 10x =$

(A) −4.04
(B) 0
(C) 4
(D) 4.04
(E) 40.4

Questions 8-9 refer to the following definition.

For any positive integer k, let $\boxed{k}$ represent the greatest odd integer that divides k; for example $\boxed{36} = 9$.

8. $\boxed{30} =$

(A) 5 (B) 6 (C) 10 (D) 15 (E) 25

9. Which of the following is equal to $\boxed{2^9}$?

(A) 1 (B) 2 (C) 2^3 (D) 2^6 (E) 2^9

10. Several people are standing in a straight line. Starting at one end of the line, Bill is counted as the 5th person and, starting at the other end, he is counted as the 12th person. How many people are in the line?

(A) 15
(B) 16
(C) 17
(D) 18
(E) 19

11. If $\frac{x}{y}$ is a fraction greater than 1, which of the following must be less than 1 ?

(A) $\frac{2y}{x}$

(B) $\frac{x}{2y}$

(C) $\sqrt{\frac{x}{y}}$

(D) $\frac{y}{x}$

(E) $\left(\frac{x}{y}\right)^2$

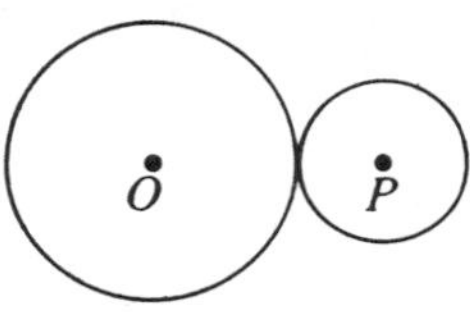

12. In the figure above, the circles with centers O and P have radii of 5 and 3, respectively, and have exactly one point in common. If a circle C (not shown) is drawn such that O is its center and P is on its circumference, what is the radius of circle C ?

(A) 8 (B) 10 (C) 11 (D) 16
(E) It cannot be determined from the information given.

GO ON TO THE NEXT PAGE

13. $\left[(2x^2y^3)^2\right]^3 =$

(A) $4x^4y^6$ (B) $12x^4y^6$ (C) $64x^4y^6$
(D) $64x^{12}y^{18}$ (E) $64x^{64}y^{216}$

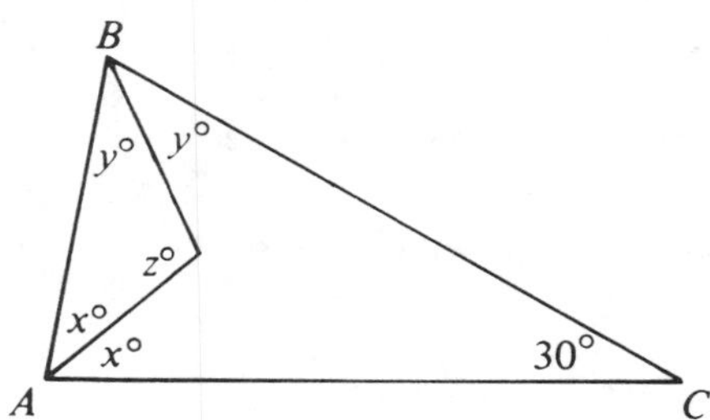

14. In the figure above, if $\angle BAC = 80^\circ$, then $z =$

(A) 100
(B) 105
(C) 110
(D) 120
(E) 125

15. If $\left(\frac{2}{10}\right)^3$ is equal to q thousandths, what is the value of q ?

(A) 5 (B) 6 (C) 8 (D) 23 (E) 32

16. If Town A is 300 kilometers due east of Town B and Town C is 400 kilometers due south of Town B, then the shortest distance, in kilometers, from Town A to Town C is

(A) 450
(B) 500
(C) 550
(D) 600
(E) 700

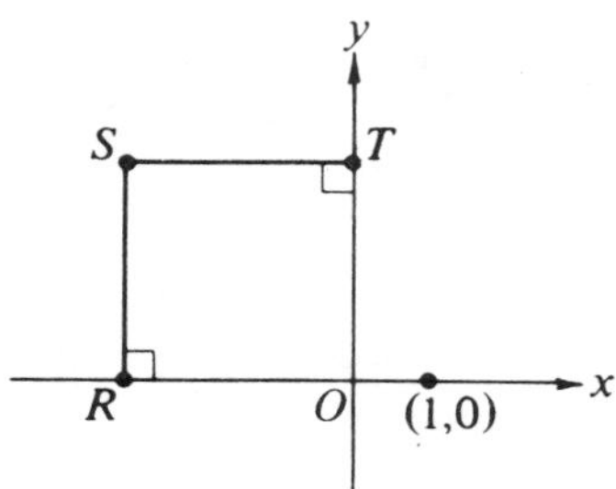

17. In the figure above, $RS = ST$ and the coordinates of S are $(k, 3)$. What is the value of k ?

(A) -3 (B) $-\sqrt{3}$ (C) 0 (D) $\sqrt{3}$ (E) 3

18. Car I averages 30 miles per gallon of gasoline while car II averages 25 miles per gallon. If gasoline costs \$2 per gallon, how much more would the gasoline cost for a 600-mile trip in car II than in car I ?

(A) \$16
(B) \$12
(C) \$10
(D) \$8
(E) \$6

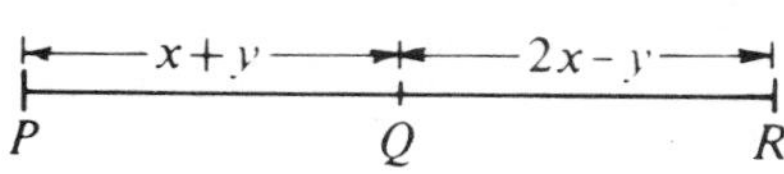

19. Segment PR is divided into two segments with lengths as shown above. If Q is the midpoint of PR, which of the following statements must be true?

(A) $x = 0$ (B) $x = \frac{1}{2}y$ (C) $x = \frac{2}{3}y$

(D) $x = y$ (E) $x = 2y$

GO ON TO THE NEXT PAGE

20. What is the perimeter of a square that has the same area as a circle that has circumference 1 ?

(A) $4\sqrt{\pi}$

(B) $\frac{2}{\sqrt{\pi}}$

(C) $\frac{1}{2\sqrt{\pi}}$

(D) $\frac{1}{\pi}$

(E) 1

21. The average (arithmetic mean) of n numbers is 10 and the average of 5 of these numbers is 8. In terms of n, what is the average of the remaining numbers?

(A) $\frac{10n + 40}{5}$

(B) $\frac{10n - 40}{5}$

(C) $\frac{40 - 10n}{5}$

(D) $\frac{40 - 10n}{n - 5}$

(E) $\frac{10n - 40}{n - 5}$

22. A train started at station S and has been traveling r miles per hour for t hours. In terms of r and t, how many miles from station S had the train traveled $\frac{3t}{4}$ hours ago?

(A) $\frac{rt}{12}$

(B) $\frac{3rt}{4}$

(C) rt

(D) $\frac{4rt}{3}$

(E) $\frac{rt}{4}$

23. If $2x + y = 15$ and $x + 2y = -3$, then $2x + 2y =$

(A) 8
(B) 12
(C) 18
(D) 24
(E) 36

24. If r is a positive integer and the ratio $\frac{r}{s}$ is $\frac{1}{3}$, which of the following could be the value of $\frac{r^2}{s}$?

I. $\frac{1}{3}$

II. 1

III. $\frac{4}{3}$

(A) None
(B) I only
(C) I and II only
(D) I and III only
(E) I, II, and III

25. What is the number of different pairs of parallel edges on a cubical wooden block?

(A) 18 (B) 12 (C) 8 (D) 6 (E) 4

IF YOU FINISH BEFORE TIME IS CALLED, YOU MAY CHECK YOUR WORK ON THIS SECTION ONLY. DO NOT TURN TO ANY OTHER SECTION IN THE TEST. **STOP**

SECTION 5	Time—30 minutes 35 Questions	In this section solve each problem, using any available space on the page for scratchwork. Then decide which is the best of the choices given and fill in the corresponding oval on the answer sheet.

The following information is for your reference in solving some of the problems.

Circle of radius r: Area $= \pi r^2$; Circumference $= 2\pi r$
The number of degrees of arc in a circle is 360.
The measure in degrees of a straight angle is 180.

Definition of symbols:
$=$ is equal to $\leq$ is less than or equal to
$\neq$ is unequal to $\geq$ is greater than or equal to
$<$ is less than $\parallel$ is parallel to
$>$ is greater than $\perp$ is perpendicular to

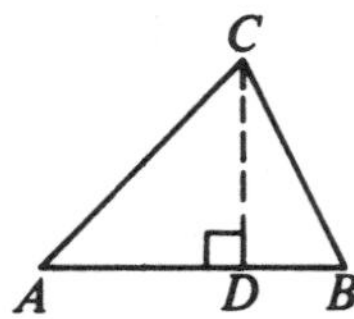

Triangle: The sum of the measures in degrees of the angles of a triangle is 180.
If $\angle CDA$ is a right angle, then

(1) area of $\triangle ABC = \frac{AB \times CD}{2}$

(2) $AC^2 = AD^2 + DC^2$

Note: Figures that accompany problems in this test are intended to provide information useful in solving the problems. They are drawn as accurately as possible EXCEPT when it is stated in a specific problem that its figure is not drawn to scale. All figures lie in a plane unless otherwise indicated. All numbers used are real numbers.

1. If $x = m - n$ and $y = n - m$, what is $x - y$ when $m = 6$ and $n = 6$?

(A) −12 (B) 0 (C) 6 (D) 12 (E) 24

Questions 2-3 refer to the following price list.

Number of Donuts	Total Price
1	\$0.40
Box of 6	\$1.89
Box of 12	\$3.59

2. Of the following, which is the closest approximation of the cost per donut when one purchases a box of 6?

(A) \$0.20 (B) \$0.30 (C) \$0.40
(D) \$0.50 (E) \$0.60

3. What would be the least amount of money needed to purchase exactly 21 donuts?

(A) \$5.88
(B) \$6.68
(C) \$7.19
(D) \$7.38
(E) \$8.40

4. If x and y are positive integers and $x + y = 12$, what is the greatest possible value of xy?

(A) 11 (B) 12 (C) 32 (D) 36 (E) 144

$$\begin{array}{r} R\,S \\ +\,S\,R \\ \hline 5\,5 \end{array}$$

5. In the addition problem above, $0 < S < 5$ and $0 < R < 5$. How many different integer values of S are possible?

(A) One
(B) Two
(C) Three
(D) Four
(E) Five

6. $\sqrt{\frac{\sqrt{16}}{4}} =$

(A) 1 (B) $\sqrt{2}$ (C) 2 (D) $2\sqrt{2}$ (E) 4

7. If $x \neq 0$ and $3x^2 - 12x = 0$, what is the value of x?

(A) −9
(B) −4
(C) 3
(D) 4
(E) 9

GO ON TO THE NEXT PAGE

5

Questions 8-27 each consist of two quantities, one in Column A and one in Column B. You are to compare the two quantities and on the answer sheet fill in oval

- **A** if the quantity in Column A is greater;
- **B** if the quantity in Column B is greater;
- **C** if the two quantities are equal;
- **D** if the relationship cannot be determined from the information given.

AN E RESPONSE WILL NOT BE SCORED.

EXAMPLES

	Column A	Column B	Answers
E1.	2×6	$2 + 6$	● Ⓑ Ⓒ Ⓓ Ⓔ
E2.	$180 - x$	y	Ⓐ Ⓑ ● Ⓓ Ⓔ
E3.	$p - q$	$q - p$	Ⓐ Ⓑ Ⓒ ● Ⓔ

(E2 figure: a line meeting a horizontal line, forming angles $x°$ and $y°$.)

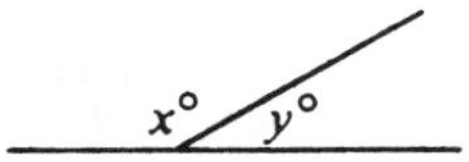

Notes:

1. In certain questions, information concerning one or both of the quantities to be compared is centered above the two columns.
2. In a given question, a symbol that appears in both columns represents the same thing in Column A as it does in Column B.
3. Letters such as x, n, and k stand for real numbers.

	Column A	Column B
8.	2^{16}	1^{32}
9.	$3.7 + 2.6 + 7$	$\frac{73.7 + 72.6}{10}$

A fair coin is tossed 2 times.

	Column A	Column B
10.	The chances of getting 2 heads	The chances of getting no heads

$5t > 3s$

	Column A	Column B
11.	t	s

In the last step of an arithmetic problem, John added 15 to the value he had obtained so far, when he should have subtracted 30. He made no other mistakes.

	Column A	Column B
12.	The correct answer to the problem	John's answer to the problem
13.	4×5^{13}	5×4^{13}

$\frac{x}{y} = \frac{1}{6}$

	Column A	Column B
14.	y	$6x$

	Column A	Column B

x is an integer.

	Column A	Column B
15.	The greatest possible value of $4 - x^2$	5

x, y, and z are equal to 1, 2, and 3, but not necessarily in that order. $y > x$

	Column A	Column B
16.	$y + z - x$	2

The number of employees in department J is 3 less than 5 times the number of employees in department P. There are n employees in department P.

	Column A	Column B
17.	The number of employees in department J	$5n - 3$

$x^2 - 13x + 42 = 0$

	Column A	Column B
18.	x	8

The list price of a watch is x dollars.

	Column A	Column B
19.	The price of the watch at 25 percent off the list price	$0.75x$ dollars

GO ON TO THE NEXT PAGE

SUMMARY DIRECTIONS FOR COMPARISON QUESTIONS

Answer:
A if the quantity in Column A is greater;
B if the quantity in Column B is greater;
C if the two quantities are equal;
D if the relationship cannot be determined from the information given.

AN E RESPONSE WILL NOT BE SCORED.

	Column A	Column B
20.	$\dfrac{1}{\frac{10}{7} - 1}$	2

$\frac{7}{8} < x < \frac{8}{7}$

	Column A	Column B
21.	x	$\frac{10}{9}$

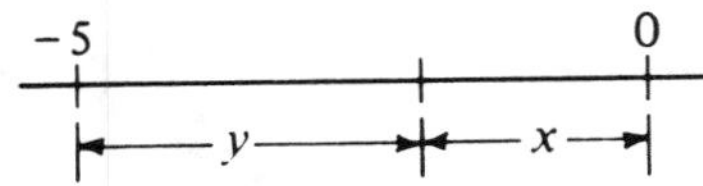

x and y are lengths of segments on the number line above.

	Column A	Column B
22.	x	$5 - y$

Polygon X has equal sides and equal angles. The perimeter of polygon X is 10.

	Column A	Column B
23.	The number of sides of polygon X	5

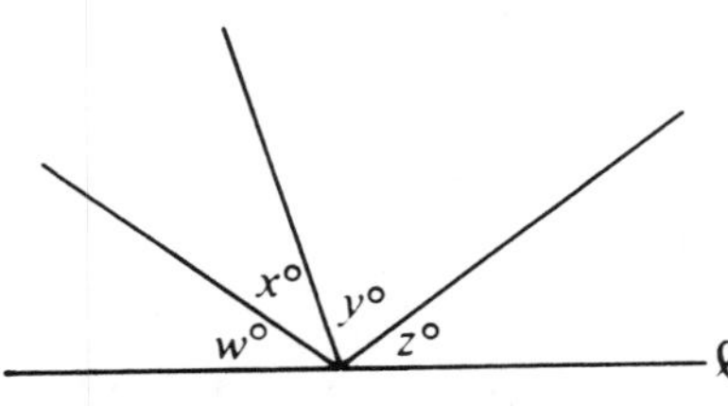

$w = x = z$ and $\frac{y}{z} = \frac{2}{1}$

	Column A	Column B
24.	y	70

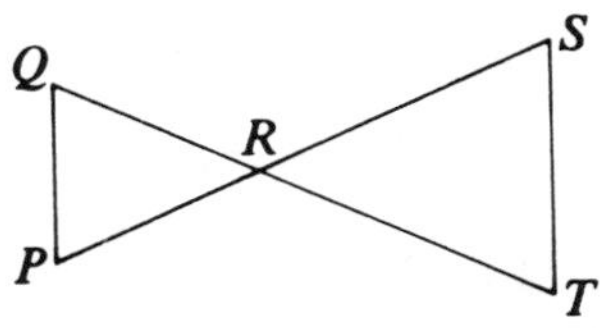

Note: Figure not drawn to scale.

Line segments QT and PS intersect at point R.
$PQ \parallel ST$

	Column A	Column B
25.	The length of QR	The length of PR

$x > y > 0$

	Column A	Column B
26.	$x^2 - y^2$	$x^2 - y$

10 millimeters = 1 centimeter

	Column A	Column B
27.	The area of a square that measures 5 centimeters on a side	10 times the area of a square that measures 5 millimeters on a side

GO ON TO THE NEXT PAGE

Solve each of the remaining problems in this section using any available space for scratchwork. Then decide which is the best of the choices given and fill in the corresponding oval on the answer sheet.

28. Which of the following equals the ratio of $2\frac{1}{2}$ days to 7 days?

(A) 2:35
(B) 2:9
(C) 2:7
(D) 5:14
(E) 5:9

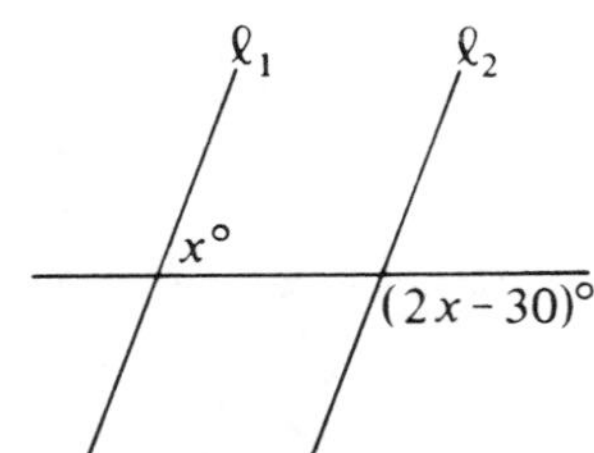

29. In the figure above, if $\ell_1 \parallel \ell_2$, then $x =$

(A) 30 (B) 50 (C) 70 (D) 105 (E) 210

30. If $(1{,}000 + 6)^2 = 10^6 + n$, then $n =$

(A) 36
(B) 6,036
(C) 12,006
(D) 12,036
(E) 60,036

31. If the sum of two angles of a parallelogram is 100°, what is the average (arithmetic mean) of the measures of the other two angles?

(A) 50°
(B) 90°
(C) 130°
(D) 180°
(E) 260°

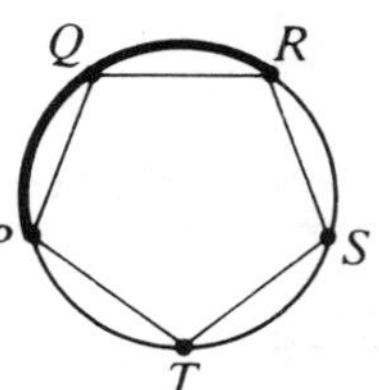

32. In the figure above, inscribed polygon $PQRST$ is equilateral. If the diameter of the circle is 10, then the length of arc PQR is

(A) 10π (B) 4π (C) 2π (D) $\frac{4\pi}{5}$ (E) $\frac{2\pi}{5}$

33. According to the formula $F = \frac{9}{5}C + 32$, if the Fahrenheit (F) temperature increased 27°, by how many degrees would the Celsius (C) temperature be increased?

(A) 9° (B) 15° (C) 47°
(D) $48\frac{3}{5}°$ (E) 59°

34. A square and an equilateral triangle have perimeters S and T, respectively. If s and t are the respective lengths of a side of the square and a side of the triangle, then, in terms of their perimeters, $s - t =$

(A) $\frac{S - T}{7}$
(B) $\frac{4T - 3S}{7}$
(C) $\frac{3S - 4T}{7}$
(D) $\frac{4T - 3S}{12}$
(E) $\frac{3S - 4T}{12}$

35. If 3 percent of $(x + y)$ is 12 and x is a negative integer, what is the <u>least</u> possible value of y?

(A) 5 (B) 41 (C) 399 (D) 400 (E) 401

IF YOU FINISH BEFORE TIME IS CALLED, YOU MAY CHECK YOUR WORK ON THIS SECTION ONLY. DO NOT TURN TO ANY OTHER SECTION IN THE TEST. **STOP**

SECTION 6 | **Time—30 minutes 45 Questions** | For each question in this section, choose the best answer and fill in the corresponding oval on the answer sheet.

Each question below consists of a word in capital letters, followed by five lettered words or phrases. Choose the word or phrase that is most nearly opposite in meaning to the word in capital letters. Since some of the questions require you to distinguish fine shades of meaning, consider all the choices before deciding which is best.

Example:

GOOD: (A) sour (B) bad (C) red (D) hot (E) ugly

Ⓐ ● Ⓒ Ⓓ Ⓔ

1. DISMANTLE: (A) recall (B) approve (C) rebuild (D) embrace (E) dwell

2. HIDEOUS: (A) careful (B) economical (C) independent (D) delightful (E) assenting

3. COMPLEX: (A) elementary (B) distinct (C) precise (D) immature (E) reasonable

4. ABUSIVENESS: (A) retaliation (B) perception (C) estrangement (D) cordiality (E) exclusivity

5. INOPPORTUNE: (A) optional (B) stratified (C) methodical (D) insistent (E) convenient

6. EMBED: (A) cool down (B) keep pure (C) energize (D) exalt (E) extract

7. CORRUGATED: (A) narrow (B) heavy (C) smooth (D) firm (E) split

8. MORBIDITY: (A) fervor (B) meditation (C) indifference (D) fearlessness (E) wholesomeness

9. ILLUSTRIOUS: (A) abstract (B) idle (C) ill-tempered (D) infamous (E) persistent

10. VOLUMINOUS: (A) indistinct (B) slight (C) inaudible (D) courteous (E) misconceived

11. EQUANIMITY: (A) dedication (B) unselfishness (C) innocence (D) lack of composure (E) lack of success

12. INCONSEQUENTIAL: (A) transitional (B) natural (C) flawless (D) lively (E) pivotal

13. CONSONANCE: (A) contempt (B) discord (C) coarseness (D) extreme uncertainty (E) mindless repetition

14. VERBOSE: (A) energetic (B) relaxed (C) exotic (D) complimentary (E) terse

15. BURGEON: (A) vary (B) wither (C) move freely (D) leave alone (E) act cautiously

Each sentence below has one or two blanks, each blank indicating that something has been omitted. Beneath the sentence are five lettered words or sets of words. Choose the word or set of words that, when inserted in the sentence, best fits the meaning of the sentence as a whole.

Example:

Although its publicity has been ----, the film itself is intelligent, well-acted, handsomely produced, and altogether ----.

(A) tasteless. .respectable (B) extensive. .moderate (C) sophisticated. .amateur (D) risqué. .crude (E) perfect. .spectacular

● Ⓑ Ⓒ Ⓓ Ⓔ

16. Although the shock of the accident had temporarily hindered his ability to think rationally, his instincts and sense of morality somehow seemed ----.

(A) intact (B) affected (C) unreachable (D) inconsistent (E) unresponsive

17. Metabolic by-products of oxygen are so ---- that breathing organisms have developed elaborate defense systems against them.

(A) insignificant (B) useful (C) toxic (D) unpredictable (E) necessary

18. Before the 1930's, the knowledge one could give children would last them their working lives, whereas today the technological revolution often renders familiar scientific developments ---- overnight.

(A) valid (B) expedient (C) obsolete (D) immortal (E) memorable

19. Ideally, every election ought to be ---- by a majority of ---- citizens, but it sometimes happens that the outcome is determined by those people who know least about politics.

(A) revoked. .esteemed (B) proposed. .prominent (C) regulated. .local (D) conducted. .ordinary (E) decided. .informed

20. She is one of the most ---- public figures in the country today, disarmingly candid and seemingly fearless of any consequences.

(A) prudent (B) agreeable (C) outspoken (D) indecisive (E) discerning

Each passage below is followed by questions based on its content. Answer the questions following each passage on the basis of what is stated or implied in that passage.

During the 1840's, some doubts were cast on the applications of Newton's theory of gravitation to problems of planetary motion when it was found that the planet Uranus was not following the orbit it should under the influence of gravitation. There seemed only one solution, and this was to assume that there must be yet another planet, farther out, affecting Uranus by its own gravitational pull. To calculate where such a planet should be and how massive it must be to account for the disturbances suffered by Uranus was an enormously difficult task. However, two mathematicians tackled the problem—Urbain Leverrier in France and John Adams in England. Both were successful and both obtained the same result: in 1846 observations were made of the place in the sky where they had predicted another planet would be seen and the planet Neptune was discovered.

After some years it was realized that this planet, too, showed irregularities in its orbit. But by then Newton's basic theory was too well established to be cast aside, and yet another planet was computed to be the cause. The computations followed the lines of those of Adams and Leverrier and were mostly carried out by the American astronomer Percival Lowell, who searched for the planet from his observatory in Arizona. But Lowell had no success with his observations and, when he died in 1916, the quest for the planet was dropped for a time. In 1930 Clyde Tombaugh found it close to the calculated position.

Pluto's discovery seemed another proof of Newtonian principles. But there was still an additional case of difficulty, and this was the behavior of Mercury. The rather oval orbit of this planet was found to rotate, but at a speed greater than that which Newtonian gravitation would lead one to expect. This fact had been appreciated by Leverrier, and he computed an orbit for a disturbing planet nearer to the Sun than Mercury. He announced his results in September 1859 and showed that the effects on Mercury's orbit could be caused by a planet of Mercury's size orbiting the Sun at half its distance. Soon afterward, an amateur astronomer claimed that he had already observed the new planet. Leverrier, who duplicated these results, claimed that the observations were the proof he needed. He named the planet Vulcan.

Though subsequent claims of successful observations were made by professional astronomers, a careful check in March 1877 and October 1882, when Vulcan should have been observed moving across the face of the Sun, showed nothing. Leverrier's conclusion about Vulcan could no longer be accepted. It remained for Einstein's 1916 theory of relativity to account almost exactly for Mercury's orbit.

21. According to the passage, the validity of Newton's gravitational theory was supported by which of the following?

    I. The discovery of the cause of the irregularity of Uranus' orbit
    II. The final explanation of unexpected characteristics of Mercury's orbit
    III. The presence of Pluto as predicted by mathematical computations

    (A) I only (B) II only (C) I and II only (D) I and III only (E) I, II, and III

22. According to the passage, John Adams predicted which of the following?

    (A) The existence of Uranus
    (B) The location of Neptune
    (C) The rotation of Pluto
    (D) The location of Vulcan
    (E) The oval orbit of Mercury

23. The author implies that reported sightings of Vulcan were most likely the result of

    (A) insufficient thoroughness in interpreting evidence
    (B) inadequate instructions provided by Leverrier's theory
    (C) interference from the planet Mercury, which eclipsed Vulcan
    (D) dominance of the field by amateur astronomers
    (E) misinterpretations of data that Newton had collected

24. According to the passage, the implications of Newton's theory of gravitation were adequate to account for which of the following?

    I. Neptune's orbit
    II. Pluto's orbit
    III. Mercury's orbit

    (A) I only (B) II only (C) III only (D) I and II only (E) I, II, and III

25. Which of the following titles is most suitable for the passage?

    (A) How Planets Are Sighted
    (B) Why Newton Was Wrong
    (C) Newton's Gravitational Theory and the Discovery of Planets
    (D) Development of Astronomical Theories in the Nineteenth Century
    (E) The Role of Mathematics in Astronomy

GO ON TO THE NEXT PAGE

Law and morality are closely related, and interact in a highly complex way; moreover, there always exists the possibility of serious divergence in a given situation between the duty imposed by law and that imposed by morality. There are three main attitudes that may be adopted toward the possibility of such a divergence, and these are encapsulated here.

First, it may be said that law and morality must necessarily coincide either because morality dictates the actual content of human law, as in the case of the Hebrew and Calvinist theocracies, or alternatively because morality is itself merely what the law lays down. The first alternative leads to the proposition that only morality is valid and that nothing that does not conform to it can be regarded as binding. The second alternative has been propounded by many eminent philosophers. Hobbes, for instance, argued that morality itself means nothing more than obeying the law, so that "unjust law" is a contradiction in terms. Hegel's mystical theory of the superiority of the state over the individual proposed that the individual could claim no higher right than to obey the law of the state of which he or she forms an insignificant part.

The second attitude asserts that law and morality are distinct, but that morality provides a touchstone for the validity of merely human law. Conflicts therefore need to be resolved, at least in the last resort, in favor of morality. Broadly speaking this approach to morality has, beginning with the Greeks, been discussed in Western jurisprudence mostly in terms of a so-called law of nature, which is regarded as containing precepts of a higher order, whether divinely ordained or part of the material world. This doctrine has been linked with the idea of the "natural rights" of the individual, which has played so large a role in democratic thought since the American and the French revolutions.

Third, there is the approach that treats the autonomy of law and morality as exclusive, so that neither can resolve questions of validity save in its own sphere. This theory is commonly referred to as "legal positivism." It insists that the validity of a legal rule can depend solely on legal criteria, just as moral validity depends on such criteria as are necessary or appropriate to a system of morality. Those who support this view hold that any conflict between the two spheres cannot impugn the validity of human law or alter the duty of legal obedience, though it may give rise to the moral problem of whether the law ought to be changed. And, in extreme cases, a conflict between legal and moral duty may have to be resolved in accordance with the conscience of individuals and their moral courage to defy a law that they believe to be contrary to what is morally right or just.

26. It can be inferred that throughout the passage the term "human law" refers to law that is

(A) established by legislative agents
(B) conceived in the spirit of compassion
(C) comprehensible to most lay people
(D) meant to govern all behavior
(E) hostile to spiritual concerns

27. It can be inferred from the passage that in a theocracy the law is

(A) the exclusive domain of priests
(B) the ultimate mystery of faith
(C) a matter of relative unimportance
(D) a reflection of ethical precepts
(E) a precondition of advanced spirituality

28. It can be inferred that "the idea of the 'natural rights' of the individual" (lines 35-36) plays a great role in revolutionary democratic thought because that idea

(A) forces one to disregard all traditional restraints
(B) calls for the abolition of religious institutions
(C) attacks the validity of all nonscientific social theories
(D) implies that anarchy is humanity's native condition
(E) justifies the infraction of repressive laws

29. It can be inferred from the passage that a legal positivist would consider which of the following to be logically possible?

I. An act that is morally reprehensible but legally correct
II. An act that is morally correct but legally reprehensible
III. An act that is morally reprehensible and legally reprehensible

(A) II only
(B) III only
(C) I and III only
(D) II and III only
(E) I, II, and III

30. According to the passage, "in extreme cases" (line 51) legal positivism allows for the possibility of

(A) irrational behavior
(B) altruistic sacrifice
(C) inspiring leadership
(D) civil disobedience
(E) religious fanaticism

GO ON TO THE NEXT PAGE

6

Select the word or set of words that best completes each of the following sentences.

31. Recent legislative action will ---- the Pine Barrens from random and harmful growth while conversely ensuring that orderly and sound commercial development will not be ----.

(A) protect. .halted (B) remove. .slowed (C) defend. .continued (D) isolate. .undertaken (E) preserve. .allowed

32. As a young man, Jean Toomer spoke of his desire to integrate the seemingly ---- elements of his racial heritage so that they might ----, rather than oppose, each other.

(A) archaic. .reprove (B) contrary. .complement (C) dissimilar. .dispel (D) baffling. .exceed (E) inverted. .induce

33. Mary Cassatt, an Impressionist painter, was the epitome of the ---- American: a native of Philadelphia who lived most of her life in Paris.

(A) conservative (B) provincial (C) benevolent (D) prophetic (E) expatriate

34. Long after science has recognized that appearances are relative, many people nevertheless continue to consider them ----.

(A) illusive (B) uncertain (C) absolute (D) dependent (E) exceptional

35. Because it has always ---- so many of life's pleasures, this sect finds it difficult to ---- its membership in today's hedonistic atmosphere.

(A) endorsed. .placate
(B) forbidden. .deplete
(C) proscribed. .augment
(D) denounced. .alienate
(E) condoned. .supplement

Each question below consists of a related pair of words or phrases, followed by five lettered pairs of words or phrases. Select the lettered pair that best expresses a relationship similar to that expressed in the original pair.

Example:

YAWN : BOREDOM :: (A) dream : sleep (B) anger : madness (C) smile : amusement (D) face : expression (E) impatience : rebellion

Ⓐ Ⓑ ● Ⓓ Ⓔ

36. CLOCK:MINUTE :: (A) ruler:centimeter (B) sundial:shadow (C) arc:ellipse (D) product:shelf life (E) quart:capacity

37. LAWYER:CLIENT ::
(A) doctor:surgeon
(B) admiral:sailor
(C) judge:defendant
(D) musician:audience
(E) tutor:student

38. CHILL:COLD :: (A) parch:dry (B) crush:soft (C) freeze:white (D) graze:opaque (E) scrub:hard

39. RECUPERATE:HEALTH ::
(A) repent:wickedness
(B) respond:medication
(C) regret:opportunity
(D) revive:consciousness
(E) revenge:assault

40. LEGEND:MAP :: (A) volume:manual (B) career:biography (C) glossary:text (D) column:article (E) issue:print

41. RIFLE:MUNITIONS ::
(A) band:instruments
(B) cash:merchandise
(C) tool:measurement
(D) spatula:utensils
(E) dumbbell:calisthenics

42. CONFLAGRATION:FIRE :: (A) precaution:danger (B) jubilee:celebration (C) challenge:perfection (D) defense:attack (E) ornamentation:communication

43. HIATUS:ACTIVITY :: (A) link:chain (B) day:eternity (C) mesh:net (D) intermission:play (E) revision:edition

44. LIONIZE:CELEBRITY :: (A) tyrannize:ruler (B) ostracize:outcast (C) demoralize:censor (D) idolize:worshipper (E) familiarize:guide

45. CHARISMATIC:LOYALTY ::
(A) crass:sophistication
(B) odious:repugnance
(C) famous:superiority
(D) pessimistic:expectation
(E) melodramatic:contradiction

IF YOU FINISH BEFORE TIME IS CALLED, YOU MAY CHECK YOUR WORK ON THIS SECTION ONLY. DO NOT TURN TO ANY OTHER SECTION IN THE TEST. **STOP**

Correct Answers for Scholastic Aptitude Test Form Code 4I			
VERBAL		MATHEMATICAL	
Section 1	Section 6	Section 3	Section 5
1. B	1. C	1. C	1. B
2. A	2. D	2. E	2. B
3. B	3. A	3. E	3. B
4. E	4. D	4. D	4. D
5. D	5. E	5. B	5. D
6. C	6. E	6. B	6. A
7. B	7. C	7. C	7. D
8. A	8. E	8. D	*8. A
9. B	9. D	9. A	*9. B
10. C	10. B	10. B	*10. C
11. A	11. D	11. D	*11. D
12. C	12. E	12. A	*12. B
13. E	13. B	13. D	*13. A
14. B	14. E	14. B	*14. C
15. D	15. B	15. C	*15. B
16. D	16. A	16. B	*16. D
17. A	17. C	17. A	*17. C
18. E	18. C	18. D	*18. B
19. D	19. E	19. E	*19. C
20. B	20. C	20. B	*20. A
21. D	21. D	21. E	*21. D
22. C	22. B	22. E	*22. C
23. A	23. A	23. A	*23. D
24. A	24. D	24. E	*24. A
25. E	25. C	25. A	*25. D
26. C	26. A		*26. D
27. C	27. D		*27. A
28. E	28. E		28. D
29. B	29. E		29. C
30. B	30. D		30. D
31. E	31. A		31. C
32. D	32. B		32. B
33. C	33. E		33. B
34. D	34. C		34. E
35. A	35. C		35. E
36. A	36. A		
37. A	37. E		
38. D	38. A		
39. E	39. D		
40. B	40. C		
	41. D		
	42. B		
	43. D		
	44. B		
	45. B		

*Indicates four-choice questions. (All of the other questions are five-choice.)

The Scoring Process

Machine-scoring is done in three steps:

- *Scanning.* Your answer sheet is "read" by a scanning machine and the oval you filled in for each question is recorded on a computer tape.
- *Scoring.* The computer compares the oval filled in for each question with the correct response. Each correct answer receives one point; omitted questions do not count toward your score. For each wrong answer, a fraction of a point is subtracted to correct for random guessing. For questions with five answer choices, one-fourth of a point is subtracted for each wrong response; for questions with four answer choices, one-third of a point is subtracted for each wrong response. The SAT-verbal test has 85 questions with five answer choices each. If, for example, a student has 44 right, 32 wrong, and 9 omitted, the resulting raw score is determined as follows:

  $$44 \text{ right} - \frac{32 \text{ wrong}}{4} = 44 - 8 = 36 \text{ raw score points}$$

  Obtaining raw scores frequently involves the rounding of fractional numbers to the nearest whole number. For example, a raw score of 36.25 is rounded to 36, the nearest whole number. A raw score of 36.50 is rounded upward to 37.
- *Converting to reported scaled score.* Raw test scores are then placed on the College Board scale of 200 to 800 through a process that adjusts scores to account for minor differences in difficulty among different editions of the test. This process, known as equating, is performed so that a student's reported score is not affected by the edition of the test taken nor by the abilities of the group with whom the student takes the test. As a result of placing SAT scores on the College Board scale, scores earned by students at different times can be compared. For example, an SAT-verbal score of 400 on a test taken at one administration indicates the same level of developed verbal ability as a 400 score obtained on a different edition of the test taken at another time.

How to Score the Test

SAT-Verbal Sections 1 and 6

Step A: Count the number of correct answers for *section 1* and record the number in the space provided on the worksheet on the next page. Then do the same for the incorrect answers. (Do not count omitted answers.) To determine subtotal A, use the formula:

$$\text{number correct} - \frac{\text{number incorrect}}{4} = \text{subtotal A}$$

Step B: Count the number of correct answers and the number of incorrect answers for *section 6* and record the numbers in the spaces provided on the worksheet. To determine subtotal B, use the formula:

$$\text{number correct} - \frac{\text{number incorrect}}{4} = \text{subtotal B}$$

Step C: To obtain C, add subtotal A to subtotal B, keeping any decimals. Enter the resulting figure on the worksheet.

Step D: To obtain D, your raw verbal score, round C to the nearest whole number. (For example, any number from 44.50 to 45.49 rounds to 45.) Enter the resulting figure on the worksheet.

Step E: To find your reported SAT-verbal score, look up the total raw verbal score you obtained in step D in the conversion table on page 94. Enter this figure on the worksheet.

SAT-Mathematical Sections 3 and 5

Step A: Count the number of correct answers and the number of incorrect answers for *section 3* and record the numbers in the spaces provided on the worksheet. To determine the subtotal A, use the formula:

$$\text{number correct} - \frac{\text{number incorrect}}{4} = \text{subtotal A}$$

Step B: Count the number of correct answers and the number of incorrect answers for the *five-choice questions (questions 1 through 7 and 28 through 35) in section 5* and record the numbers in the spaces provided on the worksheet. To determine the subtotal B, use the formula:

$$\text{number correct} - \frac{\text{number incorrect}}{4} = \text{subtotal B}$$

Step C: Count the number of correct answers and the number of incorrect answers for the *four-choice questions (questions 8 through 27) in section 5* and record the numbers in the spaces provided on the worksheet. To determine the subtotal C, use the formula:

$$\text{number correct} - \frac{\text{number incorrect}}{3} = \text{subtotal C}$$

Step D: To obtain D, add subtotal A, subtotal B, and subtotal C, keeping any decimals. Enter the resulting figure on the worksheet.

Step E: To obtain E, your raw mathematical score, round D to the nearest whole number. (For example, any number from 44.50 to 45.49 rounds to 45.) Enter the resulting figure on the worksheet.

Step F: To find your reported SAT-mathematical score, look up the total raw mathematical score you obtained in E in the conversion table on page 94. Enter this figure on the worksheet.

SAT SCORING WORKSHEET

SAT-Verbal Sections

A. Section 1: ________ (no. correct) − ¼ (________) (no. incorrect) = ________ subtotal A

B. Section 6: ________ (no. correct) − ¼ (________) (no. incorrect) = ________ subtotal B

C. Total unrounded raw score (Total A + B) ________ C

D. Total rounded raw score (Rounded to nearest whole number) ________ D

E. SAT-verbal reported scaled score (See the conversion table on page 94.) [ ] SAT-verbal score

SAT-Mathematical Sections

A. Section 3: ________ (no. correct) − ¼ (________) (no. incorrect) = ________ subtotal A

B. Section 5: Questions 1 through 7 and 28 through 35 (5-choice) ________ (no. correct) − ¼ (________) (no. incorrect) = ________ subtotal B

C. Section 5: Questions 8 through 27 (4-choice) ________ (no. correct) − ⅓ (________) (no. incorrect) = ________ subtotal C

D. Total unrounded raw score (Total A + B + C) ________ D

E. Total rounded raw score (Rounded to nearest whole number) ________ E

F. SAT-mathematical reported scaled score (See the conversion table on page 94.) [ ] SAT-math score

Score Conversion Table
Scholastic Aptitude Test
Form Code 4I

Raw Score	College Board Reported Score		Raw Score	College Board Reported Score	
	SAT-Verbal	SAT-Math		SAT-Verbal	SAT-Math
85	800		40	460	600
84	780		39	450	590
83	760		38	450	580
82	750		37	440	570
81	740		36	430	570
80	730		35	430	560
79	730		34	420	550
78	720		33	410	540
77	710		32	410	530
76	700		31	400	520
75	690		30	390	510
74	690		29	390	500
73	680		28	380	500
72	670		27	370	490
71	660		26	370	480
70	660		25	360	470
69	650		24	350	460
68	640		23	350	450
67	630		22	340	440
66	630		21	330	440
65	620		20	330	430
64	610		19	320	420
63	610		18	310	410
62	600		17	310	400
61	590		16	300	390
60	590	800	15	290	380
59	580	780	14	290	380
58	570	770	13	280	370
57	570	760	12	270	360
56	560	750	11	270	350
55	550	740	10	260	340
54	550	730	9	260	340
53	540	720	8	250	330
52	540	710	7	240	320
51	530	700	6	240	310
50	520	690	5	230	300
49	520	680	4	220	300
48	510	670	3	220	290
47	500	660	2	210	280
46	500	650	1	200	270
45	490	640	0	200	270
44	490	640	–1	200	260
43	480	630	–2	200	250
42	470	620	–3	200	250
41	470	610	–4	200	240
			–5	200	230
			–6	200	220
			–7	200	220
			–8	200	210
			–9 or below	200	200

COLLEGE BOARD — SCHOLASTIC APTITUDE TEST and Test of Standard Written English Side 1

Use a No. 2 pencil only. Be sure each mark is dark and completely fills the intended oval. Completely erase any errors or stray marks.

1. YOUR NAME: (Print) ______ Last ______ First ______ M.I.

SIGNATURE: ______ **DATE:** ___/___/___

HOME ADDRESS: (Print) ______ Number and Street

______ City ______ State ______ Zip Code

CENTER: (Print) ______ City ______ State ______ Center Number

IMPORTANT: Please fill in items 2 and 3 exactly as shown on the back cover of your test book.

FOR ETS USE ONLY

2. TEST FORM (Copy from back cover of your test book.)

3. FORM CODE (Copy and grid as shown on back cover of your test book.)

First column: 0 1 2 3 4 5 6 7 8 9

Letter columns: A B C D E F G H I / J K L M N O P Q R / S T U V W X Y Z

Number columns (3): 0 1 2 3 4 5 6 7 8 9

4. REGISTRATION NUMBER (Copy from your Admission Ticket.)

Seven columns: 0 1 2 3 4 5 6 7 8 9

5. YOUR NAME

First 4 letters of last name | First Init. | Mid. Init.

Each column: A B C D E F G H I J K L M N O P Q R S T U V W X Y Z

6. DATE OF BIRTH

Month	Day		Year	
Jan.				
Feb.				
Mar.	0	0	0	0
Apr.	1	1	1	1
May	2	2	2	2
June	3	3	3	3
July		4	4	4
Aug.		5	5	5
Sept.		6	6	6
Oct.		7	7	7
Nov.		8		8
Dec.		9		9

7. SEX

Female

Male

8. TEST BOOK SERIAL NUMBER (Copy from front cover of your test book.)

Start with number 1 for each new section. If a section has fewer than 50 questions, leave the extra answer spaces blank.

SECTION 1

1	A	B	C	D	E	26	A	B	C	D	E
2	A	B	C	D	E	27	A	B	C	D	E
3	A	B	C	D	E	28	A	B	C	D	E
4	A	B	C	D	E	29	A	B	C	D	E
5	A	B	C	D	E	30	A	B	C	D	E
6	A	B	C	D	E	31	A	B	C	D	E
7	A	B	C	D	E	32	A	B	C	D	E
8	A	B	C	D	E	33	A	B	C	D	E
9	A	B	C	D	E	34	A	B	C	D	E
10	A	B	C	D	E	35	A	B	C	D	E
11	A	B	C	D	E	36	A	B	C	D	E
12	A	B	C	D	E	37	A	B	C	D	E
13	A	B	C	D	E	38	A	B	C	D	E
14	A	B	C	D	E	39	A	B	C	D	E
15	A	B	C	D	E	40	A	B	C	D	E
16	A	B	C	D	E	41	A	B	C	D	E
17	A	B	C	D	E	42	A	B	C	D	E
18	A	B	C	D	E	43	A	B	C	D	E
19	A	B	C	D	E	44	A	B	C	D	E
20	A	B	C	D	E	45	A	B	C	D	E
21	A	B	C	D	E	46	A	B	C	D	E
22	A	B	C	D	E	47	A	B	C	D	E
23	A	B	C	D	E	48	A	B	C	D	E
24	A	B	C	D	E	49	A	B	C	D	E
25	A	B	C	D	E	50	A	B	C	D	E

SECTION 2

1	A	B	C	D	E	26	A	B	C	D	E
2	A	B	C	D	E	27	A	B	C	D	E
3	A	B	C	D	E	28	A	B	C	D	E
4	A	B	C	D	E	29	A	B	C	D	E
5	A	B	C	D	E	30	A	B	C	D	E
6	A	B	C	D	E	31	A	B	C	D	E
7	A	B	C	D	E	32	A	B	C	D	E
8	A	B	C	D	E	33	A	B	C	D	E
9	A	B	C	D	E	34	A	B	C	D	E
10	A	B	C	D	E	35	A	B	C	D	E
11	A	B	C	D	E	36	A	B	C	D	E
12	A	B	C	D	E	37	A	B	C	D	E
13	A	B	C	D	E	38	A	B	C	D	E
14	A	B	C	D	E	39	A	B	C	D	E
15	A	B	C	D	E	40	A	B	C	D	E
16	A	B	C	D	E	41	A	B	C	D	E
17	A	B	C	D	E	42	A	B	C	D	E
18	A	B	C	D	E	43	A	B	C	D	E
19	A	B	C	D	E	44	A	B	C	D	E
20	A	B	C	D	E	45	A	B	C	D	E
21	A	B	C	D	E	46	A	B	C	D	E
22	A	B	C	D	E	47	A	B	C	D	E
23	A	B	C	D	E	48	A	B	C	D	E
24	A	B	C	D	E	49	A	B	C	D	E
25	A	B	C	D	E	50	A	B	C	D	E

Q1362-04

I.N. 575008 — 110VV58P3720

(Cut here to detach.)

COLLEGE BOARD — SCHOLASTIC APTITUDE TEST and Test of Standard Written English

Side 2

Use a No. 2 pencil only. Be sure each mark is dark and completely fills the intended oval. Completely erase any errors or stray marks.

Start with number 1 for each new section. If a section has fewer than 50 questions, leave the extra answer spaces blank.

SECTION 3	SECTION 4	SECTION 5	SECTION 6
1 A B C D E	1 A B C D E	1 A B C D E	1 A B C D E
2 A B C D E	2 A B C D E	2 A B C D E	2 A B C D E
3 A B C D E	3 A B C D E	3 A B C D E	3 A B C D E
4 A B C D E	4 A B C D E	4 A B C D E	4 A B C D E
5 A B C D E	5 A B C D E	5 A B C D E	5 A B C D E
6 A B C D E	6 A B C D E	6 A B C D E	6 A B C D E
7 A B C D E	7 A B C D E	7 A B C D E	7 A B C D E
8 A B C D E	8 A B C D E	8 A B C D E	8 A B C D E
9 A B C D E	9 A B C D E	9 A B C D E	9 A B C D E
10 A B C D E	10 A B C D E	10 A B C D E	10 A B C D E
11 A B C D E	11 A B C D E	11 A B C D E	11 A B C D E
12 A B C D E	12 A B C D E	12 A B C D E	12 A B C D E
13 A B C D E	13 A B C D E	13 A B C D E	13 A B C D E
14 A B C D E	14 A B C D E	14 A B C D E	14 A B C D E
15 A B C D E	15 A B C D E	15 A B C D E	15 A B C D E
16 A B C D E	16 A B C D E	16 A B C D E	16 A B C D E
17 A B C D E	17 A B C D E	17 A B C D E	17 A B C D E
18 A B C D E	18 A B C D E	18 A B C D E	18 A B C D E
19 A B C D E	19 A B C D E	19 A B C D E	19 A B C D E
20 A B C D E	20 A B C D E	20 A B C D E	20 A B C D E
21 A B C D E	21 A B C D E	21 A B C D E	21 A B C D E
22 A B C D E	22 A B C D E	22 A B C D E	22 A B C D E
23 A B C D E	23 A B C D E	23 A B C D E	23 A B C D E
24 A B C D E	24 A B C D E	24 A B C D E	24 A B C D E
25 A B C D E	25 A B C D E	25 A B C D E	25 A B C D E
26 A B C D E	26 A B C D E	26 A B C D E	26 A B C D E
27 A B C D E	27 A B C D E	27 A B C D E	27 A B C D E
28 A B C D E	28 A B C D E	28 A B C D E	28 A B C D E
29 A B C D E	29 A B C D E	29 A B C D E	29 A B C D E
30 A B C D E	30 A B C D E	30 A B C D E	30 A B C D E
31 A B C D E	31 A B C D E	31 A B C D E	31 A B C D E
32 A B C D E	32 A B C D E	32 A B C D E	32 A B C D E
33 A B C D E	33 A B C D E	33 A B C D E	33 A B C D E
34 A B C D E	34 A B C D E	34 A B C D E	34 A B C D E
35 A B C D E	35 A B C D E	35 A B C D E	35 A B C D E
36 A B C D E	36 A B C D E	36 A B C D E	36 A B C D E
37 A B C D E	37 A B C D E	37 A B C D E	37 A B C D E
38 A B C D E	38 A B C D E	38 A B C D E	38 A B C D E
39 A B C D E	39 A B C D E	39 A B C D E	39 A B C D E
40 A B C D E	40 A B C D E	40 A B C D E	40 A B C D E
41 A B C D E	41 A B C D E	41 A B C D E	41 A B C D E
42 A B C D E	42 A B C D E	42 A B C D E	42 A B C D E
43 A B C D E	43 A B C D E	43 A B C D E	43 A B C D E
44 A B C D E	44 A B C D E	44 A B C D E	44 A B C D E
45 A B C D E	45 A B C D E	45 A B C D E	45 A B C D E
46 A B C D E	46 A B C D E	46 A B C D E	46 A B C D E
47 A B C D E	47 A B C D E	47 A B C D E	47 A B C D E
48 A B C D E	48 A B C D E	48 A B C D E	48 A B C D E
49 A B C D E	49 A B C D E	49 A B C D E	49 A B C D E
50 A B C D E	50 A B C D E	50 A B C D E	50 A B C D E

9. SIGNATURE:

FOR ETS USE ONLY	VTR	VTFS	VRR	VRFS	VVR	VVFS	WER	WEFS	M4R	M4FS	M5R	M5FS	MTFS
	VTW	VTCS	VRW	VRCS	VVW	VVCS	WEW	WECS	M4W		M5W		MTCS

SECTION 1	Time—30 minutes 45 Questions	For each question in this section, choose the best answer and fill in the corresponding oval on the answer sheet.

Each question below consists of a word in capital letters, followed by five lettered words or phrases. Choose the word or phrase that is most nearly opposite in meaning to the word in capital letters. Since some of the questions require you to distinguish fine shades of meaning, consider all the choices before deciding which is best.

Example:

GOOD: (A) sour (B) bad (C) red (D) hot (E) ugly

Ⓐ ● Ⓒ Ⓓ Ⓔ

1. PROTECT: (A) endanger (B) ignore (C) excite (D) alert (E) imprison

2. BIZARRE: (A) worthless (B) ordinary (C) humble (D) genuine (E) flexible

3. VIBRANT: (A) solvent (B) adaptable (C) constant (D) unified (E) lifeless

4. BLUNDER: (A) confess (B) persevere (C) plan jointly (D) act wisely (E) play happily

5. BULGE: (A) continuity (B) solidity (C) restoration (D) compliance (E) indentation

6. ANGULAR: (A) hollow (B) shallow (C) rotund (D) motionless (E) detached

7. MONOTONY: (A) authenticity (B) resiliency (C) opposition (D) usefulness (E) diversity

8. CONVICTION: (A) doubt (B) simplicity (C) decline (D) reflection (E) depression

9. INDEFATIGABLE: (A) distinctive (B) faithful (C) partial (D) instantly done (E) easily tired

10. BEGUILE: (A) surmise (B) ratify (C) remonstrate (D) enlighten (E) pretend

11. STYMIE: (A) exhibit (B) assist (C) evade (D) brighten (E) empty

12. CONFOUND: (A) distinguish between (B) dislodge from (C) dominate (D) terminate (E) prolong

13. DISSOLUTION: (A) integration (B) triviality (C) receptivity (D) wariness (E) supplication

14. VOLUBLE: (A) tedious (B) pertinent (C) taciturn (D) voracious (E) furtive

15. NOISOME: (A) tranquil (B) frugal (C) profuse (D) meddlesome (E) wholesome

Each sentence below has one or two blanks, each blank indicating that something has been omitted. Beneath the sentence are five lettered words or sets of words. Choose the word or set of words that, when inserted in the sentence, best fits the meaning of the sentence as a whole.

Example:

Although its publicity has been ----, the film itself is intelligent, well-acted, handsomely produced, and altogether ----.

(A) tasteless. .respectable (B) extensive. .moderate (C) sophisticated. .amateur (D) risqué. .crude (E) perfect. .spectacular

● Ⓑ Ⓒ Ⓓ Ⓔ

16. Stick insects have elongated, twig-shaped bodies that enable them to be ---- when they alight on shrubbery.

(A) devoured (B) foliated (C) nurtured (D) camouflaged (E) acclimated

17. An accurate assessment of this shore community's ---- is complicated by the ---- migrations of part-time residents.

(A) age. .historical
(B) revenue. .negligible
(C) geography. .regional
(D) population. .seasonal
(E) environment. .predictable

18. Within the tribal government of the Crow Indians, the clan system serves as a method of checks and balances that ---- the assumption of authoritarian rule by any one clan.

(A) determines (B) prevents (C) examines (D) delegates (E) incorporates

19. The research is so ---- that it leaves no part of the issue unexamined.

(A) comprehensive (B) rewarding (C) sporadic (D) economical (E) problematical

20. Mr. McNulty seems to like hardly anyone; but since his ---- is witty and controlled, his commentaries are a delight to the reader.

(A) deceit (B) malice (C) empathy (D) magnanimity (E) pomposity

GO ON TO THE NEXT PAGE

Each passage below is followed by questions based on its content. Answer the questions following each passage on the basis of what is stated or implied in that passage.

The 1920's marked a new independence in political party affiliation among Black Americans—they were ready to move in a new political direction. This direction was not, however, to the extreme left, despite the wooings of the socialists and the communists.

Notwithstanding the zeal and dedication of A. Philip Randolph and Chandler Owen, prominent Black socialists of the early 1920's, the Socialist party made little impression upon the postwar Black population. Because their entire program revolved around the working person, socialists viewed the problems of society as mainly economic rather than racial; they saw the Black person primarily as a worker and only incidentally as a "Negro." No matter how eloquent, their program was generally viewed by Black Americans as remote from their immediate needs.

The failure of the socialists to win mass support from the Black population was carefully studied by the communists. They regarded Black people as assets capable of helping to spearhead the proletarian revolution in the United States. To win the support of Black Americans, the Communist party devoted most of its efforts to practical measures rather than to indoctrination in Marxist theory.

The communists sought to recruit Black workers and then to persuade White workers to accept them. In addition, they organized in 1925 the American Negro Labor Congress, which was designed to bring all Black trade unionists together in order to strengthen the party. They also organized the International Labor Defense, a legal arm that was designed to defend communists in the courts, but that concerned itself particularly with cases involving Black people regardless of their political affiliations.

Another approach was the practicing of social equality in an effort to make Black people feel a complete personal acceptance. Still another part of their program was designed to give Black Americans responsible positions in the Communist party and to have them run for high office on the party ticket in state and national elections.

Even with such strenuous efforts the communists made few Black converts. In 1928, realizing that they must adopt a new line, the American communists launched the idea of a separate Black republic within the United States. But this idea was based on an incorrect analogy with Russia, where different areas were occupied by different races with different languages and customs. Black Americans' chief objection to the idea was its underlying assumption that Black people did not and could not fit into American life. Black Americans simply did not seem to be attuned to the communist message for reasons that are not hard to fathom.

21. The first paragraph suggests that, prior to 1920, Black Americans

(A) were not inclined to be politically active
(B) had little freedom in making political decisions
(C) had traditionally followed one political course
(D) sanctioned the activities of leftist organizations
(E) were secretive about their political alliances

22. According to the passage, the fundamental purpose for which the Communist party solicited Black members was to

(A) promote racial equality in the United States
(B) establish a separate republic for the Black population
(C) foment a working-class rebellion in the United States
(D) include Black Americans in national politics
(E) stabilize the economic situation of Black Americans

23. According to the passage, the communists de-emphasized which of the following in their attempt to persuade Black Americans to join the party?

(A) Unionization of Black workers
(B) Legal defense in the courts
(C) Promotion of social equality
(D) Inclusion in political endeavors
(E) Instruction in political theory

24. The passage as a whole is primarily concerned with

(A) describing tactics
(B) condemning attitudes
(C) interpreting reactions
(D) comparing goals
(E) accounting for results

25. The author apparently feels that the Black population's rejection of the communist plan for a separate Black republic was

(A) a surprising refusal
(B) an understandable response
(C) a self-defeating act
(D) an unreasonable reaction
(E) a clever political maneuver

GO ON TO THE NEXT PAGE

The tremendous explosion, known as the Tunguska blast, that flattened hundreds of square miles of Siberian pine forest in 1908 was probably equal in power to that of a modern thermonuclear bomb. The blasted region of the forest had an irregular shape similar to that of a butterfly. Decades later, specialists noticed an accelerated growth of trees in the region immediately surrounding the blast. Any theory describing the cause of the Tunguska blast must account for these puzzling factors.

For many years scientists just assumed that the blast had been caused by the impact of a large meteor, although no crater was ever found. After the bombings of Hiroshima and Nagasaki in 1945, suggestions were made that the otherwise enigmatic Tunguska blast had actually been an atomic explosion that had been set off by an alien vehicle from another world. The spaceship hypothesis claims that an interstellar vehicle was attempting to make a landing on Earth when its nuclear power plant accidentally detonated. The hull of the ship acted like a Claymore mine, shaping the charge into the irregular pattern. As at Hiroshima and Nagasaki, radiation caused the accelerated growth of trees around the bomb site.

The generally accepted hypothesis, however, is that the Tunguska blast was caused by the impact of a cometary nucleus with Earth. The explosion of the comet, which occurred at an altitude of several miles above the ground, was caused when the tremendous kinetic energy of the onrushing comet was converted into heat by its passage through Earth's atmosphere.

Proponents of the comet hypothesis also suggest that the forest fire ignited by the thermal pulse of the blast caused the accelerated growth of trees around the blast site by clearing the undergrowth and fertilizing the soil. In fact, a Soviet survey team discovered that the accelerated growth did indeed follow the outline of the burned areas quite well—even though some unburned areas were quite close to ground zero, and some burned areas were quite distant.

Comet hypothesis advocates also contend that a combination of sonic boom and detonation were quite sufficient to account for the seemingly odd shape of the flattened area. Dynamics specialists in Moscow attempted to recreate the shock waves of the original event, assuming that the passage of the object through the air produced a supersonic shock wave, and that at the end of this trail a detonation wave resulted from the sudden disintegration of the comet. The specialists strung explosives along a string suspended above a "forest" of miniature match sticks. When the explosives were set off, the match sticks were smashed down in a beautiful butterfly pattern.

26. The main purpose of the passage is to discuss the

(A) explosive power of comets
(B) puzzling cause of the Tunguska blast
(C) role of atomic energy in explosions
(D) major features of the Tunguska blast
(E) attempts to recreate the Tunguska blast

27. The passage suggests that which of the following would indicate that the Tunguska blast was caused by a meteor, rather than a spaceship exploding above the Earth?

I. The presence of a crater in the area
II. Evidence of accelerated tree growth in the area surrounding the blast
III. A circular pattern of destruction in the area surrounding the blast

(A) I only (B) III only (C) I and II only (D) II and III only (E) I, II, and III

28. According to the comet hypothesis, the Tunguska blast occurred when the

(A) forest fire produced by the heat of the comet ignited the comet nucleus
(B) impact of the comet's nucleus against the Earth's surface caused the comet to explode
(C) extremely high temperature of the comet heated up the atmospheric gases surrounding it to the point that they exploded
(D) tremendous speed of the comet through the Earth's atmosphere created so much heat that the comet nucleus suddenly disintegrated
(E) supersonic shock wave produced by the comet's flight through the atmosphere caused the explosive material in the comet to detonate

29. Which of the following best describes the author's tone in the discussion of the comet hypothesis?

(A) Amused (B) Defensive (C) Impartial (D) Sarcastic (E) Overstated

30. If the experiment described in the last paragraph helps support the comet hypothesis, all of the following assumptions must be made EXCEPT:

(A) A series of small explosions will produce an effect similar to that of a supersonic shock wave.
(B) A supersonic shock wave will cause the object that created it to disintegrate.
(C) A "forest" of matchsticks will behave in much the same way as trees in an ordinary forest.
(D) The disintegration of a comet could create a detonation blast.
(E) A falling comet can travel through the Earth's atmosphere at a speed sufficient to cause a supersonic shock wave.

GO ON TO THE NEXT PAGE

1

Select the word or set of words that best completes each of the following sentences.

31. Some historians have been searching so diligently for the ---- of modern culture that they have reduced the Renaissance period to little more than ---- the present.

(A) justification. .an antithesis to
(B) influence. .a paradigm for
(C) perils. .a duplication of
(D) inspiration. .a climax of
(E) origins. .a prelude to

32. The ancient politicians were masters of carefully disguised ---- that almost always reached the discerning part of their audience, but left them free to pretend innocence and good will.

(A) enthusiasm (B) vacuities (C) accolades (D) insinuations (E) policies

33. To ---- the ravages of acid rain, the curators moved the statues that once ---- the monument's facade to the safety of a museum.

(A) imperil. .defaced (B) perpetuate. .enhanced (C) belittle. .surrounded (D) forestall. .adorned (E) protect. .comprised

34. The senator chose to incur dislike rather than ---- her principles to win favor with the public.

(A) gratify (B) endorse (C) accuse (D) compromise (E) advertise

35. Her vague sense of ---- grew into anxiety and then alarm when she discovered that her initial doubts about the success of the undertaking were well founded.

(A) foreboding (B) remorse (C) anticipation (D) intrigue (E) complacency

Each question below consists of a related pair of words or phrases, followed by five lettered pairs of words or phrases. Select the lettered pair that best expresses a relationship similar to that expressed in the original pair.

Example:

YAWN : BOREDOM :: (A) dream : sleep (B) anger : madness (C) smile : amusement (D) face : expression (E) impatience : rebellion

Ⓐ Ⓑ ● Ⓓ Ⓔ

36. INFLATE : BIGGER :: (A) expel : shorter (B) extend : longer (C) extract : wider (D) expose : softer (E) expunge : lighter

37. CHART : NAVIGATOR :: (A) novel : reader (B) log : captain (C) map : motorist (D) pedigree : dog (E) graph : mathematician

38. SIEVE : DRAINING :: (A) paper : writing (B) oven : cleaning (C) faucet : washing (D) film : developing (E) filter : separating

39. POKER : CARDS :: (A) racetrack : horses (B) lottery : dice (C) roulette : wheel (D) football : points (E) dealer : odds

40. BRUSH : TOUCH :: (A) glimpse : see (B) study : read (C) chatter : speak (D) dodge : run (E) finger : point

41. MARBLE : SCULPTURE :: (A) canvas : portrait (B) slivers : kaleidoscope (C) upholstery : sofa (D) glass : goblet (E) glue : collage

42. CLOUDBURST : RAINFALL :: (A) ashes : fire (B) sunbeam : warmth (C) ripple : wave (D) drizzle : mist (E) gust : wind

43. FOOLHARDY : BOLD :: (A) cruel : disobedient (B) discontented : smug (C) gullible : trusting (D) fearful : heroic (E) helpless : sympathetic

44. UPROARIOUS : FUNNY ::
(A) mysterious : alarming
(B) outrageous : improper
(C) anxious : serene
(D) thunderous : rainy
(E) ponderous : tired

45. PRESCIENT : FORESIGHT ::
(A) obstinate : compliance
(B) oblivious : awareness
(C) assiduous : diligence
(D) renounced : preference
(E) superficial : appeal

IF YOU FINISH BEFORE TIME IS CALLED, YOU MAY CHECK YOUR WORK ON THIS SECTION ONLY. DO NOT TURN TO ANY OTHER SECTION IN THE TEST. **STOP**

SECTION 2	Time—30 minutes 25 Questions	In this section solve each problem, using any available space on the page for scratchwork. Then decide which is the best of the choices given and fill in the corresponding oval on the answer sheet.

The following information is for your reference in solving some of the problems.

Circle of radius r: Area $= \pi r^2$; Circumference $= 2\pi r$
The number of degrees of arc in a circle is 360.
The measure in degrees of a straight angle is 180.

Definition of symbols:

$=$ is equal to	$\leq$ is less than or equal to
$\neq$ is unequal to	$\geq$ is greater than or equal to
$<$ is less than	$\parallel$ is parallel to
$>$ is greater than	$\perp$ is perpendicular to

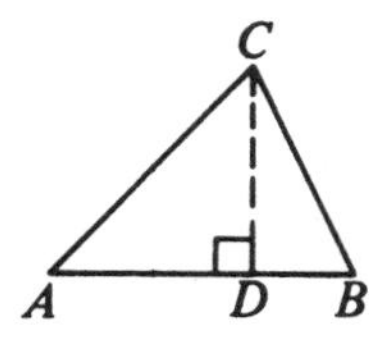

Triangle: The sum of the measures in degrees of the angles of a triangle is 180.

If $\angle CDA$ is a right angle, then

(1) area of $\triangle ABC = \frac{AB \times CD}{2}$

(2) $AC^2 = AD^2 + DC^2$

Note: Figures that accompany problems in this test are intended to provide information useful in solving the problems. They are drawn as accurately as possible EXCEPT when it is stated in a specific problem that its figure is not drawn to scale. All figures lie in a plane unless otherwise indicated. All numbers used are real numbers.

1. $\frac{0.25 + 0.25 + 0.25 + 0.25}{4} =$

(A) 0.025 (B) 0.125 (C) 0.25
(D) 0.50 (E) 0.75

2. Jack goes to the store and, after spending a total of 75 cents to buy 15 identical erasers, has no money left. If he then decides he needs 2 pencils at 15 cents each, how many erasers must he exchange?

(A) Two (B) Four (C) Six
(D) Eight (E) Ten

3. Which of the following is (are) true?

I. $(10 - 5) - 3 = 10 - (5 - 3)$
II. $(2 \times 3) \times 5 = 2 \times (3 \times 5)$
III. $(2 + 3) + 5 = 2 + (3 + 5)$

(A) I only (B) II only (C) III only
(D) I and III (E) II and III

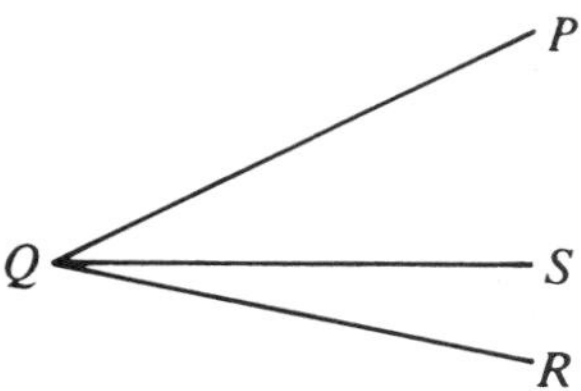

Note: Figure not drawn to scale.

4. In the figure above, the measure of $\angle SQR$ is $\frac{2}{5}$ the measure of $\angle PQR$. If the measure of $\angle PQR$ is $\frac{2}{3}$ the measure of a right angle, what is the measure of $\angle SQR$?

(A) 24°
(B) 36°
(C) 48°
(D) 60°
(E) 96°

GO ON TO THE NEXT PAGE

5. For what positive value of x does $\frac{4}{x} = \frac{x}{16}$?

(A) 2
(B) 8
(C) 20
(D) 32
(E) 64

6. The decimal representation for $1{,}000 + 1 + \frac{1}{1{,}000}$ is

(A) 1,000.1001
(B) 1,000.101
(C) 1,001.0001
(D) 1,001.001
(E) 1,001.01

7. If $p = 15$, then $\frac{p^2 + 2p}{p} =$

(A) 3
(B) 15
(C) 17
(D) 45
(E) 227

8. What is the circumference of a circle with radius π ?

(A) π (B) 2π (C) π^2 (D) 4π (E) $2\pi^2$

9. What is the least positive integer divisible by the numbers 2, 3, 4, and 5 ?

(A) 30 (B) 40 (C) 60 (D) 90 (E) 120

10. Three children each weigh 100 pounds or less. Their average (arithmetic mean) weight is 80 pounds. If one of them weighs 80 pounds, what is the least possible weight, in pounds, of a child in the group?

(A) 1
(B) 50
(C) 60
(D) 70
(E) 80

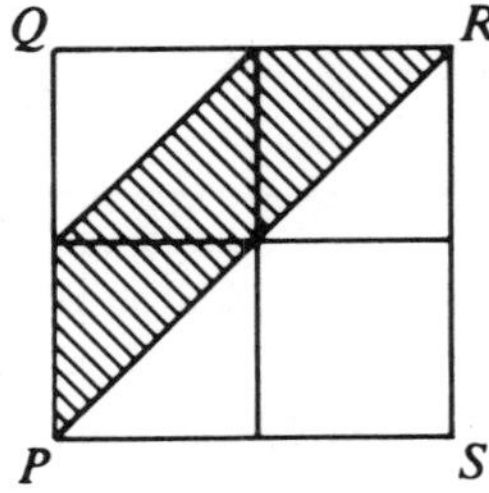

11. In the figure above, square $PQRS$ is divided into four smaller squares. If the area of the shaded region is 3, what is the area of $PQRS$?

(A) 8 (B) 7 (C) 6 (D) 5 (E) 1

---

12. If x and y are negative integers and $x < y$, which of the following is greatest?

(A) xy (B) $-xy$ (C) $x - y$
(D) $x + y$ (E) $x^3 + y$

13. The Smith Metal Company's old machine makes 300 bolts per hour. Its new machine makes 450 bolts per hour. If both machines begin running at the same time, how many minutes will it take the two machines to make a combined total of 900 bolts?

(A) 36
(B) 72
(C) 120
(D) 144
(E) 180

GO ON TO THE NEXT PAGE

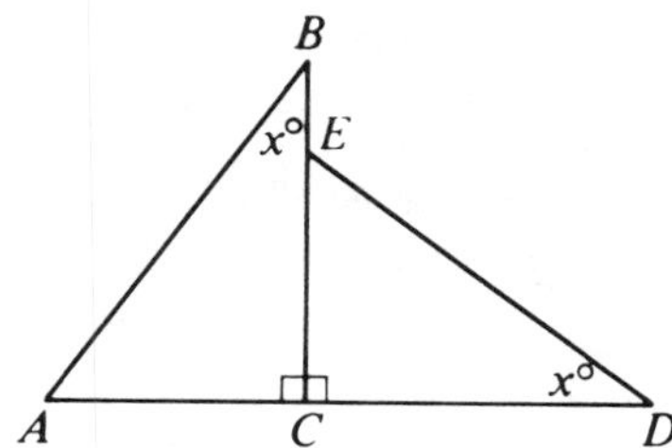

14. In the figure above, if $AB = 5$, $AC = 3$, and $BC = CD$, then $BE =$

(A) 1 (B) 2 (C) 3 (D) 4 (E) 5

15. Jane buys one goldfish and two guppies for \$3.00. Dave buys two goldfish and four guppies for \$6.00. If goldfish cost x dollars each and guppies cost y dollars each, what is the value of x ?

(A) \$0.50
(B) \$0.80
(C) \$1.00
(D) \$1.20
(E) It cannot be determined from the information given.

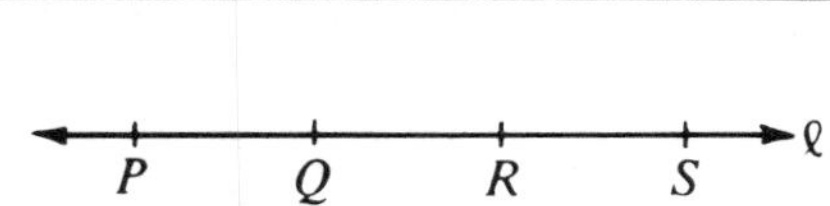

Note: Figure not drawn to scale.

16. Points $P, Q, R,$ and S are on line ℓ in the order shown. If Q is the midpoint of segment PS and if $RS = 4$ and $PQ = 7$, then $PR =$

(A) 3
(B) 10
(C) 11
(D) 14
(E) 18

Questions 17-18 refer to the following definition.

For all positive integers x,

$$\boxed{x} = \frac{1}{2}x, \text{ if } x \text{ is even;}$$

$$\boxed{x} = 2x, \text{ if } x \text{ is odd.}$$

17. $\boxed{1 + 5} =$

(A) 2 (B) 3 (C) 6 (D) 12 (E) 24

18. For a positive integer q, which of the following equals $\boxed{4q + 1}$?

(A) $2q + \frac{1}{2}$

(B) $2q + 1$

(C) $2q + 2$

(D) $8q + 1$

(E) $8q + 2$

19. There are x exposures on a certain roll of film. The cost of the roll of film is d dollars, and the cost to develop the film is c cents per exposure. What is the cost, in dollars, to purchase and develop the roll of film?

(A) $\frac{cx}{100} + d$

(B) $\frac{dx}{100} + c$

(C) $\frac{cdx}{100}$

(D) $cx + 100d$

(E) $100dx + c$

GO ON TO THE NEXT PAGE

$$2, 0, 4, 0, 6, 0, 8, 0$$

20. If x and y represent any two unequal numbers from the list above, how many different values are possible for xy ?

(A) Four (B) Five (C) Six
(D) Seven (E) Eight

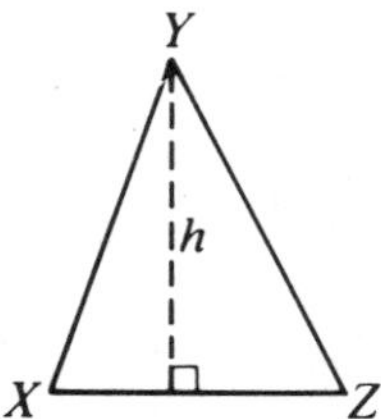

21. In ΔXYZ above, the length of XZ is $\frac{6}{7}$ of the length of altitude h. What is the area of ΔXYZ in terms of h ?

(A) $\frac{h^2}{3}$

(B) $\frac{3h^2}{7}$

(C) $\frac{3h}{7}$

(D) $\frac{6h^2}{7}$

(E) $\frac{12h^2}{7}$

22. If x and y are two different integers and the product $35xy$ is the square of an integer, which of the following could be equal to xy ?

(A) 5
(B) 70
(C) 105
(D) 140
(E) 350

23. Of 220 stamps in a certain stamp collection, exactly 60 were United States stamps and 110 were canceled. If 60 percent of the United States stamps were canceled, how many of the stamps were both not United States stamps and not canceled?

(A) 36
(B) 50
(C) 74
(D) 86
(E) 110

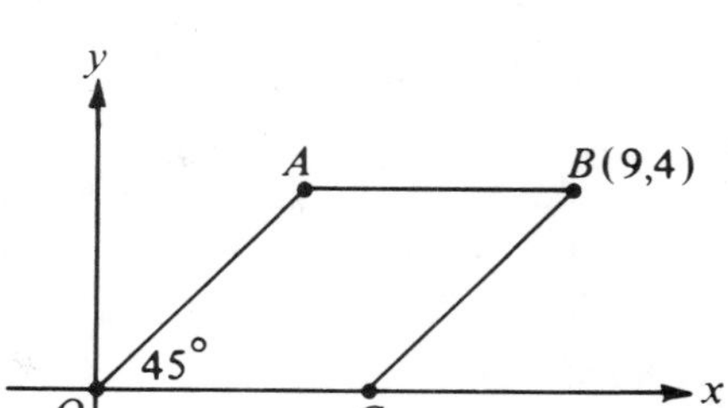

24. In the figure above, what is the perimeter of parallelogram $OABC$?

(A) $10 + 4\sqrt{2}$
(B) $10 + 8\sqrt{2}$
(C) 18
(D) 36
(E) It cannot be determined from the information given.

25. A pilot surveys a flat circular area represented by 4π square inches on a map. If 1 inch on the map represents 60 miles, how many square miles does the pilot survey?

(A) 15π (B) 240π (C) 900π
(D) $7{,}200\pi$ (E) $14{,}400\pi$

IF YOU FINISH BEFORE TIME IS CALLED, YOU MAY CHECK YOUR WORK ON THIS SECTION ONLY. DO NOT TURN TO ANY OTHER SECTION IN THE TEST. **STOP**

SECTION 4 **Time—30 minutes 40 Questions**

For each question in this section, choose the best answer and fill in the corresponding oval on the answer sheet.

Each question below consists of a word in capital letters, followed by five lettered words or phrases. Choose the word or phrase that is most nearly opposite in meaning to the word in capital letters. Since some of the questions require you to distinguish fine shades of meaning, consider all the choices before deciding which is best.

Example:

GOOD: (A) sour (B) bad (C) red (D) hot (E) ugly

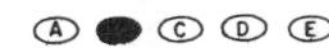

1. FERTILE: (A) tiresome (B) unsettled (C) methodical (D) continuous (E) unproductive

2. APPREHEND: (A) apply for (B) turn loose (C) obey regulations (D) perform (E) obstruct

3. ZEAL:
(A) loss of virtue
(B) respect for others
(C) appreciation for beauty
(D) lack of enthusiasm
(E) fear of interference

4. ERRATIC: (A) compact (B) irresistible (C) consistent (D) clearly heard (E) formally received

5. ADORN: (A) dislike (B) distrust (C) move away (D) prove useless (E) make unattractive

6. DECLIVITY: (A) ascending slope (B) general aptitude (C) extreme passivity (D) detriment (E) waste

7. UNCONDITIONAL: (A) commensurate (B) qualified (C) organized (D) identifiable (E) endurable

8. JETTISON: (A) ambush (B) command (C) lead astray (D) slow down (E) bring aboard

9. SUMPTUOUS: (A) moist (B) close (C) paltry (D) showing disfavor (E) seeking change

10. DECORUM: (A) impropriety (B) admonition (C) simplicity (D) indignation (E) embellishment

Each sentence below has one or two blanks, each blank indicating that something has been omitted. Beneath the sentence are five lettered words or sets of words. Choose the word or set of words that, when inserted in the sentence, best fits the meaning of the sentence as a whole.

Example:

Although its publicity has been ----, the film itself is intelligent, well-acted, handsomely produced, and altogether ----.

(A) tasteless. . respectable (B) extensive. . moderate (C) sophisticated. . amateur (D) risqué. . crude (E) perfect. . spectacular

● Ⓑ Ⓒ Ⓓ Ⓔ

11. Because heroin is regarded as the most ---- drug threat to society, there has been a much more ---- effort to develop treatment for heroin addicts than for other drug users.

(A) incidental. .general
(B) trivial. .concerted
(C) serious. .concentrated
(D) obvious. .tentative
(E) dangerous. .disastrous

12. How can we learn to ---- the situation as right and proper when the whole tendency of our thought and interest carries us in ---- direction?

(A) defend. .an evident (B) reject. .a parallel (C) protest. .a reverse (D) accept. .a contrary (E) enjoy. .a reciprocal

13. She contributed to the project after much ----, and then only because she realized that its failure would ---- all previous progress.

(A) procrastination. .accelerate
(B) consultation. .reaffirm
(C) inattention. .overlook
(D) hesitation. .negate
(E) resentment. .emphasize

14. Mexico's discovery of oil created a nation-wide economic ---- that ---- many Mexican-American scientists and engineers to take jobs with thriving Mexican companies.

(A) failure. .convinced (B) upturn. .required (C) boom. .induced (D) prosperity. .doomed (E) slump. .inspired

15. The practice of ---- coins that end up on edge in a coin-flipping experiment illustrates one method of dealing with the ambiguous case within a ---- system.

(A) ignoring. .classification
(B) destroying. .production
(C) minting. .logical
(D) cleaning. .scientific
(E) saving. .fiscal

Each question below consists of a related pair of words or phrases, followed by five lettered pairs of words or phrases. Select the lettered pair that best expresses a relationship similar to that expressed in the original pair.

Example:

YAWN : BOREDOM :: (A) dream : sleep (B) anger : madness (C) smile : amusement (D) face : expression (E) impatience : rebellion

Ⓐ Ⓑ ● Ⓓ Ⓔ

16. PARACHUTE : AIRPLANE :: (A) trunk : tree (B) lifeboat : ship (C) knapsack : school (D) trampoline : tent (E) elevator : floor

17. PULSE : HEART :: (A) pitch : music (B) nerve : brain (C) tick : clock (D) motor : engine (E) blood : artery

18. MOMENT : ETERNITY :: (A) light : beam (B) darkness : sun (C) space : time (D) water : ocean (E) point : infinity

19. CATHEDRAL : CHAPEL :: (A) mortar : bricks (B) landscape : views (C) horizon : sky (D) shelf : tier (E) city : village

20. ANARCHIST : LAWS :: (A) partisan : allegiance (B) federalist : union (C) pacifist : war (D) insurgent : rebellion (E) despot : leadership

21. CARICATURE : PORTRAIT :: (A) parody : poem (B) clown : jester (C) medley : symphony (D) episode : tragedy (E) opera : soprano

22. RACONTEUR : ANECDOTES :: (A) editor : books (B) screenwriter : credits (C) comedian : jokes (D) lecturer : digressions (E) actor : roles

23. DEADPAN : EMOTION ::
(A) distrustful : alertness
(B) lethargic : energy
(C) mobile : movement
(D) ambivalent : precision
(E) petty : openness

24. INTRACTABLE : OBEY :: (A) modest : hide (B) forlorn : comfort (C) cynical : sneer (D) steadfast : change (E) pompous : proclaim

25. SWINDLER : DUPE :: (A) embezzler : thief (B) robber : cash (C) bully : weakling (D) magician : illusion (E) advertiser : hoax

GO ON TO THE NEXT PAGE

Each passage below is followed by questions based on its content. Answer the questions following each passage on the basis of what is stated or implied in that passage.

Pterosaurs (from the Greek for "winged lizard") appeared and died out with the dinosaurs, after a long history of nearly 140 million years. They ranged from sparrow-sized flutterers to giant soarers with wingspans of nearly forty feet.

The flying abilities of pterosaurs have never been fully appreciated. Although pterosaurs have been represented traditionally as clumsy gliders, with leathery curtain-like wings, new evidence suggests that they were strong and graceful fliers. Unlike bats' wings, those of pterosaurs were narrow and gull-like and extended along the body wall only to the limits of the pelvis. We know pterosaurs were powerful flappers by the enormous bony expansion of the breastbone, which covers most of the chest region and has a deep keel for attachment of the flight muscles. The bones of the upper arm are also well developed to support flight musculature, and are perforated at their ends by tiny pores, as in birds. (These pores, called pneumatic foramina, allow the expansion of the respiratory surface of the lungs into the bones, to increase the animal's ability to receive oxygen and breathe out carbon dioxide, thus maintaining the high metabolic rate that flight requires.) In addition, the bones are hollow and unusually thin. Skeletal lightness by itself might be an adaptation merely for gliding, but no gliding animal has these other modifications for flight. Add to all this the recent discovery of a kind of hairy covering on a pterosaur found in the Soviet Union, and one can only conclude that pterosaurs, the first fliers, were warm-blooded, active animals long before the birds arose from dinosaurs: not cold-blooded, or slow, or awkward at all.

26. The passage as a whole is an attempt to

(A) distinguish the flight strategies of pterosaurs from those of birds and bats
(B) revise the conventional view of the pterosaur's airborne behavior
(C) introduce an innovative approach to the study of flight physiology
(D) determine the features necessary for the development of flight capabilities
(E) trace the origin of diverse winged creatures to a common ancestor

27. The passage states that pterosaurs differed from bats with respect to

(A) aesthetic appeal (B) flying altitude
(C) nocturnal habits (D) skeletal lightness
(E) wing structure

28. The discussion of the "pneumatic foramina" (line 19) suggests that flying is an activity that

(A) demands a large expenditure of energy
(B) places great stress on the skeletal structure
(C) is more efficient than other means of locomotion
(D) involves still-obscure biochemical processes
(E) has reached its maximum point of development

GO ON TO THE NEXT PAGE

Her image accompanied me even in places the most hostile to romance. On Saturday evenings when my aunt went marketing I had to go to carry some of the parcels. We walked through the flaring streets, jostled by drunken men and bargaining women, amid the curses of laborers, the shrill litanies of shop-boys who stood on guard by the barrels of pigs' cheeks, the nasal chanting of street-singers, who sang a "come-all-you" about O'Donovan Rossa, or a ballad about the troubles of our native land. These noises converged in a single sensation of life for me: I imagined that I bore my chalice safely through a throng of foes. Her name sprang to my lips at moments in strange prayers and praises which I myself did not understand. My eyes were often full of tears (I could not tell why) and at times a flood from my heart seemed to pour itself out into my bosom. I thought little of the future. I did not know whether I would ever speak to her or not or, if I spoke to her, how I could tell her of my confused adoration. But my body was like a harp and her words and gestures were like fingers running upon the wires.

29. It can be inferred from the passage that places that are "the most hostile to romance" (lines 1-2) are places that are characterized chiefly by

(A) monotonous tranquillity
(B) imminent danger
(C) routine bustle
(D) illusory conviviality
(E) desolate remoteness

30. All of the following are implied contrasts in the passage EXCEPT

(A) religious chants and litanies *versus* the actual sounds of shop-boys and street-singers
(B) a sack of goods from the market *versus* a personal symbol of reverence
(C) the oaths of workers *versus* the unspoken prayers and praises of the boy
(D) tearful eyes *versus* a flood from the heart
(E) wordless emotions *versus* senseless babble

31. In the context of the passage, the image of the chalice (line 11) suggests all of the following EXCEPT

(A) the purity of the boy's feelings
(B) the sacredness of the boy's imagined relationship
(C) something to be guarded amid some danger
(D) a sacrifice for the benefit of all
(E) the superior level on which the boy places the girl

32. In which of the following sentences does the descriptive focus of the passage shift most dramatically?

(A) "We walked . . . our native land." (lines 4-9)
(B) "These noises . . . throng of foes." (lines 9-11)
(C) "My eyes . . . into my bosom." (lines 13-16)
(D) "I thought little of the future." (line 16)
(E) "I did not know . . . confused adoration." (lines 16-18)

GO ON TO THE NEXT PAGE

The fundamental distinction between the professional historian and the amateur lies in the intellectual treatment of the questions asked. This is not always an easy distinction to make, for it is not identical with that between those who earn their living by the study of history and those who engage in it as an avocation. The distinction I have in mind rests between the person who has learned the job and the person who, sometimes with touches of genius, comes to it in a happy spirit of untrained enterprise: crudely, the distinction between those who have grasped that research means assimilating the various and often very tiresome relics of the past and those who think that research means reading a lot of books. Examples of both are found inside as well as outside the academic profession.

The hallmark of the amateur is a failure of instinctive understanding. This expresses itself most clearly in a readiness to see the exceptional in the commonplace and to find the unusual ordinary. The amateur shows a tendency to find the past, or parts of it, quaint; the professional is totally incapable of this. On the other hand, the professional, truly understanding an age from the inside—living with its attitudes and prejudices—can also judge it; refusal to judge is quite as amateurish a characteristic as willingness to judge by the wrong, because anachronistic, standards. By all these criteria, Lord Acton appears an amateur, and so he was, a prince of amateurs. Very wide reading and self-consciously deep thinking may have attended him; but he was forever expressing distress or surprise at some turn in the story, was alternately censorious and uncomprehending, suspected conspiracies and deep plots everywhere. In short, he lived in history as a stranger, a visitor from Mars.

The professional lives in history as a contemporary, though a contemporary equipped with immunity, hindsight, and arrogant superiority—a visitor from the Inquisition. How is such professionalism created? G. M. Young once offered celebrated advice: read in a period until you hear its people speak. But this is amateurishness of a drastic kind, because it is superficially professional. Who ever knew or understood people just because he heard them speak? The truth is that one must read them, study their creations, and think about them until one knows what they are going to say next.

33. The passage can best be described as which of the following?

(A) A passionate plea for revision of historical methodology
(B) A satirical look at the limitations of one type of scholar
(C) A portrait of a famous but ultimately unsuccessful historian
(D) A consideration of the problems inherent in studying the past
(E) A discussion of what the author considers desirable and undesirable in a historian

34. According to the passage, the chief characteristic of the professional historian is

(A) a fixed desire to instruct others about history
(B) a natural attraction to exotic practices
(C) a profound comprehension of a past age
(D) an intransigent feeling of outrage at ancient injustice
(E) an implicit rejection of contemporary life

35. Which of the following best describes the reference to Lord Acton in lines 26-33 ?

(A) It illustrates a general type through the case of an individual.
(B) It supports a previous statement with generally accepted facts.
(C) It presents a standard of excellence for all historians.
(D) It demonstrates that past historians were not well trained.
(E) It offers a balanced view of the habits of certain historians.

36. All of the following are cited in the passage as common to the amateur historian EXCEPT

(A) extensive reading with insufficient focus
(B) profound meditation with dubious results
(C) indifference to genuinely important facts
(D) exclusion from the academic community
(E) alienation from the period under study

37. The author compares the professional with the amateur historian through the metaphor of two distinctly different

(A) tamers of the same wilderness
(B) subjects of the same ruler
(C) participants in the same contest
(D) travelers to the same place
(E) spectators at the same play

GO ON TO THE NEXT PAGE

Much of our thinking consists of trains of images suggested one by another, of a sort of spontaneous reverie in which the links between the terms are either "contiguity" or "similarity." As a rule, in this sort of irresponsible thinking, the terms that happen to be coupled together are concrete rather than abstract ones. A sunset may call up the vessel's deck from which I saw one last summer, the companions of my voyage, my arrival into port, etc.; or it may make me think of solar myths, of Hercules' funeral pyre, of Homer, of the Greek alphabet, etc. If habitual contiguities predominate, we have a prosaic mind; if rare contiguities, or similarities, have free play, we call the person fanciful, poetic, or witty. But the thought is of matters taken in their entirety. Having been thinking of one, we find later that we are thinking of another, to which we have been lifted along, we hardly know how. If an abstract quality figures in the procession, it arrests our attention but for a moment and fades into something else and is never very abstract. Thus, in thinking of the sun myths, we may have a gleam of admiration at the gracefulness of the mythologies of early civilizations or a moment of disgust at the narrowness of modern interpreters. But, in the main, we think less of qualities than of whole things. The upshot of it may be that we are reminded of some practical duty; we write a letter to a friend, or we study our Greek lesson. Our thought is rational and leads to a rational act, but it can hardly be called reasoning in a strict sense of the term.

38. The author most probably calls the kind of thinking described in the passage "irresponsible" (line 4) because it

(A) lacks originality
(B) is fundamentally immoral
(C) fails to abstract from specific images
(D) ignores the realities of the present
(E) is not consciously analytical

39. The author claims that the thought process by which people connect one image or term to another is

(A) either analytical or poetic
(B) neither spontaneous nor rational
(C) not clearly understood by them
(D) wholly determined by the nature of their formal education
(E) deliberately directed toward achieving a practical outcome

40. Which of the following elements is most central to the thought process described in the passage?

(A) Rationalization (B) Association
(C) Memorization (D) Analysis
(E) Innovation

IF YOU FINISH BEFORE TIME IS CALLED, YOU MAY CHECK YOUR WORK ON THIS SECTION ONLY. DO NOT TURN TO ANY OTHER SECTION IN THE TEST. **STOP**

SECTION 5 Time—30 minutes 35 Questions

In this section solve each problem, using any available space on the page for scratchwork. Then decide which is the best of the choices given and fill in the corresponding oval on the answer sheet.

The following information is for your reference in solving some of the problems.

Circle of radius r: Area $= \pi r^2$; Circumference $= 2\pi r$
The number of degrees of arc in a circle is 360.
The measure in degrees of a straight angle is 180.

Definition of symbols:
$=$ is equal to
$\neq$ is unequal to
$<$ is less than
$>$ is greater than
$\leqq$ is less than or equal to
$\geqq$ is greater than or equal to
$\parallel$ is parallel to
$\perp$ is perpendicular to

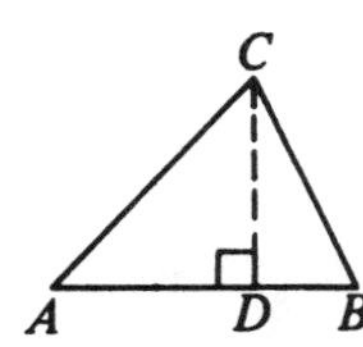

Triangle: The sum of the measures in degrees of the angles of a triangle is 180.
If $\angle CDA$ is a right angle, then

(1) area of $\triangle ABC = \frac{AB \times CD}{2}$

(2) $AC^2 = AD^2 + DC^2$

Note: Figures that accompany problems in this test are intended to provide information useful in solving the problems. They are drawn as accurately as possible EXCEPT when it is stated in a specific problem that its figure is not drawn to scale. All figures lie in a plane unless otherwise indicated. All numbers used are real numbers.

1. If $x + 3 = 6$ and $x + y = 8$, then $y =$

(A) -1 (B) 2 (C) 5 (D) 6 (E) 11

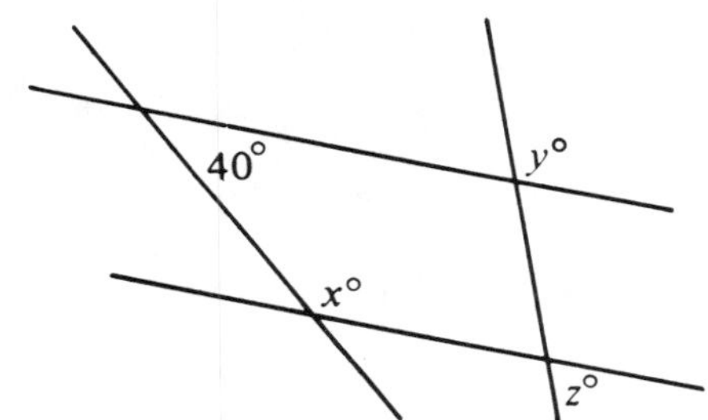

2. In the figure above, if $y + z = 180$, then $x =$

(A) 40 (B) 50 (C) 120 (D) 140 (E) 180

The sum of $3x$ and 5 is equal to the product of x and $\frac{1}{3}$.

3. Which of the following equations gives the relationship stated in the problem above?

(A) $3x = \frac{1}{3}x + 5$

(B) $5(3x) = x + \frac{1}{3}$

(C) $3(x + 5) = \frac{1}{3}x$

(D) $3x + 5 = x \div \frac{1}{3}$

(E) $3x + 5 = \frac{1}{3}x$

4. Eric has \$3.50. Of this amount, he owes his mother 14 percent and his sister 76 percent. How much will he have left after he pays these debts?

(A) \$0.10
(B) \$0.35
(C) \$0.70
(D) \$0.72
(E) \$0.84

5. The cube above has a number on each of its six faces. If the sum of the numbers on each pair of opposite faces is 10, what is the sum of the numbers on the faces not shown?

(A) 8 (B) 10 (C) 12 (D) 14 (E) 16

6. If $4x - 2 = 10$, then $1 - 2x =$

(A) -5
(B) -3
(C) 2
(D) 3
(E) 5

7. Which of the following could be the remainders when 4 consecutive positive integers are each divided by 3 ?

(A) 1, 2, 3, 1 (B) 1, 2, 3, 4 (C) 0, 1, 2, 3
(D) 0, 1, 2, 0 (E) 0, 2, 3, 0

GO ON TO THE NEXT PAGE

5

Questions 8-27 each consist of two quantities, one in Column A and one in Column B. You are to compare the two quantities and on the answer sheet fill in oval

- **A** if the quantity in Column A is greater;
- **B** if the quantity in Column B is greater;
- **C** if the two quantities are equal;
- **D** if the relationship cannot be determined from the information given.

AN E RESPONSE WILL NOT BE SCORED.

EXAMPLES

	Column A	Column B	Answers
E1.	2×6	$2 + 6$	● Ⓑ Ⓒ Ⓓ Ⓔ
E2.	$180 - x$	y	Ⓐ Ⓑ ● Ⓓ Ⓔ
E3.	$p - q$	$q - p$	Ⓐ Ⓑ Ⓒ ● Ⓔ

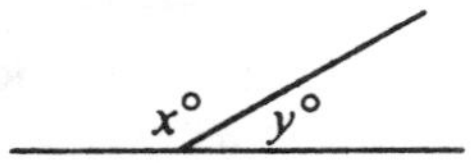

Notes:

1. In certain questions, information concerning one or both of the quantities to be compared is centered above the two columns.
2. In a given question, a symbol that appears in both columns represents the same thing in Column A as it does in Column B.
3. Letters such as x, n, and k stand for real numbers.

	Column A	Column B
8.	$0.3 + 0.09$	$0.3 + 0.009$

$c = 0$

9.	$a(b + c)$	ab

There are 26 chairs arranged in rows so that the first row has 5 chairs and each successive row has one more chair than the row immediately preceding it.

10.	The number of rows of chairs	5

11.	An even number multiplied by 2	An odd number multiplied by 2

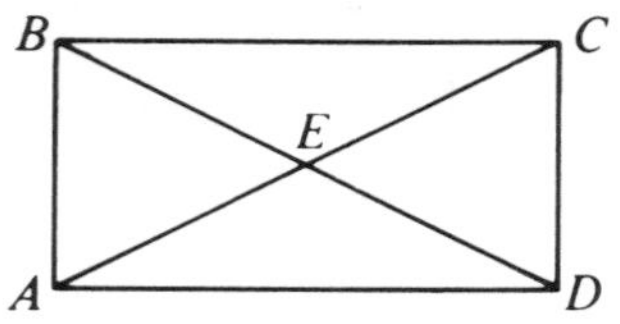

12.	The total number of triangles that can be named in the figure above	6

$r > s > t > 0$

13.	$r - t$	$s - t$

Column A	Column B

$P = \{1, 3, 5, 6\}$
$Q = \{2, 4, 6, 7, 9\}$

14.	A number that is a member of set P but not of set Q	A number that is a member of both sets P and Q

$8t - 8 = 40$
$9u - 9 = 45$

15.	t	u

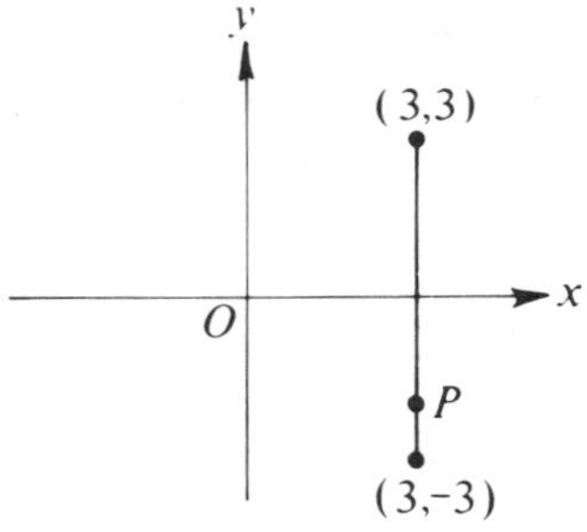

16.	The y-coordinate of point P	-4

$x^2 + kx + 12 = 0$
k is a positive integer.

17.	k	7

GO ON TO THE NEXT PAGE

SUMMARY DIRECTIONS FOR COMPARISON QUESTIONS

Answer:
- A if the quantity in Column A is greater;
- B if the quantity in Column B is greater;
- C if the two quantities are equal;
- D if the relationship cannot be determined from the information given.

AN E RESPONSE WILL NOT BE SCORED.

	Column A	Column B
	$6 \times 10^n = 3 \times 20 \times 100$	
18.	n	2

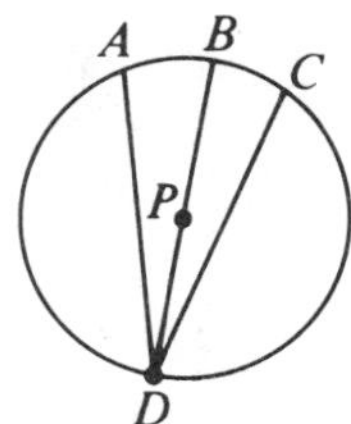

P is the center of the circle.

	Column A	Column B
19.	$AD \times CD$	$BD \times BD$

The ratio of 3 to 6 equals the ratio of $\sqrt{x}$ to 4.

	Column A	Column B
20.	x	4

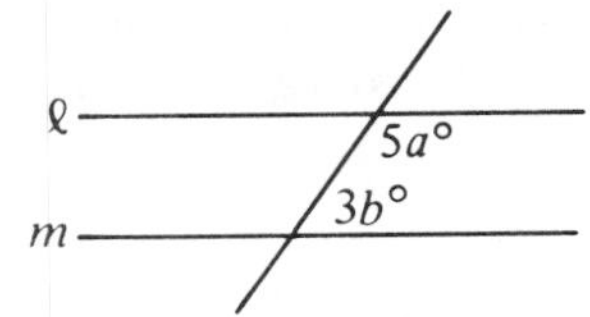

Note: Figure not drawn to scale.

$\ell \parallel m$

	Column A	Column B
21.	a	b
22.	$\dfrac{1}{2 - \frac{7}{4}}$	$2 + \dfrac{7}{4}$

$-9 \leqq x \leqq -2$

	Column A	Column B
23.	The greatest possible value of $18x$	The least possible value of $4x$

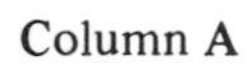

	Column A	Column B
	$a > 0$	
24.	a^{100}	$a^{1,000}$

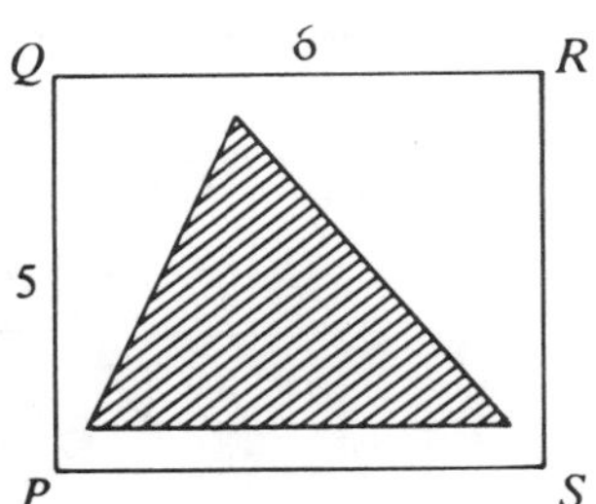

	Column A	Column B
25.	Area of the shaded triangle inside rectangle $PQRS$	15

The sum of the lengths of three sides of rectangle R is 18. One side of R has length 4.

	Column A	Column B
26.	Perimeter of R	22

$x + y = 3z$

$xyz \neq 0$

	Column A	Column B
27.	The average (arithmetic mean) of $x, y,$ and z	$\dfrac{4z}{3}$

GO ON TO THE NEXT PAGE

Solve each of the remaining problems in this section using any available space for scratchwork. Then decide which is the best of the choices given and fill in the corresponding oval on the answer sheet.

28. The weight of the tea in a box of 100 identical tea bags is 8 ounces. What is the weight, in ounces, of the tea in one bag?

(A) 0.04 (B) 0.08 (C) 0.125
(D) 0.8 (E) 1.25

29. If $\frac{1}{3x} = 9$, then $3x =$

(A) 27 (B) 3 (C) $\frac{1}{3}$ (D) $\frac{1}{9}$ (E) $\frac{1}{27}$

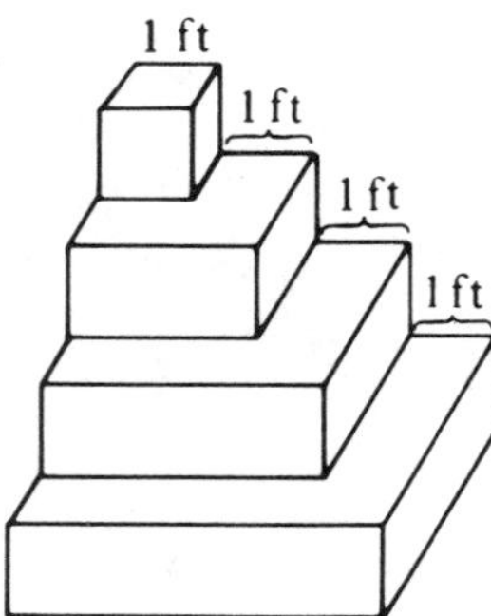

30. The figure above shows the dimensions of a pedestal constructed of 4 layers of marble. Each layer is 1 foot high and has a square base. How many cubic feet of marble make up the pedestal?

(A) 14 (B) 16 (C) 30 (D) 36 (E) 80

31. How many positive integers less than 30 are equal to 5 times an <u>even</u> integer?

(A) Two
(B) Three
(C) Four
(D) Five
(E) Six

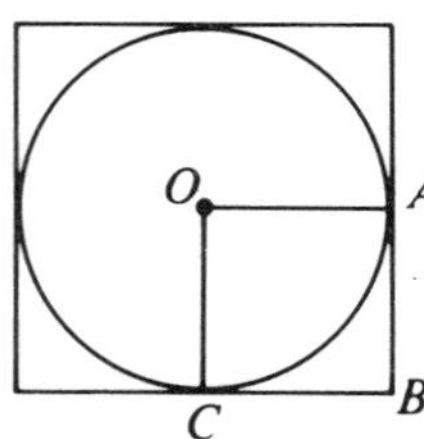

32. In the figure above, if the area of square $OABC$ is 2, what is the area of the circle with center O ?

(A) $\frac{\pi}{4}$ (B) $\pi\sqrt{2}$ (C) 2π (D) 4π (E) 16π

33. One cup of vinegar and 1 cup of oil are added to 2 cups of an original vinegar-and-oil salad dressing. If the yield is 4 cups of dressing that is $\frac{1}{3}$ vinegar by volume, what fraction of the original dressing was vinegar?

(A) $\frac{1}{6}$

(B) $\frac{1}{3}$

(C) $\frac{1}{4}$

(D) $\frac{1}{2}$

(E) $\frac{2}{3}$

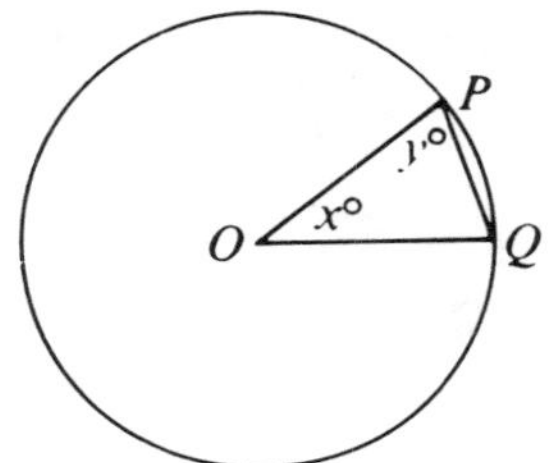

34. In the circle above with center O, if $0 < x < 40$, what are all possible values of y ?

(A) $40 < y < 60$
(B) $50 < y < 70$
(C) $60 < y < 90$
(D) $70 < y < 90$
(E) $y > 70$

35. If $x = 5^y$ and $y = z + 1$, what is $\frac{x}{5}$ in terms of z ?

(A) z
(B) $z + 1$
(C) 5^z
(D) $5^z + 1$
(E) 5^{z+1}

IF YOU FINISH BEFORE TIME IS CALLED, YOU MAY CHECK YOUR WORK ON THIS SECTION ONLY. DO NOT TURN TO ANY OTHER SECTION IN THE TEST. **STOP**

Correct Answers for Scholastic Aptitude Test Form Code 5D

VERBAL		MATHEMATICAL	
Section 1	Section 4	Section 2	Section 5
1. A	1. E	1. C	1. C
2. B	2. B	2. C	2. D
3. E	3. D	3. E	3. E
4. D	4. C	4. A	4. B
5. E	5. E	5. B	5. E
6. C	6. A	6. D	6. A
7. E	7. B	7. C	7. D
8. A	8. E	8. E	*8. A
9. E	9. C	9. C	*9. C
10. D	10. A	10. C	*10. B
11. B	11. C	11. A	*11. D
12. A	12. D	12. A	*12. A
13. A	13. D	13. B	*13. A
14. C	14. C	14. A	*14. B
15. E	15. A	15. E	*15. C
16. D	16. B	16. B	*16. A
17. D	17. C	17. B	*17. D
18. B	18. E	18. E	*18. A
19. A	19. E	19. A	*19. B
20. B	20. C	20. D	*20. C
21. C	21. A	21. B	*21. D
22. C	22. C	22. D	*22. A
23. E	23. B	23. D	*23. C
24. A	24. D	24. B	*24. D
25. B	25. C	25. E	*25. B
26. B	26. B		*26. D
27. A	27. E		*27. C
28. D	28. A		28. B
29. C	29. C		29. D
30. B	30. D		30. C
31. E	31. D		31. A
32. D	32. B		32. C
33. D	33. E		33. A
34. D	34. C		34. D
35. A	35. A		35. C
36. B	36. D		
37. C	37. D		
38. E	38. E		
39. C	39. C		
40. A	40. B		
41. D			
42. E			
43. C			
44. B			
45. C			

*Indicates four-choice questions. (All of the other questions are five-choice.)

The Scoring Process

Machine-scoring is done in three steps:

- *Scanning.* Your answer sheet is "read" by a scanning machine and the oval you filled in for each question is recorded on a computer tape.
- *Scoring.* The computer compares the oval filled in for each question with the correct response. Each correct answer receives one point; omitted questions do not count toward your score. For each wrong answer, a fraction of a point is subtracted to correct for random guessing. For questions with five answer choices, one-fourth of a point is subtracted for each wrong response; for questions with four answer choices, one-third of a point is subtracted for each wrong response. The SAT-verbal test has 85 questions with five answer choices each. If, for example, a student has 44 right, 32 wrong, and 9 omitted, the resulting raw score is determined as follows:

  $$44 \text{ right} - \frac{32 \text{ wrong}}{4} = 44 - 8 = 36 \text{ raw score points}$$

  Obtaining raw scores frequently involves the rounding of fractional numbers to the nearest whole number. For example, a raw score of 36.25 is rounded to 36, the nearest whole number. A raw score of 36.50 is rounded upward to 37.
- *Converting to reported scaled score.* Raw test scores are then placed on the College Board scale of 200 to 800 through a process that adjusts scores to account for minor differences in difficulty among different editions of the test. This process, known as equating, is performed so that a student's reported score is not affected by the edition of the test taken nor by the abilities of the group with whom the student takes the test. As a result of placing SAT scores on the College Board scale, scores earned by students at different times can be compared. For example, an SAT-verbal score of 400 on a test taken at one administration indicates the same level of developed verbal ability as a 400 score obtained on a different edition of the test taken at another time.

How to Score the Test

SAT-Verbal Sections 1 and 4

Step A: Count the number of correct answers for *section 1* and record the number in the space provided on the worksheet on the next page. Then do the same for the incorrect answers. (Do not count omitted answers.) To determine subtotal A, use the formula:

$$\text{number correct} - \frac{\text{number incorrect}}{4} = \text{subtotal A}$$

Step B: Count the number of correct answers and the number of incorrect answers for *section 4* and record the numbers in the spaces provided on the worksheet. To determine subtotal B, use the formula:

$$\text{number correct} - \frac{\text{number incorrect}}{4} = \text{subtotal B}$$

Step C: To obtain C, add subtotal A to subtotal B, keeping any decimals. Enter the resulting figure on the worksheet.

Step D: To obtain D, your raw verbal score, round C to the nearest whole number. (For example, any number from 44.50 to 45.49 rounds to 45.) Enter the resulting figure on the worksheet.

Step E: To find your reported SAT-verbal score, look up the total raw verbal score you obtained in step D in the conversion table on page 118. Enter this figure on the worksheet.

SAT-Mathematical Sections 2 and 5

Step A: Count the number of correct answers and the number of incorrect answers for *section 2* and record the numbers in the spaces provided on the worksheet. To determine the subtotal A, use the formula:

$$\text{number correct} - \frac{\text{number incorrect}}{4} = \text{subtotal A}$$

Step B: Count the number of correct answers and the number of incorrect answers for the *five-choice questions (questions 1 through 7 and 28 through 35) in section 5* and record the numbers in the spaces provided on the worksheet. To determine the subtotal B, use the formula:

$$\text{number correct} - \frac{\text{number incorrect}}{4} = \text{subtotal B}$$

Step C: Count the number of correct answers and the number of incorrect answers for the *four-choice questions (questions 8 through 27) in section 5* and record the numbers in the spaces provided on the worksheet. To determine the subtotal C, use the formula:

$$\text{number correct} - \frac{\text{number incorrect}}{3} = \text{subtotal C}$$

Step D: To obtain D, add subtotal A, subtotal B, and subtotal C, keeping any decimals. Enter the resulting figure on the worksheet.

Step E: To obtain E, your raw mathematical score, round D to the nearest whole number. (For example, any number from 44.50 to 45.49 rounds to 45.) Enter the resulting figure on the worksheet.

Step F: To find your reported SAT-mathematical score, look up the total raw mathematical score you obtained in E in the conversion table on page 118. Enter this figure on the worksheet.

SAT SCORING WORKSHEET

SAT-Verbal Sections

A. Section 1:	________ no. correct	− ¼	(________) no. incorrect	=	________ subtotal A
B. Section 4:	________ no. correct	− ¼	(________) no. incorrect	=	________ subtotal B
C. Total unrounded raw score (Total A + B)					________ C
D. Total rounded raw score (Rounded to nearest whole number)					________ D
E. SAT-verbal reported scaled score (See the conversion table on page 118.)					[ ] SAT-verbal score

SAT-Mathematical Sections

A. Section 2:	________ no. correct	− ¼	(________) no. incorrect	=	________ subtotal A
B. Section 5: Questions 1 through 7 and 28 through 35 (5-choice)	________ no. correct	− ¼	(________) no. incorrect	=	________ subtotal B
C. Section 5: Questions 8 through 27 (4-choice)	________ no. correct	− ⅓	(________) no. incorrect	=	________ subtotal C
D. Total unrounded raw score (Total A + B + C)					________ D
E. Total rounded raw score (Rounded to nearest whole number)					________ E
F. SAT-mathematical reported scaled score (See the conversion table on page 118.)					[ ] SAT-math score

Score Conversion Table
Scholastic Aptitude Test
Form Code 5D

Raw Score	College Board Reported Score		Raw Score	College Board Reported Score	
	SAT-Verbal	SAT-Math		SAT-Verbal	SAT-Math
85	800		40	460	590
84	780		39	450	580
83	770		38	440	570
82	760		37	440	560
81	750		36	430	550
80	740		35	430	540
79	730		34	420	530
78	720		33	410	520
77	710		32	410	510
76	700		31	400	500
75	700		30	400	490
74	690		29	390	480
73	680		28	380	480
72	670		27	380	470
71	660		26	370	460
70	650		25	360	450
69	650		24	350	440
68	640		23	350	430
67	630		22	340	420
66	620		21	330	410
65	620		20	330	400
64	610		19	320	400
63	600		18	310	390
62	590		17	300	380
61	590		16	300	370
60	580	800	15	290	360
59	570	780	14	280	350
58	560	760	13	270	350
57	560	750	12	270	340
56	550	740	11	260	330
55	550	730	10	250	320
54	540	720	9	250	320
53	530	710	8	240	310
52	530	700	7	230	300
51	520	690	6	230	290
50	510	680	5	220	290
49	510	670	4	220	280
48	500	660	3	210	270
47	500	650	2	200	260
46	490	640	1	200	260
45	490	630	0	200	250
44	480	620	−1	200	240
43	470	610	−2	200	230
42	470	610	−3	200	230
41	460	600	−4	200	220
			−5	200	210
			−6 or below	200	200

(Cut here to detach.)

COLLEGE BOARD — SCHOLASTIC APTITUDE TEST and Test of Standard Written English

Side 1

Use a No. 2 pencil only. Be sure each mark is dark and completely fills the intended oval. Completely erase any errors or stray marks.

1. YOUR NAME: (Print) Last First M.I.

SIGNATURE: DATE: / /

HOME ADDRESS: (Print) Number and Street

City State Zip Code

CENTER: (Print) City State Center Number

IMPORTANT: Please fill in items 2 and 3 exactly as shown on the back cover of your test book.

FOR ETS USE ONLY

2. TEST FORM (Copy from back cover of your test book.)

3. FORM CODE (Copy and grid as shown on back cover of your test book.)

4. REGISTRATION NUMBER (Copy from your Admission Ticket.)

5. YOUR NAME

First 4 letters of last name | First Init. | Mid. Init.

6. DATE OF BIRTH

Month | Day | Year

Jan. Feb. Mar. Apr. May June July Aug. Sept. Oct. Nov. Dec.

7. SEX

Female

Male

8. TEST BOOK SERIAL NUMBER (Copy from front cover of your test book.)

Start with number 1 for each new section. If a section has fewer than 50 questions, leave the extra answer spaces blank.

SECTION 1

1–50 (A) (B) (C) (D) (E)

SECTION 2

1–50 (A) (B) (C) (D) (E)

Q1362-04

I.N. 575008 — 110VV58P3720

COLLEGE BOARD — SCHOLASTIC APTITUDE TEST and Test of Standard Written English Side 2

Use a No. 2 pencil only. Be sure each mark is dark and completely fills the intended oval. Completely erase any errors or stray marks.

Start with number 1 for each new section. If a section has fewer than 50 questions, leave the extra answer spaces blank.

No.	SECTION 3	SECTION 4	SECTION 5	SECTION 6
1	A B C D E	A B C D E	A B C D E	A B C D E
2	A B C D E	A B C D E	A B C D E	A B C D E
3	A B C D E	A B C D E	A B C D E	A B C D E
4	A B C D E	A B C D E	A B C D E	A B C D E
5	A B C D E	A B C D E	A B C D E	A B C D E
6	A B C D E	A B C D E	A B C D E	A B C D E
7	A B C D E	A B C D E	A B C D E	A B C D E
8	A B C D E	A B C D E	A B C D E	A B C D E
9	A B C D E	A B C D E	A B C D E	A B C D E
10	A B C D E	A B C D E	A B C D E	A B C D E
11	A B C D E	A B C D E	A B C D E	A B C D E
12	A B C D E	A B C D E	A B C D E	A B C D E
13	A B C D E	A B C D E	A B C D E	A B C D E
14	A B C D E	A B C D E	A B C D E	A B C D E
15	A B C D E	A B C D E	A B C D E	A B C D E
16	A B C D E	A B C D E	A B C D E	A B C D E
17	A B C D E	A B C D E	A B C D E	A B C D E
18	A B C D E	A B C D E	A B C D E	A B C D E
19	A B C D E	A B C D E	A B C D E	A B C D E
20	A B C D E	A B C D E	A B C D E	A B C D E
21	A B C D E	A B C D E	A B C D E	A B C D E
22	A B C D E	A B C D E	A B C D E	A B C D E
23	A B C D E	A B C D E	A B C D E	A B C D E
24	A B C D E	A B C D E	A B C D E	A B C D E
25	A B C D E	A B C D E	A B C D E	A B C D E
26	A B C D E	A B C D E	A B C D E	A B C D E
27	A B C D E	A B C D E	A B C D E	A B C D E
28	A B C D E	A B C D E	A B C D E	A B C D E
29	A B C D E	A B C D E	A B C D E	A B C D E
30	A B C D E	A B C D E	A B C D E	A B C D E
31	A B C D E	A B C D E	A B C D E	A B C D E
32	A B C D E	A B C D E	A B C D E	A B C D E
33	A B C D E	A B C D E	A B C D E	A B C D E
34	A B C D E	A B C D E	A B C D E	A B C D E
35	A B C D E	A B C D E	A B C D E	A B C D E
36	A B C D E	A B C D E	A B C D E	A B C D E
37	A B C D E	A B C D E	A B C D E	A B C D E
38	A B C D E	A B C D E	A B C D E	A B C D E
39	A B C D E	A B C D E	A B C D E	A B C D E
40	A B C D E	A B C D E	A B C D E	A B C D E
41	A B C D E	A B C D E	A B C D E	A B C D E
42	A B C D E	A B C D E	A B C D E	A B C D E
43	A B C D E	A B C D E	A B C D E	A B C D E
44	A B C D E	A B C D E	A B C D E	A B C D E
45	A B C D E	A B C D E	A B C D E	A B C D E
46	A B C D E	A B C D E	A B C D E	A B C D E
47	A B C D E	A B C D E	A B C D E	A B C D E
48	A B C D E	A B C D E	A B C D E	A B C D E
49	A B C D E	A B C D E	A B C D E	A B C D E
50	A B C D E	A B C D E	A B C D E	A B C D E

9. SIGNATURE: ______________________

FOR ETS USE ONLY	VTR	VTFS	VRR	VRFS	VVR	VVFS	WER	WEFS	M4R	M4FS	M5R	M5FS	MTFS
	VTW	VTCS	VRW	VRCS	VVW	VVCS	WEW	WECS	M4W		M5W		MTCS

SECTION 1 | **Time—30 minutes** **40 Questions** | For each question in this section, choose the best answer and fill in the corresponding oval on the answer sheet.

Each question below consists of a word in capital letters, followed by five lettered words or phrases. Choose the word or phrase that is most nearly opposite in meaning to the word in capital letters. Since some of the questions require you to distinguish fine shades of meaning, consider all the choices before deciding which is best.

Example:

GOOD: (A) sour (B) bad (C) red (D) hot (E) ugly

Ⓐ ● Ⓒ Ⓓ Ⓔ

1. SURPLUS: (A) shortage (B) criticism (C) heated argument (D) sudden victory (E) thorough review

2. VAGUE: (A) abundant (B) correct (C) definite (D) stable (E) petty

3. COLLABORATE: (A) pay attention (B) issue orders (C) become simpler (D) gain strength (E) work alone

4. NONCOMBATANT: (A) forerunner (B) inhabitant (C) eccentric (D) warrior (E) expert

5. POROUS: (A) inclement (B) impermeable (C) concentrated (D) perishable (E) uncongealed

6. EXTRADITE: (A) stimulate (B) underemphasize (C) become specialized (D) withhold wages from (E) grant asylum to

7. SOPHOMORIC: (A) charitable (B) profound (C) accidental (D) histrionic (E) straightforward

8. DEBILITATE: (A) reveal (B) decorate (C) sustain (D) put forth (E) give approval

9. PRODIGAL: (A) antagonist (B) successor (C) grouch (D) underweight person (E) thrifty individual

10. PRECOCIOUS: (A) elusive (B) isolated (C) understandable (D) proven (E) backward

Each sentence below has one or two blanks, each blank indicating that something has been omitted. Beneath the sentence are five lettered words or sets of words. Choose the word or set of words that, when inserted in the sentence, best fits the meaning of the sentence as a whole.

Example:

Although its publicity has been ----, the film itself is intelligent, well-acted, handsomely produced, and altogether ----.

(A) tasteless. .respectable (B) extensive. .moderate (C) sophisticated. .amateur (D) risqué. .crude (E) perfect. .spectacular

● Ⓑ Ⓒ Ⓓ Ⓔ

11. The summer's ---- drought has brought about a ---- shedding of leaves.

    (A) torrid. .nonexistent
    (B) inconsequential. .disastrous
    (C) rainy. .colorful
    (D) severe. .premature
    (E) unusual. .traditional

12. At the age of forty-five, with a worldwide reputation and an as yet unbroken string of notable successes to her credit, Carson was at the ---- of her career.

    (A) paradigm (B) zenith (C) fiasco (D) periphery (E) inception

13. The fact that they cherished religious objects more than most of their other possessions ---- the ---- role of religion in their lives.

    (A) demonstrates. .crucial
    (B) obliterates. .vital
    (C) limits. .daily
    (D) concerns. .informal
    (E) denotes. .varying

GO ON TO THE NEXT PAGE

14. The alarm voiced by the committee investigating the incident had a ---- effect, for its dire predictions motivated people to take precautions that ---- an ecological disaster.

(A) trivial. .prompted
(B) salutary. .averted
(C) conciliatory. .supported
(D) beneficial. .exacerbated
(E) perverse. .vanquished

15. After the First World War, a large decrease in Mexican immigration to the United States occurred because the wartime ---- of immigration restrictions was ----.

(A) waiver. .rescinded
(B) enactment. .overturned
(C) abolition. .endorsed
(D) repeal. .guaranteed
(E) execution. .relaxed

Each question below consists of a related pair of words or phrases, followed by five lettered pairs of words or phrases. Select the lettered pair that best expresses a relationship similar to that expressed in the original pair.

Example:

YAWN : BOREDOM :: (A) dream : sleep
(B) anger : madness (C) smile : amusement
(D) face : expression (E) impatience : rebellion

16. FOOTSTOOL : FOOT :: (A) desk : floor
(B) table : hand (C) bench : chair
(D) pillow : head (E) pencil : pocket

17. CANOE : RAPIDS :: (A) plane : turbulence
(B) truck : garage (C) oar : rowboat
(D) factory : automation (E) pond : stream

18. IRON : BLACKSMITH :: (A) gold : miser
(B) clay : potter (C) food : gourmet
(D) steel : industrialist (E) silver : miner

19. ACRE : LAND :: (A) distance : space
(B) speed : movement (C) gallon : liquid
(D) degree : thermometer (E) year : birthday

20. CONVENE : ASSEMBLY :: (A) borrow : library
(B) reprove : defiance (C) contrast : shadow
(D) implicate : court (E) compile : collection

21. COMPATRIOTS : COUNTRY ::
(A) transients : home
(B) kinsfolk : family
(C) competitors : team
(D) performers : audience
(E) figureheads : government

22. ENTREATY : REQUEST ::
(A) conviction : opinion
(B) theory : truth
(C) success : persistence
(D) debate : compromise
(E) hope : future

23. COVEN : WITCHES :: (A) tavern : bartenders
(B) altar : clergy (C) amulet : vampires
(D) castle : royalty (E) choir : singers

24. STALWART : STRENGTH ::
(A) penniless : wealth (B) portly : girth
(C) persuasive : depth (D) pernicious : health
(E) precious : mirth

25. OPALESCENT : IRIDESCENCE ::
(A) magnetic : repulsion
(B) garish : drabness
(C) flushed : ruddiness
(D) effervescent : stagnation
(E) fluorescent : darkness

GO ON TO THE NEXT PAGE

Each passage below is followed by questions based on its content. Answer the questions following each passage on the basis of what is stated or implied in that passage.

"What's that cry of deadly pain?" his sister drawled from the back seat. "Oh, it's you," she said. "Well, well, we have the artist with us again. How utterly utterly." She had a decidedly nasal voice.

He didn't answer her or turn his head. He had learned that much. Never answer her.

"Mary George!" his mother said sharply. "Asbury is sick. Leave him alone."

"What's wrong with him?" Mary George asked.

"There's the house!" his mother said as if they were all blind but her. It rose on the crest of the hill—a white two-story farmhouse with a wide porch and pleasant columns. She always approached it with a feeling of pride and she had said more than once to Asbury, "You have a home here that half those people up there would give their eyeteeth for!"

She had been once to the terrible place where he lived in New York. They had gone up five flights of dark stone steps, past open garbage cans on every landing, to arrive finally at two damp rooms and a closet with a toilet in it. "You wouldn't live like this at home," she had muttered.

"No!" he'd said with an ecstatic look, "it wouldn't be possible!"

She pulled the car into the side drive. "Home again, home again jiggity jig!" she said.

Asbury groaned.

"The artist arrives at death row," Mary George said.

26. Which of the following best describes the tone of the question in line 1 ?

(A) Despair (B) Confusion (C) Ridicule (D) Genuine alarm (E) Cautious curiosity

27. In context, which of the following best describes the feelings expressed by Asbury's statement in lines 22-23 ?

(A) Deranged hatred
(B) Defiant elation
(C) Resentful anger
(D) Defeated resignation
(E) Apathetic satisfaction

28. Based on the information in the passage, which of the following best describes the mother?

(A) Angry at her children's cynical and bickering manner but envious of their intelligence and sharp wit
(B) Aware of the individuality of each of her children and approving of their life-styles
(C) Anxious about her children's interests and welfare and convinced that she knows what is best for them
(D) Somber in viewing her life and pessimistically dwelling on the unpleasant and the depressing
(E) Successful in achieving her goals in life but unconcerned with what others think about her family

GO ON TO THE NEXT PAGE

The reading passages in this test are brief excerpts or adaptations of excerpts from published material. The ideas contained in them do not necessarily represent the opinions of the College Board or Educational Testing Service. To make the text suitable for testing purposes, we may in some cases have altered the style, contents, or point of view of the original.

From a vantage point in space, an observer could see that the Earth is engaged in a variety of motions. First, there is its rotation on its own axis, causing the alternation of day and night. This rotation, however, is not altogether steady. Primarily because of the Moon's gravitational action, the Earth's axis wobbles like that of an ill-spun top. In this motion, called "precession," the North and South Poles each trace out the base of a cone in space, completing a circle every 25,800 years. In addition, as the Sun and the Moon change their positions with respect to the Earth, their changing gravitational effects result in a slight "nodding" of the Earth's axis, called "nutation," which is superimposed on precession. The Earth completes one of these "nods" every 18.6 years.

The Earth also, of course, revolves around the Sun, in a 6-million-mile journey that takes 365.25 days. The shape of this orbit is an ellipse, but it is not the center of the Earth that follows the elliptical path. Earth and Moon behave like an asymmetrical dumbbell, and it is the center of mass of this dumbbell that traces the ellipse around the Sun. The center of the Earth-Moon mass lies about 3,000 miles away from the center of the Earth, and the Earth thus moves in an S-curve that crosses and recrosses its orbital path. Then too, the Earth accompanies the Sun in the Sun's movements: first, through its local star cloud, and second, in a great sweep around the "hub" of its galaxy, the Milky Way, that takes 200 million years to complete.

29. Which of the following best describes the main subject of the passage?

(A) The various types of the Earth's motions
(B) Past changes in the Earth's position
(C) The predictability of the Earth's orbit
(D) Oddities of the Earth's rotation on its axis
(E) The Moon's gravitational effect on the Earth

30. The passage is most likely directed toward an audience of

(A) geologists
(B) astronauts
(C) aircraft navigators
(D) meteorologists interested in weather prediction
(E) persons with little technical knowledge of astronomy

31. Which of the following techniques does the author use in order to make the descriptions of motion clear?

I. Comparisons with familiar objects
II. Reference to geometric forms
III. Allusions to the works of other authors

(A) I only
(B) II only
(C) I and II only
(D) I and III only
(E) I, II, and III

32. The passage indicates that a single cycle of which of the following motions is completed in the shortest period of time?

(A) Nutation
(B) Precession
(C) The Earth's rotation on its axis
(D) The Earth's revolution around the Sun
(E) The Sun's movement around the hub of the Milky Way

GO ON TO THE NEXT PAGE

Poetry is not like reasoning, a power to be exerted according to the determination of the will. A person cannot say, "I will compose poetry." The greatest poet even cannot say it: for the mind in creation is as a fading coal, which some invisible influence, like an inconstant wind, awakens to transitory brightness: this power arises from within, like the color of a flower which fades and changes as it is developed, and the conscious portions of our natures are unprophetic either of its approach or its departure. Could this influence be durable in its original purity and force, it is impossible to predict the greatness of the results; but when composition begins, inspiration is already on the decline, and the most glorious poetry that has ever been communicated to the world is probably a feeble shadow of the original conception of the poet. I appeal to the great poets of the present day, whether it be not an error to assert that the finest passages of poetry are produced by labor and study. The toil and the delay recommended by critics, can be justly interpreted to mean no more than a careful observation of the inspired moments, and an artificial connection of the spaces between their suggestions by the intertexture of conventional expressions; a necessity only imposed by the limitedness of the poetical faculty itself.

33. The comparison of "the mind in creation" to "a fading coal" touched by the wind (lines 4-5) emphasizes which of the following?

(A) The infinite variety of the intellect
(B) The inability of the mind to reason consistently
(C) The nourishment that poetry gives the mind
(D) The fleeting nature of inspiration
(E) The passionate quality of poetry

34. The author appeals to "the great poets of the present day" (line 16) to support the view that

(A) poets are made not born
(B) great poetry can be written only by people of great intellect
(C) familiarity with literary tradition is essential to poetic greatness
(D) modern poets are at least as talented as classical authors
(E) diligent effort and training do not produce the best poetry

35. By the "limitedness of the poetical faculty" (lines 23-24), the author means a poet's

(A) failure to comprehend the importance of study for poetic composition
(B) inability to sustain inspiration for long periods
(C) inability to understand the nature of inspiration
(D) reluctance to compose longer poetical works
(E) failure to make extensive use of traditional expression in poetry

Even if history is viewed from other than equalitarian perspectives, and it is granted that differentials in economic rewards are morally justified and socially useful, it is impossible to justify the degree of inequality which complex societies inevitably create by the increased centralization of power that develops with more elaborate civilizations. The literature of all ages is filled with rational and moral justifications for these inequalities, but most of them are specious. If superior abilities and services to society deserve special rewards, it may be regarded as axiomatic that the rewards are always higher than the services warrant. No impartial authority determines the rewards. The people of power who control society grant these perquisites to themselves. Whenever special ability is not associated with power, as in the case of modern professionals, the excess of income over the average is ridiculously low in comparison with that of the economic overlords, who are the real centers of power in an industrial society.

Most rational and social justifications for unequal privilege are clearly afterthoughts. The facts are created by the disproportion of power that exists in a given social system. The justifications are usually dictated by the desire of the powerful to hide the nakedness of their greed and by the inclination of society to veil the brutal facts of human life from itself. This inclination is rather pathetic but understandable, since the facts of collective life easily rob the average individual of confidence in the human enterprise. The inevitable hypocrisy that is associated with all of the collective activities of the human race springs chiefly from this source: individuals have a moral code that makes the actions of society an outrage to their conscience. They therefore invent romantic and moral interpretations of the real facts, preferring to obscure rather than reveal the true character of their collective behavior. Sometimes they are as anxious to offer moral justifications for the brutalities from which they suffer as for those which they commit. The fact that the hypocrisy of group behavior expresses itself not only in terms of self-justification but in terms of moral justification of human behavior in general symbolizes one of the tragedies of the human spirit: its inability to conform its collective life to its individual ideals. As individuals, people believe that they ought to love and serve each other and establish justice toward each other. As economic and national groups, they take for themselves whatever their power can command.

36. The author refers to "modern professionals" (line 16) as examples of those who

(A) have the potential to become economic overlords
(B) are least likely to rebel against an unjust society
(C) can achieve incomes far in excess of the benefits they can give society
(D) lack the power to reward themselves excessively for their special abilities
(E) are unable to develop their special abilities for the greatest social good

37. According to the passage, those who would defend current levels of inequality in society are usually motivated by

(A) naïve idealism
(B) self-protective dishonesty
(C) an earnest concern for the well-being of others
(D) an obsessive desire for progress
(E) fear of reprisals from those in power

38. According to the passage, the origin of the "inevitable hypocrisy" (line 29) is

(A) a pervasive misunderstanding of the means by which inequalities in society can be reduced
(B) the dissimilarity in the moral codes of the individuals who constitute a large society
(C) the disparity between the individual's moral code and that of the larger society
(D) human inability to develop any sense of what a moral code should be
(E) the demands of an unselfish society on individuals who are innately selfish

39. The author's tone in the passage is that of a person attempting to

(A) urge the reader to take specific action
(B) ridicule previous analyses of an issue
(C) evaluate a theory without making a judgment
(D) explain an unfortunate and unrecognized truth
(E) defend a previously attacked theory

40. As described by the author, the average individual is all of the following EXCEPT

(A) defiant (B) compassionate
(C) hypocritical (D) self-deceptive
(E) unjustly treated

IF YOU FINISH BEFORE TIME IS CALLED, YOU MAY CHECK YOUR WORK ON THIS SECTION ONLY. DO NOT TURN TO ANY OTHER SECTION IN THE TEST. **STOP**

SECTION 3 Time—30 minutes 25 Questions

In this section solve each problem, using any available space on the page for scratchwork. Then decide which is the best of the choices given and fill in the corresponding oval on the answer sheet.

The following information is for your reference in solving some of the problems.

Circle of radius r: Area $= \pi r^2$; Circumference $= 2\pi r$
The number of degrees of arc in a circle is 360.
The measure in degrees of a straight angle is 180.

Definition of symbols:

$=$ is equal to	$\leq$ is less than or equal to
$\neq$ is unequal to	$\geq$ is greater than or equal to
$<$ is less than	$\parallel$ is parallel to
$>$ is greater than	$\perp$ is perpendicular to

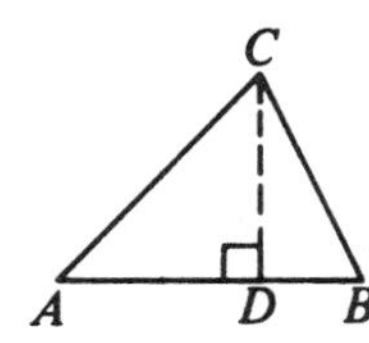

Triangle: The sum of the measures in degrees of the angles of a triangle is 180.
If $\angle CDA$ is a right angle, then

(1) area of $\triangle ABC = \frac{AB \times CD}{2}$

(2) $AC^2 = AD^2 + DC^2$

Note: Figures that accompany problems in this test are intended to provide information useful in solving the problems. They are drawn as accurately as possible EXCEPT when it is stated in a specific problem that its figure is not drawn to scale. All figures lie in a plane unless otherwise indicated. All numbers used are real numbers.

1. If $x + 3 = 13$, what does $x - 5$ equal?

(A) 5 (B) 8 (C) 10 (D) 11 (E) 15

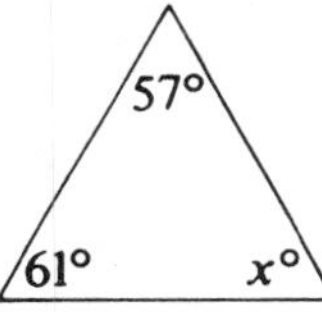

2. In the triangle above, $x =$

(A) 59 (B) 60 (C) 61 (D) 62 (E) 63

3. If $y = 2x - 3$, then $-2y =$

(A) $5x + 3$
(B) $5x - 3$
(C) $2x + 6$
(D) $-4x - 6$
(E) $-4x + 6$

4. If $x > -3$, then $x + 4$ could equal

(A) 2 (B) 1 (C) 0 (D) -6 (E) -8

5. The odometer of a new automobile functions improperly and registers only 2 miles for every 3 miles driven. If the odometer indicates 48 miles, how many miles has the automobile actually been driven?

(A) 144 (B) 72 (C) 64 (D) 32 (E) 24

6. If $\sqrt{16} = 2^k$, what is the value of k ?

(A) 1 (B) 2 (C) 3 (D) 4 (E) 8

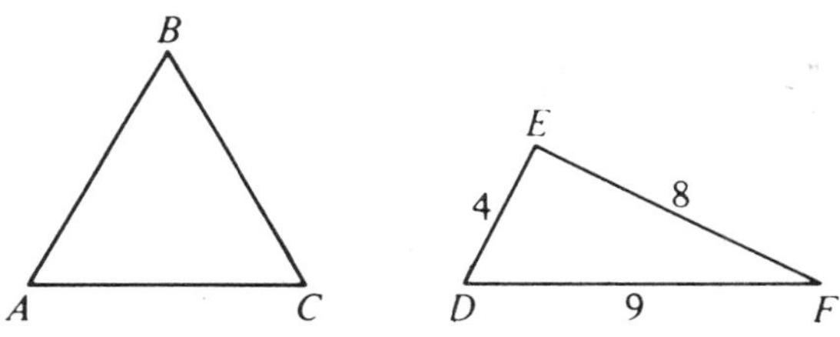

7. For the triangles above, the perimeter of $\triangle ABC$ equals the perimeter of $\triangle DEF$. If $\triangle ABC$ is equilateral, what is the length of side AB ?

(A) 4 (B) 5 (C) 7 (D) 9 (E) 15

GO ON TO THE NEXT PAGE

8. If $q < r < s < t$ where r and s are odd integers and q and t are even integers, what is the least possible value of $t - q$?

(A) 3 (B) 4 (C) 6 (D) 7 (E) 8

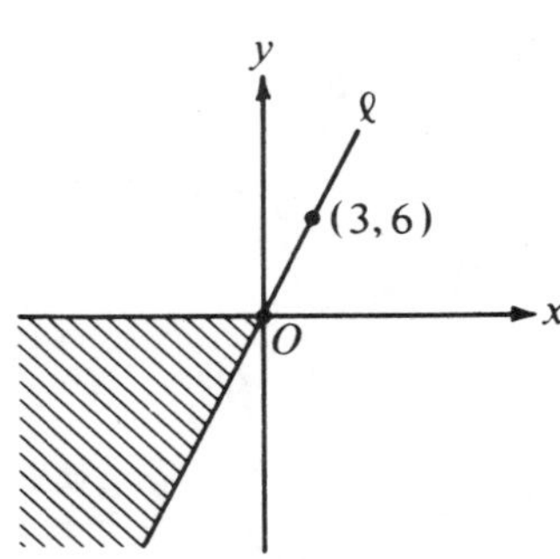

9. Of the following, which are the coordinates of a point that is located in the shaded region of the graph shown above?

(A) (−4, −5) (B) (−4, 5) (C) (−5, −12)
(D) (−5, 10) (E) (5, −10)

---

10. If P was the number of Persian soldiers at the battle of Marathon and G was the number of Greek soldiers at that battle, which of the following equations can represent the statement "The number of Persian soldiers was 3 times the number of Greek soldiers"?

(A) $3P = 3G$
(B) $P = G + 3$
(C) $P + 3 = G$
(D) $G = 3P$
(E) $P = 3G$

Questions 11-13 refer to the following definition.

Let # be defined by the equation
$a \# b = ab + a + b$ for all numbers a and b.

11. $2 \# 5 =$

(A) 7 (B) 10 (C) 17 (D) 20 (E) 32

12. If $10 \# h = 98$, then $h =$

(A) 8
(B) 9
(C) 10
(D) 11
(E) 12

13. For what value of x is the statement $x \# y = x$ always true?

(A) −2
(B) −1
(C) 0
(D) 1
(E) 2

---

14. The sum of the digits of a two-digit integer is 12. If the units' digit is one-half the tens' digit, then the two-digit integer is

(A) 26
(B) 48
(C) 62
(D) 84
(E) 93

GO ON TO THE NEXT PAGE

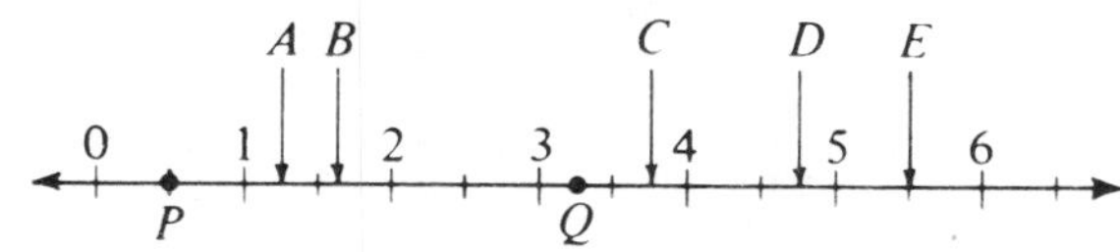

15. If P and Q are numbers on the number line above, which of the points shown best represents $P \times Q$?

(A) A (B) B (C) C (D) D (E) E

$$\frac{5,\blacksquare 81}{23} = N$$

16. In the fraction above, the four-digit numerator has one digit covered by ■. If N is a whole number, which of the following could be the value of N?

(A) 244 (B) 245 (C) 246
(D) 247 (E) 248

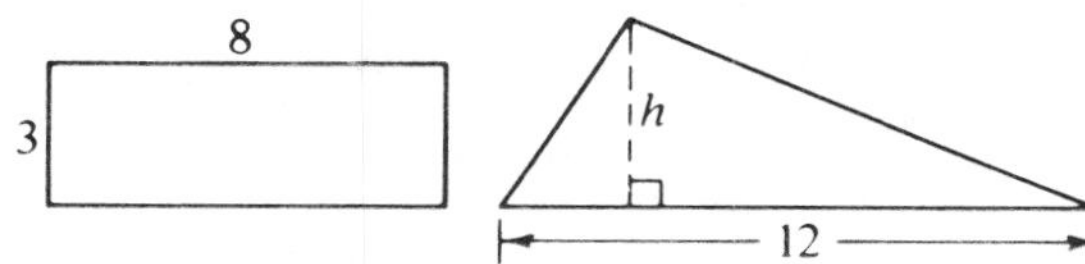

17. In the figures above, if the area of the rectangle is equal to the area of the triangle, then $h =$

(A) 1
(B) 2
(C) 3
(D) 4
(E) 5

18. If the degree measures of the four angles of a quadrilateral are in the ratio 1 : 2 : 3 : 4, what is the degree measure of the largest angle?

(A) 36 (B) 90 (C) 144
(D) 160 (E) 180

19. A person paid a total of \$700 for shirts priced at \$9 and \$13 each. If the person purchased two \$13 shirts for every \$9 shirt, what was the total number of shirts purchased?

(A) 20
(B) 23
(C) 40
(D) 60
(E) 68

20. If 1 jar + 5 cups = 1 tub and
if 3 jars + 2 cups = 2 tubs,
how many cups equal a tub?

(A) 8
(B) 11
(C) 13
(D) 15
(E) 18

GO ON TO THE NEXT PAGE

21. Points Q and R are on segment PS, which has length 24. If PQ is half as long as QS, and QR is 3 times as long as RS, how long is RS ?

(A) 2
(B) 3
(C) 4
(D) 8
(E) 12

22. If United States imports increased 20 percent and exports decreased 10 percent during a certain year, the ratio of imports to exports at the end of the year was how many times the ratio at the beginning of the year?

(A) $\frac{12}{11}$

(B) $\frac{4}{3}$

(C) $\frac{11}{8}$

(D) $\frac{3}{2}$

(E) 2

23. If $xy = 1$, then y is the reciprocal of x. Which of the following equals the average (arithmetic mean) of x and its reciprocal?

(A) $\frac{x^2 + 1}{2x}$

(B) $\frac{x + 1}{2x}$

(C) $\frac{x^2 + 2}{2x}$

(D) $\frac{2x^2 + 2}{x}$

(E) $\frac{x^2 + 1}{x}$

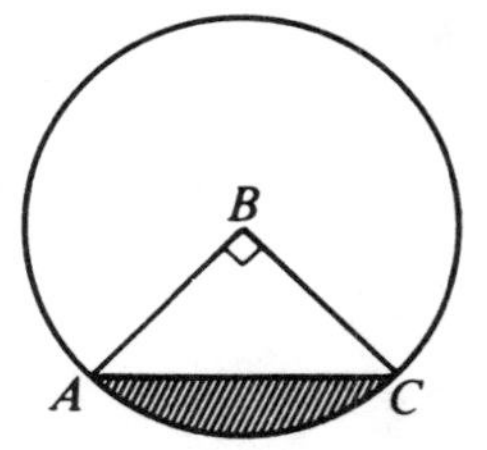

24. In the figure above, B is the center of the circle with radius 6. What is the area of the shaded region?

(A) 9π

(B) $36 - 9\pi$

(C) $36\pi - 18$

(D) $18 - \frac{9\pi}{2}$

(E) $9\pi - 18$

---

25. The sum of the first 1,000 positive integers is 500,500. What is the sum of the first 2,000 positive integers?

(A) 1,001,000
(B) 1,500,500
(C) 2,000,000
(D) 2,001,000
(E) 2,500,500

IF YOU FINISH BEFORE TIME IS CALLED, YOU MAY CHECK YOUR WORK ON THIS SECTION ONLY. DO NOT TURN TO ANY OTHER SECTION IN THE TEST.	**STOP**

SECTION 5	Time—30 minutes 35 Questions	In this section solve each problem, using any available space on the page for scratchwork. Then decide which is the best of the choices given and fill in the corresponding oval on the answer sheet.

The following information is for your reference in solving some of the problems.

Circle of radius r: Area $= \pi r^2$; Circumference $= 2\pi r$
The number of degrees of arc in a circle is 360.
The measure in degrees of a straight angle is 180.

Definition of symbols:

$=$ is equal to	$\leq$ is less than or equal to
$\neq$ is unequal to	$\geq$ is greater than or equal to
$<$ is less than	$\parallel$ is parallel to
$>$ is greater than	$\perp$ is perpendicular to

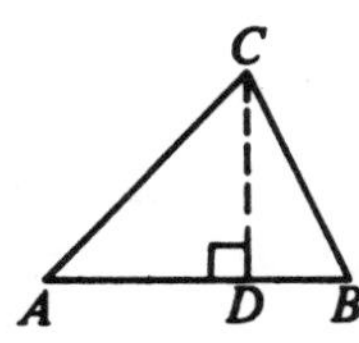

Triangle: The sum of the measures in degrees of the angles of a triangle is 180.
If $\angle CDA$ is a right angle, then

(1) area of $\triangle ABC = \dfrac{AB \times CD}{2}$

(2) $AC^2 = AD^2 + DC^2$

Note: Figures that accompany problems in this test are intended to provide information useful in solving the problems. They are drawn as accurately as possible EXCEPT when it is stated in a specific problem that its figure is not drawn to scale. All figures lie in a plane unless otherwise indicated. All numbers used are real numbers.

1. Amelia has saved \$80 to buy a stereo that costs a total of \$220. If her take-home pay is \$4 an hour, how many hours will she have to work in order to have just enough to buy the stereo?

   (A) 35
   (B) 40
   (C) 45
   (D) 50
   (E) 55

2. On a certain map, the distance of 100 miles is represented by 1 inch. What is the distance represented by 2.4 inches on this map?

   (A) 200.4 mi
   (B) 204.0 mi
   (C) 225.0 mi
   (D) 233.3 mi
   (E) 240.0 mi

3. Three students have a total of 25 pencils among them. If the first student has 32 percent of the pencils and the second student has 48 percent of the pencils, how many pencils does the third student have?

   (A) 5 (B) 6 (C) 8 (D) 9 (E) 10

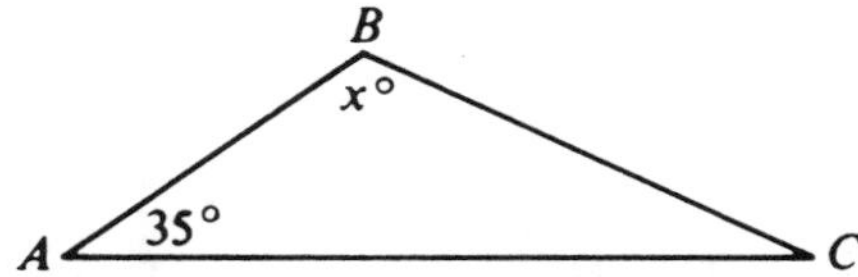

Note: Figure not drawn to scale.

4. In $\triangle ABC$ above, if $AB = BC$, then $x =$

   (A) 35 (B) 55 (C) 70 (D) 110 (E) 135

5. $\frac{5}{12}$ of $3 \times 6 \times 4 =$

   (A) 6 (B) 10 (C) 20 (D) 24 (E) 30

6. If $ax + 3 = 7$ and $bx + 5 = 12$, what is the value of $\frac{a}{b}$?

   (A) $\frac{3}{11}$ (B) $\frac{4}{7}$ (C) $\frac{7}{12}$ (D) $\frac{10}{17}$ (E) $\frac{3}{5}$

7. Twenty-eight identical boxes are stacked so that each layer above the bottom layer consists of 1 box fewer than the layer immediately below it. The top layer contains only 1 box. How many layers make up the stack?

   (A) Eight
   (B) Seven
   (C) Six
   (D) Five
   (E) Four

GO ON TO THE NEXT PAGE

5

Questions 8-27 each consist of two quantities, one in Column A and one in Column B. You are to compare the two quantities and on the answer sheet fill in oval

- A if the quantity in Column A is greater;
- B if the quantity in Column B is greater;
- C if the two quantities are equal;
- D if the relationship cannot be determined from the information given.

AN E RESPONSE WILL NOT BE SCORED.

EXAMPLES

	Column A	Column B	Answers
E1.	2×6	$2 + 6$	● Ⓑ Ⓒ Ⓓ Ⓔ
E2.	$180 - x$	y	Ⓐ Ⓑ ● Ⓓ Ⓔ
E3.	$p - q$	$q - p$	Ⓐ Ⓑ Ⓒ ● Ⓔ

(E2 figure: angles $x°$ and $y°$ on a straight line)

Notes:

1. In certain questions, information concerning one or both of the quantities to be compared is centered above the two columns.
2. In a given question, a symbol that appears in both columns represents the same thing in Column A as it does in Column B.
3. Letters such as x, n, and k stand for real numbers.

	Column A	Column B
8.	$5^2 - 3^2$	2^2

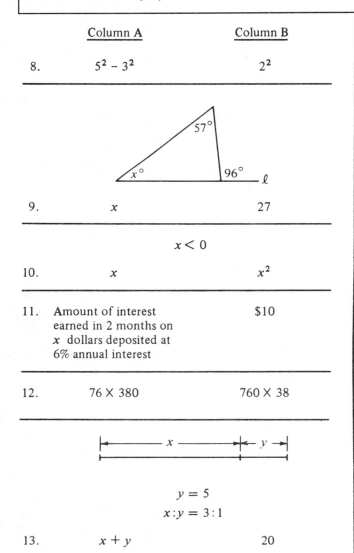

(Figure: triangle with angles $57°$, $x°$ and exterior angle $96°$ on line ℓ)

	Column A	Column B
9.	x	27

$x < 0$

	Column A	Column B
10.	x	x^2
11.	Amount of interest earned in 2 months on x dollars deposited at 6% annual interest	\$10
12.	76 X 380	760 X 38

(Figure: segment divided into lengths x and y)

$y = 5$

$x:y = 3:1$

	Column A	Column B
13.	$x + y$	20

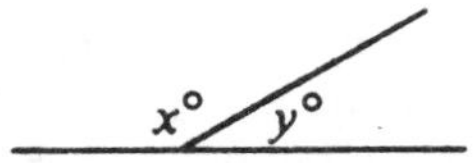

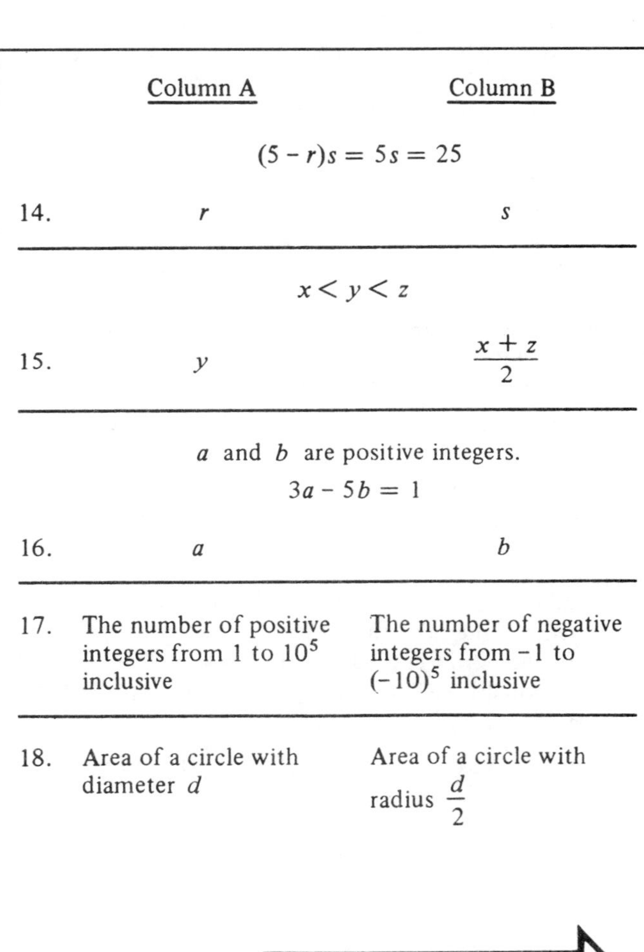

	Column A	Column B

$(5 - r)s = 5s = 25$

	Column A	Column B
14.	r	s

$x < y < z$

	Column A	Column B
15.	y	$\frac{x + z}{2}$

a and b are positive integers.

$3a - 5b = 1$

	Column A	Column B
16.	a	b
17.	The number of positive integers from 1 to 10^5 inclusive	The number of negative integers from -1 to $(-10)^5$ inclusive
18.	Area of a circle with diameter d	Area of a circle with radius $\frac{d}{2}$

GO ON TO THE NEXT PAGE

SUMMARY DIRECTIONS FOR COMPARISON QUESTIONS

Answer:
- A if the quantity in Column A is greater;
- B if the quantity in Column B is greater;
- C if the two quantities are equal;
- D if the relationship cannot be determined from the information given.

AN E RESPONSE WILL NOT BE SCORED.

	Column A	Column B

k is an integer greater than 1.

19. $k^2 + k^3$ | k^4

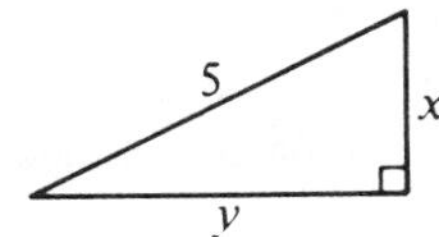

$y = 2x$

20. x | 3

21. The time it would take a car to travel 50 miles at an average speed of 55 miles per hour | The time it would take a car to travel 55 miles at an average speed of 50 miles per hour

p, q, and r are consecutive integers and $pqr = 0$.

22. The greatest of p, q, and r | 0

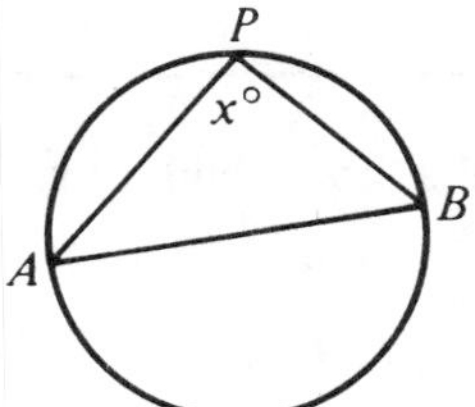

Note: Figure not drawn to scale.

AB is any chord of the circle.
P is a point on the circle.

23. x | 90

	Column A	Column B

$x \neq -1$

24. $\dfrac{4x^2 + 8x + 4}{(x + 1)^2}$ | 4

A 2-kilogram solid cube has edges of length 10 centimeters. (Assume uniform density.)

25. The length of an edge of a 4-kilogram solid cube made from the identical material | 20 centimeters

26. $\dfrac{1}{1 - (0.6)^3}$ | 1

27. The greatest power of 2 that is a factor of n, where $n = 2^2 \cdot 3 + 2^2 \cdot 7$ | The greatest power of 2 that is a factor of k, where $k = 2 \cdot 3 + 2 \cdot 5$

GO ON TO THE NEXT PAGE

Solve each of the remaining problems in this section using any available space for scratchwork. Then decide which is the best of the choices given and fill in the corresponding oval on the answer sheet.

28. If 1.39962 is rounded to the nearest thousandth, how many of its digits will remain unchanged?

(A) One (B) Two (C) Three
(D) Four (E) Five

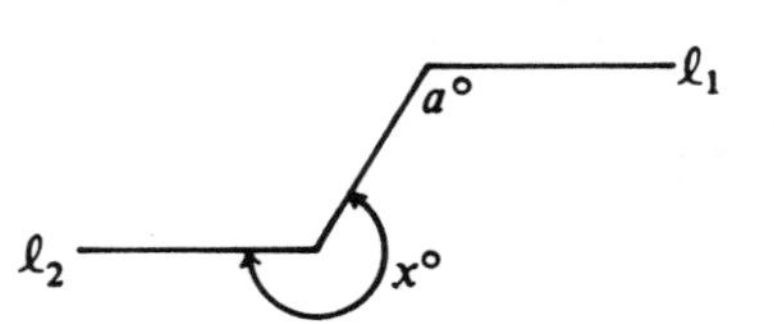

29. In the figure above, if $\ell_1 \parallel \ell_2$, what is the value of x in terms of a?

(A) $180 - a$
(B) $180 + a$
(C) $270 - a$
(D) $360 + a$
(E) $360 - a$

30. If 25 squares, each painted one of the solid colors red, green, yellow, or blue, are lined up side by side in a single row so that no two adjacent squares are the same color and there is at least one square of each color, what is the maximum possible number of blue squares?

(A) 9 (B) 10 (C) 11 (D) 12 (E) 13

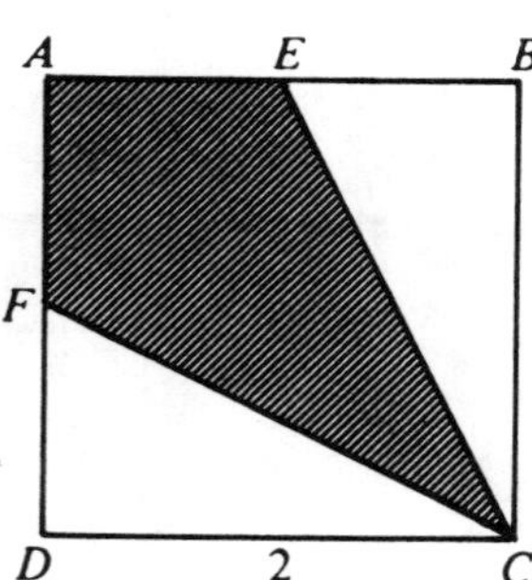

31. In the figure above, $ABCD$ is a square with side of length 2. If E is the midpoint of line segment AB and F is the midpoint of line segment AD, then the area of quadrilateral $CFAE$ is

(A) 1 (B) $\frac{3}{2}$ (C) 2 (D) $\frac{7}{2}$ (E) 4

32. What is the result when the sum of the odd integers from 1 to 29, inclusive, is subtracted from the sum of the even integers from 2 to 30, inclusive?

(A) 0
(B) 1
(C) 15
(D) 16
(E) 30

33. If k and h are constants and $x^2 + kx + 7$ factors into $(x + 1)(x + h)$, what is the value of k?

(A) 0 (B) 1 (C) 7 (D) 8
(E) It cannot be determined from the information given.

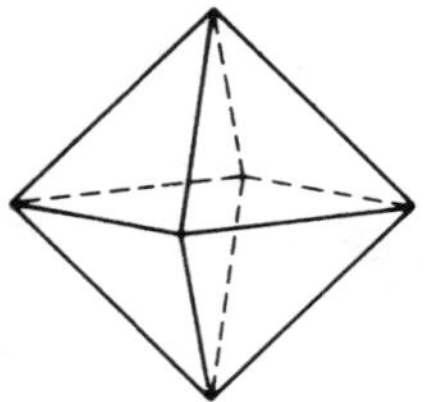

34. The octahedron shown above is a solid figure whose eight equal faces are equilateral triangles, each with perimeter 5. The sum of the lengths of all the edges of the octahedron is

(A) $13\frac{1}{3}$ (B) 20 (C) $26\frac{2}{3}$
(D) 40 (E) 60

35. It takes Bill $2m$ minutes to complete form A, which has q questions, and $3m$ minutes to complete form B, which has $\frac{1}{2}q$ questions. If Bill answers all of the questions, his average (arithmetic mean) time to answer a form B question is how many minutes longer than his average time to answer a form A question?

(A) $\frac{4m}{q}$ (B) $\frac{10m}{3q}$ (C) $\frac{2m}{q}$
(D) $3mq$ (E) $\frac{1}{2}mq$

IF YOU FINISH BEFORE TIME IS CALLED, YOU MAY CHECK YOUR WORK ON THIS SECTION ONLY. DO NOT TURN TO ANY OTHER SECTION IN THE TEST. **STOP**

SECTION 6	Time—30 minutes 45 Questions	For each question in this section, choose the best answer and fill in the corresponding oval on the answer sheet.

Each question below consists of a word in capital letters, followed by five lettered words or phrases. Choose the word or phrase that is most nearly opposite in meaning to the word in capital letters. Since some of the questions require you to distinguish fine shades of meaning, consider all the choices before deciding which is best.

Example:

GOOD: (A) sour (B) bad (C) red (D) hot (E) ugly

Ⓐ ● Ⓒ Ⓓ Ⓔ

1. RESTRAINT: (A) accuracy (B) secrecy (C) efficiency (D) freedom (E) protection

2. MUSTY: (A) fragrant (B) mobile (C) irregular (D) optional (E) tranquil

3. IRRITATE: (A) completely deny (B) apply fluid (C) strongly affect (D) work off (E) calm down

4. SUBTLE: (A) valuable (B) mellow (C) spacious (D) obvious (E) similar

5. INCENTIVE: (A) excuse (B) failure (C) discouragement (D) advice (E) interruption

6. FOCUSED: (A) distant (B) muddled (C) occasional (D) incomplete (E) proven

7. VIRTUOSO: (A) unprincipled schemer (B) unskilled beginner (C) idealistic reformer (D) staunch supporter (E) enthusiastic tutor

8. SERPENTINE: (A) serious (B) periodic (C) harsh (D) straight (E) tangential

9. CHASTEN: (A) communicate (B) reward (C) accompany (D) misjudge (E) disown

10. ORNATE: (A) nameless (B) austere (C) fragile (D) authentic (E) marred

11. ATROPHY: (A) justify (B) thrive (C) retreat (D) repel (E) insist

12. CULPABLE: (A) impossible (B) pleasing (C) insincere (D) reasonable (E) blameless

13. EFFACE: (A) entrap (B) condense (C) oppose (D) consider improper (E) make conspicuous

14. PENCHANT: (A) rigidity (B) disinclination (C) arrogance (D) levity (E) insensitivity

15. ECLECTIC: (A) of high price (B) of sound mind (C) of enormous merit (D) from concrete details (E) from one source

Each sentence below has one or two blanks, each blank indicating that something has been omitted. Beneath the sentence are five lettered words or sets of words. Choose the word or set of words that, when inserted in the sentence, best fits the meaning of the sentence as a whole.

Example:

Although its publicity has been ----, the film itself is intelligent, well-acted, handsomely produced, and altogether ----.

(A) tasteless. .respectable (B) extensive. .moderate (C) sophisticated. .amateur (D) risqué. .crude (E) perfect. .spectacular

● Ⓑ Ⓒ Ⓓ Ⓔ

16. The job allowed no relaxation, but Jackson enjoyed ---- and welcomed the challenge of dealing with the variety of problems that came across her desk every day.

(A) leisure (B) monotony (C) pressure (D) privacy (E) inertia

17. Scientists are studying the birth and growth of thunderstorms to discover what causes the difference between showers that enable crops to ---- and ---- storms that cause floods and erosion.

(A) flourish. .violent (B) wither. .damaging (C) grow. .harmless (D) parch. .severe (E) multiply. .essential

18. The ballet stage is a bright, seemingly weightless world where gravity is continually being ---- by the dancers.

(A) prolonged (B) reapportioned (C) unbalanced (D) reflected (E) defied

19. A dictatorship ---- its citizens to be docile and finds it expedient to make outcasts of those who do not ----.

(A) forces. .rebel (B) expects. .disobey (C) requires. .conform (D) allows. .withdraw (E) forbids. .agree

20. Granted that McMurphy was frequently ----, it is still hard to believe in him as a profound political or economic thinker.

(A) arbitrary (B) taciturn (C) perfunctory (D) perceptive (E) intemperate

Each passage below is followed by questions based on its content. Answer the questions following each passage on the basis of what is stated or implied in that passage.

Dr. Lloyd A. Hall (1894-1971) was a pioneer of American food chemistry, a field that burgeoned in the period between the two world wars. He was born in Elgin, Illinois, the grandson of a free Black man who settled in Chicago in 1837. Hall studied at Northwestern University and the University of Chicago, and was chief chemist and director of research at Griffith Laboratories from 1925 to his retirement in 1959.

Hall's interests in food technology and industrial chemistry were varied; he held over one hundred patents on products and methods he had invented. One area that occupied much of his research was the sterilization of foods and food additives. Even today, many people believe that spices help preserve foods. Hall found, to the contrary, that many of the spices marketed (such as cloves, cinnamon, ginger, paprika, allspice, and sage) were teeming with bacteria, molds, and yeasts. Even dried vegetables and herbs (onion powder and garlic powder) were guilty of contaminating food. Meat packers who added spices and seasonings to their meat products were actually contaminating them.

Hall undertook long and exhaustive research into the question of how to sterilize these foodstuffs effectively and at the same time preserve their appearance, quality, and flavor. Spices darkened when heated in air; they lost their flavor and aroma when subjected to evaporation or oxidation. Sterilizing spices with dry or moist heat above 240°F ruined the color and flavor of the spices so as to make them unmarketable.

After experimenting with a number of chemicals, Hall hit on ethylene oxide, a gas whose ability to kill insects was well known. Hall now used it to kill germs in foodstuffs. First, however, the chemical had to penetrate the foodstuff in order to reach the germs. This was difficult because the moisture and gases present on the surface and in the interior of the substances to be sterilized prevented the entrance of the ethylene oxide. Hall solved this problem by subjecting the foodstuff to a vacuum, a technique that removed moisture and rid the surfaces and interior of the foodstuff of any gases. In this way, the foodstuff was activated to take up the sterilizing gas. Hall then introduced the ethylene oxide into the vacuum chamber for the period of time necessary to sterilize the material; conditions of time and temperature differed according to the microorganism to be killed.

The introduction of sterilized spices to the meatpacking industry did much to revolutionize it. Hall's process was also applied to medicines, medical supplies, cosmetics, and other products. Sterilization with ethylene oxide became a very large business; Hall's method and its derivatives remain in general use today.

21. The passage is primarily concerned with

(A) describing a scientific advance achieved by Hall
(B) referring to scientific impasses that plagued Hall
(C) correcting a misconception about food preservation
(D) suggesting the breadth of Hall's career
(E) tracing the progress of food technology in this century

22. The passage suggests that, until Hall's breakthrough, all available methods of spice sterilization were impractical because they

(A) were too costly for use in mass production
(B) were suspected of posing health risks to consumers
(C) failed to yield results that were consistent
(D) made the product less attractive to the eye and palate
(E) sterilized only the surface of the spices

23. According to the passage, subjecting spices to a vacuum was crucial because this process made possible the

(A) prevention of further contamination by airborne matter
(B) extraction of the contaminants from the foodstuff
(C) precise control of conditions like time and temperature
(D) replication of the experiment by independent researchers
(E) impregnation of the foodstuff with ethylene oxide

24. It can be inferred that Hall's method for introducing ethylene oxide into foodstuffs worked because the gas

(A) occupied the spaces left vacant by the previously extracted gases and moisture
(B) was subjected to pressure many times that of the atmosphere
(C) displayed a natural affinity for any moisture-free substance
(D) became active when the temperature of the vacuum chamber was raised
(E) expanded in proportion to the time it remained in the vacuum chamber

25. The passage suggests that Hall's process was important for which of the following reasons?

I. It helped improve sanitary standards in the meat-processing industry.
II. It proved useful in areas unrelated to the food industry.
III. It enabled Hall to get funds for research into other problems.

(A) I only (B) I and II only (C) I and III only (D) II and III only (E) I, II, and III

It is only recently, in the 1930's, that parents and teachers have ceased taking childhood and adolescence for granted. Rather than press the child into an inflexible educational mold, they have at last begun to fit education to the needs of the child. To this new task they were spurred by two forces: the growth of the science of psychology and the increasing, or at least more visible, maladjustments of youth. Psychologists alerted society to its need to gain knowledge about the ways in which children develop, about the stages through which they pass, and about the kinds of behavior adults might reasonably expect of a two-month-old baby or a two-year-old child. At the same time, the fulminations from the pulpit, the loudly voiced laments of the social philosopher, the records of juvenile courts and social agencies all demanded that something be done about the stage which science had named adolescence. The growing spectacle of a younger generation rejecting respected home standards and conventional religious values was a social phenomenon that worried even the least thoughtful among us. To adults, adolescents seemed cut adrift, without anchorage.

In American civilization, with its many immigrant strains, its dozens of conflicting standards of conduct, its hundreds of religious sects, and its shifting economic conditions, this unsettled, disturbed status of youth was more apparent than in the older, more settled civilizations. American conditions challenged the psychologist, the educator, and the social philosopher to propose acceptable explanations of the plight of children as they mature. Now a great mass of literature about adolescence is flooding bookshops as theoretical psychologists try to account for the restlessness of youth. Popular works by psychologists identify the various causes of the conflict and distress felt by young people, characterizing adolescence as the period in which idealism flowers and rebellion against authority waxes strong, a period when difficulties and conflicts are absolutely inevitable.

Many experimental psychologists, however, whose work is based on empirical data, do not subscribe to these views. Instead, they claim, "We have very little data. We are only just learning when a baby's eyes will first follow a light. How can we presume to define the needs of a developed personality, about which we know nothing?"

26. The author's primary purpose in this passage is to

(A) discuss a growth of interest in the problems of adolescence
(B) call for more psychological research in the area of adolescent behavior
(C) explore the ways of dealing with the problems of adolescents
(D) examine the various sources of conflict that confront adolescents
(E) define adolescence on the basis of psychological research

27. Which of the following does the author consider a major advance resulting from the increasing awareness of the problems of adolescence?

(A) Increased sensitivity in juvenile court systems
(B) A decline in the number of psychologically disturbed youths
(C) More flexible standards in religious organizations
(D) The revision of educational practices
(E) The growing influence of experimental psychologists

28. The phrase "cut adrift, without anchorage" (lines 21-22) is used in the passage to mean that adolescents

(A) receive insufficient advice from parents
(B) thrive on rebellion and risk
(C) have difficulty earning respect from adults
(D) espouse philosophies that they will later regret
(E) have no standards to replace the ones they rejected

29. It can be inferred from the passage that experimental psychologists are more interested than theoretical psychologists in

(A) carefully examining all aspects of human behavior before attempting to draw conclusions about adolescence
(B) formulating theories about the role of the adolescent in contemporary society
(C) sincerely helping adolescents learn to identify and cope with their most profound problems
(D) administering help to individuals rather than advising groups of people
(E) observing adolescent behavior from a historical point of view

30. The author's attitude toward the problems of adolescence can best be described as one of

(A) increasing apprehension
(B) objective reflection
(C) deep-rooted frustration
(D) condescending amusement
(E) open confusion

GO ON TO THE NEXT PAGE

Select the word or set of words that best completes each of the following sentences.

31. Are we to become mere ----, watching the panorama without personal involvement, our senses dulled, our capacity to ---- undeveloped?
(A) captives. .submit (B) imitators. .observe (C) bystanders. .act (D) entertainers. .relax (E) disciples. .assist

32. Although laboratory scientists often find themselves performing routine functions, their training should indicate to them ways in which their knowledge can be applied in ---- manner.
(A) an overt (B) a practical (C) an original (D) a professional (E) a systematic

33. Because the situation called for immediate action, I ---- my natural inclination to consider the issues with ---- before making a decision.
(A) controlled. .improvidence
(B) followed. .circumspection
(C) repudiated. .expediency
(D) resisted. .deliberation
(E) accepted. .imprudence

34. In the nineteenth century many literary critics saw themselves as stern, authoritarian figures defending society against the ---- of those ---- beings called authors.
(A) depravities. .wayward
(B) atrocities. .exemplary
(C) merits. .ineffectual
(D) kudos. .antagonistic
(E) indictments. .reticent

35. Because he felt intimidated in his new position, he was ---- divulging his frank opinions of company proposals.
(A) scurrilous about (B) candid in (C) chary of (D) fervid about (E) precipitate in

Each question below consists of a related pair of words or phrases, followed by five lettered pairs of words or phrases. Select the lettered pair that best expresses a relationship similar to that expressed in the original pair.

Example:

YAWN : BOREDOM :: (A) dream : sleep (B) anger : madness (C) smile : amusement (D) face : expression (E) impatience : rebellion

Ⓐ Ⓑ ● Ⓓ Ⓔ

36. BLUEPRINT : BUILDING :: (A) trunk : tree (B) skin : hand (C) watch : time (D) photograph : camera (E) pattern : dress

37. DECISION : JUDGE :: (A) evidence : jury (B) verdict : defendant (C) examination : teacher (D) diagnosis : doctor (E) election : candidate

38. ALUMINUM : METAL :: (A) alloy : element (B) steel : tin (C) hydrogen : water (D) oxygen : gas (E) diamond : ring

39. REHEARSAL : PLAY :: (A) draft : essay (B) manual : process (C) applause : performance (D) recital : concert (E) journal : news

40. TALON : HAWK :: (A) horn : bull (B) fang : snake (C) claw : tiger (D) tail : monkey (E) shell : tortoise

41. APOLOGY : RUEFUL ::
(A) confession : inquisitive
(B) request : grateful
(C) recommendation : censorious
(D) boast : proud
(E) taunt : timid

42. DEFECTOR : CAUSE :: (A) counterfeiter : money (B) deserter : army (C) critic : book (D) advertiser : sale (E) intruder : meeting

43. STUPEFACTION : ALERT ::
(A) vexation : curious
(B) contention : grave
(C) perplexity : courteous
(D) apprehension : optimistic
(E) enlightenment : wise

44. CUPIDITY : WEALTH :: (A) affection : passion (B) intelligence : wit (C) mourning : death (D) gluttony : food (E) audacity : fear

45. TACIT : WORDS ::
(A) visible : scenes (B) inevitable : facts (C) colorful : hues (D) suspicious : clues (E) unanimous : disagreements

IF YOU FINISH BEFORE TIME IS CALLED, YOU MAY CHECK YOUR WORK ON THIS SECTION ONLY. DO NOT TURN TO ANY OTHER SECTION IN THE TEST. **STOP**

Correct Answers for Scholastic Aptitude Test Form Code 5E			
VERBAL		**MATHEMATICAL**	
Section 1	**Section 6**	**Section 3**	**Section 5**
1. A	1. D	1. A	1. A
2. C	2. A	2. D	2. E
3. E	3. E	3. E	3. A
4. D	4. D	4. A	4. D
5. B	5. C	5. B	5. E
6. E	6. B	6. B	6. B
7. B	7. B	7. C	7. B
8. C	8. D	8. B	*8. A
9. E	9. B	9. A	*9. A
10. E	10. B	10. E	*10. B
11. D	11. B	11. C	*11. D
12. B	12. E	12. A	*12. C
13. A	13. E	13. B	*13. C
14. B	14. B	14. D	*14. B
15. A	15. E	15. B	*15. D
16. D	16. C	16. D	*16. A
17. A	17. A	17. D	*17. C
18. B	18. E	18. C	*18. C
19. C	19. C	19. D	*19. B
20. E	20. D	20. C	*20. B
21. B	21. A	21. C	*21. B
22. A	22. D	22. B	*22. D
23. E	23. E	23. A	*23. D
24. B	24. A	24. E	*24. C
25. C	25. B	25. D	*25. B
26. C	26. A		*26. A
27. B	27. D		*27. B
28. C	28. E		28. A
29. A	29. A		29. E
30. E	30. B		30. E
31. C	31. C		31. C
32. C	32. C		32. C
33. D	33. D		33. D
34. E	34. A		34. B
35. B	35. C		35. A
36. D	36. E		
37. B	37. D		
38. C	38. D		
39. D	39. A		
40. A	40. C		
	41. D		
	42. B		
	43. D		
	44. D		
	45. E		

*Indicates four-choice questions. (All of the other questions are five-choice.)

The Scoring Process

Machine-scoring is done in three steps:

- *Scanning.* Your answer sheet is "read" by a scanning machine and the oval you filled in for each question is recorded on a computer tape.
- *Scoring.* The computer compares the oval filled in for each question with the correct response. Each correct answer receives one point; omitted questions do not count toward your score. For each wrong answer, a fraction of a point is subtracted to correct for random guessing. For questions with five answer choices, one-fourth of a point is subtracted for each wrong response; for questions with four answer choices, one-third of a point is subtracted for each wrong response. The SAT-verbal test has 85 questions with five answer choices each. If, for example, a student has 44 right, 32 wrong, and 9 omitted, the resulting raw score is determined as follows:

  $$44 \text{ right} - \frac{32 \text{ wrong}}{4} = 44 - 8 = 36 \text{ raw score points}$$

  Obtaining raw scores frequently involves the rounding of fractional numbers to the nearest whole number. For example, a raw score of 36.25 is rounded to 36, the nearest whole number. A raw score of 36.50 is rounded upward to 37.
- *Converting to reported scaled score.* Raw test scores are then placed on the College Board scale of 200 to 800 through a process that adjusts scores to account for minor differences in difficulty among different editions of the test. This process, known as equating, is performed so that a student's reported score is not affected by the edition of the test taken nor by the abilities of the group with whom the student takes the test. As a result of placing SAT scores on the College Board scale, scores earned by students at different times can be compared. For example, an SAT-verbal score of 400 on a test taken at one administration indicates the same level of developed verbal ability as a 400 score obtained on a different edition of the test taken at another time.

How to Score the Test

SAT-Verbal Sections 1 and 6

Step A: Count the number of correct answers for *section 1* and record the number in the space provided on the worksheet on the next page. Then do the same for the incorrect answers. (Do not count omitted answers.) To determine subtotal A, use the formula:

$$\text{number correct} - \frac{\text{number incorrect}}{4} = \text{subtotal A}$$

Step B: Count the number of correct answers and the number of incorrect answers for *section 6* and record the numbers in the spaces provided on the worksheet. To determine subtotal B, use the formula:

$$\text{number correct} - \frac{\text{number incorrect}}{4} = \text{subtotal B}$$

Step C: To obtain C, add subtotal A to subtotal B, keeping any decimals. Enter the resulting figure on the worksheet.

Step D: To obtain D, your raw verbal score, round C to the nearest whole number. (For example, any number from 44.50 to 45.49 rounds to 45.) Enter the resulting figure on the worksheet.

Step E: To find your reported SAT-verbal score, look up the total raw verbal score you obtained in step D in the conversion table on page 142. Enter this figure on the worksheet.

SAT-Mathematical Sections 3 and 5

Step A: Count the number of correct answers and the number of incorrect answers for *section 3* and record the numbers in the spaces provided on the worksheet. To determine the subtotal A, use the formula:

$$\text{number correct} - \frac{\text{number incorrect}}{4} = \text{subtotal A}$$

Step B: Count the number of correct answers and the number of incorrect answers for the *five-choice questions (questions 1 through 7 and 28 through 35) in section 5* and record the numbers in the spaces provided on the worksheet. To determine the subtotal B, use the formula:

$$\text{number correct} - \frac{\text{number incorrect}}{4} = \text{subtotal B}$$

Step C: Count the number of correct answers and the number of incorrect answers for the *four-choice questions (questions 8 through 27) in section 5* and record the numbers in the spaces provided on the worksheet. To determine the subtotal C, use the formula:

$$\text{number correct} - \frac{\text{number incorrect}}{3} = \text{subtotal C}$$

Step D: To obtain D, add subtotal A, subtotal B, and subtotal C, keeping any decimals. Enter the resulting figure on the worksheet.

Step E: To obtain E, your raw mathematical score, round D to the nearest whole number. (For example, any number from 44.50 to 45.49 rounds to 45.) Enter the resulting figure on the worksheet.

Step F: To find your reported SAT-mathematical score, look up the total raw mathematical score you obtained in E in the conversion table on page 142. Enter this figure on the worksheet.

SAT SCORING WORKSHEET

SAT-Verbal Sections

A. Section 1: ______ no. correct − ¼ (______ no. incorrect) = ______ subtotal A

B. Section 6: ______ no. correct − ¼ (______ no. incorrect) = ______ subtotal B

C. Total unrounded raw score (Total A + B) ______ C

D. Total rounded raw score (Rounded to nearest whole number) ______ D

E. SAT-verbal reported scaled score (See the conversion table on page 142.) [ ] SAT-verbal score

SAT-Mathematical Sections

A. Section 3: ______ no. correct − ¼ (______ no. incorrect) = ______ subtotal A

B. Section 5: Questions 1 through 7 and 28 through 35 (5-choice) ______ no. correct − ¼ (______ no. incorrect) = ______ subtotal B

C. Section 5: Questions 8 through 27 (4-choice) ______ no. correct − ⅓ (______ no. incorrect) = ______ subtotal C

D. Total unrounded raw score (Total A + B + C) ______ D

E. Total rounded raw score (Rounded to nearest whole number) ______ E

F. SAT-mathematical reported scaled score (See the conversion table on page 142.) [ ] SAT-math score

Score Conversion Table
Scholastic Aptitude Test
Form Code 5E

Raw Score	College Board Reported Score		Raw Score	College Board Reported Score	
	SAT-Verbal	SAT-Math		SAT-Verbal	SAT-Math
85	800		40	460	600
84	780		39	450	590
83	760		38	450	580
82	750		37	440	570
81	740		36	430	570
80	730		35	430	560
79	720		34	420	550
78	710		33	420	540
77	700		32	410	530
76	700		31	400	520
75	690		30	400	510
74	680		29	390	500
73	670		28	380	490
72	670		27	370	480
71	660		26	370	470
70	660		25	360	460
69	650		24	350	450
68	640		23	350	440
67	640		22	340	440
66	630		21	330	430
65	620		20	330	420
64	620		19	320	410
63	610		18	310	400
62	600		17	310	390
61	600		16	300	380
60	590	800	15	290	370
59	580	780	14	290	370
58	580	760	13	280	360
57	570	750	12	270	350
56	560	740	11	260	340
55	560	730	10	260	330
54	550	720	9	250	330
53	540	710	8	240	320
52	540	700	7	240	310
51	530	690	6	230	300
50	530	680	5	220	290
49	520	670	4	220	280
48	510	670	3	210	270
47	510	660	2	200	270
46	500	650	1	200	260
45	490	640	0	200	250
44	490	630	–1	200	240
43	480	620	–2	200	230
42	470	620	–3	200	220
41	470	610	–4	200	210
			–5 or below	200	200

COLLEGE BOARD — SCHOLASTIC APTITUDE TEST and Test of Standard Written English — Side 1

Use a No. 2 pencil only. Be sure each mark is dark and completely fills the intended oval. Completely erase any errors or stray marks.

1. YOUR NAME: (Print) ______ Last ______ First ______ M.I.

SIGNATURE: ______ **DATE:** ___ / ___ / ___

HOME ADDRESS: (Print) ______ Number and Street

______ City ______ State ______ Zip Code

CENTER: (Print) ______ City ______ State ______ Center Number

IMPORTANT: Please fill in items 2 and 3 exactly as shown on the back cover of your test book.

FOR ETS USE ONLY

2. TEST FORM (Copy from back cover of your test book.)

3. FORM CODE (Copy and grid as shown on back cover of your test book.)

4. REGISTRATION NUMBER (Copy from your Admission Ticket.)

5. YOUR NAME

First 4 letters of last name | First Init. | Mid. Init.

6. DATE OF BIRTH

Month | Day | Year

Jan. Feb. Mar. Apr. May June July Aug. Sept. Oct. Nov. Dec.

7. SEX

Female

Male

8. TEST BOOK SERIAL NUMBER (Copy from front cover of your test book.)

(Cut here to detach.)

Start with number 1 for each new section. If a section has fewer than 50 questions, leave the extra answer spaces blank.

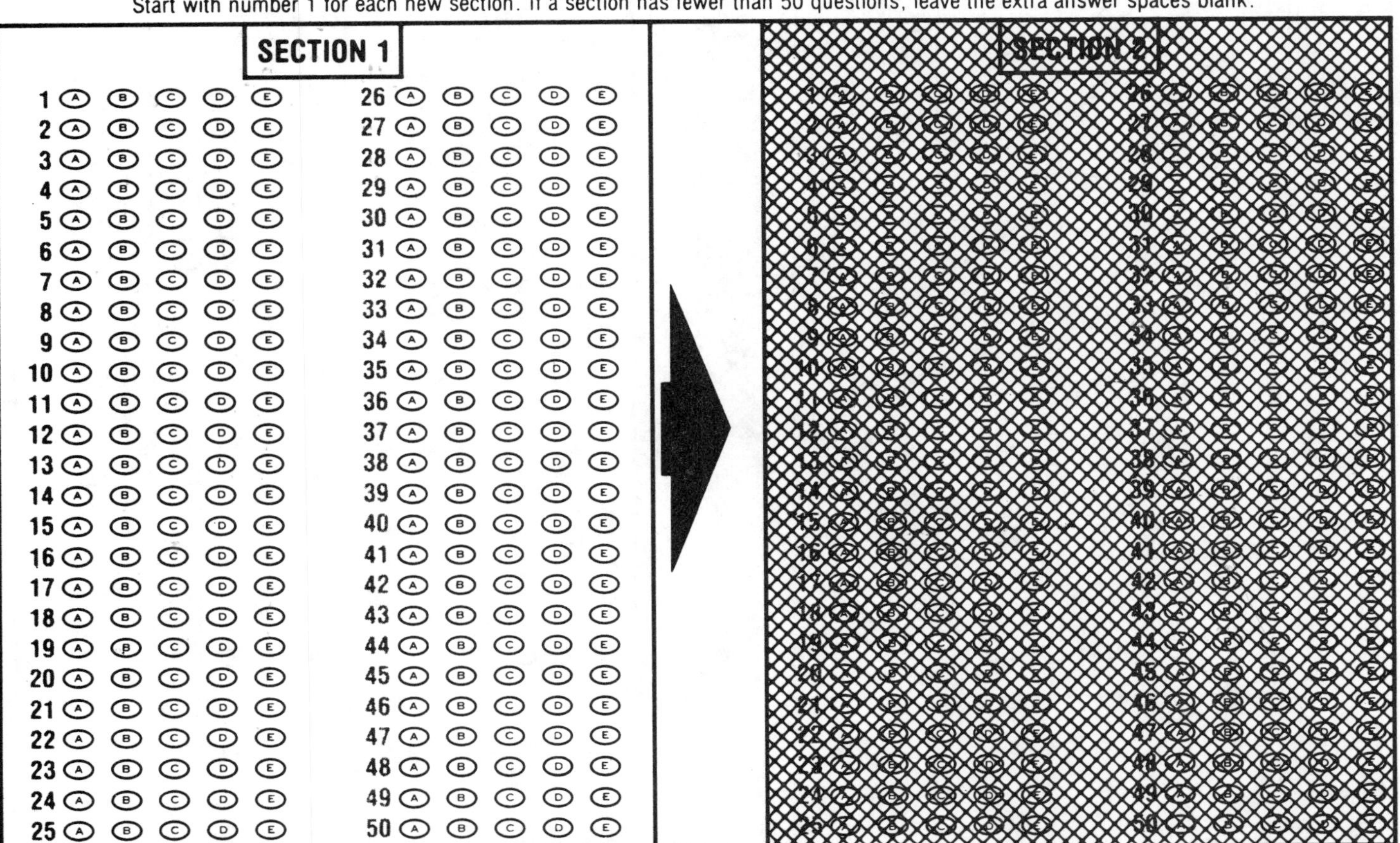

SECTION 1

SECTION 2

Q1362-04

I.N. 575008 — 110VV58P3720

COLLEGE BOARD — SCHOLASTIC APTITUDE TEST and Test of Standard Written English Side 2

Use a No. 2 pencil only. Be sure each mark is dark and completely fills the intended oval. Completely erase any errors or stray marks.

Start with number 1 for each new section. If a section has fewer than 50 questions, leave the extra answer spaces blank.

	SECTION 3	SECTION 4	SECTION 5	SECTION 6
1	A B C D E	A B C D E	A B C D E	A B C D E
2	A B C D E	A B C D E	A B C D E	A B C D E
3	A B C D E	A B C D E	A B C D E	A B C D E
4	A B C D E	A B C D E	A B C D E	A B C D E
5	A B C D E	A B C D E	A B C D E	A B C D E
6	A B C D E	A B C D E	A B C D E	A B C D E
7	A B C D E	A B C D E	A B C D E	A B C D E
8	A B C D E	A B C D E	A B C D E	A B C D E
9	A B C D E	A B C D E	A B C D E	A B C D E
10	A B C D E	A B C D E	A B C D E	A B C D E
11	A B C D E	A B C D E	A B C D E	A B C D E
12	A B C D E	A B C D E	A B C D E	A B C D E
13	A B C D E	A B C D E	A B C D E	A B C D E
14	A B C D E	A B C D E	A B C D E	A B C D E
15	A B C D E	A B C D E	A B C D E	A B C D E
16	A B C D E	A B C D E	A B C D E	A B C D E
17	A B C D E	A B C D E	A B C D E	A B C D E
18	A B C D E	A B C D E	A B C D E	A B C D E
19	A B C D E	A B C D E	A B C D E	A B C D E
20	A B C D E	A B C D E	A B C D E	A B C D E
21	A B C D E	A B C D E	A B C D E	A B C D E
22	A B C D E	A B C D E	A B C D E	A B C D E
23	A B C D E	A B C D E	A B C D E	A B C D E
24	A B C D E	A B C D E	A B C D E	A B C D E
25	A B C D E	A B C D E	A B C D E	A B C D E
26	A B C D E	A B C D E	A B C D E	A B C D E
27	A B C D E	A B C D E	A B C D E	A B C D E
28	A B C D E	A B C D E	A B C D E	A B C D E
29	A B C D E	A B C D E	A B C D E	A B C D E
30	A B C D E	A B C D E	A B C D E	A B C D E
31	A B C D E	A B C D E	A B C D E	A B C D E
32	A B C D E	A B C D E	A B C D E	A B C D E
33	A B C D E	A B C D E	A B C D E	A B C D E
34	A B C D E	A B C D E	A B C D E	A B C D E
35	A B C D E	A B C D E	A B C D E	A B C D E
36	A B C D E	A B C D E	A B C D E	A B C D E
37	A B C D E	A B C D E	A B C D E	A B C D E
38	A B C D E	A B C D E	A B C D E	A B C D E
39	A B C D E	A B C D E	A B C D E	A B C D E
40	A B C D E	A B C D E	A B C D E	A B C D E
41	A B C D E	A B C D E	A B C D E	A B C D E
42	A B C D E	A B C D E	A B C D E	A B C D E
43	A B C D E	A B C D E	A B C D E	A B C D E
44	A B C D E	A B C D E	A B C D E	A B C D E
45	A B C D E	A B C D E	A B C D E	A B C D E
46	A B C D E	A B C D E	A B C D E	A B C D E
47	A B C D E	A B C D E	A B C D E	A B C D E
48	A B C D E	A B C D E	A B C D E	A B C D E
49	A B C D E	A B C D E	A B C D E	A B C D E
50	A B C D E	A B C D E	A B C D E	A B C D E

9. SIGNATURE:

FOR ETS USE ONLY	VTR	VTFS	VRR	VRFS	VVR	VVFS	WER	WEFS	M4R	M4FS	M5R	M5FS	MTFS
	VTW	VTCS	VRW	VRCS	VVW	VVCS	WEW	WECS	M4W		M5W		MTCS

TEST 5—FORM CODE 5X

SECTION 1 — Time—30 minutes — 40 Questions

For each question in this section, choose the best answer and fill in the corresponding oval on the answer sheet.

Each question below consists of a word in capital letters, followed by five lettered words or phrases. Choose the word or phrase that is most nearly opposite in meaning to the word in capital letters. Since some of the questions require you to distinguish fine shades of meaning, consider all the choices before deciding which is best.

Example:

GOOD: (A) sour (B) bad (C) red (D) hot (E) ugly

Ⓐ ● Ⓒ Ⓓ Ⓔ

1. SWELL: (A) diminish in size (B) enrich in content (C) demote in rank (D) forbid (E) deny

2. VIGOR: (A) misfortune (B) defeat (C) weakness (D) sentiment (E) thriftiness

3. WHIM: (A) good deed (B) serious purpose (C) brief announcement (D) crude expression (E) strong argument

4. WARRANTED: (A) unbelievable (B) undetermined (C) unjustified (D) undigested (E) unmistakable

5. ADHERENT: (A) liar (B) dissenter (C) judge (D) informer (E) buffoon

6. INTERMINABLE:
(A) rudely interrupted
(B) sparsely settled
(C) repeated and monotonous
(D) short and limited
(E) swift and skillful

7. REBUFF: (A) hasten (B) waste (C) deceive (D) embrace (E) conclude

8. ABSTEMIOUS: (A) silent (B) intelligent (C) disturbed (D) gluttonous (E) skeptical

9. ESOTERIC: (A) theoretical (B) exotic (C) sane (D) symptomatic (E) obvious

10. ASSIDUOUS:
(A) idle and inattentive
(B) furtive and stealthy
(C) boring and disappointing
(D) insolent and unpopular
(E) solitary and laconic

Each sentence below has one or two blanks, each blank indicating that something has been omitted. Beneath the sentence are five lettered words or sets of words. Choose the word or set of words that, when inserted in the sentence, best fits the meaning of the sentence as a whole.

Example:

Although its publicity has been ----, the film itself is intelligent, well-acted, handsomely produced, and altogether ----.

(A) tasteless. .respectable (B) extensive. .moderate (C) sophisticated. .amateur (D) risqué. .crude (E) perfect. .spectacular

● Ⓑ Ⓒ Ⓓ Ⓔ

11. American pioneers moved west with tremendous hope, but often only ---- awaited them, given the ---- realities of the new land.

(A) excitement. .bleak (B) disillusionment. .harsh (C) success. .strenuous (D) surprise. .golden (E) failure. .abundant

12. Nontraditional use of sand paintings was first viewed by many Navaho people with dismay and is still a matter of ----.

(A) practicality (B) publicity (C) controversy (D) convenience (E) skill

13. Most of her letters to prominent Victorians have been destroyed, but those that are ---- are highly valued by scholars for their biographical content.

(A) archaic (B) literate (C) extant (D) vulnerable (E) optional

14. Under the ---- influence of current formalistic theories, thinking has lost all openness and its main aim now is to ---- preconceived ideas.

(A) contemporary. .challenge
(B) pluralistic. .surpass
(C) scrupulous. .renounce
(D) indeterminate. .appraise
(E) dogmatic. .confirm

15. Watson attributes the success of his rivals to the public's lack of ----, forgetting that his own reputation rests on the ---- of that public.

(A) insight. .hypocrisy
(B) erudition. .intervention
(C) discrimination. .approbation
(D) adventurousness. .authority
(E) information. .anticipation

GO ON TO THE NEXT PAGE

1

Each question below consists of a related pair of words or phrases, followed by five lettered pairs of words or phrases. Select the lettered pair that best expresses a relationship similar to that expressed in the original pair.

Example:

YAWN : BOREDOM :: (A) dream : sleep (B) anger : madness (C) smile : amusement (D) face : expression (E) impatience : rebellion

16. ALBUM : PHOTOGRAPHS :: (A) trial : briefs (B) board : directors (C) meeting : agendas (D) scrapbook : clippings (E) checkbook : money

17. STOMACH : DIGEST :: (A) eyes : dilate (B) muscles : cramp (C) arteries : bleed (D) teeth : chew (E) bones : break

18. SIGNATURE : CONSENT ::
(A) employment : qualification
(B) writing : publication
(C) intellect : education
(D) wave : gesture
(E) nod : agreement

19. DRILL : HOLE :: (A) air : window (B) ax : tree (C) hammer : nail (D) string : bundle (E) plow : furrow

20. SEETHE : ANGER :: (A) smile : shame (B) writhe : nonchalance (C) precede : event (D) view : vision (E) glow : happiness

21. MOLT : FEATHERS :: (A) shear : wool (B) shed : hair (C) lop : branches (D) drop : stitch (E) fur : pelt

22. INDEFATIGABLE : ENERGY :: (A) hopeful : success (B) steadfast : loyalty (C) courageous : anxiety (D) careless : safety (E) aggressive : exuberance

23. ACCLAIM : ADMIRER :: (A) imitate : leader (B) rehearse : performer (C) censure : denouncer (D) destroy : bungler (E) inquire : accuser

24. GARRULOUS : TALK ::
(A) extravagant : spend
(B) loquacious : joke
(C) enthusiastic : stimulate
(D) antagonistic : retreat
(E) ruthless : sympathize

25. ACTORS : TROUPE :: (A) criminals : coterie (B) demagogues : junta (C) politicians : clique (D) scientists : equipment (E) soldiers : phalanx

GO ON TO THE NEXT PAGE

Each passage below is followed by questions based on its content. Answer the questions following each passage on the basis of what is stated or implied in that passage.

Human blood cells originate within the bone marrow, in a highly complicated process, at the rate of hundreds of billions of cells a day. Both red and white blood cells – along with colorless, disc-shaped particles called platelets – are suspended in an amber fluid called plasma. Scientists have learned how to generate these blood cells outside the human body, using a living mouse as a "factory."

The "mouse factory" system was developed in a laboratory where scientists constructed a device called a diffusion chamber. The sides of the chamber were made of fine filter paper with openings too small for cells to escape, but large enough to let fluid in. Human bone marrow cells, which form blood cells, were placed in the chamber which was then implanted inside the mouse's abdominal cavity. There it floated surrounded by all the vital fluids and nutrients necessary for cell growth. In a few weeks millions of blood cells were grown in this living laboratory, each one eventually differentiating into one of the various types found in normal bone marrow.

Not only does this chamber system permit scientists to study more closely the complex blood-forming activities that go on deep inside bone marrow, but it also may ultimately lead to improved treatment of blood diseases by providing more information about their origin. The chamber method may someday be a useful means of transplanting marrow in patients afflicted by such diseases as leukemia, a cancer of the blood-forming tissue, and anemia, a disease marked by a deficiency of red blood cells.

26. The main point of the passage is to

(A) debate the advantages and disadvantages of the "mouse factory"
(B) examine the role of laboratory mice in experiments
(C) discuss a technique for studying blood cell formation
(D) explain the role of human blood cells
(E) give an example of cell transplantation from a human to an animal

27. According to the passage, which of the following statements about human blood cells is true?

(A) They are a vital constituent of plasma.
(B) They are indistinguishable from platelets.
(C) They cannot exist outside of the human body.
(D) They are disc-shaped and colorless.
(E) They are produced in the bone marrow.

28. According to the author, the possible future benefits of the diffusion chamber include all of the following EXCEPT

(A) information about the causes of certain blood diseases
(B) data on blood cell formation in bone marrow
(C) treatment for some blood-related diseases
(D) reproduction of more complex types of human cells
(E) transplantation of bone marrow into humans

GO ON TO THE NEXT PAGE

The reading passages in this test are brief excerpts or adaptations of excerpts from published material. The ideas contained in them do not necessarily represent the opinions of the College Board or Educational Testing Service. To make the text suitable for testing purposes, we may in some cases have altered the style, contents, or point of view of the original.

I am making this statement as an act of willful defiance of military authority, because I believe that the war is being deliberately prolonged by those who have the power to end it. I am a soldier, convinced that I am acting on behalf of soldiers. I believe that this war, upon which I entered as a war of defense and liberation, has now become a war of aggression and conquest. I believe that the purposes for which I and my fellow soldiers entered upon this war should have been so clearly stated as to have made it impossible to change them. Had this been done, surely the goals which motivated our mobilization would now be attainable by negotiation. I have seen and endured the sufferings of the troops, and I can no longer be a party to the prolonging of these sufferings for ends which I believe to be evil and unjust. I am not protesting against the military leaders who conduct the war, but against the political leaders whose errors and hypocrisies cheapen the sacrifices of our fighting men. For the sake of those lives which are being sacrificed even as I write, I make this protest against the deception practiced upon all our fighting men. I also hope that my protest may help to destroy the callous complacency with which the majority of those at home regard the continuation of agonies which do not touch them and which they have not sufficient imagination to realize.

29. The passage suggests that the author would support which of the following views?

I. Soldiers should not be forced to defend a cause they see as wrong.
II. War should be recognized as immoral because of the suffering it causes.
III. Foreign policies set by a few should not be blindly accepted by all.

(A) I only (B) III only (C) I and II only (D) I and III only (E) I, II, and III

30. According to the author, which of the following is true of the politicians in charge of the war?

(A) They have been dishonest about their goals and have acted incompetently.
(B) They have shown far too little concern for public opinion.
(C) They lack both experience and enthusiasm.
(D) They need to establish their independence from military authority.
(E) They need to put greater effort into motivating the troops to fight.

31. If the author were to continue the passage, which of the following additional statements would best support the charge of "callous complacency" (lines 24-25) brought against the civilian population?

(A) There can be no doubt that the majority of the public shares my opposition to the war.
(B) It is often difficult to prove either public complacency or public concern.
(C) Whenever I hear people discuss the war, their criticisms are negative, never constructive.
(D) Editorialists and public speakers rarely ask why we are fighting the war.
(E) When soldiers are home on leave, they are often seen mingling with civilians.

32. The author's presentation is marked by an element of

(A) callousness (B) didacticism (C) sentimentalism (D) opportunism (E) fatalism

GO ON TO THE NEXT PAGE

Certain individuals, usually called professors, are charged with the duty of examining the construction of the plants, animals, and soils which are the instruments of a great orchestra. Each professor selects one instrument and spends his or her career taking it apart and describing its strings and sounding board, a process of dismemberment called research.

Professors may pluck the strings of their own instruments but never those of another, and if they listen for the music their instruments make, they must do so in secret. They are restrained by an ironbound taboo that decrees that the construction of instruments is the domain of science, while the detection of harmony is the domain of poets.

Of course, professors serve science and science serves progress—so well, in fact, that many intricate instruments are stepped upon and broken in the rush to spread progress around the world.

Science obviously contributes moral as well as material blessings to the world. Its great moral contribution is the scientific point of view, which, in essence, means doubting everything except facts. One of the facts cherished by science is the belief that every river needs more people, and all people need more inventions, and hence more science. The good life, according to science, depends on the indefinite extension of this chain of logic. That the good life on any river may likewise depend on the perception and preservation of its music largely has escaped the notice of science.

33. The "great orchestra" (line 4) is used as a metaphor for

(A) human nature
(B) a large university
(C) the natural world
(D) the aesthetic aspects of music
(E) the intricacy of scientific research

34. The author apparently views the "chain of logic" (line 28) as

(A) logically persuasive
(B) morally uplifting
(C) theoretically intricate
(D) scientifically impractical
(E) potentially dangerous

35. Which of the following best states the main idea of the passage?

(A) There are important similarities between the scientific method and the creation of music.
(B) The scientific method provides only a partial understanding of nature.
(C) If material progress is to continue, scientists must ignore the allure of the poetic.
(D) Material progress is destructive and attempts to further it should be stopped.
(E) Professors of the arts as well as the sciences must emphasize the teaching of scientific logic.

GO ON TO THE NEXT PAGE

As Newman passed on with his host he asked who the Duchess might be. "The greatest lady in France!" the Marquis hereupon reservedly replied. He then presented his prospective brother-in-law to some twenty other persons of both sexes, selected apparently for some recognized value of name or fame or attitude. In some cases their honors were written in a good round hand on the countenance of the wearer; in others Newman was thankful for such help as his companion's impressively brief intimation contributed to the discovery of them. Every one gave Newman extreme attention, every one lighted up for him regardless, as he would have said, of expense, every one was enchanted to make his acquaintance, every one looked at him with that fraudulent intensity of good society which puts out its bountiful hand but keeps the fingers closed over the coin. If the Marquis was going about as a bear-leader, if the fiction of Beauty and the Beast was supposed to show thus its companion piece, the general impression appeared that the bear was a very fair imitation of humanity.

It was handsome to be treated with so much explicit politeness, of course. It was handsome to meet civilities as pointed as witticisms, and to hear them so syllabled and articulated that they suggested handfuls of crisp counted notes pushed over by a banker's clerk. It was handsome of clever Frenchwomen—they all seemed clever—to turn their backs to their partners for a good look at the slightly gaunt outsider whom Claire de Cintré was to marry, and then shine on the subject as if they quite understood.

At last Newman caught the eye of the Marquis fixed on him inscrutably, and checked himself. "Am I behaving like a blamed fool?" he wondered. "Am I stepping about like a terrier on its hind legs?" At this moment he perceived Mrs. Tristram at the other side of the room and made his way to her.

"Am I holding my head too high and opening my mouth too wide?" he demanded. "Do I look as if they were saying 'Catch!' and I were snapping down what they throw me and licking my lips?"

"You look like all very successful men—fatuous without knowing it. Women triumph with more tact, just as they suffer with more grace. I've been watching you for the last ten minutes, and I've been watching M. de Bellegarde. He doesn't like what he has to do."

"The more credit to him for putting it through," Newman returned. "But I shall be generous. I shan't trouble him any more. Only I'm very happy. I can't stand still here. Please take my arm and we'll go for a walk."

36. The passage indicates that one purpose of the reception is to

(A) introduce the Marquis to Newman's acquaintances
(B) introduce Newman to acquaintances of the Marquis
(C) celebrate Newman's engagement to Mrs. Tristram
(D) celebrate Newman's arrival in France
(E) honor the Marquis on his birthday

37. According to the passage, Newman considers the people at the reception to be all of the following EXCEPT

(A) sophisticated (B) genuinely cordial (C) faultlessly proper (D) attentive (E) flattering

38. Which of the following best conveys the meaning of the statement "their honors were written in a good round hand on the countenance of the wearer" (lines 7-9)?

(A) They looked candid and cheerful.
(B) Their behavior was elegant and proper.
(C) They introduced themselves in a respectful manner.
(D) Their expressions all began to seem equally dignified and aloof.
(E) Their importance was obvious to any observer.

39. The questions that Newman addresses to Mrs. Tristram reveal his

(A) unease (B) cleverness (C) arrogance (D) anger (E) incautiousness

40. Which of the following can be inferred from the passage about Claire de Cintré and the Marquis?

(A) Neither is particularly comfortable in the company at the reception.
(B) It is unusual for them both to be found at the same party.
(C) They were formerly married to one another.
(D) They are sister and brother.
(E) They are daughter and father.

IF YOU FINISH BEFORE TIME IS CALLED, YOU MAY CHECK YOUR WORK ON THIS SECTION ONLY. DO NOT TURN TO ANY OTHER SECTION IN THE TEST. **STOP**

SECTION 3	Time—30 minutes 25 Questions	In this section solve each problem, using any available space on the page for scratchwork. Then decide which is the best of the choices given and fill in the corresponding oval on the answer sheet.

The following information is for your reference in solving some of the problems.

Circle of radius r: Area $= \pi r^2$; Circumference $= 2\pi r$
The number of degrees of arc in a circle is 360.
The measure in degrees of a straight angle is 180.

Definition of symbols:
$=$ is equal to
$\neq$ is unequal to
$<$ is less than
$>$ is greater than
$\leq$ is less than or equal to
$\geq$ is greater than or equal to
$\parallel$ is parallel to
$\perp$ is perpendicular to

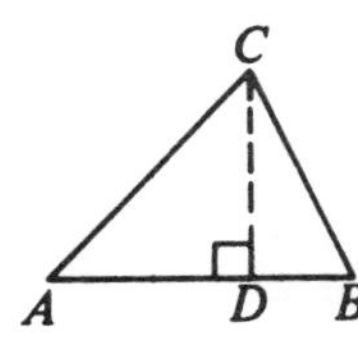

Triangle: The sum of the measures in degrees of the angles of a triangle is 180.
If $\angle CDA$ is a right angle, then

(1) area of $\triangle ABC = \frac{AB \times CD}{2}$

(2) $AC^2 = AD^2 + DC^2$

Note: Figures that accompany problems in this test are intended to provide information useful in solving the problems. They are drawn as accurately as possible EXCEPT when it is stated in a specific problem that its figure is not drawn to scale. All figures lie in a plane unless otherwise indicated. All numbers used are real numbers.

1. If $\frac{1}{x+1} = \frac{1}{2}$, then $x =$

(A) 2 (B) 1 (C) 0 (D) -1 (E) -2

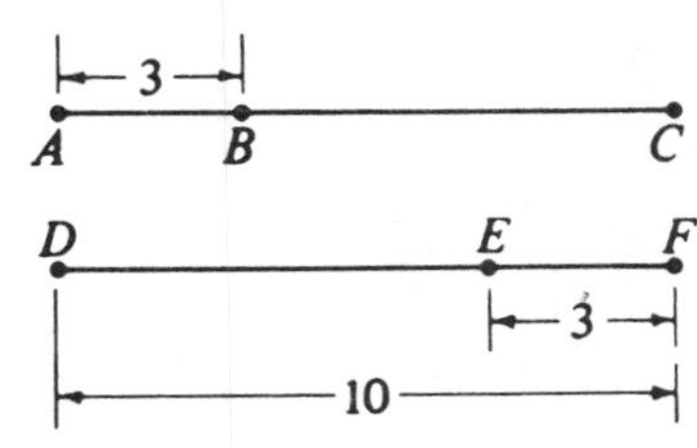

2. In the figure above, if $AC = DF = 10$, then $BC + DE =$

(A) 6 (B) 7 (C) 13 (D) 14 (E) 17

3. $\dfrac{2+3+6}{\frac{1}{2}+\frac{1}{3}+\frac{1}{6}} =$

(A) 3
(B) 11
(C) 49
(D) 66
(E) 121

4. If $x = -3$, then $(x+3)^2 - 3x =$

(A) -6 (B) -3 (C) 0 (D) 6 (E) 9

5. $\frac{2}{4} \times \frac{3}{6} \times \frac{4}{8} \times \frac{5}{10} =$

(A) $\frac{1}{2}$ (B) $\frac{1}{4}$ (C) $\frac{1}{8}$ (D) $\frac{1}{16}$ (E) $\frac{1}{32}$

6. What is 10 percent of 20 percent of $\frac{3}{2}$?

(A) 0.003
(B) 0.03
(C) 0.045
(D) 0.45
(E) 0.6

7. If $2^y = 8$ and $y = \frac{x}{2}$, then $x =$

(A) 6 (B) 5 (C) 4 (D) 3 (E) 2

GO ON TO THE NEXT PAGE

$$\begin{array}{r} 7X \\ +X1 \\ \hline 1Y7 \end{array}$$

8. The correct addition problem above shows the sum of two 2-digit numbers. If X and Y represent different nonzero digits, then $Y =$

(A) 1 (B) 3 (C) 6 (D) 7 (E) 8

9. What is the least number of squares with area 9 needed to cover completely, without overlap, a square with side of length 9 ?

(A) 2 (B) 3 (C) 4 (D) 9 (E) 12

10. Which of the following equations are equivalent?

I. $2x + 4y = 8$
II. $3x + 6y = 12$
III. $4x + 8y = 8$
IV. $6x + 12y = 16$

(A) I and II only
(B) I and III only
(C) II and III only
(D) II and IV only
(E) I, II, and III

11. If the length of a rectangle is $x + 1$ and its area is 1, which of the following must be its width?

(A) 1

(B) $\frac{1}{2}$

(C) $\frac{1}{1-x}$

(D) $\frac{1}{x}$

(E) $\frac{1}{1+x}$

12. All numbers divisible by both 4 and 15 are also divisible by which of the following?

(A) 6
(B) 8
(C) 18
(D) 24
(E) 45

TEMPERATURES IN CITY X ON DECEMBER 6	
6 a.m.	10° below zero
8 a.m.	2° below zero
10 a.m.	15° above zero

13. The average (arithmetic mean) of the temperatures shown in the table above is

(A) 2° below zero
(B) 1° below zero
(C) 1° above zero
(D) 3° above zero
(E) 5° above zero

14. A uniform rate of 720 flicks per revolution and 20 revolutions per hour is the same as a rate of how many flicks per second?

(A) 4
(B) 5
(C) 24
(D) 36
(E) 240

GO ON TO THE NEXT PAGE

15. If the average (arithmetic mean) of 7 numbers is $7n$, then in terms of n the sum of these 7 numbers is

(A) $\frac{n}{7}$ (B) $7n$ (C) $\frac{49}{n}$ (D) $\frac{n}{49}$ (E) $49n$

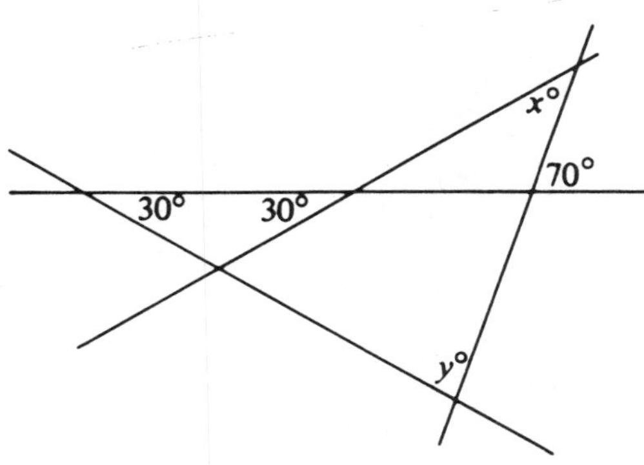

16. If four lines intersect as shown in the figure above, what is the value of $x + y$?

(A) 140 (B) 130 (C) 120
(D) 110 (E) 100

17. If $x > 1$, the value of which of the following expressions must increase as x increases?

I. $1 - \frac{1}{x}$

II. $\sqrt{x}$

III. $\frac{1}{x^2}$

(A) I only (B) II only (C) I and II only
(D) II and III only (E) I, II, and III

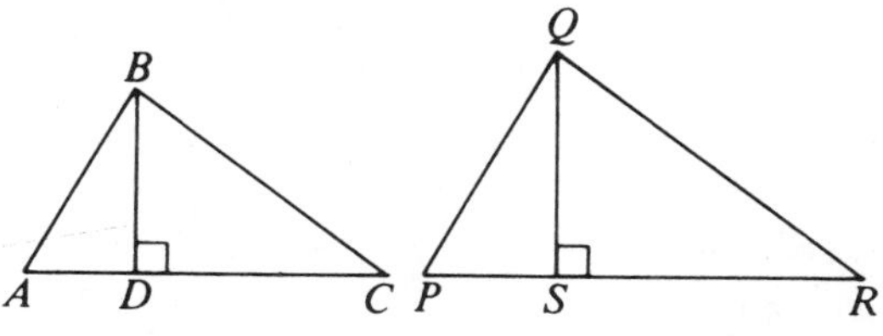

Note: Figures not drawn to scale.

18. The length of side PR of $\triangle PQR$ is 3 times the length of side AC of $\triangle ABC$. If the length of QS is twice the length of BD, the area of $\triangle PQR$ is how many times the area of $\triangle ABC$?

(A) $\frac{2}{3}$ (B) $\frac{3}{2}$ (C) 3 (D) 5 (E) 6

19. If the tenth number in a list of numbers is 27 and if each number after the first number in the list is 5 less than the number immediately preceding it, what is the fifth number in the list?

(A) 72
(B) 52
(C) 47
(D) 7
(E) 2

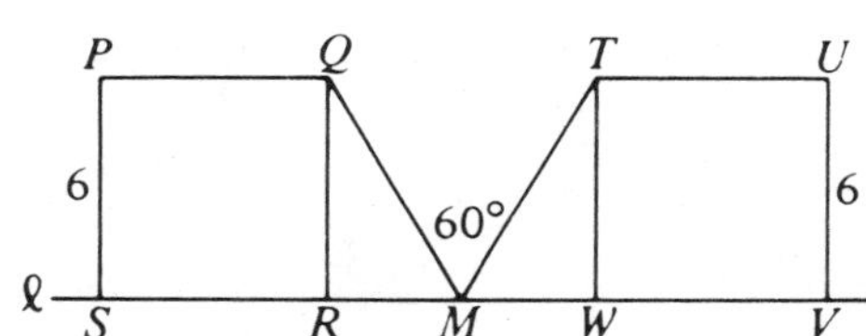

20. The figure above shows squares $PQRS$ and $TUVW$, each with side of length 6, that lie on line ℓ. If $RM = MW$, then $RW =$

(A) $2\sqrt{3}$ (B) 6 (C) $4\sqrt{3}$
(D) $6\sqrt{2}$ (E) 10

GO ON TO THE NEXT PAGE

21. A well 100 meters deep is drilled at the base of a mountain 1,000 meters high whose peak is 2,000 meters above sea level. How many meters above sea level is the bottom of the well?

(A) 900
(B) 1,000
(C) 1,100
(D) 1,900
(E) 2,100

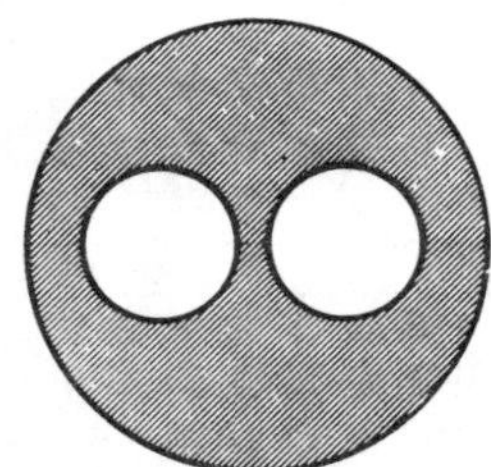

22. In the figure above, if the radii of the two smaller circles are each equal to $\frac{1}{3}$ of the radius of the larger circle, then the ratio $\frac{\text{area of shaded region}}{\text{area of larger circle}} =$

(A) $\frac{8}{9}$ (B) $\frac{7}{9}$ (C) $\frac{2}{3}$ (D) $\frac{4}{9}$ (E) $\frac{1}{3}$

23. The daytime telephone rate between two cities is 90 cents for the first 3 minutes and c cents for each additional minute. The total charge is reduced 65 percent on calls made after 11:00 p.m. The cost in <u>dollars</u> of a 30-minute call made after 11:00 p.m. between these two cities is

(A) $0.35(0.90) + 27c$
(B) $0.35(0.90 + 0.27c)$
(C) $0.35(0.90 + 9c)$
(D) $0.65(0.90 + 27c)$
(E) $0.65(0.90 + 0.30c)$

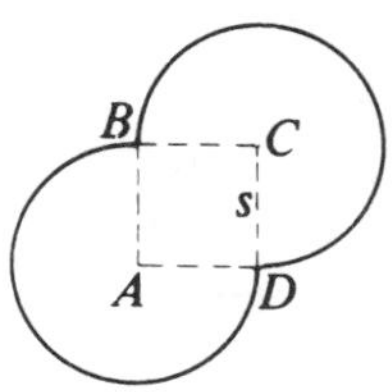

24. The figure above shows portions of two circles with centers at A and C, respectively, and square $ABCD$ with side of length s. What is the perimeter of the curved figure in terms of s?

(A) $\frac{4}{3}\pi s$ (B) $\frac{3}{2}\pi s$ (C) $2\pi s$

(D) $3\pi s$ (E) $4\pi s$

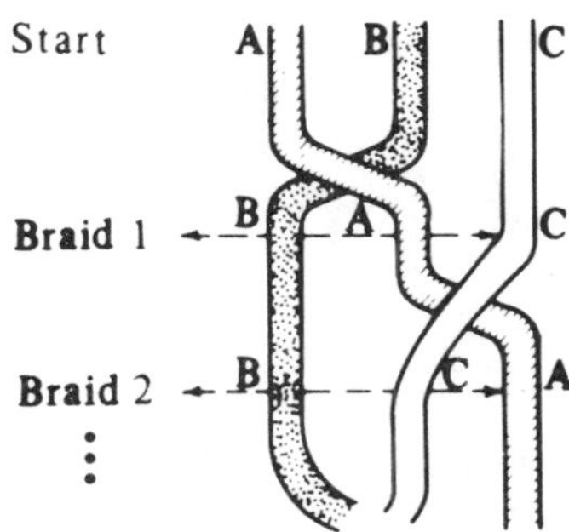

25. In the figure above, three wires are braided. That is, by starting in the order A, B, C, the outer left wire A is brought over wire B to the middle position forming the order shown in braid 1, then the outer right wire C is brought to the new middle position forming the order shown in braid 2, and so on, alternately bringing each new left and right wire to the middle. What is the number of the braid (not shown) that first repeats the original order A, B, C ?

(A) 3 (B) 4 (C) 5 (D) 6 (E) 7

IF YOU FINISH BEFORE TIME IS CALLED, YOU MAY CHECK YOUR WORK ON THIS SECTION ONLY. DO NOT TURN TO ANY OTHER SECTION IN THE TEST. **STOP**

SECTION 5 — Time—30 minutes, 35 Questions

In this section solve each problem, using any available space on the page for scratchwork. Then decide which is the best of the choices given and fill in the corresponding oval on the answer sheet.

The following information is for your reference in solving some of the problems.

Circle of radius r: Area $= \pi r^2$; Circumference $= 2\pi r$
The number of degrees of arc in a circle is 360.
The measure in degrees of a straight angle is 180.

Definition of symbols:

$=$ is equal to	$\leqq$ is less than or equal to
$\neq$ is unequal to	$\geqq$ is greater than or equal to
$<$ is less than	$\parallel$ is parallel to
$>$ is greater than	$\perp$ is perpendicular to

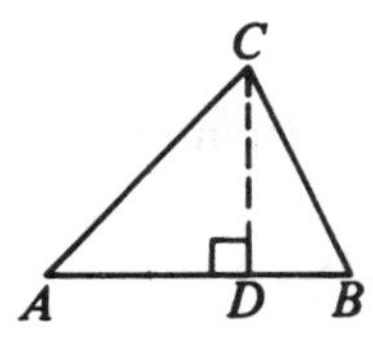

Triangle: The sum of the measures in degrees of the angles of a triangle is 180.
If $\angle CDA$ is a right angle, then

(1) area of $\triangle ABC = \dfrac{AB \times CD}{2}$

(2) $AC^2 = AD^2 + DC^2$

Note: Figures that accompany problems in this test are intended to provide information useful in solving the problems. They are drawn as accurately as possible EXCEPT when it is stated in a specific problem that its figure is not drawn to scale. All figures lie in a plane unless otherwise indicated. All numbers used are real numbers.

1. Of the following, which product is greatest?

(A) $22 \times 22 \times 222$
(B) $22 \times 22 \times 22$
(C) $2 \times 2 \times 22 \times 222$
(D) $2 \times 222 \times 22$
(E) $2 \times 2 \times 2 \times 2 \times 2 \times 2$

2. The following are coordinates of points in the XY-plane. Which of these points is nearest the origin?

(A) $(0, -1)$
(B) $\left(0, \frac{1}{2}\right)$
(C) $\left(\frac{1}{2}, -\frac{1}{2}\right)$
(D) $\left(\frac{1}{2}, \frac{1}{2}\right)$
(E) $(-1, -1)$

3. If 100 grams is half the mass of one object and twice the mass of another, the mass of the heavier object is how many grams more than the mass of the lighter object?

(A) 50
(B) 75
(C) 100
(D) 150
(E) 200

$A = \{3, 6, 9\}$
$B = \{5, 7, 9\}$
$C = \{7, 8, 9\}$

4. If three different numbers are selected, one from each of the sets shown above, what is the greatest sum that these three numbers could have?

(A) 22 (B) 23 (C) 24 (D) 25 (E) 27

5. How many different integer pairs (x, y) satisfy the equation $\dfrac{x}{y} = \dfrac{1}{2}$?

(A) One (B) Two (C) Three (D) Four
(E) More than four

6. If $3x + y = 18$ and x is an odd positive integer, which of the following must be true?

I. y is an odd integer.
II. y is a positive integer.
III. y is a multiple of 3.

(A) I only (B) II only (C) III only
(D) I and III (E) II and III

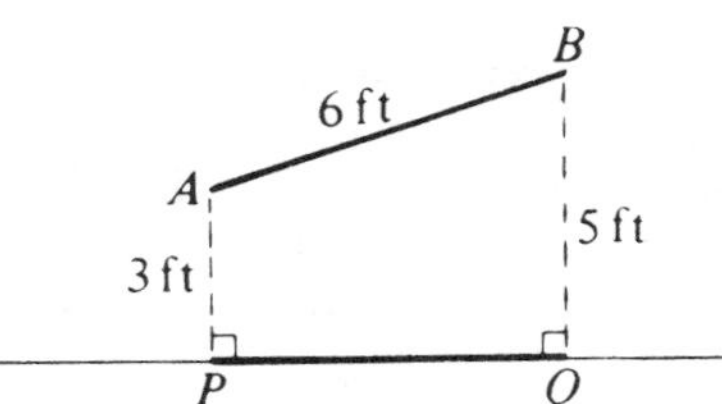

7. In the figure above, a straight stick AB casts a shadow PQ on a flat table. What is the length, in feet, of PQ?

(A) 4 (B) 4.5 (C) 5
(D) $3\sqrt{3}$ (E) $4\sqrt{2}$

GO ON TO THE NEXT PAGE

5

Questions 8-27 each consist of two quantities, one in Column A and one in Column B. You are to compare the two quantities and on the answer sheet fill in oval

- **A** if the quantity in Column A is greater;
- **B** if the quantity in Column B is greater;
- **C** if the two quantities are equal;
- **D** if the relationship cannot be determined from the information given.

AN E RESPONSE WILL NOT BE SCORED.

EXAMPLES

	Column A	Column B	Answers
E1.	2×6	$2 + 6$	● Ⓑ Ⓒ Ⓓ Ⓔ
	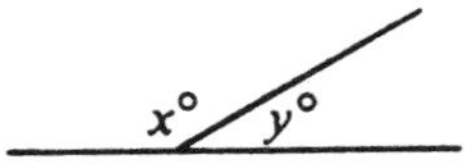		
E2.	$180 - x$	y	Ⓐ Ⓑ ● Ⓓ Ⓔ
E3.	$p - q$	$q - p$	Ⓐ Ⓑ Ⓒ ● Ⓔ

Notes:

1. In certain questions, information concerning one or both of the quantities to be compared is centered above the two columns.
2. In a given question, a symbol that appears in both columns represents the same thing in Column A as it does in Column B.
3. Letters such as x, n, and k stand for real numbers.

	Column A	Column B
8.	$-2(-8)$	$-2 + (-8)$

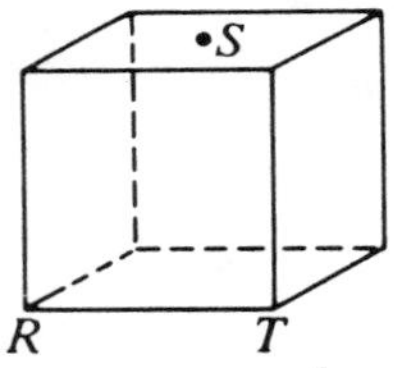

Point S is at the center of the top face of the cube.

	Column A	Column B
9.	The distance from S to R	The distance from S to T
10.	$2^2 + 3^2$	5^2

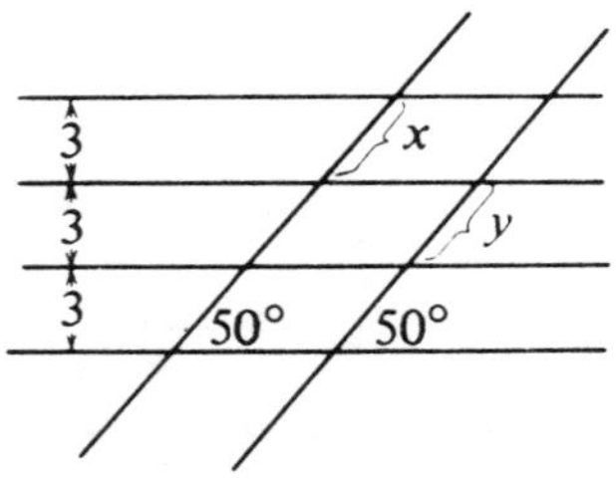

Four parallel lines are intersected by two other lines.

	Column A	Column B
11.	$\frac{y}{x}$	$\frac{x}{y}$

	Column A	Column B

7 less than $3x$ is 53.

12.	x	18

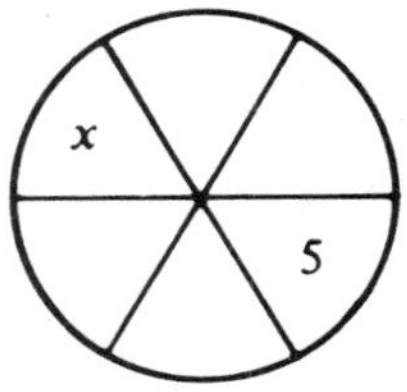

Each of the six sectors in the circle above is assigned a number such that the sum of the numbers in any two sectors adjacent to each other is 9.

13.	x	5

GO ON TO THE NEXT PAGE

SUMMARY DIRECTIONS FOR COMPARISON QUESTIONS

Answer:
A if the quantity in Column A is greater;
B if the quantity in Column B is greater;
C if the two quantities are equal;
D if the relationship cannot be determined from the information given.

AN E RESPONSE WILL NOT BE SCORED.

	Column A	Column B
	$y > x$ $y < -2$	
14.	x	0
15.	The result after rounding 2.481 to the nearest tenth	The result after rounding 2.493 to the nearest tenth
	The ratio of men to women in a room is $\frac{4}{5}$.	
16.	The total number of men and women in the room	9
	$n = 27$	
17.	The tens' digit of the product $10n$	5
	Let the operation ϕ have the property that $x \phi y = y \phi x$. $1 \phi 2 = 6$	
18.	$2 \phi 1$	7
	Rose has more money than Juanita, Juanita has less money than Sam, and Sam has less money than Rose.	
19.	Amount of money Rose has	The combined total of the amounts that Sam and Juanita have
	$(r + 6)(r + k) = r^2 + 9r + 18$	
20.	k	6
	In a bag containing exactly 200 marbles, 30 are white, 60 are black, and the remainder are red.	
21.	The percent of marbles in the bag that are red	60%

	Column A	Column B
	The perimeter of equilateral triangle T is equal to the perimeter of square S.	
22.	Length of a side of T	Length of a side of S
23.	$\frac{4.02}{0.2}$	$\frac{402}{20}$
	n is a positive integer and $n(n + 1)(n + 2) = 210$.	
24.	$n + 1$	7
	A box contains a number of discs each marked with a number less than 10. A disc is chosen without looking.	
25.	The probability of choosing a disc numbered 4 from the box	The probability of choosing a disc numbered 5 from the box

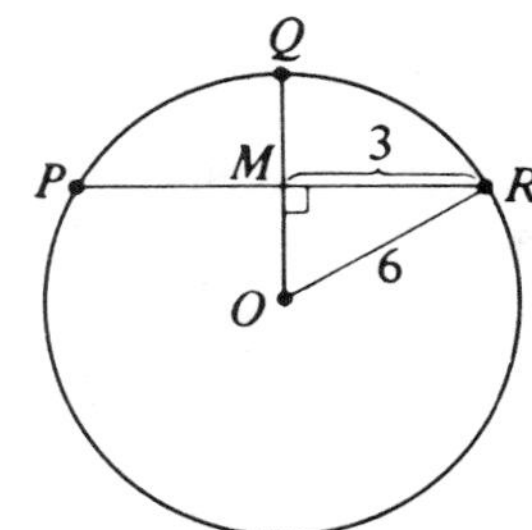

Note: Figure not drawn to scale.

P, Q, and R are points on the circle with center O. PR and OQ are line segments.

	Column A	Column B
26.	The length of OM	The length of MQ

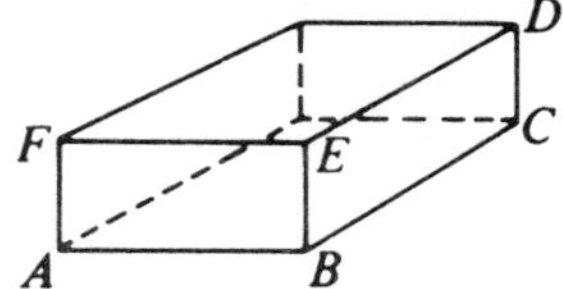

Note: Figure not drawn to scale.

The area of face $ABEF$ of the rectangular solid is 12 and the area of face $BCDE$ is 8.

	Column A	Column B
27.	The volume of the rectangular solid	24

GO ON TO THE NEXT PAGE

Solve each of the remaining problems in this section using any available space for scratchwork. Then decide which is the best of the choices given and fill in the corresponding oval on the answer sheet.

28. Of the following, the least number is

(A) $-\frac{1}{10}$ (B) $-\frac{1}{100}$ (C) $-\frac{11}{1,000}$

(D) $-\frac{1}{9}$ (E) $\frac{1}{1,000}$

29. What is the total value, in cents, of x coins worth 5 cents each and $x + 7$ coins worth 10 cents each?

(A) $15x + 70$ (B) $15x + 7$ (C) $10x + 75$

(D) $6x + 7$ (E) $2x + 7$

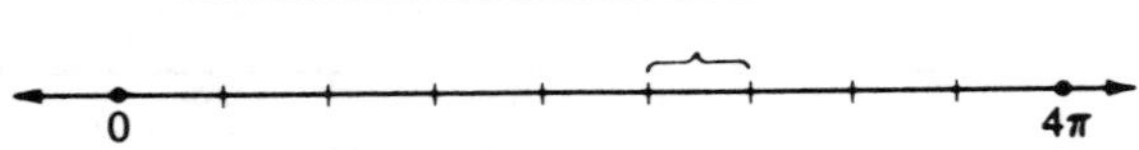

30. On the number line shown, the segment from 0 to 4π is divided into 9 intervals of equal length. Which of the following numbers would be in the sixth interval indicated above?

(A) $\frac{4\pi}{3}$ (B) $\frac{13\pi}{7}$ (C) 2π (D) $\frac{12\pi}{5}$ (E) 3π

31. If a plane intersects a cube, which of the following can be the shape of the intersection?

I. A rectangle
II. A quadrilateral with exactly two parallel sides
III. A triangle

(A) None (B) I only (C) III only

(D) I and II only (E) I, II, and III

32. If $(5.5 \times 10^2) \times (8.0 \times 10^3) = 4.4 \times 10^y$, then $y =$

(A) 2
(B) 3
(C) 4
(D) 5
(E) 6

33. If $\overset{\frown}{x}$ represents the area of a semicircle with diameter x, then $\overset{\frown}{2} + \overset{\frown}{4} =$

(A) $\overset{\frown}{3}$

(B) $\overset{\frown}{5}$

(C) $\overset{\frown}{3\sqrt{2}}$

(D) $\overset{\frown}{2\sqrt{5}}$

(E) $\overset{\frown}{6}$

34. Two partners divide a profit of \$3,000 so that the difference between the two amounts is $\frac{1}{3}$ of their average (arithmetic mean). What is the ratio of the larger to the smaller amount?

(A) 7:5 (B) 5:1 (C) 4:3

(D) 3:2 (E) 3:1

35. If $0 < p < r$ and if p is equal to $\frac{3}{10}$ of r, then r is what percent <u>more</u> than p?

(A) 30% (B) $33\frac{1}{3}$% (C) 70%

(D) 230% (E) $233\frac{1}{3}$%

IF YOU FINISH BEFORE TIME IS CALLED, YOU MAY CHECK YOUR WORK ON THIS SECTION ONLY. DO NOT TURN TO ANY OTHER SECTION IN THE TEST. **STOP**

SECTION 6	Time—30 minutes 45 Questions	For each question in this section, choose the best answer and fill in the corresponding oval on the answer sheet.

Each question below consists of a word in capital letters, followed by five lettered words or phrases. Choose the word or phrase that is most nearly opposite in meaning to the word in capital letters. Since some of the questions require you to distinguish fine shades of meaning, consider all the choices before deciding which is best.

Example:

GOOD: (A) sour (B) bad (C) red (D) hot (E) ugly

Ⓐ ● Ⓒ Ⓓ Ⓔ

1. SUMMON: (A) link together (B) send away (C) remain calm (D) subtract (E) promote

2. HARMONY: (A) injustice (B) conflict (C) weakness (D) deception (E) omission

3. TRIVIA: (A) actual values (B) original sources (C) individual cases (D) expected results (E) important matters

4. FUSE: (A) destroy (B) burn (C) preserve (D) divide (E) scald

5. HEFTY: (A) wise (B) slight (C) cheerful (D) cooperative (E) indecisive

6. OPPORTUNE: (A) inappropriately timed (B) illegally transported (C) indefinite (D) invariable (E) incredible

7. FLUID: (A) dull (B) ruddy (C) jerky (D) drowsy (E) growing

8. ABBREVIATE: (A) foretell (B) protract (C) perfect (D) proceed (E) arrange

9. QUIESCENT: (A) secretive (B) active (C) mannerly (D) spiritual (E) miniature

10. DIMINUTION: (A) classification (B) escalation (C) brightness (D) separation (E) consciousness

11. EXCISE: (A) reply (B) clarify (C) illuminate (D) insert (E) comply

12. HIGH-HANDED: (A) thrifty (B) solemn (C) servile (D) eccentric (E) dishonest

13. CENSURE: (A) excite (B) repay (C) increase (D) expedite (E) praise

14. CIRCUMSPECT: (A) lonely (B) selfish (C) reckless (D) powerful (E) remorseful

15. PENURY: (A) haste (B) silence (C) enmity (D) apathy (E) opulence

Each sentence below has one or two blanks, each blank indicating that something has been omitted. Beneath the sentence are five lettered words or sets of words. Choose the word or set of words that, when inserted in the sentence, best fits the meaning of the sentence as a whole.

Example:

Although its publicity has been ----, the film itself is intelligent, well-acted, handsomely produced, and altogether ----.

(A) tasteless. . respectable (B) extensive. . moderate (C) sophisticated. . amateur (D) risqué. . crude (E) perfect. . spectacular

● Ⓑ Ⓒ Ⓓ Ⓔ

16. The government attempts to protect farm laborers from the ---- of pesticides through warning labels printed in several languages.

(A) uses (B) shock (C) degrees (D) dangers (E) crime

17. Investigation of the epidemic involved determining what was ---- about the people who were affected, what made them differ from those who remained well.

(A) chronic (B) unique (C) fortunate (D) misunderstood (E) historical

18. She announced that, because the company is financially hard-pressed, ---- at all levels is ----.

(A) austerity. .urged
(B) paucity. .avoidable
(C) bankruptcy. .maintained
(D) luxury. .predicted
(E) sacrifice. .discouraged

19. We can never know what is ---- until we have tried without success to avoid it.

(A) futile (B) inevitable (C) fallacious (D) inconstant (E) expedient

20. Cunningham is no ----; on the contrary, there is a certain ---- in his acceptance of the political pieties of our time.

(A) rebel. .defiance
(B) conformist. .apathy
(C) zealot. .complacency
(D) conservative. .orderliness
(E) hypocrite. .deceptiveness

GO ON TO THE NEXT PAGE

6

Each passage below is followed by questions based on its content. Answer the questions following each passage on the basis of what is stated or implied in that passage.

Benjamin Banneker, mathematician, astronomer, clock-maker, and surveyor, was born a free Black man in Maryland in 1731. Among Banneker's extraordinary accomplishments was a series of almanacs, the first of which he published in 1791. A study of his journal of astronomy and a comparison of his notes with his published almanacs provide a revealing documentation of how he taught himself astronomy. A reader who is willing to do some work can detect the occasional errors Banneker made and can also see how, in the laborious process of self-instruction, he was able to correct them.

An ephemeris, or astronomical almanac, is calculated from a series of basic computations required to establish the positions of the Sun, Moon, and planets each year; these computations then become the basis for other calculations. A comparison of Banneker's manuscript journal with his published ephemerides reveals his method. First, he had to make a reckoning of the calendar, one of the major preoccupations of the almanac-maker. He then entered the times of sunrise and sunset, and listed the important religious and noteworthy days of each month in an outline he had previously prepared. No basis can be identified for the method Banneker used for weather predictions, since no working notes or clues relating to them have survived. Before proceeding with the remainder of the calculations, Banneker customarily awaited the arrival of the new edition of the *Nautical Almanac*, from which he extracted some of his preliminary data.

The vast amount of work required to calculate an eclipse made Banneker's accomplishments all the more impressive. He had to make at least sixty-eight mathematical calculations to produce the ten elements required to construct a single eclipse diagram. Banneker learned to conserve his efforts by making constructions only for eclipses visible in the Baltimore-Washington area in which his almanacs would be sold. After all the eclipses for a particular year had been calculated, he drew and labeled each with a descriptive statement that would be inserted in the published almanac.

Before venturing to make his own calculations, a competent philomath must have mastered a good deal of the text of an authoritative writer on the subject, such as Ferguson or Leadbetter. Banneker had the work of both available to him. He suffered from an embarrassment of riches, however, because of the conflicting instructions occasionally presented by the two authors for the same type of computation.

The contents of Banneker's journal and notes are unique records of an eighteenth-century almanac-maker, as they provide a clear exposition of the method by which almanacs were calculated during this period of American scientific history.

21. Which of the following titles best summarizes the content of the passage?

(A) How to Calculate an Eclipse
(B) The History of Almanac-Making in America
(C) The Life and Work of Benjamin Banneker
(D) Benjamin Banneker's Influence on Eighteenth-Century Astronomy
(E) Astronomical Endeavors of Benjamin Banneker

22. According to the author, Banneker's technique for predicting weather was not described in the passage because

(A) weather predictions were not accurate in the eighteenth century
(B) weather conditions were not considered astronomical phenomena during Banneker's time
(C) no record remains of Banneker's method for predicting weather
(D) Banneker used other almanacs as the source of his information about the weather
(E) no weather predictions were included in Banneker's almanacs

23. According to the information in the passage, which of the following statements about Leadbetter and Ferguson is true?

(A) They were overrated as authorities on astronomy.
(B) They did not know about each other's work.
(C) They did not agree on certain matters of methodology.
(D) They were less meticulous in their calculations than was Banneker.
(E) They were more concerned with eclipses than with other aspects of astronomy.

24. Banneker's notes and journal would probably be particularly useful to a person interested in doing research on which of the following?

I. Scientific discoveries during the eighteenth century
II. The development of astronomy in the United States
III. Eighteenth-century almanacs

(A) II only (B) III only (C) I and II only
(D) I and III only (E) II and III only

25. The author apparently regards Banneker's skills as an almanac-maker as

(A) extraordinary, because Banneker had no formal training in astronomy
(B) innovative, because Banneker adapted his work to the needs of a particular geographic region
(C) minimal, because Banneker sometimes relied on other almanacs
(D) amateurish, because of the errors Banneker made in his calculations
(E) commonplace, because many people in the eighteenth century made weather predictions

But is there, as certain continental critics have insisted, an "American novel," a specific subvariety of the form? If we turn to these critics for a definition, we come on such terms as "neorealist," "hard-boiled," "naive," and "anti-traditional"—terms derived from a standard view of America as an "anticulture," an eternally maintained preserve of primitivism. This view (notoriously exemplified by André Gide) ends by finding in Dashiell Hammett the same values as in William Faulkner, and is more a symptom of European cultural malaise than a useful critical distinction. It is tempting to insist on the pat rebuttal that, far from being an anticulture, we are merely a branch of Western culture, and that there is no "American novel," only local variants of the standard European kinds of fiction: American sentimental, American gothic, American historical romance, etc. Certainly no single subgenre of the novel was invented in the United States. Yet the peculiarities of our variants seem more interesting and important than their resemblances to the parent forms.

There is a real sense in which our prose fiction is immediately distinguishable from that of Europe, though this is a fact that is difficult for Americans (oddly defensive and flustered in its presence) to confess. In this sense, our novels seem not primitive, perhaps, but innocent, unfallen in a disturbing way, almost juvenile. Many great works of American fiction are notoriously at home in the children's section of the library, their level of sentimentality precisely that of a preadolescent. That is part of what we mean when we talk about the incapacity of American novelists to develop; in a compulsive way they return to a limited world of experience, usually associated with childhood, writing the same books over and over again until they lapse into silence or self-parody.

Merely finding a language, learning to talk in a land where there are no conventions of conversation, no special class idioms, and no dialogue between classes, no continuing literary language—this exhausts American writers. They are forever beginning, saying for the first time (without real tradition there can never be a second time) what it is like to stand alone before nature, or in a city as appallingly lonely as any virgin forest. They face, moreover, another problem, which has resulted in a failure of feeling and imagination perceptible at the heart of even our most notable works. Our great novelists, though experts on indignity and assault, on loneliness and terror, tend to avoid treating the passionate encounter of a man and woman, which we expect at the center of a novel. Indeed they rather shy away from permitting in their fictions the presence of any full-fledged mature woman.

26. Which of the following questions is the author most interested in discussing in the passage?

(A) Why do American writers reflect an "anti-culture"?
(B) What are the unique characteristics of the American novel?
(C) How is the American novel similar to the European novel?
(D) Have European critics reacted favorably to American novels?
(E) Which subgenres of the novel are most respected by American critics?

27. The author suggests which of the following about André Gide's criticism of the American novel?

(A) It is based on a study of too few American novelists.
(B) It includes a useful definition of the novel.
(C) It is not typical of most continental critics.
(D) It denies the differences between European and American novels.
(E) It is a reflection of his background.

28. According to the author, which of the following topics is (are) often treated by American novelists?

I. Adult passion
II. Youthful experience
III. Social class struggles

(A) II only
(B) I and II only
(C) I and III only
(D) II and III only
(E) I, II, and III

29. According to the author, the American novelist is hampered by

(A) a desire to imitate European writers
(B) the structural demands of the novel form
(C) an inability to portray dignified characters
(D) the ignorance or antagonism of literary critics in America
(E) a lack of distinct differences in speech patterns among American classes

30. Which of the following best describes the author's attitude toward American writers in the last sentence of the passage?

(A) Boastful (B) Prudish (C) Pedantic (D) Nostalgic (E) Disparaging

GO ON TO THE NEXT PAGE

6

Select the word or set of words that best completes each of the following sentences.

31. Despite the efforts of conservationists to save the tiger, many biologists sadly agree that this ---- has probably come too late.

(A) prospect (B) problem (C) knowledge (D) concern (E) assessment

32. The ---- treatment necessitated by the study's broad geographical scope makes it ---- for the reader to understand thoroughly any particular African custom.

(A) superficial. .difficult
(B) purposeful. .superfluous
(C) scholarly. .imperative
(D) supplementary. .rewarding
(E) eloquent. .critical

33. Overindulgence, fatigue, and worry are the three ---- of civilization that probably do most to ---- the natural defenses of the body.

(A) products. .sustain (B) enemies. .influence (C) victims. .damage (D) delinquents. .exploit (E) concomitants. .undermine

34. Most people will struggle mightily to stop change, or at least to ---- its effects on them.

(A) enhance (B) initiate (C) distort (D) defend (E) mitigate

35. Cut adrift from the structured authority ---- the whole ritual of grading and certification, certain faculty members saw the new program as a monumental ---- in which nothing was any longer considered sacred.

(A) afforded by. .heresy
(B) counteracted by. .fantasy
(C) anchored to. .preservation
(D) relieved by. .hoax
(E) attributed to. .relic

Each question below consists of a related pair of words or phrases, followed by five lettered pairs of words or phrases. Select the lettered pair that best expresses a relationship similar to that expressed in the original pair.

Example:

YAWN : BOREDOM :: (A) dream : sleep (B) anger : madness (C) smile : amusement (D) face : expression (E) impatience : rebellion

Ⓐ Ⓑ ● Ⓓ Ⓔ

36. ICE PACK : SWELLING :: (A) magnet : attraction (B) tourniquet : bleeding (C) bulb : illumination (D) thermometer : fever (E) funnel : pouring

37. NOVELIST : FICTION :: (A) detective : crime (B) carpenter : lumber (C) aggression : dominance (D) composer : music (E) book : pages

38. ILLOGICAL : CONFUSION ::
(A) profound : laughter
(B) revolting : sympathy
(C) astounding : amazement
(D) obscure : contrast
(E) deliberate : vitality

39. THIMBLE : FINGER :: (A) apron : clothes (B) ruler : line (C) bracelet : ring (D) saw : wood (E) needle : thread

40. SHORTHAND : RAPIDITY :: (A) typing : diligence (B) stenography : aptitude (C) art : simplicity (D) paper : penmanship (E) code : secrecy

41. DOODLE : DRAW :: (A) coddle : pamper (B) meddle : interfere (C) waddle : run (D) prattle : talk (E) protest : argue

42. CLOSEFISTED : SKINFLINT :: (A) inane : scapegoat (B) immoral : daredevil (C) impetuous : hothead (D) irresolute : spitfire (E) inarticulate : busybody

43. VOLATILE : VAPORIZED :: (A) oily : dried (B) edible : wilted (C) concave : curved (D) diverse : concentrated (E) combustible : ignited

44. CONTRACTION : LETTER ::
(A) period : sentence
(B) retraction : complaint
(C) explanation : understanding
(D) ellipsis : word
(E) compromise : agreement

45. DELETERIOUS : HARM :: (A) menacing : tranquillity (B) voluntary : coercion (C) suspicious : guilt (D) wearisome : fatigue (E) meritorious : wealth

IF YOU FINISH BEFORE TIME IS CALLED, YOU MAY CHECK YOUR WORK ON THIS SECTION ONLY. DO NOT TURN TO ANY OTHER SECTION IN THE TEST. **STOP**

Correct Answers for Scholastic Aptitude Test Form Code 5X

VERBAL		MATHEMATICAL	
Section 1	**Section 6**	**Section 3**	**Section 5**
1. A	1. B	1. B	1. A
2. C	2. B	2. D	2. B
3. B	3. E	3. B	3. D
4. C	4. D	4. E	4. C
5. B	5. B	5. D	5. E
6. D	6. A	6. B	6. D
7. D	7. C	7. A	7. E
8. D	8. B	8. B	*8. A
9. E	9. B	9. D	*9. C
10. A	10. B	10. A	*10. B
11. B	11. D	11. E	*11. C
12. C	12. C	12. A	*12. A
13. C	13. E	13. C	*13. B
14. E	14. C	14. A	*14. B
15. C	15. E	15. E	*15. C
16. D	16. D	16. C	*16. D
17. D	17. B	17. C	*17. A
18. E	18. A	18. E	*18. B
19. E	19. B	19. B	*19. D
20. E	20. C	20. C	*20. B
21. B	21. E	21. A	*21. B
22. B	22. C	22. B	*22. A
23. C	23. C	23. B	*23. C
24. A	24. E	24. D	*24. B
25. E	25. A	25. D	*25. D
26. C	26. B		*26. A
27. E	27. E		*27. D
28. D	28. A		28. D
29. D	29. E		29. A
30. A	30. E		30. D
31. D	31. D		31. E
32. B	32. A		32. E
33. C	33. E		33. D
34. E	34. E		34. A
35. B	35. A		35. E
36. B	36. B		
37. B	37. D		
38. E	38. C		
39. A	39. A		
40. D	40. E		
	41. D		
	42. C		
	43. E		
	44. D		
	45. D		

*Indicates four-choice questions. (All of the other questions are five-choice.)

The Scoring Process

Machine-scoring is done in three steps:

- *Scanning.* Your answer sheet is "read" by a scanning machine and the oval you filled in for each question is recorded on a computer tape.
- *Scoring.* The computer compares the oval filled in for each question with the correct response. Each correct answer receives one point; omitted questions do not count toward your score. For each wrong answer, a fraction of a point is subtracted to correct for random guessing. For questions with five answer choices, one-fourth of a point is subtracted for each wrong response; for questions with four answer choices, one-third of a point is subtracted for each wrong response. The SAT-verbal test has 85 questions with five answer choices each. If, for example, a student has 44 right, 32 wrong, and 9 omitted, the resulting raw score is determined as follows:

$$44 \text{ right} - \frac{32 \text{ wrong}}{4} = 44 - 8 = 36 \text{ raw score points}$$

  Obtaining raw scores frequently involves the rounding of fractional numbers to the nearest whole number. For example, a raw score of 36.25 is rounded to 36, the nearest whole number. A raw score of 36.50 is rounded upward to 37.
- *Converting to reported scaled score.* Raw test scores are then placed on the College Board scale of 200 to 800 through a process that adjusts scores to account for minor differences in difficulty among different editions of the test. This process, known as equating, is performed so that a student's reported score is not affected by the edition of the test taken nor by the abilities of the group with whom the student takes the test. As a result of placing SAT scores on the College Board scale, scores earned by students at different times can be compared. For example, an SAT-verbal score of 400 on a test taken at one administration indicates the same level of developed verbal ability as a 400 score obtained on a different edition of the test taken at another time.

How to Score the Test

SAT-Verbal Sections 1 and 6

Step A: Count the number of correct answers for *section 1* and record the number in the space provided on the worksheet on the next page. Then do the same for the incorrect answers. (Do not count omitted answers.) To determine subtotal A, use the formula:

$$\text{number correct} - \frac{\text{number incorrect}}{4} = \text{subtotal A}$$

Step B: Count the number of correct answers and the number of incorrect answers for *section 6* and record the numbers in the spaces provided on the worksheet. To determine subtotal B, use the formula:

$$\text{number correct} - \frac{\text{number incorrect}}{4} = \text{subtotal B}$$

Step C: To obtain C, add subtotal A to subtotal B, keeping any decimals. Enter the resulting figure on the worksheet.

Step D: To obtain D, your raw verbal score, round C to the nearest whole number. (For example, any number from 44.50 to 45.49 rounds to 45.) Enter the resulting figure on the worksheet.

Step E: To find your reported SAT-verbal score, look up the total raw verbal score you obtained in step D in the conversion table on page 166. Enter this figure on the worksheet.

SAT-Mathematical Sections 3 and 5

Step A: Count the number of correct answers and the number of incorrect answers for *section 3* and record the numbers in the spaces provided on the worksheet. To determine the subtotal A, use the formula:

$$\text{number correct} - \frac{\text{number incorrect}}{4} = \text{subtotal A}$$

Step B: Count the number of correct answers and the number of incorrect answers for the *five-choice questions (questions 1 through 7 and 28 through 35) in section 5* and record the numbers in the spaces provided on the worksheet. To determine the subtotal B, use the formula:

$$\text{number correct} - \frac{\text{number incorrect}}{4} = \text{subtotal B}$$

Step C: Count the number of correct answers and the number of incorrect answers for the *four-choice questions (questions 8 through 27) in section 5* and record the numbers in the spaces provided on the worksheet. To determine the subtotal C, use the formula:

$$\text{number correct} - \frac{\text{number incorrect}}{3} = \text{subtotal C}$$

Step D: To obtain D, add subtotal A, subtotal B, and subtotal C, keeping any decimals. Enter the resulting figure on the worksheet.

Step E: To obtain E, your raw mathematical score, round D to the nearest whole number. (For example, any number from 44.50 to 45.49 rounds to 45.) Enter the resulting figure on the worksheet.

Step F: To find your reported SAT-mathematical score, look up the total raw mathematical score you obtained in E in the conversion table on page 166. Enter this figure on the worksheet.

SAT SCORING WORKSHEET

SAT-Verbal Sections

A. Section 1: ________ no. correct − ¼ (________ no. incorrect) = ________ subtotal A

B. Section 6: ________ no. correct − ¼ (________ no. incorrect) = ________ subtotal B

C. Total unrounded raw score (Total A + B) ________ C

D. Total rounded raw score (Rounded to nearest whole number) ________ D

E. **SAT-verbal reported scaled score (See the conversion table on page 166.)** [ ] SAT-verbal score

SAT-Mathematical Sections

A. Section 3: ________ no. correct − ¼ (________ no. incorrect) = ________ subtotal A

B. Section 5: Questions 1 through 7 and 28 through 35 (5-choice) ________ no. correct − ¼ (________ no. incorrect) = ________ subtotal B

C. Section 5: Questions 8 through 27 (4-choice) ________ no. correct − ⅓ (________ no. incorrect) = ________ subtotal C

D. Total unrounded raw score (Total A + B + C) ________ D

E. Total rounded raw score (Rounded to nearest whole number) ________ E

F. **SAT-mathematical reported scaled score (See the conversion table on page 166.)** [ ] SAT-math score

Score Conversion Table
Scholastic Aptitude Test
Form Code 5X

Raw Score	College Board Reported Score SAT-Verbal	College Board Reported Score SAT-Math	Raw Score	College Board Reported Score SAT-Verbal	College Board Reported Score SAT-Math
85	800		40	460	620
84	780		39	460	610
83	770		38	450	600
82	760		37	440	590
81	750		36	440	580
80	740		35	430	570
79	730		34	430	560
78	720		33	420	550
77	710		32	410	540
76	700		31	410	530
75	690		30	400	520
74	680		29	390	510
73	670		28	390	500
72	660		27	380	490
71	650		26	370	490
70	640		25	370	480
69	630		24	360	470
68	630		23	350	460
67	620		22	350	450
66	610		21	340	440
65	610		20	330	430
64	600		19	330	420
63	600		18	320	410
62	590		17	310	410
61	580		16	310	400
60	580	800	15	300	390
59	570	790	14	300	380
58	570	780	13	290	370
57	560	770	12	280	370
56	560	760	11	280	360
55	550	750	10	270	350
54	540	740	9	270	340
53	540	730	8	260	330
52	530	720	7	250	330
51	530	710	6	250	320
50	520	700	5	240	310
49	520	700	4	230	300
48	510	690	3	230	290
47	500	680	2	220	290
46	500	670	1	210	280
45	490	660	0	200	270
44	490	650	−1	200	260
43	480	640	−2	200	250
42	480	630	−3	200	240
41	470	620	−4	200	230
			−5	200	230
			−6	200	220
			−7	200	210
			−8 or below	200	200

COLLEGE BOARD — SCHOLASTIC APTITUDE TEST and Test of Standard Written English **Side 1**

Use a No. 2 pencil only. Be sure each mark is dark and completely fills the intended oval. Completely erase any errors or stray marks.

1. YOUR NAME: (Print) ______ Last ______ First ______ M.I.

SIGNATURE: ______ **DATE:** ___ / ___ / ___

HOME ADDRESS: (Print) ______ Number and Street

______ City ______ State ______ Zip Code

CENTER: (Print) ______ City ______ State ______ Center Number

5. YOUR NAME

First 4 letters of last name | First Init. | Mid. Init.

A B C D E F G H I J K L M N O P Q R S T U V W X Y Z

IMPORTANT: Please fill in items 2 and 3 exactly as shown on the back cover of your test book.

FOR ETS USE ONLY

2. TEST FORM (Copy from back cover of your test book.)

3. FORM CODE (Copy and grid as shown on back cover of your test book.)

0 1 2 3 4 5 6 7 8 9 | A B C D E F G H I | J K L M N O P Q R | S T U V W X Y Z | 0 1 2 3 4 5 6 7 8 9 | 0 1 2 3 4 5 6 7 8 9 | 0 1 2 3 4 5 6 7 8 9

4. REGISTRATION NUMBER (Copy from your Admission Ticket.)

0 1 2 3 4 5 6 7 8 9 (seven columns)

6. DATE OF BIRTH

Month	Day		Year	
Jan.				
Feb.				
Mar.	0	0	0	0
Apr.	1	1	1	1
May	2	2	2	2
June	3	3	3	3
July		4	4	4
Aug.		5	5	5
Sept.		6	6	6
Oct.		7	7	7
Nov.		8		8
Dec.		9		9

7. SEX

Female

Male

8. TEST BOOK SERIAL NUMBER (Copy from front cover of your test book.)

Start with number 1 for each new section. If a section has fewer than 50 questions, leave the extra answer spaces blank.

SECTION 1

1 A B C D E
2 A B C D E
3 A B C D E
4 A B C D E
5 A B C D E
6 A B C D E
7 A B C D E
8 A B C D E
9 A B C D E
10 A B C D E
11 A B C D E
12 A B C D E
13 A B C D E
14 A B C D E
15 A B C D E
16 A B C D E
17 A B C D E
18 A B C D E
19 A B C D E
20 A B C D E
21 A B C D E
22 A B C D E
23 A B C D E
24 A B C D E
25 A B C D E
26 A B C D E
27 A B C D E
28 A B C D E
29 A B C D E
30 A B C D E
31 A B C D E
32 A B C D E
33 A B C D E
34 A B C D E
35 A B C D E
36 A B C D E
37 A B C D E
38 A B C D E
39 A B C D E
40 A B C D E
41 A B C D E
42 A B C D E
43 A B C D E
44 A B C D E
45 A B C D E
46 A B C D E
47 A B C D E
48 A B C D E
49 A B C D E
50 A B C D E

SECTION 2

1 A B C D E
2 A B C D E
3 A B C D E
4 A B C D E
5 A B C D E
6 A B C D E
7 A B C D E
8 A B C D E
9 A B C D E
10 A B C D E
11 A B C D E
12 A B C D E
13 A B C D E
14 A B C D E
15 A B C D E
16 A B C D E
17 A B C D E
18 A B C D E
19 A B C D E
20 A B C D E
21 A B C D E
22 A B C D E
23 A B C D E
24 A B C D E
25 A B C D E
26 A B C D E
27 A B C D E
28 A B C D E
29 A B C D E
30 A B C D E
31 A B C D E
32 A B C D E
33 A B C D E
34 A B C D E
35 A B C D E
36 A B C D E
37 A B C D E
38 A B C D E
39 A B C D E
40 A B C D E
41 A B C D E
42 A B C D E
43 A B C D E
44 A B C D E
45 A B C D E
46 A B C D E
47 A B C D E
48 A B C D E
49 A B C D E
50 A B C D E

(Cut here to detach.)

Q1362-04

I.N. 575008 — 110VV58P3720

COLLEGE BOARD — SCHOLASTIC APTITUDE TEST and Test of Standard Written English Side 2

Use a No. 2 pencil only. Be sure each mark is dark and completely fills the intended oval. Completely erase any errors or stray marks.

Start with number 1 for each new section. If a section has fewer than 50 questions, leave the extra answer spaces blank.

	SECTION 3	SECTION 4	SECTION 5	SECTION 6
1	A B C D E	A B C D E	A B C D E	A B C D E
2	A B C D E	A B C D E	A B C D E	A B C D E
3	A B C D E	A B C D E	A B C D E	A B C D E
4	A B C D E	A B C D E	A B C D E	A B C D E
5	A B C D E	A B C D E	A B C D E	A B C D E
6	A B C D E	A B C D E	A B C D E	A B C D E
7	A B C D E	A B C D E	A B C D E	A B C D E
8	A B C D E	A B C D E	A B C D E	A B C D E
9	A B C D E	A B C D E	A B C D E	A B C D E
10	A B C D E	A B C D E	A B C D E	A B C D E
11	A B C D E	A B C D E	A B C D E	A B C D E
12	A B C D E	A B C D E	A B C D E	A B C D E
13	A B C D E	A B C D E	A B C D E	A B C D E
14	A B C D E	A B C D E	A B C D E	A B C D E
15	A B C D E	A B C D E	A B C D E	A B C D E
16	A B C D E	A B C D E	A B C D E	A B C D E
17	A B C D E	A B C D E	A B C D E	A B C D E
18	A B C D E	A B C D E	A B C D E	A B C D E
19	A B C D E	A B C D E	A B C D E	A B C D E
20	A B C D E	A B C D E	A B C D E	A B C D E
21	A B C D E	A B C D E	A B C D E	A B C D E
22	A B C D E	A B C D E	A B C D E	A B C D E
23	A B C D E	A B C D E	A B C D E	A B C D E
24	A B C D E	A B C D E	A B C D E	A B C D E
25	A B C D E	A B C D E	A B C D E	A B C D E
26	A B C D E	A B C D E	A B C D E	A B C D E
27	A B C D E	A B C D E	A B C D E	A B C D E
28	A B C D E	A B C D E	A B C D E	A B C D E
29	A B C D E	A B C D E	A B C D E	A B C D E
30	A B C D E	A B C D E	A B C D E	A B C D E
31	A B C D E	A B C D E	A B C D E	A B C D E
32	A B C D E	A B C D E	A B C D E	A B C D E
33	A B C D E	A B C D E	A B C D E	A B C D E
34	A B C D E	A B C D E	A B C D E	A B C D E
35	A B C D E	A B C D E	A B C D E	A B C D E
36	A B C D E	A B C D E	A B C D E	A B C D E
37	A B C D E	A B C D E	A B C D E	A B C D E
38	A B C D E	A B C D E	A B C D E	A B C D E
39	A B C D E	A B C D E	A B C D E	A B C D E
40	A B C D E	A B C D E	A B C D E	A B C D E
41	A B C D E	A B C D E	A B C D E	A B C D E
42	A B C D E	A B C D E	A B C D E	A B C D E
43	A B C D E	A B C D E	A B C D E	A B C D E
44	A B C D E	A B C D E	A B C D E	A B C D E
45	A B C D E	A B C D E	A B C D E	A B C D E
46	A B C D E	A B C D E	A B C D E	A B C D E
47	A B C D E	A B C D E	A B C D E	A B C D E
48	A B C D E	A B C D E	A B C D E	A B C D E
49	A B C D E	A B C D E	A B C D E	A B C D E
50	A B C D E	A B C D E	A B C D E	A B C D E

9. SIGNATURE:

FOR ETS USE ONLY	VTR	VTFS	VRR	VRFS	VVR	VVFS	WER	WEFS	M4R	M4FS	M5R	M5FS	MTFS
	VTW	VTCS	VRW	VRCS	VVW	VVCS	WEW	WECS	M4W		M5W		MTCS

SECTION 1	Time—30 minutes 45 Questions	For each question in this section, choose the best answer and fill in the corresponding oval on the answer sheet.

Each question below consists of a word in capital letters, followed by five lettered words or phrases. Choose the word or phrase that is most nearly opposite in meaning to the word in capital letters. Since some of the questions require you to distinguish fine shades of meaning, consider all the choices before deciding which is best.

Example:

GOOD: (A) sour (B) bad (C) red (D) hot (E) ugly

Ⓐ ● Ⓒ Ⓓ Ⓔ

1. OBEDIENT: (A) bitter (B) unhappy (C) grotesque (D) unruly (E) dangerous

2. DIFFUSE: (A) bring together (B) make habitual (C) leave unattended (D) openly admire (E) seldom heed

3. PAMPER: (A) magnify (B) conceal (C) discipline (D) reclaim (E) confuse

4. PUCKERED: (A) ancient (B) smooth (C) zigzag (D) pale (E) thin

5. HYPOCRISY: (A) sincerity (B) remorse (C) enthusiasm (D) persistence (E) anxiety

6. GHASTLY: (A) appealing (B) noisy (C) generous (D) casual (E) approving

7. ANTIPATHY: (A) urgency (B) idiosyncrasy (C) competence (D) constant repetition (E) strong affection

8. PERTURBATION: (A) hardiness (B) alacrity (C) frankness (D) serenity (E) obstinacy

9. CONSTRICT: (A) suspend (B) regard (C) invert (D) distend (E) exclude

10. SANCTIFY: (A) amplify (B) threaten (C) taint (D) separate (E) release

11. REGIMEN: (A) unpopular policy (B) unofficial agent (C) impractical solution (D) unsystematic activity (E) disaffected group

12. SOMBER: (A) light in color (B) quick to understand (C) unable to sleep (D) resistant to change (E) small in size

13. DECADENT: (A) enormously wealthy (B) remarkably charming (C) ruthless (D) distinctive (E) flourishing

14. INTRINSIC: (A) extensive (B) shoddy (C) divided (D) simple (E) extraneous

15. FECUND: (A) gradual (B) adaptable (C) external (D) untroubled (E) barren

GO ON TO THE NEXT PAGE

Each sentence below has one or two blanks, each blank indicating that something has been omitted. Beneath the sentence are five lettered words or sets of words. Choose the word or set of words that, when inserted in the sentence, best fits the meaning of the sentence as a whole.

Example:

Although its publicity has been ----, the film itself is intelligent, well-acted, handsomely produced, and altogether ----.

(A) tasteless. .respectable (B) extensive. .moderate (C) sophisticated. .amateur (D) risqué. .crude (E) perfect. .spectacular

● Ⓑ Ⓒ Ⓓ Ⓔ

16. The strong affinity of these wild sheep for mountains is not ----: mountain slopes represent ---- because they effectively limit the ability of less agile predators to pursue the sheep.

(A) useful. .peril
(B) accidental. .security
(C) instinctive. .attainment
(D) restrained. .nourishment
(E) surprising. .inferiority

17. An author whose only ---- is a biography, he has been dismissed by its critics as a mere reporter who recorded the brilliant wit of another and thereby gained a ---- fame of his own.

(A) failure. .belated
(B) justification. .tragic
(C) accomplishment. .spurious
(D) collaboration. .complete
(E) enterprise. .deserved

18. Hastings is deeply contemptuous of the ---- world; his notions have obliged him to live a life of ----.

(A) practical. .utility (B) sensual. .gratification (C) ethereal. .inspiration (D) public. .solitude (E) depraved. .abandon

19. Convinced that they themselves ---- relevant knowledge, most of that country's citizens consigned political judgments to experts and technocrats, thereby reducing themselves to ----.

(A) commanded. .tyrants
(B) possessed. .witnesses
(C) disseminated. .automatons
(D) required. .representatives
(E) lacked. .spectators

20. In some animal species, differences between opposite sexes are so ---- that it is very difficult to tell that the male and female are ----.

(A) measurable. .distinct
(B) minute. .similar
(C) obvious. .indistinguishable
(D) extreme. .related
(E) trivial. .identical

21. In her opening statement, the defense attorney told the jury that she would prove how one fact that appears to conflict with another may actually be ---- it.

(A) superior to (B) contradictory to (C) detrimental to (D) incompatible with (E) reconcilable with

22. If his methods were autocratic and his manner imperious, these were ---- and frequently even ---- as attributes becoming a monarch.

(A) criticized. .glorified
(B) overlooked. .ignored
(C) discussed. .denounced
(D) tolerated. .applauded
(E) encouraged. .dismissed

23. A fear of ----, prevalent among nineteenth-century educators, was evident in their frequent exhortations on the need to protect adolescents from the premature acquisition of knowledge and abilities.

(A) isolation (B) illiteracy (C) precocity (D) barbarity (E) frivolity

24. Because Alvin Ailey's choreography combines elements from traditions as different from each other as African folk dance and classical European ballet, his approach has been aptly termed ----.

(A) eclectic (B) intense (C) impromptu (D) theoretical (E) conventional

25. Like most political ---- in the United States, this newly coined phrase designates a ---- of groups and programs whose parts do not fit together seamlessly.

(A) labels. .mosaic (B) symbols. .symmetry (C) parties. .discord (D) slogans. .milestone (E) entities. .violation

GO ON TO THE NEXT PAGE

Each passage below is followed by questions based on its content. Answer all questions following a passage on the basis of what is stated or implied in that passage.

Two kinds of electric force operate between atoms or molecules: an attractive force, which is effective over a limited range (a few times the atom's or molecule's diameter), and a highly repulsive force, which is effective over a much shorter range. In the solid state, the forces between atoms or molecules determine the structure. When two atoms or molecules are about one hundred-millionth of an inch apart, these two forces cancel each other out, establishing a point of equilibrium and causing atoms or molecules to vibrate slightly toward and away from each other, as if held by invisible springs.

A small bar of iron looks solid, but the component atoms of the iron are entirely separate, suspended in space. Each of the individual atoms is vibrating unceasingly toward and away from each one of its neighbors. As they hang in space, the atoms form the intersections of a regular latticework. In iron, the lattice is composed of tiny cubes with an atom at each corner and one in the middle. Other substances have lattices with sides forming a variety of geometrical shapes which give each element its peculiar internal structure. When an object is broken, it normally separates along the lines of the lattice.

An increase in temperature speeds up the average velocity of molecular vibration within solids just as it does in gases. Each swinging movement of a single molecule, under the influence of added heat, is wider and faster and increases the average molecular separation. In other words, a solid object generally expands as a whole when the temperature is increased. As the additional heat forces the vibrating movement of the tightly bound molecules to become wilder and wilder, a point is reached at which some of the molecules begin to burst away from the binding forces exerted by their neighbors—they slip out of the regular latticework. With further heat, more molecules escape their captivity. As the rigid order begins to diminish, whole clusters of molecules begin to slip past each other. Finally the substance is no longer a solid, and the resultant breakdown of order is a process called melting.

When internal fluidity is fully achieved, the molecules are said to be in the liquid state. In liquids, the molecules hurtle in and then out of each other's areas of influence. Thus the force of a single molecule on another can be exerted for only the briefest time. Neighbors appear and disappear in millionths of a second. In liquids, as in solids, the addition of heat increases the average space between molecular centers. The observation that both liquids and solids generally expand with the addition of heat is best explained by the kinetic theory.

The reading passages in this test are brief excerpts or adaptations of excerpts from published material. The ideas contained in them do not necessarily represent the opinions of the College Board or Educational Testing Service. To make the text suitable for testing purposes, we may in some cases have altered the style, contents, or point of view of the original.

26. The primary focus of the passage is on

(A) how liquid substances alter when changing to the solid state
(B) how forces among molecules determine the structure of matter
(C) the shapes disrupted by lattices of atoms
(D) the advantages of equilibrium in liquids
(E) the dominance of the repulsive force in the solid state

27. Which of the following best describes what happens to the latticework of iron when iron changes from a solid to a liquid state?

(A) It recombines into larger cubes.
(B) Its sides shift to form other geometric shapes.
(C) It vibrates.
(D) It shrinks.
(E) It disappears.

28. According to the passage, a substance is very near its melting point when which of the following occurs?

(A) A change in temperature speeds up the average velocity of molecular vibration.
(B) Whole clusters of molecules begin to slip past one another.
(C) An object separates along the lines of the lattice.
(D) The attractive and repulsive forces cancel each other out.
(E) The component atoms are completely separated from one another.

GO ON TO THE NEXT PAGE

29. It can be inferred from the passage that internal fluidity has been fully achieved when which of the following conditions exists?

    (A) More and more molecules escape their captivity.
    (B) Heat increases the average space between molecular centers.
    (C) Forces are effectively exerted by any particular molecule on another for only a very brief time.
    (D) The vibrating movement of the tightly bound molecules becomes wilder and wilder.
    (E) The lattice assumes a different geometric shape.

30. The passage indicates that which of the following statements is true of both a solid and a liquid?

    (A) The addition of heat generally increases the average space between molecular centers.
    (B) The lattice is composed of tiny cubes with an atom at each corner and one in the middle.
    (C) The molecules hurtle in and then out of each other's areas of influence.
    (D) Each swinging movement of a single molecule is wider and wider.
    (E) The attractive force is always stronger than the repulsive force.

GO ON TO THE NEXT PAGE

The constant reference point for some Chicano historians is the Indian heritage, whether it be Mayan, Aztec, or Pueblo. Because Chicanos are mestizos, they possess an Indian background; I do not quarrel with this. What I do object to is the rejection of our European past. The history of America since the European conquest has been shaped by European factors adjusted to the American environment. Chicanos are a product of this adjustment, and we cannot understand our culture or our history without recognizing this fact.

This is not to suggest that we should go to the extreme of calling ourselves Spanish, Spanish Americans, or Hispanos. The fact is we are Mexicans. This distinction was overlooked by the historian Bolton, for example. In an article published in 1930, he made the point that the Southwest was the "meeting place and fusing place of two streams of European civilization, one coming from the south (the Spanish), the other from the north (the English)." In describing the Spanish influence there, Bolton mentioned the fact that states, rivers, mountains possessed Spanish names. "Many towns have Spanish quarters," he wrote, "where the life of the old days goes on, and where one can always hear the soft Castilian tongue."

Now, Chicanos know there are very few, if any, places in the Southwest where the "soft Castilian tongue" can be heard! The point, of course, is that Bolton did not recognize that the civilization existing in the Southwest at the time of the United States conquest in 1848 was not Spanish, but Mexican. It was, therefore, a mestizo society—one that had fused the Indian elements with the Spanish ones to create a distinct national culture. De Gandia recognizes the existence of national cultures, such as the Mexican, but at the same time acknowledges that not only the culture of Mexico, but also the political, economic, and social currents of the Mexican experience were for the most part European in origin. And this is what we have to understand.

We can be proud of being Mexican or Chicano and, at the same time, recognize and try to understand the European influence, thereby coming to know ourselves better. I am not saying we should be proud of our European heritage—that is up to each individual. What I am saying is that to neglect it is to neglect reality.

Leopoldo Zea, the Mexican philosopher, writes that "Mexicanism in itself cannot be a legitimate goal, but only a point of departure, a means toward a broader and more responsible task." What Zea says about "Mexicanism" is also true for "Chicanismo"; it is not a goal, but a means. And, I submit, it is a means toward a universal understanding of people. We look at ourselves and at others for the purpose of comprehending the human condition.

31. The passage primarily addresses itself to which of the following questions?

(A) What is the most appropriate cultural perspective for the study of Chicano history?
(B) Which cultural tradition of the Chicano heritage is the most interesting?
(C) How are Chicano writers influenced by their Indian heritage?
(D) Why should scholars learn to distinguish between "Mexicanism" and "Chicanismo"?
(E) Which of the Indian traditions most directly influenced Chicano history?

32. The author's position on the European heritage of Chicano culture can be described as which of the following?

(A) An assertion of its paramount importance to Indian culture
(B) A denial of its usefulness as an aid to understanding Chicano heritage
(C) A recognition of its relevance to Chicano history
(D) An analysis of the values and goals that it represents
(E) An acknowledgment of its pervasive influence and praise for its contributions

33. The passage suggests that the author would probably consider which of the following most helpful in presenting a realistic account of Chicano history?

(A) An essay that traced elements of Indian culture in modern Mexico
(B) A book that examined the interaction between Indian and European cultures in Mexico
(C) An article that celebrated the Indian civilization before the Colonial era
(D) A diary that recorded the life of a young Chicano a hundred years ago
(E) A dissertation that listed all known sites of ancient Mayan cities

GO ON TO THE NEXT PAGE

34. The author's discussion of Bolton develops the primary point of the passage by

(A) emphasizing the inaccuracy of a culturally narrow view of Chicano history
(B) demonstrating the direct relevance of European culture to Chicano identity
(C) illustrating the temptation of most historians to misrepresent reality
(D) questioning the importance of varying linguistic patterns
(E) affirming the necessity of discussion between European and Indian scholars

35. Which of the following best describes the function of the last paragraph in the passage?

(A) It adds further details to the statements made previously.
(B) It defines previously implicit assumptions about the European heritage.
(C) It presents a personal view of historical facts presented earlier.
(D) It illustrates the passage's generalizations about Chicano culture.
(E) It justifies the field of study discussed in the rest of the passage.

Each question below consists of a related pair of words or phrases, followed by five lettered pairs of words or phrases. Select the lettered pair that best expresses a relationship similar to that expressed in the original pair.

Example:

YAWN:BOREDOM :: (A) dream:sleep (B) anger:madness (C) smile:amusement (D) face:expression (E) impatience:rebellion

Ⓐ Ⓑ ● Ⓓ Ⓔ

36. NEEDLE : KNITTING :: (A) finger : sewing (B) sign : painting (C) throat : singing (D) hurdle : running (E) chisel : carving

37. SUBMERGE : WATER :: (A) parch : soil (B) bury : earth (C) suffocate : air (D) disperse : gas (E) extinguish : fire

38. APPAREL : SHIRT :: (A) sheep : wool (B) foot : shoe (C) light : camera (D) belt : buckle (E) jewelry : ring

39. INFURIATE : DISPLEASE :: (A) release : drop (B) oppress : swelter (C) drench : moisten (D) stir : respond (E) conceive : imagine

40. PROPHETIC : FUTURE ::
(A) incredible : belief
(B) contemporary : time
(C) visionary : reality
(D) historical : past
(E) revolutionary : fashion

41. STRATAGEM : OUTWIT ::
(A) prototype : design
(B) variation : change
(C) decoy : lure
(D) riddle : solve
(E) charade : guess

42. SHACKLE : MOVEMENT :: (A) weapon : protection (B) anchor : ship (C) rudder : direction (D) alarm : warning (E) gag : speech

43. CHARLATAN : EXPERTISE :: (A) glutton : food (B) orator : lecture (C) braggart : impression (D) liar : truth (E) performer : idleness

44. WANDERLUST : TRAVEL :: (A) fantasy : indulge (B) innocence : confess (C) ignorance : know (D) digression : speak (E) avarice : acquire

45. EXTRICATE : QUAGMIRE :: (A) liberate : captivity (B) rescue : lifeboat (C) defer : decision (D) eradicate : swamp (E) strain : filter

IF YOU FINISH BEFORE TIME IS CALLED, YOU MAY CHECK YOUR WORK ON THIS SECTION ONLY. DO NOT TURN TO ANY OTHER SECTION IN THE TEST. **STOP**

SECTION 2	**Time—30 minutes 25 Questions**	**In this section solve each problem, using any available space on the page for scratchwork. Then decide which is the best of the choices given and fill in the corresponding oval on the answer sheet.**

The following information is for your reference in solving some of the problems.

Circle of radius r: Area $= \pi r^2$; Circumference $= 2\pi r$
The number of degrees of arc in a circle is 360.
The measure in degrees of a straight angle is 180.

Definition of symbols:

$=$ is equal to	$\leq$ is less than or equal to
$\neq$ is unequal to	$\geq$ is greater than or equal to
$<$ is less than	$\parallel$ is parallel to
$>$ is greater than	$\perp$ is perpendicular to

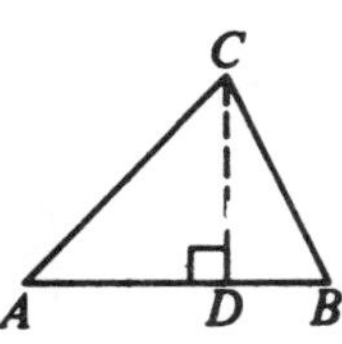

Triangle: The sum of the measures in degrees of the angles of a triangle is 180.

If $\angle CDA$ is a right angle, then

(1) area of $\triangle ABC = \frac{AB \times CD}{2}$

(2) $AC^2 = AD^2 + DC^2$

Note: Figures that accompany problems in this test are intended to provide information useful in solving the problems. They are drawn as accurately as possible EXCEPT when it is stated in a specific problem that its figure is not drawn to scale. All figures lie in a plane unless otherwise indicated. All numbers used are real numbers.

1. Bill weighs exactly twice as much as his brother Fred. If Bill's weight is between 95 and 120 pounds, then Fred's weight CANNOT be equal to which of the following?

(A) 47
(B) 50
(C) 52
(D) 55
(E) 57

2. Ten oranges cost \$1.25. At this rate, if 2 oranges are purchased and paid for with a \$5.00 bill, what is the correct change? (Assume no tax.)

(A) \$0.75
(B) \$1.25
(C) \$3.50
(D) \$3.75
(E) \$4.75

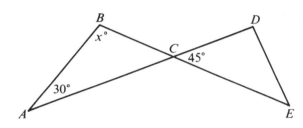

3. In the figure above, what is the value of x ?

(A) 75
(B) 90
(C) 95
(D) 105
(E) 110

GO ON TO THE NEXT PAGE

4. A man travels 150 miles in 3 hours. If he continues at this rate, how many miles will he travel in the next 2 hours?

(A) 50
(B) 100
(C) 250
(D) 300
(E) 900

5. $\frac{1}{2}\cdot\frac{2}{3}\cdot\frac{3}{4}\cdot\frac{4}{5}\cdot\frac{5}{6}\cdot\frac{6}{7} =$

(A) $\frac{1}{7}$

(B) $\frac{3}{7}$

(C) $\frac{21}{27}$

(D) $\frac{6}{7}$

(E) $\frac{7}{8}$

6. If $x = 2$ and $y = -1$, what is the value of $\frac{x - y}{x + y}$?

(A) -3

(B) -1

(C) $\frac{1}{3}$

(D) 1

(E) 3

x	$2x - 1$
0	-1
2	3
a	11

7. In the table shown above, $a =$

(A) 21
(B) 20
(C) 10
(D) 6
(E) 4

GO ON TO THE NEXT PAGE

8. $\sqrt{25 - 9} =$

(A) 2
(B) 4
(C) 8
(D) 16
(E) 32

9. If $6,565 = 65(x + 1)$, then $x =$

(A) 10
(B) 11
(C) 100
(D) 101
(E) 1,001

10. A number is formed by arranging the digits of 1,985 in descending order and another number is formed by arranging these digits in ascending order. The difference between these two newly formed numbers is

(A) 8,372
(B) 8,362
(C) 8,272
(D) 8,262
(E) 3,906

11. A drugstore had a promotion in which $0.50 was refunded to customers for each $10.00 spent on merchandise. If a customer spent $20.00 on merchandise during this promotion, the refund was equal to what percent of the amount spent?

(A) $1\frac{1}{4}\%$

(B) $2\frac{1}{2}\%$

(C) 5%

(D) 25%

(E) 50%

12. In $\triangle RST$, $\angle S$ is a right angle and $\angle R$ is 10° greater than $\angle T$. What is the measure of $\angle T$?

(A) 40°
(B) 45°
(C) 50°
(D) 55°
(E) 80°

GO ON TO THE NEXT PAGE

13. Abby cuts each of $n + 3$ apple pies into 5 pieces. In terms of n, what is the total number of pieces of pie?

(A) $\frac{n}{5} + \frac{3}{5}$

(B) $\frac{n}{5} + 3$

(C) $n + 15$

(D) $5n + 3$

(E) $5n + 15$

14. For a certain hot water heater, the increase in heating expenses is directly proportional to the increase in water-temperature setting. If heating expenses increase by $24 when the water-temperature setting increases by 20 degrees Fahrenheit, by how much will heating expenses increase if the water-temperature setting is increased by 15 degrees Fahrenheit?

(A) $16
(B) $18
(C) $19
(D) $20
(E) $21

15. If an integer is added to its square, the units' digit of this sum could be

(A) 1
(B) 2
(C) 3
(D) 4
(E) 5

16. If a circle with a circumference of 20 has two overlapping arcs with lengths of 16 and 14, respectively, what is the LEAST possible total length of the overlap of the two arcs?

(A) 2
(B) 4
(C) 6
(D) 10
(E) 12

GO ON TO THE NEXT PAGE

Questions 17-19 refer to the following information.

A computer is programmed to read a positive integer n and carry out the following instructions repeatedly until a value of 1 is obtained.

If n is even, then the new value of n is $\frac{n}{2}$.

If n is odd, then the new value of n is $3n + 1$.

For example, if the first value of n is 14, the second value of n is 7 and the third value is 22. The process continues and the results are printed in the following form.

value #1 = 14
value #2 = 7
value #3 = 22
. .
. .
. .

The process stops when a value of 1 is obtained.

17. If the first value of n is 40, what is the fifth value of n?

(A) 2
(B) 5
(C) 10
(D) 16
(E) 91

18. For which of the following first values of n is the instruction "the new value of n is $3n + 1$" never carried out?

(A) 100
(B) 80
(C) 64
(D) 48
(E) 25

19. When the first value of n is 27, the 112th value is 1. When the first value of n is 54, which value is 1?

(A) 56th
(B) 58th
(C) 111th
(D) 113th
(E) 224th

20. If a circle with center at the origin passes through the point (0, 5), through which of the following points does it also pass?

(A) $(2, \sqrt{21})$
(B) (4, 5)
(C) $(5, \sqrt{21})$
(D) (5, 5)
(E) (5, 12)

21. If 12 eggs cost x cents and 20 slices of bacon cost y cents, what is the cost, in cents, of 2 eggs and 4 slices of bacon?

(A) $\frac{xy}{30}$
(B) $\frac{x + 2y}{30}$
(C) $\frac{5x + 3y}{60}$
(D) $\frac{5x + 6y}{30}$
(E) $\frac{6x + 5y}{30}$

22. Each "word" in a special code is a three-digit number. If no word in the code can begin with a 1 or a 0, what is the greatest number of different words the code can contain?

(A) 28
(B) 512
(C) 800
(D) 900
(E) 1,000

GO ON TO THE NEXT PAGE

23. In a windowless, cube-shaped storage room, the ceiling and 4 walls, including a door, are completely painted. The floor is not painted. If the painted area is equal to 80 square meters, what is the volume of the room, in cubic meters?

(A) 16
(B) 20
(C) 64
(D) 256
(E) 400

24. Two cylindrical candles of the same height and diameter burn at the same uniform rate. Each takes 4 hours to be consumed. If the first candle is lit at 8:00 p.m. and the second at 9:00 p.m., at what time will the second candle be exactly 3 times as tall as the first?

(A) 9:30 p.m.
(B) 10:00 p.m.
(C) 10:30 p.m.
(D) 11:00 p.m.
(E) 11:30 p.m.

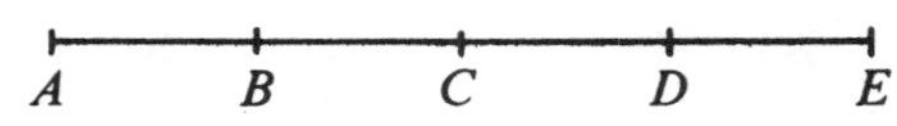

Note: Figure not drawn to scale.

25. On line segment AE above, if the lengths of AC, BD, and CE are equal, which of the following must be true?

I. C is the midpoint of AE.
II. B is the midpoint of AC.
III. BC and DE are equal in length.

(A) I only
(B) III only
(C) I and II only
(D) I and III only
(E) I, II, and III

IF YOU FINISH BEFORE TIME IS CALLED, YOU MAY CHECK YOUR WORK ON THIS SECTION ONLY. DO NOT TURN TO ANY OTHER SECTION IN THE TEST. **STOP**

SECTION 4 Time—30 minutes 40 Questions

For each question in this section, choose the best answer and fill in the corresponding oval on the answer sheet.

Each question below consists of a word in capital letters, followed by five lettered words or phrases. Choose the word or phrase that is most nearly opposite in meaning to the word in capital letters. Since some of the questions require you to distinguish fine shades of meaning, consider all the choices before deciding which is best.

Example:

GOOD: (A) sour (B) bad (C) red (D) hot (E) ugly

Ⓐ ● Ⓒ Ⓓ Ⓔ

1. TURBULENCE: (A) misconduct (B) calmness (C) sincerity (D) flexibility (E) prominence

2. MALICE: (A) familiarity (B) confidence (C) kindheartedness (D) good health (E) artistic talent

3. EXPANSIVE: (A) gracious (B) reserved (C) meticulous (D) unpopular (E) irresponsible

4. LACKADAISICAL: (A) unwholesome (B) unreliable (C) honest (D) energetic (E) pleasant

5. PALTRY: (A) frugal (B) impartial (C) superior (D) desperate (E) prudish

6. CORROBORATE: (A) challenge (B) adorn (C) display privately (D) restore completely (E) leave secretly

7. EXTEMPORANEOUS:
(A) obviously rehearsed
(B) correctly estimated
(C) rarely perceived
(D) accurately balanced
(E) extremely awkward

8. DIVEST: (A) ascend (B) confide (C) implicate (D) lapse (E) endow

9. COHERE: (A) splinter (B) absorb (C) detest (D) ignore (E) reproach

10. CELERITY: (A) slowness (B) foolishness (C) hardness (D) coldness (E) unhappiness

Each sentence below has one or two blanks, each blank indicating that something has been omitted. Beneath the sentence are five lettered words or sets of words. Choose the word or set of words that, when inserted in the sentence, best fits the meaning of the sentence as a whole.

Example:

Although its publicity has been ----, the film itself is intelligent, well-acted, handsomely produced, and altogether ----.

(A) tasteless. .respectable (B) extensive. .moderate (C) sophisticated. .amateur (D) risqué. .crude (E) perfect. .spectacular

● Ⓑ Ⓒ Ⓓ Ⓔ

11. A judgment made before all the facts are known must be called ----.

(A) harsh (B) deliberate (C) sensible (D) premature (E) fair

12. Because science is a discipline in which error is best discovered by peer review, it is appropriate that knowledgeable readers of scientific articles ---- what appear to be ---- interpretations of data.

(A) uphold. .untenable
(B) fabricate. .implausible
(C) ignore. .infallible
(D) question. .improbable
(E) praise. .equivocal

13. Although she knew that ---- was considered unfashionable in some circles, curator Estela Delgado was ---- to express her joy at the public's generous contributions to the two museums.

(A) exuberance. .unwilling
(B) restraint. .compelled
(C) spontaneity. .prepared
(D) decorum. .eager
(E) enthusiasm. .unashamed

GO ON TO THE NEXT PAGE

14. The author ---- the idea that someone would revive the incidents of his early life, and so he instructed his friends and associates to ---- any potential biographer.

(A) ridiculed. .respect (B) deplored. .forgive (C) abhorred. .frustrate (D) savored. .avoid (E) dismissed. .dissuade

15. The new instrument proved to be of little usefulness to the geologists; because it had no midrange sensitivity, it only registered disturbances that were either inconsequential or ----.

(A) cataclysmic (B) improbable (C) subjective (D) instantaneous (E) unintelligible

Each question below consists of a related pair of words or phrases, followed by five lettered pairs of words or phrases. Select the lettered pair that best expresses a relationship similar to that expressed in the original pair.

Example:

YAWN:BOREDOM :: (A) dream:sleep (B) anger:madness (C) smile:amusement (D) face:expression (E) impatience:rebellion

16. CYLINDRICAL : ROLLER ::
(A) mechanical : engine (B) spherical : globe (C) protruding : knob (D) nuclear : reactor (E) circular : path

17. PATENT : INVENTION :: (A) trigger : firearm (B) key : lock (C) vault : money (D) copyright : book (E) door : building

18. SWEEP : FLOOR :: (A) pave : street (B) wipe : table (C) prune : shrub (D) repair : car (E) mow : lawn

19. LARYNX : NECK :: (A) joint : elbow (B) heart : chest (C) splint : bone (D) cavity : tooth (E) indigestion : stomach

20. EXCOMMUNICATION : CHURCH ::
(A) expulsion : school (B) sermon : congregation (C) execution : victim (D) dismissal : student (E) extortion : business

21. EMIT : ODOR :: (A) reflect : shadow (B) radiate : heat (C) incline : angle (D) discharge : vent (E) measure : size

22. COMPOST : FERTILIZE :: (A) topsoil : erode (B) scalpel : suture (C) anchor : hold (D) detergent : stain (E) thermostat : install

23. SKULK : MOVE :: (A) blink : wink (B) weep : grieve (C) peek : observe (D) shake : quiver (E) cower : withdraw

24. STAGE : PLAY :: (A) rostrum : speech (B) camera : film (C) orchestra : band (D) theater : drama (E) hall : dance

25. OBDURATE : PERSUADE ::
(A) incorrigible : reform
(B) dour : displease
(C) crass : offend
(D) despondent : provoke
(E) gullible : convince

GO ON TO THE NEXT PAGE

Each passage below is followed by questions based on its content. Answer all questions following a passage on the basis of what is stated or implied in that passage.

Uncle Harold claimed that he had been shot right between the eyes, in France, during the First World War. He told me so himself.

"Right between the eyes," he said. "See this scar?"

"I don't see any scar," I said.

"It's probably faded by now," he said. "It's been a long time ago."

It didn't matter that my mother called him "the biggest liar God ever sent down the pike." I found him irresistible. It was his refusal to spoil a good story by slavish adherence to fact that enchanted me.

He was not a tall man, but the Marines had taught him to carry himself erectly and to measure people with the grave, cool arrogance of authority. Though he now shoveled dirt for a living, he was always immaculately manicured by the time he sat down to supper. In this polished man of the world—suits pressed to razor sharpness, every hair in place—I began to detect a hidden boy, in spirit not unlike myself, though with a love for mischief which had been subdued in me by too much melancholy striving to satisfy my mother's notions of manhood.

I understood that Uncle Harold was not a liar but a teller of stories and a romantic. I no longer received his stories with total credulity, but listened for the pleasure of watching his imagination at play. We were two romancers whose desire for something more fanciful than the humdrum of our drab neighborhood was beyond the grasp of unimaginative people like my mother.

26. Which of the following titles is most suitable for the passage?

    (A) Uncle Harold's Childhood and Adulthood
    (B) A Polished Man of the World
    (C) Hardships of a Struggling Family
    (D) My Career as a Storyteller
    (E) Not a Liar But a Romantic

27. The passage implies that as the boy learned the truth, his reaction to Uncle Harold's stories became one of

    (A) delight in the flamboyance of his uncle's imagination
    (B) respect for the danger in his uncle's earlier experiences
    (C) disappointment in the deliberate deceptions practiced by his uncle
    (D) regret for the persistent habits of his uncle
    (E) resentment at the disturbing immaturity displayed by his uncle

28. The relationship between Uncle Harold and the author is best described as one of

    (A) writer and reviewer
    (B) director and actor
    (C) employer and employee
    (D) friendly rivals
    (E) kindred spirits

GO ON TO THE NEXT PAGE

We are accustomed to thinking that great leaps forward in history occur because someone came up with a better way of doing things. Actually, these so-called better ways are in reality only different ways of doing things occasioned by the need to adjust to less easily exploitable sources of energy. Textbooks generally attribute the transition from the medieval era to the modern age to a great awakening of the human mind, and scholars debate the significance of the Protestant Reformation, the rise of the bourgeoisie, and the opening of trade routes in the great metamorphosis that occurred, but few admit that the fundamental cause of the Industrial Revolution was a switch from one energy base to another.

Today the sight of open countryside in Europe makes it difficult to imagine that in the fourth century a dense forest blanketed the continent from the Alps to the Carpathian Mountains. Wood in abundance provided the energy for the medieval way of life. A steady increase in the human population, however, between the ninth and twelfth centuries spurred the opening up of large tracts of land for cultivation, greatly reducing the available supply of wood. By the thirteenth century, wood had become so scarce that a search for alternative sources of energy began, eventually leading to coal.

Since it is more difficult to mine and process coal than it is to cut down trees, the switch from wood to coal initiated a long series of technological innovations. The process of mining coal, for example, was facilitated by the introduction of the steam engine. Such innovations laid the foundation for the industrial era that emerged.

29. The primary purpose of the passage is to

(A) support a theory
(B) criticize a method
(C) defend a way of life
(D) refute an opponent
(E) predict a trend

30. The passage suggests that the Industrial Revolution might not have happened as it did were it not for the

(A) competitiveness among technologically minded inventors
(B) emergence of commercialism and the middle class
(C) inefficient management of resources before the fourth century
(D) exorbitant price of high-quality wood in the thirteenth century
(E) steady rise in population from the ninth to the twelfth century

31. Which of the following maxims is most compatible with the view of change that is presented in the passage?

(A) There is nothing new under the sun.
(B) All is for the best in the best of all possible worlds.
(C) Little strokes fell great oaks.
(D) Necessity is the mother of invention.
(E) Human history is a history of ideas.

GO ON TO THE NEXT PAGE

About 10,000 years ago, as glaciers retreated into Canada, North America lost most of its large animals. The casualty list included mammoths, many species of horses and camels, the giant beaver, and others, totaling over 100 species. The question of what caused this late Pleistocene extinction has provoked a storm of controversy.

One widely held hypothesis is that sudden climatic change was responsible for the abrupt extinctions. My own hypothesis is that prehistoric human hunters were responsible. This view is neither new nor widely held. To discount the hypothesis one need simply identify a major wave of extinctions anywhere in the world in the late Pleistocene age prior to the hunters' arrival. To date, such evidence has not been found. In fact, the chronological sequence of extinction closely follows human footsteps, occurring first in Africa and southern Asia, next in Australia, then through northern Eurasia and into North and South America, much later in the West Indies, and finally, during the last 1,000 years, in Madagascar and New Zealand. The pattern shows that late Pleistocene extinction did not occur in all locations at the same time, as it would have if there had been a sudden climatic change or perhaps a cataclysmic destruction of the Earth's atmosphere by lethal radiation from cosmic-ray bombardment, another common hypothesis. Since no synchronous destruction of plants or of plant communities is known, the long-held belief that climatic change caused the extinction lacks credibility.

32. The central argument of the passage is that

(A) all the evidence points to the arrival of humans in North America about 10,000 years ago
(B) large animals became extinct in North America 10,000 years ago
(C) sudden climatic change does not affect the survival of a species
(D) no species became extinct before the arrival of human hunters
(E) human hunters caused the extinction of large animals in the late Pleistocene age

33. According to the passage, which of the following is (are) true of the author's hypothesis?

I. The author is the first person to propose it.
II. No evidence has yet been found to disprove it conclusively.
III. Few scholars interested in the subject have endorsed it.

(A) I only (B) I and II only
(C) I and III only (D) II and III only
(E) I, II, and III

34. According to the passage, which of the following would invalidate the author's argument?

(A) The discovery of major Pleistocene extinctions that occurred before the arrival of humans
(B) Evidence that a bombardment of cosmic rays had occurred after humans had reached North America
(C) Proof that North America has experienced little climatic change
(D) Discovery of a species of large animal that survived the arrival of humans in North America
(E) Proof that humans had come to North America from Europe

35. All of the following are central to the author's argument EXCEPT:

(A) The number of species of large animals native to North America decreased.
(B) Cosmic-ray bombardment would have affected every place on Earth at the same time.
(C) Many animals became extinct before the late Pleistocene age.
(D) Prehistoric humans hunted large animals.
(E) A dramatic and widespread climatic change would destroy both plant and animal species.

GO ON TO THE NEXT PAGE

An architect's stupidity is more dangerous than any other, for its inescapable influence crushes the sensitive individual by the disorder of proportions. It is not a matter of good taste or bad; it is a matter of the site that exhausts, that envenoms, that debases, that casts its spells and curses in silence, in secret. A hotel, a ship can cause strange ravages. You cannot trace the source of the discomfort that dissipates your resources, but your soul slowly stiffens and loses its adaptability. The malaise is impossible to analyze. At first you laugh at ugliness; it intrigues you, revolts you. Gradually it poisons you; your organism refuses to prosper; it squints, it limps, it dies.

In most cases the picturesque and the fantastic overcome us with fatigue and boredom. Forms, lines, and colors exert a power that the Occidental controls but imperfectly, and that the Oriental uses to achieve specific and predetermined effects. An Indian temple, a Chinese pagoda can hypnotize, bewitch, excite, lull, all by the use of volumes, curves, perspectives.

A monument that *serves*, or that has served, never fatigues us. The Colosseum served, the Acropolis served, the Sphinx served, ... That is why they delight us. It is not necessary to know what they served *for*, or to take advantage of their services. The fact that they were born of a need, that a purpose directed those who built them and obliged them to submit to certain rules, clears these monuments of all disorder, all frivolity. Whether they were intended to astound, to thank, to overpower, to assure the survival of the dead by the resemblance of a double, or, by that resemblance, to terrify tomb robbers, the point of departure is not a matter of chance. The great epochs never confront us with works of aesthetes. A scarecrow frightens birds, not us, but the very necessity of achieving a successful result inspires the farmer who devises it, dispensing him from being decorative. That is the beauty of the scarecrow. And of African masks, totems, the Sphinxes of Egypt.

Powerful and almost always secret motives are to be found at the origin of a thousand details that weave the seething beauty of nature. A singularity may appear gratuitous to us, but its expressive force always conceals roots. The same holds for the Orient, its architecture, its art; once we know the source of its nuances we no longer find them odd, quaint. The tourists who travel there must realize that they are passing through a ritual of which they understand nothing. Let this realization make them wary of judging, and strip them once and for all of our Western impertinence. Let nothing that disconcerts them make them smile; let them respect signs that lose all their decorative naïveté as soon as our minds divine their meaning.

36. It can be inferred from the passage that an ill-conceived building is especially offensive because of the

(A) insidiousness with which it impinges on one's consciousness
(B) undeserved profit its owner is likely to realize
(C) irrevocable harm it can do to the public's perception of architecture
(D) demolition of better buildings to make way for its construction
(E) impossibility of improving even its least problematic features

37. A stylistic device by which the author emphasizes the effects of oppressive architecture on a sensitive individual is the

(A) accumulation of short verb phrases
(B) juxtaposition of contradictory statements
(C) alternation between points of view
(D) response to implied rhetorical questions
(E) repetition of adjectives with negative connotations

38. The author argues that the monuments that delight us are those that

(A) were created to endure for thousands of years
(B) are similar to those our own era might create
(C) were built to serve a particular social purpose
(D) are inherently interesting by virtue of their proportions
(E) were intended to mystify all who encountered them

39. It can be inferred from the final paragraph that the author believes people who consider unfamiliar art or architecture merely curious or quaint to have

(A) no hope of enjoying foreign travel
(B) a seriously uninformed attitude
(C) no potential for any spiritual growth
(D) a need to be entertained rather than impressed
(E) no understanding of human nature

40. The passage as a whole combines

(A) an analysis of history with an evaluation of creativity
(B) a personal reminiscence with general observations
(C) a description of monuments with prescriptions for travel
(D) a theory of architecture with an appreciation of the East
(E) a critique of the West with a nostalgic evocation of the past

IF YOU FINISH BEFORE TIME IS CALLED, YOU MAY CHECK YOUR WORK ON THIS SECTION ONLY. DO NOT TURN TO ANY OTHER SECTION IN THE TEST. **STOP**

SECTION 5	Time—30 minutes 35 Questions	In this section solve each problem, using any available space on the page for scratchwork. Then decide which is the best of the choices given and fill in the corresponding oval on the answer sheet.

The following information is for your reference in solving some of the problems.

Circle of radius r: Area $= \pi r^2$; Circumference $= 2\pi r$
The number of degrees of arc in a circle is 360.
The measure in degrees of a straight angle is 180.

Definition of symbols:

$=$ is equal to	$\leq$ is less than or equal to
$\neq$ is unequal to	$\geq$ is greater than or equal to
$<$ is less than	$\parallel$ is parallel to
$>$ is greater than	$\perp$ is perpendicular to

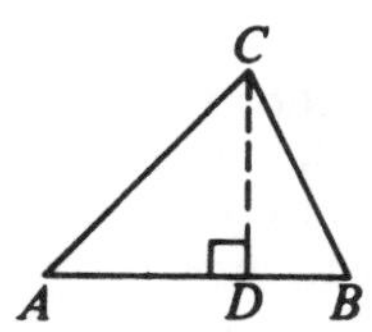

Triangle: The sum of the measures in degrees of the angles of a triangle is 180.
If $\angle CDA$ is a right angle, then

(1) area of $\triangle ABC = \frac{AB \times CD}{2}$

(2) $AC^2 = AD^2 + DC^2$

Note: Figures that accompany problems in this test are intended to provide information useful in solving the problems. They are drawn as accurately as possible EXCEPT when it is stated in a specific problem that its figure is not drawn to scale. All figures lie in a plane unless otherwise indicated. All numbers used are real numbers.

1. If $r = 3$, then $(2r)^2 =$

(A) 10
(B) 12
(C) 18
(D) 25
(E) 36

2. If $x + y = 10$ and $x - y = 2$, then $xy =$

(A) 24
(B) 20
(C) 16
(D) 12
(E) 8

3. Brand X granola bars are packed 12 to a box, and each granola bar supplies 2 grams of protein. How many such boxes of granola bars would supply 72 grams of protein?

(A) 3
(B) 10
(C) 12
(D) 24
(E) 36

4. $9 + \frac{9}{100} + \frac{9}{10{,}000} =$

(A) 9.99
(B) 9.909
(C) 9.099
(D) 9.0909
(E) 9.0099

GO ON TO THE NEXT PAGE

(6)	4
9	7
(8)	5
(4)	13
8	6

5. In the figure above, the average (arithmetic mean) of the numbers in each column is k. If the three circled numbers are moved from the left to the right column, which of the following combinations of numbers can then be moved from the right to the left column so that k remains the average of the numbers in each column?

(A) 6, 13
(B) 4, 5, 6
(C) 4, 7, 5
(D) 4, 7, 6
(E) 7, 5, 6

6. The figure above shows an accurate clock. If Eric leaves his office exactly 3 hours and 20 minutes after the time shown, which of the following will be the measure of the angle that the minute hand forms with the hour hand when Eric leaves his office?

(A) 60°
(B) 90°
(C) 120°
(D) 150°
(E) 180°

7. The ratio of the length of a rectangular floor to its width is 3:2. If the length of the floor is 12 meters, what is the perimeter of the floor, in meters?

(A) 20
(B) 40
(C) 60
(D) 96
(E) 120

GO ON TO THE NEXT PAGE

Questions 8-27 each consist of two quantities, one in Column A and one in Column B. You are to compare the two quantities and on the answer sheet fill in oval

A if the quantity in Column A is greater;
B if the quantity in Column B is greater;
C if the two quantities are equal;
D if the relationship cannot be determined from the information given.

AN E RESPONSE WILL NOT BE SCORED.

EXAMPLES

	Column A	Column B	Answers
E1.	2×6	$2 + 6$	
	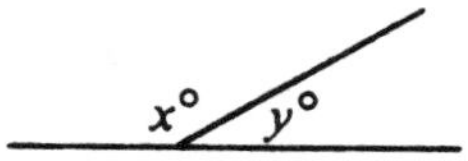		
E2.	$180 - x$	y	
E3.	$p - q$	$q - p$	

Notes:

1. In certain questions, information concerning one or both of the quantities to be compared is centered above the two columns.
2. In a given question, a symbol that appears in both columns represents the same thing in Column A as it does in Column B.
3. Letters such as x, n, and k stand for real numbers.

	Column A	Column B
8.	$(-2)(-8)$	$(-2) + (-8)$
9.	$(3 \times 10^5) + (4 \times 10^3)$	$(3 \times 10^5) + (5 \times 10^2)$
10.	The number of days in 8 weeks	The number of hours in $2\frac{1}{2}$ days

$a < 0$

11.	$\frac{1}{6}$	$\frac{1}{a^2}$

In 1983 Dealer X sold 270 more cars than in 1982.

12.	The number of cars each  represents	100
13.	$\frac{1}{2} \times \frac{1}{2}$	$\frac{\frac{1}{2}}{2}$

	Column A	Column B

$$\frac{x}{12} = \frac{5}{11}$$

14.	x	5

$$\begin{array}{r} 23 \\ 16 \\ 57 \\ +\ x \\ \hline 108 \end{array} \qquad \begin{array}{r} 23 \\ 16 \\ 27 \\ +\ y \\ \hline 108 \end{array}$$

15.	x	y

P and Q are two points on the circumference of a circle with center O.

16.	Length of PO	Length of QO

$a^3 = b^3$

17.	ab	a^2

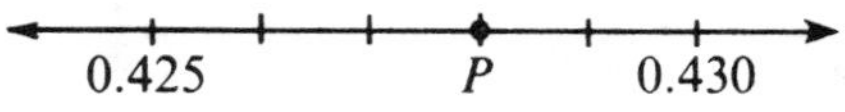

The tick marks on the number line are equally spaced.

18.	The coordinate of point P	0.4256
19.	$2(x - 4y)$	$2x - 4y$

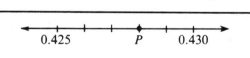

GO ON TO THE NEXT PAGE

5

SUMMARY DIRECTIONS FOR COMPARISON QUESTIONS

Answer: A if the quantity in Column A is greater;
B if the quantity in Column B is greater;
C if the two quantities are equal;
D if the relationship cannot be determined from the information given.

AN E RESPONSE WILL NOT BE SCORED.

	Column A	Column B

$s = 6q$, where q is a positive integer, and $s = 2r$, where r is a positive integer.

20. s — 12

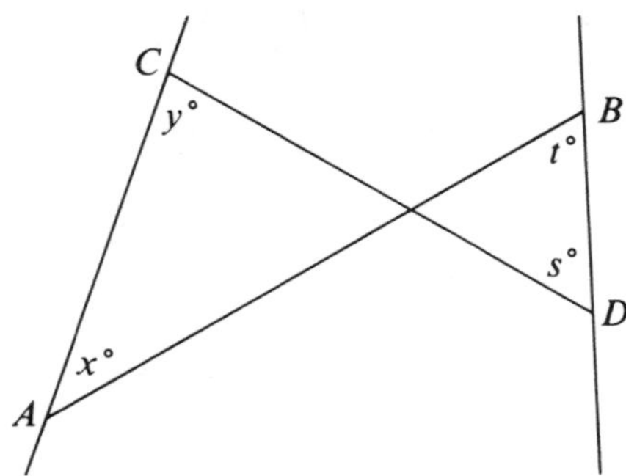

Line segments AB and CD intersect as shown.

21. $x + y$ — $s + t$

$x - y > 0$
$x + y < 0$

22. y — 0

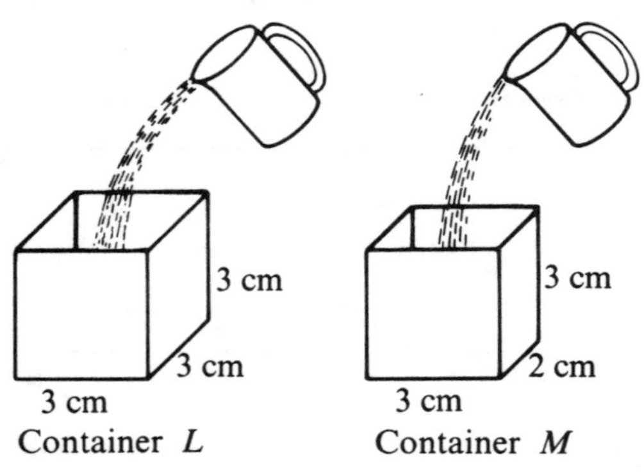

X cubic centimeters of water was poured into each of the empty rectangular containers above. The containers rest on a level surface.

$0 < X < 18$

23. The height of the water in container L — The height of the water in container M

	Column A	Column B

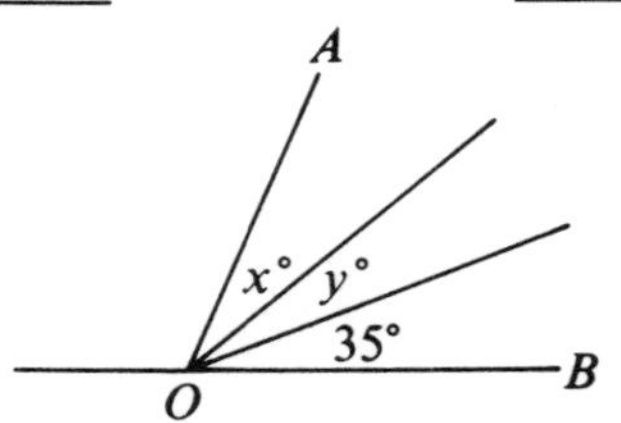

Note: Figure not drawn to scale.
$\angle AOB = 80°$ and $y > 10$

24. x — 35

$x > 0$

25. $3 + \dfrac{1}{x + \frac{1}{2} + \frac{1}{4}}$ — 4

26. The greatest possible number of points common to a triangle and a circle — 3

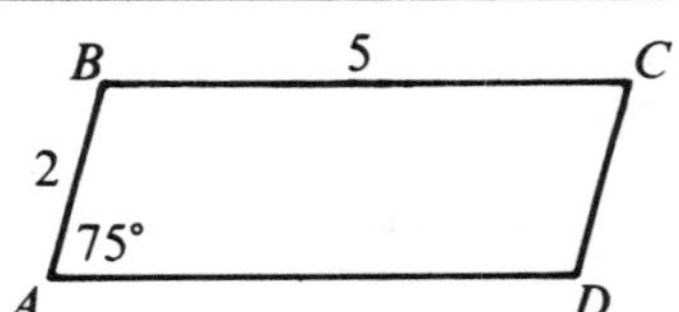

27. The area of parallelogram $ABCD$ — 10

GO ON TO THE NEXT PAGE

Solve each of the remaining problems in this section using any available space for scratchwork. Then decide which is the best of the choices given and fill in the corresponding oval on the answer sheet.

28. A triangle has sides with lengths $x - 2$, $2x - 3$, and $x + 1$. If the perimeter of the triangle is 20, what is the length of its longest side?

(A) 9
(B) 8
(C) 7
(D) 6
(E) 5

Questions 29-30 refer to the following definition.

S is the set of all integers that can be written as $n^2 + 1$ where n is a nonzero integer.

29. Which of the following integers is in S?

(A) 16
(B) 28
(C) 35
(D) 39
(E) 50

30. If x and y are two different integers in S, which of the following must be the square of an integer?

I. $(x - 1)(y - 1)$
II. $4(x - 1)$
III. $x^2 + y^2$

(A) None
(B) I only
(C) II only
(D) III only
(E) I and II

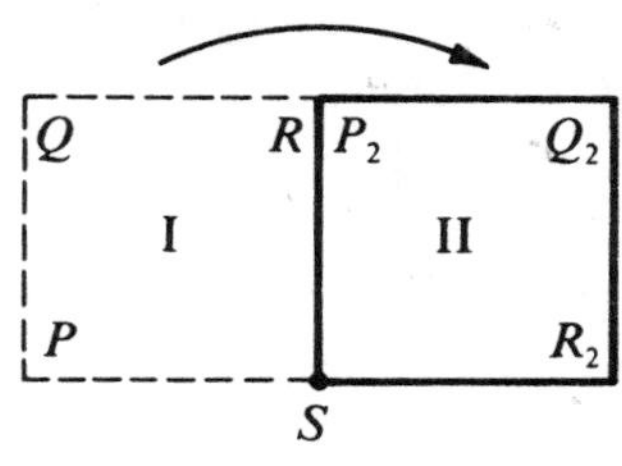

31. In the figure above, square $PQRS$, initially in position I, has been rotated clockwise about point S to position II. If P_2, Q_2, and R_2 are the second positions of P, Q, and R, respectively, and if a side of the square is 1, what is the length of the path followed by P in rotating to P_2?

(A) $\frac{\pi}{4}$
(B) 1
(C) $\frac{\pi}{2}$
(D) 2
(E) π

32. If x and y are positive integers, x divided by 7 leaves a remainder of 3, and y divided by 7 leaves a remainder of 4, what is the remainder when xy is divided by 7?

(A) 0
(B) 1
(C) 2
(D) 5
(E) 6

GO ON TO THE NEXT PAGE

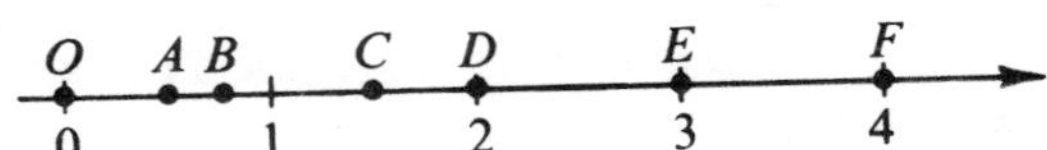

33. On the number line above, the ratio of distance OB to distance OA is closest to which of the following distance ratios?

(A) $\frac{OC}{OB}$

(B) $\frac{OD}{OB}$

(C) $\frac{OE}{OD}$

(D) $\frac{OE}{OC}$

(E) $\frac{OF}{OD}$

34. The average (arithmetic mean) weight of 3 boxes is $75\frac{1}{3}$ pounds. If each box weighs at least 74 pounds, what is the greatest possible weight, in pounds, of one of these boxes?

(A) 75
(B) 76
(C) 77
(D) 78
(E) 79

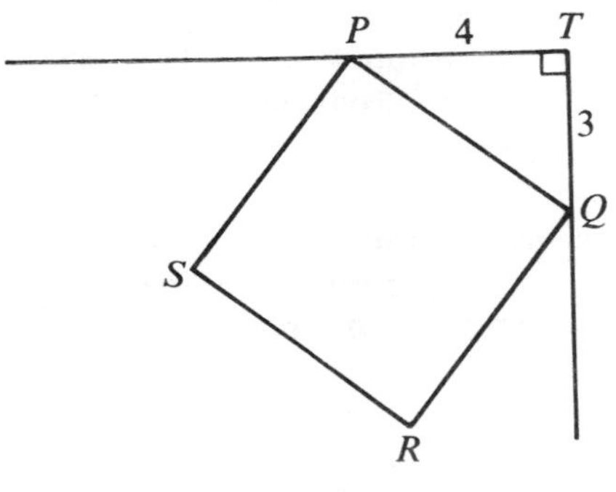

35. In the figure above, if $PQRS$ is a square, $PT \perp QT$, $QT = 3$, and $PT = 4$, then $RT =$

(A) $5\sqrt{2}$
(B) $2\sqrt{15}$
(C) $\sqrt{58}$
(D) $\sqrt{65}$
(E) $\sqrt{66}$

IF YOU FINISH BEFORE TIME IS CALLED, YOU MAY CHECK YOUR WORK ON THIS SECTION ONLY. DO NOT TURN TO ANY OTHER SECTION IN THE TEST. **STOP**

Correct Answers for Scholastic Aptitude Test Form Code 6K			
VERBAL		MATHEMATICAL	
Section 1	Section 4	Section 2	Section 5
1. D	1. B	1. A	1. E
2. A	2. C	2. E	2. A
3. C	3. B	3. D	3. A
4. B	4. D	4. B	4. D
5. A	5. C	5. A	5. E
6. A	6. A	6. E	6. E
7. E	7. A	7. D	7. B
8. D	8. E	8. B	*8. A
9. D	9. A	9. C	*9. A
10. C	10. A	10. D	*10. B
11. D	11. D	11. C	*11. D
12. A	12. D	12. A	*12. A
13. E	13. E	13. E	*13. C
14. E	14. C	14. B	*14. A
15. E	15. A	15. B	*15. B
16. B	16. B	16. D	*16. C
17. C	17. D	17. D	*17. C
18. D	18. B	18. C	*18. A
19. E	19. B	19. D	*19. D
20. D	20. A	20. A	*20. D
21. E	21. B	21. D	*21. C
22. D	22. C	22. C	*22. B
23. C	23. C	23. C	*23. B
24. A	24. A	24. E	*24. B
25. A	25. A	25. D	*25. D
26. B	26. E		*26. A
27. E	27. A		*27. B
28. B	28. E		28. A
29. C	29. A		29. E
30. A	30. E		30. E
31. A	31. D		31. C
32. C	32. E		32. D
33. B	33. D		33. C
34. A	34. A		34. D
35. E	35. C		35. C
36. E	36. A		
37. B	37. A		
38. E	38. C		
39. C	39. B		
40. D	40. D		
41. C			
42. E			
43. D			
44. E			
45. A			

*Indicates four-choice questions. (All of the other questions are five-choice.)

The Scoring Process

Machine-scoring is done in three steps:

- *Scanning.* Your answer sheet is "read" by a scanning machine and the oval you filled in for each question is recorded on a computer tape.
- *Scoring.* The computer compares the oval filled in for each question with the correct response. Each correct answer receives one point; omitted questions do not count toward your score. For each wrong answer, a fraction of a point is subtracted to correct for random guessing. For questions with five answer choices, one-fourth of a point is subtracted for each wrong response; for questions with four answer choices, one-third of a point is subtracted for each wrong response. The SAT-verbal test has 85 questions with five answer choices each. If, for example, a student has 44 right, 32 wrong, and 9 omitted, the resulting raw score is determined as follows:

$$\text{44 right} - \frac{\text{32 wrong}}{4} = 44 - 8 = \text{36 raw score points}$$

Obtaining raw scores frequently involves the rounding of fractional numbers to the nearest whole number. For example, a raw score of 36.25 is rounded to 36, the nearest whole number. A raw score of 36.50 is rounded upward to 37.

- *Converting to reported scaled score.* Raw test scores are then placed on the College Board scale of 200 to 800 through a process that adjusts scores to account for minor differences in difficulty among different editions of the test. This process, known as equating, is performed so that a student's reported score is not affected by the edition of the test taken nor by the abilities of the group with whom the student takes the test. As a result of placing SAT scores on the College Board scale, scores earned by students at different times can be compared. For example, an SAT-verbal score of 400 on a test taken at one administration indicates the same level of developed verbal ability as a 400 score obtained on a different edition of the test taken at another time.

How to Score the Test

SAT-Verbal Sections 1 and 4

Step A: Count the number of correct answers for *section 1* and record the number in the space provided on the worksheet on the next page. Then do the same for the incorrect answers. (Do not count omitted answers.) To determine subtotal A, use the formula:

$$\text{number correct} - \frac{\text{number incorrect}}{4} = \text{subtotal A}$$

Step B: Count the number of correct answers and the number of incorrect answers for *section 4* and record the numbers in the spaces provided on the worksheet. To determine subtotal B, use the formula:

$$\text{number correct} - \frac{\text{number incorrect}}{4} = \text{subtotal B}$$

Step C: To obtain C, add subtotal A to subtotal B, keeping any decimals. Enter the resulting figure on the worksheet.

Step D: To obtain D, your raw verbal score, round C to the nearest whole number. (For example, any number from 44.50 to 45.49 rounds to 45.) Enter the resulting figure on the worksheet.

Step E: To find your reported SAT-verbal score, look up the total raw verbal score you obtained in step D in the conversion table on page 196. Enter this figure on the worksheet.

SAT-Mathematical Sections 2 and 5

Step A: Count the number of correct answers and the number of incorrect answers for *section 2* and record the numbers in the spaces provided on the worksheet. To determine the subtotal A, use the formula:

$$\text{number correct} - \frac{\text{number incorrect}}{4} = \text{subtotal A}$$

Step B: Count the number of correct answers and the number of incorrect answers for the *five-choice questions (questions 1 through 7 and 28 through 35) in section 5* and record the numbers in the spaces provided on the worksheet. To determine the subtotal B, use the formula:

$$\text{number correct} - \frac{\text{number incorrect}}{4} = \text{subtotal B}$$

Step C: Count the number of correct answers and the number of incorrect answers for the *four-choice questions (questions 8 through 27) in section 5* and record the numbers in the spaces provided on the worksheet. To determine the subtotal C, use the formula:

$$\text{number correct} - \frac{\text{number incorrect}}{3} = \text{subtotal C}$$

Step D: To obtain D, add subtotal A, subtotal B, and subtotal C, keeping any decimals. Enter the resulting figure on the worksheet.

Step E: To obtain E, your raw mathematical score, round D to the nearest whole number. (For example, any number from 44.50 to 45.49 rounds to 45.) Enter the resulting figure on the worksheet.

Step F: To find your reported SAT-mathematical score, look up the total raw mathematical score you obtained in E in the conversion table on page 196. Enter this figure on the worksheet.

SAT SCORING WORKSHEET

FORM CODE 6K

SAT-Verbal Sections

A. Section 1: ____________ − ¼ (____________) = ____________
no. correct — no. incorrect — subtotal A

B. Section 4: ____________ − ¼ (____________) = ____________
no. correct — no. incorrect — subtotal B

C. Total unrounded raw score (Total A + B) ____________ C

D. Total rounded raw score (Rounded to nearest whole number) ____________ D

E. SAT-verbal reported scaled score (See the conversion table on page 196.) [ ] SAT-verbal score

SAT-Mathematical Sections

A. Section 2: ____________ − ¼ (____________) = ____________
no. correct — no. incorrect — subtotal A

B. Section 5: Questions 1 through 7 and 28 through 35 (5-choice) ____________ − ¼ (____________) = ____________
no. correct — no. incorrect — subtotal B

C. Section 5: Questions 8 through 27 (4-choice) ____________ − ⅓ (____________) = ____________
no. correct — no. incorrect — subtotal C

D. Total unrounded raw score (Total A + B + C) ____________ D

E. Total rounded raw score (Rounded to nearest whole number) ____________ E

F. SAT-mathematical reported scaled score (See the conversion table on page 196.) [ ] SAT-math score

Score Conversion Table
Scholastic Aptitude Test
Form Code 6K

Raw Score	College Board Reported Score		Raw Score	College Board Reported Score	
	SAT-Verbal	SAT-Math		SAT-Verbal	SAT-Math
85	800		40	460	590
84	780		39	450	580
83	760		38	440	570
82	750		37	440	560
81	740		36	430	550
80	730		35	430	540
79	720		34	420	530
78	710		33	410	520
77	700		32	410	510
76	700		31	400	500
75	690		30	390	490
74	680		29	390	480
73	670		28	380	480
72	660		27	380	470
71	650		26	370	460
70	650		25	360	450
69	640		24	360	440
68	630		23	350	430
67	620		22	340	420
66	620		21	340	410
65	610		20	330	410
64	600		19	320	400
63	600		18	320	390
62	590		17	310	380
61	580		16	300	370
60	580	800	15	300	360
59	570	780	14	290	360
58	560	770	13	280	350
57	560	760	12	280	340
56	550	750	11	270	330
55	540	740	10	260	320
54	540	730	9	250	320
53	530	720	8	250	310
52	530	710	7	240	300
51	520	690	6	230	290
50	510	690	5	230	280
49	510	680	4	220	280
48	500	670	3	210	270
47	500	660	2	200	260
46	490	650	1	200	250
45	480	640	0	200	250
44	480	630	–1	200	240
43	470	620	–2	200	230
42	470	610	–3	200	220
41	460	600	–4	200	210
			–5	200	210
			–6 or below	200	200

(Cut here to detach.)

COLLEGE BOARD — SCHOLASTIC APTITUDE TEST and Test of Standard Written English

Side 1

Use a No. 2 pencil only. Be sure each mark is dark and completely fills the intended oval. Completely erase any errors or stray marks.

1.

YOUR NAME: (Print) ______ Last ______ First ______ M.I.

SIGNATURE: ______ **DATE:** ___ / ___ / ___

HOME ADDRESS: (Print) ______ Number and Street

______ City ______ State ______ Zip Code

CENTER: (Print) ______ City ______ State ______ Center Number

IMPORTANT: Please fill in items 2 and 3 exactly as shown on the back cover of your test book.

FOR ETS USE ONLY

2. TEST FORM (Copy from back cover of your test book.)

3. FORM CODE (Copy and grid as shown on back cover of your test book.)

0	A	J	S	0	0	0
1	B	K	T	1	1	1
2	C	L	U	2	2	2
3	D	M	V	3	3	3
4	E	N	W	4	4	4
5	F	O	X	5	5	5
6	G	P	Y	6	6	6
7	H	Q	Z	7	7	7
8	I	R		8	8	8
9				9	9	9

4. REGISTRATION NUMBER (Copy from your Admission Ticket.)

0	0	0	0	0	0	0
1	1	1	1	1	1	1
2	2	2	2	2	2	2
3	3	3	3	3	3	3
4	4	4	4	4	4	4
5	5	5	5	5	5	5
6	6	6	6	6	6	6
7	7	7	7	7	7	7
8	8	8	8	8	8	8
9	9	9	9	9	9	9

5. YOUR NAME

First 4 letters of last name | First Init. | Mid. Init.

A B C D E F G H I J K L M N O P Q R S T U V W X Y Z (in each of the six columns)

6. DATE OF BIRTH

Month	Day		Year	
Jan.				
Feb.				
Mar.	0	0	0	0
Apr.	1	1	1	1
May	2	2	2	2
June	3	3	3	3
July		4	4	4
Aug.		5	5	5
Sept.		6	6	6
Oct.		7	7	7
Nov.		8		8
Dec.		9		9

7. SEX

Female

Male

8. TEST BOOK SERIAL NUMBER (Copy from front cover of your test book.)

Start with number 1 for each new section. If a section has fewer than 50 questions, leave the extra answer spaces blank.

SECTION 1

1–50: A B C D E (each question)

SECTION 2

1–50: A B C D E (each question)

Q1362-04

I.N. 575008 — 110VV58P3720

COLLEGE BOARD — SCHOLASTIC APTITUDE TEST and Test of Standard Written English Side 2

Use a No. 2 pencil only. Be sure each mark is dark and completely fills the intended oval. Completely erase any errors or stray marks.

Start with number 1 for each new section. If a section has fewer than 50 questions, leave the extra answer spaces blank.

	SECTION 3	SECTION 4	SECTION 5	SECTION 6
1	A B C D E	A B C D E	A B C D E	A B C D E
2	A B C D E	A B C D E	A B C D E	A B C D E
3	A B C D E	A B C D E	A B C D E	A B C D E
4	A B C D E	A B C D E	A B C D E	A B C D E
5	A B C D E	A B C D E	A B C D E	A B C D E
6	A B C D E	A B C D E	A B C D E	A B C D E
7	A B C D E	A B C D E	A B C D E	A B C D E
8	A B C D E	A B C D E	A B C D E	A B C D E
9	A B C D E	A B C D E	A B C D E	A B C D E
10	A B C D E	A B C D E	A B C D E	A B C D E
11	A B C D E	A B C D E	A B C D E	A B C D E
12	A B C D E	A B C D E	A B C D E	A B C D E
13	A B C D E	A B C D E	A B C D E	A B C D E
14	A B C D E	A B C D E	A B C D E	A B C D E
15	A B C D E	A B C D E	A B C D E	A B C D E
16	A B C D E	A B C D E	A B C D E	A B C D E
17	A B C D E	A B C D E	A B C D E	A B C D E
18	A B C D E	A B C D E	A B C D E	A B C D E
19	A B C D E	A B C D E	A B C D E	A B C D E
20	A B C D E	A B C D E	A B C D E	A B C D E
21	A B C D E	A B C D E	A B C D E	A B C D E
22	A B C D E	A B C D E	A B C D E	A B C D E
23	A B C D E	A B C D E	A B C D E	A B C D E
24	A B C D E	A B C D E	A B C D E	A B C D E
25	A B C D E	A B C D E	A B C D E	A B C D E
26	A B C D E	A B C D E	A B C D E	A B C D E
27	A B C D E	A B C D E	A B C D E	A B C D E
28	A B C D E	A B C D E	A B C D E	A B C D E
29	A B C D E	A B C D E	A B C D E	A B C D E
30	A B C D E	A B C D E	A B C D E	A B C D E
31	A B C D E	A B C D E	A B C D E	A B C D E
32	A B C D E	A B C D E	A B C D E	A B C D E
33	A B C D E	A B C D E	A B C D E	A B C D E
34	A B C D E	A B C D E	A B C D E	A B C D E
35	A B C D E	A B C D E	A B C D E	A B C D E
36	A B C D E	A B C D E	A B C D E	A B C D E
37	A B C D E	A B C D E	A B C D E	A B C D E
38	A B C D E	A B C D E	A B C D E	A B C D E
39	A B C D E	A B C D E	A B C D E	A B C D E
40	A B C D E	A B C D E	A B C D E	A B C D E
41	A B C D E	A B C D E	A B C D E	A B C D E
42	A B C D E	A B C D E	A B C D E	A B C D E
43	A B C D E	A B C D E	A B C D E	A B C D E
44	A B C D E	A B C D E	A B C D E	A B C D E
45	A B C D E	A B C D E	A B C D E	A B C D E
46	A B C D E	A B C D E	A B C D E	A B C D E
47	A B C D E	A B C D E	A B C D E	A B C D E
48	A B C D E	A B C D E	A B C D E	A B C D E
49	A B C D E	A B C D E	A B C D E	A B C D E
50	A B C D E	A B C D E	A B C D E	A B C D E

9. SIGNATURE:

FOR ETS USE ONLY	VTR	VTFS	VRR	VRFS	VVR	VVFS	WER	WEFS	M4R	M4FS	M5R	M5FS	MTFS
	VTW	VTCS	VRW	VRCS	VVW	VVCS	WEW	WECS	M4W		M5W		MTCS

TEST 7—FORM CODE 7A 1 1 1 1 1 1 1 1

SECTION 1 | Time—30 minutes 45 Questions | For each question in this section, choose the best answer and fill in the corresponding oval on the answer sheet.

Each question below consists of a word in capital letters, followed by five lettered words or phrases. Choose the word or phrase that is most nearly opposite in meaning to the word in capital letters. Since some of the questions require you to distinguish fine shades of meaning, consider all the choices before deciding which is best.

Example:

GOOD: (A) sour (B) bad (C) red (D) hot (E) ugly

Ⓐ ● Ⓒ Ⓓ Ⓔ

1. LINK: (A) disturb (B) depart (C) disallow (D) disconnect (E) discredit

2. EQUILIBRIUM: (A) brevity (B) vulnerability (C) prominence (D) imbalance (E) angularity

3. ROBUST: (A) fortunate (B) opinionated (C) frail (D) crass (E) carefree

4. AFFIRMATION: (A) commonality (B) plurality (C) negation (D) transmission (E) concession

5. IMMACULATE: (A) obvious (B) stained (C) prolonged (D) meaningful (E) customary

6. FEASIBLE: (A) inexpensive (B) inconspicuous (C) unworkable (D) morally wrong (E) easily forgotten

7. LISTLESS: (A) rude (B) energetic (C) undesirable (D) decisive (E) uninformed

8. RECONCILIATION: (A) impetuosity (B) vigilance (C) initiation (D) foolishness (E) alienation

9. SCINTILLATING: (A) dull (B) moral (C) loud (D) exact (E) shaky

10. DIMINUTION: (A) agreement (B) hazard (C) construction (D) enlargement (E) brightness

11. STYMIE: (A) please (B) assist (C) purify (D) spare (E) engage

12. PRECURSOR: (A) descendant (B) supporter (C) beneficiary (D) subordinate (E) convert

13. PUERILE: (A) modest (B) definitive (C) mature (D) serene (E) private

14. DROSS: (A) gratitude (B) consistency (C) candor (D) valuable matter (E) current rate

15. FORSWEAR: (A) treat confidentially (B) embrace eagerly (C) handle carefully (D) think optimistically (E) wander aimlessly

GO ON TO THE NEXT PAGE

Each sentence below has one or two blanks, each blank indicating that something has been omitted. Beneath the sentence are five lettered words or sets of words. Choose the word or set of words that, when inserted in the sentence, best fits the meaning of the sentence as a whole.

Example:

Although its publicity has been ----, the film itself is intelligent, well-acted, handsomely produced, and altogether ----.

(A) tasteless. .respectable (B) extensive. .moderate (C) sophisticated. .amateur (D) risqué. .crude (E) perfect. .spectacular

● Ⓑ Ⓒ Ⓓ Ⓔ

16. The supposedly ---- defenses on the country's eastern border became ---- when the enemy discovered the defenses could be avoided by an approach from the north.

(A) obsolete. .modern
(B) flexible. .impassable
(C) inexpensive. .vital
(D) impregnable. .worthless
(E) independent. .isolated

17. In the past, Black scientists and researchers received scant credit for their achievements, but today their contributions are more widely ----.

(A) inferred (B) acknowledged (C) elaborated (D) standardized (E) envied

18. Fairly incompetent himself, he tended to favor those who were even less ---- than he was and who therefore were not ---- to him or his authority.

(A) capable. .a threat (B) efficient. .a boost (C) qualified. .an asset (D) weak. .a danger (E) inferior. .a risk

19. Even those who do not ---- Robinson's views ---- him as a candidate who has courageously refused to compromise his convictions.

(A) shrink from. .condemn
(B) concur with. .recognize
(C) profit from. .dismiss
(D) disagree with. .envision
(E) dissent from. .remember

20. After observing several vicious territorial fights, Jane Goodall had to revise her earlier opinion that these particular primates were always ---- animals.

(A) ignorant (B) inquisitive (C) responsive (D) cruel (E) peaceful

21. Although his opinions are ----, his word is not gospel and his report will not be without its ----.

(A) valid. .adherents
(B) personal. .partisans
(C) respected. .critics
(D) familiar. .negotiators
(E) confusing. .misinterpreters

22. Traditional Native American storytellers acted as ---- of their tribes' repertory of tales and, as such, were especially valued for their ability to ---- material familiar to their audiences.

(A) gatherers. .invent
(B) detractors. .celebrate
(C) performers. .dramatize
(D) inheritors. .debase
(E) guardians. .corrupt

23. Although often victims of circumstance, the heroines of Shakespearean comedy tend to be ---- women, usually ready with a clever stratagem or verbal ploy for getting out of a difficult situation.

(A) imperious (B) suffering (C) excitable (D) resourceful (E) precocious

24. The language of Anne Spencer's poetry conveys an impression of ---- that can be misleading: just when a poem seems to be echoing routine feelings, the diction suddenly sharpens to embody fresh and unexpected ideas.

(A) frivolity (B) triteness (C) diversity (D) lyricism (E) precision

25. Our fear of being branded ---- if we do not unquestioningly accept new fashions forestalls dismissal of much recent art that is merely novel and momentarily ----.

(A) tolerant. .appealing
(B) contemporary. .interesting
(C) impulsive. .unsettling
(D) reactionary. .seductive
(E) insensitive. .defective

GO ON TO THE NEXT PAGE

Each passage below is followed by questions based on its content. Answer the questions following each passage on the basis of what is stated or implied in that passage.

Kangaroos are fascinating creatures because they differ so much from the usual notion of what constitutes a mammal. Kangaroos rear their young in a pouch and they hop. The explanation often given for these odd features is simply that kangaroos are marsupials and marsupials are primitive mammals. This is no answer, but reflects an impression that seems to have arisen, particularly among people who live in the Northern Hemisphere, from statements made about the Virginia opossum, the only marsupial in North America. The opossum is frequently described as an archaic primitive mammal, little changed since the time of dinosaurs. There is perhaps some basis for such statements: fossils of marsupials that coexisted with dinosaurs toward the end of the Mesozoic era, some 100 million years ago, have been classified as belonging to the same genus as that of the Virginia opossum. But even if the opossum can in some ways be considered a "living fossil," the same cannot be inferred for the kangaroo. These Australian marsupials of the Macropodidae (literally, "big feet") family represent a recent specialized adaptation to a changing environment. Macropodidae evolved from small forest-dwelling browsing animals into predominantly open-range grazing ones. Their rise was probably related to the spread of grassland in the interior of Australia in the Miocene epoch, between 10 and 15 million years ago.

There are indications that all mammals are descended from a mammal-like reptile that lived late in the Triassic period, more than 200 million years ago. Soon thereafter, about 180 million years ago, the stocks leading to two groups of mammals separated. One group was the prototherians, which consists of egg-laying monotremes such as the platypus. The other group was the therians, which includes the marsupial and the placental animals. Information from a variety of sources suggests the marsupials developed in North America and were the dominant therians there for most of the Cretaceous period, or until about 70 million years ago.

The placentals apparently developed initially in Asia and only reached North America late in the Cretaceous period, when there was no oceanic barrier betwen the two landmasses. Competition with the invading placentals has been suggested as the reason for the great marsupial extinction, but other causes may have been involved, since this was also the time when dinosaurs finally died out.

Tracing the evolution of the tiny insect-eating marsupials of the Cretaceous period in North America to the grasslands of Australia was aided by evidence supporting the theories of continental drift. They probably migrated via the Central American bridge to South America and from there to Australia when South America was linked to Australia by Antarctica. Whatever the form of the earliest Australian marsupials, by the start of the Miocene epoch, 25 million years ago, the process of differentiation had established their major groups. One of these groups was the Macropodidae.

26. The primary focus of the passage is on
    (A) events characteristic of geological time periods
    (B) evidence that marsupials coexisted with dinosaurs
    (C) the evolutionary history of kangaroos
    (D) the nonmammalian features of kangaroos
    (E) the importance of placental fossils in geological research

27. According to the passage, which of the following events happened first?
    (A) Marsupials of the same genus as the Virginia opossum coexisted with dinosaurs.
    (B) The stocks leading to two groups of mammals separated.
    (C) The Macropodidae evolved into open-range grazing animals.
    (D) The marsupials were the dominant mammals in North America.
    (E) South America, Australia, and Antarctica separated.

28. Based on information in the passage, kangaroos could be classified as
    (A) insect-eating marsupials
    (B) mammal-like monotremes
    (C) monotreme prototherians
    (D) marsupial prototherians
    (E) marsupial therians

GO ON TO THE NEXT PAGE

The reading passages in this test are brief excerpts or adaptations of excerpts from published material. The ideas contained in them do not necessarily represent the opinions of the College Board or Educational Testing Service. To make the text suitable for testing purposes, we may in some cases have altered the style, contents, or point of view of the original.

29. Which of the following statements about the mammal-like reptile mentioned at the beginning of the second paragraph can be inferred from the information given in the passage?

(A) It was the dominant animal in the Triassic period.
(B) It was the ancestor of many other species.
(C) It was more similar to the therians than to the prototherians.
(D) It lived only in certain regions of North America.
(E) Its diet was similar to that of the Virginia opossum.

30. In developing the passage, the author does all of the following EXCEPT

(A) cite a specific source
(B) refute a mistaken notion
(C) define terms
(D) speculate about causes
(E) relate independent occurrences

GO ON TO THE NEXT PAGE

Tomás Rivera's book entitled . . .*and the earth did not part* is difficult to describe. It is not a novel in the conventional sense, but then neither is it a mere collection of stories and sketches. The book contains a set of twelve thematically unified stories—symbolic of the twelve months of the year—framed at the beginning by an introductory selection entitled "The Lost Year," and at the end by a summarizing selection entitled "Under the House." Preceding each of these pieces except "The Lost Year" is a brief anecdote, now directed backward (echoing or commenting on the thematic concerns of the preceding narrative), now pointed forward (prefacing the narrative that follows). Sometimes the anecdote does not relate directly either to what immediately precedes or to what follows, but instead echoes or reechoes values, motifs, themes, or judgments found elsewhere in the book. The effect is incremental. Through the reinforcement, variation, and amplification provided by the twelve stories and thirteen anecdotes, a picture of the community is gradually filled. In the summarizing selection, the entire experience is synthesized and brought to a thematic conclusion through the consciousness of the central character.

The central figure—presumably the author's alter ego—is the unnamed hero of the two frame pieces. Though it may be conjectured that this central figure is the same one who moves through some of the other selections in the book, direct and explicit identification of the characters in the stories with the central figure is of minor importance, for the overall impression created by the book is not of an individual but a group experience. The various persons of the stories, the experiences and the landscapes of these lives, belong unmistakably to the hero's past. The emphasis, however, remains on the general experience, communal and social rather than individual and personal. Even in the two frame selections at the beginning and end, the protagonist's voice is not that of an individual hero intent on discovering and expressing his own subjective reality, but that of a Mexican American in the significant process of discovering and embracing representatively his community's experience and culture. The end toward which the narrative is directed is one of social identity.

The hero of the frame pieces plays no explicitly active part in the book. He serves merely as the "rememberer," the central figure—however unrealized he may appear as a fully developed character—around whom Rivera weaves his thematic tapestry. At the beginning the hero is confused, alone, frightened, and disoriented. He is the one for whom the year is lost. The succeeding twelve stories and thirteen anecdotes compose his effort to reclaim a past. At the end of the book he has become the synthesizer and commentator, the one who discovers his "lost year."

31. The primary purpose of the passage is to

(A) summarize the plot of a novel
(B) describe the main characters in a book
(C) discuss the distinctive features of a literary work
(D) present the moral lesson learned by the hero of a novel
(E) compare and contrast different stories in a collection

32. The author of the passage is LEAST sure of which of the following?

(A) Whether the central character is seeking a social identity
(B) Whether the central character of the frame pieces appears in the other selections
(C) What state of mind the protagonist is in at the beginning of the novel
(D) Which society is being portrayed in the stories and anecdotes
(E) Why there are exactly twelve stories with common themes

33. According to the passage, the different anecdotes and stories in Rivera's work are unified by which of the following?

I. A shared theme
II. A temporal arrangement
III. The repetition and expansion of particular ideas

(A) I only (B) III only (C) I and II only (D) II and III only (E) I, II, and III

34. As described in the passage, the function of the central character of the book is primarily to

(A) express the author's criticism of society and the modern world
(B) convey a uniquely personal view of a bewildering series of events
(C) interconnect the elements of the book by providing a thematic focus
(D) confirm the impression of despair established by other major characters
(E) balance the extreme views presented by the minor characters

GO ON TO THE NEXT PAGE

35. It can be inferred from the passage that Rivera's novel is best characterized as

(A) a representation of Mexican-American culture
(B) an insightful satire on American culture and politics
(C) a comic treatment of social issues affecting Mexican Americans
(D) a traditional literary work depicting radical social changes
(E) a book that appeals primarily to readers of mystery novels

Each question below consists of a related pair of words or phrases, followed by five lettered pairs of words or phrases. Select the lettered pair that <u>best</u> expresses a relationship similar to that expressed in the original pair.

Example:

YAWN:BOREDOM :: (A) dream:sleep (B) anger:madness (C) smile:amusement (D) face:expression (E) impatience:rebellion

Ⓐ Ⓑ ● Ⓓ Ⓔ

36. GLAUCOMA : EYE :: (A) emphysema : lung (B) anemia : strength (C) obesity : weight (D) ventricle : heart (E) circulation : artery

37. CHARGE : BATTERY :: (A) melt : candle (B) wind up : clock (C) paddle : canoe (D) steer : wheel (E) turn on : switch

38. SHEEP : BLEAT :: (A) bear : den (B) fish : bait (C) whale : spout (D) horse : neigh (E) cow : grass

39. BRIDGE : GORGE :: (A) railing : balcony (B) tunnel : mountain (C) chimney : roof (D) stream : cavern (E) desert : quicksand

40. COURIER : MESSAGE :: (A) soldier : battle (B) student : knowledge (C) prophet : revelation (D) judge : law (E) athlete : prowess

41. QUIBBLE : OBJECT :: (A) boggle : decide (B) wail : cry (C) dawdle : hurry (D) exclaim : state (E) bicker : quarrel

42. DELECTABLE : FOOD :: (A) expensive : money (B) attractive : magnetism (C) delicate : health (D) distilled : water (E) engaging : personality

43. CARICATURE : FACE :: (A) amusement : formality (B) parody : poem (C) cartoon : politics (D) rhyme : verse (E) ridicule : clown

44. PARRY : BLOW :: (A) compile : evidence (B) mediate : dispute (C) instigate : argument (D) deflect : criticism (E) delineate : issue

45. MISNOMER : NAME :: (A) malcontent : person (B) malapropism : word (C) maze : network (D) euphemism : insult (E) stereotype : role

IF YOU FINISH BEFORE TIME IS CALLED, YOU MAY CHECK YOUR WORK ON THIS SECTION ONLY. DO NOT TURN TO ANY OTHER SECTION IN THE TEST. **STOP**

SECTION 2	Time—30 minutes 25 Questions	In this section solve each problem, using any available space on the page for scratchwork. Then decide which is the best of the choices given and fill in the corresponding oval on the answer sheet.

The following information is for your reference in solving some of the problems.

Circle of radius r: Area $= \pi r^2$; Circumference $= 2\pi r$
The number of degrees of arc in a circle is 360.
The measure in degrees of a straight angle is 180.

Definition of symbols:

$=$ is equal to	$\leq$ is less than or equal to
$\neq$ is unequal to	$\geq$ is greater than or equal to
$<$ is less than	$\parallel$ is parallel to
$>$ is greater than	$\perp$ is perpendicular to

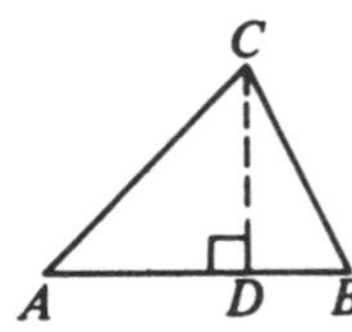

Triangle: The sum of the measures in degrees of the angles of a triangle is 180.
If $\angle CDA$ is a right angle, then

(1) area of $\triangle ABC = \frac{AB \times CD}{2}$

(2) $AC^2 = AD^2 + DC^2$

Note: Figures that accompany problems in this test are intended to provide information useful in solving the problems. They are drawn as accurately as possible EXCEPT when it is stated in a specific problem that its figure is not drawn to scale. All figures lie in a plane unless otherwise indicated. All numbers used are real numbers.

1. Jim's annual take-home pay is \$13,200. If this amount is paid in 12 equal monthly payments, how much does Jim receive each month?

(A) \$101
(B) \$110
(C) \$1,010
(D) \$1,100
(E) \$1,200

2. Which of the following CANNOT be written as the sum of two negative numbers?

(A) -4
(B) $-2\sqrt{2}$
(C) $-\frac{1}{2}$
(D) $-\frac{1}{8}$
(E) 2

3. Model A of a machine produces 300 parts per hour and model B produces 450 parts per hour. If a company has 3 model A machines and 1 model B machine, how many parts can the company produce in one hour?

(A) 750
(B) 900
(C) 1,350
(D) 1,650
(E) 2,250

4. If the length of a side of a square is 0.25, what is the perimeter of the square?

(A) 0.0625
(B) 0.50
(C) 0.75
(D) 1.00
(E) 2.50

GO ON TO THE NEXT PAGE

5. If the price of a computer was decreased from $1,000 to $750, by what percent was the price decreased?

(A) 25%

(B) $33\frac{1}{3}\%$

(C) $66\frac{2}{3}\%$

(D) 75%

(E) 250%

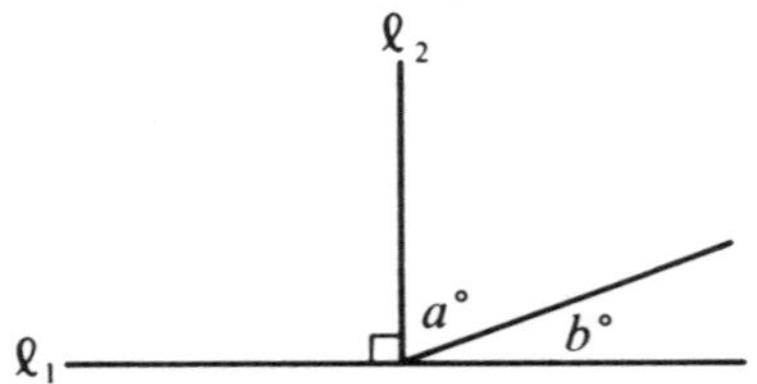

Note: Figure not drawn to scale.

6. In the figure above, $\ell_1 \perp \ell_2$. Which of the following must be true?

I. $a = 70$
II. If $a = 70$, then $b = 20$.
III. If $b = 20$, then $a = 70$.

(A) I only
(B) II only
(C) III only
(D) II and III only
(E) I, II, and III

7. Pat has 1,114 pennies in a jar. What is the least number of pennies that Pat should remove so that she would be able to divide the remaining pennies equally among 3 of her friends?

(A) 0
(B) 1
(C) 2
(D) 3
(E) 4

8. If the sum of two consecutive odd integers is 24, what is their product?

(A) 48
(B) 130
(C) 143
(D) 156
(E) 195

9. In a recipe for sugar cookies, the ratio of flour to sugar is 3:2. If the recipe is doubled in order to make twice the number of cookies, the ratio of flour to sugar will be

(A) 3:1
(B) 2:1
(C) 3:2
(D) 1:1
(E) 3:4

10. Al has $5. If the cost of pads of paper ranges from 60 cents to 90 cents per pad, what is the greatest number of pads that he can buy?

(A) 9
(B) 8
(C) 7
(D) 6
(E) 5

11. If the lengths of the sides of squares S and T are $\sqrt{5}$ and $\sqrt{7}$, respectively, then the area of T minus the area of S is

(A) $\sqrt{2}$

(B) 2

(C) 4

(D) 24

(E) 35

12. What is the average (arithmetic mean) of 3^2, 4^2, and 5^2?

(A) 12

(B) $12\frac{2}{3}$

(C) 16

(D) $16\frac{2}{3}$

(E) 25

GO ON TO THE NEXT PAGE

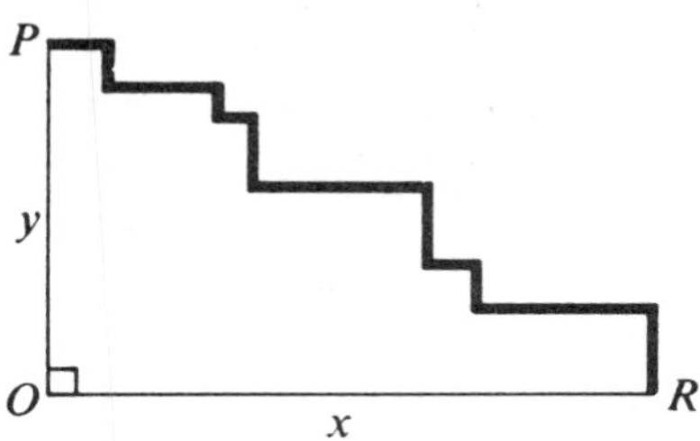

13. In the figure above, the heavy broken line from P to R is composed of line segments that are parallel either to OR or OP. If the length of OR is x and the length of OP is y, what is the total length of the heavy broken line from P to R?

(A) $\sqrt{x^2 + y^2}$
(B) $x + y$
(C) $2(x + y)$
(D) $x^2 + y^2$
(E) $(x + y)^2$

14. The sum of two integers is 72. If the integers are in a ratio of 3:5, what is the value of the greater integer?

(A) 38
(B) 39
(C) 40
(D) 45
(E) 48

15. How many cubical blocks, each with edge of 4 centimeters, are needed to fill a rectangular box with inside dimensions 20 centimeters by 24 centimeters by 32 centimeters?

(A) 38
(B) 96
(C) 192
(D) 240
(E) 384

16. If $x - 3$ is 1 greater than y, then $x + 10$ is how much greater than y?

(A) 6
(B) 7
(C) 8
(D) 13
(E) 14

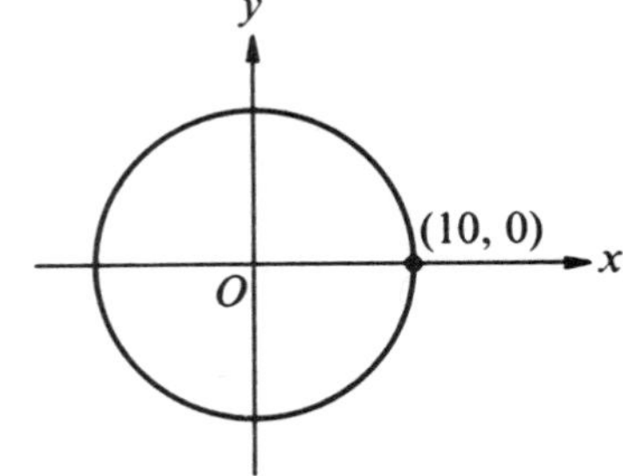

17. In the figure above, if O is the center of the circle, which of the following points lies outside the circle?

(A) $(-7, -8)$
(B) $(-7, 7)$
(C) $(8, -6)$
(D) $(8, 5)$
(E) $(9, 4)$

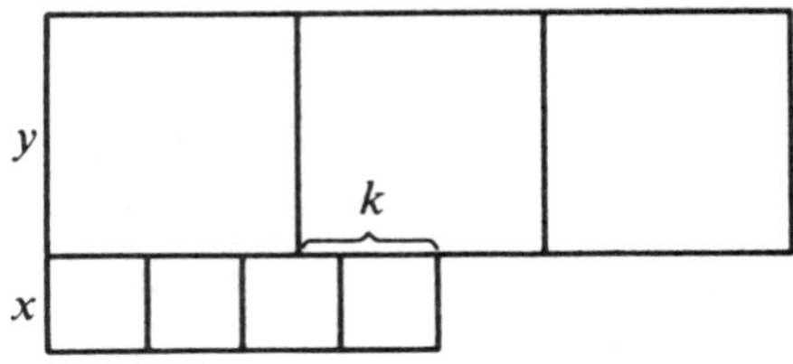

18. The figure above is made up of 4 squares with sides of length x and 3 squares with sides of length y. In terms of x and y, what does k equal?

(A) $4x - y$
(B) $2y - 4x$
(C) $3y - 2x$
(D) $3y - 3x$
(E) $3y - 4x$

19. A train leaves the station at 11 a.m. traveling at the rate of 40 miles per hour. A faster train leaves the same station at 1 p.m. that afternoon and travels in the same direction on a parallel track at a rate of 60 miles per hour. At what time will the faster train overtake the slower one?

(A) 3 p.m.
(B) 4 p.m.
(C) 5 p.m.
(D) 6 p.m.
(E) 7 p.m.

GO ON TO THE NEXT PAGE

20. If x and y are integers greater than zero and $x + y = 12$, what is the least possible value of $x - y$?

(A) -12
(B) -11
(C) -10
(D) -1
(E) 0

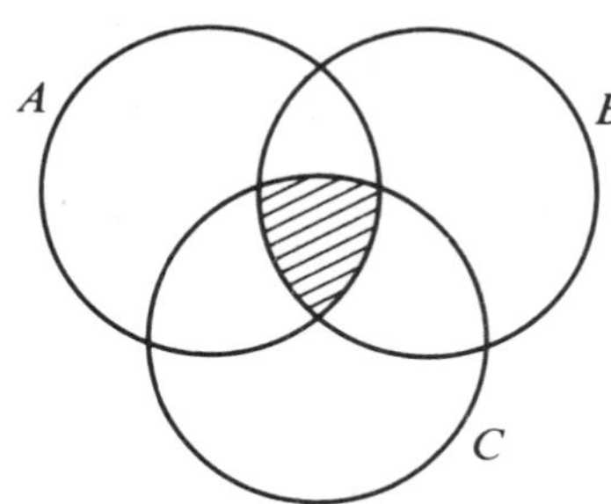

21. In the figure above, circular region A represents the set of all numbers of the form $2m$, circular region B represents the set of all numbers of the form n^2, and circular region C represents the set of all numbers of the form 10^k, where m, n, and k are positive integers. Which of the following numbers belongs in the set represented by the shaded region?

(A) 2
(B) 4
(C) 10
(D) 25
(E) 100

22. Triangles ABC and ABD share side AB. Triangle ABC has area Q and triangle ABD has area R. If AD is longer than AC and BD is longer than BC, which of the following could be true?

I. $R > Q$
II. $R = Q$
III. $R < Q$

(A) I only
(B) III only
(C) I and II only
(D) I and III only
(E) I, II, and III

23. For any real number x, define $\boxed{x}$ as the least non-negative number such that $x + \boxed{x}$ is an integer. For example, $\boxed{2.8} = 0.2$, since $2.8 + 0.2 = 3$. What is the value of $0.4 - \boxed{0.4}$?

(A) -0.6
(B) -0.2
(C) 0
(D) 0.6
(E) 1

24. If n is a positive integer, then $(4^n)^2 =$

(A) 2^{4n}
(B) 2^{2n^2}
(C) 4^{n+2}
(D) 4^{n^2}
(E) $16n^2$

25. If $\frac{a^2 - 4}{(a - 2)^2} = b$ and $a \neq 2$, what is the value of a in terms of b?

(A) $\frac{2 + b}{2 - b}$
(B) $\frac{4}{b - 1}$
(C) $\frac{b + 2}{b - 2}$
(D) $2\sqrt{\frac{1 + b}{1 - b}}$
(E) $\frac{2 + 2b}{b - 1}$

IF YOU FINISH BEFORE TIME IS CALLED, YOU MAY CHECK YOUR WORK ON THIS SECTION ONLY. DO NOT TURN TO ANY OTHER SECTION IN THE TEST. **STOP**

SECTION 4

Time—30 minutes
40 Questions

For each question in this section, choose the best answer and fill in the corresponding oval on the answer sheet.

Each question below consists of a word in capital letters, followed by five lettered words or phrases. Choose the word or phrase that is most nearly opposite in meaning to the word in capital letters. Since some of the questions require you to distinguish fine shades of meaning, consider all the choices before deciding which is best.

Example:

GOOD: (A) sour (B) bad (C) red (D) hot (E) ugly

Ⓐ ● Ⓒ Ⓓ Ⓔ

1. EVACUATE: (A) compel (B) fill (C) delay (D) fix (E) tighten

2. WATERY: (A) agitated (B) polluted (C) filtered (D) thick (E) warm

3. ROUSE: (A) succeed (B) discover (C) dry off (D) place together (E) lull to sleep

4. COMPREHENSIVE: (A) restorative (B) adaptable (C) apprehensive (D) narrowly focused (E) rigidly enforced

5. UNKEMPT: (A) neat (B) slim (C) creative (D) sociable (E) generous

6. JAUNTY: (A) depressed (B) natural (C) unpopular (D) distorted (E) satiated

7. APPEND: (A) deny (B) damage (C) delete (D) straighten (E) solidify

8. REPLETE: (A) self-evident (B) ill-provided (C) irregularly shaped (D) awkwardly placed (E) carefully restored

9. CARP: (A) ponder (B) destroy (C) treat seriously (D) accomplish without effort (E) accept without complaint

10. PENURY: (A) symmetry (B) frequency (C) wealth (D) honor (E) innocence

Each sentence below has one or two blanks, each blank indicating that something has been omitted. Beneath the sentence are five lettered words or sets of words. Choose the word or set of words that, when inserted in the sentence, best fits the meaning of the sentence as a whole.

Example:

Although its publicity has been ----, the film itself is intelligent, well-acted, handsomely produced, and altogether ----.

(A) tasteless. .respectable (B) extensive. .moderate (C) sophisticated. .amateur (D) risqué. .crude (E) perfect. .spectacular

● Ⓑ Ⓒ Ⓓ Ⓔ

11. His frequent stage appearances during those few years, though they brought him more ----, hardly added to his ---- as an actor.

(A) fame. .development
(B) money. .activity
(C) admirers. .popularity
(D) joy. .years
(E) regret. .responsibility

12. Contemporary novelist Alice Walker is quite the opposite of ----; through the ability of her heroines to rise above tragic setbacks, she expresses the belief that people can take charge of their destinies.

(A) an optimist (B) an idealist (C) a moralizer (D) a fatalist (E) a competitor

13. The world, accustomed to ---- whenever governments change hands, expected rioting and bloodshed; but the transition of power was remarkably ----.

(A) turmoil. .chaotic
(B) harmony. .orderly
(C) ceremony. .solemn
(D) violence. .uneventful
(E) splendor. .unpopular

GO ON TO THE NEXT PAGE

14. Researchers studying dieters conclude that exercise should be an ---- to any decrease in calorie intake, noting that efforts to lose weight without regular physical activity are usually ----.

(A) alternative. .sustained
(B) equivalent. .misguided
(C) incentive. .notable
(D) adjunct. .doomed
(E) impediment. .detrimental

15. Most doctors say that to deny the ---- link between cigarette smoking and lung disease is to make a mockery of the statistical evidence that so clearly ---- the connection.

(A) significant. .undermines
(B) causal. .demonstrates
(C) meager. .refutes
(D) questionable. .acknowledges
(E) residual. .suppresses

Each question below consists of a related pair of words or phrases, followed by five lettered pairs of words or phrases. Select the lettered pair that best expresses a relationship similar to that expressed in the original pair.

Example:

YAWN:BOREDOM :: (A) dream:sleep
(B) anger:madness (C) smile:amusement
(D) face:expression (E) impatience:rebellion

16. SLINGSHOT : STONE :: (A) pistol : trigger
(B) missile : rocket (C) bow : arrow
(D) firecracker : fuse (E) knife : blade

17. COMPASS : DIRECTION :: (A) tent : shelter
(B) scale : weight (C) watch : dial
(D) thunder : noise (E) camera : film

18. RIND : LEMON :: (A) shell : egg
(B) slice : bread (C) pit : seed
(D) tree : apple (E) cream : milk

19. CHOIR : SING :: (A) herd : stampede
(B) class : instruct (C) court : testify
(D) team : cheer (E) troupe : act

20. PRESUME : ASCERTAIN :: (A) garble : express
(B) help : rescue (C) theorize : prove
(D) propel : halt (E) idealize : believe

21. PURSE : LIPS :: (A) bend : knee
(B) knit : brow (C) grimace : eye
(D) speak : tongue (E) stretch : neck

22. IDOLATRY : ADMIRATION ::
(A) absurdity : enjoyment
(B) thanklessness : patronage
(C) exasperation : annoyance
(D) intimacy : solitude
(E) eccentricity : conformity

23. NECROMANCY : SORCERER ::
(A) boredom : sophisticate
(B) ambition : politician
(C) legislation : governor
(D) verdict : jury
(E) quackery : charlatan

24. HAIRDRESSER : COIFFURE ::
(A) model : photograph
(B) tailor : garment
(C) beautician : cosmetology
(D) pharmacist : illness
(E) artist : studio

25. MAGNATE : POWER ::
(A) novice : youth (B) miser : generosity
(C) paragon : excellence (D) sentry : protection
(E) student : knowledge

GO ON TO THE NEXT PAGE

Each passage below is followed by questions based on its content. Answer the questions following each passage on the basis of what is stated or implied in that passage.

Carruthers was an artist. He was also a clerk in the Foreign Office. His reputation as a writer was distinguished; he was not interested in the vulgar, and to sell well would possibly have damaged his career. I could not surmise what had induced him to invite me to have coffee with him. It is true he was alone, but I should have supposed he found his thoughts excellent company, and I could not believe he imagined that I had anything to say that would interest him. Nevertheless I could not but see that he was doing his dreary best to be affable. We talked for a moment of common friends in London. Our conversation did not go easily and I made up my mind that as soon as I civilly could I would leave. Presently I had an odd sensation that he was conscious of this and was desperately anxious not to give me the opportunity. I was surprised. I noticed that whenever I paused he broke in with a new topic. He was trying to find something to interest me so that I should stay. He was straining every nerve to be agreeable. Surely he could not be lonely; he must know plenty of people with whom he could have spent the evening. He talked with a sort of harsh eagerness as though he were afraid of a moment's silence. It was very strange. Though I did not like him, though he meant nothing to me and to be with him irked me somewhat, I was against my will a trifle interested.

26. Which of the following best characterizes the existing relationship between Carruthers and the narrator?

(A) Close friends
(B) Former colleagues
(C) Distant relatives
(D) Casual acquaintances
(E) Political opponents

27. The "opportunity" mentioned in line 16 is best interpreted as the opportunity for

(A) the narrator to respond to Carruthers
(B) the narrator to depart from Carruthers' presence
(C) the narrator to change the topic of conversation
(D) Carruthers to confess his problems to the narrator
(E) Carruthers to change the topic of the conversation

28. The primary purpose of the passage is to

(A) relate an incident
(B) explain a custom
(C) refuse an invitation
(D) transcribe a conversation
(E) evaluate a career

GO ON TO THE NEXT PAGE

Imagine a portion of space far removed from all appreciable masses. Next, imagine in this portion of space a large closed chest resembling a room with a man inside. Gravitation naturally does not exist for this person; upon slightest impact with the floor, he moves toward the ceiling. On the outside of the lid of the chest is a hook with rope attached. Now imagine that a "being" begins to pull on this rope with constant force; the chest moves "upward" with a uniformly accelerated motion.

But how does the person in the chest regard the process? In the accelerated frame of reference of the chest, he is suddenly standing exactly as anyone stands on Earth. When he releases an object from his hand, it approaches the floor with an accelerated relative motion. He will further ascertain that, whatever kind of object he experiments with, its acceleration toward the floor is always of the same magnitude. Relying on his knowledge of gravity, the man concludes that he and the chest are now within the influence of a constant gravitational field.

Ought we to smile and say that this person errs in his conclusion? We must rather admit that his interpretation violates neither reason nor known mechanical laws. Even though the chest is being accelerated, we can nevertheless regard it as being at rest. This hypothetical case thus suggests for us the validity of the principle that a gravitational field can be equivalent in every respect to an accelerated frame of reference in which gravity is absent.

29. The primary purpose of the passage is to

(A) discuss a complex problem and its solution
(B) present a new theory and suggest several ways of testing it
(C) give background information on recent discoveries
(D) provide a basis for choosing between two hypotheses
(E) illustrate the validity of a general principle

30. The author's attitude toward the reasoning displayed by the person inside the chest is best described as one of

(A) sympathetic understanding
(B) reluctant acceptance
(C) apologetic embarrassment
(D) cynical skepticism
(E) amused dismissal

31. Which of the following best describes the method by which the author develops the passage?

(A) Generalization followed by support
(B) Argument followed by rebuttal
(C) Statement of fact followed by theories and laws
(D) Controversial proposal followed by debate
(E) Extended example followed by thesis

GO ON TO THE NEXT PAGE

The form of rural England as it is today is largely the result of an agricultural revolution that took place between about 1760 and 1815. The central point of this critical period was the enclosure of the open fields traditionally used by each village. The changes have a poignant interest because, in the early nineteenth century, disaster fell upon the English village. How much was this disaster a result of the agricultural revolution? Controversy raged round the question of enclosures in the eighteenth century and rages round it still, controversy that has obscured as well as illuminated the issue of enclosures. In the past, the controversy became acute in times of dearth and distress, and those involved in the dispute were apt to put the blame for hard times on everything they disliked: enclosures, rich farmers, dealers in grain, speculators, the consumption of tea, and luxury—the last being a vague and question-begging term.

In the eighteenth century, the controversy over enclosures was confused by a belief that the population was shrinking rapidly, although it was actually increasing faster than ever before. Two things gave rise to the belief: first, a fall in the number of deaths (due really to the fall in the death rate) and, second, a decline in the exportation of grain. About 1773 England ceased to be a grain-exporting country on a large scale. This development was really a result of the increased consumption of a larger population and of an enormous increase in the number of horses used to provide improved transport. But the decline in deaths and in grain exports was attributed, at the time, to "depopulation and luxury," and it was argued that this (imaginary) decline in the population and food supply was brought about by enclosures. As usual there were the exceptional cases that could be cited in support of an unsound generalization. The well-known line in Goldsmith's *The Deserted Village*, "Where wealth accumulates and men decay," sums up the contentions of a number of dreary pamphlets. But though in most cases the population of villages increased after enclosures, as the food supply certainly did, the number of farms often decreased.

Although the enclosures of the sixteenth and early seventeenth centuries had been for sheepfarming and the production of wool and did definitely lead to depopulation of villages, the enclosures of the eighteenth century were for improved agriculture. Mixed farming and an advanced rotation system resulted in crops that provided food for stock and more stock produced manure for more and better crops. Moreover, with the new Norfolk rotation and turnip cultivation, sandy wastes were turned into rich arable land. These innovations brought about a revolution in agriculture.

32. The passage can best be described as an
    (A) explanation of the political climate that provoked enclosure in England
    (B) explanation of incorrect assumptions about the effects of enclosures
    (C) inquiry about a particularly bad time of famine in England
    (D) analysis of England's falling population rate
    (E) analysis of the effects of methods of farming on agricultural exports

33. Which of the following best describes the author's attitude toward "those involved in the dispute" (lines 13-14) ?
    (A) Admiration of their persistent search for the truth
    (B) Compassion for the seriousness of their plight
    (C) Confusion in assessing the value of their beliefs
    (D) Criticism of their simple view of a complex situation
    (E) Rage at the disorder they caused in their own time

34. The author believes that enclosures made at which of the following times led to depopulation of villages in England?
    I. The sixteenth century
    II. The early seventeenth century
    III. The eighteenth century
    (A) I only
    (B) III only
    (C) I and II only
    (D) II and III only
    (E) I, II, and III

35. The author cites a line from Goldsmith's *The Deserted Village* to illustrate
    (A) a theory similar to that held by the author
    (B) a popular unfounded conclusion held in eighteenth-century England
    (C) an exception to the statements made by most eighteenth-century writers
    (D) the views of many modern historians about eighteenth-century England
    (E) the influence of Goldsmith's writing on opinions in eighteenth-century England

36. It can be inferred from the passage that one effect of the Norfolk rotation was
    (A) an increase in agricultural production
    (B) an increase in grain exports
    (C) a decrease in population
    (D) a decrease in livestock
    (E) a decrease in food consumption in England

GO ON TO THE NEXT PAGE

It is perhaps ironic that in today's hypertechnological climate there flourish, if only fleetingly, "theories" or "systems" that pretend to scientific status. Cynics argue that people are free to lavish money on anything they wish, and laugh at books about out-of-body travel, astrological predictions generated by computers, and diets purporting to double the human lifespan. It is unfortunate, however, when people substitute sham remedies for effective medical or psychiatric treatment. Also regrettable is the ignorance pseudoscientific fads abet: a benighted public may fall prey to spurious doctrines promoted by political forces that exploit credulity.

The best way to counter pseudoscience is to distinguish between authentic research and humbug. Two criteria apply. One is a scale of the degree to which a theory has been confirmed. At one end of the scale are theories almost certainly false, like the view that an embryo retains in its memory conversations its mother has held. Toward the middle are theories advanced as working hypotheses, like current efforts to describe the ultimate composition of atomic particles. At the other end are theories almost certainly true, like the belief that the Earth is a slightly compressed sphere.

The second criterion is a scale of personal competence, ranging from brilliant professionalism to gross ineptitude. That there are scientists of debatable competence ought not to obscure the fact that certain self-styled scientists are cranks. The label "crank" is justified neither by the novelty of the cranks' views nor by the neurotic motivation behind their theories, but by the failure of those theories to meet the standards by which all theories are judged. Whoever maintains views that contradict all available evidence and offer no reason for serious consideration is rightly exposed and dismissed.

37. The passage as a whole constitutes

(A) a demolition of certain dearly held popular misconceptions
(B) an attempt to criticize the standards scientists use to judge theories
(C) a personal attack on well-known purveyors of groundless claims
(D) an analysis of the methods by which frauds deceive people
(E) an admonition concerning false notions masquerading as science

38. The comment in line 30 about "neurotic motivation" suggests that, in the author's view, such motivation

(A) is as common among reputable scientists as it is among cranks
(B) is not a pertinent criterion for determining what is pseudoscience
(C) is too complex for even modern psychiatry to illuminate
(D) might remain hidden even from a crank's closest colleagues
(E) may be a stimulus to creative individuals in nonscientific fields

39. The author's attitude toward pseudoscience is a mixture of

(A) concern and disapproval
(B) scorn and despair
(C) vindication and amusement
(D) confusion and revulsion
(E) puzzlement and insolence

40. The author does all of the following in considering pseudoscience EXCEPT

(A) provide common examples of it
(B) allude to its dangerous consequences
(C) grant it a limited usefulness
(D) compare it to authentic science
(E) suggest methods for discerning it

IF YOU FINISH BEFORE TIME IS CALLED, YOU MAY CHECK YOUR WORK ON THIS SECTION ONLY. DO NOT TURN TO ANY OTHER SECTION IN THE TEST. **STOP**

SECTION 5	Time—30 minutes 35 Questions	In this section solve each problem, using any available space on the page for scratchwork. Then decide which is the best of the choices given and fill in the corresponding oval on the answer sheet.

The following information is for your reference in solving some of the problems.

Circle of radius r: Area $= \pi r^2$; Circumference $= 2\pi r$
The number of degrees of arc in a circle is 360.
The measure in degrees of a straight angle is 180.

Definition of symbols:

- $=$ is equal to
- $\neq$ is unequal to
- $<$ is less than
- $>$ is greater than
- $\leq$ is less than or equal to
- $\geq$ is greater than or equal to
- $\parallel$ is parallel to
- $\perp$ is perpendicular to

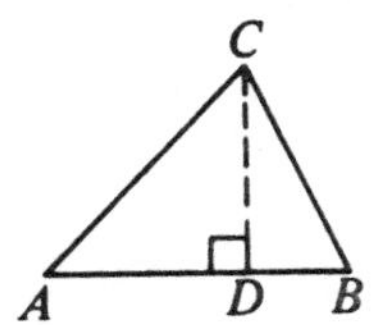

Triangle: The sum of the measures in degrees of the angles of a triangle is 180.

If $\angle CDA$ is a right angle, then

(1) area of $\triangle ABC = \frac{AB \times CD}{2}$

(2) $AC^2 = AD^2 + DC^2$

Note: Figures that accompany problems in this test are intended to provide information useful in solving the problems. They are drawn as accurately as possible EXCEPT when it is stated in a specific problem that its figure is not drawn to scale. All figures lie in a plane unless otherwise indicated. All numbers used are real numbers.

1. If $x + 3x + 5x = -9$, then $x =$

(A) -1

(B) $-\frac{1}{9}$

(C) 0

(D) $\frac{1}{9}$

(E) 81

2. If the following numbers were graphed on a number line, which would be closest to zero?

(A) $-\frac{16}{3}$

(B) $\frac{7}{2}$

(C) 5

(D) -3

(E) $\frac{11}{2}$

3. If $\frac{a}{b} = 4$, $\frac{b}{c} = 5$, and $c = 2$, what is the value of a?

(A) $\frac{5}{4}$

(B) $\frac{5}{2}$

(C) 10

(D) 20

(E) 40

4. The average (arithmetic mean) of three numbers is 7. If the sum of two of the numbers is 16, then the third number is

(A) 4
(B) 5
(C) 6
(D) 7
(E) 8

GO ON TO THE NEXT PAGE

5. $a \cdot 3 \cdot b^2 \cdot \frac{1}{2} =$

(A) a^3b
(B) $1.5ab^2$
(C) $1.5a^2b^2$
(D) $3ab$
(E) $6ab^2$

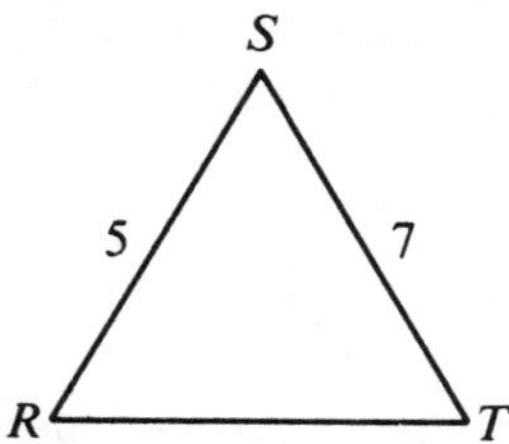

Note: Figure not drawn to scale.

6. If the perimeter of $\triangle RST$ above is 3 times the length of RS, then $RT =$

(A) 3
(B) 5
(C) 8
(D) 9
(E) 10

7. Let the symbol (x) represent the number of different pairs of positive integers whose product is x. For example, (16) = 3, since there are 3 different pairs of positive integers whose product is 16:

$$16 \times 1, \ 8 \times 2, \text{ and } 4 \times 4.$$

What does (36) equal?

(A) 5
(B) 6
(C) 8
(D) 10
(E) 12

GO ON TO THE NEXT PAGE

Questions 8-27 each consist of two quantities, one in Column A and one in Column B. You are to compare the two quantities and on the answer sheet fill in oval

A if the quantity in Column A is greater;
B if the quantity in Column B is greater;
C if the two quantities are equal;
D if the relationship cannot be determined from the information given.

AN E RESPONSE WILL NOT BE SCORED.

	EXAMPLES Column A	Column B	Answers
E1.	2×6	$2 + 6$	● Ⓑ Ⓒ Ⓓ Ⓔ
E2.	$180 - x$	y	Ⓐ Ⓑ ● Ⓓ Ⓔ
E3.	$p - q$	$q - p$	Ⓐ Ⓑ Ⓒ ● Ⓔ

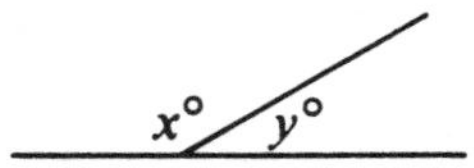

(E2 figure: a line with a ray forming angles $x°$ and $y°$.)

Notes:

1. In certain questions, information concerning one or both of the quantities to be compared is centered above the two columns.
2. In a given question, a symbol that appears in both columns represents the same thing in Column A as it does in Column B.
3. Letters such as x, n, and k stand for real numbers.

	Column A	Column B
8.	$\frac{3}{4} + \frac{1}{3}$	$\frac{4}{7}$

$$\begin{array}{r} P15 \\ \times\ Q5 \\ \hline 2075 \\ 2490 \\ \hline 26{,}975 \end{array}$$

P and Q represent digits in the correctly solved multiplication problem above.

9.	P	Q

$$\frac{4}{6} = \frac{a}{9}$$

$$\frac{3}{12} = \frac{b}{12}$$

10.	a	b

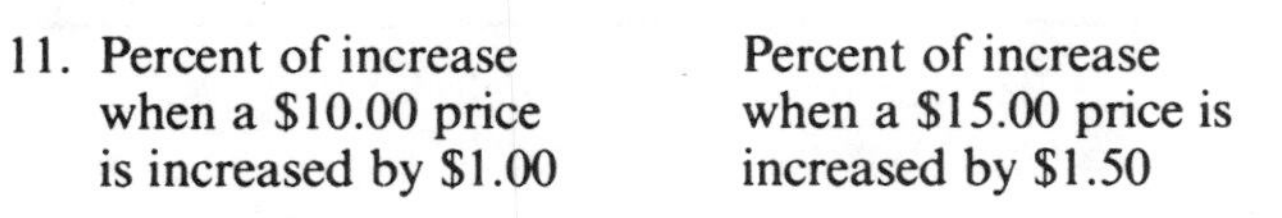

11.	Percent of increase when a \$10.00 price is increased by \$1.00	Percent of increase when a \$15.00 price is increased by \$1.50

$x + 2y = 6$ and $5y = 10$

12.	x	y

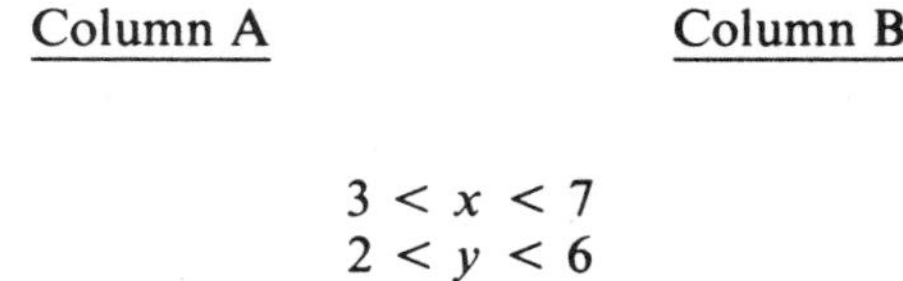

$3 < x < 7$
$2 < y < 6$

	Column A	Column B
13.	$x - y$	5
14.	$0 \cdot 1 \cdot 2 \cdot 3 \cdot 4 \cdot 5 \cdot 6$	$0 \cdot 1 \cdot 2 \cdot 3 \cdot 4 \cdot 5 \cdot 6 \cdot 7$

x is one less than a multiple of 4.
y is a prime number.

15.	x	y

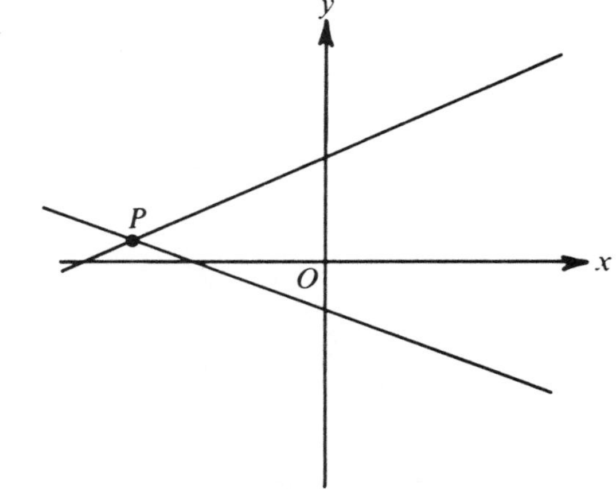

16.	The x-coordinate of point P	The y-coordinate of point P

GO ON TO THE NEXT PAGE

5

SUMMARY DIRECTIONS FOR COMPARISON QUESTIONS

Answer:
- A if the quantity in Column A is greater;
- B if the quantity in Column B is greater;
- C if the two quantities are equal;
- D if the relationship cannot be determined from the information given.

AN E RESPONSE WILL NOT BE SCORED.

	Column A	Column B

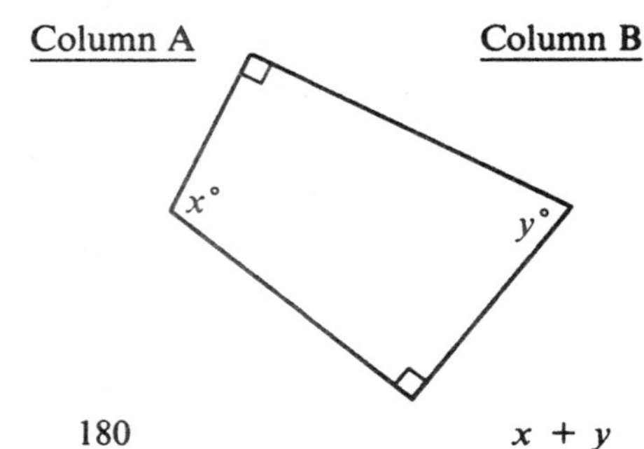

17. 180 | $x + y$

18. The cost per orange, if a 4-pound bag of oranges costs \$1.59 | \$0.16

$x > y > 0$

19. $\frac{2y + x}{2}$ | $y + x$

$ab \neq 0$

20. a^2b^2 | $(-ab)^2$

$y^2 = x$

$y > 0$

21. x | 1

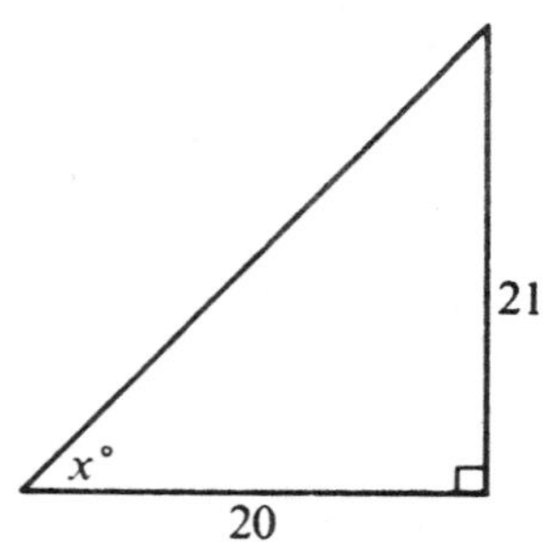

22. x | 45

	Column A	Column B

Charles and David live the same walking distance from school. It took Charles and David 20 minutes and 15 minutes, respectively, to walk directly from home to school without stopping.

23. Average number of kilometers per hour at which Charles walked | Average number of kilometers per hour at which David walked

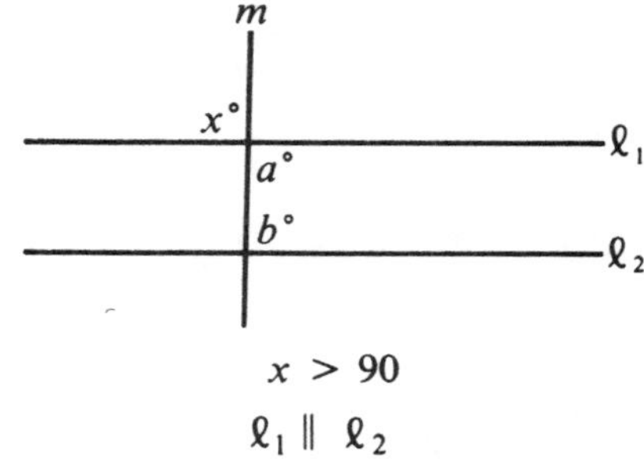

$x > 90$

$\ell_1 \parallel \ell_2$

24. a | b

25. Sum of all integers from -5 to 25 inclusive | Sum of all integers from 6 to 25 inclusive

$y \neq 0$

26. $y + y^2$ | $y^2 - y$

x is the circumference of circle O.
y is the diameter of circle O.

27. x | $3y$

GO ON TO THE NEXT PAGE

Solve each of the remaining problems in this section using any available space for scratchwork. Then decide which is the best of the choices given and fill in the corresponding oval on the answer sheet.

28. If on a certain day there were only 28 of 32 students present for a gym class, what percent of the class was absent?

(A) 4%
(B) 12.5%
(C) 25%
(D) 28%
(E) 87.5%

29. If neither a nor b is an integer, which of the following could be an integer?

I. $\frac{a}{b}$

II. $a \cdot b$

III. $\sqrt{a + b}$

(A) None
(B) I only
(C) II only
(D) I and II only
(E) I, II, and III

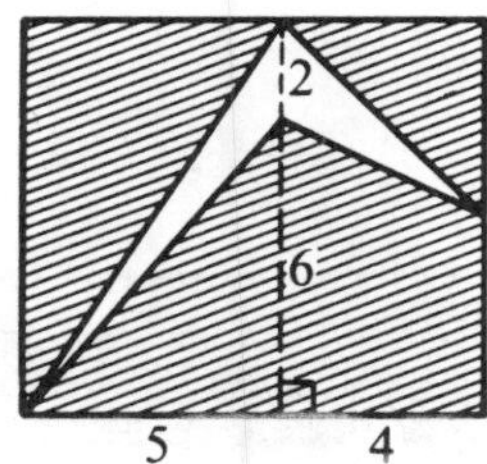

30. In the rectangle above, what is the area of the unshaded region?

(A) 36
(B) 27
(C) 18
(D) 12
(E) 9

31. If $\frac{v}{w} + \frac{x}{y} = z$, $v = 3x$, and $w = 2y$, what is the value of $\frac{2z}{5}$ in terms of x and y?

(A) $\frac{2x}{3y}$

(B) $\frac{2y}{3x}$

(C) $\frac{x}{y}$

(D) $\frac{y}{x}$

(E) $\frac{5x}{2y}$

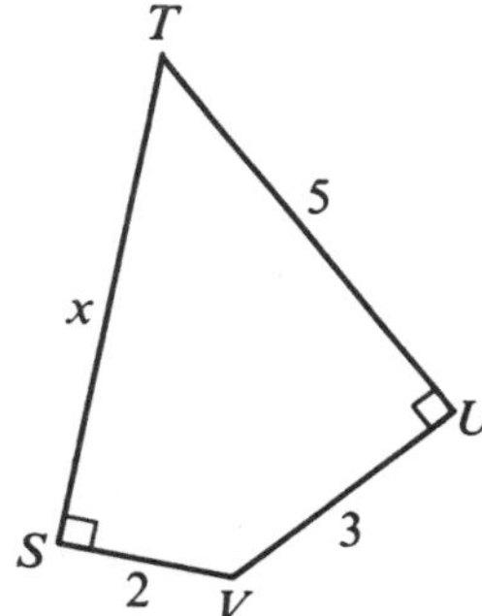

32. In the figure above, $x =$

(A) 7

(B) 6

(C) $4\sqrt{2}$

(D) $\sqrt{30}$

(E) $\sqrt{34} - \sqrt{2}$

GO ON TO THE NEXT PAGE

33. The radius of a unicycle wheel is 1 foot. When the unicycle travels continuously in one direction for 500 feet, the wheel makes v revolutions. Of the following, which is the best approximation of v ?

(A) 80
(B) 160
(C) 310
(D) 3,140
(E) 6,280

20 m

5 m

34. The rectangle above is a diagram of the fencing surrounding an animal pen 20 meters by 5 meters. If an additional 4 square meters is to be enclosed by moving just one side of the pen, while retaining its rectangular shape, what is the least possible number of meters of additional fencing needed?

(A) 2.0
(B) 1.6
(C) 1.0
(D) 0.8
(E) 0.4

35. Let P be the product of the first 10 positive integers. If $\frac{P}{10^x}$ is an integer, what is the maximum possible value of x ?

(A) 1
(B) 2
(C) 4
(D) 5
(E) 10

IF YOU FINISH BEFORE TIME IS CALLED, YOU MAY CHECK YOUR WORK ON THIS SECTION ONLY. DO NOT TURN TO ANY OTHER SECTION IN THE TEST. **STOP**

Correct Answers for Scholastic Aptitude Test Form Code 7A

VERBAL		MATHEMATICAL	
Section 1	**Section 4**	**Section 2**	**Section 5**
1. D	1. B	1. D	1. A
2. D	2. D	2. E	2. D
3. C	3. E	3. C	3. E
4. C	4. D	4. D	4. B
5. B	5. A	5. A	5. B
6. C	6. A	6. D	6. A
7. B	7. C	7. B	7. A
8. E	8. B	8. C	*8. A
9. A	9. E	9. C	*9. B
10. D	10. C	10. B	*10. A
11. B	11. A	11. B	*11. C
12. A	12. D	12. D	*12. C
13. C	13. D	13. B	*13. B
14. D	14. D	14. D	*14. C
15. B	15. B	15. D	*15. D
16. D	16. C	16. E	*16. B
17. B	17. B	17. A	*17. C
18. A	18. A	18. A	*18. D
19. B	19. E	19. C	*19. B
20. E	20. C	20. C	*20. C
21. C	21. B	21. E	*21. D
22. C	22. C	22. E	*22. A
23. D	23. E	23. B	*23. B
24. B	24. B	24. A	*24. A
25. D	25. C	25. E	*25. C
26. C	26. D		*26. D
27. B	27. B		*27. A
28. E	28. A		28. B
29. B	29. E		29. E
30. A	30. A		30. E
31. C	31. E		31. C
32. B	32. B		32. D
33. E	33. D		33. A
34. C	34. C		34. E
35. A	35. B		35. B
36. A	36. A		
37. B	37. E		
38. D	38. B		
39. B	39. A		
40. C	40. C		
41. E			
42. E			
43. B			
44. D			
45. B			

*Indicates four-choice questions. (All of the other questions are five-choice.)

The Scoring Process

Machine-scoring is done in three steps:

- *Scanning.* Your answer sheet is "read" by a scanning machine and the oval you filled in for each question is recorded on a computer tape.
- *Scoring.* The computer compares the oval filled in for each question with the correct response. Each correct answer receives one point; omitted questions do not count toward your score. For each wrong answer, a fraction of a point is subtracted to correct for random guessing. For questions with five answer choices, one-fourth of a point is subtracted for each wrong response; for questions with four answer choices, one-third of a point is subtracted for each wrong response. The SAT-verbal test has 85 questions with five answer choices each. If, for example, a student has 44 right, 32 wrong, and 9 omitted, the resulting raw score is determined as follows:

$$44 \text{ right} - \frac{32 \text{ wrong}}{4} = 44 - 8 = 36 \text{ raw score points}$$

Obtaining raw scores frequently involves the rounding of fractional numbers to the nearest whole number. For example, a raw score of 36.25 is rounded to 36, the nearest whole number. A raw score of 36.50 is rounded upward to 37.

- *Converting to reported scaled score.* Raw test scores are then placed on the College Board scale of 200 to 800 through a process that adjusts scores to account for minor differences in difficulty among different editions of the test. This process, known as equating, is performed so that a student's reported score is not affected by the edition of the test taken nor by the abilities of the group with whom the student takes the test. As a result of placing SAT scores on the College Board scale, scores earned by students at different times can be compared. For example, an SAT-verbal score of 400 on a test taken at one administration indicates the same level of developed verbal ability as a 400 score obtained on a different edition of the test taken at another time.

How to Score the Test

SAT-Verbal Sections 1 and 4

Step A: Count the number of correct answers for *section 1* and record the number in the space provided on the worksheet on the next page. Then do the same for the incorrect answers. (Do not count omitted answers.) To determine subtotal A, use the formula:

$$\text{number correct} - \frac{\text{number incorrect}}{4} = \text{subtotal A}$$

Step B: Count the number of correct answers and the number of incorrect answers for *section 4* and record the numbers in the spaces provided on the worksheet. To determine subtotal B, use the formula:

$$\text{number correct} - \frac{\text{number incorrect}}{4} = \text{subtotal B}$$

Step C: To obtain C, add subtotal A to subtotal B, keeping any decimals. Enter the resulting figure on the worksheet.

Step D: To obtain D, your raw verbal score, round C to the nearest whole number. (For example, any number from 44.50 to 45.49 rounds to 45.) Enter the resulting figure on the worksheet.

Step E: To find your reported SAT-verbal score, look up the total raw verbal score you obtained in step D in the conversion table on page 224. Enter this figure on the worksheet.

SAT-Mathematical Sections 2 and 5

Step A: Count the number of correct answers and the number of incorrect answers for *section 2* and record the numbers in the spaces provided on the worksheet. To determine the subtotal A, use the formula:

$$\text{number correct} - \frac{\text{number incorrect}}{4} = \text{subtotal A}$$

Step B: Count the number of correct answers and the number of incorrect answers for the *five-choice questions (questions 1 through 7 and 28 through 35) in section 5* and record the numbers in the spaces provided on the worksheet. To determine the subtotal B, use the formula:

$$\text{number correct} - \frac{\text{number incorrect}}{4} = \text{subtotal B}$$

Step C: Count the number of correct answers and the number of incorrect answers for the *four-choice questions (questions 8 through 27) in section 5* and record the numbers in the spaces provided on the worksheet. To determine the subtotal C, use the formula:

$$\text{number correct} - \frac{\text{number incorrect}}{3} = \text{subtotal C}$$

Step D: To obtain D, add subtotal A, subtotal B, and subtotal C, keeping any decimals. Enter the resulting figure on the worksheet.

Step E: To obtain E, your raw mathematical score, round D to the nearest whole number. (For example, any number from 44.50 to 45.49 rounds to 45.) Enter the resulting figure on the worksheet.

Step F: To find your reported SAT-mathematical score, look up the total raw mathematical score you obtained in E in the conversion table on page 224. Enter this figure on the worksheet.

SAT SCORING WORKSHEET

FORM CODE 7A

SAT-Verbal Sections

A. Section 1:	______ no. correct	$-\frac{1}{4}$	(______) no. incorrect	=	______ subtotal A
B. Section 4:	______ no. correct	$-\frac{1}{4}$	(______) no. incorrect	=	______ subtotal B
C. Total unrounded raw score (Total A + B)					______ C
D. Total rounded raw score (Rounded to nearest whole number)					______ D
E. SAT-verbal reported scaled score (See the conversion table on page 224.)					[ ] SAT-verbal score

SAT-Mathematical Sections

A. Section 2:	______ no. correct	$-\frac{1}{4}$	(______) no. incorrect	=	______ subtotal A
B. Section 5: Questions <u>1 through 7</u> and <u>28 through 35</u> (5-choice)	______ no. correct	$-\frac{1}{4}$	(______) no. incorrect	=	______ subtotal B
C. Section 5: Questions <u>8 through 27</u> (4-choice)	______ no. correct	$-\frac{1}{3}$	(______) no. incorrect	=	______ subtotal C
D. Total unrounded raw score (Total A + B + C)					______ D
E. Total rounded raw score (Rounded to nearest whole number)					______ E
F. SAT-mathematical reported scaled score (See the conversion table on page 224.)					[ ] SAT-math score

Score Conversion Table
Scholastic Aptitude Test
Form Code 7A

Raw Score	College Board Reported Score		Raw Score	College Board Reported Score	
	SAT-Verbal	SAT-Math		SAT-Verbal	SAT-Math
85	800		40	460	600
84	780		39	450	590
83	770		38	450	580
82	760		37	440	570
81	750		36	430	560
80	740		35	430	560
79	730		34	420	550
78	720		33	420	540
77	710		32	410	530
76	700		31	400	520
75	690		30	400	510
74	680		29	390	500
73	680		28	380	490
72	670		27	380	490
71	660		26	370	480
70	650		25	360	470
69	650		24	360	460
68	640		23	350	450
67	630		22	340	440
66	620		21	340	430
65	620		20	330	430
64	610		19	320	420
63	600		18	320	410
62	590		17	310	400
61	590		16	300	390
60	580	800	15	290	390
59	570	780	14	290	380
58	570	770	13	280	370
57	560	760	12	270	360
56	560	750	11	270	350
55	550	740	10	260	350
54	540	730	9	250	340
53	540	720	8	240	330
52	530	710	7	240	320
51	530	700	6	230	310
50	520	690	5	220	300
49	510	680	4	210	290
48	510	670	3	200	290
47	500	660	2	200	280
46	500	650	1	200	270
45	490	640	0	200	260
44	480	630	−1	200	250
43	480	620	−2	200	240
42	470	620	−3	200	230
41	470	610	−4	200	220
			−5	200	220
			−6	200	210
			−7 or below	200	200

COLLEGE BOARD — SCHOLASTIC APTITUDE TEST and Test of Standard Written English Side 1

Use a No. 2 pencil only. Be sure each mark is dark and completely fills the intended oval. Completely erase any errors or stray marks.

1.
YOUR NAME: (Print) ______ Last ______ First ______ M.I.

SIGNATURE: ______ **DATE:** __/__/__

HOME ADDRESS: (Print) ______ Number and Street

______ City ______ State ______ Zip Code

CENTER: (Print) ______ City ______ State ______ Center Number

IMPORTANT: Please fill in items 2 and 3 exactly as shown on the back cover of your test book.

FOR ETS USE ONLY

2. TEST FORM (Copy from back cover of your test book.)

3. FORM CODE (Copy and grid as shown on back cover of your test book.)

4. REGISTRATION NUMBER (Copy from your Admission Ticket.)

5. YOUR NAME

First 4 letters of last name | First Init. | Mid. Init.

6. DATE OF BIRTH

Month | Day | Year

Jan. Feb. Mar. Apr. May June July Aug. Sept. Oct. Nov. Dec.

7. SEX

Female

Male

8. TEST BOOK SERIAL NUMBER (Copy from front cover of your test book.)

Start with number 1 for each new section. If a section has fewer than 50 questions, leave the extra answer spaces blank.

SECTION 1

SECTION 2

Q1362-04

I.N. 575008 — 110VV58P3720

(Cut here to detach.)

COLLEGE BOARD — SCHOLASTIC APTITUDE TEST and Test of Standard Written English Side 2

Use a No. 2 pencil only. Be sure each mark is dark and completely fills the intended oval. Completely erase any errors or stray marks.

Start with number 1 for each new section. If a section has fewer than 50 questions, leave the extra answer spaces blank.

SECTION 3	SECTION 4	SECTION 5	SECTION 6
1 Ⓐ Ⓑ Ⓒ Ⓓ Ⓔ	1 Ⓐ Ⓑ Ⓒ Ⓓ Ⓔ	1 Ⓐ Ⓑ Ⓒ Ⓓ Ⓔ	1 Ⓐ Ⓑ Ⓒ Ⓓ Ⓔ
2 Ⓐ Ⓑ Ⓒ Ⓓ Ⓔ	2 Ⓐ Ⓑ Ⓒ Ⓓ Ⓔ	2 Ⓐ Ⓑ Ⓒ Ⓓ Ⓔ	2 Ⓐ Ⓑ Ⓒ Ⓓ Ⓔ
3 Ⓐ Ⓑ Ⓒ Ⓓ Ⓔ	3 Ⓐ Ⓑ Ⓒ Ⓓ Ⓔ	3 Ⓐ Ⓑ Ⓒ Ⓓ Ⓔ	3 Ⓐ Ⓑ Ⓒ Ⓓ Ⓔ
4 Ⓐ Ⓑ Ⓒ Ⓓ Ⓔ	4 Ⓐ Ⓑ Ⓒ Ⓓ Ⓔ	4 Ⓐ Ⓑ Ⓒ Ⓓ Ⓔ	4 Ⓐ Ⓑ Ⓒ Ⓓ Ⓔ
5 Ⓐ Ⓑ Ⓒ Ⓓ Ⓔ	5 Ⓐ Ⓑ Ⓒ Ⓓ Ⓔ	5 Ⓐ Ⓑ Ⓒ Ⓓ Ⓔ	5 Ⓐ Ⓑ Ⓒ Ⓓ Ⓔ
6 Ⓐ Ⓑ Ⓒ Ⓓ Ⓔ	6 Ⓐ Ⓑ Ⓒ Ⓓ Ⓔ	6 Ⓐ Ⓑ Ⓒ Ⓓ Ⓔ	6 Ⓐ Ⓑ Ⓒ Ⓓ Ⓔ
7 Ⓐ Ⓑ Ⓒ Ⓓ Ⓔ	7 Ⓐ Ⓑ Ⓒ Ⓓ Ⓔ	7 Ⓐ Ⓑ Ⓒ Ⓓ Ⓔ	7 Ⓐ Ⓑ Ⓒ Ⓓ Ⓔ
8 Ⓐ Ⓑ Ⓒ Ⓓ Ⓔ	8 Ⓐ Ⓑ Ⓒ Ⓓ Ⓔ	8 Ⓐ Ⓑ Ⓒ Ⓓ Ⓔ	8 Ⓐ Ⓑ Ⓒ Ⓓ Ⓔ
9 Ⓐ Ⓑ Ⓒ Ⓓ Ⓔ	9 Ⓐ Ⓑ Ⓒ Ⓓ Ⓔ	9 Ⓐ Ⓑ Ⓒ Ⓓ Ⓔ	9 Ⓐ Ⓑ Ⓒ Ⓓ Ⓔ
10 Ⓐ Ⓑ Ⓒ Ⓓ Ⓔ	10 Ⓐ Ⓑ Ⓒ Ⓓ Ⓔ	10 Ⓐ Ⓑ Ⓒ Ⓓ Ⓔ	10 Ⓐ Ⓑ Ⓒ Ⓓ Ⓔ
11 Ⓐ Ⓑ Ⓒ Ⓓ Ⓔ	11 Ⓐ Ⓑ Ⓒ Ⓓ Ⓔ	11 Ⓐ Ⓑ Ⓒ Ⓓ Ⓔ	11 Ⓐ Ⓑ Ⓒ Ⓓ Ⓔ
12 Ⓐ Ⓑ Ⓒ Ⓓ Ⓔ	12 Ⓐ Ⓑ Ⓒ Ⓓ Ⓔ	12 Ⓐ Ⓑ Ⓒ Ⓓ Ⓔ	12 Ⓐ Ⓑ Ⓒ Ⓓ Ⓔ
13 Ⓐ Ⓑ Ⓒ Ⓓ Ⓔ	13 Ⓐ Ⓑ Ⓒ Ⓓ Ⓔ	13 Ⓐ Ⓑ Ⓒ Ⓓ Ⓔ	13 Ⓐ Ⓑ Ⓒ Ⓓ Ⓔ
14 Ⓐ Ⓑ Ⓒ Ⓓ Ⓔ	14 Ⓐ Ⓑ Ⓒ Ⓓ Ⓔ	14 Ⓐ Ⓑ Ⓒ Ⓓ Ⓔ	14 Ⓐ Ⓑ Ⓒ Ⓓ Ⓔ
15 Ⓐ Ⓑ Ⓒ Ⓓ Ⓔ	15 Ⓐ Ⓑ Ⓒ Ⓓ Ⓔ	15 Ⓐ Ⓑ Ⓒ Ⓓ Ⓔ	15 Ⓐ Ⓑ Ⓒ Ⓓ Ⓔ
16 Ⓐ Ⓑ Ⓒ Ⓓ Ⓔ	16 Ⓐ Ⓑ Ⓒ Ⓓ Ⓔ	16 Ⓐ Ⓑ Ⓒ Ⓓ Ⓔ	16 Ⓐ Ⓑ Ⓒ Ⓓ Ⓔ
17 Ⓐ Ⓑ Ⓒ Ⓓ Ⓔ	17 Ⓐ Ⓑ Ⓒ Ⓓ Ⓔ	17 Ⓐ Ⓑ Ⓒ Ⓓ Ⓔ	17 Ⓐ Ⓑ Ⓒ Ⓓ Ⓔ
18 Ⓐ Ⓑ Ⓒ Ⓓ Ⓔ	18 Ⓐ Ⓑ Ⓒ Ⓓ Ⓔ	18 Ⓐ Ⓑ Ⓒ Ⓓ Ⓔ	18 Ⓐ Ⓑ Ⓒ Ⓓ Ⓔ
19 Ⓐ Ⓑ Ⓒ Ⓓ Ⓔ	19 Ⓐ Ⓑ Ⓒ Ⓓ Ⓔ	19 Ⓐ Ⓑ Ⓒ Ⓓ Ⓔ	19 Ⓐ Ⓑ Ⓒ Ⓓ Ⓔ
20 Ⓐ Ⓑ Ⓒ Ⓓ Ⓔ	20 Ⓐ Ⓑ Ⓒ Ⓓ Ⓔ	20 Ⓐ Ⓑ Ⓒ Ⓓ Ⓔ	20 Ⓐ Ⓑ Ⓒ Ⓓ Ⓔ
21 Ⓐ Ⓑ Ⓒ Ⓓ Ⓔ	21 Ⓐ Ⓑ Ⓒ Ⓓ Ⓔ	21 Ⓐ Ⓑ Ⓒ Ⓓ Ⓔ	21 Ⓐ Ⓑ Ⓒ Ⓓ Ⓔ
22 Ⓐ Ⓑ Ⓒ Ⓓ Ⓔ	22 Ⓐ Ⓑ Ⓒ Ⓓ Ⓔ	22 Ⓐ Ⓑ Ⓒ Ⓓ Ⓔ	22 Ⓐ Ⓑ Ⓒ Ⓓ Ⓔ
23 Ⓐ Ⓑ Ⓒ Ⓓ Ⓔ	23 Ⓐ Ⓑ Ⓒ Ⓓ Ⓔ	23 Ⓐ Ⓑ Ⓒ Ⓓ Ⓔ	23 Ⓐ Ⓑ Ⓒ Ⓓ Ⓔ
24 Ⓐ Ⓑ Ⓒ Ⓓ Ⓔ	24 Ⓐ Ⓑ Ⓒ Ⓓ Ⓔ	24 Ⓐ Ⓑ Ⓒ Ⓓ Ⓔ	24 Ⓐ Ⓑ Ⓒ Ⓓ Ⓔ
25 Ⓐ Ⓑ Ⓒ Ⓓ Ⓔ	25 Ⓐ Ⓑ Ⓒ Ⓓ Ⓔ	25 Ⓐ Ⓑ Ⓒ Ⓓ Ⓔ	25 Ⓐ Ⓑ Ⓒ Ⓓ Ⓔ
26 Ⓐ Ⓑ Ⓒ Ⓓ Ⓔ	26 Ⓐ Ⓑ Ⓒ Ⓓ Ⓔ	26 Ⓐ Ⓑ Ⓒ Ⓓ Ⓔ	26 Ⓐ Ⓑ Ⓒ Ⓓ Ⓔ
27 Ⓐ Ⓑ Ⓒ Ⓓ Ⓔ	27 Ⓐ Ⓑ Ⓒ Ⓓ Ⓔ	27 Ⓐ Ⓑ Ⓒ Ⓓ Ⓔ	27 Ⓐ Ⓑ Ⓒ Ⓓ Ⓔ
28 Ⓐ Ⓑ Ⓒ Ⓓ Ⓔ	28 Ⓐ Ⓑ Ⓒ Ⓓ Ⓔ	28 Ⓐ Ⓑ Ⓒ Ⓓ Ⓔ	28 Ⓐ Ⓑ Ⓒ Ⓓ Ⓔ
29 Ⓐ Ⓑ Ⓒ Ⓓ Ⓔ	29 Ⓐ Ⓑ Ⓒ Ⓓ Ⓔ	29 Ⓐ Ⓑ Ⓒ Ⓓ Ⓔ	29 Ⓐ Ⓑ Ⓒ Ⓓ Ⓔ
30 Ⓐ Ⓑ Ⓒ Ⓓ Ⓔ	30 Ⓐ Ⓑ Ⓒ Ⓓ Ⓔ	30 Ⓐ Ⓑ Ⓒ Ⓓ Ⓔ	30 Ⓐ Ⓑ Ⓒ Ⓓ Ⓔ
31 Ⓐ Ⓑ Ⓒ Ⓓ Ⓔ	31 Ⓐ Ⓑ Ⓒ Ⓓ Ⓔ	31 Ⓐ Ⓑ Ⓒ Ⓓ Ⓔ	31 Ⓐ Ⓑ Ⓒ Ⓓ Ⓔ
32 Ⓐ Ⓑ Ⓒ Ⓓ Ⓔ	32 Ⓐ Ⓑ Ⓒ Ⓓ Ⓔ	32 Ⓐ Ⓑ Ⓒ Ⓓ Ⓔ	32 Ⓐ Ⓑ Ⓒ Ⓓ Ⓔ
33 Ⓐ Ⓑ Ⓒ Ⓓ Ⓔ	33 Ⓐ Ⓑ Ⓒ Ⓓ Ⓔ	33 Ⓐ Ⓑ Ⓒ Ⓓ Ⓔ	33 Ⓐ Ⓑ Ⓒ Ⓓ Ⓔ
34 Ⓐ Ⓑ Ⓒ Ⓓ Ⓔ	34 Ⓐ Ⓑ Ⓒ Ⓓ Ⓔ	34 Ⓐ Ⓑ Ⓒ Ⓓ Ⓔ	34 Ⓐ Ⓑ Ⓒ Ⓓ Ⓔ
35 Ⓐ Ⓑ Ⓒ Ⓓ Ⓔ	35 Ⓐ Ⓑ Ⓒ Ⓓ Ⓔ	35 Ⓐ Ⓑ Ⓒ Ⓓ Ⓔ	35 Ⓐ Ⓑ Ⓒ Ⓓ Ⓔ
36 Ⓐ Ⓑ Ⓒ Ⓓ Ⓔ	36 Ⓐ Ⓑ Ⓒ Ⓓ Ⓔ	36 Ⓐ Ⓑ Ⓒ Ⓓ Ⓔ	36 Ⓐ Ⓑ Ⓒ Ⓓ Ⓔ
37 Ⓐ Ⓑ Ⓒ Ⓓ Ⓔ	37 Ⓐ Ⓑ Ⓒ Ⓓ Ⓔ	37 Ⓐ Ⓑ Ⓒ Ⓓ Ⓔ	37 Ⓐ Ⓑ Ⓒ Ⓓ Ⓔ
38 Ⓐ Ⓑ Ⓒ Ⓓ Ⓔ	38 Ⓐ Ⓑ Ⓒ Ⓓ Ⓔ	38 Ⓐ Ⓑ Ⓒ Ⓓ Ⓔ	38 Ⓐ Ⓑ Ⓒ Ⓓ Ⓔ
39 Ⓐ Ⓑ Ⓒ Ⓓ Ⓔ	39 Ⓐ Ⓑ Ⓒ Ⓓ Ⓔ	39 Ⓐ Ⓑ Ⓒ Ⓓ Ⓔ	39 Ⓐ Ⓑ Ⓒ Ⓓ Ⓔ
40 Ⓐ Ⓑ Ⓒ Ⓓ Ⓔ	40 Ⓐ Ⓑ Ⓒ Ⓓ Ⓔ	40 Ⓐ Ⓑ Ⓒ Ⓓ Ⓔ	40 Ⓐ Ⓑ Ⓒ Ⓓ Ⓔ
41 Ⓐ Ⓑ Ⓒ Ⓓ Ⓔ	41 Ⓐ Ⓑ Ⓒ Ⓓ Ⓔ	41 Ⓐ Ⓑ Ⓒ Ⓓ Ⓔ	41 Ⓐ Ⓑ Ⓒ Ⓓ Ⓔ
42 Ⓐ Ⓑ Ⓒ Ⓓ Ⓔ	42 Ⓐ Ⓑ Ⓒ Ⓓ Ⓔ	42 Ⓐ Ⓑ Ⓒ Ⓓ Ⓔ	42 Ⓐ Ⓑ Ⓒ Ⓓ Ⓔ
43 Ⓐ Ⓑ Ⓒ Ⓓ Ⓔ	43 Ⓐ Ⓑ Ⓒ Ⓓ Ⓔ	43 Ⓐ Ⓑ Ⓒ Ⓓ Ⓔ	43 Ⓐ Ⓑ Ⓒ Ⓓ Ⓔ
44 Ⓐ Ⓑ Ⓒ Ⓓ Ⓔ	44 Ⓐ Ⓑ Ⓒ Ⓓ Ⓔ	44 Ⓐ Ⓑ Ⓒ Ⓓ Ⓔ	44 Ⓐ Ⓑ Ⓒ Ⓓ Ⓔ
45 Ⓐ Ⓑ Ⓒ Ⓓ Ⓔ	45 Ⓐ Ⓑ Ⓒ Ⓓ Ⓔ	45 Ⓐ Ⓑ Ⓒ Ⓓ Ⓔ	45 Ⓐ Ⓑ Ⓒ Ⓓ Ⓔ
46 Ⓐ Ⓑ Ⓒ Ⓓ Ⓔ	46 Ⓐ Ⓑ Ⓒ Ⓓ Ⓔ	46 Ⓐ Ⓑ Ⓒ Ⓓ Ⓔ	46 Ⓐ Ⓑ Ⓒ Ⓓ Ⓔ
47 Ⓐ Ⓑ Ⓒ Ⓓ Ⓔ	47 Ⓐ Ⓑ Ⓒ Ⓓ Ⓔ	47 Ⓐ Ⓑ Ⓒ Ⓓ Ⓔ	47 Ⓐ Ⓑ Ⓒ Ⓓ Ⓔ
48 Ⓐ Ⓑ Ⓒ Ⓓ Ⓔ	48 Ⓐ Ⓑ Ⓒ Ⓓ Ⓔ	48 Ⓐ Ⓑ Ⓒ Ⓓ Ⓔ	48 Ⓐ Ⓑ Ⓒ Ⓓ Ⓔ
49 Ⓐ Ⓑ Ⓒ Ⓓ Ⓔ	49 Ⓐ Ⓑ Ⓒ Ⓓ Ⓔ	49 Ⓐ Ⓑ Ⓒ Ⓓ Ⓔ	49 Ⓐ Ⓑ Ⓒ Ⓓ Ⓔ
50 Ⓐ Ⓑ Ⓒ Ⓓ Ⓔ	50 Ⓐ Ⓑ Ⓒ Ⓓ Ⓔ	50 Ⓐ Ⓑ Ⓒ Ⓓ Ⓔ	50 Ⓐ Ⓑ Ⓒ Ⓓ Ⓔ

9. SIGNATURE:

FOR ETS USE ONLY	VTR	VTFS	VRR	VRFS	VVR	VVFS	WER	WEFS	M4R	M4FS	M5R	M5FS	MTFS
	VTW	VTCS	VRW	VRCS	VVW	VVCS	WEW	WECS	M4W		M5W		MTCS

SECTION 1 Time—30 minutes 40 Questions

For each question in this section, choose the best answer and fill in the corresponding oval on the answer sheet.

Each question below consists of a word in capital letters, followed by five lettered words or phrases. Choose the word or phrase that is most nearly opposite in meaning to the word in capital letters. Since some of the questions require you to distinguish fine shades of meaning, consider all the choices before deciding which is best.

Example:

GOOD: (A) sour (B) bad (C) red (D) hot (E) ugly

Ⓐ ● Ⓒ Ⓓ Ⓔ

1. HUMANE: (A) tiny (B) yearning (C) proud (D) merciless (E) ordinary

2. COMMENCE: (A) treat as an equal (B) bring to an end (C) suspect (D) reject (E) arrange

3. SOMBER: (A) large (B) solid (C) rigid (D) thin (E) bright

4. PROCRASTINATION: (A) promptness (B) contraction (C) austerity (D) suppression (E) disclaimer

5. PRIMEVAL: (A) diminutive (B) secondary (C) carelessly guarded (D) recently developed (E) easily forgotten

6. ASCENDANCY: (A) offspring (B) decline (C) wisdom (D) emigration (E) deprivation

7. OPACITY: (A) diversity (B) viscosity (C) obsolescence (D) translucence (E) fluency

8. MUNDANE: (A) archaic (B) otherworldly (C) minute (D) unemotional (E) oppressive

9. TRIGGER: (A) improve (B) adapt (C) check (D) sharpen (E) defend

10. SPURN: (A) examine (B) initiate (C) detract from (D) request of (E) cleave to

Each sentence below has one or two blanks, each blank indicating that something has been omitted. Beneath the sentence are five lettered words or sets of words. Choose the word or set of words that, when inserted in the sentence, best fits the meaning of the sentence as a whole.

Example:

Although its publicity has been ----, the film itself is intelligent, well-acted, handsomely produced, and altogether ----.

(A) tasteless. .respectable (B) extensive. .moderate (C) sophisticated. .amateur (D) risqué. .crude (E) perfect. .spectacular

● Ⓑ Ⓒ Ⓓ Ⓔ

11. Once Murphy left home for good, he wrote no letters to his worried mother; he did not, therefore, live up to her picture of him as her ---- son.

(A) misunderstood (B) elusive (C) destructive (D) persuasive (E) dutiful

12. We can no longer treat American foreign policy as ---- subject, sufficient unto itself; we must recognize its impact on the rest of the world.

(A) an isolated (B) an assenting (C) an unwieldy (D) a mandatory (E) a subordinate

13. Refuting the claim that the surest way to reduce anger is to express it, the author asserts that ---- anger can actually increase its ----.

(A) denying. .impact
(B) understanding. .importance
(C) overcoming. .likelihood
(D) venting. .intensity
(E) voicing. .benefits

GO ON TO THE NEXT PAGE

14. If the contention of some cognitive psychologists that it is possible for anesthetized patients to ---- gains credence, then there may be less ---- among surgeons during operations.

(A) revive. .haste (B) respond. .constraint (C) suffer. .anxiety (D) hear. .banter (E) recover. .miscalculation

15. The comic excesses and inventiveness praised by the critics of Percival Everett's first novel are virtually absent in his second, replaced by ---- that verges on bluntness.

(A) a superfluity (B) a terseness (C) an exuberance (D) a poignancy (E) a fertility

Each question below consists of a related pair of words or phrases, followed by five lettered pairs of words or phrases. Select the lettered pair that best expresses a relationship similar to that expressed in the original pair.

Example:

YAWN:BOREDOM :: (A) dream:sleep (B) anger:madness (C) smile:amusement (D) face:expression (E) impatience:rebellion

Ⓐ Ⓑ ● Ⓓ Ⓔ

16. FINGER : KNUCKLE :: (A) jaw : tooth (B) ankle : knee (C) arm : elbow (D) hand : palm (E) eye : eyelid

17. LITIGATION : COURT :: (A) decoration : house (B) surgery : hospital (C) migration : travel (D) graduation : course (E) improvisation : role

18. OPPRESS : FREEDOM ::
(A) enlighten : knowledge
(B) confine : movement
(C) corrupt : reputation
(D) regulate : order
(E) demote : reprimand

19. FLUIDS : DEHYDRATION :: (A) squint : eyestrain (B) sleepiness : hypnosis (C) protein : nutrition (D) uproar : protest (E) strength : exhaustion

20. PULPIT : PODIUM :: (A) choir : chapel (B) offering : altar (C) pew : bench (D) hymn : organ (E) hood : robe

21. VOTER : ELECTORATE :: (A) student : professor (B) lawyer : jury (C) passenger : bus (D) teacher : faculty (E) civilian : army

22. INVIGORATE : VIM ::
(A) entice : glamour
(B) embarrass : poise
(C) embolden : courage
(D) embrace : aloofness
(E) entreat : generosity

23. TATTERS : CLOTHING :: (A) mulch : garden (B) slag : iron (C) rubble : edifice (D) weed : garden (E) disease : body

24. AUDACIOUS : RESTRAINT ::
(A) passionate : concern
(B) impudent : courtesy
(C) profound : reverence
(D) persevering : danger
(E) ingenious : design

25. MATCHLESS : PEER :: (A) fearless : enemy (B) priceless : object (C) doubtless : certainty (D) flawless : blemish (E) painless : injury

GO ON TO THE NEXT PAGE

Each passage below is followed by questions based on its content. Answer all questions following a passage on the basis of what is stated or implied in that passage.

The invention of the piano was determined by inherent defects in both the clavichord and the harpsichord. The harpsichord did not allow for the execution of dynamics, that is, for playing either loudly or softly, whereas the clavichord allowed a modest range of dynamics but could not generate a tone nearly as loud as that of the harpsichord. A remedy was provided by the Italian harpsichord-maker Bartolommeo Cristofori, who in 1709 built the first hammer-action keyboard instrument. Cristofori called his original instrument the "piano-forte," meaning that it could be played both softly and loudly. An improved model of the pianoforte included an escapement mechanism that "threw" each free-swinging hammer upward at the strings and also a back-check that regulated the hammer's downward return. An individual damper connected to the action of the hammer was provided for each note.

A later innovation involved the frame. Constant striving for greater sonority had led to the use of very heavy strings, and the point was reached at which the wooden frames of the earlier pianos could no longer withstand the tension. In 1855 the German-born Henry Steinway brought out a grand piano with a cast-iron frame that has served as a model for all subsequent piano frames. Although minor refinements are constantly being introduced, there have been no fundamental changes in the design or construction of pianos since 1855.

26. This passage is primarily concerned with the

(A) origin of the Cristofori hammer action
(B) defects of the clavichord and harpsichord
(C) necessity of a hammer-action keyboard
(D) development of the pianoforte and the modern piano
(E) performance standards of eighteenth-century keyboard instruments

27. The passage suggests that Steinway built the cast-iron frame because it

(A) increased the durability of the piano
(B) could be more easily reproduced
(C) was readily adaptable to classical piano design
(D) was bound to arouse great popular demand
(E) made the piano less bulky and obtrusive

28. The author would probably agree with all of the following statements about the piano EXCEPT that

(A) its design is likely to change radically in the near future
(B) its development was brought about by tonal considerations
(C) Cristofori's prototype underwent several modifications
(D) contemporary piano frames derive from a nineteenth-century improvement
(E) the use of heavy strings damaged the wooden frames of early pianos

GO ON TO THE NEXT PAGE

The reading passages in this test are brief excerpts or adaptations of excerpts from published material. The ideas contained in them do not necessarily represent the opinions of the College Board or Educational Testing Service. To make the text suitable for testing purposes, we may in some cases have altered the style, contents, or point of view of the original.

Arthur Charles Prohack came downstairs at eight-thirty, as usual; and found breakfast ready in the empty dining room. He was a fairly tall man, with a big head, pronounced features, and a beard. His characteristic expression denoted benevolence based on an ironic realization of the humanity of human nature. He had been for more than twenty years at the Treasury, in which organism he had now attained a certain importance.

He was proud of the Treasury's war record. Other departments of state had swollen to amazing dimensions during the war. The Treasury, while its work had been multiplied a hundredfold, had increased its personnel by only a negligible percentage. It was the cheapest of all the departments, the most efficient, and the most powerful. The War Office, the Admiralty, and perhaps one other department presided over by a personality whom the Prime Minister feared did certainly defy and even ignore the Treasury. But the remaining departments might scheme as much as they liked—they could do nothing until the Treasury had approved their enterprises. Modest Mr. Prohack was among the chief arbiters of destiny for them.

In the end the war was not lost, and Mr. Prohack reckoned that he personally, by the exercise of courage in the face of grave danger, had saved for the country five hundred and forty-six millions of the country's money. At any rate he had exercised a real influence over the conduct of the war. Despite all this, the great public had never heard of him.

29. Which of the following is most likely to be the essence of Mr. Prohack's "realization" (lines 5-6) ?

(A) People are by definition weak and fallible.
(B) People are capable of unique achievements.
(C) People should recognize their inner strengths.
(D) People's most basic instinct is togetherness.
(E) People sometimes behave like vicious animals.

30. The phrase "exercise of courage" (line 24) most likely refers to Mr. Prohack's

(A) military exploits
(B) influence over the public
(C) political manipulations
(D) reputation as a great leader
(E) financial decisions

31. The author uses which of the following to describe Mr. Prohack?

I. Details of Mr. Prohack's physical appearance
II. Comments made about Mr. Prohack by others
III. Beliefs held by Mr. Prohack

(A) I only
(B) II only
(C) I and II only
(D) I and III only
(E) I, II, and III

GO ON TO THE NEXT PAGE

The traditional Navajo calendar differs from that of the Pueblos in several ways. Traditional Navajos derive their livelihood primarily from ranching and move from place to place, unlike the Pueblos, who live in one building year-round. These differences between the Pueblos and the Navajos are reflected in their use of celestial motions for reckoning a calendar. The Navajos depend on the stars, de-emphasizing the Sun and the Moon. Their star-watching skills are developed to the point that they know when to prepare their fields, plant corn, and start their harvest. It may seem surprising to think of the Navajos as agriculturists, since they are known as sheep- and cattle-herders; however, the Navajos have tilled the land since they first moved to the Southwest.

The Navajos' use of the constellation Dilyehe is one illustration of how the Navajos use the rising and setting stars as calendar markers. The fact that this constellation reappears near the time of summer solstice has made it useful as a calendar device throughout the world. When Dilyehe is first sighted in the early morning sky to the northeast after having been absent from the night sky for several months, the Navajos know that it is too late to plant and still be able to harvest before the first frost. In late September near the autumnal equinox, at about ten o'clock at night, Dilyehe rises in the northeast, and the Navajos know that the first autumn frost is not far off. During the fall and winter nights, Dilyehe's position can be used instead of a clock.

Functional reasons related to the ancient Navajo lifestyle may explain the Navajos' assumption that the stars are a more useful standard for constructing a calendar than the Sun is. The fixed nature of the stars' positions makes them appropriate for people who move from one location to another with the seasons. The Pueblo system of determining important dates by tracing the position of the Sun at certain times of the day throughout every year is one that requires a fixed horizon and therefore a fixed place from which to view it. While the Pueblo Sun chiefs relied on a horizon calendar dependent on the geographical position of their own pueblos, Navajo calendar-makers developed methods that were not place-specific and could be carried in one's memory to many locations. Thus, as archaeologists have noted, while the ancient Pueblos have left astronomical structures such as windows placed at an angle specifically oriented toward the position of the Sun at a certain moment on a given day of the year, the ancient Navajos, because they had no need of fixed cues, have left little physical evidence of their observation of the sky.

32. The author would most likely agree with which of the following statements about the Pueblo calendar?

(A) It relies heavily on the position of the Sun as well as on that of the stars.
(B) It depends on the Sun's position relative to fixed dwellings.
(C) It makes seasonal calculations of the Sun's position unnecessary.
(D) It requires that the position of the Sun be calculated by several Sun chiefs.
(E) It is checked against time markers determined by sightings of certain constellations.

33. The author's description of the practical reasons for the ancient Navajos' dependence on the stars for calendar-making is apparently based on

(A) informed speculation
(B) written narrative histories
(C) mathematical computations
(D) observations by modern astronomers
(E) personal experience in calendar-making

34. According to the passage, which of the following best explains the differences between the Navajo and Pueblo calendars?

(A) The Navajos and the Pueblos traditionally have basically different ways of life.
(B) The Pueblos live in a more southerly region than do the Navajos.
(C) The religious system of the Navajos is based on the Sun and Moon rather than on the stars.
(D) The farming techniques of the Navajos are different from those of the Pueblos.
(E) The constellations the Navajos use for navigation are different from those the Pueblos use.

35. Which of the following can be inferred from the passage about the use of the night sky for constructing a calendar?

(A) It is feasible at certain times of the year.
(B) It is characteristic of many peoples in the world.
(C) It was practiced solely by nomadic peoples.
(D) It is the most accurate way to mark seasonal changes.
(E) It is less reliable than the use of the Sun and the Moon for such a purpose.

36. According to the passage, the ancient Navajos left little physical evidence of their knowledge of astronomy because their

(A) stargazing equipment was often lost during seasonal migration
(B) calendar was constructed with perishable materials
(C) observations were not dependent on permanent structures
(D) calendar was developed only recently in their history
(E) method of astronomical observation varied with each generation

Intercellular adhesions are important in a wide variety of organisms, from bacteria to humans. Organelles of adhesion are thought to provide certain bacteria with devices for securing nutrients and facilitating genetic exchange. In higher organisms, adhesive forces are presumed to be of prime importance during embryonic development and in maintaining distinct structural features of tissues in the adult. Intercellular adhesion also facilitates such diverse processes as fertilization, nutrient absorption, and excretion, and the presence of receptors on animal cell surfaces allows infection by viruses and bacteria to occur. Moreover, the normal adhesive properties of a cell may be lost or modified under abnormal conditions, such as when transformation to malignancy occurs.

Despite the importance of intercellular adhesion, experimental data defining the phenomenon in molecular terms are largely lacking. This paucity of information has generated abundant hypotheses on the chemical nature of cellular adhesion. For example, one hypothesis originated with the observation that glycosyl transferases, enzymes that catalyze the transfer of sugars to appropriate acceptor glycoproteins or glycolipids, are associated with the surface membranes of certain animal cells. The suggestion was advanced that cell adhesion may result from the interactions between the glycosyl transferases associated with one cell and the surface glycosyl acceptors of another cell. Since each glycosyl transferase exhibits specificity for its acceptor molecule, highly specific cell interactions would be possible. Because this hypothesis can account for the high degree of specificity observed in cell recognition, it is an appealing one.

37. It can be inferred from the passage that adhesion is vital to both bacteria and higher organisms in which of the following functions?

(A) Organizing basic cellular structure
(B) Regulating cellular growth rate
(C) Stabilizing the genetic complement of each cell
(D) Providing a means of communication within each cell
(E) Securing suitable nutrients from an external source

38. The author addresses which of the following points directly in describing the glycosyl transferase hypothesis?

(A) The highly specific nature of the enzyme/acceptor interaction
(B) The chemical nature of the enzyme/cell membrane association
(C) The structure of cells that have glycosyl transferases
(D) The molecular nature of the sugars that are transferred
(E) The types of acceptor glycoproteins in the enzyme/acceptor interaction

39. The passage reports that which of the following hypotheses has been proposed about the role of gylcosyl transferases?

(A) They allow infections by viruses and bacteria to occur.
(B) They are the primary receptors of certain animal cells.
(C) They react with sugar molecules to effect the creation of proteins.
(D) They are involved in cell adhesion via interaction with acceptors.
(E) They actively seek out certain acceptor glycoproteins and glycolipids.

40. The information in the passage indicates that the glycosyl transferase hypothesis represents which of the following stages in the establishment of a theory?

(A) Purely speculative consideration of extreme possibilities
(B) Acceptance of a theory characterized by scientific validity
(C) Compilation of information from diverse sources
(D) Verification of an explanation by laboratory experiments
(E) Conjecture based on observed phenomena

IF YOU FINISH BEFORE TIME IS CALLED, YOU MAY CHECK YOUR WORK ON THIS SECTION ONLY. DO NOT TURN TO ANY OTHER SECTION IN THE TEST. **STOP**

SECTION 2 Time—30 minutes 35 Questions

In this section solve each problem, using any available space on the page for scratchwork. Then decide which is the best of the choices given and fill in the corresponding oval on the answer sheet.

The following information is for your reference in solving some of the problems.

Circle of radius r: Area $= \pi r^2$; Circumference $= 2\pi r$
The number of degrees of arc in a circle is 360.
The measure in degrees of a straight angle is 180.

Definition of symbols:

$=$ is equal to	$\leq$ is less than or equal to
$\neq$ is unequal to	$\geq$ is greater than or equal to
$<$ is less than	$\parallel$ is parallel to
$>$ is greater than	$\perp$ is perpendicular to

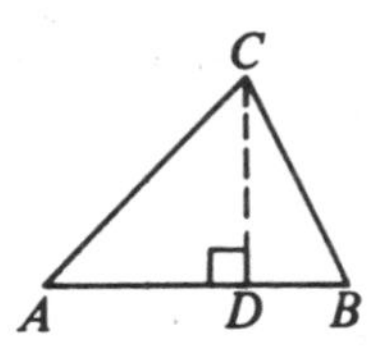

Triangle: The sum of the measures in degrees of the angles of a triangle is 180.

If $\angle CDA$ is a right angle, then

(1) area of $\triangle ABC = \frac{AB \times CD}{2}$

(2) $AC^2 = AD^2 + DC^2$

Note: Figures that accompany problems in this test are intended to provide information useful in solving the problems. They are drawn as accurately as possible EXCEPT when it is stated in a specific problem that its figure is not drawn to scale. All figures lie in a plane unless otherwise indicated. All numbers used are real numbers.

1. What number exceeds 17 by the same amount that 56 exceeds 38 ?

   (A) 25
   (B) 35
   (C) 38
   (D) 45
   (E) 77

2. Which of the following has the least number of factors?

   (A) 20
   (B) 26
   (C) 35
   (D) 47
   (E) 63

3. Pat must pay a 6 percent state sales tax and a 2 percent city sales tax on school supplies. If the price of the supplies before taxes is \$30.00, what is the total amount that Pat must pay in sales taxes?

   (A) \$0.24
   (B) \$0.90
   (C) \$1.80
   (D) \$2.40
   (E) \$2.60

4. If $3x = 4y = 24$, then $x + y =$

   (A) 12
   (B) 14
   (C) 18
   (D) 32
   (E) 48

5. If x and y are negative integers, which of the following must be positive?

   (A) $x + y$
   (B) $x - y$
   (C) $y - x$
   (D) $-(x - y)$
   (E) $-(x + y)$

GO ON TO THE NEXT PAGE

Questions 6-7 refer to the following definition.

Let [m] represent the set of all positive integers that are not multiples of integer m.

For example, [3] represents the set {1, 2, 4, 5, 7, 8, 10, 11, . . .}.

---

6. Which of the following sets has no members?

   (A) [1]

   (B) [2]

   (C) [10]

   (D) [13]

   (E) [1,000]

7. If y is in set [5] and in set [2], then, of the following, y could be

   (A) 25
   (B) 26
   (C) 28
   (D) 29
   (E) 30

GO ON TO THE NEXT PAGE

Questions 8-27 each consist of two quantities, one in Column A and one in Column B. You are to compare the two quantities and on the answer sheet fill in oval

A if the quantity in Column A is greater;
B if the quantity in Column B is greater;
C if the two quantities are equal;
D if the relationship cannot be determined from the information given.

AN E RESPONSE WILL NOT BE SCORED.

EXAMPLES

	Column A	Column B	Answers
E1.	2×6	$2 + 6$	● Ⓑ Ⓒ Ⓓ Ⓔ
	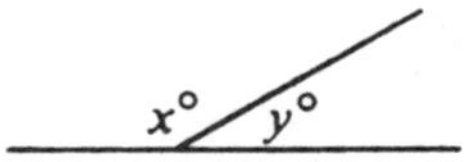		
E2.	$180 - x$	y	Ⓐ Ⓑ ● Ⓓ Ⓔ
E3.	$p - q$	$q - p$	Ⓐ Ⓑ Ⓒ ● Ⓔ

Notes:

1. In certain questions, information concerning one or both of the quantities to be compared is centered above the two columns.
2. In a given question, a symbol that appears in both columns represents the same thing in Column A as it does in Column B.
3. Letters such as x, n, and k stand for real numbers.

	Column A	Column B
8.	$(0.5)(0.5)$	$\frac{25}{100}$

In a certain game, points are assigned to a word as follows: each "a" is worth 2 points, each "e" is worth 1 point, and all other letters are worth 0 points.

	Column A	Column B
9.	The sum of the points assigned to the word "leader"	The sum of the points assigned to the word "abash"

Greg scored 90 on each of his first 3 tests and 95 on each of his last 2 tests.

	Column A	Column B
10.	The average (arithmetic mean) of Greg's scores for these 5 tests	92.5
11.	Number of brand X cookies in an 800-gram package	Number of brand Y cookies in an 850-gram package

The rate for a telephone call between City A and City B is 50 cents for the first minute and 30 cents for each additional minute.

	Column A	Column B
12.	Cost of a 6-minute phone call between City A and City B	\$3.00

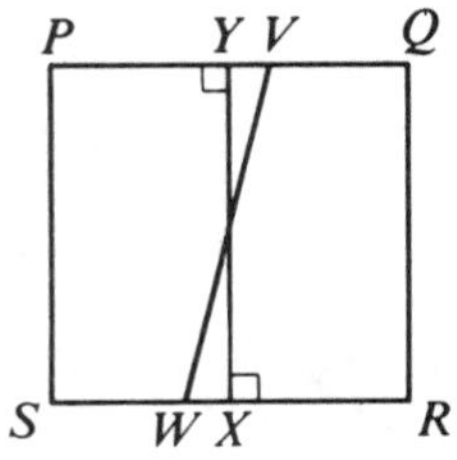

$PQRS$ is a square.

	Column A	Column B
13.	Length of SR	Length of VW
14.	$(x + 2y) - (2x + y)$	$x + y$

In $\triangle ABC$, side AB has length 6 and side BC has length 4.

	Column A	Column B
15.	The length of side AC	8
16.	$\frac{1}{2^{12}}$	$\frac{1}{2^{10}}$

$$2x = 10^3$$

	Column A	Column B
17.	$\frac{x}{5}$	50

GO ON TO THE NEXT PAGE

SUMMARY DIRECTIONS FOR COMPARISON QUESTIONS

Answer: A if the quantity in Column A is greater;
B if the quantity in Column B is greater;
C if the two quantities are equal;
D if the relationship cannot be determined from the information given.

AN E RESPONSE WILL NOT BE SCORED.

Column A	Column B

Let 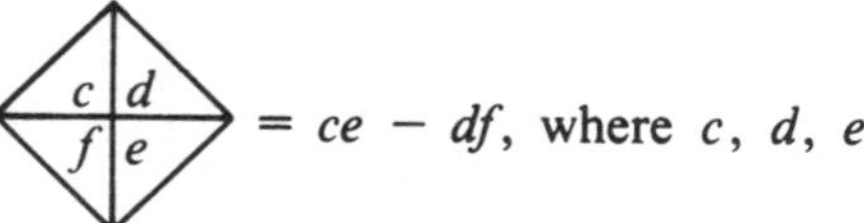

$= ce - df$, where c, d, e, and f are integers.

18. 

 0

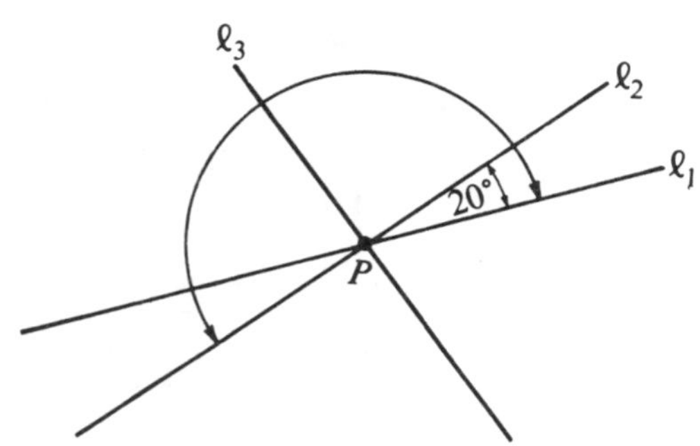

The lines ℓ_1, ℓ_2, and ℓ_3 intersect in point P.

19. The degree measure of the large marked angle — 200°

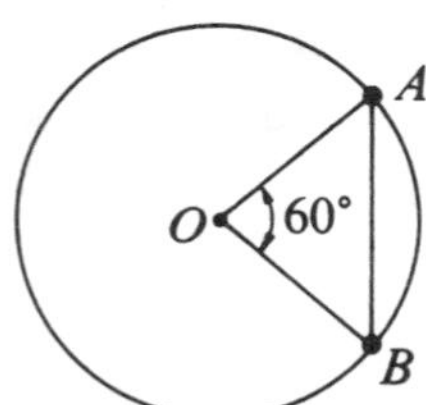

Note: Figure not drawn to scale.

O is the center and OA and OB are radii of the circle.

20. Length of OB — Length of AB

21. The maximum number of tubes of caulking costing \$2.98 each that can be bought for \$15 (Assume no tax.) — The maximum number of tubes of caulking costing \$3.24 each that can be bought for \$20 (Assume no tax.)

Column A	Column B

$x = \frac{1}{4}$

22. $\sqrt{x} - x$ — 0

$2t < w < 4t$

23. w — $3t$

$x + y = 3$
and
$x - y = 4$

24. x — 3

r and s are even positive integers and
$20 < rs < 25$

25. Number of possible values of product rs — 2

k is an integer.

26. The number of distinct prime numbers that are factors of k — The number of distinct prime numbers that are factors of k^2

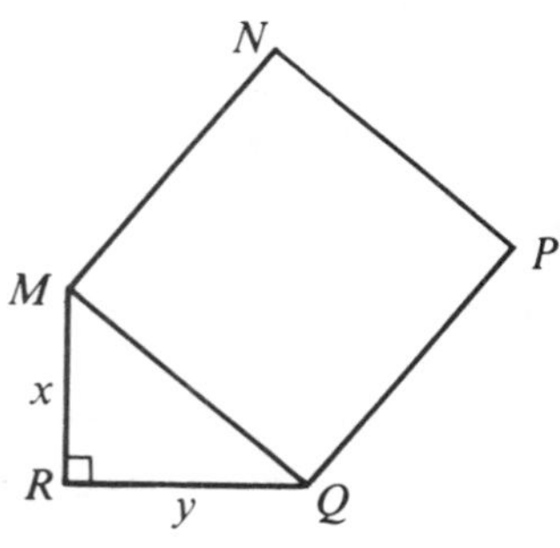

$MNPQ$ is a square.
$x < y$

27. The area of $MNPQ$ — Four times the area of right triangle MQR

GO ON TO THE NEXT PAGE

Solve each of the remaining problems in this section using any available space for scratchwork. Then decide which is the best of the choices given and fill in the corresponding oval on the answer sheet.

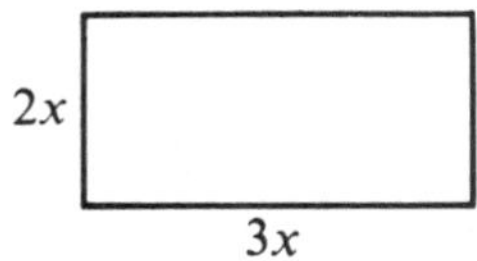

28. If the perimeter of the rectangle above is 80, what is the value of x ?

(A) 4
(B) 8
(C) 10
(D) 12
(E) 16

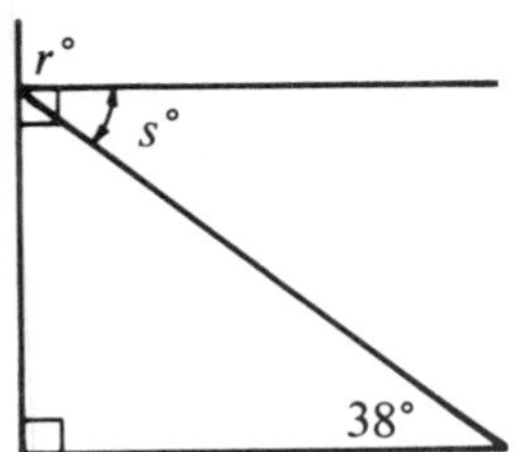

29. In the figure above, what is the value of $r + s$?

(A) 112
(B) 118
(C) 122
(D) 128
(E) 142

30. If 16 is written as the product of three integers, each greater than 1, what is the sum of those three integers?

(A) 6
(B) 8
(C) 10
(D) 11
(E) 18

31. If a 2-digit positive integer A is represented by $10x + y$ where x is the tens' digit and y is the units' digit, then the number of integers between A and $10A$ (not including A and $10A$) can be represented as

(A) $90x + 10y$
(B) $90x + 11y$
(C) $90x + 9y - 1$
(D) $90x + 9y + 1$
(E) $90x + 10y + 1$

32. What is the area of the largest circle that can be inscribed in a semicircular region of radius r ?

(A) $\frac{\pi r^2}{4}$

(B) $\frac{\pi r^2}{3}$

(C) $\frac{\pi r^2}{2}$

(D) $\frac{2}{3}\pi r^2$

(E) $\frac{3}{4}\pi r^2$

33. If the average (arithmetic mean) of 3 integers is 15 and the sum of the two greater numbers is 42, which of the following must be true?

I. The two greater numbers are each divisible by the least.
II. The least number is 3.
III. The second greatest number is 15.

(A) I only
(B) II only
(C) III only
(D) I and II
(E) II and III

GO ON TO THE NEXT PAGE

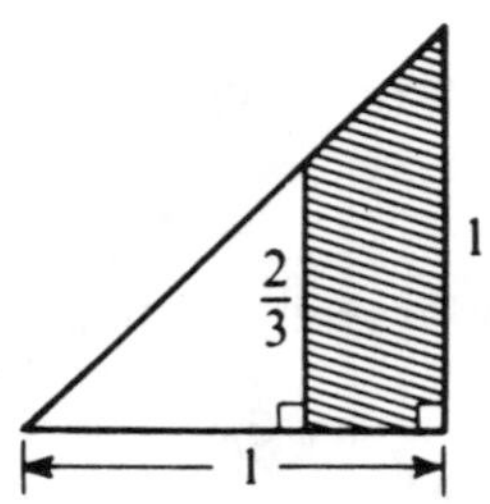

34. In the figure above, what is the area of the shaded region?

(A) $\frac{5}{36}$

(B) $\frac{5}{18}$

(C) $\frac{1}{3}$

(D) $\frac{5}{12}$

(E) $\frac{5}{6}$

35. In Linden College there are 75 more women than men enrolled. If there are n men enrolled, then, in terms of n, what percent of those enrolled are men?

(A) $\frac{n}{n + 75}\%$

(B) $\frac{n}{2n + 75}\%$

(C) $\frac{n}{100(2n + 75)}\%$

(D) $\frac{100n}{n + 75}\%$

(E) $\frac{100n}{2n + 75}\%$

IF YOU FINISH BEFORE TIME IS CALLED, YOU MAY CHECK YOUR WORK ON THIS SECTION ONLY. DO NOT TURN TO ANY OTHER SECTION IN THE TEST. **STOP**

SECTION 3 Time—30 minutes 45 Questions

For each question in this section, choose the best answer and fill in the corresponding oval on the answer sheet.

Each question below consists of a word in capital letters, followed by five lettered words or phrases. Choose the word or phrase that is most nearly opposite in meaning to the word in capital letters. Since some of the questions require you to distinguish fine shades of meaning, consider all the choices before deciding which is best.

Example:

GOOD: (A) sour (B) bad (C) red (D) hot (E) ugly

Ⓐ ● Ⓒ Ⓓ Ⓔ

1. DELICATE: (A) coarse (B) intricate (C) scary (D) timely (E) colorful

2. HOSTILITY: (A) honesty (B) capability (C) peaceableness (D) perseverance (E) decisiveness

3. UNLEASH: (A) consume (B) withhold (C) improve (D) maltreat (E) remind

4. LUSTROUS: (A) passive (B) uninformative (C) inexpensive (D) dull (E) cold

5. IRONHANDED: (A) tightfisted (B) well-founded (C) openmouthed (D) kind and yielding (E) graceful and precise

6. GNARL: (A) evacuate (B) liquefy (C) bridge (D) polish and brighten (E) smooth and straighten

7. SPECIFICITY: (A) communication (B) universality (C) density (D) rebirth (E) distraction

8. TEMPESTUOUS: (A) responsible (B) predictable (C) tranquil (D) prodigious (E) tentative

9. WAN: (A) attentive (B) definite (C) capable (D) full of vitality (E) extremely noisy

10. HYPERBOLE: (A) insensitivity (B) parallelism (C) contrast (D) grievance (E) understatement

11. PLACATE: (A) dread (B) question (C) finish (D) anger (E) promote

12. SALUBRIOUS: (A) unhealthful (B) unskilled (C) inefficient (D) difficult to understand (E) hard to please

13. DUPLICITY: (A) adequacy (B) gloominess (C) solitude (D) frankness (E) lenience

14. CONSECRATE: (A) curtail (B) demolish (C) exonerate (D) extricate (E) profane

15. DISAFFECTED: (A) permanent (B) loyal (C) articulate (D) probable (E) rational

GO ON TO THE NEXT PAGE

Each sentence below has one or two blanks, each blank indicating that something has been omitted. Beneath the sentence are five lettered words or sets of words. Choose the word or set of words that, when inserted in the sentence, best fits the meaning of the sentence as a whole.

Example:

Although its publicity has been ----, the film itself is intelligent, well-acted, handsomely produced, and altogether ----.

(A) tasteless. .respectable (B) extensive. .moderate (C) sophisticated. .amateur (D) risqué. .crude (E) perfect. .spectacular

● Ⓑ Ⓒ Ⓓ Ⓔ

16. By the time the troops arrived, the river had become so choked with ice as to be ---- even with small boats.

(A) indiscernible (B) impassable (C) unreliable (D) ineradicable (E) immeasurable

17. Stabilized by Queen Elizabeth I in 1561, the British pound sterling retained its value until well into the twentieth century, while its variable European counterparts ---- dramatically.

(A) revived (B) fluctuated (C) prospered (D) adjusted (E) accumulated

18. Very few adults boast that no one can understand a word they say, but quite a few seem proud of ---- handwriting.

(A) elegant (B) stylized (C) indecipherable (D) unusual (E) legible

19. To the professor, who assumed that a great degree of ---- should always attend youth, the young man had already been too ----.

(A) modesty. .presumptuous
(B) enthusiasm. .independent
(C) innocence. .naïve
(D) humility. .emotional
(E) optimism. .successful

20. Since the explanations offered are ---- to the exposition, it would be unfair to treat them as ---- parts of the studies under consideration.

(A) tangential. .subsidiary
(B) irrelevant. .superfluous
(C) referable. .correspondent
(D) incidental. .essential
(E) crucial. .immutable

21. Despite their ---- proportions, the murals of Diego Rivera give his Mexican compatriots the sense that their history is ---- and human in scale, not remote and larger than life.

(A) monumental. .accessible
(B) focused. .prolonged
(C) vast. .ancient
(D) realistic. .extraneous
(E) narrow. .overwhelming

22. The popular appeal of detective stories that feature ---- depictions of crime can be attributed to readers' attraction to ---- violence.

(A) somber. .trivialized
(B) prurient. .expurgated
(C) euphemistic. .explicit
(D) sordid. .glamorous
(E) lurid. .sensationalized

23. Although cultural anthropologists have shown some interest in individual biographies, writing that describes particular lives is ---- in their science, which is devoted to cultural truths and ---- representations.

(A) popular. .schematic
(B) conventional. .formal
(C) sporadic. .collective
(D) incongruous. .solitary
(E) suspect. .fictional

24. Their ideal was to combine individual liberty with material equality, a goal that has not yet been realized and that may be as ---- as transmutation of lead into gold.

(A) chimerical (B) indispensable (C) historical (D) cynical (E) inharmonious

25. A lifelong foe of deceit, he has spent nearly four decades ---- the claims of spurious psychics and alerting parapsychological researchers to the dangers of ----.

(A) construing. .intolerance
(B) distorting. .spirituality
(C) inflating. .methodology
(D) debunking. .credulity
(E) reproving. .rationalism

GO ON TO THE NEXT PAGE

Each passage below is followed by questions based on its content. Answer all questions following a passage on the basis of what is stated or implied in that passage.

Verbicide, the murder of a word, happens in many ways. Inflation is one of the commonest; those who taught us to say "awfully" for "very," "tremendous" for "great," "sadism" for "cruelty," and "unthinkable" for "undesirable" were guilty. Another way is verbiage, by which I here mean the use of a word as a promise to pay that is never going to be kept. The use of "significant" as if it were an absolute, and with no intention of ever telling us what the thing so described is significant of, is an example. People often commit verbicide because they want to snatch a word as a party banner, to appropriate its selling quality. Verbicide was committed when "liberal" and "conservative" were pressed into service as political catchwords. But the greatest cause of verbicide is the fact that most people are obviously far more eager to express their approval and disapproval of things than to describe them. Hence the tendency of words to first become less descriptive and more evaluative; then to become evaluative, while still retaining some hint of the sort of goodness or badness implied; and to end up by being purely evaluative—useless synonyms for "good" or for "bad." "Rotten" has become so completely a synonym for "bad" that we now have to say "the meat has gone bad" when we want to say that it is rotten.

I am not suggesting that we can by a radical purism repair any of the losses that have already occurred. It may not, however, be entirely useless to resolve that we ourselves will never commit verbicide. If modern critical usage seems to be initiating a process that might finally make "adolescent" and "contemporary" mere synonyms for "bad" and "good"—and stranger things have happened—we should banish them from our vocabulary. Our conversation will have little effect; but if we get into print—perhaps especially if we are leading writers, reviewers, or reporters—we can help to contain some disastrous vogue word, can encourage innovations that are discriminative, and decry those that only blur. Care should be taken because many things the press prints today will be taken up by the great mass of speakers in a few years.

I cannot resist closing with an adaptation of a couplet we used to see in some parks:

Let no one say, and say it to your shame,
That there was meaning here before you came.

26. The author is mainly concerned with the
   (A) erosion of standards in the teaching of English
   (B) distortion of language and what might be done about it
   (C) determined effort some people make to destroy their own language
   (D) difference between everyday speech and expository writing
   (E) emerging need for a self-regulated league of writers

27. The author, in complaining about the "use of 'significant' as if it were an absolute" (lines 7-8), is probably referring to those who use that word to mean
   (A) important (B) desirable (C) logical
   (D) complex (E) daring

28. According to the author, the greatest cause of verbicide is people's desire to
   (A) appear more sophisticated than they are
   (B) avoid the mundane realities of life
   (C) adorn their speech with exotic words
   (D) convey their feelings about particular objects
   (E) sway others to their point of view

29. The author deplores verbicide chiefly because it
   (A) robs words of their descriptive power
   (B) makes words obsolete prematurely
   (C) forces people to create unneeded words
   (D) encourages sloganeering in politics
   (E) enables charlatans to deceive the public

30. The author develops the first paragraph by
   (A) drawing conclusions from implied premises
   (B) making assertions and then illustrating them
   (C) contrasting several facts with one another
   (D) offering hypothetical situations with a common point
   (E) suggesting proposals and then qualifying them

GO ON TO THE NEXT PAGE

Originally, Mars was probably surrounded by a protoatmosphere of reducing gases, such as methane and ammonia, and must have exuded great quantities of water vapor and carbon dioxide. The planet had a force of gravity sufficient to keep all the gases except the light hydrogen from escaping into space, as all the gases of our Moon did. Because of Mars's greater distance from the Sun, the cooling and condensation of water vapor would have taken place more rapidly than on Earth. For a geologically brief time, oceans probably formed in the basins that are now filled with dust. There is no plausible reason why life could not have developed in these primeval oceans as it did in the oceans of Earth. However, the course of evolution on the two planets would have diverged early in their history. No matter how much oxygen was released, a biologically determined, oxygen-rich atmosphere comparable to that which results from the process of photosynthesis probably could never have formed on Mars. It is unlikely that the oxygen content of the Martian atmosphere, and the accompanying formation of ozone in sunlight would ever have risen to a level sufficient to protect organisms from ultraviolet light so that they could live on dry land.

One explanation stems from the size of the planet. The Earth had a force of gravity strong enough to form a dense iron core; Mars did not. On Mars, a larger proportion of iron in relation to the planet's mass lies closer to the surface. Water vapor molecules were split into oxygen and hydrogen by the ultraviolet portion of solar radiation. While the light hydrogen escaped into space, the highly reactive oxygen promptly combined with the iron on the surface to form iron oxides. These same processes probably took place during the early history of the Earth. But on Earth there was proportionately less iron on the surface, so that a certain amount of oxygen was left over to enrich the atmosphere. The conversion of some oxygen to ozone led to the blocking of ultraviolet radiation which prevented the further dissociation of water vapor and of liquid water, and also protected life forms. On Mars oxygen atoms released into the atmosphere were almost immediately consumed again. A self-regulating process that would have shielded the water from ultraviolet radiation probably could not get started. As the water vapor in the Martian atmosphere was dissociated, the iron crust of Mars was gradually oxidized. The iron oxides and iron hydroxides formed give Mars its characteristic reddish or "rusted" appearance.

31. Which of the following is the best title for the passage?

(A) The Formation of Iron Oxides
(B) Evaporation of the Martian Oceans
(C) Early Life of Earth and Mars
(D) Development of the Martian Atmosphere
(E) Atmospheric Ozone and Ultraviolet Radiation

32. The passage suggests that which of the following could have happened on both Mars and Earth?

I. Dissociation of water vapor
II. Oxidation of iron on the planet's surface
III. Development of marine organisms

(A) I only
(B) II only
(C) I and III only
(D) II and III only
(E) I, II, and III

33. The discussion in the passage is based on which of the following general assumptions about chemical interactions?

(A) Catalysis of chemical reactions is inhibited by low temperatures.
(B) Generation of water vapor requires high atmospheric pressure.
(C) Fusion of hydrogen and oxygen takes place constantly.
(D) Binding between iron and oxygen is accelerated in low gravity.
(E) Reactions among chemical elements are consistent from planet to planet.

34. According to the passage, the characteristic color of Mars is a result of

(A) absorption of ultraviolet light
(B) oxidation of a metallic element
(C) concentration of organic compounds
(D) consolidation of land masses
(E) accumulation of cloud cover

35. The author's discussion of the possibility of life on Mars is best described as

(A) speculation within the limits of scientific knowledge
(B) criticism of unwarranted assumptions
(C) analysis of past misconceptions
(D) extrapolation from recent discoveries
(E) explication of facts accepted by prominent scientists

GO ON TO THE NEXT PAGE

Each question below consists of a related pair of words or phrases, followed by five lettered pairs of words or phrases. Select the lettered pair that best expresses a relationship similar to that expressed in the original pair.

Example:

YAWN:BOREDOM :: (A) dream:sleep (B) anger:madness (C) smile:amusement (D) face:expression (E) impatience:rebellion

Ⓐ Ⓑ ● Ⓓ Ⓔ

36. WALLS : CORNER :: (A) leaves : tree (B) rugs : mat (C) bones : joint (D) faucets : drain (E) keys : typewriter

37. CLAW : SCRATCH :: (A) hoof : walk (B) tail : dangle (C) fang : bite (D) bristle : clean (E) beak : chirp

38. FISH : AQUARIUM :: (A) tree : forest (B) plant : greenhouse (C) keeper : zoo (D) hedge : garden (E) star : planetarium

39. ACT : PLAY :: (A) song : music (B) rhyme : poem (C) page : novel (D) chapter : book (E) scenery : performance

40. HECKLE : DISAPPROVAL :: (A) suggest : assertion (B) snub : evasion (C) confront : agreement (D) concede : point (E) boast : pride

41. REAM : PAPER :: (A) chaff : wheat (B) echo : sound (C) bolt : cloth (D) flax : linen (E) ton : weight

42. EMBELLISH : ORNAMENT :: (A) chasten : culprit (B) close : gap (C) season : spice (D) wrap : gift (E) squander : fortune

43. SPITEFUL : MALEVOLENCE ::
(A) curt : grandiloquence
(B) incisive : pomposity
(C) envious : possession
(D) glum : despondency
(E) remorseful : innocence

44. BOLD : FOOLHARDY :: (A) lively : enthusiastic (B) natural : synthetic (C) generous : spendthrift (D) wise : thoughtful (E) creative : childlike

45. TIRADE : ABUSIVE :: (A) confession : earnest (B) elegy : mournful (C) epic : miniature (D) accolade : humble (E) compliment : obsequious

IF YOU FINISH BEFORE TIME IS CALLED, YOU MAY CHECK YOUR WORK ON THIS SECTION ONLY. DO NOT TURN TO ANY OTHER SECTION IN THE TEST. **STOP**

SECTION 4 Time—30 minutes 25 Questions

In this section solve each problem, using any available space on the page for scratchwork. Then decide which is the best of the choices given and fill in the corresponding oval on the answer sheet.

The following information is for your reference in solving some of the problems.

Circle of radius r: Area $= \pi r^2$; Circumference $= 2\pi r$
The number of degrees of arc in a circle is 360.
The measure in degrees of a straight angle is 180.

Definition of symbols:

$=$ is equal to	$\leq$ is less than or equal to
$\neq$ is unequal to	$\geq$ is greater than or equal to
$<$ is less than	$\parallel$ is parallel to
$>$ is greater than	$\perp$ is perpendicular to

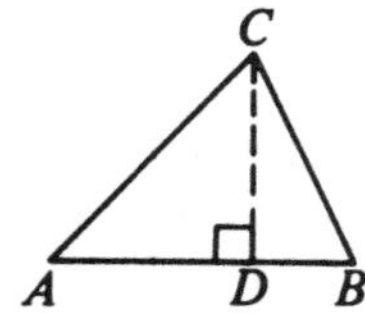

Triangle: The sum of the measures in degrees of the angles of a triangle is 180.

If $\angle CDA$ is a right angle, then

(1) area of $\triangle ABC = \dfrac{AB \times CD}{2}$

(2) $AC^2 = AD^2 + DC^2$

Note: Figures that accompany problems in this test are intended to provide information useful in solving the problems. They are drawn as accurately as possible EXCEPT when it is stated in a specific problem that its figure is not drawn to scale. All figures lie in a plane unless otherwise indicated. All numbers used are real numbers.

1. A runner's time for an 800-meter race was 1 minute 57.2 seconds. The following week the runner's time for the same distance was 1 minute 55.5 seconds. By what number of seconds did the runner improve her time?

(A) 0.7
(B) 1.3
(C) 1.7
(D) 2.3
(E) 2.7

2. If $a^2 > b^2$, which of the following could be the values of a and b?

(A) $a = -5,\ b = 0$

(B) $a = -3,\ b = -4$

(C) $a = 0,\ b = -1$

(D) $a = \frac{3}{4},\ b = 1$

(E) $a = 1,\ b = -2$

3. Classified ads cost \$2.50 per 30 words at *City Newspaper*. How many words must be deleted from the text of a 75-word classified ad to reduce the cost to \$5.00 ?

(A) 5
(B) 15
(C) 20
(D) 30
(E) 60

4. If $x = 10^2 - 8^2$ and $y = 10^2 - 6^2$, then $\sqrt{x} - \sqrt{y} =$

(A) -2

(B) $\sqrt{2} - 2$

(C) $2 - \sqrt{2}$

(D) 1

(E) 2

GO ON TO THE NEXT PAGE

5. Multiplying which of the following by the nonzero number $\frac{6 - 2x}{9}$ will give a product of 1 ?

(A) $9(6 - 2x)$

(B) $9(2x - 6)$

(C) $\frac{9}{6 - 2x}$

(D) $\frac{9}{2x - 6}$

(E) $\frac{2x - 6}{9}$

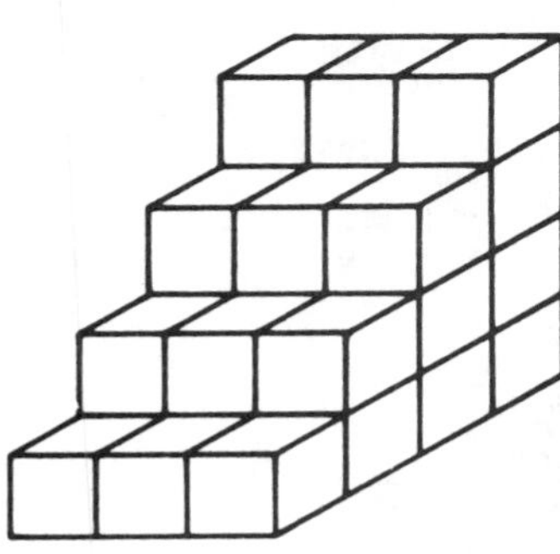

6. A solid set of steps made of concrete blocks of equal size is shown above. How many of these blocks would be needed to build 2 such sets of steps?

(A) 30
(B) 48
(C) 60
(D) 64
(E) 68

7. A recipe calls for 1 cup of nuts, 5 cups of chocolate chips, and $\frac{1}{3}$ cup of raisins. Which of the following gives the ratio of nuts to chips to raisins?

(A) 1:5:3
(B) 1:5:1
(C) 3:5:1
(D) 3:15:1
(E) 5:15:1

8. If $4(9) = 3(x - 1)$, then $x =$

(A) 9
(B) 10
(C) 11
(D) 12
(E) 13

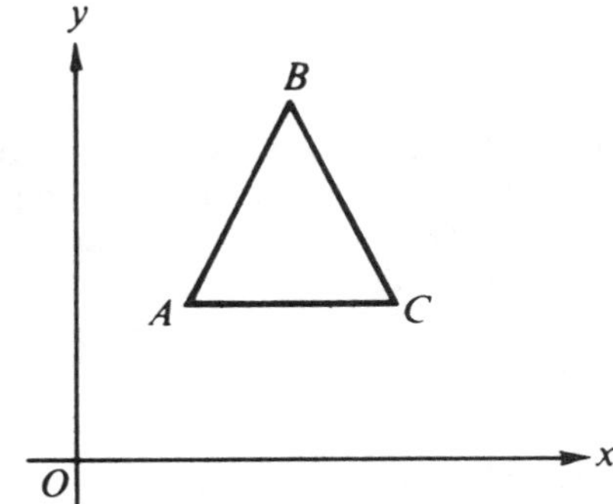

Note: Figure not drawn to scale.

9. In $\triangle ABC$ shown above, $AB = BC$ and base AC is equal to the altitude of the triangle from point B. If the coordinates of points A and C are (2,5) and (6,5), respectively, which of the following could be the coordinates of point B ?

(A) (2,7)
(B) (2,8)
(C) (2,9)
(D) (4,8)
(E) (4,9)

GO ON TO THE NEXT PAGE

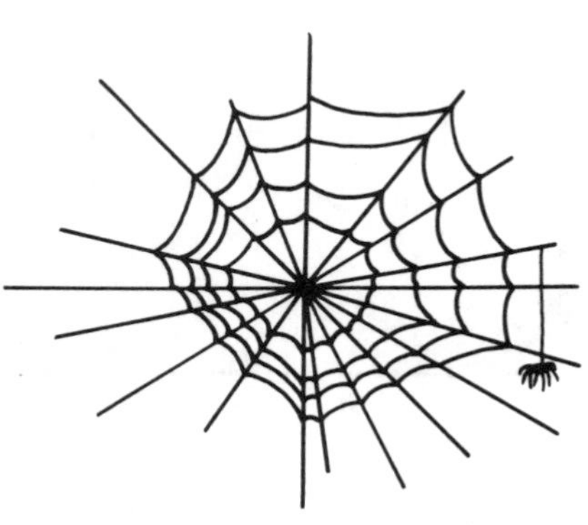

10. In the spiderweb above, 18 straight threads meet at the center. What is the average (arithmetic mean) measure, in degrees, of the 18 nonoverlapping angles about the center?

(A) 18
(B) 20
(C) 22
(D) 25
(E) 28

11. In a certain game, eleven targets are numbered 1 to 11 and the number of points scored is equal to the sum of the numbers on the targets hit. If each target is hit exactly once and if Player M hits each odd-numbered target and Player L hits each even-numbered target, M's total score is how many points greater than L's?

(A) 0
(B) 2
(C) 3
(D) 4
(E) 6

12. If x is between $1 - \frac{1}{5}$ and $1 + \frac{1}{5}$, then x could equal each of the following EXCEPT

(A) 1
(B) $\frac{5}{4}$
(C) $\frac{9}{10}$
(D) $\frac{10}{11}$
(E) $\frac{101}{100}$

Questions 13-14 refer to the following definition.

Define "→" by the equations below.

$$a \rightarrow b = a + 2b, \text{ if } a > b.$$

$$a \rightarrow b = \frac{a - b}{2}, \text{ if } a \leqq b.$$

13. What is the value of $3 \rightarrow 5$?

(A) -2
(B) -1
(C) 4
(D) 11
(E) 13

14. Which of the following equal(s) 0 ?

I. $2 \rightarrow -1$
II. $3 \rightarrow 3$
III. $5 \rightarrow -5$

(A) I only
(B) II only
(C) I and II only
(D) II and III only
(E) I, II, and III

GO ON TO THE NEXT PAGE

15. The weight of a sack of grain plus $\frac{1}{3}$ of this weight is equal to 24 pounds. What is the weight of the sack of grain, in pounds?

(A) 18
(B) 16
(C) 14
(D) 8
(E) 6

P Q R

16. In the figure above, if $PR = 5x - 3$ and $PQ = 2x - 6$, what is QR in terms of x ?

(A) $7x - 9$
(B) $3x - 9$
(C) $3x - 3$
(D) $3x + 3$
(E) $-3x + 3$

17. If the lengths of the sides of a triangle are x, $x + 1$, and $x + 2$, which of the following is a possible measure for the angle opposite the side with length x ?

(A) 58°
(B) 60°
(C) 61°
(D) 62°
(E) 89°

18. If the sum of $\frac{1}{2}$ of an even integer and $\frac{2}{3}$ of the next consecutive even integer is equal to 27, what is the odd integer between these two even integers?

(A) 13
(B) 17
(C) 23
(D) 25
(E) 26

23, 16, 19, 21, 15

19. If each of the five numbers above were decreased by x, the average (arithmetic mean) of the resulting set of 5 numbers would be 18. The value of x is

(A) $\frac{1}{5}$
(B) $\frac{2}{5}$
(C) $\frac{3}{5}$
(D) $\frac{4}{5}$
(E) 1

GO ON TO THE NEXT PAGE

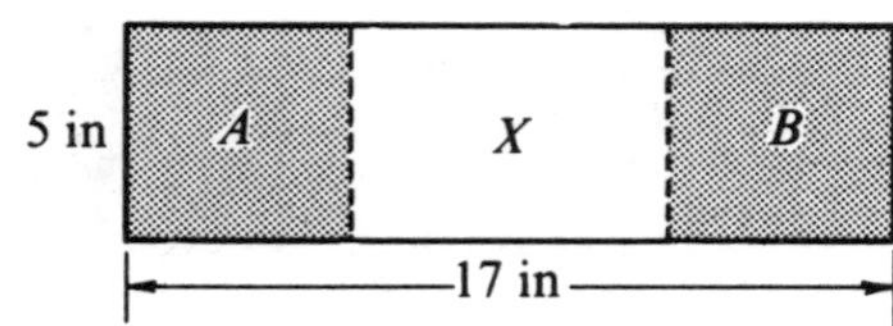

20. In the rectangle above, the shaded square regions A and B are to be folded along the broken lines onto rectangular region X. What will be the area, in square inches, of the part of A that overlaps with B?

(A) 5
(B) 10
(C) 15
(D) 20
(E) 25

21. A car traveling at an average rate of 55 kilometers per hour made a trip in 6 hours. If it had traveled at an average rate of 50 kilometers per hour, the trip would have taken how many minutes longer?

(A) 15
(B) 25
(C) 30
(D) 35
(E) 36

22. Of the following, which has the greatest value when $x = 0.000001$?

(A) $\frac{1}{x}$

(B) $\frac{1}{2}x$

(C) x

(D) $\sqrt{x}$

(E) x^2

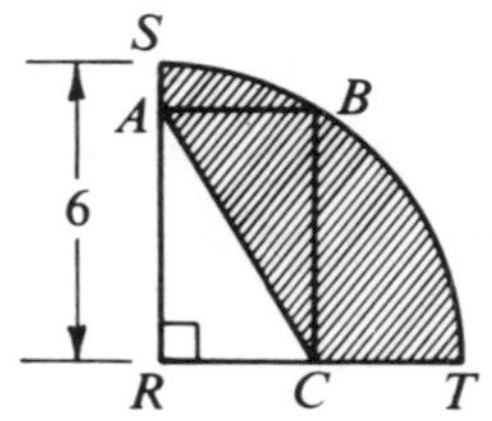

23. In the figure above, arc SBT is one quarter of a circle with center R and radius 6. If the length plus the width of rectangle $ABCR$ is 8, then the perimeter of the shaded region is

(A) $8 + 3\pi$
(B) $10 + 3\pi$
(C) $14 + 3\pi$
(D) $1 + 6\pi$
(E) $12 + 6\pi$

24. If $x + y = t$ and $x - y = v$, then, in terms of t and v, which of the following is equal to xy ?

(A) tv

(B) $\frac{t - v}{2}$

(C) $\frac{t + v}{2}$

(D) $\frac{t^2 - v^2}{2}$

(E) $\frac{t^2 - v^2}{4}$

$$v,\ w,\ x,\ 25$$

25. In the sequence above, when any one of the first three terms is subtracted from the term immediately following it, the result equals $v - 1$. What is the value of v ?

(A) 6

(B) $\frac{25}{4}$

(C) 7

(D) 8

(E) 16

IF YOU FINISH BEFORE TIME IS CALLED, YOU MAY CHECK YOUR WORK ON THIS SECTION ONLY. DO NOT TURN TO ANY OTHER SECTION IN THE TEST. **STOP**

Correct Answers for Scholastic Aptitude Test Form Code 7B			
VERBAL		**MATHEMATICAL**	
Section 1	**Section 3**	**Section 4**	**Section 2**
1. D	1. A	1. C	1. B
2. B	2. C	2. A	2. D
3. E	3. B	3. B	3. D
4. A	4. D	4. A	4. B
5. D	5. D	5. C	5. E
6. B	6. E	6. C	6. A
7. D	7. B	7. D	7. D
8. B	8. C	8. E	*8. C
9. C	9. D	9. E	*9. C
10. E	10. E	10. B	*10. B
11. E	11. D	11. E	*11. D
12. A	12. A	12. B	*12. B
13. D	13. D	13. B	*13. B
14. D	14. E	14. C	*14. D
15. B	15. B	15. A	*15. D
16. C	16. B	16. D	*16. B
17. B	17. B	17. A	*17. A
18. B	18. C	18. C	*18. A
19. E	19. A	19. D	*19. C
20. C	20. D	20. C	*20. C
21. D	21. A	21. E	*21. B
22. C	22. E	22. A	*22. A
23. C	23. C	23. B	*23. D
24. B	24. A	24. E	*24. A
25. D	25. D	25. C	*25. B
26. D	26. B		*26. C
27. A	27. A		*27. A
28. A	28. D		28. B
29. A	29. A		29. D
30. E	30. B		30. B
31. D	31. D		31. C
32. B	32. E		32. A
33. A	33. E		33. B
34. A	34. B		34. B
35. B	35. A		35. E
36. C	36. C		
37. E	37. C		
38. A	38. B		
39. D	39. D		
40. E	40. E		
	41. C		
	42. C		
	43. D		
	44. C		
	45. B		

*Indicates four-choice questions. (All of the other questions are five-choice.)

The Scoring Process

Machine-scoring is done in three steps:

- *Scanning.* Your answer sheet is "read" by a scanning machine and the oval you filled in for each question is recorded on a computer tape.
- *Scoring.* The computer compares the oval filled in for each question with the correct response. Each correct answer receives one point; omitted questions do not count toward your score. For each wrong answer, a fraction of a point is subtracted to correct for random guessing. For questions with five answer choices, one-fourth of a point is subtracted for each wrong response; for questions with four answer choices, one-third of a point is subtracted for each wrong response. The SAT-verbal test has 85 questions with five answer choices each. If, for example, a student has 44 right, 32 wrong, and 9 omitted, the resulting raw score is determined as follows:

$$44 \text{ right} - \frac{32 \text{ wrong}}{4} = 44 - 8 = 36 \text{ raw score points}$$

Obtaining raw scores frequently involves the rounding of fractional numbers to the nearest whole number. For example, a raw score of 36.25 is rounded to 36, the nearest whole number. A raw score of 36.50 is rounded upward to 37.

- *Converting to reported scaled score.* Raw test scores are then placed on the College Board scale of 200 to 800 through a process that adjusts scores to account for minor differences in difficulty among different editions of the test. This process, known as equating, is performed so that a student's reported score is not affected by the edition of the test taken nor by the abilities of the group with whom the student takes the test. As a result of placing SAT scores on the College Board scale, scores earned by students at different times can be compared. For example, an SAT-verbal score of 400 on a test taken at one administration indicates the same level of developed verbal ability as a 400 score obtained on a different edition of the test taken at another time.

How to Score the Test

SAT-Verbal Sections 1 and 3

Step A: Count the number of correct answers for *section 1* and record the number in the space provided on the worksheet on the next page. Then do the same for the incorrect answers. (Do not count omitted answers.) To determine subtotal A, use the formula:

$$\text{number correct} - \frac{\text{number incorrect}}{4} = \text{subtotal A}$$

Step B: Count the number of correct answers and the number of incorrect answers for *section 3* and record the numbers in the spaces provided on the worksheet. To determine subtotal B, use the formula:

$$\text{number correct} - \frac{\text{number incorrect}}{4} = \text{subtotal B}$$

Step C: To obtain C, add subtotal A to subtotal B, keeping any decimals. Enter the resulting figure on the worksheet.

Step D: To obtain D, your raw verbal score, round C to the nearest whole number. (For example, any number from 44.50 to 45.49 rounds to 45.) Enter the resulting figure on the worksheet.

Step E: To find your reported SAT-verbal score, look up the total raw verbal score you obtained in step D in the conversion table on page 252. Enter this figure on the worksheet.

SAT-Mathematical Sections 4 and 2

Step A: Count the number of correct answers and the number of incorrect answers for *section 4* and record the numbers in the spaces provided on the worksheet. To determine the subtotal A, use the formula:

$$\text{number correct} - \frac{\text{number incorrect}}{4} = \text{subtotal A}$$

Step B: Count the number of correct answers and the number of incorrect answers for the *five-choice questions (questions 1 through 7 and 28 through 35) in section 2* and record the numbers in the spaces provided on the worksheet. To determine the subtotal B, use the formula:

$$\text{number correct} - \frac{\text{number incorrect}}{4} = \text{subtotal B}$$

Step C: Count the number of correct answers and the number of incorrect answers for the *four-choice questions (questions 8 through 27) in section 2* and record the numbers in the spaces provided on the worksheet. To determine the subtotal C, use the formula:

$$\text{number correct} - \frac{\text{number incorrect}}{3} = \text{subtotal C}$$

Step D: To obtain D, add subtotal A, subtotal B, and subtotal C, keeping any decimals. Enter the resulting figure on the worksheet.

Step E: To obtain E, your raw mathematical score, round D to the nearest whole number. (For example, any number from 44.50 to 45.49 rounds to 45.) Enter the resulting figure on the worksheet.

Step F: To find your reported SAT-mathematical score, look up the total raw mathematical score you obtained in E in the conversion table on page 252. Enter this figure on the worksheet.

SAT SCORING WORKSHEET

SAT-Verbal Sections

A. Section 1:	______ no. correct	− ¼	(______) no. incorrect	=	______ subtotal A
B. Section 3:	______ no. correct	− ¼	(______) no. incorrect	=	______ subtotal B
C. Total unrounded raw score (Total A + B)					______ C
D. Total rounded raw score (Rounded to nearest whole number)					______ D
E. SAT-verbal reported scaled score (See the conversion table on page 252.)					[ ] SAT-verbal score

SAT-Mathematical Sections

A. Section 4:	______ no. correct	− ¼	(______) no. incorrect	=	______ subtotal A
B. Section 2: Questions 1 through 7 and 28 through 35 (5-choice)	______ no. correct	− ¼	(______) no. incorrect	=	______ subtotal B
C. Section 2: Questions 8 through 27 (4-choice)	______ no. correct	− ⅓	(______) no. incorrect	=	______ subtotal C
D. Total unrounded raw score (Total A + B + C)					______ D
E. Total rounded raw score (Rounded to nearest whole number)					______ E
F. SAT-mathematical reported scaled score (See the conversion table on page 252.)					[ ] SAT-math score

Score Conversion Table
Scholastic Aptitude Test
Form Code 7B

Raw Score	College Board Reported Score		Raw Score	College Board Reported Score	
	SAT-Verbal	SAT-Math		SAT-Verbal	SAT-Math
85	800		40	460	590
84	780		39	450	580
83	770		38	450	570
82	760		37	440	560
81	750		36	430	550
80	740		35	430	550
79	730		34	420	540
78	720		33	420	530
77	720		32	410	520
76	710		31	400	510
75	700		30	400	500
74	690		29	390	490
73	680		28	380	480
72	680		27	380	470
71	670		26	370	470
70	660		25	360	460
69	650		24	360	450
68	650		23	350	440
67	640		22	340	430
66	630		21	340	420
65	620		20	330	420
64	620		19	320	410
63	610		18	320	400
62	600		17	310	390
61	600		16	300	380
60	590	800	15	290	370
59	580	780	14	290	370
58	570	760	13	280	360
57	570	750	12	270	350
56	560	750	11	270	340
55	550	740	10	260	330
54	550	730	9	250	330
53	540	720	8	250	320
52	530	710	7	240	310
51	530	700	6	230	300
50	520	690	5	220	290
49	520	680	4	220	280
48	510	670	3	210	270
47	500	660	2	210	270
46	500	650	1	200	260
45	490	640	0	200	250
44	480	630	–1	200	240
43	480	620	–2	200	230
42	470	610	–3	200	220
41	470	600	–4	200	220
			–5	200	210
			–6 or below	200	200

COLLEGE BOARD — SCHOLASTIC APTITUDE TEST and Test of Standard Written English   Side 1

Use a No. 2 pencil only. Be sure each mark is dark and completely fills the intended oval. Completely erase any errors or stray marks.

1.
YOUR NAME: (Print) ____ Last ____ First ____ M.I.

SIGNATURE: ____ DATE: __ / __ / __

HOME ADDRESS: (Print) ____ Number and Street

____ City ____ State ____ Zip Code

CENTER: (Print) ____ City ____ State ____ Center Number

IMPORTANT: Please fill in items 2 and 3 exactly as shown on the back cover of your test book.

FOR ETS USE ONLY

2. TEST FORM (Copy from back cover of your test book.)

3. FORM CODE (Copy and grid as shown on back cover of your test book.)

0	A	J	S	0	0	0
1	B	K	T	1	1	1
2	C	L	U	2	2	2
3	D	M	V	3	3	3
4	E	N	W	4	4	4
5	F	O	X	5	5	5
6	G	P	Y	6	6	6
7	H	Q	Z	7	7	7
8	I	R		8	8	8
9				9	9	9

4. REGISTRATION NUMBER (Copy from your Admission Ticket.)

0	0	0	0	0	0	0
1	1	1	1	1	1	1
2	2	2	2	2	2	2
3	3	3	3	3	3	3
4	4	4	4	4	4	4
5	5	5	5	5	5	5
6	6	6	6	6	6	6
7	7	7	7	7	7	7
8	8	8	8	8	8	8
9	9	9	9	9	9	9

5. YOUR NAME

First 4 letters of last name | First Init | Mid Init

A B C D E F G H I J K L M N O P Q R S T U V W X Y Z (in each of the six columns)

6. DATE OF BIRTH

Month	Day		Year	
Jan.				
Feb.				
Mar.	0	0	0	0
Apr.	1	1	1	1
May	2	2	2	2
June	3	3	3	3
July		4	4	4
Aug.		5	5	5
Sept.		6	6	6
Oct.		7	7	7
Nov.		8		8
Dec.		9		9

7. SEX

Female

Male

8. TEST BOOK SERIAL NUMBER (Copy from front cover of your test book.)

Start with number 1 for each new section. If a section has fewer than 50 questions, leave the extra answer spaces blank.

SECTION 1

Questions 1–50, each with answer ovals A B C D E.

SECTION 2

Questions 1–50, each with answer ovals A B C D E.

(Cut here to detach.)

Q1362-04

I.N. 575008 — 110VV58P3720

COLLEGE BOARD — SCHOLASTIC APTITUDE TEST and Test of Standard Written English

Side 2

Use a No. 2 pencil only. Be sure each mark is dark and completely fills the intended oval. Completely erase any errors or stray marks.

Start with number 1 for each new section. If a section has fewer than 50 questions, leave the extra answer spaces blank.

SECTION 3	SECTION 4	SECTION 5	SECTION 6
1 A B C D E	1 A B C D E	1 A B C D E	1 A B C D E
2 A B C D E	2 A B C D E	2 A B C D E	2 A B C D E
3 A B C D E	3 A B C D E	3 A B C D E	3 A B C D E
4 A B C D E	4 A B C D E	4 A B C D E	4 A B C D E
5 A B C D E	5 A B C D E	5 A B C D E	5 A B C D E
6 A B C D E	6 A B C D E	6 A B C D E	6 A B C D E
7 A B C D E	7 A B C D E	7 A B C D E	7 A B C D E
8 A B C D E	8 A B C D E	8 A B C D E	8 A B C D E
9 A B C D E	9 A B C D E	9 A B C D E	9 A B C D E
10 A B C D E	10 A B C D E	10 A B C D E	10 A B C D E
11 A B C D E	11 A B C D E	11 A B C D E	11 A B C D E
12 A B C D E	12 A B C D E	12 A B C D E	12 A B C D E
13 A B C D E	13 A B C D E	13 A B C D E	13 A B C D E
14 A B C D E	14 A B C D E	14 A B C D E	14 A B C D E
15 A B C D E	15 A B C D E	15 A B C D E	15 A B C D E
16 A B C D E	16 A B C D E	16 A B C D E	16 A B C D E
17 A B C D E	17 A B C D E	17 A B C D E	17 A B C D E
18 A B C D E	18 A B C D E	18 A B C D E	18 A B C D E
19 A B C D E	19 A B C D E	19 A B C D E	19 A B C D E
20 A B C D E	20 A B C D E	20 A B C D E	20 A B C D E
21 A B C D E	21 A B C D E	21 A B C D E	21 A B C D E
22 A B C D E	22 A B C D E	22 A B C D E	22 A B C D E
23 A B C D E	23 A B C D E	23 A B C D E	23 A B C D E
24 A B C D E	24 A B C D E	24 A B C D E	24 A B C D E
25 A B C D E	25 A B C D E	25 A B C D E	25 A B C D E
26 A B C D E	26 A B C D E	26 A B C D E	26 A B C D E
27 A B C D E	27 A B C D E	27 A B C D E	27 A B C D E
28 A B C D E	28 A B C D E	28 A B C D E	28 A B C D E
29 A B C D E	29 A B C D E	29 A B C D E	29 A B C D E
30 A B C D E	30 A B C D E	30 A B C D E	30 A B C D E
31 A B C D E	31 A B C D E	31 A B C D E	31 A B C D E
32 A B C D E	32 A B C D E	32 A B C D E	32 A B C D E
33 A B C D E	33 A B C D E	33 A B C D E	33 A B C D E
34 A B C D E	34 A B C D E	34 A B C D E	34 A B C D E
35 A B C D E	35 A B C D E	35 A B C D E	35 A B C D E
36 A B C D E	36 A B C D E	36 A B C D E	36 A B C D E
37 A B C D E	37 A B C D E	37 A B C D E	37 A B C D E
38 A B C D E	38 A B C D E	38 A B C D E	38 A B C D E
39 A B C D E	39 A B C D E	39 A B C D E	39 A B C D E
40 A B C D E	40 A B C D E	40 A B C D E	40 A B C D E
41 A B C D E	41 A B C D E	41 A B C D E	41 A B C D E
42 A B C D E	42 A B C D E	42 A B C D E	42 A B C D E
43 A B C D E	43 A B C D E	43 A B C D E	43 A B C D E
44 A B C D E	44 A B C D E	44 A B C D E	44 A B C D E
45 A B C D E	45 A B C D E	45 A B C D E	45 A B C D E
46 A B C D E	46 A B C D E	46 A B C D E	46 A B C D E
47 A B C D E	47 A B C D E	47 A B C D E	47 A B C D E
48 A B C D E	48 A B C D E	48 A B C D E	48 A B C D E
49 A B C D E	49 A B C D E	49 A B C D E	49 A B C D E
50 A B C D E	50 A B C D E	50 A B C D E	50 A B C D E

9. SIGNATURE:

FOR ETS USE ONLY	VTR	VTFS	VRR	VRFS	VVR	VVFS	WER	WEFS	M4R	M4FS	M5R	M5FS	MTFS
	VTW	VTCS	VRW	VRCS	VVW	VVCS	WEW	WECS	M4W		M5W		MTCS

SECTION 1	Time—30 minutes 35 Questions	In this section solve each problem, using any available space on the page for scratchwork. Then decide which is the best of the choices given and fill in the corresponding oval on the answer sheet.

The following information is for your reference in solving some of the problems.

Circle of radius r: Area $= \pi r^2$; Circumference $= 2\pi r$
The number of degrees of arc in a circle is 360.
The measure in degrees of a straight angle is 180.

Definition of symbols:

$=$ is equal to	$\leq$ is less than or equal to
$\neq$ is unequal to	$\geq$ is greater than or equal to
$<$ is less than	$\parallel$ is parallel to
$>$ is greater than	$\perp$ is perpendicular to

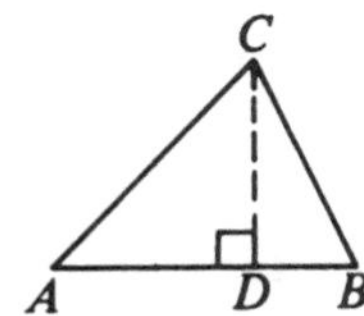

Triangle: The sum of the measures in degrees of the angles of a triangle is 180.
If $\angle CDA$ is a right angle, then

(1) area of $\triangle ABC = \frac{AB \times CD}{2}$

(2) $AC^2 = AD^2 + DC^2$

Note: Figures that accompany problems in this test are intended to provide information useful in solving the problems. They are drawn as accurately as possible EXCEPT when it is stated in a specific problem that its figure is not drawn to scale. All figures lie in a plane unless otherwise indicated. All numbers used are real numbers.

1. If $\frac{x-1}{5} + 1 = 2$, then $x =$

(A) −2
(B) 4
(C) 6
(D) 10
(E) 16

2. Julie runs 4 kilometers every Monday, Wednesday, and Friday and 6 kilometers every Tuesday, Thursday, and Saturday. If she runs 40 kilometers each week, how many kilometers does she run every Sunday?

(A) 4
(B) 5
(C) 6
(D) 8
(E) 10

8	16	24	32
4	8	y	16
2	x	6	8
1	2	3	4

3. In the rectangular array of numbers above, each number above the bottom row is equal to twice the number immediately below it. What is the value of xy?

(A) 4
(B) 12
(C) 36
(D) 48
(E) 56

4. In a video game, 10 spaceships from planet A engaged in a battle with 10 spaceships from planet B, during which exactly 7 spaceships were destroyed. If only 4 of the spaceships from planet A survived the battle, how many spaceships from planet B were destroyed during the battle?

(A) One
(B) Four
(C) Five
(D) Six
(E) Nine

GO ON TO THE NEXT PAGE

$-1, 1, 3, \ldots$

5. The first three numbers in a sequence of 1,000 numbers are shown above. Every number of this sequence after these first three numbers is the sum of the three immediately preceding numbers. For example, the fourth number of this sequence is $-1+1+3=3$, the fifth number is $1+3+3=7$, and so on. How many numbers in this sequence are even?

(A) None
(B) One
(C) Two
(D) Three
(E) More than three

6. What is the value of $\sqrt{4x^2-4xy+y^2}$ when $x=3$ and $y=5$?

(A) 1
(B) $\sqrt{11}$
(C) 7
(D) 11
(E) 49

7. If the area of a rectangle is 24 and the ratio $\frac{\text{width}}{\text{length}}=\frac{2}{3}$, then the length of the rectangle is

(A) 3
(B) 4
(C) 6
(D) 8
(E) 12

GO ON TO THE NEXT PAGE

Questions 8-27 each consist of two quantities, one in Column A and one in Column B. You are to compare the two quantities and on the answer sheet fill in oval

A if the quantity in Column A is greater;
B if the quantity in Column B is greater;
C if the two quantities are equal;
D if the relationship cannot be determined from the information given.

AN E RESPONSE WILL NOT BE SCORED.

EXAMPLES

	Column A	Column B	Answers
E1.	2×6	$2 + 6$	● Ⓑ Ⓒ Ⓓ Ⓔ
E2.	$180 - x$	y	Ⓐ Ⓑ ● Ⓓ Ⓔ
E3.	$p - q$	$q - p$	Ⓐ Ⓑ Ⓒ ● Ⓔ

Notes:

1. In certain questions, information concerning one or both of the quantities to be compared is centered above the two columns.
2. In a given question, a symbol that appears in both columns represents the same thing in Column A as it does in Column B.
3. Letters such as x, n, and k stand for real numbers.

	Column A	Column B
8.	1	$\frac{1}{2} + \frac{1}{4} + \frac{1}{8}$
9.	x^2y^4	1

Bag A contains 20 marbles, exactly 9 of which are white. Bag B contains 10 marbles, exactly 5 of which are white. One marble is drawn at random from each bag.

	Column A	Column B
10.	The probability that the marble from bag A is white	The probability that the marble from bag B is white
11.	$\frac{3}{75}$	$\frac{4}{100}$
12.	The distance between the tips of the hands of a clock indicating 8:30	The distance between the tips of the hands of the same clock indicating 9:00

Nan has n coins and Charles has 3 less than 5 times the number of coins that Nan has.

	Column A	Column B
13.	The number of coins that Charles has	$5n + 3$

$$\frac{x + x + x}{3} = 5$$

	Column A	Column B
14.	$\frac{x + x + x + x}{4}$	5

	Column A	Column B
15.	x	50
16.	$\frac{2}{7} + \frac{3}{7}$	$\frac{2 + 3}{7 + 7}$

$$x + y < 8$$

	Column A	Column B
17.	x	7

$$k < 0$$

	Column A	Column B
18.	$k^2 - k^3 + k^4$	0

GO ON TO THE NEXT PAGE

SUMMARY DIRECTIONS FOR COMPARISON QUESTIONS

Answer: A if the quantity in Column A is greater;
B if the quantity in Column B is greater;
C if the two quantities are equal;
D if the relationship cannot be determined from the information given.

AN E RESPONSE WILL NOT BE SCORED.

	Column A	Column B
19.	The number of solutions to the equation $5x = 0$	The number of solutions to the equation $0 \cdot y = 5$

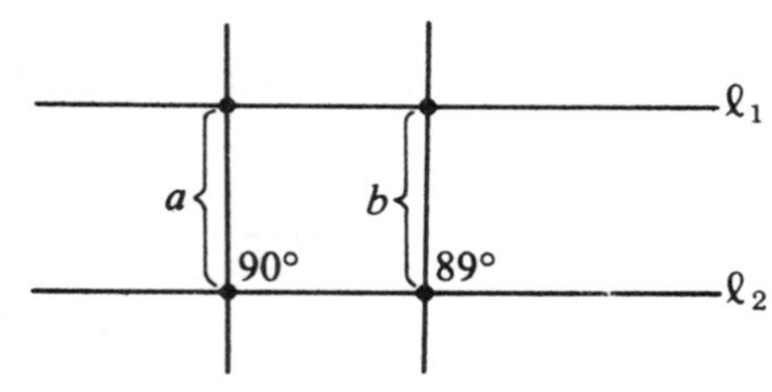

$\ell_1 \parallel \ell_2$

	Column A	Column B
20.	a	b
21.	The number of positive odd integer factors of 26	The number of positive even integer factors of 26

$x = \frac{2y}{3}$ and $x = y - 1$

	Column A	Column B
22.	x	2

The area of a square is K square meters and its perimeter is M meters.

	Column A	Column B
23.	K	M

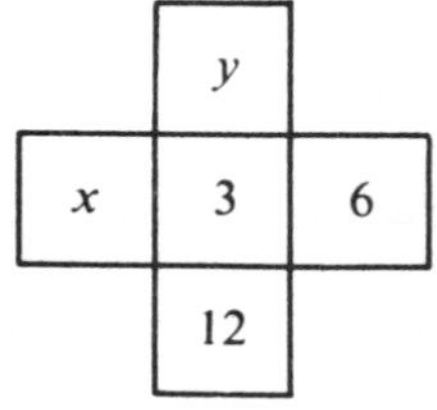

The product of the three numbers in the row is equal to the product of the three numbers in the column.

	Column A	Column B
24.	$2y - x$	0
25.	$x^2 - 5x - 6$	$6 + 5x - x^2$

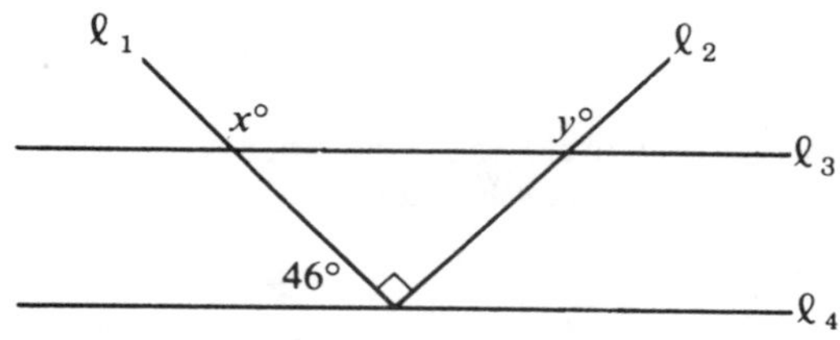

$\ell_3 \parallel \ell_4$

	Column A	Column B
26.	x	y

$y > 0$

	Column A	Column B
27.	The number of seconds in y hours	$60y$

GO ON TO THE NEXT PAGE

Solve each of the remaining problems in this section using any available space for scratchwork. Then decide which is the best of the choices given and fill in the corresponding oval on the answer sheet.

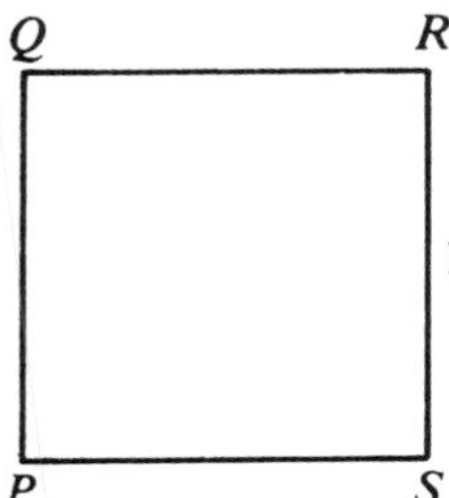

28. In the square above with side of length 1 unit, a point starts at vertex P and moves along the sides of the square in a clockwise direction. If the point travels a distance of exactly 487 units, where will the point be?

(A) P
(B) Q
(C) R
(D) S
(E) Not at a vertex

29. If a taxicab driver charges \$0.60 for the first $\frac{1}{3}$ mile and \$0.40 for each $\frac{2}{5}$ mile, or part thereof, after that, a ride costing \$3.80 could be at most how many miles long?

(A) $3\frac{8}{15}$

(B) $3\frac{11}{15}$

(C) $3\frac{13}{15}$

(D) 4

(E) $4\frac{1}{3}$

30. What is the average (arithmetic mean) of all the multiples of 10 from 10 to 90, inclusive?

(A) 40
(B) 45
(C) 50
(D) 55
(E) 90

x^2 xy
xy a^2 ab
ab s^2 st
st t^2

31. In the square above, if the ten nonoverlapping regions have the areas shown, which of the following is equal to y?

(A) $x + t$
(B) $s + t$
(C) $a + s + t$
(D) $b + s + t$
(E) $a + b + s$

GO ON TO THE NEXT PAGE

32. $\sqrt{2}$ percent of $3\sqrt{2} =$

(A) 0.06

(B) 0.3

(C) $\frac{1}{3}$

(D) 6

(E) $33\frac{1}{3}$

33. The sum of the areas of the faces of a cube is 300 square inches. The volume of this cube, in cubic inches, is

(A) $125\sqrt{2}$
(B) $250\sqrt{2}$
(C) $300\sqrt{2}$
(D) 2,500
(E) 125,000

34. If s denotes the sum of the integers from 1 to 30 inclusive, and t denotes the sum of the integers from 31 to 60 inclusive, what is the value of $t - s$?

(A) 30
(B) 31
(C) 180
(D) 450
(E) 900

35. $\frac{8^5 - 8^4}{7} =$

(A) $\frac{1}{7}$

(B) $\frac{8}{7}$

(C) 8^3

(D) $\frac{8^4}{7}$

(E) 8^4

IF YOU FINISH BEFORE TIME IS CALLED, YOU MAY CHECK YOUR WORK ON THIS SECTION ONLY. DO NOT TURN TO ANY OTHER SECTION IN THE TEST. **STOP**

SECTION 2 | **Time—30 minutes 40 Questions** | For each question in this section, choose the best answer and fill in the corresponding oval on the answer sheet.

Each question below consists of a word in capital letters, followed by five lettered words or phrases. Choose the word or phrase that is most nearly opposite in meaning to the word in capital letters. Since some of the questions require you to distinguish fine shades of meaning, consider all the choices before deciding which is best.

Example:

GOOD: (A) sour (B) bad (C) red (D) hot (E) ugly

Ⓐ ● Ⓒ Ⓓ Ⓔ

1. RUFFLE: (A) begin (B) increase (C) smooth (D) speak clearly (E) act promptly

2. FINESSE: (A) submission (B) tendency (C) contentment (D) indulgence (E) awkwardness

3. FEISTY: (A) devoted and loyal (B) subdued and peaceful (C) honest (D) knowledgeable (E) thorough

4. GARBLE: (A) agree on (B) subtract from (C) make clear (D) act cautiously (E) provide abundantly

5. DETRIMENT: (A) recurrence (B) disclosure (C) resemblance (D) enhancement (E) postponement

6. SECTARIAN: (A) unethical (B) exhilarating (C) broad-minded (D) modernistic (E) good-natured

7. CONTEND: (A) divulge (B) confound (C) discourage (D) concede (E) discharge

8. BURNISH: (A) reduce gradually (B) soften slightly (C) make dull (D) destroy (E) moisten

9. TEPID: (A) passionate (B) grandiose (C) carefree (D) faintly reminiscent (E) easily apprehended

10. SURFEIT: (A) shortage (B) confidence (C) inconsistency (D) quick temper (E) established practice

Each sentence below has one or two blanks, each blank indicating that something has been omitted. Beneath the sentence are five lettered words or sets of words. Choose the word or set of words that, when inserted in the sentence, best fits the meaning of the sentence as a whole.

Example:

Although its publicity has been ----, the film itself is intelligent, well-acted, handsomely produced, and altogether ----.

(A) tasteless. .respectable (B) extensive. .moderate (C) sophisticated. .amateur (D) risqué. .crude (E) perfect. .spectacular

● Ⓑ Ⓒ Ⓓ Ⓔ

11. Some insects rely on camouflage to capture their prey; certain colorful assassin bugs, for instance, become virtually ---- on flower petals of similar hue.

(A) irrepressible (B) invisible (C) indestructible (D) defenseless (E) colorless

12. Looking on the world with reverence and wonder, landscape photographers cross deserts and descend into live volcanoes to share their ---- with others.

(A) duty (B) silence (C) awe (D) gloom (E) energy

13. Although the acreage involved in a national boundary dispute may seem insignificant, even the slightest ---- in a country's alleged border appears ---- to that nation, a threat to its security.

(A) inconsistency. .felicitous
(B) variation. .trivial
(C) rigidity. .traumatic
(D) change. .favorable
(E) breach. .ominous

14. It is a curious fact that soothsayers are, virtually each and every one, ---- souls, ---- to the status quo and resistant to change.

    (A) consistent..opposed
    (B) innovative..committed
    (C) conciliatory..hostile
    (D) conservative..dedicated
    (E) progressive..unsympathetic

15. Those unschooled in the latest theories of art will be frustrated by Ms. Kaplan's arcane brochure because they will find it all but ----.

    (A) antithetical (B) unintelligible (C) unimpressive (D) masterful (E) predictable

Each question below consists of a related pair of words or phrases, followed by five lettered pairs of words or phrases. Select the lettered pair that <u>best</u> expresses a relationship similar to that expressed in the original pair.

Example:

YAWN:BOREDOM :: (A) dream:sleep (B) anger:madness (C) smile:amusement (D) face:expression (E) impatience:rebellion

16. COUNTERFEIT:MONEY ::
    (A) complication:stratagem
    (B) masquerade:costume
    (C) forgery:signature
    (D) bluff:gamble
    (E) camouflage:equipment

17. SALT:MINERAL :: (A) cocoa:coffee (B) lead:pencil (C) cinnamon:spice (D) sugar:cane (E) coal:mine

18. PUCKER:LIPS :: (A) tremble:fear (B) pout:anger (C) pat:back (D) hunch:shoulders (E) stare:object

19. CHANT:SPEAK :: (A) listen:hear (B) wince:avoid (C) pinch:touch (D) blink:see (E) march:walk

20. ARCHIVE:DOCUMENTS ::
    (A) museum:artifacts
    (B) orchestra:instruments
    (C) courthouse:sentences
    (D) theater:performances
    (E) library:borrowers

21. ACRID:TASTE :: (A) faint:odor (B) numb:touch (C) raucous:sound (D) hazy:sight (E) giddy:feeling

22. IMPECCABLE:FAULT ::
    (A) immortal:life
    (B) impoverished:wealth
    (C) imperceptible:vision
    (D) insolvent:debt
    (E) imperious:disobedience

23. IMPASSE:ESCAPE :: (A) bastion:defense (B) detour:travel (C) stalemate:victory (D) handicap:contest (E) prevention:cure

24. BICKER:PETTY :: (A) banter:playful (B) smirk:sincere (C) flaunt:open (D) grumble:merry (E) assault:sudden

25. DIMINUTIVE:STATURE :: (A) dainty:taste (B) juvenile:humor (C) slender:girth (D) shy:disposition (E) fleet:endurance

GO ON TO THE NEXT PAGE

Each passage below is followed by questions based on its content. Answer all questions following a passage on the basis of what is stated or implied in that passage.

Mr. Frampton took no interest in the amenities of life. Nor did he appear very interested in his daughter. In his secret heart he regarded his child as responsible for her mother's death, for the woman had outlived her daughter's birth by only a few months, and though not an unkind man, he felt vaguely hostile to her, as if she had deliberately usurped her mother's place. He was a cold, cautious, crafty man of affairs, with so little imagination, even in his business, that it was not until his employer promoted him from the position of a trusted subordinate to that of official partner that his industry and thrift received anything like their merited recognition. Mr. Frampton ate whatever was placed before him and drank whatever was in his decanter. He used the same bed, the same carpets, the same curtains, the same chairs, the same cushions, that he had bought for his wife, of whom he was idolatrously fond, when he was an underpaid clerk in Cattistock's office. Peg had only once in her life seen her father really angry and that was when she had bought at a fancy-work bazaar a brilliant oriental-looking cover for their faded drawing-room sofa. Nor, even then, had his anger been shown in any way except by his getting very red. But as he was always extremely sallow, this event was as startling to Peg as would have been the hoisting of a Russian flag by a battleship in Portland Harbour. Mr. Frampton removed the cover from the sofa, folded it up very carefully, and hung it over the bottom of the banisters.

26. According to the passage, Mr. Frampton's attitude toward his wife was one of

(A) brooding suspicion
(B) excessive adoration
(C) anxious possessiveness
(D) aloof tolerance
(E) fatherly affection

27. The author implies that Mr. Frampton eventually won promotion because of his

(A) reliability (B) initiative (C) generosity (D) self-denial (E) idealism

28. According to the passage, Mr. Frampton's attitude toward his daughter was one of

(A) blind devotion
(B) protective concern
(C) timid fellowship
(D) suppressed resentment
(E) distrustful jealousy

GO ON TO THE NEXT PAGE

The reading passages in this test are brief excerpts or adaptations of excerpts from published material. The ideas contained in them do not necessarily represent the opinions of the College Board or Educational Testing Service. To make the text suitable for testing purposes, we may in some cases have altered the style, contents, or point of view of the original.

The notion that in the United States elected officials have exclusive responsibility for making public policy is false. Already twenty-three states have adopted a procedure called the initiative. This procedure allows voters to participate in making law by petitioning to place on the ballot a law previously proposed by the legislature. If the number of signatures required by law is secured for the petition, the proposed law can be put before the voters, who then can adopt or reject it.

Although, according to pollsters, the American public today is better educated and more politically sophisticated than ever before, we cannot be certain that Americans have not lost interest in and commitment to the spirit of democracy when so many of them choose not to vote in national elections. Perhaps those who do not vote are disillusioned by the inability of politicians to act. If a national initiative were adopted, it would fulfill a need for increased citizen participation in the policymaking process. The initiative would provide a mechanism, now nonexistent at the federal level, for letting citizens establish public policy when legislators fail to act, as can happen when powerful pressure groups block adoption of legislation involving controversial issues.

Of course, a national initiative would not cure all our national ills, and Congress would continue to pass nearly all our laws. But the mere existence of the initiative would, perhaps, cause public officials to listen more closely to the voice of the people and increase both voter interest and voter participation by injecting more issues into campaigns.

29. The main purpose of the passage is to

(A) criticize the failure of elected officials to act
(B) urge voters to become better informed about important political decisions
(C) describe the process by which federal law is made
(D) affirm the political sophistication of the American populace
(E) advocate the federal government's adoption of the initiative

30. It can be inferred that the author believes that the strength of a democracy can be measured by the

(A) political involvement of its citizens
(B) moral responsibility of its elected officials
(C) stability of its constitution
(D) cooperation among different levels of government
(E) political sophistication of its voters

31. The author suggests that a national initiative would do all of the following EXCEPT

(A) allow citizens to express their opinions about proposed legislation
(B) encourage public officials to pay more attention to public opinion
(C) increase voter turnout
(D) transfer principal legislative power from Congress to voters
(E) make political campaigns more issue-oriented

GO ON TO THE NEXT PAGE

Scientists searching for extraterrestrials by listening for their radio transmissions face the formidable task of looking at millions of stars before they can have any probability of success, and this supposes the unlikely optimum situation in which the "others" have high-powered signals aimed continuously toward Earth. Most current approaches to the search for extraterrestrial intelligence (SETI) are therefore based on observing a large number of stars simultaneously, in the hope of detecting very powerful transmissions. The choice of frequencies at which to listen is ingenious. The absorption and reemission of radiation by gases in the Earth's atmosphere creates a wall of noise in the radio spectrum, which is difficult for radio telescopes to penetrate. There is a quiet area, however, between 1,000 and 10,000 megahertz (MHz). This range includes the 1,420 MHz band, one of the frequencies at which hydrogen, the major constituent of the universe, emits radiation. At 1,662 MHz the frequency range also contains an emission frequency of the hydroxyl ion—a hydrogen atom bound to an oxygen atom. Between these two frequencies is the quietest part of the radio spectrum as seen from the Earth's surface. Since this radio window is bound by constituents of the water molecule, it has been poetically dubbed the "water hole"—the traditional meeting place of different species. It seems reasonable to suppose that intelligent beings biologically similar to us would follow the same logic and choose to broadcast in this region.

32. The primary purpose of the passage is to
    - (A) speculate on the existence of extraterrestrial life
    - (B) promote the scientific search for extraterrestrial life
    - (C) discuss the search for extraterrestrials through the monitoring of radio waves from space
    - (D) define the radio frequencies at which scientists broadcast signals into space
    - (E) stress the significance of the radio telescope in modern astronomy

33. Which of the following statements about the hydrogen emission frequency mentioned by the author is supported by the passage?
    - (A) It happens to be near one end of the quietest part of the radio spectrum as perceived at the Earth's surface.
    - (B) It makes it unnecessary for astronomers searching for extraterrestrials to view many stars simultaneously.
    - (C) It requires that radio telescopes be fixed at frequencies above 1,662 MHz.
    - (D) It clears the Earth's atmosphere of dense water molecules.
    - (E) It directs radio signals away from possible extraterrestrial life.

34. Which of the following is NOT used by the author in developing the passage?
    - (A) Discussion of the current search for extraterrestrials
    - (B) Evaluation of one way to narrow the search for extraterrestrials
    - (C) Definition of a problem associated with radio telescopes
    - (D) Description of the cause of hydroxyl ion emission
    - (E) Explanation of the term "water hole"

35. According to the passage, the quietest part of the radio spectrum is called the "water hole" for which of the following reasons?
    - I. Its boundaries are marked by emission frequencies of components of the water molecule.
    - II. It is a region in which humans might receive radio signals from extraterrestrials.
    - III. It is something for which scientists have been desperately searching.

    (A) I only (B) II only (C) I and II only (D) I and III only (E) I, II, and III

GO ON TO THE NEXT PAGE

For more than a century we have lived with the contrasting images of the American character that Thomas Jefferson and Alexis de Tocqueville visualized. For Jefferson, the American was an equalitarian, an agrarian democrat, an independent individualist, and an idealist. For Tocqueville, a French observer of American life, the American was in many respects quite different.

Although Tocqueville, like Jefferson, had no doubt of the depth of the American commitment to equality and therefore to democracy, he perceived an America far removed from Jefferson's dream of a democracy in which love of equality and love of liberty go together. "Liberty," Tocqueville wrote, "is not the chief object of [Americans'] desires; equality is their idol . . . and they would rather perish than lose it." To Tocqueville, the dangers inherent in equality were severe. While acknowledging that in rare circumstances equality and freedom might "meet and blend," he noted that for the most part equality encouraged conformity and discouraged individualism, regimented opinion and inhibited dissent. This, he observed, was the case in America, where the same equality that rendered the individual independent of each fellow citizen, taken one by one, exposed the individual alone and unprotected to the enormous influence of the opinion of the majority. Because of the principle of equality, Tocqueville wrote, "freedom of opinion does not exist in America." The American character, in fact, evidenced a conformity so extreme that individuality and even liberty were endangered.

To this picture of the American as a conformist, Tocqueville added his condemnation of the American as a materialist. Though not alone in his criticism of the materialistic aspects of American life, Tocqueville was the first to link materialism with equality, as he had already linked conformity. The craving for physical comforts, he wrote, "is the prominent and indelible feature of democratic times." In America the craving had become a passion. "I know of no country, indeed, where the love of money has taken stronger hold on the affections of men."

The discrepancy between Jefferson's and Tocqueville's images of the American character is so great that one wonders whether their seemingly nearly antithetical versions of the American can be reconciled in any way or whether the warnings of those who have spoken against the whole concept of national character should be heeded. The latter view has been fueled by the fact that many generalizations about national groups have been derived not from any dispassionate observation or quest for truth but from superheated patriotism that sought to glorify one national group by invidious comparison with other national groups.

36. The author's main purpose in the passage is to

(A) disparage past attempts to define the American character
(B) discuss the contrasts inherent in two views of the American character
(C) deny the existence of observable national traits
(D) show that the complexity of the American character defies consistent explanation
(E) reveal the dubious reasons frequently motivating portrayals of national character

37. Which of the following statements about Tocqueville is most strongly supported by the passage?

(A) His views reflected his misunderstanding of American democracy.
(B) He was original in his analysis of the social effects of American political belief.
(C) His views of America were favorable because of his foreign birth.
(D) He was antagonistic to all aspects of the democratic trends of his time.
(E) His views reflected his enthusiasm for Jefferson's agrarian democratic ideals.

38. The passage suggests that the author finds Jefferson's and Tocqueville's views of American society

(A) strongly influenced by European philosophy
(B) at variance in every respect
(C) illustrative of traditional American thought
(D) of interest merely as historical oddities
(E) still worthy of intellectual consideration

39. The passage suggests that Jefferson would most likely have agreed with which of the following views held by Tocqueville?

(A) Americans put equality before liberty.
(B) Americans resist subservience to other individuals.
(C) Freedom of opinion does not exist in America.
(D) Democracy encourages materialism.
(E) Equality discourages individualism.

40. The author uses the last paragraph primarily to

(A) cast doubt on the personal integrity of both Jefferson and Tocqueville
(B) intimate that Jefferson's views derived from "superheated patriotism"
(C) assail the invidious comparisons implied in Jefferson's and Tocqueville's views
(D) question the validity of the notion that nations can be characterized by particular traits
(E) point to the need for a new method of observation in order to arrive at truthful portraits of national character

IF YOU FINISH BEFORE TIME IS CALLED, YOU MAY CHECK YOUR WORK ON THIS SECTION ONLY. DO NOT TURN TO ANY OTHER SECTION IN THE TEST. **STOP**

SECTION 3 Time—30 minutes 25 Questions

In this section solve each problem, using any available space on the page for scratchwork. Then decide which is the best of the choices given and fill in the corresponding oval on the answer sheet.

The following information is for your reference in solving some of the problems.

Circle of radius r: Area $= \pi r^2$; Circumference $= 2\pi r$
The number of degrees of arc in a circle is 360.
The measure in degrees of a straight angle is 180.

Definition of symbols:

$=$ is equal to	$\leq$ is less than or equal to
$\neq$ is unequal to	$\geq$ is greater than or equal to
$<$ is less than	$\parallel$ is parallel to
$>$ is greater than	$\perp$ is perpendicular to

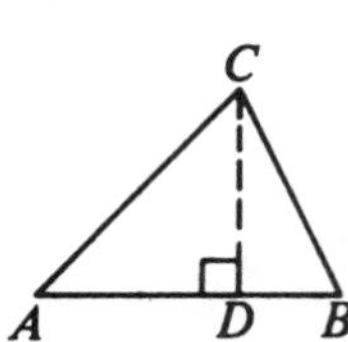

Triangle: The sum of the measures in degrees of the angles of a triangle is 180.
If $\angle CDA$ is a right angle, then

(1) area of $\triangle ABC = \frac{AB \times CD}{2}$

(2) $AC^2 = AD^2 + DC^2$

Note: Figures that accompany problems in this test are intended to provide information useful in solving the problems. They are drawn as accurately as possible EXCEPT when it is stated in a specific problem that its figure is not drawn to scale. All figures lie in a plane unless otherwise indicated. All numbers used are real numbers.

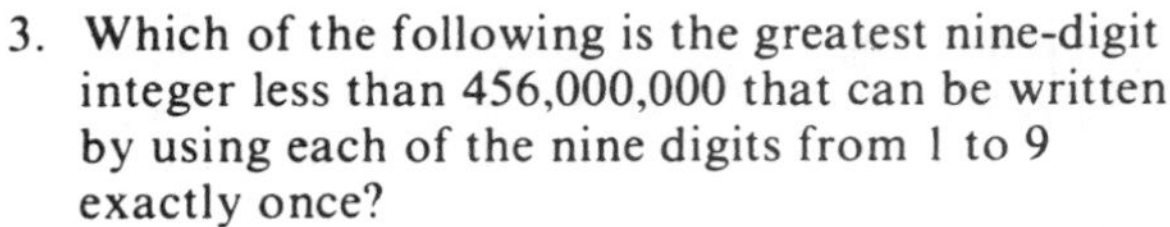

1. $6 + \frac{4(9+1)}{5} =$

   (A) 26

   (B) 20

   (C) 14

   (D) $13\frac{1}{5}$

   (E) $8\frac{4}{5}$

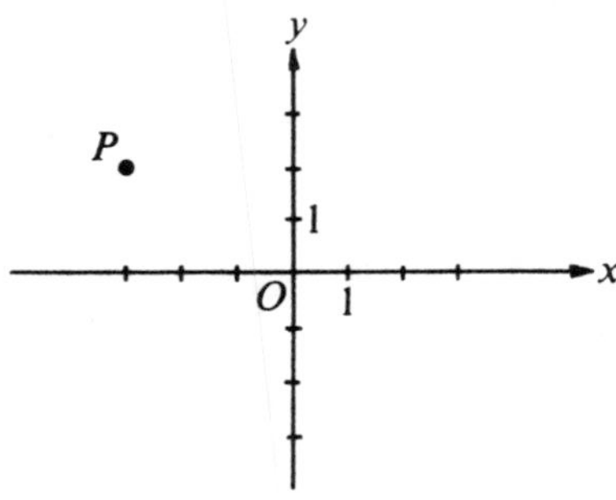

2. In the figure above, what are the coordinates of point P?

   (A) (3, −2)
   (B) (2, 3)
   (C) (−2, 3)
   (D) (−3, 2)
   (E) (−3, −2)

3. Which of the following is the greatest nine-digit integer less than 456,000,000 that can be written by using each of the nine digits from 1 to 9 exactly once?

   (A) 455,999,999
   (B) 455,987,654
   (C) 454,987,321
   (D) 453,987,651
   (E) 453,987,621

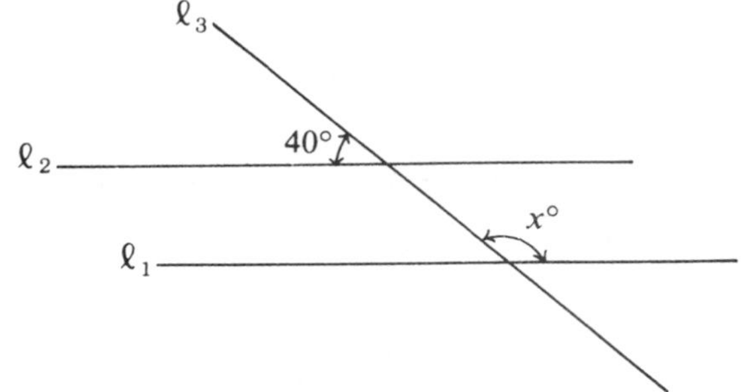

4. In the figure above, if $\ell_1 \parallel \ell_2$, what is the value of x?

   (A) 120
   (B) 130
   (C) 140
   (D) 150
   (E) 160

GO ON TO THE NEXT PAGE

5. Tom had 18 comic books, while Diane and Helen had none. Tom gave $\frac{1}{3}$ of the comic books to Diane who passed $\frac{1}{3}$ of these books along to Helen. If Tom then gave Helen $\frac{1}{3}$ of the books he had left, how many comic books did Helen receive from Tom and Diane?

(A) 6
(B) 5
(C) 4
(D) 3
(E) 2

6. If n is an odd integer, which of the following expressions must represent an even integer?

I. $n+2$
II. $2n$
III. n^2

(A) I only
(B) II only
(C) III only
(D) I and II only
(E) I, II, and III

7. If the notation used in the expressions 2_{123} and 2_{245} is defined as follows:

$$2_{123} = 2^1 + 2^2 + 2^3 = 14 \text{ and}$$
$$2_{245} = 2^2 + 2^4 + 2^5 = 52,$$

then $2_{135} =$

(A) 42 (B) 66 (C) 270
(D) 512 (E) 2^{135}

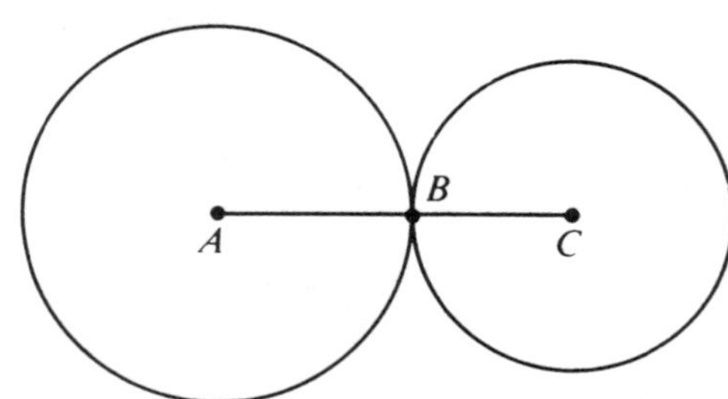

Note: Figure not drawn to scale.

8. In the figure above, point B is on line segment AC, and $AC = 6$. If the circumference of the circle with center A is twice the circumference of the circle with center C, what is the length of BC?

(A) 1
(B) 2
(C) 3
(D) 4
(E) 6

9. Of the following, which is greatest?

(A) 0.05×2
(B) 0.02×5
(C) $\frac{2}{0.05}$
(D) $\frac{0.05}{2}$
(E) $\frac{5}{0.02}$

10. Conveyer belt R travels at 45 feet per minute and conveyer belt S travels at 30 feet per minute. A given point on R would travel how many more feet in one hour than a given point on S?

(A) 15
(B) 900
(C) 1,800
(D) 2,700
(E) 4,500

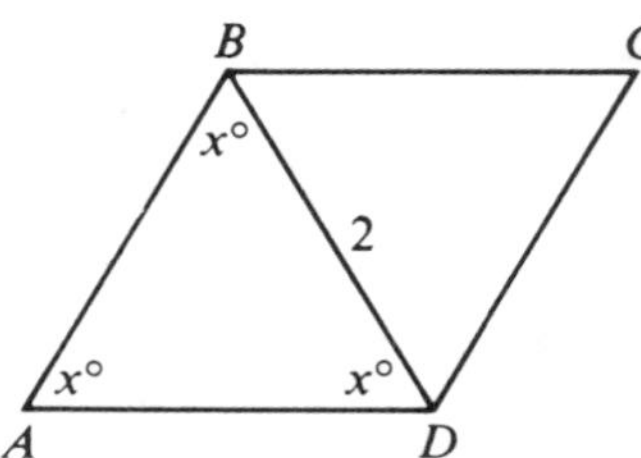

11. What is the perimeter of parallelogram $ABCD$ in the figure above?

(A) 8
(B) $4\sqrt{3}$
(C) 6
(D) 4
(E) $2\sqrt{3}$

12. If 40 percent of x is 18, then 20 percent of $2x$ is

(A) 90
(B) 45
(C) 36
(D) 18
(E) 9

GO ON TO THE NEXT PAGE

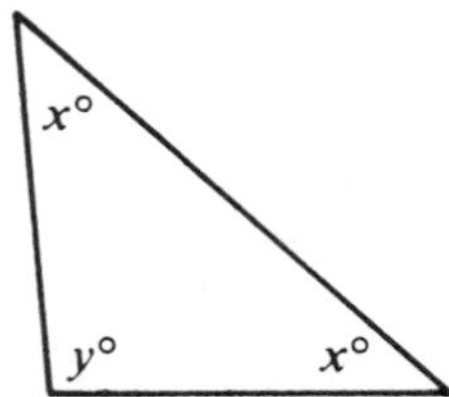

Note: Figure not drawn to scale.

13. In the triangle above, if $80 \leq y \leq 100$, which of the following must be true?

(A) $30 \leq x \leq 40$
(B) $40 \leq x \leq 50$
(C) $50 \leq x \leq 60$
(D) $60 \leq x \leq 70$
(E) $70 \leq x \leq 80$

14. The present ages, in years, of three brothers are three consecutive even integers. Four years ago the sum of their ages was 30 years. What is the present age in years of the youngest brother?

(A) 6
(B) 8
(C) 10
(D) 12
(E) 14

15. If $x + y = 6$, $x - z = 3$, and $x = 2$, then $z - y =$

(A) 3
(B) −1
(C) −2
(D) −3
(E) −5

16. In the figure above, segment PT has length 36, Q is the midpoint of PR, R is the midpoint of QS, and S is the midpoint of QT. What is the length of segment QS?

(A) 7.2
(B) 12.2
(C) 12.4
(D) 14.2
(E) 14.4

17. If a, b, and c are positive integers such that $a < b < c$ and $abc = 50$, then the least possible value of c is

(A) 25
(B) 10
(C) 5
(D) 2
(E) 1

18. A perfect square is an integer whose square root is an integer. The numbers 16, 25, and 36 are perfect squares. If a and b are perfect squares, which of the following is NOT necessarily a perfect square?

(A) $25a$
(B) a^2
(C) a^3
(D) ab
(E) $a - b$

19. If $S = \left\{\frac{1}{5}, \frac{1}{4}, \frac{1}{3}, \frac{2}{3}, \frac{3}{4}, \frac{4}{5}\right\}$ and x and y are elements of S, what is the maximum possible value of $3x - 3y$?

(A) $\frac{9}{10}$
(B) $\frac{7}{5}$
(C) $\frac{3}{2}$
(D) $\frac{9}{5}$
(E) 3

20. On a given day there are 12 trains to City X with an average (arithmetic mean) of 1,400 commuters per train. If the number of trains were cut to 7 and the total number of commuters remained the same, there would be an average of how many more commuters per train?

(A) 600
(B) 800
(C) 1,000
(D) 1,600
(E) 2,400

GO ON TO THE NEXT PAGE

21. A 3 by 4 rectangle is inscribed in a circle. What is the area of the circle?

(A) 6.25π
(B) 9π
(C) 12.25π
(D) 16π
(E) 25π

22. Three numbers when added in pairs give the sums 15, 18, and 21. The average (arithmetic mean) of the 3 numbers is

(A) 3
(B) 9
(C) 12
(D) 15
(E) 18

23. If $z = -x$ and $x \neq 0$, what are all values of y for which $(x + y)^2 + (y + z)^2 = 2x^2$?

(A) 0
(B) 0, 1
(C) −1, 0, 1
(D) All positive numbers
(E) There are no values of y for which the equation is true.

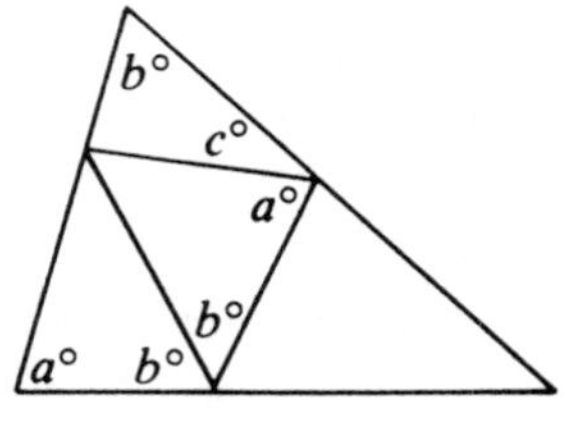

24. In the figure above, what is the value of c in terms of a and b?

(A) $a + 3b - 180$
(B) $2a + 2b - 180$
(C) $180 - a - b$
(D) $360 - a - b$
(E) $360 - 2a - 3b$

25. Which of the following is closest in value to 3.14159?

(A) $\frac{314}{100}$
(B) $\frac{1,571}{500}$
(C) $\frac{3,141}{1,000}$
(D) $\frac{15,708}{5,000}$
(E) $\frac{31,415}{10,000}$

IF YOU FINISH BEFORE TIME IS CALLED, YOU MAY CHECK YOUR WORK ON THIS SECTION ONLY. DO NOT TURN TO ANY OTHER SECTION IN THE TEST. **STOP**

SECTION 4 | **Time—30 minutes** **45 Questions** | For each question in this section, choose the best answer and fill in the corresponding oval on the answer sheet.

Each question below consists of a word in capital letters, followed by five lettered words or phrases. Choose the word or phrase that is most nearly opposite in meaning to the word in capital letters. Since some of the questions require you to distinguish fine shades of meaning, consider all the choices before deciding which is best.

Example:

GOOD: (A) sour (B) bad (C) red (D) hot (E) ugly

Ⓐ ● Ⓒ Ⓓ Ⓔ

1. ALERT: (A) mistaken (B) inattentive (C) aloof (D) insulting (E) helpful

2. EQUILIBRIUM: (A) saturation (B) independence (C) isolation (D) oppression (E) imbalance

3. VIBRANCY: (A) innocence (B) immaturity (C) arrogance (D) lifelessness (E) hostility

4. PRECEDE: (A) come after (B) remain loyal (C) act decisively (D) move away from (E) fail to inform

5. MINUSCULE: (A) gigantic (B) slippery (C) diverse (D) valid (E) united

6. SUBSIDE: (A) extract (B) divide (C) rise (D) plan (E) enter

7. DEXTEROUS: (A) clumsy (B) large (C) formal (D) menacing (E) plentiful

8. BELLIGERENCY: (A) pain (B) silence (C) homeliness (D) elegance (E) peace

9. PREVALENT: (A) disproportionate (B) inconvenient (C) superficial (D) uncommon (E) simple

10. SANCTION: (A) prohibit (B) convert (C) divulge (D) allot (E) contaminate

11. INCEPTION: (A) termination (B) vulnerability (C) vacillation (D) acceptance (E) coherence

12. DEBASE: (A) startle (B) elevate (C) encircle (D) replace (E) assemble

13. CARNAL: (A) fragrant (B) lengthy (C) factual (D) spiritual (E) antiquated

14. SINUOUS: (A) beneficial (B) authentic (C) attractive (D) straight (E) pungent

15. MUNIFICENCE: (A) disloyalty (B) stinginess (C) dispersion (D) simplicity (E) vehemence

GO ON TO THE NEXT PAGE

Each sentence below has one or two blanks, each blank indicating that something has been omitted. Beneath the sentence are five lettered words or sets of words. Choose the word or set of words that, when inserted in the sentence, best fits the meaning of the sentence as a whole.

Example:

Although its publicity has been ----, the film itself is intelligent, well-acted, handsomely produced, and altogether ----.

(A) tasteless. . respectable (B) extensive. . moderate (C) sophisticated. . amateur (D) risqué. . crude (E) perfect. . spectacular

● Ⓑ Ⓒ Ⓓ Ⓔ

16. Scientists have always recognized that deforestation will have an impact on the immediate environment, but they now warn that cutting down large forests can ---- problems on a much wider scale.

(A) generate (B) isolate (C) disturb (D) curtail (E) document

17. A group of Black American fighter pilots known as the Red Tail Angels has the ---- of never having lost any of the bombers it escorted on missions over Europe in the Second World War.

(A) onus (B) distinction (C) imperative (D) potential (E) assignment

18. Although they must rely on ---- and accumulation of facts, historians also need ---- in order to understand the evidence they gather.

(A) omission..diligence
(B) curiosity..confusion
(C) observation..imagination
(D) objectivity..neutrality
(E) ignorance..sympathy

19. Convinced that the vote of women workers would ---- social legislation that it favored, the American Federation of Labor supported woman suffrage as early as 1886.

(A) replace (B) counterbalance (C) disguise (D) confuse (E) promote

20. In cartography the elimination of a certain amount of detail is the ---- of achieving clarity; accordingly, the most ---- maps in this atlas tend to be the simplest.

(A) foundation..detailed
(B) enemy..concise
(C) price..comprehensible
(D) hazard..ornate
(E) predecessor..technical

21. The land can hardly be considered ----, for the steep hills retain little of the summer rains and the soil is ----.

(A) unprofitable..inactive
(B) barren..overused
(C) arable..thin
(D) luxuriant..fertile
(E) impractical..arid

22. Certain book reviewers have become increasingly reverential toward the very idea of writing, as if the mere writing of a book ---- a ---- act or a selfless public service.

(A) involved..blasphemous
(B) repudiated..gallant
(C) constituted..virtuous
(D) trivialized..ceremonious
(E) embodied..perverse

23. Some settlers planned to return eventually to their homeland, ---- that geography made easy and that left them ---- to seek permanent residency in the new land.

(A) a mandate..reluctant
(B) a pledge..committed
(C) a quandary..unmotivated
(D) an ambivalence..inspired
(E) an intention..disinclined

24. Elegant chess moves, complex musical melodies, and brilliant mathematical theorems share this trait: each has idiosyncratic nuances that seem ---- on reflection but are impossible to ----.

(A) correct..devise
(B) obvious..overlook
(C) animated..assess
(D) spontaneous..duplicate
(E) inevitable..anticipate

25. Traditional stories concerning the marvels of the medieval cities and empires of western Sudan were ultimately based on historical fact; thus while the stories ----, they did not actually ----.

(A) embroidered..invent
(B) criticized..comment
(C) documented..evaluate
(D) fabricated..judge
(E) entertained..investigate

GO ON TO THE NEXT PAGE

Each passage below is followed by questions based on its content. Answer the questions following each passage on the basis of what is stated or implied in that passage.

The immune system fights invading particles, known as antigens, through the action of specialized white blood cells called lymphocytes. When a foreign particle is injected into an animal, a few lymphocytes are able to recognize the particular antigen. They promptly begin to divide rapidly and to manufacture specific antibodies to fight against the antigen. The animal becomes sensitized or immune to this antigen and stays that way indefinitely.

When this phenomenon was first discovered, it was thought that the lymphocytes confronting the foreign particle were somehow taught what to do by the encounter. Researchers theorized that each cell, naïve to begin with, learned from contact with the antigen how to make exactly the right antibody needed to combat the foreign particle. This notion, the "instructive" theory, has now been replaced by what is called the "clonal selection" theory of immune response, which is supported by an immense body of reliable research. According to this theory, lymphocytes are created knowing what to look for, and they roam the blood and tissues seeking the specific antigens that match their particular receptors. When a lymphocyte meets its complementary antigen, it promptly enlarges and begins dividing rapidly. The result is a clone of identical cells, all prepared to synthesize the particular antibody needed.

Among the billions of lymphocytes in a young animal are individual cells capable of recognizing the molecular configuration of almost anything, including synthetic compounds never before seen in nature. The populations of these cells, and the extent of their collective repertoire, greatly increase as the animal matures, probably as the result of rearrangements of genes in the cells that give rise to lymphocytes. The system works with astonishing efficiency because of the high mobility of the recognizing cells, their large numbers, and their capacity to amplify the antibody production quickly by replicating just the cells that are needed for the occasion.

Yet from the point of view of any individual lymphocyte, the immune system must look like nothing but one mistake after another. When an antigen appears, it is recognizable to only a small minority of the cell population; for all the rest of the cells, attempts to identify the antigen are a waste of time, motion, and effort. Also, there are chances of making major blunders, endangering the whole organism. The formation of flawed lymphocytes that cannot distinguish between indigenous and foreign particles can bring about the devastating diseases of autoimmunity. Blind spots, or gaps of recognition, can exist so that certain strains of animals are genetically unable to recognize the foreignness of certain bacteria and viruses. Despite such potential failures, however, the immune system on the whole is remarkably efficient and adaptable.

26. Which of the following would be the most appropriate title for the passage?
    - (A) Theories About Antigen Formation
    - (B) The Weaknesses of the Immune System
    - (C) The Molecular Configuration of Lymphocytes
    - (D) The Nature of the Immune System
    - (E) Experimental Research on the Immune System

27. According to the passage, the immune response typically involves which of the following?
    - I. Frequent autoimmune reactions
    - II. Production of antibodies
    - III. Rapid cell division

    (A) I only (B) II only (C) I and II only (D) II and III only (E) I, II, and III

28. It can be inferred that all of the following statements are consistent with both the "instructive" theory and the "clonal selection" theory EXCEPT:
    - (A) Antibodies play a critical role in protecting the body against infection.
    - (B) Each lymphocyte has an innate ability to recognize only one type of antigen.
    - (C) Lymphocytes manufacture antibodies after identifying an invading antigen.
    - (D) Lymphocytes multiply rapidly by making duplicates of themselves.
    - (E) Only a certain type of antibody is able to fight each specific antigen.

GO ON TO THE NEXT PAGE

29. In the last paragraph, the author is primarily concerned with

    (A) correcting the misconception that lymphocytes are capable of making major blunders
    (B) praising the immune system for its ability to compensate for occasional errors
    (C) attacking the inability of the "clonal selection" theory to explain the wastefulness of the immune system
    (D) weighing impartially the merits of conflicting explanations of the immune response
    (E) qualifying a generally positive view of the efficiency of the immune system

30. According to the "clonal selection" theory, all of the following contribute to the efficiency of the immune system EXCEPT the

    (A) capacity of each lymphocyte to produce antibodies against all antigens
    (B) ability of the immune system to increase dramatically its production of needed antibodies
    (C) fact that only the necessary cells are cloned when an antigen invades
    (D) existence of billions of available lymphocytes
    (E) high mobility of lymphocytes

GO ON TO THE NEXT PAGE

Until the sixties, the growth of Chicano literature had been hampered by the general unwillingness of most publishers in the United States to issue such works—particularly those in Spanish—on the assumption that they had too limited an appeal to be profitable. In 1967, however, Quinto Sol Publications was established in Berkeley, California, to provide a forum for Chicano writers. The success of Quinto Sol led to the opening of other Chicano publishing houses. The result has been a burst of Chicano literary activity.

The writers of the Quinto Sol school are characterized by a literary style that contrasts sharply with that of earlier Mexican-American writers such as Niggli, Suárez, and Villarreal. The irony and the tone of controlled disappointment are replaced by more intense emotions, sometimes by an almost violent sense of outrage. The careful explication, born of a desire to acquaint Anglo-American readers with the Mexican culture of the United States, is generally absent from the works of the Quinto Sol authors. The Quinto Sol group wrote primarily for a select audience that shared their experiences; they felt no need, therefore, to justify their culture.

Although authors like Suárez and Villarreal had written sensitively on Chicano subjects in English, their styles and techniques were in no important ways different from those of Anglo-American writers. But the Quinto Sol writers often rejected Anglo-American literary models and instead turned southward and adopted the literary conventions of authors such as Rulfo, Borges, and García Márquez. The Quinto Sol writers not only reaffirmed their ties to the cultures of contemporary Latin America but also rediscovered, as Mexican artists had earlier in the century, their Aztec heritage. They invoked Aztec philosophy and metaphors and were particularly attracted to the concept of Aztlán, the ancestral home of the Aztecs, which lay somewhere in the American Southwest. Some scholars have quibbled that the concept of Aztlán is historically inaccurate, but they miss the point: its importance is symbolic, in that it provides Chicanos with a deeper and more intimate sense of cultural continuity.

Finally, the Quinto Sol writers developed a variety of linguistic techniques with which to express their cultural distinctiveness. In the past, Mexican-American writers had written in conventional Spanish or English, while a few writers such as Mena and Niggli (and Villarreal to a lesser degree) tried to re-create the flavor of Spanish in English, occasionally employing the original Spanish for special effect. But these new authors aimed to reproduce Chicano speech exactly. They used not only conventional Spanish and English but various regional dialects of both languages and combinations of all of these. Their distinctive usage has produced gratifying results, particularly in poetry.

31. The primary purpose of the passage is to
    - (A) define the characteristics of what the author considers to be a new school of Chicano writers
    - (B) encourage publishers to solicit more works of literature by Chicano writers
    - (C) convey the reactions of contemporary Chicano writers to current Mexican-American literature
    - (D) emphasize the common literary heritage of all Spanish-speaking peoples
    - (E) describe the influence of Aztec culture on contemporary Chicano literature

32. According to the passage, publishers in the United States were initially reluctant to issue works of Chicano literature because they assumed that
    - (A) such action would establish a legal precedent
    - (B) publishers in Mexico would issue the works
    - (C) little money would be earned by selling the works
    - (D) the general public preferred earlier Mexican-American literature
    - (E) poetry cannot be adequately translated into another language

33. The author's response to critics who question the historical validity of Aztlán is to
    - (A) reveal the critics' lack of credibility
    - (B) dismiss their objection as irrelevant
    - (C) enlist the support of critics with differing views
    - (D) present archaeological evidence of Aztlán's existence
    - (E) argue that myths usually have a historical basis

34. All of the following statements about the writer Niggli are made in the passage EXCEPT that she
    - (A) wrote about Mexican-American culture
    - (B) made use of irony in her works
    - (C) sometimes used Spanish phrases in her works
    - (D) inspired the works of Quinto Sol writers
    - (E) assumed that many of her readers were Anglo-Americans

35. In discussing the Quinto Sol writers, the author uses all of the following EXCEPT
    - (A) generalizations
    - (B) references to earlier writers
    - (C) discussion of linguistic techniques
    - (D) examination of a specific work
    - (E) examples of cultural influence

GO ON TO THE NEXT PAGE

Each question below consists of a related pair of words or phrases, followed by five lettered pairs of words or phrases. Select the lettered pair that best expresses a relationship similar to that expressed in the original pair.

Example:

YAWN : BOREDOM :: (A) dream : sleep (B) anger : madness (C) smile : amusement (D) face : expression (E) impatience : rebellion

Ⓐ Ⓑ ● Ⓓ Ⓔ

36. SCULPTOR:STATUES :: (A) cook:spices (B) tailor:clothes (C) jockey:horses (D) detective:crimes (E) dressmaker:fabric

37. BANDAGE:LACERATION ::
(A) ambulance:transportation
(B) alcohol:antiseptic
(C) cast:fracture
(D) transfusion:blood
(E) oxygen:shock

38. PEDAL:FOOT :: (A) thimble:finger (B) crutch:leg (C) knob:hand (D) belt:waist (E) pillow:head

39. ABBREVIATE:WORD :: (A) quote:passage (B) condense:book (C) duplicate:copy (D) translate:language (E) conclude:argument

40. PILOT:STEER :: (A) chef:dine (B) boss:obey (C) lawyer:retain (D) guard:protect (E) soldier:command

41. AMORPHOUS:FORM :: (A) verifiable:proof (B) contagious:disease (C) analogous:parallel (D) anonymous:name (E) convergent:length

42. RHETORIC:DISCOURSE :: (A) algebra:symmetry (B) harmony:rhythm (C) astronomy:lenses (D) physics:optics (E) logic:reasoning

43. DISSEMINATE:INFORMATION :: (A) disburse:funds (B) disown:family (C) dispute:position (D) dispel:anxieties (E) dissipate:energy

44. FALLOW:LAND :: (A) smooth:surface (B) idle:machinery (C) polluted:water (D) polished:metal (E) productive:mind

45. MNEMONIC:MEMORY ::
(A) derivative:painting
(B) self-governing:establishment
(C) corporeal:body
(D) parochial:open-mindedness
(E) recurrent:dream

IF YOU FINISH BEFORE TIME IS CALLED, YOU MAY CHECK YOUR WORK ON THIS SECTION ONLY. DO NOT TURN TO ANY OTHER SECTION IN THE TEST. **STOP**

Correct Answers for Scholastic Aptitude Test
Form Code 7W

VERBAL		MATHEMATICAL	
Section 2	**Section 4**	**Section 3**	**Section 1**
1. C	1. B	1. C	1. C
2. E	2. E	2. D	2. E
3. B	3. D	3. E	3. D
4. C	4. A	4. C	4. A
5. D	5. A	5. A	5. A
6. C	6. C	6. B	6. A
7. D	7. A	7. A	7. C
8. C	8. E	8. B	*8. A
9. A	9. D	9. E	*9. D
10. A	10. A	10. B	*10. B
11. B	11. A	11. A	*11. C
12. C	12. B	12. D	*12. B
13. E	13. D	13. B	*13. B
14. D	14. D	14. D	*14. C
15. B	15. B	15. E	*15. B
16. C	16. A	16. E	*16. A
17. C	17. B	17. B	*17. D
18. D	18. C	18. E	*18. A
19. E	19. E	19. D	*19. A
20. A	20. C	20. C	*20. B
21. C	21. C	21. A	*21. C
22. B	22. C	22. B	*22. C
23. C	23. E	23. A	*23. D
24. A	24. E	24. E	*24. C
25. C	25. A	25. D	*25. D
26. B	26. D		*26. B
27. A	27. D		*27. A
28. D	28. B		28. D
29. E	29. E		29. A
30. A	30. A		30. C
31. D	31. A		31. C
32. C	32. C		32. A
33. A	33. B		33. B
34. D	34. D		34. E
35. C	35. D		35. E
36. B	36. B		
37. B	37. C		
38. E	38. C		
39. B	39. B		
40. D	40. D		
	41. D		
	42. E		
	43. A		
	44. B		
	45. C		

*Indicates four-choice questions. (All of the other questions are five-choice.)

The Scoring Process

Machine-scoring is done in three steps:

- *Scanning.* Your answer sheet is "read" by a scanning machine and the oval you filled in for each question is recorded on a computer tape.
- *Scoring.* The computer compares the oval filled in for each question with the correct response. Each correct answer receives one point; omitted questions do not count toward your score. For each wrong answer, a fraction of a point is subtracted to correct for random guessing. For questions with five answer choices, one-fourth of a point is subtracted for each wrong response; for questions with four answer choices, one-third of a point is subtracted for each wrong response. The SAT-verbal test has 85 questions with five answer choices each. If, for example, a student has 44 right, 32 wrong, and 9 omitted, the resulting raw score is determined as follows:

$$44 \text{ right} - \frac{32 \text{ wrong}}{4} = 44 - 8 = 36 \text{ raw score points}$$

Obtaining raw scores frequently involves the rounding of fractional numbers to the nearest whole number. For example, a raw score of 36.25 is rounded to 36, the nearest whole number. A raw score of 36.50 is rounded upward to 37.

- *Converting to reported scaled score.* Raw test scores are then placed on the College Board scale of 200 to 800 through a process that adjusts scores to account for minor differences in difficulty among different editions of the test. This process, known as equating, is performed so that a student's reported score is not affected by the edition of the test taken nor by the abilities of the group with whom the student takes the test. As a result of placing SAT scores on the College Board scale, scores earned by students at different times can be compared. For example, an SAT-verbal score of 400 on a test taken at one administration indicates the same level of developed verbal ability as a 400 score obtained on a different edition of the test taken at another time.

How to Score the Test

SAT-Verbal Sections 2 and 4

Step A: Count the number of correct answers for *section 2* and record the number in the space provided on the worksheet on the next page. Then do the same for the incorrect answers. (Do not count omitted answers.) To determine subtotal A, use the formula:

$$\text{number correct} - \frac{\text{number incorrect}}{4} = \text{subtotal A}$$

Step B: Count the number of correct answers and the number of incorrect answers for *section 4* and record the numbers in the spaces provided on the worksheet. To determine subtotal B, use the formula:

$$\text{number correct} - \frac{\text{number incorrect}}{4} = \text{subtotal B}$$

Step C: To obtain C, add subtotal A to subtotal B, keeping any decimals. Enter the resulting figure on the worksheet.

Step D: To obtain D, your raw verbal score, round C to the nearest whole number. (For example, any number from 44.50 to 45.49 rounds to 45.) Enter the resulting figure on the worksheet.

Step E: To find your reported SAT-verbal score, look up the total raw verbal score you obtained in step D in the conversion table on page 280. Enter this figure on the worksheet.

SAT-Mathematical Sections 3 and 1

Step A: Count the number of correct answers and the number of incorrect answers for *section 3* and record the numbers in the spaces provided on the worksheet. To determine the subtotal A, use the formula:

$$\text{number correct} - \frac{\text{number incorrect}}{4} = \text{subtotal A}$$

Step B: Count the number of correct answers and the number of incorrect answers for the *five-choice questions (questions 1 through 7 and 28 through 35) in section 1* and record the numbers in the spaces provided on the worksheet. To determine the subtotal B, use the formula:

$$\text{number correct} - \frac{\text{number incorrect}}{4} = \text{subtotal B}$$

Step C: Count the number of correct answers and the number of incorrect answers for the *four-choice questions (questions 8 through 27) in section 1* and record the numbers in the spaces provided on the worksheet. To determine the subtotal C, use the formula:

$$\text{number correct} - \frac{\text{number incorrect}}{3} = \text{subtotal C}$$

Step D: To obtain D, add subtotal A, subtotal B, and subtotal C, keeping any decimals. Enter the resulting figure on the worksheet.

Step E: To obtain E, your raw mathematical score, round D to the nearest whole number. (For example, any number from 44.50 to 45.49 rounds to 45.) Enter the resulting figure on the worksheet.

Step F: To find your reported SAT-mathematical score, look up the total raw mathematical score you obtained in E in the conversion table on page 280. Enter this figure on the worksheet.

SAT SCORING WORKSHEET

SAT-Verbal Sections

A. Section 2:	______ no. correct	− ¼	(______) no. incorrect	=	______ subtotal A
B. Section 4:	______ no. correct	− ¼	(______) no. incorrect	=	______ subtotal B
C. Total unrounded raw score (Total A + B)					______ C
D. Total rounded raw score (Rounded to nearest whole number)					______ D
E. SAT-verbal reported scaled score (See the conversion table on page 280.)					[ ] SAT-verbal score

SAT-Mathematical Sections

A. Section 3:	______ no. correct	− ¼	(______) no. incorrect	=	______ subtotal A
B. Section 1: Questions 1 through 7 and 28 through 35 (5-choice)	______ no. correct	− ¼	(______) no. incorrect	=	______ subtotal B
C. Section 1: Questions 8 through 27 (4-choice)	______ no. correct	− ⅓	(______) no. incorrect	=	______ subtotal C
D. Total unrounded raw score (Total A + B + C)					______ D
E. Total rounded raw score (Rounded to nearest whole number)					______ E
F. SAT-mathematical reported scaled score (See the conversion table on page 280.)					[ ] SAT-math score

Score Conversion Table
Scholastic Aptitude Test
Form Code 7W

Raw Score	College Board Reported Score		Raw Score	College Board Reported Score	
	SAT-Verbal	SAT-Math		SAT-Verbal	SAT-Math
85	800		40	450	600
84	780		39	450	590
83	760		38	440	580
82	750		37	430	580
81	740		36	430	570
80	730		35	420	560
79	730		34	410	550
78	720		33	410	540
77	710		32	400	530
76	710		31	390	520
75	700		30	380	510
74	690		29	380	500
73	680		28	370	490
72	670		27	360	480
71	660		26	360	470
70	660		25	350	460
69	650		24	340	450
68	640		23	340	450
67	630		22	330	440
66	630		21	320	430
65	620		20	310	420
64	610		19	310	410
63	610		18	300	400
62	600		17	290	390
61	590		16	290	380
60	580	800	15	280	380
59	580	780	14	270	370
58	570	760	13	260	360
57	560	750	12	260	350
56	560	740	11	250	340
55	550	730	10	240	330
54	540	720	9	240	320
53	540	720	8	230	310
52	530	710	7	220	310
51	520	700	6	220	300
50	520	690	5	210	290
49	510	680	4	200	280
48	500	670	3	200	270
47	500	670	2	200	260
46	490	660	1	200	260
45	490	650	0	200	250
44	480	640	–1	200	240
43	470	630	–2	200	230
42	470	620	–3	200	230
41	460	610	–4	200	220
			–5	200	210
			–6	200	210
			–7 or below	200	200

(Cut here to detach.)

COLLEGE BOARD — SCHOLASTIC APTITUDE TEST and Test of Standard Written English — Side 1

Use a No. 2 pencil only. Be sure each mark is dark and completely fills the intended oval. Completely erase any errors or stray marks.

1. YOUR NAME: (Print) ______ Last ______ First ______ M.I.

SIGNATURE: ______ **DATE:** ___/___/___

HOME ADDRESS: (Print) ______ Number and Street

______ City ______ State ______ Zip Code

CENTER: (Print) ______ City ______ State ______ Center Number

IMPORTANT: Please fill in items 2 and 3 exactly as shown on the back cover of your test book.

FOR ETS USE ONLY

2. TEST FORM (Copy from back cover of your test book.)

3. FORM CODE (Copy and grid as shown on back cover of your test book.)

0	A	J	S	0	0	0
1	B	K	T	1	1	1
2	C	L	U	2	2	2
3	D	M	V	3	3	3
4	E	N	W	4	4	4
5	F	O	X	5	5	5
6	G	P	Y	6	6	6
7	H	Q	Z	7	7	7
8	I	R		8	8	8
9				9	9	9

4. REGISTRATION NUMBER (Copy from your Admission Ticket.)

0–9 in each of 7 columns

5. YOUR NAME

First 4 letters of last name | First Init. | Mid. Init.

A–Z in each column

6. DATE OF BIRTH

Month	Day		Year	
Jan.				
Feb.				
Mar.	0	0	0	0
Apr.	1	1	1	1
May	2	2	2	2
June	3	3	3	3
July		4	4	4
Aug.		5	5	5
Sept.		6	6	6
Oct.		7	7	7
Nov.		8		8
Dec.		9		9

7. SEX

Female

Male

8. TEST BOOK SERIAL NUMBER (Copy from front cover of your test book.)

Start with number 1 for each new section. If a section has fewer than 50 questions, leave the extra answer spaces blank.

SECTION 1

1–50: A B C D E for each question

SECTION 2

1–50: A B C D E for each question

Q1362-04

I.N. 575008 — 110VV58P3720

COLLEGE BOARD — SCHOLASTIC APTITUDE TEST and Test of Standard Written English Side 2

Use a No. 2 pencil only. Be sure each mark is dark and completely fills the intended oval. Completely erase any errors or stray marks.

Start with number 1 for each new section. If a section has fewer than 50 questions, leave the extra answer spaces blank.

	SECTION 3	SECTION 4	SECTION 5	SECTION 6
1	A B C D E	A B C D E	A B C D E	A B C D E
2	A B C D E	A B C D E	A B C D E	A B C D E
3	A B C D E	A B C D E	A B C D E	A B C D E
4	A B C D E	A B C D E	A B C D E	A B C D E
5	A B C D E	A B C D E	A B C D E	A B C D E
6	A B C D E	A B C D E	A B C D E	A B C D E
7	A B C D E	A B C D E	A B C D E	A B C D E
8	A B C D E	A B C D E	A B C D E	A B C D E
9	A B C D E	A B C D E	A B C D E	A B C D E
10	A B C D E	A B C D E	A B C D E	A B C D E
11	A B C D E	A B C D E	A B C D E	A B C D E
12	A B C D E	A B C D E	A B C D E	A B C D E
13	A B C D E	A B C D E	A B C D E	A B C D E
14	A B C D E	A B C D E	A B C D E	A B C D E
15	A B C D E	A B C D E	A B C D E	A B C D E
16	A B C D E	A B C D E	A B C D E	A B C D E
17	A B C D E	A B C D E	A B C D E	A B C D E
18	A B C D E	A B C D E	A B C D E	A B C D E
19	A B C D E	A B C D E	A B C D E	A B C D E
20	A B C D E	A B C D E	A B C D E	A B C D E
21	A B C D E	A B C D E	A B C D E	A B C D E
22	A B C D E	A B C D E	A B C D E	A B C D E
23	A B C D E	A B C D E	A B C D E	A B C D E
24	A B C D E	A B C D E	A B C D E	A B C D E
25	A B C D E	A B C D E	A B C D E	A B C D E
26	A B C D E	A B C D E	A B C D E	A B C D E
27	A B C D E	A B C D E	A B C D E	A B C D E
28	A B C D E	A B C D E	A B C D E	A B C D E
29	A B C D E	A B C D E	A B C D E	A B C D E
30	A B C D E	A B C D E	A B C D E	A B C D E
31	A B C D E	A B C D E	A B C D E	A B C D E
32	A B C D E	A B C D E	A B C D E	A B C D E
33	A B C D E	A B C D E	A B C D E	A B C D E
34	A B C D E	A B C D E	A B C D E	A B C D E
35	A B C D E	A B C D E	A B C D E	A B C D E
36	A B C D E	A B C D E	A B C D E	A B C D E
37	A B C D E	A B C D E	A B C D E	A B C D E
38	A B C D E	A B C D E	A B C D E	A B C D E
39	A B C D E	A B C D E	A B C D E	A B C D E
40	A B C D E	A B C D E	A B C D E	A B C D E
41	A B C D E	A B C D E	A B C D E	A B C D E
42	A B C D E	A B C D E	A B C D E	A B C D E
43	A B C D E	A B C D E	A B C D E	A B C D E
44	A B C D E	A B C D E	A B C D E	A B C D E
45	A B C D E	A B C D E	A B C D E	A B C D E
46	A B C D E	A B C D E	A B C D E	A B C D E
47	A B C D E	A B C D E	A B C D E	A B C D E
48	A B C D E	A B C D E	A B C D E	A B C D E
49	A B C D E	A B C D E	A B C D E	A B C D E
50	A B C D E	A B C D E	A B C D E	A B C D E

9. SIGNATURE: ____________________

FOR ETS USE ONLY	VTR	VTFS	VRR	VRFS	VVR	VVFS	WER	WEFS	M4R	M4FS	M5R	M5FS	MTFS
	VTW	VTCS	VRW	VRCS	VVW	VVCS	WEW	WECS	M4W		M5W		MTCS

SECTION 1	Time—30 minutes 25 Questions	In this section solve each problem, using any available space on the page for scratchwork. Then decide which is the best of the choices given and fill in the corresponding oval on the answer sheet.

The following information is for your reference in solving some of the problems.

Circle of radius r: Area $= \pi r^2$; Circumference $= 2\pi r$
The number of degrees of arc in a circle is 360.
The measure in degrees of a straight angle is 180.

Definition of symbols:

$=$ is equal to	$\leqq$ is less than or equal to
$\neq$ is unequal to	$\geqq$ is greater than or equal to
$<$ is less than	$\parallel$ is parallel to
$>$ is greater than	$\perp$ is perpendicular to

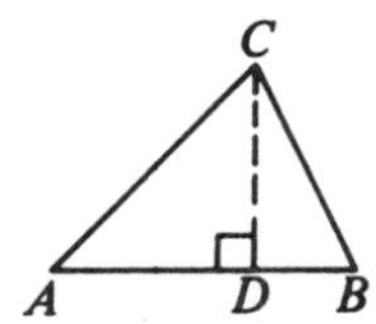

Triangle: The sum of the measures in degrees of the angles of a triangle is 180.

If $\angle CDA$ is a right angle, then

(1) area of $\triangle ABC = \dfrac{AB \times CD}{2}$

(2) $AC^2 = AD^2 + DC^2$

Note: Figures that accompany problems in this test are intended to provide information useful in solving the problems. They are drawn as accurately as possible EXCEPT when it is stated in a specific problem that its figure is not drawn to scale. All figures lie in a plane unless otherwise indicated. All numbers used are real numbers.

1. If $a = 4$ and $2b + c = 5$, then $2a + 2b + c =$

(A) 13 (B) 14 (C) 15 (D) 16 (E) 17

2. If the total cost of 12 equally priced typewriters is \$2,160, what is the total cost of 9 of these typewriters?

(A) \$1,080
(B) \$1,260
(C) \$1,440
(D) \$1,620
(E) \$1,800

ℓ

3. If ℓ is to be a line of symmetry when the unfinished pattern above is completed, which of the following placements of dots could complete the pattern?

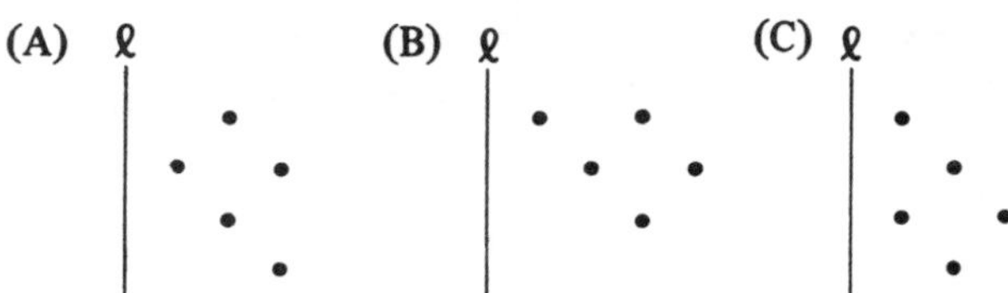

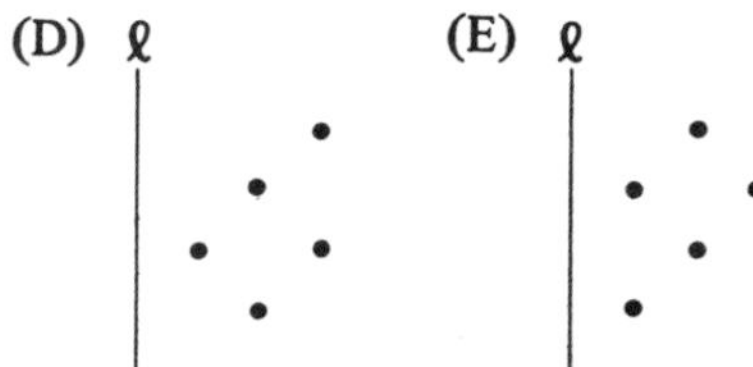

GO ON TO THE NEXT PAGE

4. If x is 5 less than the product of 9 and y and if $y = 4$, then what is the value of x?

(A) −31 (B) −11 (C) 11 (D) 31
(E) It cannot be determined from the information given.

10, 20, 30, 40, 50

5. The average (arithmetic mean) of the five numbers above is NOT equal to the average of

(A) 10 and 50
(B) 20 and 40
(C) 10, 20, and 40
(D) 10, 30, and 50
(E) 20, 30, and 40

6. A classroom with a square floor and vertical walls has 1 wall with windows and 3 walls without windows. If the windows do not reach the ceiling, what percent of the total wall space of the room could consist of windows? (Assume the walls are equal in height.)

(A) Less than 25%
(B) 25%
(C) Between 25 and 50%
(D) 50%
(E) More than 50%

7. C is the midpoint of line segment AE and B is the midpoint of line segment AC. If D is a point between A and E so that the length of AB equals the length of DE, what is the ratio $\frac{\text{length of } CD}{\text{length of } AC}$?

(A) $\frac{4}{1}$

(B) $\frac{2}{1}$

(C) $\frac{3}{4}$

(D) $\frac{1}{2}$

(E) $\frac{1}{4}$

8. If $(4-3)(3-2)(2-1)x = (1-2)(2-3)(3-4)$, then $x =$

(A) −2 (B) −1 (C) 0 (D) 1 (E) 2

9. In a game in which there are 7 sticks on a table, the player who removes the last stick wins. If two players take turns at removing at least 1 but no more than 4 sticks at each turn, how many sticks must the first player remove on the first turn in order to be certain that he can take the last stick?

(A) 1
(B) 2
(C) 3
(D) 4
(E) 5

10. If $\frac{x}{y} = \frac{1}{2}$ and $\frac{w}{z} = 4$, what is the value of $\frac{x}{z}$?

(A) $\frac{1}{8}$

(B) $\frac{1}{2}$

(C) 2

(D) 8

(E) It cannot be determined from the information given.

11. How deep will the sand be in a rectangular sandbox with inside dimensions 300 centimeters long, 200 centimeters wide, and 20 centimeters deep if 600,000 cubic centimeters of sand is evenly distributed in it?

(A) 1 cm
(B) 2 cm
(C) 10 cm
(D) 12 cm
(E) 20 cm

GO ON TO THE NEXT PAGE

12. Pat can paint a certain model house in 1 day while Chris takes 2 days to paint the same type of house. If they work independently at their own respective rates, what is the greatest number of houses of this type that the two can completely finish painting in 5 days?

(A) 5
(B) 7
(C) 8
(D) 10
(E) 15

13. Seventeen different points are to be located on the circumference of a circle and each point is to be connected to all other points by line segments. At most, how many of the segments thus formed can be diameters of the circle?

(A) 8 (B) 9 (C) 16 (D) 17 (E) 34

Questions 14-16 refer to the following number line in which the letters represent consecutive integers.

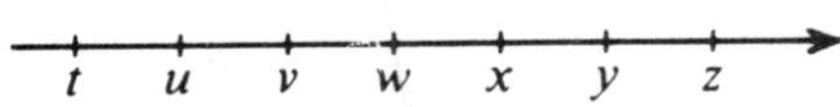

14. $w - u =$

(A) 1 (B) 2 (C) 3 (D) 4 (E) 5

15. In terms of u, the sum $u + w + y =$

(A) $3u + 2$
(B) $3u + 3$
(C) $3u + 4$
(D) $3u + 5$
(E) $3u + 6$

16. If $v^2 - t^2 = 24$, then $w^2 - u^2 =$

(A) 28
(B) 24
(C) 20
(D) 18
(E) 16

17. At a fruit stand, 1 quart of strawberries costs x dollars. However, if you pick the berries yourself, 4 quarts costs $3x$ dollars. In terms of x, how many dollars do you save by picking 8 quarts yourself rather than buying 8 quarts at the fruit stand?

(A) $2x$ (B) $4x$ (C) $6x$ (D) $8x$ (E) $16x$

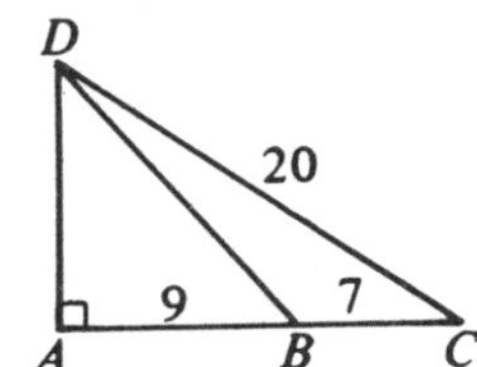

Note: Figure not drawn to scale.

18. In the figure above, what is the length of BD ?

(A) 12 (B) 13 (C) 14 (D) 15 (E) 16

19. If $y = \frac{3}{2x}$ and $wy = \frac{3}{4x}$ for $x \neq 0$, then $w =$

(A) 4 (B) 2 (C) $\frac{1}{2}$ (D) $\frac{1}{4}$ (E) $\frac{1}{8}$

20. In a group of 75 students, 23 are enrolled in algebra, 39 are enrolled in music, and 18 are enrolled in both algebra and music. How many students are not enrolled in either course?

(A) 5
(B) 13
(C) 18
(D) 21
(E) 31

GO ON TO THE NEXT PAGE

21. If the perimeter of a rectangle is 9 times its width, then its length is how many times its width?

(A) $2\frac{1}{2}$

(B) 3

(C) $3\frac{1}{2}$

(D) 4

(E) $4\frac{1}{2}$

22. If $x = 2y = 3z$, then the average (arithmetic mean) of x, y, and z in terms of x is

(A) $2x$

(B) $\frac{11x}{6}$

(C) $\frac{7x}{5}$

(D) $\frac{11x}{18}$

(E) $\frac{x}{2}$

23. If 30 percent of $2x$ is multiplied by 2 percent of x, the result is what percent of $3x^2$?

(A) 0.2%
(B) 0.4%
(C) 0.6%
(D) 1.2%
(E) 2.5%

24. After running 3,000 meters on a circular path, a runner is at her starting point. The radius of her circular path could be which of the following?

I. $\frac{1{,}500}{\pi}$ meters

II. $\frac{750}{\pi}$ meters

III. $\frac{250}{\pi}$ meters

(A) I only (B) I and II only (C) I and III only (D) II and III only (E) I, II, and III

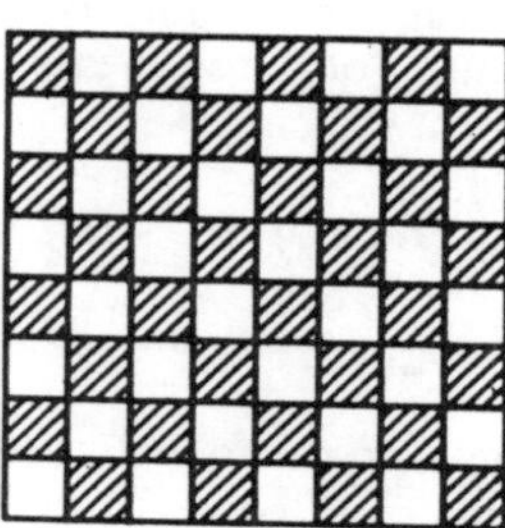

25. What is the greatest number of 4×4 squares that can be traced out along the existing line segments of the 8×8 checkerboard shown above?

(A) 8 (B) 10 (C) 16 (D) 25 (E) 36

IF YOU FINISH BEFORE TIME IS CALLED, YOU MAY CHECK YOUR WORK ON THIS SECTION ONLY. DO NOT TURN TO ANY OTHER SECTION IN THE TEST. **STOP**

SECTION 2 Time—30 minutes 45 Questions

For each question in this section, choose the best answer and fill in the corresponding oval on the answer sheet.

Each question below consists of a word in capital letters, followed by five lettered words or phrases. Choose the word or phrase that is most nearly opposite in meaning to the word in capital letters. Since some of the questions require you to distinguish fine shades of meaning, consider all the choices before deciding which is best.

Example:

GOOD: (A) sour (B) bad (C) red (D) hot (E) ugly

Ⓐ ● Ⓒ Ⓓ Ⓔ

1. AVOID: (A) arouse (B) purify (C) modify (D) push down (E) seek out
2. FOOLPROOF: (A) unavailable (B) uneventful (C) easy to leave (D) likely to fail (E) able to act
3. PREPOSTEROUS: (A) urgent (B) visible (C) dangerous (D) interesting (E) reasonable
4. SWELTERING: (A) cool (B) lean (C) healing (D) forgiving (E) flowing
5. ALLY: (A) agent (B) foil (C) peer (D) mob (E) foe
6. HEADLONG: (A) cautious (B) wealthy (C) hopeful (D) powerful (E) innocent
7. EXOTIC: (A) exalted (B) deprived (C) ethical (D) native (E) fierce
8. ENCODE: (A) mar (B) offend (C) decipher (D) wear away (E) postpone action
9. OBLIVION: (A) wisdom (B) willingness (C) remembrance (D) directness (E) tact
10. VIABLE: (A) unworkable (B) unknown (C) unnecessary (D) natural (E) wayward
11. ELUCIDATE: (A) implant (B) becloud (C) offer (D) relax (E) remain
12. INCEPTION: (A) efficiency (B) foresight (C) conclusion (D) inquiry (E) condolence
13. SCINTILLATION: (A) imbalance (B) resonance (C) dullness (D) synthesis (E) preservation
14. ASSUAGE: (A) exemplify (B) exacerbate (C) immerse (D) replicate (E) revere
15. DESULTORY: (A) methodical (B) preliminary (C) superfluous (D) inventive (E) abusive

Each sentence below has one or two blanks, each blank indicating that something has been omitted. Beneath the sentence are five lettered words or sets of words. Choose the word or set of words that, when inserted in the sentence, best fits the meaning of the sentence as a whole.

Example:

Although its publicity has been ----, the film itself is intelligent, well-acted, handsomely produced, and altogether ----.

(A) tasteless. .respectable (B) extensive. .moderate (C) sophisticated. .amateur (D) risqué. .crude (E) perfect. .spectacular

● Ⓑ Ⓒ Ⓓ Ⓔ

16. The aspect of this symphony that most astonished its early listeners was its ----; it was nearly twice as long as any symphony written up to that date.

    (A) sonority (B) duration (C) dynamism (D) richness (E) gravity

17. They did their best to avoid getting embroiled in the quarrel, preferring to maintain their ---- as long as possible.

    (A) subjectivity (B) suspense (C) interest (D) decisiveness (E) neutrality

18. Some scientists ---- that biofeedback is a valuable means of controlling our biological processes at will, while others dismiss it as a ---- .

    (A) argue. .gimmick (B) agree. .discovery (C) deny. .distortion (D) lament. .danger (E) proclaim. .pleasure

19. Although this book about Black American poets is, in general, accurate and consistent, it presents some ---- arguments that it never really ----.

    (A) similar. .reconciles (B) precise. .clarifies (C) conflicting. .states (D) paradoxical. .resolves (E) erroneous. .adopts

20. She deplored his manners, telling her friends that his conduct was the ---- of good behavior.

    (A) epitome (B) distillation (C) antithesis (D) composite (E) counterpart

Each passage below is followed by questions based on its content. Answer all questions following a passage on the basis of what is stated or implied in that passage.

The biological "clock," an internal property possessed by many organisms, has become the subject of considerable interest in recent years. A biological clock is of such obvious adaptive value that one can expect that many organisms must be equipped with it. However, only recently has the very widespread occurrence of such living clocks been pointed out. This development of the subject has in part been stimulated by discoveries that internal clocks play an essential role in several aspects of plant and animal behavior and physiology. For example, animal directional orientation—which is involved in migratory activities, homing, and other behavioral activities—involves an internal biological clock. The fascinating phenomena of bird navigation are far from being completely explained, but it has now been demonstrated that orientation is accomplished by an internal clock working in conjunction with celestial clues such as the sun, moon, and stars and some other cues that researchers are presently exploring.

Another manifestation of the existence of a biological clock is one in which plants and animals are able to perceive the seasons of the year by accurately measuring the changing day length. Examples of this phenomenon, which is generally called photoperiodism, are probably familiar to almost everyone. The flowering of plants depends in many cases on the length of the night: whether a plant blooms characteristically in the spring, or fall, or summer is intimately related to the duration and timing of light and dark conditions. Photoperiodic time measurements can also be accomplished by animals. In the lower animals, particularly insects, many developmental processes are responsive to the light-dark cycles; and in the higher animals, breeding activities, growth, and the initiation of the migratory drive are examples of photoinduced activities. In all cases, the response that is induced may depend to a slight extent on factors other than the relative length of day and night, but the one common feature of these phenomena is that in some way the organism is responsive to the length of the day or night. In this sense it possesses an internal clock.

21. In this passage, the author is primarily concerned with
    (A) describing experiments that have proved the existence of a biological clock in animals
    (B) discussing some theories that explain the composition of biological clocks
    (C) discussing the relationship between photoperiodism and plant physiology
    (D) citing some of the evidence supporting the importance of biological clocks
    (E) explaining ways in which animal orientation plays a part in evolution

The reading passages in this test are brief excerpts or adaptations of excerpts from published material. The ideas contained in them do not necessarily represent the opinions of the College Board or Educational Testing Service. To make the text suitable for testing purposes, we may in some cases have altered the style, contents, or point of view of the original.

22. Which of the following best describes the author's view of the existence of biological clocks?
    (A) The existence of such clocks is an accepted fact.
    (B) Although such clocks probably exist, there is no evidence to prove it.
    (C) Manifestations of the occurrence of such clocks can usually be explained in other ways.
    (D) Very few such clocks have been observed.
    (E) It is not likely that such clocks exist.

23. It can be inferred from the passage that the author considers photoperiodism to be a phenomenon that is
    (A) of interest only to biologists
    (B) likely to occur only under rare circumstances
    (C) commonly exhibited in many species of organisms
    (D) important primarily in the study of plant life
    (E) unaffected by the working of biological clocks

24. According to the passage, the recent increase in interest in the study of biological clocks is primarily the result of the discovery of the
    (A) processes governing all the workings of such clocks
    (B) ways of controlling such clocks
    (C) varied occurrence and widespread importance of such clocks
    (D) importance of such clocks in animal migration
    (E) relationship of such clocks in flowering plants to the rate of growth

25. On the basis of the information in the passage, which of the following is LEAST likely to be a phenomenon involving a biological clock?
    (A) Certain turtles nest at the same place during the same season each year.
    (B) Some animals hibernate during the winter months.
    (C) Growing plants tend to bend toward the light.
    (D) Egg production is increased by increasing the hours of illumination to which hens are exposed.
    (E) Some pigeons are able to return to their bases even when they have been taken far away from them.

GO ON TO THE NEXT PAGE

A curious but understandable thing happened in the eighteenth century. By then, cities had done well enough for Europeans, mediating between them and many harsh aspects of nature, so that something became popularly possible which previously had been a rarity—sentimentalization of nature, or at any rate, sentimentalization of a rustic relationship with nature. Marie Antoinette playing milkmaid was an expression of this sentimentality on one plane. The romantic idea of the "noble savage" was an even sillier one, on another plane. So, in the New World, was Jefferson's intellectual rejection of cities of free artisans and mechanics, and his dream of an ideal republic of self-reliant rural yeomen—an odd dream for a man whose land was tilled by slaves.

In real life, peasants were the least free of all people—bound by tradition, ridden by caste, fettered by superstitions, riddled by suspicion and foreboding of whatever was strange. "City air makes free" was the medieval saying, when city air literally did make free the runaway serf. City air still makes free the runaways from company towns, from factory-farms, from subsistence farms, from migrant picker routes, from mining villages, from one-class suburbs.

Owing to the mediation of cities, it became popularly possible to regard "nature" as benign, ennobling, and pure. Opposed to all this fictionalized purity, nobility, and beneficence, cities, not being fictions, could be considered as seats of malignancy and, obviously, the enemies of nature. And once people begin looking at nature as if it were a nice big St. Bernard dog for the children, what could be more natural than the desire to bring this sentimental pet into the city so that the city might get some nobility, purity, and beneficence by association?

There are dangers in sentimentalizing nature. Most sentimental ideas imply, at bottom, a deep if unacknowledged disrespect. It is no accident that inveterate sentimentalizers about nature can be, at one and the same time, voracious and disrespectful destroyers of wild and rural countryside.

It is neither love for nature nor respect for nature that leads to this schizophrenic attitude. Instead, it is a sentimental desire to toy, rather patronizingly, with some insipid, standardized, suburbanized shadow of nature—apparently in sheer disbelief that we and our cities, just by virtue of being, are also a legitimate part of nature and involved with it in much deeper and more inescapable ways than grass trimming, sunbathing, and contemplative uplift. And so, each day, several thousand more acres of our countryside are eaten by the bulldozers, covered by pavement, dotted with suburbanites who have killed the thing they thought they came to find.

26. The author's argument is structured around the essential conflict she perceives between

(A) past and present
(B) reality and distortion
(C) city and nature
(D) aristocrats and serfs
(E) creation and destruction

27. According to the author, sentimentalization was made possible because

(A) prominent people espoused the idea
(B) medieval concepts of the city were outdated
(C) nature is truly ennobling and pure
(D) cities protected people from nature's brutal realities
(E) people sought freedom from the trials of city living

28. According to the passage, those who sentimentalize nature are to be criticized for their

(A) imitation of aristocratic attitudes
(B) disregard for the nobility and purity of the city
(C) failure to see the city as a part of nature
(D) acceptance of medieval biases against the city
(E) lack of adequate knowledge of an actual city

29. The author apparently believes that for something to be "natural" it is sufficient that it be

(A) present in the world
(B) extant before the appearance of humans
(C) maintained in a pristine condition
(D) beneficial to life
(E) considered so by a majority

30. The author regards the urge to sentimentalize nature as

(A) novel (B) waning (C) opportunistic
(D) instinctive (E) deluded

GO ON TO THE NEXT PAGE

Select the word or set of words that best completes each of the following sentences.

31. Land, if it is well chosen, can be an excellent investment because the amount of land is ---- whereas the population is always growing.

(A) constant (B) inordinate (C) precarious (D) traditional (E) irrelevant

32. The quality that distinguishes serious scientists and scholars is perhaps the ---- of their curiosity, which causes them to spend months or even years on a single quest.

(A) arrogance (B) remoteness (C) futility (D) spontaneity (E) persistence

33. Ms. Harte's book must be classified as ----; it is not fiction, legend, or sociology, but a work rich in well-authenticated facts of America's ----.

(A) history. .past (B) myth. .folktales (C) narrative. .problems (D) feminist. .heroes (E) imagination. .society

34. Gradually ----, though seldom ----, he eventually won a few honors that helped to compensate for years of hardship and neglect.

(A) ostracized. .published
(B) approached. .accosted
(C) accepted. .applauded
(D) copied. .imitated
(E) idolized. .glorified

35. Continuing her search for rare and elusive animal subjects, photographer Hope Ryden found the ---- of the bobcat to be a challenge; sometimes it took her days to locate one.

(A) belligerence (B) proliferation (C) furtiveness (D) vacillation (E) gregariousness

Each question below consists of a related pair of words or phrases, followed by five lettered pairs of words or phrases. Select the lettered pair that best expresses a relationship similar to that expressed in the original pair.

Example:

YAWN : BOREDOM :: (A) dream : sleep (B) anger : madness (C) smile : amusement (D) face : expression (E) impatience : rebellion

Ⓐ Ⓑ ● Ⓓ Ⓔ

36. SALESPERSON : MERCHANDISE ::
(A) mechanic : garage (B) merchant : bank (C) writer : research (D) captain : vessel (E) broker : stock

37. TOP-HEAVY : STABILITY ::
(A) thickset : size
(B) haphazard : change
(C) steadfast : vitality
(D) waterlogged : buoyancy
(E) able-bodied : strength

38. COMPONENT : CONFIGURATION ::
(A) spoke : rim (B) border : conflict (C) brick : mortar (D) star : constellation (E) weight : scale

39. INARTICULATE : SPEECH ::
(A) inefficient : apathy
(B) incessant : activity
(C) unpredictable : time
(D) uncoordinated : movement
(E) immune : health

40. AVIARY : BIRDS :: (A) sty : pigs (B) garden : butterflies (C) swamp : mosquitoes (D) tree : squirrels (E) net : fish

41. REMISSION : DISEASE ::
(A) submission : defeat
(B) abatement : storm
(C) inhibition : personality
(D) anxiety : attack
(E) hiatus : interruption

42. EULOGY : PRAISE ::
(A) defamation : description
(B) masquerade : appearance
(C) tirade : disapproval
(D) escapade : emigration
(E) debate : indifference

43. CURMUDGEON : CANTANKEROUS ::
(A) braggart : courageous (B) hypocrite : devout (C) reprobate : chaste (D) simpleton : foolish (E) ingrate : charitable

44. ANOMALY : RULE ::
(A) revelation : future outcome
(B) deviation : accepted norm
(C) retaliation : spontaneous action
(D) fantasy : pleasant dream
(E) hypothesis : desired result

45. PROCRASTINATOR : DILATORY ::
(A) mediator : partial
(B) charlatan : deceitful
(C) recluse : hostile
(D) contemporary : ephemeral
(E) adversary : vociferous

IF YOU FINISH BEFORE TIME IS CALLED, YOU MAY CHECK YOUR WORK ON THIS SECTION ONLY. DO NOT TURN TO ANY OTHER SECTION IN THE TEST. **STOP**

SECTION 3

Time—30 minutes
35 Questions

In this section solve each problem, using any available space on the page for scratchwork. Then decide which is the best of the choices given and fill in the corresponding oval on the answer sheet.

The following information is for your reference in solving some of the problems.

Circle of radius r: Area $= \pi r^2$; Circumference $= 2\pi r$
The number of degrees of arc in a circle is 360.
The measure in degrees of a straight angle is 180.

Triangle: The sum of the measures in degrees of the angles of a triangle is 180.
If $\angle CDA$ is a right angle, then

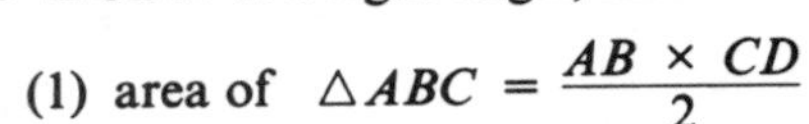

(1) area of $\triangle ABC = \frac{AB \times CD}{2}$

(2) $AC^2 = AD^2 + DC^2$

Definition of symbols:

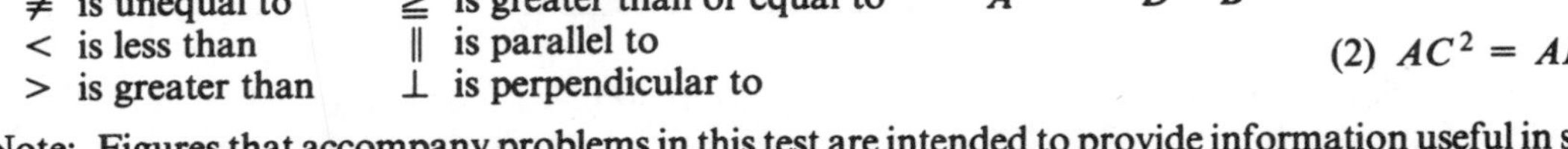

$=$	is equal to	$\leq$	is less than or equal to
$\neq$	is unequal to	$\geq$	is greater than or equal to
$<$	is less than	$\parallel$	is parallel to
$>$	is greater than	$\perp$	is perpendicular to

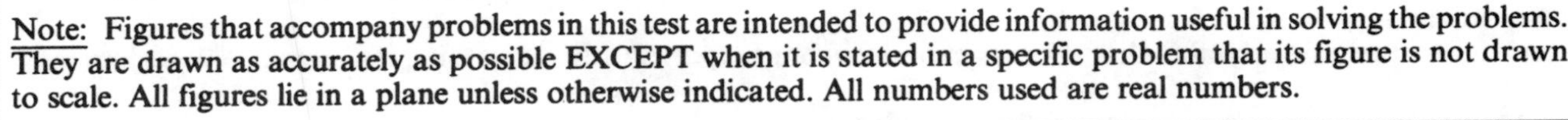

Note: Figures that accompany problems in this test are intended to provide information useful in solving the problems. They are drawn as accurately as possible EXCEPT when it is stated in a specific problem that its figure is not drawn to scale. All figures lie in a plane unless otherwise indicated. All numbers used are real numbers.

1. If $\frac{a}{2} + 1 = 3$, then $a =$

   (A) 2 (B) 4 (C) 5 (D) 6 (E) 8

2. If x is an integer and $0 < 6x < 16$, what are all possible values of x?

   (A) 0 only
   (B) 1 only
   (C) 2 only
   (D) 0 and 1
   (E) 1 and 2

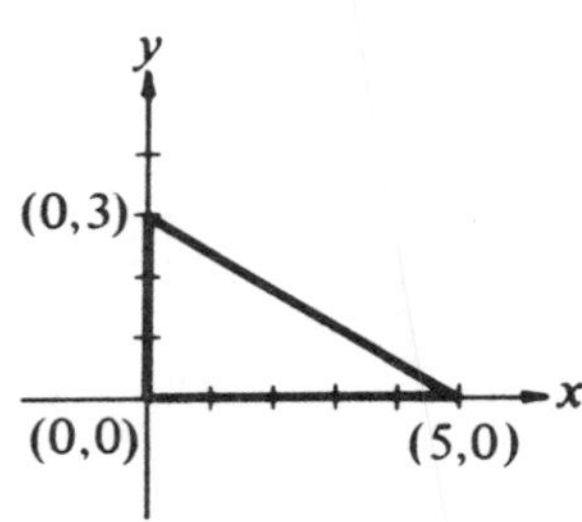

3. What is the area of the triangle in the figure above?

   (A) 4.0 (B) 7.5 (C) 8.0
   (D) 8.5 (E) 15.0

4. If 5 is the average (arithmetic mean) of x, 5, and 5, then $x =$

   (A) −15 (B) −5 (C) 0 (D) 5 (E) 15

5. Which of the following must be true for all integers a, b, and c?

   I. $a - 0 = a$
   II. $a - b = b - a$
   III. $(a - b) - c = a - (b - c)$

   (A) I only (B) II only (C) III only
   (D) I and II (E) II and III

6. If the measures of the angles of a triangle are $x°$, $(x + 10)°$, and $(x - 40)°$, what is the measure of the smallest of these angles?

   (A) 10°
   (B) 20°
   (C) 30°
   (D) 70°
   (E) 80°

7. If $\frac{s}{t} = -1$, then $\frac{t}{s} - \frac{2s}{t} =$

   (A) −2 (B) −1 (C) 0 (D) 1 (E) 2

GO ON TO THE NEXT PAGE

Questions 8-27 each consist of two quantities, one in Column A and one in Column B. You are to compare the two quantities and on the answer sheet fill in oval

A if the quantity in Column A is greater;
B if the quantity in Column B is greater;
C if the two quantities are equal;
D if the relationship cannot be determined from the information given.

AN E RESPONSE WILL NOT BE SCORED.

EXAMPLES

	Column A	Column B	Answers
E1.	2×6	$2 + 6$	● Ⓑ Ⓒ Ⓓ Ⓔ
E2.	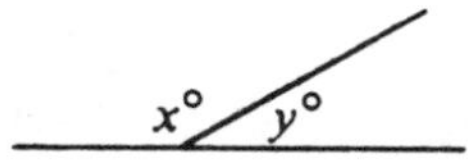 $180 - x$	y	Ⓐ Ⓑ ● Ⓓ Ⓔ
E3.	$p - q$	$q - p$	Ⓐ Ⓑ Ⓒ ● Ⓔ

Notes:

1. In certain questions, information concerning one or both of the quantities to be compared is centered above the two columns.
2. In a given question, a symbol that appears in both columns represents the same thing in Column A as it does in Column B.
3. Letters such as x, n, and k stand for real numbers.

	Column A	Column B
8.	$\frac{4}{5}$ of 5	$\frac{5}{4}$ of 4

$x + y = 0$

$x = -3$

9.	y	0

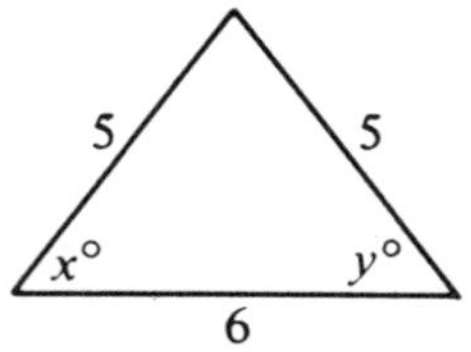

10.	x	y
11.	$\frac{1}{5} + \frac{4}{10}$	$\frac{2}{5} + \frac{2}{10}$

$x < 5$

$y < 15$

12.	x	y

$3x + y = 10$

13.	$6x + 2y$	16

	Column A	Column B

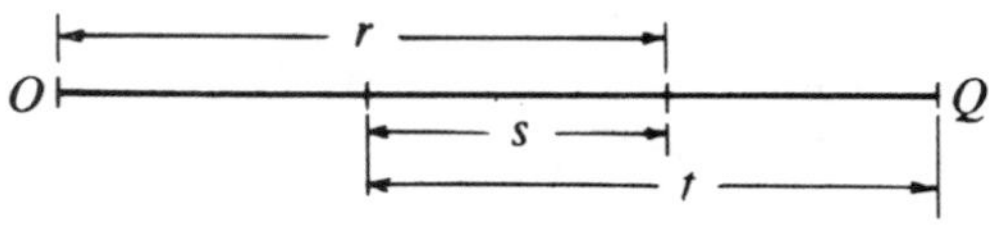

14.	Length OQ	$r + t - s$
15.	$\frac{1}{10}$	5%

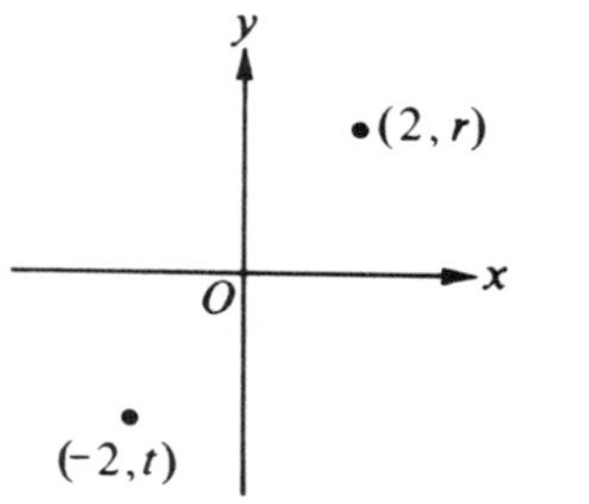

Note: Figure not drawn to scale.

16.	$2r$	$-2t$
17.	$x^2 - 16$	$x^2 - 25$

GO ON TO THE NEXT PAGE

SUMMARY DIRECTIONS FOR COMPARISON QUESTIONS

Answer: A if the quantity in Column A is greater;
B if the quantity in Column B is greater;
C if the two quantities are equal;
D if the relationship cannot be determined from the information given.

AN E RESPONSE WILL NOT BE SCORED.

	Column A	Column B

The formula for the volume of a right circular cylinder is $V = \pi r^2 h$.

18.	The volume of a right circular cylinder with $r = 4$ and $h = 8$	The volume of a right circular cylinder with $r = 8$ and $h = 4$

A number greater than or equal to x is defined to be an "exey" number. The number 10 is not exey.

19.	x	10

$0 < r < s < t < u < v < w$

20.	$r + t + v$	$s + u + w$

Marker X is 3 kilometers from Marker Y and Marker Z is 4 kilometers from Marker Y.

21.	Distance from Marker Z to Marker X	Distance from Marker X to Marker Y

A pentagon has five sides.

22.	The sum of the degree measures of all interior angles of a pentagon if all sides are equal in length	The sum of the degree measures of all interior angles of a pentagon if the sides are unequal in length

Column A	Column B

Child	Weight (in pounds)
Steve	x
Carol	60
Bev	50
Jim	y
Paul	90

The average (arithmetic mean) of the weights of the five children listed above is 70 pounds.

23.	$x + y$	140

When an integer x is divided by 7, the remainder is 6.
When an integer y is divided by 6, the remainder is 5.

24.	x	y

$x = \frac{2}{3}r$, $y = \frac{5}{12}r$, and $z = \frac{2}{5}y$

25.	x	$4z$

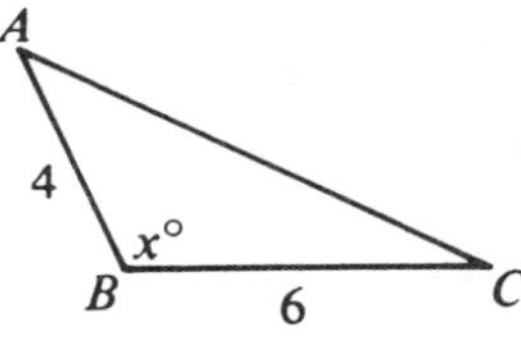

$90 < x < 180$

26.	Area of $\triangle ABC$	12

x is a positive integer.
y is a positive integer.

27.	2^{x+y}	$2^x + 2^y$

GO ON TO THE NEXT PAGE

Solve each of the remaining problems in this section using any available space for scratchwork. Then decide which is the best of the choices given and fill in the corresponding oval on the answer sheet.

28. Which of the following fractions is greater than $\frac{1}{2}$ but less than $\frac{2}{3}$?

(A) $\frac{5}{12}$ (B) $\frac{6}{12}$ (C) $\frac{7}{12}$ (D) $\frac{8}{12}$ (E) $\frac{9}{12}$

29. When it is 7:00 a.m. in Seattle, it is 10:00 a.m. in Philadelphia. A plane is scheduled to leave Philadelphia at 11:30 a.m. (Philadelphia time) and to arrive in Seattle at 4:15 p.m. (Seattle time). How many hours are scheduled for the trip?

(A) $4\frac{3}{4}$ (B) $5\frac{3}{4}$ (C) $6\frac{1}{4}$ (D) $7\frac{1}{4}$ (E) $7\frac{3}{4}$

30. $\frac{3.4(10^6)}{1.7(10^2)} =$

(A) $20(10^3)$
(B) $[2(10)]^4$
(C) 20^3
(D) $20(10^4)$
(E) $2(10^8)$

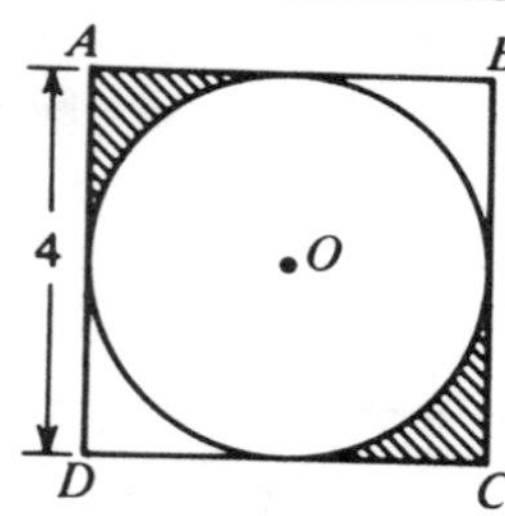

31. In the figure above, a circle with center O is inscribed in square $ABCD$. What is the total area of the shaded regions?

(A) $4 - \frac{\pi}{2}$ (B) $8 - 2\pi$ (C) $8 - \frac{3\pi}{2}$

(D) $16 - 4\pi$ (E) $16 - 2\pi$

32. In a certain sport in which there are no ties a team has a won:lost ratio of 7:5. If the team has played n games, which of the following is equal to the difference between the number of wins and the number of losses?

(A) $\frac{n}{2}$ (B) $\frac{n}{4}$ (C) $\frac{n}{6}$ (D) $\frac{n}{8}$ (E) $\frac{n}{12}$

33. Two lists of 5 consecutive positive integers contain exactly one integer in common. The sum of the 5 integers on one list is how much greater than the sum on the other?

(A) 4
(B) 5
(C) 10
(D) 20
(E) It cannot be determined from the information given.

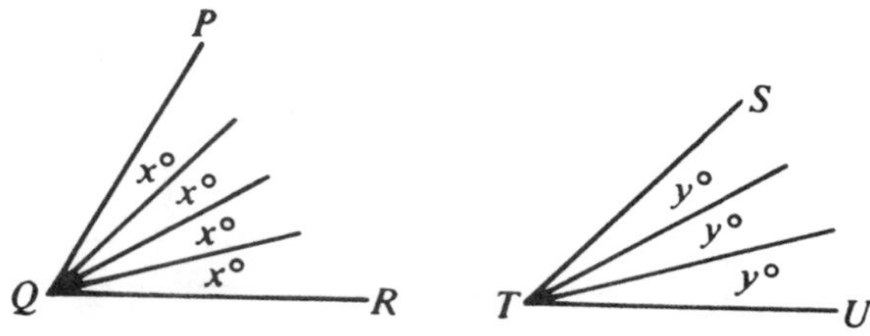

Note: Figure not drawn to scale.

34. In the figure above, if $\angle PQR = 2\angle STU$, then $\frac{x}{y} =$

(A) $\frac{2}{3}$ (B) $\frac{3}{4}$ (C) $\frac{3}{2}$ (D) $\frac{4}{3}$ (E) $\frac{8}{3}$

35. As a fee for his service, a miller kept 10 percent of the flour he ground for a customer. If the customer got 1 ton, how many tons did the miller grind?

(A) $1\frac{1}{11}$

(B) $1\frac{1}{10}$

(C) $1\frac{1}{9}$

(D) $1\frac{1}{8}$

(E) $1\frac{1}{7}$

IF YOU FINISH BEFORE TIME IS CALLED, YOU MAY CHECK YOUR WORK ON THIS SECTION ONLY. DO NOT TURN TO ANY OTHER SECTION IN THE TEST. **STOP**

SECTION 4 **Time—30 minutes 40 Questions**

For each question in this section, choose the best answer and fill in the corresponding oval on the answer sheet.

Each question below consists of a word in capital letters, followed by five lettered words or phrases. Choose the word or phrase that is most nearly opposite in meaning to the word in capital letters. Since some of the questions require you to distinguish fine shades of meaning, consider all the choices before deciding which is best.

Example:

GOOD: (A) sour (B) bad (C) red (D) hot (E) ugly

Ⓐ ● Ⓒ Ⓓ Ⓔ

1. VERIFY: (A) multiply (B) qualify (C) prove false (D) render inadequate (E) seem impossible

2. REPELLENT: (A) discovery (B) antidote (C) segment (D) origin (E) lure

3. IMPULSIVE:
(A) planned in advance
(B) arrived at independently
(C) easily challenged
(D) acknowledged
(E) unproductive

4. MISCARRY: (A) unload (B) dismount (C) contend (D) succeed (E) pretend

5. LIABILITY: (A) asset (B) precedent (C) exchange (D) preconceived idea (E) well-founded accusation

6. INEBRIATED: (A) risky (B) sober (C) stingy (D) foul (E) secretive

7. PUGNACITY:
(A) authenticity
(B) disposition
(C) willingness to experiment
(D) dislike of falsehood
(E) disinclination to fight

8. ARABLE: (A) shallow (B) flat (C) irrigated (D) known for variety (E) unfit for plowing

9. CONVOKE: (A) dissolve (B) transmit (C) oblige (D) kindle (E) disable

10. INCLUSIVE: (A) narrow (B) persistent (C) repetitive (D) disputable (E) unavailable

Each sentence below has one or two blanks, each blank indicating that something has been omitted. Beneath the sentence are five lettered words or sets of words. Choose the word or set of words that, when inserted in the sentence, best fits the meaning of the sentence as a whole.

Example:

Although its publicity has been ----, the film itself is intelligent, well-acted, handsomely produced, and altogether ----.

(A) tasteless. . respectable (B) extensive. . moderate (C) sophisticated. . amateur (D) risqué. . crude (E) perfect. . spectacular

● Ⓑ Ⓒ Ⓓ Ⓔ

11. The book is now regarded as ---- because of its ---- in predicting economic trends.
(A) prophetic. .accuracy
(B) incomprehensible. .consistency
(C) successful. .neglect
(D) controversial. .monotony
(E) incoherent. .proficiency

12. A society confronted by new problems but unable to meet them shows a ---- to cling to the past, seeking emotional security in a reaffirmation of ----.
(A) reluctance. .conservatism
(B) resolve. .progress
(C) compulsion. .reform
(D) zeal. .transition
(E) tendency. .tradition

GO ON TO THE NEXT PAGE

13. The name "Ojibwa," originally an allusion to the distinctive puckered seam of a moccasin, was so ---- by the Europeans who transcribed it that it appeared in print as "Chippewa."

(A) exalted (B) garbled (C) imitated (D) abbreviated (E) perpetuated

14. Though most of the experimental data seemed to be confirmatory, her spirited skepticism kept her from ---- that still-debated theory.

(A) poring over (B) fabricating (C) expounding on (D) modulating (E) subscribing to

15. The strength of liberal democracy owes a considerable debt to the nineteenth-century romantics who ---- civil liberties and the --- of suffrage.

(A) advocated. .repression
(B) thwarted. .acceptance
(C) vindicated. .prohibition
(D) championed. .extension
(E) challenged. ratification

Each question below consists of a related pair of words or phrases, followed by five lettered pairs of words or phrases. Select the lettered pair that <u>best</u> expresses a relationship similar to that expressed in the original pair.

Example:

YAWN:BOREDOM :: (A) dream:sleep (B) anger:madness (C) smile:amusement (D) face:expression (E) impatience:rebellion

Ⓐ Ⓑ ● Ⓓ Ⓔ

16. FOX:CHICKEN COOP :: (A) artist:museum (B) robber:bank (C) priest:church (D) keeper:zoo (E) sparrow:nest

17. DOOR:WALL :: (A) toll:road (B) guard:border (C) gate:fence (D) bridge:river (E) key:lock

18. SAIL:MAST :: (A) coat:hanger (B) paint:wall (C) flag:flagpole (D) leaf:tree (E) ribbon:hair

19. RETROSPECTION:PAST ::
(A) imagination:reality
(B) expectation:future
(C) spontaneity:newness
(D) measurement:eternity
(E) preservation:antiquity

20. WISP:SMOKE :: (A) sliver:wood (B) droplet:sponge (C) chimney:fire (D) flood:water (E) seed:sprout

21. INTOLERABLE:ENDURED ::
(A) educable:comprehended
(B) peerless:surpassed
(C) figurative:delineated
(D) surreptitious:concealed
(E) detrimental:hurt

22. MUFFLE:SOUND :: (A) dampen:enthusiasm (B) resolve:quandary (C) resent:intrusion (D) deceive:vision (E) abet:progress

23. INSOLVENT:FUNDS ::
(A) infirm:flaws
(B) immoral:desires
(C) impoverished:debts
(D) ineligible:qualifications
(E) independent:rights

24. CONVENTIONAL:CONFORM ::
(A) rational:retaliate (B) neutral:incite (C) polite:intrude (D) insincere:dissemble (E) exceptional:notice

25. SHIP:FOUNDER :: (A) invention:discover (B) mule:kick (C) canoe:paddle (D) airplane:crash (E) submarine:launch

GO ON TO THE NEXT PAGE

Each passage below is followed by questions based on its content. Answer all questions following a passage on the basis of what is stated or implied in that passage.

Imagine listening to an orchestra out in space. Then imagine that space filled with ordinary air, the material medium necessary for sound to be transmitted from the instruments of the orchestra to our eardrums. Sound leaving each instrument in the form of waves spreads in all directions. If there is nothing to absorb the energy of the waves, they travel on forever, but their intensity diminishes as they travel farther from their source. The natural law of diminution is in effect. Nevertheless, the harmonics of sound remain constant. That is, the pitches of notes sounded by the orchestra remain the same even as the amount of sound diminishes.

Although distance does not affect the quality of the sound, other factors do. One factor is the ear that hears the sound. It treats different pitches in different ways. When sounds are faint, the ear is more sensitive to treble notes than to bass. Bass notes, though, are more likely to reach the ear than treble notes, when, with our orchestra back on Earth now, an obstacle such as a pillar blocks the short treble waves more fully than the longer bass waves. Bass sound waves also reflect more effectively off the ground and travel more successfully through solid materials. Sound waves that do not travel through may be said to be absorbed by the solid material. We may conclude from all of this information that the acoustical experts who plan a concert hall have a highly complex task. Or we may conclude that we should hire more flutes and violins for our earthly orchestra than for our heavenly one.

26. One can infer from the request in line 1 that the author wishes to

(A) allow the reader to hear music from the same vantage point as a conductor
(B) establish the contradictory notions of direction and endless space
(C) emphasize the universal appeal of great music
(D) prevent the reader from thinking of sound waves as a visual phenomenon
(E) suggest a situation in which sound waves would meet no interference

27. According to the passage, the "natural law of diminution" (lines 9-10) concerns which of the following?

(A) The size of an instrument
(B) The energy of sound waves
(C) The length of a sound wave
(D) The rate of absorption of sound
(E) The failure to focus sound waves in one direction

28. Which of the following judgments is implied in the author's second conclusion (lines 29-32)?

(A) Large orchestras are better than small instrumental groups.
(B) Sounds from treble instruments are more beautiful than those from bass instruments.
(C) Balance of sound in an orchestra is desirable.
(D) Melody is more important than harmony.
(E) Good acoustics are not worth their high cost.

GO ON TO THE NEXT PAGE

A profound and bullying impudence emanated from Thomas Frazier, like steam escaping from a hot valve. In his grunts, his refusal of the older man's efforts to please, he was making a comment upon the life and work of Johnson Palmer. Frazier, a young "action" painter, was shrugging off Palmer's conservative portraits of lonely-eyed children, his nostalgic scenes of summer lawns where some abandoned object always lay sadly in the background. Whatever the merits of the two men's work, they faced each other in a condition of steadfast hostility, like the appropriate antagonism of the Army and Navy teams on the football field.

Palmer was spare and courteous, Frazier choleric and boastful. Palmer's confidence, over the years, had become as thin as his body. The two were now meeting through the efforts of their friend Buck Sampson, who, in blundering charity and innocence, had made one of those perilous suggestions that burn the souls of sensitive egoists: that Palmer purchase one of Frazier's canvases. Sampson had brought forth his proposal as only incidentally a financial aid to the young man; dollars, he felt, were a sort of spiritual coin that carried with them a boost to a hungry pride. Sampson had not realized the truth, that the older painter was a good deal more in need of boosting than the younger. Disappointment and decline of expectation had settled upon Palmer. True, he was more "known" than Frazier, but Frazier had all the fresh bark and bluster, the blowing bravado of a beginner who had attached himself to a new school.

29. The passage is primarily concerned with which of the following?

(A) Comparing the work of conservative and action painters
(B) Presenting the tensions that existed between Frazier and Palmer
(C) Creating stereotypes of the artistic character
(D) Revealing the difficult lives of struggling artists
(E) Describing the effect of Palmer's personality on Frazier

30. The unspoken "comment" (line 4) made by Frazier suggests that he

(A) has reason to fear Palmer's success
(B) envies Palmer's hard-won independence
(C) is contemptuous of Palmer
(D) respects Palmer, but only as an artist
(E) knows that Palmer is jealous of his background and talents

31. Which of the following best describes Thomas Frazier?

(A) An embittered creative genius
(B) A mercenary youth
(C) A confident and acclaimed artist
(D) A cocksure newcomer
(E) A vindictive revolutionary

GO ON TO THE NEXT PAGE

By the mid-1920's, archaeologists knew much about the Anasazi (a Navajo name meaning "Ancient Ones") who lived in Chaco Canyon, New Mexico, a thousand years ago: they occupied thirteen giant pueblos; their population may have reached 15,000; they were highly skilled in masonry. But archaeologists did not know why the Anasazi had built retaining walls, or why they had carved wide, shallow depressions, or why they built stairways into the cliffs; or why, in the desert far from their communities, they had put up innlike way houses. Nor did archaeologists know why the Anasazi had laboriously built what appeared to be a system of water control.

The first breakthrough came in the late 1960's when an archaeologist investigating that system came upon strange features that did not appear to be canals. Behind the largest pueblo he noticed two parallel lines of rocks that looked like borders of a garden path. Following them, he came to what was apparently a stone ramp giving easy access to the top of a cliff. It seemed possible that many features previously regarded as water-control structures might be parts of an ancient system of roads.

In 1971, archaeologists discovered numerous stairways in the canyon walls, suggesting a transportation system far larger than they had imagined. They found confirmation a problem, however, for few such roads were visible from the ground. It was recalled that aerial photographs had been taken in 1929 by Charles Lindbergh, and the investigation was continued. In aerial photographs, distracting detail dissolves and scattered points merge into lines. Photographic evidence was startling: it was immediately apparent that the Anasazi roadways were not isolated avenues but part of a network of ancient pedestrian highways.

After they had learned everything possible from studying aerial photographs with the unaided eye, archaeologists began work in the laboratory with a stereoscope, an instrument using two overlapping photographs to create a three-dimensional view. Infrared film, which shows vegetation in bright pink and red patterns, revealed several previously undiscovered stretches of road. Multispectral imaging, by photographing the same scene simultaneously with several cameras fitted with different filters, added more information. And an electronic device invented by astronomers which enhances faint features by deepening their shadows doubled the number of known roadways.

Next came what archaeologists call gathering "ground truth." Dusty roadway segments, some almost thirty miles long, were walked along, measured, and photographed. Almost all of the major highways were a precise nine meters wide, and all roads had a dish-shaped cross section, which might have resulted from the pressure of many feet. Ground truth also revealed that some of Chaco Canyon's prime enigmas were part of the roadway network.

By 1975, archaeologists had mapped a complex web of some two hundred miles of roads, some extending as much as sixty-five miles to other major Anasazi centers, and others heading toward destinations yet to be discovered.

32. Which of the following questions is most fully answered by the passage?

(A) When was the first Anasazi community established in Chaco Canyon?
(B) How were the Anasazi roadways discovered and studied?
(C) Why were way houses built in remote parts of the desert?
(D) Why do some of the roads studied have no particular destination?
(E) How did the Anasazi ensure an adequate supply of water?

33. From the information given in the passage, it appears that archaeologists for many years could not explain some Anasazi structures because of

(A) adherence to a misleading interpretation
(B) insufficient opportunities to gather data
(C) aversion to the physical work of exploration
(D) partial disintegration of ancient buildings
(E) reluctance to use new laboratory methods

34. Judging from the information given in the passage, a contemporary archaeologist would most likely interpret the "wide, shallow depressions" (lines 8-9) as which of the following?

(A) Collection ponds for rainwater
(B) Isolated visible portions of ancient roadways
(C) Subterranean storage areas for food
(D) Remnants of a cliff staircase
(E) Pockets of land once cultivated

35. The passage neither states nor suggests that the Anasazi society had

(A) elected government officials
(B) frequent communication between settlements
(C) standardized units of measurement
(D) proficiency in engineering skills
(E) populations organized in large communities

36. Which of the following is the most suitable title for the passage?

(A) The First American Highway
(B) Digging in the Desert
(C) The History of the Anasazi
(D) Solving an Archaeological Puzzle
(E) The Birth of an Archaeological Theory

GO ON TO THE NEXT PAGE

In most modern instances, interpretation amounts to the philistine refusal to leave the work of art alone. Real art tends to make us nervous. By reducing the work of art to its content and then interpreting that, one tames the work of art. Interpretation makes art manageable, conformable.

The philistinism of interpretation is more rife in literature than in any other art. For decades now, literary critics have understood it to be their task to translate the elements of the poem or play or novel or story into something else. Sometimes writers will be so uneasy before the naked power of their art that they will install within the work itself—albeit with a little shyness, a touch of the good taste of irony—the clear and explicit interpretation of it. And if an author is not so cooperative, the critic is only too happy to perform the job.

The work of Kafka, for example, has been subjected to a mass ravishment by no less than three armies of interpreters. Those who read Kafka as a social allegory see case studies of the frustrations and insanity of modern bureaucracy. Those who read Kafka as a psychoanalytic allegory see desperate revelations of Kafka's fear of his father. Those who read Kafka as religious allegory explain that Joseph K. in *The Trial* is being judged by the inexorable and mysterious justice of God.

37. Which of the following statements is (are) consistent with the author's ideas as presented in the passage?

I. The value of a work of art lies in its total effect.
II. Art is a sometimes disturbing form of expression.
III. Every artist has a message and interpreters must find it.

(A) I only (B) II only (C) I and II only (D) I and III only (E) I, II and III

38. It can be inferred that the author believes most critics respond to a writer's art by

(A) relating the work to the most pressing social problems of the time
(B) interpreting the ways that the writer's work tends to make readers nervous and uneasy
(C) ignoring the work of art and interpreting the writer's life
(D) focusing only on the writer's style and method of presentation
(E) placing it within an established framework of assumptions and values

39. According to the passage, some writers who are uneasy with the power of their own work react by

(A) providing built-in explanations of its meaning
(B) creating modern fables to analyze important issues of the day
(C) adapting their art to include many different elements for interpretation
(D) using allegories to mask the true meaning of their art
(E) misleading critics through false explanations of their art

40. The author's attitude toward modern critics can best be characterized as

(A) oblivious (B) disdainful (C) sympathetic (D) hopeful (E) amused

IF YOU FINISH BEFORE TIME IS CALLED, YOU MAY CHECK YOUR WORK ON THIS SECTION ONLY. DO NOT TURN TO ANY OTHER SECTION IN THE TEST. **STOP**

Correct Answers for Scholastic Aptitude Test Form Code 7X			
VERBAL		**MATHEMATICAL**	
Section 2	**Section 4**	**Section 1**	**Section 3**
1. E	1. C	1. A	1. B
2. D	2. E	2. D	2. E
3. E	3. A	3. E	3. B
4. A	4. D	4. D	4. D
5. E	5. A	5. C	5. A
6. A	6. B	6. A	6. C
7. D	7. E	7. D	7. D
8. C	8. E	8. B	*8. B
9. C	9. A	9. B	*9. A
10. A	10. A	10. E	*10. C
11. B	11. A	11. C	*11. C
12. C	12. E	12. B	*12. D
13. C	13. B	13. A	*13. A
14. B	14. E	14. B	*14. C
15. A	15. D	15. E	*15. A
16. B	16. B	16. A	*16. D
17. E	17. C	17. A	*17. A
18. A	18. C	18. D	*18. B
19. D	19. B	19. C	*19. A
20. C	20. A	20. E	*20. B
21. D	21. B	21. C	*21. D
22. A	22. A	22. D	*22. C
23. C	23. D	23. B	*23. A
24. C	24. D	24. E	*24. D
25. C	25. D	25. D	*25. C
26. B	26. E		*26. B
27. D	27. B		*27. D
28. C	28. C		28. C
29. A	29. B		29. E
30. E	30. C		30. A
31. A	31. D		31. B
32. E	32. B		32. C
33. A	33. A		33. D
34. C	34. B		34. C
35. C	35. A		35. C
36. E	36. D		
37. D	37. C		
38. D	38. E		
39. D	39. A		
40. A	40. B		
41. B			
42. C			
43. D			
44. B			
45. B			

*Indicates four-choice questions. (All of the other questions are five-choice.)

The Scoring Process

Machine-scoring is done in three steps:

- *Scanning.* Your answer sheet is "read" by a scanning machine and the oval you filled in for each question is recorded on a computer tape.
- *Scoring.* The computer compares the oval filled in for each question with the correct response. Each correct answer receives one point; omitted questions do not count toward your score. For each wrong answer, a fraction of a point is subtracted to correct for random guessing. For questions with five answer choices, one-fourth of a point is subtracted for each wrong response; for questions with four answer choices, one-third of a point is subtracted for each wrong response. The SAT-verbal test has 85 questions with five answer choices each. If, for example, a student has 44 right, 32 wrong, and 9 omitted, the resulting raw score is determined as follows:

$$44 \text{ right} - \frac{32 \text{ wrong}}{4} = 44 - 8 = 36 \text{ raw score points}$$

Obtaining raw scores frequently involves the rounding of fractional numbers to the nearest whole number. For example, a raw score of 36.25 is rounded to 36, the nearest whole number. A raw score of 36.50 is rounded upward to 37.

- *Converting to reported scaled score.* Raw test scores are then placed on the College Board scale of 200 to 800 through a process that adjusts scores to account for minor differences in difficulty among different editions of the test. This process, known as equating, is performed so that a student's reported score is not affected by the edition of the test taken nor by the abilities of the group with whom the student takes the test. As a result of placing SAT scores on the College Board scale, scores earned by students at different times can be compared. For example, an SAT-verbal score of 400 on a test taken at one administration indicates the same level of developed verbal ability as a 400 score obtained on a different edition of the test taken at another time.

How to Score the Test

SAT-Verbal Sections 2 and 4

Step A: Count the number of correct answers for *section 2* and record the number in the space provided on the worksheet on the next page. Then do the same for the incorrect answers. (Do not count omitted answers.) To determine subtotal A, use the formula:

$$\text{number correct} - \frac{\text{number incorrect}}{4} = \text{subtotal A}$$

Step B: Count the number of correct answers and the number of incorrect answers for *section 4* and record the numbers in the spaces provided on the worksheet. To determine subtotal B, use the formula:

$$\text{number correct} - \frac{\text{number incorrect}}{4} = \text{subtotal B}$$

Step C: To obtain C, add subtotal A to subtotal B, keeping any decimals. Enter the resulting figure on the worksheet.

Step D: To obtain D, your raw verbal score, round C to the nearest whole number. (For example, any number from 44.50 to 45.49 rounds to 45.) Enter the resulting figure on the worksheet.

Step E: To find your reported SAT-verbal score, look up the total raw verbal score you obtained in step D in the conversion table on page 304. Enter this figure on the worksheet.

SAT-Mathematical Sections 1 and 3

Step A: Count the number of correct answers and the number of incorrect answers for *section 1* and record the numbers in the spaces provided on the worksheet. To determine the subtotal A, use the formula:

$$\text{number correct} - \frac{\text{number incorrect}}{4} = \text{subtotal A}$$

Step B: Count the number of correct answers and the number of incorrect answers for the *five-choice questions (questions 1 through 7 and 28 through 35) in section 3* and record the numbers in the spaces provided on the worksheet. To determine the subtotal B, use the formula:

$$\text{number correct} - \frac{\text{number incorrect}}{4} = \text{subtotal B}$$

Step C: Count the number of correct answers and the number of incorrect answers for the *four-choice questions (questions 8 through 27) in section 3* and record the numbers in the spaces provided on the worksheet. To determine the subtotal C, use the formula:

$$\text{number correct} - \frac{\text{number incorrect}}{3} = \text{subtotal C}$$

Step D: To obtain D, add subtotal A, subtotal B, and subtotal C, keeping any decimals. Enter the resulting figure on the worksheet.

Step E: To obtain E, your raw mathematical score, round D to the nearest whole number. (For example, any number from 44.50 to 45.49 rounds to 45.) Enter the resulting figure on the worksheet.

Step F: To find your reported SAT-mathematical score, look up the total raw mathematical score you obtained in E in the conversion table on page 304. Enter this figure on the worksheet.

SAT SCORING WORKSHEET

SAT-Verbal Sections

A. Section 2: ______ (no. correct) − ¼ (______) (no. incorrect) = ______ subtotal A

B. Section 4: ______ (no. correct) − ¼ (______) (no. incorrect) = ______ subtotal B

C. Total unrounded raw score (Total A + B) ______ C

D. Total rounded raw score (Rounded to nearest whole number) ______ D

E. SAT-verbal reported scaled score (See the conversion table on page 304.) [ ] SAT-verbal score

SAT-Mathematical Sections

A. Section 1: ______ (no. correct) − ¼ (______) (no. incorrect) = ______ subtotal A

B. Section 3: Questions 1 through 7 and 28 through 35 (5-choice) ______ (no. correct) − ¼ (______) (no. incorrect) = ______ subtotal B

C. Section 3: Questions 8 through 27 (4-choice) ______ (no. correct) − ⅓ (______) (no. incorrect) = ______ subtotal C

D. Total unrounded raw score (Total A + B + C) ______ D

E. Total rounded raw score (Rounded to nearest whole number) ______ E

F. SAT-mathematical reported scaled score (See the conversion table on page 304.) [ ] SAT-math score

Score Conversion Table
Scholastic Aptitude Test
Form Code 7X

Raw Score	College Board Reported Score		Raw Score	College Board Reported Score	
	SAT-Verbal	SAT-Math		SAT-Verbal	SAT-Math
85	800		40	460	610
84	780		39	450	600
83	760		38	450	590
82	750		37	440	580
81	740		36	430	570
80	730		35	430	570
79	720		34	420	560
78	710		33	410	550
77	710		32	410	540
76	700		31	400	530
75	690		30	390	520
74	680		29	390	510
73	680		28	380	510
72	670		27	370	500
71	660		26	370	490
70	660		25	360	480
69	650		24	350	470
68	640		23	350	460
67	630		22	340	450
66	630		21	330	440
65	620		20	330	430
64	610		19	320	430
63	610		18	310	420
62	600		17	310	410
61	590		16	300	400
60	590	800	15	290	390
59	580	780	14	290	380
58	570	760	13	280	370
57	570	750	12	270	370
56	560	740	11	270	360
55	550	740	10	260	350
54	550	730	9	250	340
53	540	720	8	250	330
52	540	710	7	240	320
51	530	700	6	230	310
50	520	690	5	230	310
49	520	690	4	220	300
48	510	680	3	210	290
47	500	670	2	210	280
46	500	660	1	200	270
45	490	650	0	200	270
44	480	640	–1	200	260
43	480	640	–2	200	250
42	470	630	–3	200	240
41	460	620	–4	200	230
			–5	200	220
			–6	200	210
			–7 or below	200	200